320.509 Sel
Self, Robert O., 1968-
All in the family : the
realignment of American
democracy s

34028080825806
CYF $30.00   ocn768728945
                    09/26/12

3 4028 08
HARRIS COUNTY P

W9-AJO-814

ALSO BY ROBERT O. SELF

American Babylon: Race and the Struggle for Postwar Oakland

America's History (coauthor with James A. Henretta and Rebecca Edwards)

ALL IN THE
FAMILY

ALL IN THE FAMILY

THE REALIGNMENT OF AMERICAN DEMOCRACY SINCE THE 1960s

ROBERT O. SELF

HILL AND WANG

A DIVISION OF FARRAR, STRAUS AND GIROUX

NEW YORK

Hill and Wang
A division of Farrar, Straus and Giroux
18 West 18th Street, New York 10011

Copyright © 2012 by Robert O. Self
All rights reserved
Distributed in Canada by D&M Publishers, Inc.
Printed in the United States of America
First edition, 2012

Library of Congress Cataloging-in-Publication Data
Self, Robert O., 1968–
    All in the family : the realignment of American democracy since the 1960s /
Robert O. Self. — First edition.
        pages   cm
    Includes index.
    ISBN 978-0-8090-9502-5 (alk. paper)
    1. Social values—Political aspects—United States.   2. Families—Political
aspects—United States.   3. United States—Social conditions—1945–   4. United
States—Politics and government—1945–1989.   5. United States—Politics and
government—1989–   I. Title.

HN90.M6 S437 2012
320.50973'09045—dc23

                                                                2011051271

Designed by Jonathan D. Lippincott

www.fsgbooks.com

10   9   8   7   6   5   4   3   2   1

FOR MY FAMILY

CONTENTS

ALL IN THE
FAMILY

PROLOGUE

Between the 1960s and the 2000s, Americans went to war with one another. They fought with words and images, through politics and the law, over what made women and men full citizens of the nation. Across three generations, they questioned everything from women's role in the labor market to their control over reproduction, from men's role as breadwinners to whether they could love each other and marry, and all manner of other explosive issues surrounding gender, sex, and family. By the dawn of the twenty-first century, the contest over civic conceptions of gender roles and sexuality had become deeply etched in competing narratives of national identity. How one understood feminism, abortion, gay rights, welfare, and "family values" signaled one's political allegiances. This book is about how that fight was joined and came to propel the tumultuous transformation of American political culture.

From this vantage point, the arc of history between 1964 and 2004 is clear. In the mid-1960s, a new generation of American social movements, inspired by and often dependent on the black freedom struggle, asserted government's responsibility to ensure equality not just for racial minorities but also for women and sexual minorities. Though hardly united, those movements sought an expansion of the nation's definition of full citizenship and, ultimately, of its social contract. By the turn of the century, this vision had not disappeared—indeed, elements of it had been enshrined in law—but it now competed with family values for Americans' political loyalties. If "equal rights" had been the driving force of American politics in one era, three decades on, "family values" had usurped that position. Those who espoused family values did not reject the equal rights framework in its entirety, but they dismissed elemental features of what it had come to mean, and they put the full force of their considerable political movement behind foreclosing the extent of transformation. Their efforts shifted not just electoral politics but the entire culture of American democracy rightward.[1]

Behind the competing visions of American life were two ideas with far-reaching political consequences: citizens have *a* sex and they *have* sex. Prior to the second half of the twentieth century, the United States, like most societies in the West, rarely recognized the first proposition. Citizens were not imbued with the gender differences assigned by biology. The universal subject of modern democracies was assumed to be a white heterosexual male. Americans did recognize the second proposition, but its implications were hidden behind the all-important distinction between public and private so long employed to divide political from domestic life in classic political thinking. Even as the state regulated everything from women's reproduction to sexual behavior and marriage, sex and sexuality were imagined as private. They were thought to have no meaningful relationship to democratic citizenship. Sporadic political insurgencies over more than a century, led by women and sexual outsiders, had ensured that these inherited assumptions did not go utterly unchallenged. Still, in 1964, when this book begins, powerful assumptions about patriarchal order and heterosexuality shaped society and guided public policy.[2]

Struggles over gender and sexuality necessarily fixed on the place of the family in American politics and culture. The white middle-class nuclear family headed by a patriotic and heterosexual male was central to political contest throughout this period. The idea of that family conveyed such power it is best thought of as a national mythology. Even as that mythology was called into question by women and gay men and lesbians, alongside in various ways the black freedom and the antiwar movements, it remained an abstraction able to determine the political success of left, right, and center. Thus who controlled that mythology mattered. In the 1960s, New Frontier and Great Society liberals such as Lyndon Johnson, Daniel Patrick Moynihan, and Sargent Shriver crafted social and economic policies they believed would make this idealized nuclear family, which had been the object of liberal concern since the New Deal, attainable for more Americans than ever before. They hoped to assist families economically, and I call their collective efforts "breadwinner liberalism."

By 2004, the nuclear family was a conservative emblem, heralded by figures such as George W. Bush, Ann Coulter, and Pat Robertson, and instead of crafting policies to extend opportunity to new segments of society, conservatives endeavored to defend families from what they cast as moral threats. They sought to protect idealized families from moral harm, and I call their collective efforts "breadwinner conservatism." Over these four decades, conservatives won back the power to define the mythological American family, and in the process the Great Society pledge to assist families became the New Right pledge to protect them.

The fact that the ideal nuclear family was never truly representative of how most Americans lived was immaterial. The conflict over this political and ideological fiction was very real: it drove the larger transformation of American democracy over three generations, remaking a center-left social welfare polity established between 1934 and 1972 as the center-right free-market system that emerged from 1973 to 2004.

This transformation was initiated by sixties social movements that challenged the liberal version of the idealized nuclear family by demanding rights not imagined by existing legal and political institutions. Feminists, gay men and lesbians, and nonconformists of all sorts formed organizations such as the Mattachine Society, the National Organization for Women, and the National Welfare Rights Organization. Together such organizations upended existing gender and sexual norms and redefined the public and private spheres of American life. They challenged male privilege, fought for women's equality, and invented the term "sexual politics" to describe the struggle over women's—and later, all—bodies. They brought sexual difference "out of the closet" and pushed for an end to the social and legal banishment of nonheterosexuals. In the broadest sense, they forced Americans to engage in debates about the meaning of manhood and womanhood, what it is to be sexual, what it means to construct families, and what all of these matters have to do with politics and the nation. Their impatient demands and urgent protestations were never limited solely to equal rights, especially among radicals, who pushed for deep and fundamental changes in white male, heterosexual society, but those who channeled their efforts into demands for rights were most able to win influence over law and public policy.[3]

Despite the many victories they won and the importance of their legacy for succeeding generations of Americans, sixties social movements provoked the rise of a powerful new politics on the right: breadwinner conservatism. This politics, which originated in Richard Nixon's notion of the "silent majority" in the late sixties and in the fevered call to arms of Catholics and evangelical Christians in the seventies, found its ultimate expression in opposition to the broad liberal left's idea of expanded citizenship—of an expanded body politic. Conservative activists and politicians, led by George Wallace, Phyllis Schlafly, and Jerry Falwell, among many others, and energized by the legalization of abortion, the demands of feminists, the expansion of welfare, rising crime rates, and the increasing visibility of homosexuality, cast the nuclear family as in crisis and its defense as their patriotic duty. Their views on gender, sexuality, and family made the conservative coalition that coalesced around Ronald Reagan in the 1980s possible. In fact, the way they sought to constrain government interference in an idealized private family sphere was intimately linked to the way they also sought to limit government interference in the private market. These stories are not often told together. Questions of gender, sex, and family have been isolated as part of the "culture war"—a struggle that has been seen as tangential to the politics of equality, power, and money.

The history recounted here shows that Americans rarely fought about equality, power, and money without invoking one idealized version of family or another. The narrow vision of democratic rights and citizenship defended by conservatives in the 1970s in time became the basis of conservative orthodoxy and, by the 1990s, of the nation's political center. The best way to tell this story is not through an election-by-election account of partisan tactical maneuvering and realignment, though elections and political tactics are important. Instead, what unfolds here is an argument about how American disputes over gender, sex, and family were interwoven with a much grander transformation of the national polity itself—the institutions, laws, values, political cultures, and notions of government that constitute civic life—and of how Americans conceived of the nation and the possibility of improving society.

Of course, gender and sexuality were not alone in driving political change in these decades. Race was equally a catalyst. The black freedom insurgency of the 1950s and 1960s dismantled the white supremacist southern Democratic Party, leading to a partisan realignment that saw the white South and much of the growing suburban fringe of the nation's cities vault toward the Republican Party between the 1950s and the 1990s. Black activism set in motion tectonic shifts in American political culture in the second half of the century, as the resistance to black freedom and equality reconfigured partisan loyalties in the South and in prominent northern and western cities. Moreover, the emergence of a law-and-order response to riots and rising crime rates in the late 1960s and of court-ordered school busing and affirmative action in the 1970s discredited black demands for equal rights among many millions of white Americans, regardless of political party. No serious account of political culture in these decades can proceed without taking the measure of the profound struggle over the meaning of black freedom and, ultimately, over the role that racial difference more broadly ought to play in the nation's laws and institutions.[4]

Yet race was far from the only issue restructuring post-1960s American politics. Not long after black demonstrators picketed, sat in, and marched across the country, questions of gender and sexual transformation rattled the nation with equal, and sometimes even greater, force. In many parts of the country, abortion, feminism, and gay rights, rather than racial backlash, animated the most passionate conservative activists in the 1970s and 1980s. Moreover, racial equality itself rested on questions of gender and family: many white Americans believed in the pathological gender roles and families of African Americans and, conversely, millions of black and Latino Americans were convinced that the future of their communities was linked to the strength of "traditional" families. Finally, breadwinner conservatism enjoyed the political advantage of not seeming to invoke race at all. Conservatives' defense of moral, male-breadwinner families often functioned in place of explicit racial segregationism. While race never lost its independent velocity in American life, with formal civil rights achieved by the mid-1960s, racial struggles were often displaced into a breadwinner politics of gender and family.

Rather than seeing race on one hand and gender, sex, and family on the other as distinct crucibles of political contest, we might find it more profitable to conceive of them as intertwined, always in play together in the political shifts between the 1964 Civil Rights Act and the second presidential term of George W. Bush.

•

The hinge of the history recounted in this book is the moment when liberalism came to seem to many millions of ordinary Americans more like a moral threat than an economic helping hand. That moment, which emerged in a series of developments in the 1970s and 1980s, was the product of the two competing political efforts sketched above. As the liberal left pushed to expand the circle of full citizenship to include a vast array of new gender and sexual rights, it called into question the mythological Great Society family. In response, the conservative right insisted on an ever narrower definition of gender and sexual rights and posited a moral family in need of protection as the organizing conceit of government policy. As a result, the liberal left lost political purchase on the mythology of family, while the conservative right gained political purchase on a new, ever more absolute family mythology. Acquiring strength and political acumen through the 1980s, the counterinsurgents cast themselves at the dawn of the twenty-first century as the defenders of a common-sense orthodoxy: family values.[5]

This political contest began in the mid-1960s with manhood under duress. Though always dominant, three core masculine norms—breadwinning, soldiering, and heterosexuality—came under challenge. By the second half of the decade, norms of womanhood—motherhood, domesticity, and heterosexuality—were likewise under assault. The challenges came from the liberal left: the black freedom struggle, the antiwar movement, the homophile movement, and various feminisms, among others. Collectively, they amounted to the century's most far-reaching efforts to redefine the gender and sexual components of citizenship: the rights and obligations of individual Americans, what citizens and the state owe to one another.

Manhood and womanhood were abstractions but also the foundation of public policy. Taken as a whole, the insurgencies that followed and were inspired by the black freedom movement, led by activists ranging from Pauli Murray and Shirley Chisholm to Gloria Steinem and Harvey Milk, developed three core sets of demands. First, equality in the labor market for women. The meaning of equality varied by race and class, but economic rights remained the cornerstone. Second, reproductive and sexual freedom for women. This included access to abortion, the end of forced sterilization, and new legal frameworks for rape and sexual harassment. Third, sexual rights and the end of heterosexual dominance. Radicals among the insurgents cast doubt on the efficacy of "rights" claims alone, but overwhelmingly the tenor of insurgent demands was for the broadest possible citizenship that expanded the social contract forged by earlier generations of Progressive-era, New Deal, and Great Society liberals.

Yet to cast these decades exclusively as a clash between sixties liberalism and eighties conservatism, or left and right, is to foreclose their larger political meaning in American history. Debate and contest were never neatly contained by two sides. Breadwinner liberalism was anathema to feminists, who disagreed vehemently with prominent New Frontier and Great Society liberals. White, black, and Latina women found themselves disagreeing as often as cooperating. Moreover, sexuality was a rather late, and often grudging, addition to the liberal "equal rights" framework, and for much of this period sexual difference provoked derision, even among otherwise liberal-minded Americans such as the feminist Betty Friedan. To make matters even more complex, for much of the 1960s and 1970s, gay men and lesbians (and transgender people) disagreed with one another over the direction of sexual politics. Those who pushed hardest to remake gender, sexuality, and family were hardly united in a single vision of the new society.[6]

If those who sought to remake the social order found themselves at odds with one another, the conservative counterinsurgents were not quite so complex. But they too were hardly monolithic. They were men such as North Carolina Senators Sam Ervin and Jesse Helms, the Baptist minister James Robison, and the Surgeon General under President Reagan, C. Everett Koop, and women such as the presidential candidate Ellen McCormack and the antifeminist activist Connie Marshner. Their numbers included self-declared housewives, high-profile political candidates, Catholic priests, and fire-and-brimstone Protestant ministers. When the latter brought evangelical Christianity into the political arena in the late 1970s, many of their coreligionists loudly opposed such a politicizing of faith. Plenty of Christian ministers would not abide the mixing of the public mandate of government and the private realm of belief. Saving souls and keeping families together, in their view, was the role of the church, and not public policy. An ongoing war *within* American Christianity, rather than the rise of a singular family-values ideology, characterized these decades among religious believers.

If political contest and debate transcended a left-right frame, *family* was ineluctably at the center. Yet that family was always more ideological than real. Rarely, if ever, was a single familial model followed by a majority of actual Americans. Neither the liberal discourse of the Great Society in the 1960s nor the conservative discourse about the traditional American family in the 1990s faced facts. The majority of American families were not constructed of breadwinning husbands and domestic wives at this or any moment in American history. In the middle decades of the twentieth century, the heterosexual nuclear family was a liberal political project. From the New Deal to the Great Society, social welfare liberals created a social safety net, supported labor unions, subsidized vast suburban housing tracts, and created government programs to fight poverty either entirely or in large part to strengthen male-breadwinner nuclear families or to compensate for their temporary instability. But the model of family life and organization with which they worked—in which a married man and woman established a home with only two generations present, and in which the husband worked in the paid workforce while the wife engaged solely in family labor—was largely a fiction based on middle-class ideals of the mid-twentieth century.[7]

Because the heterosexual, male-breadwinner model of family life structured middle-class ideas about domesticity and privacy, anxiety about the decline of the family preoccupied politicians, opinion-makers, and both liberal and conservative activists for decades. And because that model was so central to mid-century American industrial and consumer capitalism, its prospects for the future touched Americans of all walks of life. Some argued that family was the glue holding the social order together, while others countered that its gender arrangements and unquestioned heterosexuality restricted freedom and wrecked lives. But as the political stakes became ever more intense between the 1960s and 1990s, an irony became evident. Americans went about creating a vast array of different kinds of families—same-sex, multigenerational, multiple-breadwinner, single-mother, divorced, remarried—at the same time a political movement advocating social policies based on a narrow, obsolete, and uncommon model of the family gained traction.

This seeming contradiction was possible because the conservative definition of "family values" represented an antiwelfare-state ideology. It was consistent with attacks on social democracy, the emphasis on market-based policies, and the general advance of neoliberalism—meaning a "new" version of classical liberalism's idea of free markets—at the dawn of the twenty-first century. Advocates of gender and sexual orthodoxy blamed the state for eroding "traditional" familial and sexual norms. A safe return to those traditions, they claimed, required reducing the domestic power of the federal government. In fact, full realization of the conservative family-values agenda would have required expansion of the surveillance power of government at all levels. But this reality was less important politically than the synchronizing of gender and sexual orthodoxy with the neoliberal agenda of shrinking the welfare state and its social contract.[8]

•

To understand what was at stake in these years, certain abstractions are necessary. At its most capacious, this is a book about notions of liberal citizenship and individual rights within the longer history of U.S. politics and capitalism. Those Americans who sought new gender and sexual paradigms in these decades came up hard against not just reactionary backlash but some of liberal democracy's greatest evasions and problems. Among these, three are crucial to the book: first, the distinction between the private life of the family and the public life of the citizenry; second, the tension between liberty and equality, between the freedom to do as one wishes and the goal of social equity; and third, the problem of identity, of conceiving of a stable *subject* of democratic rights and governance. These form the pivots of each chapter.

The boundary between private and public was among the most ferociously contested issues in these decades. More than a mantra of second-wave feminism, "the personal is political" is one of the chief ideas by which democratic humanism has been advanced in the last half century. Under this broad rubric, secrets became public, and then the basis of rights. What lived in the shadows of the "private"—abortion, rape, homosexuality, sexual harassment and abuse—activists pushed into the public realm. They contended that gender and sexuality were not private matters but central to public life. The relationships that such debates have called forth—between state authority and the human body, between and among men and women, and among institutions such as marriage, the family, and the law—are constitutive of both everyday life and the economic arrangements of the nation.[9]

The tension between liberty and equality was likewise divisive. Battles over gender and sexuality in these decades invoked the state, meaning all levels of government, and its role in advancing liberty and safeguarding equality. As Americans demanded new rights, they tugged the state in two directions. In one direction, the state simply acknowledged new liberties and allowed citizens to pursue them unhindered. In the other, the state actively assisted citizens in fully exercising their newfound rights. This distinction has often been rendered as the difference between negative liberty, the right to be left alone, and positive liberty, the rights guaranteed by state action. The political arc from equal rights to family values was accompanied by a parallel arc: from a demand for positive rights and robust state action to a reluctant acceptance of negative rights and a weaker state more committed to liberty than equality.[10]

Two examples clarify the impact of this shift. To say that women ought to be free to realize their potential in the workplace is to invoke a negative right: women's freedom to do as they wish. It is different to say that in order for women to exercise this right fully, they require additional state action: guaranteed maternity leave and child care, for instance, or affirmative action in hiring. These are positive rights. A similar dynamic is at work in the realm of sexuality. To say that men and women are free to love, and engage in sex with, whomever they wish is to invoke a negative right: to be left alone. It is again different to say that full citizenship requires the state to guarantee the equality of same-sex relationships: by recognizing same-sex marriage, for instance. This is a positive right. What activists on the liberal left learned in the 1960s and 1970s is that the more a right is rendered in negative terms, the more it becomes wealth sensitive—that is, the more it disproportionately benefits members of society who already possess resources. This truism, more than anything else, both inspired insurgents to seek greater protections and divided them along economic lines.

Conflict over gender, sex, and family in these decades was thus not simply a "cultural war," if that term is meant to imply a sharp distinction between culture and political economy. Such a distinction is false and historically misleading. Debates about Americans' sexual practices and intimate lives, women's reproduction, and the nature of family are inseparable from the history of capitalism and the modern liberal state. This cannot be emphasized enough. At its heart, the social contract overseen by government mediates the relationship among individuals, social institutions such as the family, and the market. The question is not *whether* gender, sex, and family are structured and regulated by the state; the question is what kinds of regulations exist and to what end. When commentators began in the 1980s to distinguish between "cultural" or "values" conservatives and economic conservatives, they identified a distinction between political constituencies, not an underlying reality of American life.

Finally, there is the problem of identity in American democracy. Those on the liberal left who sought to reimagine the subject of democratic governance faced considerable challenges. They argued that women and men, male and female, sex and sexuality are in the end socially constituted, made by human society. As such, they can be remade. To imagine a social order in which a lesbian mother, a female physician, and a poor African American man with AIDS are all equal citizens is a noble and morally just goal. But it is not easy to bring that social order into being. To be inclusive and to live up to its professed values, the liberal left embraced multiple identities, which proved both internally divisive and especially difficult when political opponents posited fixed identities in response. Americans who argued that manhood and womanhood are largely, or even entirely, invented and thus can be reimagined faced the considerable challenge of opponents who claimed the opposite: that manhood and womanhood, sex and sexuality, are fixed and timeless. And this is to say nothing of the millions of ordinary Americans who did not see themselves as partisans in a national fight over the family and who endeavored to make sense of how the epic political battles of these decades would affect their inherited, and often cherished, ideas about manhood, womanhood, and family.

Americans rewrote the social contract over the course of the last half century to broaden women's citizenship, protect racial and sexual difference, permit greater freedom in intimate private lives, and ensure greater liberty in the construction of families. By the early 2000s, the results of the rewritten social contract had become evident, and they were decidedly mixed. Many Americans lived in a resolutely new world—where new gender roles were celebrated, sexualities of all sorts were openly accepted, and family had been redefined. But many others rejected that world, or certainly large parts of it, and fought politically to sustain a social order governed by what they called "traditional" values. Still others, largely among the working class and poor but increasingly among segments of the middle class as well, enjoyed far less choice about the kind of world they could create. Whatever the outcome for individual Americans, the battle over what it means to be an American citizen, to be a member of the body politic—from the first efforts to include "sex" in the 1964 Civil Rights Act to the 2003 *Lawrence v. Texas* decision by the Supreme Court that struck down sodomy laws—changed the political order of the nation.

Just as profoundly, this battle revealed a central limitation of American democracy. Radicals and reformers alike in this era recognized that the white heterosexual male breadwinner was an impoverished model for conceiving of a democratic subject, a modern citizen. But they struggled mightily to bring into being a political order based on anything else. The liberal left had defined its political subject—one with varying gender, sexual, racial, and class inflections—in ways that the political philosophy and institutions underlying American democracy could not fully accommodate. The liberal left could win, within limits, *freedom* to do as one pleased. But it could not win positive rights that would make such freedom meaningful to many, many Americans. Meanwhile, conservatives found themselves advocating a form of freedom—market-based, without government meddling—that was at the heart of that very political philosophy. Americans now live, whether they recognize it day to day or not, in the long shadow of that battle.

PART 1

THIS IS A MAN'S WORLD, 1964–1973

1

ARE YOU MAN ENOUGH?
SIXTIES BREADWINNER LIBERALISM

On a March morning in 1964, the day after President Lyndon Johnson announced his War on Poverty, Sargent Shriver climbed the Capitol steps to deliver a report to Congress on the Job Corps, the centerpiece of the new president's employment plan. Brother-in-law to the slain John F. Kennedy and former director of the Peace Corps, Shriver was confident that the administration's antipoverty initiative reflected sound liberal economic theory and embodied Kennedy's legacy.

Others were less convinced. "What brought about this limitation to young *men?*" the Oregon congresswoman Edith Green asked Shriver. A longtime advocate for women's rights—she had sponsored the 1963 Equal Pay Act—Green was the lone woman on the committee considering Shriver's report. "Are there not as many young women in this age group?"[1]

Shriver's response was telling: "The general purpose of these [employment] centers" was to help young men who "we hope will be heads of families." Naturally, he continued, men were charged with "supporting a family." Prepared for such an answer, Green asked if, because the military already absorbed a large number of disadvantaged young men, there was not a "greater need" to train and employ young women?[2]

The following day, Secretary of Defense Robert McNamara, the clean-cut former president of the Ford Motor Company and emblem of Camelot's masculine resolve, arrived on Capitol Hill to explain another component of the president's War on Poverty, the Pentagon's plan to "rehabilitate" half a million young men who had failed the Selective Service exam. As she had with Shriver, Green asked McNamara why the administration seemed oblivious of the problems facing women. Plenty of young women, she told the defense secretary, "are bogged down because of poverty and are disadvantaged culturally, economically, and educationally." McNamara echoed Shriver by asserting one of the assumptions of the era: "Boys are likely to be the heads of families and the primary breadwinners in the family."[3]

Breadwinning was the ideal that had supported both middle-class domesticity and working-class demands for the "family wage" since the nineteenth century. Breadwinning divided labor by gender: men's work was public, remunerative, family sustaining, while women's work was domestic, caregiving, and, if it was remunerative, supplementary to their husbands' wages. He performed market work; she performed family work. The social psychologist Morris Zelditch summed up the era's conventional wisdom in 1955, writing that "the American male, by definition, must 'provide' for his family . . . his primary function in the family is to supply 'income,' to be the 'breadwinner.'" Male breadwinning was so taken for granted that it was not even acknowledged as an ideology, as a choice. It functioned as an organizing mythology of social life and was believed to be the bedrock of a sound family and by extension a sound society. Its pervasive influence explains a great deal about how Americans struggled to shape the social order in these decades.[4]

This male head of household contracting his labor in the marketplace was more than social science and cultural touchstone, however. He drove public policy. In the 1930s he was enshrined in the New Deal welfare state, which sought to assist the breadwinner's efforts in the market. Inasmuch as the nation had developed a national employment policy—through legislation such as the 1935 Social Security and Wagner acts, the 1937 Fair Labor Standards Act, and the 1946 Employment Act—it was based on male-breadwinner ideology. The New Deal's "citizen worker" and the nuclear family he headed remained a mainstay of conventional liberal thinking and a cornerstone of the Keynesian consensus that guided 1960s economic policy, which together can be called breadwinner liberalism.[5]

For the greater part of the sixties, Green and women like her had little success in challenging breadwinner liberalism. During the heady days of Kennedy's New Frontier and Johnson's Great Society, men, and their status as citizen workers, monopolized the attention of big-picture policy thinkers. The nation's liberal establishment knew that women engaged in market work. After all, federal and state governments offered vocational programs that trained women and provided the poorest among them with needed services. But postwar liberals nonetheless consistently underestimated the growing importance of women's market labor to the fate of families and the nation. They remained well behind a curve that was to define the last third of the twentieth century: the shifting of greater and greater economic responsibilities within the American household, and in the country at large, onto the backs of women.[6]

Yet before Great Society liberalism ran headlong into the women's movement in the late sixties, the black freedom movement had already politicized the nation's breadwinners. Compelled by the surging calls for civil rights and African American equality, liberal officials, from Johnson, Shriver, and McNamara to Robert Weaver and Wilbur Cohen, came to believe that ending racial discrimination and embarking on ambitious antipoverty and affirmative action programs would allow heretofore marginalized black men to become productive workers and heads of families. They sought to expand the reach of breadwinner liberalism to encompass black men. Such efforts collided with a white working-class breadwinner ideology, which championed a presumptively race-neutral ethic of male labor and responsibility. In a paradox that would produce decades of conflict, breadwinner ideology thus became the basis for both a liberal project of racial recompense and equal opportunity and the conservative resistance provoked by that project.

Because so few Americans questioned the naturalness of the nuclear family, what most divided Great Society liberals from their opponents was the nature and extent of government assistance. Liberals' focus in the sixties on the deficiencies of male breadwinners, especially nonwhite ones, opened a political flank exploited by the opponents of civil rights and the welfare state, critics such as George Wallace or the conservative columnists Rowland Evans and Robert Novak. If men failed to become breadwinners and support families, these opponents argued, it was a personal failure, not a social one. Breadwinners *earned* their places at the heads of families; their jobs and income were products of individual effort. Government, these critics conceded, should certainly endorse market freedom for potential breadwinners, a classic "negative" right. But to take further, positive steps to ensure equality was to overextend government's mandate. The allegedly race-blind meritocratic individualism that supplanted forthright segregationism during and especially after the 1960s was a version of breadwinning that could be bent toward a distinctly conservative view of social policy. Arguments against civil rights, affirmative action, and other state interventions on behalf of people of color and poor people increasingly bore the stamp of this individualist, bootstrap version of male-breadwinner ideology. Manhood signaled many things, dependency on government not among them.[7]

As Green's dispute with Shriver and McNamara demonstrated, conservative opposition was hardly breadwinner liberalism's only obstacle. It suffered its own blinders. Breadwinner liberalism failed to come to terms with women's rapidly evolving relationship to work. It posited marriage, not the marketplace, as the vehicle for women's economic security and public standing. The nation's marketplace, the remunerative economic sphere, remained the public world of men. Financially taken care of by her husband, a woman could preoccupy herself with domestic goals, avoiding the rough-and-tumble workplace and the vagaries of the market. Such a model of the sexes, derived largely from nineteenth-century white middle-class notions of public and private spheres, never described a majority of Americans in any decade, but it grew woefully outdated as the long post-war economic boom began to fizzle in the late 1960s.[8]

Breadwinner liberalism represented the dominant liberal thinking in the early sixties. Its advocates believed it to be the best, most politically defensible alternative to socialism on the left and free-market libertarianism on the right. Yet it was far narrower than its architects imagined and therefore vulnerable to social movements that would point out its exclusions. In particular, the rising political fortunes of African Americans and women threw inherited notions of breadwinning, and therefore breadwinner liberalism, into turmoil. The centrality of the male breadwinner was such that the disputes that erupted over him, the critiques leveled at him, and the defenses marshaled on his behalf set in motion a decades-long political and cultural transformation.

•

Two distinct ways of thinking about work and family clashed in the first half of the 1960s. One focused on women. Its advocates—namely, a small but growing coterie of female trade unionists, academics, and politicians (such as Edith Green)—argued that with women constituting more than one-third of the paid workforce, the male-breadwinner ideal was becoming a historical relic. In 1962 blue- and pink-collar and professional women together contributed between one-quarter and one-third of family income in the United States, and one in ten households was headed solely by a woman (one in four among African American women). The obstacles these women faced were abundant: low wages, job and educational discrimination, sex segregation, and unaffordable child care.[9]

The second and more influential way of thinking focused on men. New Frontier and Great Society liberals worried deeply about male unemployment, the replacement of manpower by machine power in the nation's factories, and the racial discrimination that kept black men underemployed and in poverty. Though they pushed for better education and training of young working-class men of all backgrounds, they devoted their greatest attention to the reality that too many impoverished fathers, black and white, would not or could not support families. Liberals stressed the need to rehabilitate the male breadwinner—through social programs, remunerative market work, and military service—and return him to his proper place at the head of the family.[10]

Those who focused on women were divided. Since the 1940s labor union women had led the fight for higher wages and better working conditions for female workers. Sensitive to the precarious balance between women's paid work and family work, they sought a broad array of reforms aimed at helping them, especially equal pay for equal work, government-subsidized child care, and maternity leave. Their influence, though limited, came from the women's divisions of major trade unions, including auto, meatpacking, and electrical workers, female-dominated unions such as the clothing and garment workers, statewide AFL-CIO federations, and the Women's Bureau of the U.S. Department of Labor. By the early 1960s their political efforts had begun to reap small rewards. In 1961, President Kennedy fulfilled a long-standing goal of the Women's Bureau when he created the President's Commission on the Status of Women (PCSW) and appointed the labor reformer Esther Peterson to run it. And in 1963 Congress passed the Equal Pay Act, for which Peterson and other prominent labor union women had lobbied since World War II.[11]

Labor union women came from diverse backgrounds to unite over common objectives. Dollie Lowther Robinson, the daughter of southern black sharecroppers, migrated in the 1930s to New York City, where she organized a union of laundry workers. She advised the Women's Bureau in the 1940s and later earned a law degree and served as secretary of labor in New York State. Mary Callahan, a widow and mother of one, took a factory job in the electrical industry in the 1930s. She later helped win provisions for maternity leave in union contracts. Kennedy appointed her to the PCSW in 1961. Robinson and Callahan believed in women's equality to men, but they also saw an economic marketplace that exploited women and compromised their ability to be mothers. As a result, they and women like them fought for minimum wages and hours for women—so-called protective legislation—alongside maternity leave and child care, treading the fine line between a woman's freedom to work and her family responsibilities.[12]

Labor union women's support for protective laws and their reluctance to challenge sex segregation—the relegation of women into jobs men preferred not to do—left them vulnerable to charges that they did not support full workplace equality. After all, in a market where women constituted 86 percent of elementary school teachers, 97 percent of physicians' assistants and dental hygienists, and 97 percent of secretaries but less than 5 percent of lawyers and physicians, protective legislation was a limited approach to improving women's options. Women needed access to the entire occupational ladder—not special treatment as women but equal treatment as workers.[13]

This view was strongly supported by the National Woman's Party (NWP). The NWP had long disparaged the Women's Bureau and its reformist objectives. This division among feminists dated to the 1920s, when the NWP had first introduced the Equal Rights Amendment (ERA) and embraced full equality with men in the labor market. Led and supported by professional women from middle- and upper-class backgrounds—often known as equal rights feminists—the NWP chafed at the barriers to women's full participation in market work and rejected a model of female citizenship constrained by motherhood and family.[14]

Both contingents wanted to expand economic opportunity and ease the double burden of paid work and family work, but they viewed the market from different perspectives. Equal rights feminists argued that sex discrimination denied women personal fulfillment and depressed female wages across the economy. They viewed the market from the top down. Labor feminists countered that if left unprotected to compete with men in the market, women would be exploited by employers and would lose support for motherhood. They saw the market from the bottom up. The differing viewpoints stemmed from class realities. For middle-class women, the problem was forced domesticity and denial of access to the market.

For working-class women, the problem was forced market labor and the denial of full-time domesticity.[15]

However divided, women's activists generated real political momentum in the mid-sixties. They were not yet powerful enough, however, to displace deeply ingrained habits of mind, as well as economic and social theory, in which the problems of men were the overriding concern of economic policy and equal rights legislation.

To many observers, these problems appeared most acute among African Americans. In the tenets of breadwinner liberalism, black men occupied a special, troubled place. Owing to a segregated labor market and a racist labor movement, black men were unemployed at far higher rates than whites. An accomplishment of the black freedom movement was to make this a pressing national concern. "The virtual exclusion of Negroes from apprenticeship and other training programs," Herbert Hill, labor director of the NAACP, wrote in 1962, "forces them to remain as marginal employees in the economy and directly affects the economic well-being of the entire Negro community." In his 1964 book *To Be Equal*, the Urban League's Whitney Young estimated that "one million Negroes—one out of every four Negro workers—are unemployed," a crisis for African Americans and the country. "Either we make these people constructive citizens," he predicted, "or they are going to be destructive dependents." Invoking breadwinner ideology, Young worried about black families' long-term reliance on government assistance or their detachment from the labor market altogether. Dependents were not providers. They were not real men.[16]

The crisis that so disturbed Young dated to the 1940s and 1950s. Between 1945 and 1960 national black unemployment hovered around 10 percent, but it spiked to 15–18 percent in industrial cities such as Detroit, Oakland, and Chicago. Typically, young black men found themselves unemployed at twice the rate of their elders—as high as 30–40 percent in some cities. Automation, plant relocation, and racial discrimination closed much of the nation's industrial labor market to young black men for nearly two decades, even as migration from southern farms to northern cities increased. In a society based on male breadwinning, so many unemployed men did not invoke the language of crisis only because black leaders were unable to penetrate national racism and draw attention to the problem until the 1960s.[17]

Civil rights leaders were not oblivious of black women's fate in the labor market—where married black women were 50 percent more likely than married white women to work for wages—but they saw the unemployment and underemployment of men as more urgent. For many civil rights leaders, racial progress was inseparably linked to the capacity of African American families to create the male-breadwinner, female-homemaker household presumed to be enjoyed by whites. The common goal of the upwardly mobile black family involved trading a woman's domestic labor in a white home for prideful domestic labor in her own home.[18]

The long fight for fair employment based on race stretched back to the 1930s. In the middle years of that decade, the National Association for the Advancement of Colored People (NAACP) and the National Urban League (NUL) campaigned unsuccessfully to have nondiscrimination guarantees included in major New Deal legislation. A. Philip Randolph's March on Washington Movement, which won establishment of the wartime Fair Employment Practice Committee (FEPC) during World War II, was a continuation of those efforts. But Congress refused to extend the FEPC after the war. Randolph, the NAACP, and a generation of African American activists then spent two decades endeavoring to place fair employment on the national political agenda. With each passing year, the crisis in black communities grew worse.

As black leaders drew attention to the marketplace's racial bias, women's advocates attempted to draw attention to its gender bias. Among the contributors to the PCSW, the most forward thinking was the African American civil rights activist and feminist intellectual Pauli Murray, who told the commission that women should push "to extend the concept of equal protection of the law to discrimination grounded in sex and sex alone." The commission's 1963 report to the president, entitled *American Women*, fell short of Murray's ambitious agenda. Still, it far outstripped the conventional wisdom of New Frontier liberalism, calling for significant government action on behalf of women in the marketplace, in health and child care, and in property and divorce law. Presenting women as more than wives and mothers (without dismissing those roles), *American Women* introduced a new concept to liberal politics: women experienced a set of problems *because* they were women. There was no universal genderless citizen.[19]

Following Kennedy's assassination, Congress considered the Civil Rights Act, which promised equal rights to all racial groups, including labor market protections. It was, first and foremost, a response to the civil rights movement, which is more accurately called the black freedom movement, since its objectives went beyond civil standing to economic and political justice. Women's advocates monitored the bill carefully, hoping that it might advance their interests as well. But "sex" was added to its protections through an unexpected route. Howard Smith, a segregationist congressman from Virginia and chair of the powerful House Rules Committee, introduced, to provoke his political enemies and possibly defeat the bill, an amendment to add "sex" to race, color, religion, and national origin in the act's employment section. Smith told Congress that since the "bill is so imperfect, what harm will this little amendment do?"[20]

Esther Peterson was incredulous at Smith's gambit. So was Edith Green, who pointed out that "the strongest *proponents* of the sex amendment were the Southerners who were the strongest *opponents* of the equal pay for equal work legislation." Moreover, many of the members of the National Woman's Party who encouraged Smith, led by Nina Horton Avery, were themselves devoted segregationists—whites loath to see the rights of African Americans, male or female, advanced ahead of their own.[21]

Smith's sex amendment threw women's advocates into disarray. Green feared that its inclusion would either defeat the bill outright or, if the bill passed, would invalidate women's protective legislation. But Murray, who coined the term "Jane Crow," possessed a keener sense of the kinds of discrimination black women faced and believed that Title VII would do little for them without the inclusion of "sex." She urged Green in a private letter to "reflect upon the significance of this amendment for Negro women." Other proponents of the sex amendment, however, couched their support in unapologetically racist language. One southern congressman reminded his colleagues that without the amendment a white woman "would be drastically discriminated against in favor of a Negro woman," an abomination he could not sanction. The result was a strange political alliance. Pauli Murray, a dedicated black freedom and women's advocate, found herself allied with segregationists in favor of the amendment, while Green, a women's advocate and a fierce defender of black rights, opposed them both.[22]

The sex amendment remained in the bill but played little role in its ultimate fate, which hinged almost exclusively on its racial implications. To everyone save women's advocates, the Civil Rights Act's prohibition of sex discrimination was a joke. Politicians across the political spectrum considered distinctions based on sex, not their abolishment, desirable. Women's biological difference, the self-evident priority of their family work, and their "femininity" demanded such distinctions. The liberal *New Republic* wondered if "a mischievous joke perpetrated on the floor of the House of Representatives" should be taken seriously "by a responsible administrative body." Conservatives at *The Wall Street Journal* struck a similarly dismissive tone, asking readers to imagine "a shapeless, knobby-kneed male 'bunny' serving drinks" or a "matronly vice president" chasing "a male secretary." Male breadwinning determined thinking about market work and family work to such an extent that Americans by and large could not imagine women's paid labor as anything but secondary, existing in a realm of distinct and segregated "women's work." To suggest otherwise was laughable.[23]

When the Equal Employment Opportunity Commission (EEOC), charged with enforcing Title VII, began to consider the new law in 1965, its chairman, Franklin Roosevelt, Jr., placed little emphasis on sex discrimination. Addressing racial discrimination, he believed, was of far greater import. Like most liberal Americans, the leaders of the commission saw racial discrimination as unnatural and harmful and sex discrimination as natural. Given the presumptions of the era and the crisis of black male unemployment, that conclusion is understandable—and many at the time believed utterly defensible. Unknowingly and largely unintentionally, however, the insertion of "sex" into Title VII would in time prove providential, becoming in the late sixties and seventies a means by which women could make their second-class economic citizenship a question of rights. Still, it would be two years, during which time women flooded the EEOC with sex discrimination complaints and founded the National Organization for Women (NOW), before the commission even began to consider the marketplace's sex inequalities.[24]

•

The Civil Rights Act was not even a year old when a quick trio of thunderclaps struck the black freedom movement in 1965. In February, Harlem buried Malcolm X. "Malcolm was our manhood, our living, black manhood," the actor and activist Ossie Davis said in his eulogy to the overflow crowd of mourners on 125th Street. Then that spring an assistant secretary of labor under President Johnson, Daniel Patrick Moynihan, drafted *The Negro Family: The Case for National Action*, which introduced the haunting phrase "tangle of pathology" into the civil rights debate. The following August, just days after Johnson had signed the Voting Rights Act, black residents in Watts, Los Angeles, burned and looted nearly a hundred square blocks of homes and businesses. Each event drew breadwinner liberalism closer to the center of national debate about what the nation owed African Americans and what they owed the nation.[25]

Malcolm X called for black freedom "by any means necessary," but he and the Nation of Islam stressed male responsibility. A political radical, Malcolm X, owing to his religion, was a patriarchal conservative. He attributed his escape from the world of chaotic street violence to "manly" self-discipline and took after black leaders like Robert F. Williams, the North Carolina advocate of black self-defense, who told an NAACP audience in 1959 that "we as men should stand up as men and protect our women and children." Malcolm X's belief system involved adherence to a "strict moral code and discipline," including a lifetime commitment to abstain from alcohol, tobacco, narcotics, and other vices and a pledge to "shelter and protect and *respect*" black women. Malcolm X saw no contradiction between his radical politics and his conservative vision of the black family.[26]

That vision was widely shared in African American communities. In April 1963 eleven black leaders had met to draft a report for Kennedy's Commission on the Status of Women. Cernoria Johnson of the National Urban League insisted that in "trying to strengthen family life," it was imperative to address "the male, in order to bring the picture together." Dorothy Height, president of the National Council of Negro Women, concurred. "Negro women," Height said, must respond to the black man's need to feel respected "in order that he may strengthen his home." Johnson, Height, and the other middle-class women present agreed that black women needed better access to education and good jobs but stressed that the central goal of public policy ought to be securing a male breadwinner at the head of the black family. Echoing such sentiments, a black youth project director in Los Angeles told the Nation of Islam's *Muhammad Speaks*: "When a man cannot find employment which pays enough to support his family, this man becomes less than a man."[27]

Moynihan's report represented a scholarly if strained version of the same idea. Theorizing that black men were "trapped in a tangle of pathology," fathering children out of wedlock and eschewing the breadwinner role, *The Negro Family* warned that "the Negro family in the urban ghettos is crumbling." Federal policy, the report argued, should set "a new kind of national goal: the establishment of a stable Negro family." Echoing prominent social science dating to W.E.B. Du Bois's 1908 *Negro American Family* that found subsequent expression in E. Franklin Frazier's 1939

The Negro Family in the United States, Gunnar Myrdal's 1945 *American Dilemma,* and Kenneth Clark's 1965 *Dark Ghetto,* Moynihan blamed black men's abandonment of the family on joblessness, white racism, and the legacies of slavery. In the vacuum created by male flight, Moynihan observed, a matriarchy had arisen. This "deviant" family structure led to a "startling increase in welfare dependency," the "fundamental problem" in the contemporary black community.[28]

No social welfare policy should concern the country more, Moynihan concluded, than restoring black men to the breadwinning head of the family. Out of Malcolm X's mouth, the identical claim was embedded in a complex conversation among African Americans about their cultural history and collective destiny. Coming from Moynihan, it could be interpreted as another in the history of white sexual mythologies about black Americans. Indeed, Moynihan's report seemed to rationalize African Americans' second-class citizenship on the basis of their alleged familial pathology.[29]

Soon after Moynihan's assessment came the final thunderclap. On an August evening two California highway patrolmen stopped twenty-one-year-old Marquette Frye at 116th and Avalon in Watts, on the far south side of Los Angeles. Frye's mother, Rena, hurried down the street to prevent her car, which Marquette had been driving while intoxicated, from being impounded. Accounts of what happened next vary, but what is certain is that after his mother appeared, the officers took issue with Frye's behavior and handled him roughly. Brandishing guns, they faced a gathering crowd of onlookers accustomed to the indignities of routine police brutality. When Frye resisted, the white officers beat him. Rena intervened on behalf of her son, and she was promptly arrested. It was a complex drama of family, manhood, and white repression that could have taken place in virtually any black community in early-sixties America.[30]

In Watts, though, the outcome was different. News of the arrests and beating, along with wild rumors, spread up Avalon. The neighborhood erupted. Residents reacted with a wave of burning, looting, and scuffles with police that built slowly over several hours and eventually engulfed more than ninety square blocks in flames and violence for seven days. The worst riot of the twentieth century left a stunning 34 dead, 1,042 injured, and 3,952 arrested. Watts shocked whites, including a dispirited President Johnson. Disheartened African American leaders, who had celebrated the signing of the Voting Rights Act a week earlier, feared a backlash from the largely white authorities. Watts, filtered through the perspective of Moynihan, brought breadwinner liberalism to the fore as the primary crucible of debate over African Americans' place in the nation.[31]

The McCone Commission, appointed by California Governor Edmund G. Brown, convened to investigate the riot in the autumn of 1965. Moynihan's logic played a major role in its conclusions. Brown himself blamed the riot on "a scene of broken families and broken hearts, of lonely children and aimless adults." The "sickness in the center of our cities," the McCone report read, began with joblessness and thwarted ambitions, which together led to "a family whose breadwinner is chronically out of work" and "invariably a disintegrating family." Activists and politicians testified to a more complex reality, citing the long history of police brutality, housing discrimination, and other obstacles African Americans faced, but to no avail. The McCone Commission gave birth to an archetype: the rootless, unemployed, and fatherless black man prone to violence.[32]

Two months before the riot, President Johnson had also drawn heavily on Moynihan's report, then an internal administration document, for a frank and widely praised speech at Howard University. Standing before graduating seniors, representatives of the rising postwar black middle class, he touched on America's history of racial discrimination, especially "the centuries of oppression and persecution of the Negro man," which had led to the "breakdown of the Negro family structure." Ending racial oppression, he declared, would be "a chief goal of my administration, and of my program next year, and in the years to come." The section of the speech on "family breakdown" drew applause from the audience, striking a chord among men and women who could assume he did not mean them. The Howard University speech represented the rhetorical high point of the Great Society's efforts to expand breadwinner liberalism—to expand the social and economic citizenship promised in the New Deal. Away from the public eye, Johnson presented his policy goals in blunter language: "to teach these nigras that don't know anything how to work for themselves, instead of just breeding."[33]

Moynihan's report ambushed black leaders. Despite its resonance with thinking in black circles, most African Americans, as Michele Wallace later wrote, "wanted to cut Daniel Moynihan's heart out and feed it to the dogs." Responding to the report seemed imperative because members of the media, along with liberal allies and civil rights opponents alike, constantly invoked it. James Farmer, director of CORE and one of the report's most vigorous critics, spoke for many when he insisted that

"Moynihan has provided a massive academic copout for the whole white conscience."[34]

Moynihan and Watts undermined the extraordinary legislative gains of 1964 and 1965. Together the report and riot threatened the black freedom movement's still-tenuous legitimacy among whites and shifted the national discussion away from the moral legitimacy of black demands to familial arrangements in the black community. Black freedom activists had no other options but to recalibrate their message for a debate about black manhood. For in the hands of anti-civil-rights conservatives such as the South Carolina senator Strom Thurmond and the West Virginia senator Robert C. Byrd, as well as the commentators William F. Buckley, Rowland Evans, and Robert Novak, the supposed gender role pathology of impoverished African American families became an argument against, not for, greater government attention to African American rights—the opposite of what Moynihan had intended. It was not the first time, nor would it be the last, that opponents of racial equality would posit moral decline as an argument against government action in the realm of civil rights.[35]

Many commentators, black and white, viewed Moynihan through a Freudian lens of sexual psychodrama. "The breakup [of the black family]," wrote psychologist Webster Argow, "acted as a psychological castration of the male." Black men, this line of reasoning suggested, faced emasculation at the hands of whites in public and at the hands of black women in private. Castration and emasculation became such accepted metaphors for black men's status that the first generation of civil-rights-era feminists and womanists, as Alice Walker was to name them, confronted the trope out of necessity. In their 1969 essay in *Liberator*, Jean Carey Bond and Patricia Peery asked, "Has the black male been castrated?" They answered with a resounding no, but their argument—that Moynihan relied on specious gender stereotypes rooted in slavery and white supremacist thought—confirmed how thoroughly the debate over black rights had become entangled with arguments about gender roles.[36]

The Moynihan report's portrait of male unemployment as devastating to black families and communities has been vindicated. But this portrait was not revelatory in 1965, especially among African American activists. What Moynihan did get wrong was his depiction of black "matriarchy," which suffered from the gender assumptions common to most liberal social scientists of the era. He was right about the long-term consequences of absent or out-of-work fathers, but his dismissive tone toward black women struggling to keep family and home together was to haunt and constrain future political efforts to defend poor black communities.[37]

At the time of its release, however, the report's political impact trumped questions about its accuracy. Many journalists and commentators either failed to read the entire report or distilled its complex message to the enticing and sensational "tangle of pathology." Most damaging was a column by Evans and Novak that appeared on August 18 as Watts lay smoldering. Implying that family breakdown had *caused* the rioting, they ignored the report's focus on economic discrimination and the legacy of slavery and segregation. How the nation responded to the report, they concluded, "may determine whether this country is doomed to succeeding summers of guerilla warfare in our cities." By neglecting the report's indictment of slavery, Jim Crow, job discrimination, and white racism, reporters and conservative activists ignored social context and reported simply on "family breakdown" or, worse, "castration." By admitting the legacy of slavery and Jim Crow, as Moynihan did, one could see broken black families as subjects of democratic rights and amenable to government intervention. Shear that legacy away, as many conservatives chose to do, and there remained only fixed pathologies beyond help or hope.[38]

Not a few commentators since 1965 have lamented that black leaders and white liberals largely rejected the report and enforced silence on the subject for decades. In refusing to see any validity in Moynihan's work, these commentators have argued, liberals made it impossible to discuss crucial questions of black male responsibility even though many black leaders themselves acknowledged the importance of such questions. This line of reasoning is understandable, but it raises a crucial question: How could the report not have been rejected? Its transformation of a moral crusade for equal rights into a discussion of gender role pathology seemed guaranteed to disable the movement at that historical moment. In the previous eighteen months, Congress had passed the most important equality legislation in a hundred years. The president had announced both the War on Poverty and a new commitment to equality *of result* among the nation's citizens. The worst riot of the century had taken place in August. Nationally, unemployment among young black men ranged between 15 and a staggering 30 percent. All this had carried the black freedom movement to its most important crossroad since emancipation. Pushing forward would require a combination of immense political capital, wide public support, compelling moral authority, and a committed national state. Moynihan, however unwittingly and unintentionally, offered an escape hatch from that difficult work ahead. To accept a discussion at that historical moment on the terrain of moral and familial dysfunction was already to have lost the debate.

The pathologizing of African American men placed African American women in an almost untenable position. They heard from all sides that their job was to support "their men." "It was her man," wrote the Chicago psychiatrist Kermit Mehlinger, "who bore the full impact of the white man's oppression." Navigating those demands, especially in the context of an emerging women's movement led by whites, would prove treacherous for black women's advocates. But these demands would also be the starting point for a distinctly African American feminism. In 1966, at the height of the Moynihan debate, Pauli Murray wrote to the Johnson aide William Yancey to say that "by stressing the matriarchal nature of Negro family life, the Moynihan report failed to place it in the broader context of changes in American family life generally." Murray meant that American women of all kinds, black and white, pink-, blue-, and white-collar, were becoming family providers because of economic necessity. Taking the Moynihan report at face value, she cautioned, could have "the possible result that Negro males would be pitted against Negro females in a highly competitive instead of cooperative endeavor." The report, she implied, wrongly encouraged black women to step back so that black men could step up.[39]

•

Few periods in American history match the urgency of the half decade after Watts. One compelling voice that embodied the intensity of these years belonged to Stokely Carmichael, who issued his call for "black power" in a June 1966 speech in Greenwood, Mississippi. Tough-minded, erudite, and sickened by the intransigency of white authorities since the 1954 *Brown v. Board of Education* decision, Carmichael called for black unity and political power, drawing from Malcolm X, the Harlem congressman Adam Clayton Powell, Jr., and the Ghanian president Kwame Nkrumah. Black power awakened more than rage. It pulled forward the long-sought objective of self-determination, in which black communities were not supplicants of white favor but autonomous agents of their own will. In that context, black power also served as a vehicle for men to lay claim to both a heroic and a breadwinning manhood.[40]

The notion of black power stretched centuries in black consciousness. Its roots lay in the notion that African Americans ought to control their own communities, own their own assets, and set the terms of their relationship to the larger society, rather than have to live as whites instructed them to. When Carmichael called for "black people to begin to define their own goals, to lead their own organizations and to support those organizations," his words resonated with African Americans across the country whose communities had by necessity been shaped by self-help and built on a foundation of racial pride. "I would rather have a black man make forty mistakes in the next year if he was doing it out of love and unity . . . than have a white man do everything for me," Detroit's Rev. Albert Cleague wrote in 1968. Self-help was one cornerstone of black power. Another was the refusal to do the bidding of whites. When he defied the U.S. government by refusing to serve in Vietnam in 1967, Muhammad Ali said to white America: "I don't have to be what you want me to be." Black power's reclamation of manhood was therefore a double gesture. It was an assertion of humanity. But it was also an expression of a more literal manhood: the courageousness, the audacity of that assertion was a manly one.[41]

Defense of family and community against white violence had long been an African American man's responsibility. As Carmichael explained in his 1966 speech, such defense had become even more critical because of the violent turn of white authorities and vigilantes since 1954—what James Boggs called white barbarism. The Emmett Till murder in 1955, the bricks that greeted black high school students in Little Rock, Arkansas, in 1957, the savage beating and firebombing of freedom riders in 1961, Medgar Evers's murder in 1963, the killing of four black girls in Birmingham, Alabama, and three Freedom Summer volunteers in Mississippi in 1964, the mass beatings at the Edmund Pettus Bridge in Selma, Alabama, in 1965, and the murder of Sammy Younge in 1966, among countless others—the names and years invoke an era of brutal white repression. In the face of such violence, against the backdrop of the Moynihan report, a new generation of young African American men followed Carmichael in saying "enough." Their adoption of the working-class argot and exaggerated masculine bearing of the street and their refusal to please whites signaled authentic black manhood.[42]

White commentators preoccupied themselves with the meaning of Carmichael's declaration and its association with violence, especially potential violence against whites. Panic turned to hysteria in May 1967, when

Huey Newton and the Black Panthers marched legally and peacefully into the California Assembly with rifles on their hips. Most whites did not see themselves implicated in violence against African Americans and could comprehend neither the escalating rhetoric and posturing of black power nor the rioting that swept through American cities in the "long hot summers" of 1967 and 1968. The white establishment, as Paul Good wrote in *The New York Times*, "had tolerated racial injustice for a century yet denounced black power in a day." To dramatize white complicity in black misery, black power spokesmen, sometimes unwittingly and sometimes knowingly, offered evidence for the opposite conclusion: that black male anger absolved whites of responsibility and that black power was a nihilistic, hypermasculine, and destructive philosophy. Figures like Carmichael, Newton, and H. Rap Brown, among others, embodied the black manhood, oversize and outlaw, that white society mythologized and feared.[43]

If whites were preoccupied with black power's violent implications, many African Americans focused on its familial implications. Though sometimes exaggerated, black power represented, among other things, the latest iteration in the attempt by African Americans to assert "traditional" manhood and womanhood as cornerstones of black domestic life. When Malcolm X wrote about "the importance of the father-male image in the strong household," he invoked a gender ideology embraced by most Americans, but one that held special significance for black families torn asunder by the legacies of slavery and the burdens of poverty.[44]

The manifestations of this manhood varied widely. Some men, taking Eldridge Cleaver's notion of pussy power seriously, saw revolutionary black women as sexual rewards for the warrior male. In a less exploitative mode, Maulana "Ron" Karenga, who founded the political organization US in Los Angeles in 1965, conceived an Afrocentric nationalism, loosely based on what the poet Amiri Baraka called a "black value system," that promised a restored black manhood. Local organizations across the country, such as the Black Coalition in Philadelphia, Albert Cleague's nationalist Christian church, Shrine of the Black Madonna, and the Newark Congress of African People, likewise embraced a renewed black patriarchy. Many men, cognizant of the feminism emerging among black women, were careful to heap praise on their "sisters." Honorifics aside, however, most envisioned a world in which women, in the words of Karenga, would dedicate themselves to the "inspiration, education, and social development of the nation."[45]

Though one version of black power embodied renewed manhood, the call for self-determination and group consciousness inspired widespread female activism and the emergence of black feminism. It emerged in part from the untenable position Pauli Murray recognized and felt compelled to write William Yancey about. "Of course we have to help the black man," the congresswoman Shirley Chisholm said in 1969, "but not at the expense of our own personalities as women. The black man must step forward, but that doesn't mean we have to step back." For Chisholm, a Barbadian from Brooklyn whose up-front feminism elicited the ire of many male black leaders, black power was a fluid concept that embraced self-help, community organizing, and even electoral politics—not simply "manly" resistance. "Upon the rebirth of the liberation struggle in the sixties, a whole genre of 'women's place' advocates immediately relegated black women to home and babies which is almost as ugly an expression of black Anglo-Saxonism as is Nixon's concept of 'black capitalism,'" the African American feminist Linda La Rue wrote in 1970. The proper response to white supremacy, La Rue made clear, was not *male* supremacy. Many African American women agreed.[46]

Indeed, most black women saw their own work, and the work of their mothers and grandmothers, as an equally valid form of black power. "It is really disgusting to hear Black women talking about giving Black men their manhood—or allowing them to get it," wrote the African American feminist Mary Ann Weathers in 1969. What Moynihan and many male African American commentators viewed as a punishing "matriarchy" was, in reality, a long tradition of community-sustaining labor by black women. For the generation of women that began shaping black feminist consciousness between 1965 and 1970, black power was less about conspicuous masculinity than about a self-reliant black community and a revolution in gender roles.[47]

Male-dominated black power and white-dominated mainstream feminism meant that black feminists found themselves caught between the emphasis on male breadwinning and the greater social capital of whites. However, black feminists turned that seemingly narrow space into a capacious one. Weathers, La Rue, Florynce "Flo" Kennedy, Frances Beal, and Beverly Smith, among others, laid the groundwork for understanding the unique predicaments of people who were neither male nor white; others would add "heterosexual." Joining them was a growing group of women—Pauli Murray, Aileen Hernandez, Eleanor Holmes Norton, and Sadie Alexander among them—who had secured positions of influence in white-dominated organizations such as NOW or in the field of law. They issued a powerful critique of both breadwinner liberalism and the male-centered politics of black power. From liberal to radical, black feminists refused to accept manhood as the only currency of sixties activism.[48]

The prominence of male black power figures and white obsession with violence obscured the complex debate within African American communities over the role of gender within the black freedom movement. That debate was animated by a critical question: Did the liberation of black America require conventional domesticity in which men not only restored community power but reclaimed their rightful place at the head of the family? This question raged across the spectrum of the black public sphere: in the pages of the bourgeois *Ebony*, the progressive *Liberator* and *Freedomways*, the mass-market *Jet*, the intellectual *Black Scholar*; in dozens of African American newspapers; and in tens of thousands of black churches. In the way that all nationalist movements historically have been bound to one version of family life or another, so too was black power.[49]

Black power held within its wide embrace many distinct types of manhood and womanhood. These included Malcolm X's disciplined patriarchy, Shirley Chisholm's uncompromising feminism, Gloria Richardson's feminine warrior ideal, the intellectual-as-activist model of Angela Davis, Huey Newton's sexual magnetism and blatant misogyny, the welfare rights of George Wiley and Johnnie Tillmon, Albert Cleague's Christian nationalism, Flo Kennedy's audacious and unapologetic feminist politics, and Amiri Baraka's probing thought, which evolved from the beat-inspired black macho of the mid-1960s to the responsible patriarchy and Kawaida values of the Spirit House in Newark, New Jersey. Born in the crucible of mid-sixties African American agitation, but stretching deep into history, black power asserted manhood but also led to black feminism.

Each in its own way became a powerful challenge to the reigning conventions of breadwinner liberalism, because black men asserted their right to be breadwinners in white-dominated America and black women asserted their right not to be shoved aside in a male-dominated America. Though the preponderance of nationalist sentiment across a range of African American movements converged on the conviction that male-headed breadwinner nuclear families would best advance the cause of the larger black struggle, the alternatives to that ideal would in time come into their own on the American landscape. In the wake of Moynihan and Watts, however, that time remained on the horizon. In the mid-1960s, most African American leaders remained overwhelmingly preoccupied with winning recognition of black *men*'s status as breadwinners in an economy long accustomed to denying them that role.

•

Great Society liberals crafted government programs to shore up breadwinner families. President Johnson opened the War on Poverty in March 1964 by making no secret of his concern with male breadwinners, both white and black. "There are 2.3 million fatherless families in America who have inherited nothing but their father's poverty," he said. Denied breadwinning mates, single mothers sought work as domestics, service workers, and factory laborers. But these jobs, Johnson continued, could not "furnish the stability and income so sorely needed in [the] absence of an able, breadwinning father."[50]

The next year, following the riot in Watts, Vice President Hubert Humphrey voiced another prominent concern of the administration. There are, Humphrey observed, two million "jobless and technologically illiterate young men who form a great untapped labor reservoir." Without more jobs, he warned, "there is a great explosion here ready to go off." As usual, Johnson put it in characteristically blunter terms in a private conversation. The War on Poverty could take "a bunch of these young strapping boys out of these damn rioting squads . . . [and] . . . put them to work."[51]

These dual concerns—promoting nuclear families with breadwinning fathers and preventing urban unrest—stood at the center of Great Society antipoverty initiatives. Architects of the War on Poverty understood the dynamics that kept many families poor: absent fathers and low-wage jobs for women. But the programs created by the 1964 Economic Opportunity Act (EOA), the cornerstone of Johnson's war, tended to focus only on absent fathers. According to Great Society thinking, newly trained men, adapted to a job market that heretofore had marginalized them, would find breadwinning employment and stabilize families. Even better, War on Poverty funds would mollify communities on the brink of rioting and divert male energies into job training rather than brick hurling. Thus, despite the War on Poverty's broad agenda, race became an overwhelming factor in the politics of breadwinner liberalism.[52]

Poverty warriors, no matter their intentions, could not escape their own and the larger culture's ambivalence about women's relationship to the market. Women were largely an afterthought in Great Society schemes. When considered at all, they were imagined mostly as potential dependents, waiting to be enfolded into a family economy. The Neighborhood Youth Corps piled up extensive waiting lists of young women, for instance, but the national office held the program's gender breakdown constant in deference to men. The Job Corps improved some women's vocational skills when a supplemental Women's Job Corps was established at Edith Green's insistence. Upward Bound too helped a small number of disadvantaged teenage girls—about ten thousand by 1967—prepare for college. And Legal Services gave poor women access to legal assistance with housing, divorce, employment discrimination, food stamps, and welfare. Such programs were not inconsequential, but given the scale of women's market disadvantage, they proved negligible compared with the size of the problem.[53]

Welfare reform, however, not the War on Poverty, produced the most visible and controversial efforts to use government policy to shape the nuclear family's relationship to the market in the Great Society era. After taking office in 1969, President Nixon, echoing Moynihan, put it bluntly: "any system which makes it more profitable for a man not to work, or which encourages a man to desert his family rather than stay with his family, is wrong and indefensible." Welfare's supporters and critics alike by the late 1960s saw Aid to Families with Dependent Children (AFDC)—a small and until then not a particularly controversial program entering its fourth decade—as encouraging male desertion.[54]

The system's complex rules provided government support only to unmarried mothers, the most common victims of male abandonment. Moreover, back in the 1950s, as the number of African Americans on welfare rolls increased, most states had amended AFDC provisions to deny benefits to women if a "substitute father" (a boyfriend, lover, or guest) was found in the house. This opened the door to intrusive supervision of the intimate lives of welfare recipients because families on public assistance could not expect "privacy" in any traditional sense. "Midnight raids" by state welfare departments were common enforcement measures. In such a system, critics argued, fathers had every financial incentive to leave and none to stay. Welfare reformers at the national level had been at work since the 1950s to devise a program that would assist women without turning away prospective breadwinners. Like Moynihan, these critics and reformers saw themselves as New Deal or Great Society liberals mending a broken system.[55]

Reform efforts acquired a new urgency in the second half of the 1960s for four reasons. First, the logic of Moynihan and Watts had linked absent male breadwinners with women's welfare dependency and male urban violence. Second, the combination of black migration out of the South and the employment crisis in northern cities threw increasing numbers of African Americans onto state welfare rolls. Third, in the South, segregationists had been bemoaning black "illegitimacy" and family instability since the *Brown* decision, in an effort to define court-imposed school desegregation as a violation of the white community's moral "standards." And fourth, the National Welfare Rights Organization (NWRO), led largely by African American women, challenged the iniquities and indignities of AFDC, including the substitute father rule and midnight raids, while encouraging women to see welfare as a right. All four developments both racialized welfare and made it fully part of the breadwinner liberalism of the Great Society.[56]

By the late 1960s no one liked welfare: not the left, not the right, not the center, not even the recipients themselves. Liberals in the Johnson administration and Congress hoped to raise welfare benefits and encourage male responsibility, but simultaneously they pushed unwed mothers into the labor market. They thought that absent male breadwinners, the exigencies of earning a wage would elevate women out of "dependency." Welfare activists foresaw the dire consequences of this reasoning: low-wage labor at the bottom of the economy without assistance for child care. In response, they cast welfare as a right, fought the surveillance of women's personal lives, and criticized liberals for abandoning them to degrading labor that compromised their motherhood. Conservatives, with a few exceptions, wanted to end welfare altogether. They saw it as a taxpayer drain, a travesty for the nuclear family, and a subsidy to "profligate breeders" among the black poor.[57]

To cut the Gordian knot, a few months into his presidency Richard Nixon took a bold gamble that he believed would both fix and shrink the welfare system. Prodded by Moynihan, who began working for Nixon in 1969, the president endorsed the Family Assistance Plan (FAP), a proposal to provide a guaranteed minimum income to a wide range of low-income families, including both current welfare recipients and the so-called working poor. Its complicated formula would award greater income support for two-parent families and for families in which both parents worked. Single-parent homes and homes without an employed family member would receive less. The inclusion of working families was essential, the president explained in his first major domestic policy speech in August 1969: "It is morally wrong for a family that is working to try to make ends meet to receive less than the family across the street on welfare."[58]

Nixon sent the bill to Congress. A relatively enthusiastic House passed it by nearly one hundred votes, despite the opposition of the Ways and Means Committee boss Wilbur Mills (D-AR), who believed that "one possible reaction of some fathers may be to let the government take over the job of completely supporting his family." As the bill sat in the Senate committee, however, its opponents on both the left and right slowly cut it to shreds. Led by George McGovern and backed by vocal NWRO activists, the liberal left charged that the FAP's formula favored working white families over impoverished black ones, that its income supports were insufficient for families and would actually *reduce* welfare benefits in a majority of states, and that it would force poor, unskilled women into the labor market with little assistance for child care. Senate conservatives simply could not abide the idea that the federal government planned to guarantee every American family below a certain income level annual assistance—especially now that the public face of poverty was urban and black. Citing an American Conservative Union study of the FAP, the conservative columnist James Kilpatrick charged that while the present system "cultivates an attitude of permanent dependency upon the welfare state," Nixon's FAP "would be worse." By the time the Senate Finance Committee turned it down, Nixon himself had begun to renege on his tactical commitment to poor breadwinners, leaving the FAP to die.[59]

As Moynihan gravitated toward neoconservatism, he continued to insist, as he had said in 1965, that "America is the only industrial democracy in the world that does not recognize the welfare and stability of family life as a principal object of social policy." Indeed, he singled out for criticism NWRO activists who fought the FAP bill, claiming they had passed on the best political compromise they would ever see (he was right). The long drama stretching from the Moynihan report in the summer of 1965 through the FAP debates in the spring and summer of 1970 deepened the connection in the public mind between the question of black equality and the stain of state assistance to the poor. Much as it had in the 1930s, the family emerged as a public project to be debated and systematically addressed. In that context, the absent male breadwinner seemed to make a mockery of the desire of Great Society liberals to broaden the

New Deal's promise of economic security and opportunity for nuclear families. "Charity can prevent physical starvation," one Iowan wrote to Moynihan, "but it cannot nourish manhood."[60]

•

The Iowan was far from alone in his dissatisfaction with liberals' welfare policies. In the spring of 1969, as Nixon officials drafted the FAP legislation, a New York journalist named Pete Hamill redirected the national political conversation. Hamill viewed "the growing alienation and paranoia of the working-class white man," not African American or women's rights, as the political drama of the era. In an influential and incendiary article in *New York* magazine entitled "The Revolt of the White Lower Middle Class," Hamill cast the "white working class" as a bastion of idealized but hard-bitten manhood and as hostile to black progress. "Talking darkly about their grievances," these breadwinners spoke with "quiet bitterness" about the loss of their economic status while complaining that "everything is for the niggers."[61]

Hamill's piece sensationalizing white male victimization was part of a much broader impulse at the end of the 1960s to recast the story of race and gender in national political life as one about working-class white men. Its authors included academics genuinely sympathetic to white workers' legitimate anxieties, cultural commentators such as Hamill, and opportunistic politicians and right-wing strategists, such as Nixon, George Wallace, Patrick Buchanan, Spiro Agnew, and Benjamin Wattenberg. From different vantages, they sought to resolve the tensions of the decade in the exasperated and put-upon white male breadwinner. But those efforts quickly and permanently obscured whatever legitimacy white male claims had by subjecting them to exaggerated political demagoguery.

Hamill did not invent, or discover, this enduring figure in American life. Robert C. Wood, director of the Harvard-MIT Joint Center for Urban Studies, similarly fused race, class, and masculinity into an iconic portrait. "Let us consider the working American—the average white ethnic male," Wood urged in 1968. "Layoffs, reductions, automation, plant relocation remain the invisible witches at every christening . . . he sees only one destination for the minority movement—his job." As often as not, that job was understood as property. "Some men leave their sons money, some large investments," wrote an ordinary worker to *The New York Times*. "I have only one worthwhile thing to give: my trade . . . and [to] sponsor my sons for an apprenticeship." Having secured a tenuous foothold in the American economy, these men saw their jobs as family assets. "For this simple father's wish," the letter writer concluded, "it is said that I discriminate against Negroes."[62]

Hamill's article circulated in the White House and figured prominently in Nixon's hard hat strategy of 1970 and 1971. The hard hat—the white, usually "ethnic" blue-collar worker—did a great deal of political work in the early 1970s. He became the answer to the black power militant and the welfare slacker, because his humble breadwinner ambitions, his unbridled patriotism, and his unflagging work ethic were celebrated as contrasts with their unreasonable demands. His relationship to work, family, and nation reflected conventional American mythologies of the social order; his heterosexuality was implicit but would be emphasized in due course. That his and his family's economic future remained in doubt as postwar expansion ground to a halt compounded the sense of injustice.[63]

In the late summer of 1968, as dozens of cities were recovering from the riots that followed Martin Luther King's assassination, more than three thousand activists met in Philadelphia at the Third National Conference on Black Power. The conferees declared black self-determination in urban America, including black control over major cities, to be the new goal of the movement. A central tactic in that struggle would be to secure construction jobs for black men, what the NAACP labor director Herbert Hill called "manly jobs" that were deemed "especially important for negro men." Public-sector financing of interstate highways, rapid transit, new schools, and urban renewal created hundreds of thousands of jobs in the heart of major cities. The black power conference had actually arrived late to this issue. Between 1963 and 1967 construction site protests by African Americans, led by local movement activists, had taken place in New York, Philadelphia, Newark, Cleveland, Cincinnati, San Francisco, Oakland, and St. Louis. Johnson's 1965 Executive Order 11246 enabled the federal government to terminate contracts with firms that refused to take affirmative action in hiring. But as community leaders discovered, on projects as diverse as the Bay Area Rapid Transit in San Francisco and the Gateway Arch in St. Louis, no one, not even federal judges, knew precisely what "affirmative action" meant. Protesters thus had two objectives: to pressure judges and other federal officials to define "affirmative action" and to force contractors to enter into private agreements by highlighting the absence of black workers at construction sites.[64]

To white construction and building trade workers, the protests were nonsensical and offensive. Most white blue-collar workers in the 1960s were only a generation removed from the bottom of the occupational ladder and retained a striver's sensibility. They did not see themselves as privileged, nor could they understand how their holding jobs prevented other men from doing the same. They saw protesters as men who wanted something without working for it. The skilled tradesmen among them had inherited a work culture in which manliness was deeply embedded in the process of apprenticing, learning and refining a craft, and working toward an independence rare in blue-collar employment. They saw the protesters as interlopers attempting to force their way into a world that white workers believed they and their fathers had built. Access to well-paying blue-collar jobs came to be understood as a zero-sum game in which black gains came only through white losses. Such sentiments represented the feelings of entire communities.[65]

One need not imagine all white workers in this era as racists to understand the structural and rhetorical logic of the nation's job markets. Such markets have never been "free" in any meaningful sense. Jobs come through dense networks of kin, friends, communities, unions, churches, business associates, education, training, mentors, and any number of ethnic ties. Such networks have long been racialized as well—both through the intentional "Caucasian-only" kind of segregation and through the normal day-to-day life of already racially segregated communities. From the inside, these networks do not look racist. They look natural. Buttressing the apparent naturalness is the rhetoric of masculine individualism— hard work, striving, self-reliance, and merit—that permeates American life and poses individual success or failure as always earned and always deserved. It is unsurprising that white workers would defend their crafts and their jobs in these terms.[66]

Neither is it surprising that black workers would object. African American activists challenged a wide range of employers in the 1960s and early 1970s, through both protest and EEOC lawsuits, but these battles rose into national consciousness most prominently in the construction industry. Following the 1968 black power conference, major campaigns opened the following summer in Pittsburgh, Chicago, Philadelphia, Detroit, and Seattle. The Chicago Coalition for United Community Action picketed

twenty major projects, and in July 1969 seventeen members of the politicized street gang Black P. Stone Nation seized the Building Trades Council headquarters, prompting arrests and generating headlines. In Pittsburgh
picketers targeted construction on the new Three Rivers Stadium, and in
Buffalo activists protested at the new $650 million State University of New
York campus. In New York City, as construction began on the mammoth
World Trade Center, the African American contractor James Haughton
formed Fight Back and led a campaign to get black workers hired on the
project.[67]

In response, Nixon resurrected a fallow Johnson administration initiative, the Philadelphia Plan. Mandating "goals" and "timetables," the
plan introduced penalties for federal contractors who did not hire African
Americans and other workers of color in sufficient numbers. The Philadelphia Plan has long been understood as cleaving two allies in the liberal
political coalition: African Americans and trade unions. Nixon critics
have tended to see his turn to the plan as cynical manipulation, intended
to divide two constituencies that opposed him. More sympathetic observers have interpreted it either as a genuine response to African American
inequality or as a pragmatic political effort to prevent the 1969 protests
from erupting into violence on the scale of 1967 and 1968. Whatever the
administration's motives, Philadelphia Plan goals, including what many
called quotas, got bogged down in a quagmire of disputes: over how many
skilled black tradesmen existed in any given city; whether apprenticeship
programs recruited African Americans; whether contractors should be punished for the practices of unions over which they had no control; and which
branch of government had control over the contract compliance program.
Nixon's strategizing aside, the plan succeeded in defusing the dramatic
public protests within a few years by shuffling street demonstrations into
courtrooms, where affirmative action became a bureaucratic question.[68]

Most important, the construction protests and the Philadelphia Plan
represented the changing politics of breadwinner liberalism. Much as conservatives attacked welfare and the FAP as programs to distribute money to
people who did not deserve it, they cast affirmative action as awarding
preference, or "special rights," to the unqualified or undeserving. "There is
no warrant in American law or history for setting up a quota system in any
area of employment," the president of the Southern States Industrial Council told a Senate subcommittee. "The American way has been to hire the
best man for the job." Here was a still-inchoate breadwinner conservatism—

"the best man for the job"—mobilized against breadwinner liberalism in the battle over whether and how to redress racial inequality.[69]

But was "the best man for the job" such a transparent concept? In his 1965 speech at Howard, President Johnson explicitly endorsed equality of result precisely because, as he reasoned, "it is not enough just to open the gates of opportunity. All our citizens must have the ability to walk through those gates." If the relationship among unions, contractors, employers, builders, and local communities had for decades operated to exclude African Americans, locking Johnson's "gate," was not "the best man for the job" already racially predetermined?[70]

Black activists thought so. Hill told a Senate subcommittee that with black populations topping 50 percent in many major cities, it was unacceptable for African American men to hold less than 5 percent of the best-paying blue-collar jobs. A disproportionately high percentage of black workers held jobs paying close to the minimum wage, Hill explained. "These are the working poor" who live "in a permanent condition of poverty."[71]

Beneath the affirmative action conflict lay ideals that both sides took for granted. White working-class men believed that they had earned these jobs; black men believed they deserved their fair shot at them. What they had in common, as few acknowledged at the time, was an overlapping vision of breadwinning manhood. They shouted at each other across an unbridgeable divide, however. Black activists articulated a sociological view of society and the marketplace. Race, they argued again and again, had always shaped opportunity, constraining African Americans' rightful roles as men in the nation. White workers, unions, and their defenders responded with an individualist view of male breadwinning and opportunity. They disputed that "equal rights" meant white workers had to relinquish jobs they considered personal assets. The American legal system, with its overwhelming emphasis on individual and property rights—to say nothing of the political system—was poorly equipped to adjudicate such disputes.

The hard hat's political season stretched from 1969 through 1972. He divided the American working class along stark racial and gendered lines. Lifted from the amorphous "silent majority," he offered a concrete, if two-dimensional, figure in which patriotism, whiteness, and merit-based breadwinning defined the legitimate American man. He exposed the artificiality of sharp distinctions between "values" and "economics" in post-1960s

American politics. The two often became one and the same because the economic interests of white workers, like their black counterparts, were represented and understood through a politics of male breadwinning.[72]

White male breadwinning may have been a powerful force thwarting claims based on racial justice, but hard hat politics actually obscured the legitimate grievances of white blue-collar workers at the dawn of the seventies. Nixon's efforts to forge a permanent Republican majority by driving white working-class voters away from the Democratic Party met with mixed success, in part because of his administration's economic policies, which encouraged union busting and rankled devoted union members among voters. But the conflict over construction jobs, which was emblematic of struggles across the country over affirmative action, disguised larger developments. As employers sought to deal with the downturn of the early years of the seventies by pushing back against labor unions and relocating plants overseas, the American public witnessed very public battles over race, manhood, jobs, and welfare—struggles that focused grievances on workers rather than bosses and on individuals rather than broad government and corporate policy. Breadwinner liberalism would have grown increasingly unable to deliver on its promises to white men, even if their status in workplaces and the national imagination had not been challenged by black men and by women of all races.[73]

The assumptions of sixties breadwinner liberalism concealed a great deal about the road on which the country was traveling. Breadwinner ideology encouraged Americans to underestimate economic transformations, to see black demands for justice as undeserved, and to worry that women's similar demands spelled the end of the family. Thus breadwinner liberalism was vulnerable not just to assault from the left but to appropriation by the right. Stripped of its social welfare and government support components, breadwinner liberalism could fast become breadwinner *conservatism*: a defense of white male breadwinners and their nuclear families against the claims of nonwhites, women, and ultimately gay men and lesbians. The political battles of the second half of the sixties launched just such a process of transformation. Those battles would be extended deeper into national life in the coming years, as more and more Americans questioned the heterosexual white male breadwinner and his nuclear family as the only legitimate framework for organizing the rights and obligations of full citizenship, and as others scrambled to defend him anew and to make him the symbol of a revived politics on the right.

2

LAST MAN TO DIE: VIETNAM AND THE CITIZEN SOLDIER

Breadwinning was not the only norm of manhood under duress in the 1960s. It was joined by soldiering. At the start of the decade, American soldiers still stood for a shared national morality. But they were also asked to do the unthinkable: endure a blizzard of violence and kill other human beings. The tension between morality and violence was resolved, so Americans hoped, in military manhood—not just duty and patriotism but the very foundation of the nation's image. Because he is meant to be noble and the best the nation has to offer, and because he is a mirror for the nation to gaze upon itself, the soldier is by nature a public figure, his manhood subject to explicit discussion and debate. Because he was all of those things, the soldier was also a cornerstone of male-breadwinner ideology.[1]

From Pearl Harbor in 1941 to the Gulf of Tonkin in 1964, Americans imagined their soldiers striding the globe as liberty's handmaidens. During this period the wartime and peacetime drafts, alongside the emerging military-industrial complex, drew the civilian and military worlds closer together than at any time since the Civil War. To serve one's country was a duty and an honor but also believed necessary for the survival of the "free world." Beginning in the early 1960s, however, the citizen soldier came under intense national scrutiny, as the nation was asked to answer for what that soldier did in Vietnam. Under that pressure, on a peninsula a world away, and equally in the living rooms, courthouses, and college campuses of the United States, Cold War American manhood frayed, split, and ultimately came undone.[2]

That manhood was at stake in the domestic turmoil over the war was made plain on the steps of the South Boston District Court in March

1966. At the end of the first year of the war's escalation, eleven members of the antiwar group Committee for Nonviolent Action emerged from a hearing following their recent arrest at an army base. Their appearance in blue-collar Irish American South Boston had drawn a crowd of about two hundred, including fifty or so high school boys, many of whom were to be inducted into the army not long after graduation. On the steps leading out of the courthouse, four of the antiwar activists—Harvard students among them—burned their reclassification notices (having earlier burned their draft cards). The high school boys surged forward, fists clenched, and began beating the activists, leaving them "pummeled and trampled," according to press reports. During the melee a Massachusetts state representative shouted: "This wouldn't have happened if these were South Boston boys; our boys are patriotic!" It was a forecast of the central place manhood, and economic class, would assume in the debates over the war.[3]

Vietnam revealed the mythic American soldier as yet another national fiction and, as a consequence, weakened the ideal of the patriotic male head of household. Military manhood came to matter so much in the Vietnam years because both right and left drew on it to conceptualize freedom, equality, and the citizen's relationship to the state. Most Americans believed in the male citizen's duty to country, but was that duty to endure and commit violence or to question the war and abnegate violence? Once the world of the stoic, manly soldier was opened to public scrutiny and was too often found wanting, the soldiering mythology crumbled. Questioning the soldier, like questioning the breadwinner, opened up a national debate about the subject of democratic rights and governance. What changed in these years was not the experience of the soldier, which was little different from other wars, but the public consumption of that experience and the political uses to which it was put.

An illuminating act in this stirring drama starred a young army private named Joe Miles, a twenty-year-old African American from Washington, D.C., who spent a year at American University before being drafted. Reporting to South Carolina's Fort Jackson in 1968, like so many nineteen-year-old working-class kids from across the South and the eastern seaboard, Miles got his first taste of military life in eight grueling weeks of basic training.[4]

The onetime vice-chairman of the National Black Antiwar Antidraft Union, Miles was a dedicated black nationalist. On several occasions during basic training, he played Malcolm X's speeches on an old phonograph in the Fort Jackson barracks for black and Puerto Rican GIs. Their use of the black power salute led to taunts by whites and interracial scuffles. When commanding officers got word of the rising black militancy, they transferred Miles to Fort Bragg, reassigned or jailed other offenders, and curtailed enlisted men's meetings. Rather than further inflame racial conflict, however, the black and Puerto Rican soldiers inspired by Miles, now calling themselves GIs United Against the War in Vietnam, recruited sympathetic white soldiers. They submitted a petition, signed by three hundred enlisted men, demanding that their commander permit open meetings to debate the war.[5]

This broad challenge to army discipline put Fort Jackson's officer corps on edge. When GIs United members Andrew Pulley, José Rudder, and Edilberto Chaparro held a discussion about the army's harassment of them, an officer summarily ended the proceedings and sent the enlisted men back to their barracks. The assembled crowd of GIs, numbering in the hundreds, cursed and mocked the officer, dispersing reluctantly while mumbling epithets. Over subsequent days army commanders arrested eight leaders of GIs United and charged them with inciting a riot and disrespecting an officer. The Fort Jackson Eight, as they became known, claimed that it was their right to "think and to speak out against an unjust war." They were among more than a dozen dissident GI groups across the country in 1969. "We are citizens of America even if the Army would like to forget it," read the GIs United's "Statement of Aims." Rather than accept conventional soldiering manhood, the statement exposed it as an open question. In the relationship between citizens and state, these young soldiers asked, what does each owe the other?[6]

Miles and other members of GIs United were not typical soldiers, just as the antiwar activists on the steps of the Boston courthouse were not typical draftees. Most men served their required time in the military, did their best to stay out of trouble and the line of fire, and looked forward to the day when they could go home. The Fort Jackson Eight and the Boston activists *were* typical, however, of the ways American soldiers entered civilian consciousness and, ultimately, civilian politics in the late 1960s. Men's relationship to the draft, to military service, to violence, to duty and patriotism surged beyond matters of individual conscience to become matters of national political significance. Wars are geopolitical contests between nation-states. They are also testing grounds for a generation of men. As Americans argued about soldiering during the Vietnam War, they fought over inherited truths about manhood and patriotism, citizen and state. And as the war dragged on, these truths that had once bound the nation together became a wedge driving Americans apart.[7]

•

"I was going on nineteen when I got drafted," Stephen A. Howard recalled. "My mother went to the bus station to see me off to Fort Bragg for basic training, and she said, 'You'll be back a man.' " Few doubted in mid-1960s America that military service was a sure path to manhood and a claim on meaningful citizenship. World War II veterans were part of the fabric of communities across the country. Every president of the United States since Franklin Roosevelt had either served in or commanded the armed forces in war. Cold War militarism valorized the dutiful manliness of the warrior and defined the American military as an international instrument of liberty.[8]

Absent a total war that mobilized the entire society, however, the nation's armed forces were replenished by volunteer recruitment and a draft system, renewed by Congress in 1948 after a brief postwar lapse, that did not call every American male to serve his country. Married men, men with children, college and graduate students, and men in "critical" occupations were exempt from the draft for the two decades between 1948 and 1968. Furthermore, between 1968 and the end of the draft in 1973, there remained innumerable ways for middle-class men to avoid combat service. As a result, the soldiers sent to Vietnam were predominantly drawn from the working classes. As one retired army colonel put it, the war was, like most in history, "a poor boy's fight."[9]

While volunteers were the armed forces' primary source of manpower in the 1960s—more than 60 percent of men in uniform—the draft remains a useful guide to Vietnam-era conceptions of the military obligations of men. For one, the draft received the lion's share of attention in the mass media and in political debate. For another, which men the nation called to fight raised not only the question of manpower but equally the moral question of equity and the manly question of duty.[10]

The draft did not cull a representative sample of American men. Rather, it by and large selected high-school-educated men hailing from blue-collar or lower-middle-class backgrounds. As early as 1965 knowledgeable observers on both ends of the political spectrum, from *The New York*

Times to the Republican presidential candidate Barry Goldwater, decried the draft as discriminatory. In 1966, pushed by Democrats in Congress, President Johnson appointed a committee, the National Advisory Commission on Selective Service, to reconsider the draft in light of the principle of "fairness to all citizens."[11]

The resulting 1967 report, *In Pursuit of Equity*, detailed the draft's shortcomings. Selection unfairly burdened nonwhites and the working class. Stringing together exemptions and deferments, many middle-class men avoided the draft for years. Local draft boards, of which there were an astonishing four thousand, had the crucial task of assigning exemptions and deferments yet were unrepresentative of their communities and invoked wildly different standards from place to place across the country. Susceptible to pressure from influential citizens and often ignorant of the cities, towns, and neighborhoods they theoretically represented, board members were beholden largely to their own passions and prejudices. *In Pursuit of Equity* spurred a revised draft bill in 1968, which introduced the marginally more equitable lottery system. The post-1968 shift to the lottery came late, however—its effects were not felt until the war was winding down—and did not fully eliminate the opportunities for middle-class and wealthy men to escape combat service.[12]

Class and race emerged as the draft's most troubling filters to those who regarded democratic fairness as an essential feature of military service. In the first two years of official U.S. combat, 1965 and 1966, college graduates made up just 2 percent of inductees. In the second half of the decade, two million men were excused from service each year with educational exemptions, to the consternation of the Yale University president Kingman Brewster, a World War II volunteer, who called college deferments "a cynical avoidance of service" and "a tarnishing of the national spirit." Just as obvious was the draft's systematic racial bias. As late as 1967, just 1 percent of all draft board members were African American, and several southern states had no black board members at all. In communities across the country, black as well as Latino men were often drafted at rates double their proportion of the local population.[13]

Sexuality too figured in the draft's discriminatory calculus. American officials and ordinary citizens alike imagined the armed services to represent a masculinity that gay men were believed not to embody. In 1950, in the depths of early Cold War anxiety, the Senate's Hoey Committee had cited the "lack of emotional stability . . . in most sex perverts and the weakness of their moral fiber" as justification for barring gay men and lesbians from federal employment. Similar justifications appeared in military regulations, which declared that "prompt separation of known homosexuals is mandatory." By 1966 the Defense Department had officially decreed: "The homosexual is considered unsuitable for military service and is not permitted to serve in the armed forces in any capacity." Despite the incontrovertible language, the draft drew tens, if not hundreds, of thousands of closeted gay men into military service in the 1950s and 1960s (because women were not drafted, lesbians entered the service through volunteering). Most homophile activists, as early gay rights activists were known, demanded that these men and women be allowed to serve openly.[14]

The men the draft sifted out of military service were not simply the white middle and upper classes and men of questionable heterosexuality. Fully "one half of the young men" called before the Selective Service for examination were "unqualified for military service," a 1964 government report bemoaned. Entitled *One Third of a Nation* and written with significant input from Daniel Moynihan, the report was a striking documentation of American poverty. Anticipating Moynihan's 1965 report on the black family, it attributed the unsatisfactory state of the American male to unemployment, low incomes, fatherless families, and poor schools. If men were not prepared for the armed services, the report concluded, the nation had failed the men. They in turn had failed the nation by being unprepared to serve their country.[15]

By the end of 1965, Johnson had set the draft calls at thirty-five thousand per month, a threefold increase over the previous year that pressured the armed services to expand the pool of eligible men. But rather than call the middle and upper classes to do their part, the Pentagon chose to revise its eligibility standards downward. Motivated by *One Third of a Nation*, the conclusions of which were underscored by a second report, *Marginal Men and Military Service*, Secretary of Defense Robert S. McNamara announced Project 100,000 in 1966. All branches of the service were to accept the previously disqualified, thereafter known as new standards men. For McNamara, the annual addition of a hundred thousand inductees meant more troops. For Johnson, influenced by Moynihan's notion of social rehabilitation, Project 100,000 was another campaign in the War on Poverty. "Low-performing men" would receive additional training and discipline. The military would become their voucher to a better life.[16]

In the context of an escalating war and the draft's already well-known biases, however, Project 100,000 appeared less like a social uplift program than a ploy for more working-class cannon fodder. Some pundits even wondered if a cynical Johnson was anxious to get black youth off the streets after the debacle in Watts. Of the first 240,000 new standards men, more than 40 percent were black, and nearly all were, as McNamara admitted, "the poor of America." Moynihan believed in the project's ambition to make military service into an antipoverty measure; his time as an enlisted man had enabled him to attend Tufts University and had rescued many others from the Depression-era Irish Catholic slums of New York, where he had spent his youth. Yet McNamara's claim, that new standards men would "return to civilian life with skills and aptitudes which, for them and their families, will reverse the downward spiral of human decay," was disingenuous at best, because by 1966 the war was sending home 500 men a month in body bags. In theory, military discipline could be an antidote to poverty, turning men with little social capital into potential breadwinners. Lofty rhetoric from the secretary of defense, however, could not change the immutable calculus of the battlefield, where tens of thousands of those potential breadwinners died and tens of thousands left for home physically injured or psychologically scarred.[17]

The draft's racial bias, deepened by Project 100,000, compelled many African Americans, especially those drawn to black power, to reverse the black freedom movement's historical demand for greater participation in the American military. Medgar Evers had encouraged Mississippi blacks to defy the state's all-white draft boards as early as 1963, as did the Mississippi Freedom Democratic Party and the Student Nonviolent Coordinating Committee in subsequent years. The black freedom movement activist Julian Bond, elected to the Georgia legislature in 1966, was denied his seat for having announced to the press: "We are in sympathy with, and support, the men in this country who are unwilling to respond to a military draft." Amid charges that drafting black men in large numbers was "part of a plan to commit calculated genocide," an exaggerated yet resonant notion, the National Black Antiwar Antidraft Union organized opposition to the draft, and Muhammad Ali's defiance of the Selective Service System in 1967, the signature gesture of Vietnam-era black refusal, made him a national hero to late-sixties antiwar activists.[18]

Two powerful forces coursing through the nation's black communities shaped this response to the draft. The first was the model of masculinity in which manhood was affirmed in the refusal to do the bidding of whites. The second force was the Third World model of internal colonization that increasingly underlay black, as well as Puerto Rican and Chicano, nationalisms in the late sixties. People of color inside the United States, the argument went, were the domestic analogues of the Vietnamese. They were not lesser victims of U.S. imperialism because they lived within the "mother country." Stokely Carmichael proclaimed in his 1966 black power speech that "We must find the strength so that when they start grabbing us to fight their war we say, 'Hell no.'" Whereas many moderate and liberal black leaders before 1967 were restrained in their criticism of the draft and the war, radical activists had no such qualms.[19]

Vietnam led to similar conflicts within Mexican American communities, where traditions of soldiering remained strong and military manhood was highly valorized. But Chicano nationalism, with its own anticolonial and Third World roots, had begun to move away from the alignment of manhood with military service. In a major 1971 speech at Exposition Park in Los Angeles, César Chávez questioned whether "to be fully men, to gain respect from other men," the "poor, brown, and black farm workers" of America ought to "kill other farm workers in Southeast Asia." How can Mexican Americans be proud, Chávez asked, if "our sons go off to war grasping for their manhood at the end of a gun?"[20]

The draft's dilemma for gay and lesbian activists was equally vexing. One of the first coordinated multicity homophile protests took place on Armed Forces Day in May 1966, when demonstrators demanded an end to the military's homosexual ban; flyers read, "Give us the right to fight for our country!" Ironically, this challenge to heterosexual military manhood (and womanhood) occurred just two months after the largest antiwar demonstration to that point, a march of twenty-five thousand in New York City. Would homophiles continue to demand inclusion in a military increasingly under assault by youthful protesters and the emerging counterculture? There was no easy answer, and the issue divided homophile activists for much of the late sixties. Starting in 1969, gay liberationists took an antimilitary stance, but plenty of prominent gay activists insisted that however misguided the war in Vietnam might be, they would continue to fight the ban and support gay and lesbian soldiers.[21]

As challenges to the draft accumulated, class stood out as the common denominator of service. It might have been reasonable to expect that in the absence of a national emergency men would not be taken out of college or away from families that needed their financial support. Reasonable observers likewise could see education and training, especially for poor citizens, as a fair compensation for military service. Death, however, proved unreasonable and changed the calculus. Once millions of men were called upon to risk their lives in combat, the cynical view—that money seemed the only difference between those who fought and those who did not—prevailed. With mounting casualties in a faraway war, and with the majority of draftees assigned to frontline infantry units, where casualties were highest, the draft seemed to many so unfair as to border on immoral.[22]

One sure way to escape Vietnam was to avoid or resist the draft. Resisters were notoriously difficult to describe, let alone count, but cautious estimates suggest that some five to six hundred thousand American men committed punishable draft violations in the Vietnam decade. Of these, a relatively small number, between fifty and seventy-five thousand, refused induction on antiwar principles and either remained in the United States at risk of arrest or fled the country to safe havens in Canada and Sweden. Far greater numbers faked injuries or medical conditions, lied about their family or financial circumstances, purposefully flunked the army intelligence test, or simply failed to register with Selective Service. Men resisted the draft in such innumerable ways and for such a variety of reasons (the majority of which had little to do with opposition to the war) that creating a single portrait of the resister is impossible. One observer from the time noted that every young man was either a "draft evader . . . or a failed draft evader." Political draft resisters were vital to the profile of the antiwar movement, but they represented a small fraction of the hundreds of thousands of men who illegally avoided the draft.[23]

Nonetheless, organizations such as the Boston Draft Resistance Group, the Montreal Council to Aid War Resisters, and Amex Canada promoted draft resistance as civic duty, not self-preservation. Like their black power counterparts, these white-dominated organizations valorized a manhood based on defiance of the war, defining principled objection to injustice as a male citizen's first duty. In the emerging protest culture of the mid-sixties, they refused the equation of unquestioning patriotism with manhood. As young men on major college campuses in Cambridge, Madison, and Berkeley refused to serve—and sometimes symbolically burned or ripped their draft cards—they took part in a newly valorized manly resistance.

The famous poster slogan "Girls say yes to boys who say no" embodied their sexual politics. In a telling demonstration of the durability of gender stereotypes, New Left men maintained the objectification of women even as they inverted manhood.[24]

Adjustments gradually improved the fairness of the draft, but by the early 1970s few Americans considered conscription the best way to construct the national military. Called unfair by both the antiwar left and the hawkish right, the draft had lost its core credibility. On the left, draft resisters and their allies in religious, antiwar, and humanitarian groups opposed conscription on the basis of its racial bias and the immorality of the war of which it was a part. Less conspicuous than any of these groups, white working-class families in the silent majority resented the draft's class bias: while middle-class young men remained in college and, in the eyes of many, protested a war they would never have to fight, their sons went off to the killing fields. On the right, libertarians increasingly rejected compulsory service as a violation of individual liberty. In the center stood President Nixon, for whom the draft was a political, rather than an ideological, problem because it stirred antiwar passions on campuses and in the streets. Nixon had announced his plan to end the draft just weeks before the 1968 election, a typically Nixonian gambit in which he appealed to white working-class populism and simultaneously plotted to end the campus protests sparked by draft notices. The reasons and rationales diverged, but a consensus had materialized. If men were to fight and die, they ought to be sifted from the national population with a more defensible and less biased mechanism.[25]

Only two wars in American history, the Civil War and World War II, defined an entire male generation. Of the thirty million draft-age men during the Vietnam decade, a mere 10 percent actually served in the military. Of those, only 20 percent saw combat. Vietnam, and the draft in particular, raised a vital question: Which Americans should fight the nation's wars? The depth and passion with which Americans sought answers confirmed that the link between manhood and duty had already been severed, not by protesters but by the nation's system of soldier making. The title of James Fallows's memorable 1975 essay "What Did You Do in the Class War, Daddy?" summed up the impossibility of the war unifying the nation.[26]

•

If nation and manhood were interwoven, each shaping the other, what soldiers did on the battlefields of Vietnam after their induction mattered as much as the legitimacy of the draft. To make an army was a preliminary step. To send it into battle invoked another set of expectations about manhood, about the citizen as soldier. What would the military do in the nation's defense? What would it do as representatives of the nation?

One answer came early in the war. In August 1965, five months after arriving in Vietnam, the Third Marine Amphibious Force was ordered to secure the air and naval bases surrounding Da Nang, on the northern coast of South Vietnam. On a typically humid afternoon soldiers surrounded Cam Ne, a small village south of Da Nang, believed to be under the Communist National Liberation Front (NLF) control. Using grenades, Zippo cigarette lighters, and flamethrowers projecting streams of fire, the marines burned Cam Ne to the ground as women, elderly men, and children begged the soldiers to allow them to save belongings from their homes.[27]

The following night on *Evening News with Walter Cronkite*, the reporter Morley Safer provided a firsthand account of the destruction of Cam Ne for a domestic audience of millions. "Today's operation is the frustration of Vietnam in miniature," Safer explained. America can "win a military victory here, but to a Vietnamese peasant whose home is [destroyed] it will take more than presidential promises to convince him that we are on his side." One of the first eyewitness reports of what came to be seen as atrocities, the piece drew the ire of President Johnson, who accused Safer of having "shat on the flag." Cam Ne passed without much public commentary in the United States. But observant Americans could catch in the flames a first glimpse of what Vietnam would mean for their soldiering ideals.[28]

Incidents such as Cam Ne were not unusual, but neither were they the rule. Measured appraisals of the war's brutality have found little to distinguish Vietnam from the grisly combat in Europe and Asia during World War II. Even the rituals of killing—the severed heads and ears—and the close proximity of soldiers and civilians were not unknown to American soldiers in previous wars. Neither did Americans invent the style of combat in Vietnam: the French Army, the North Vietnamese Army (NVA), and the NLF had encouraged ferocious bloodletting well before American soldiers arrived on the peninsula. Atrocities perpetrated by Americans, however, stood in flagrant contrast with the nation's stated goals and purported ideals in the Cold War standoff with communism. As Safer recognized before most others, the United States might win the war but in doing so risked surrendering its moral legitimacy in the eyes of the world.

Little in Vietnam sharpened debate about soldiering manhood more than the killing of civilians. The central question was deceptively simple: Were atrocities in a guerrilla war an unfortunate by-product of a soldier's duty, or were they indications that the war had made "good boys into murderers," as the journalist Peter Barnes put it? When Robert Kennedy turned against the war in 1967, he wondered aloud on national television if "we have the right here in the United States to say that we're going to kill tens of thousands, make millions of people, as we have, millions of people refugees, *kill women and children*, as we have. I very seriously question whether we have that right." The rhetoric of American military manhood allowed that "war is hell" and that men are called to do in war what would be unthinkable in peacetime. But Vietnam required of American fighting men a kind of combat—among an agricultural population infiltrated by enemy guerrillas and where anyone, including women and children, could be a lethal combatant—that made civilian deaths inevitable. While the nation's idealized soldiers would never kill women and children, the men in the field did just that. What in other wars might be rationalized as regrettable but necessary became in Vietnam a symbol of American immorality.[29]

Securing and defending territory, the traditional measure of military success, were replaced early in Vietnam by kill ratios, which became body counts. American commanders first used kill ratios to evaluate the effectiveness of South Vietnamese units, but General William Westmoreland, commander of American forces, and other military officials seized on them as a shorthand for communicating to politicians and journalists the war's progress and the concept of counterinsurgency. Furthermore, because it was impossible, and Westmoreland reasoned undesirable, in all but a handful of cases to capture Vietnamese villages, field commanders encouraged their units to achieve high kill ratios in lieu of tactical victories. Unsurprisingly, the result was a devaluation of Vietnamese life. A war measured in bodies, in the field and at home, was a war reduced to the most elemental calculation and impossible to disguise as anything other than a competition in human slaughter.[30]

Johnson's troop buildup forestalled the collapse of South Vietnam that had seemed imminent in 1964, but by 1967 the war had degenerated into a gory stalemate. With nearly half a million American soldiers in Southeast Asia, Johnson confronted two mounting problems on the domestic front. The first was an uneasy feeling among the populace, reflected in both skeptical media coverage and Gallup polls, that the United States was no longer winning the war. Nothing turns Americans against a war quite like the prospect of losing it, and approval of Johnson's handling of the war had fallen to 50 percent by the end of 1967, a month before the North Vietnamese launched the Tet Offensive.[31]

Second on Johnson's growing list of troubles was the antiwar movement. The Spring Mobilization to End the War brought one hundred thousand protesters into the streets of San Francisco, while more than a quarter of a million followed Martin Luther King through Manhattan from Central Park to the United Nations. In October, another hundred thousand marched on the Pentagon. Stop the Draft Week created the indelible image of the draft card burner, and Muhammad Ali made national headlines by refusing induction. Antiwar protesters forced an anxious political class and a complacent populace to regard the war in new ways. Johnson absorbed the blows and counterpunched. "The enemy's hope for victory . . . is in our division, our weariness, our uncertainty," he told the country. Still, he well understood that the presidential campaign of 1968 would be a referendum on his war.[32]

In this context, two turning point events reshaped the war abroad and at home. The first came in January 1968, with the Tet Offensive, dozens of coordinated attacks against American and South Vietnamese forces that, while largely defeated, proved the NLF's resilience. Tet convinced the American public that despite the claims of Johnson, McNamara, and Westmoreland, the United States had become intractably "bogged down." Following Tet, which initiated a dominolike cascade of events leading to Johnson's withdrawal from the presidential race in March, public support for the war never exceeded 50 percent. After his election in November, Nixon spent four years pursuing a bloody withdrawal.

The second turning point came in September 1969, with the revelations of the massacre at My Lai. Fighting in Vietnam was vicious, but Americans understandably preferred to believe that they were the victims, not perpetrators, of its callousness. Press coverage of the early years of U.S. involvement stressed the professionalism of American soldiers and their disdain for the Geneva Convention violations committed by North and South Vietnamese troops alike. That veil of innocence fell definitively with My Lai. The floodgates opened, and accusations of atrocities spilled forth.[33]

Westmoreland's response to Tet had been to order, along with massive aerial assaults and napalm strikes, the systematic destruction of villages—tactics that led to the bloodiest six months of the war. In the early morning of March 16, 1968, American soldiers from the army's Twentieth Infantry entered the villages of My Lai and My Khe. Facing no armed resistance, they executed between four and five hundred men, women, and children. The massacre at My Lai and My Khe, villages believed to have harbored NLF soldiers during the offensive, were tangible outcomes of Westmoreland's new tactics.

Commanding the American soldiers in My Lai was Capt. Ernest "Mad Dog" Medina. Lt. William "Rusty" Calley, a quixotic and bombastic commander unpopular among grunts, as enlisted men were known, commanded the first platoon of Charlie Company. Medina's units had been in the field only since January but had suffered terrible casualties. Calley's platoon alone had lost nearly half its men. Already weary of the strain of guerrilla warfare—children often carried grenades, and villagers were known to booby-trap homes, dead bodies, baskets, anything that could conceal a bomb—Medina's soldiers killed everyone in the village. Many raped women and girls. A handful of soldiers refused to participate, and a helicopter pilot, Hugh Thompson, saved a dozen villagers and ordered his gunners to protect him from the rampaging GIs. On balance, however, soldiers under Medina, and especially those led by Calley, slaughtered with abandon.[34]

Concealed by army commanders, who falsely reported a "battle" to the press, the massacre took time to reach the American public. Thompson relayed the incident to his commanding officer, but it stalled in the army chain of command. Not until Ron Ridenhour, a helicopter gunner who had not been at My Lai, wrote incriminating letters to members of Congress and the secretaries of defense and state in March 1969, did the army investigate. The journalist Seymour Hersh picked up the story in the fall of 1969 and published a series on the massacre and its cover-up that appeared in newspapers around the country.[35]

Calley, placed under arrest along with Medina and several other infantrymen, instantly became the center of a furious national debate about the war. Every major weekly newsmagazine in the United States, and dozens more abroad, carried front-page stories about Calley and My Lai.

Esquire, Life, Time, and *Newsweek* each ran multiple articles and interviews. Headlines about the case splashed on the front pages of newspapers across the country and the globe, and Ronald Haeberle's photographs of the massacre in *Life* stunned and chastised the nation. Americans, *Time* observed, "must stand in the larger dock of guilt and human conscience."[36]

Every soldier at My Lai, with the exception of Calley and Medina, escaped prosecution. The Peers Commission, charged with conducting the army's official investigation, recommended legal action against two generals, four colonels, four lieutenant colonels, and four majors, but every case that was pursued was eventually dismissed. Esequiel Torres, a machine gunner under investigation for killings at My Lai, tried to subpoena Westmoreland in a symbolic but unsuccessful gambit. Medina was eventually acquitted. The insulation of the army chain of command was complete.[37]

Only Calley remained officially accountable. His trial, which lasted from November 1970 to March 1971, was a referendum on the war and American soldiering. Scapegoated by the army, Calley groped for explanations. "I had to value the lives of my troops, and I feel that was the only crime I have committed," he said, evasively. Caught between faulting his superiors—"I felt then and I still do that I acted as I was directed"—and defending them—"they [Vietnamese] were all the enemy, they were all to be destroyed"—Calley made for an unconvincing fall guy. Charged with 102 killings, now illegal murders, Calley testified that he had fired no more than a dozen rounds in total. But on March 29, 1971, he was convicted of 22 of the charges, bearing sole legal responsibility for some of the most heartless American actions of the war.[38]

However unsympathetic a figure, Calley was a victim of America's prosecution of the war in Vietnam. Born into a modest middle-class Miami suburban family in the 1950s, Calley flunked out of Palm Beach Junior College in 1963 and eventually landed at Florida East Coast Railroad as a strikebreaker. His work was erratic and generally poor, and when he was demoted at the strike's conclusion, Calley moved to an insurance company. In 1965, jobless and broke, he set off for California. Calley was an ideal candidate to be drafted: single, childless, and not in college. Upon arriving in San Francisco, he received his delinquent draft notice, turned around, and headed back to Miami. He ran out of money in Albuquerque and enlisted in the army, a "volunteer" in name only. Desperate for junior officers, the army assigned Calley to Fort Benning, where he finished officer training in 1967. It would not be long before, singularly ill suited to be a junior officer, he was headed for combat.[39]

Virtually no one in the United States saw Calley as anything but a patsy or a bungler. Nonetheless, both the antiwar left and the hawkish right invested his trial with enormous significance because it proved the core problem of the war as each side saw it. Among antiwar activists and even many otherwise fence-sitting liberals, Calley was a stooge for the real perpetrators: Johnson, Nixon, McNamara, Westmoreland, and Dean Rusk. To the right, Calley's trial and conviction demonstrated that the war effort was hamstrung by grandstanding politicians and the antiwar movement. They thought the United States was pulling its punches while wasting time prosecuting men for doing, in the words of an Alabama mayor, "nothing different from what the fighting men of World War II did." It was a sign of the times that Calley briefly offered American politics a unifying figure, if only because all sides agreed that his conviction was a farce. Polls showed that between 70 and 80 percent of Americans disapproved of it.[40]

Calley was a galvanizing figure, but he was not the war in microcosm. As gruesome as fighting in Vietnam was, hundreds of thousands of American soldiers came home never having witnessed, much less committed, an act of atrocity. Most veterans returned home and did their best to resume abandoned lives. They came home with the same physical and emotional scars, the same anxiety about mustering out, the same desire to separate from their wartime selves and resume conventional civilian existence as men in most wars.

However, the "Calley case" and "My Lai" transcended the typical, ordinary experiences of American soldiers because they came to stand for the war in the public imagination. The thousands upon thousands of letters from Americans now sitting in the Nixon Presidential Papers—CBS reported that twenty thousand arrived in just the first week—and in the archival collections of members of Congress speak not of silent, honorable men who came home and went to work in their fathers' stores or enrolled in community colleges, but of Calley and what he signaled about the war's meaning. Calley came to stand for American soldiers and for how Americans argued about manhood and its alignment with patriotism and national duty.[41]

Conservative Americans reacted to Calley's conviction with disbelief and maintained that the North Vietnamese bore ultimate responsibility for the war's brutality. Critics on the right blamed Ho Chi Minh for employing guerrilla tactics that made civilians into combatants. My Lai proved only the depravity of communism's collectivist ethos and the willingness of the NLF to throw away millions of lives in defense of an amoral ideology. For the crimes of the North Vietnamese, these critics insisted, the American military had decided to "to punish little men," such as Calley.[42]

On this basis, conservatives transformed Calley into a populist emblem of the dutiful soldier abandoned by his country. Letters and petitions poured into Fort Benning, congressional offices, and the Nixon White House following the verdict. These were part of a nationwide "Pardon Calley" campaign, strongest in the Midwest and South, launched by local public officials, radio stations, and the American Legion. The Georgia governor Jimmy Carter proclaimed April 5 "American Fighting Men's Day" and urged residents to hoist the flag. The right-wing radio preacher Rev. Carl McIntire organized a "victory rally" in Washington, D.C., where marchers appeared carrying FREE CALLEY NOW! signs. Terry Nelson's song "Battle Hymn of Lt. Calley," which sold hundreds of thousands of records in a few days, took direct aim at the antiwar movement: "While we're fighting in the jungles they were marching in the street / While we're dying in the rice fields they were helping our defeat."[43]

Calley thus emerged from the killing fields of My Lai and the subsequent media spectacle as a martyred hero of the American right. In the spring of 1971 he joined the hard hats, whose first burst of fame had come less than a year earlier, as conscripts in the emerging narrative of white male victimization. George Wallace, the populist, segregationist governor of Alabama and frequent presidential candidate, met with Calley the day after the guilty verdict and afterward spoke to a raucous crowd of two thousand of the lieutenant's supporters. Accompanying Wallace as he stepped to the podium was Lieutenant Governor Lester G. Maddox, who intoned, to applause, "God bless Lt. Calley" for fighting "in the cause of the nation." In Calley, many Americans believed they had found the real victim of the war: not Vietnam or the Vietnamese, not the nation's democratic ideals, but the American everyman, a dutiful innocent betrayed by the antiwar movement and a misguided government.[44]

Calley's heroic elevation by conservatives had deeper roots in gender and class aspects of American culture. Tolerance of violence has long been a tenet of manhood. To retreat or wince in the face of violence is to reveal feminine weakness and unmanly cowardice. Calley represented in conservative corners this ideal of manhood: he did not wince. He could be fashioned into a populist hero in many quarters, in ways peace activists could not, because a true man pledged his patriotism, accepted the possibility of violence, and performed his duty without question, all in service to nation. Peace activists, on the other hand, asserted a claim anathema to Calley's defenders: that manhood might consist in challenging, rather than defending, national righteousness and renouncing, rather than enduring, violence.

Military service was so embedded in working-class American communities that virtually everyone knew someone who had served. As one Vietnam vet explained, "you just can't imagine the pull of the military on kids from neighborhoods like mine [Pittsburgh's North Side]. Everything you'd seen and heard your whole life made it feel inevitable and right that you would do your time in the service." Calley may have been a symbol, even an abstraction, to antiwar protesters, but his fate was felt intimately in thousands of neighborhoods across the country, where military service was an unquestioned and noble part of becoming a man. In those neighborhoods it appeared that Calley was put on trial simply for being a soldier. Thus a crucial component of Calley's populist appeal was the way he could be figured as a working-class hero against the middle-class war protesters and draft resisters, whose distance from actual military service rankled people in places like the North Side of Pittsburgh.[45]

•

A counterpoint to the defense of Calley materialized a mere three weeks after the verdict, when more than eight hundred Vietnam veterans lined up in front of the Capitol building in Washington, D.C. Before thousands of spectators and rows of television cameras, one by one they stepped from among their comrades and threw their medals onto the steps. Purple Hearts, Silver and Bronze Stars, and Distinguished Service Crosses clattered against the statue of Chief Justice John Marshall. "Here's my merit badge for murder," one vet said, "from the country I betrayed by enlisting in the U.S. Army." After tossing their medals, they retreated, many in tears, to the circle of vets, where they met with the silent embraces of comrades. The spare symbolism of the gesture made it one of the war's most visceral and haunting moments.[46]

Well before the vets arrived in Washington, internal crises plagued the armed forces. In early 1970 Nixon had begun the process of Vietnamization, transferring ground combat to reluctant South Vietnamese units. Meanwhile American troop morale had fallen to appallingly low levels. With killed-in-action rates approaching World War II levels, field commanders often found themselves at the mercy of soldiers who refused to fight. Stateside, reportage of the "next My Lai" seemed always around the corner, and journalists picked up on declining morale, the increasing drug use by enlisted men, and escalating tensions between grunts and officers. *The Washington Post* reported on "an army in anguish," and *Newsweek* wondered if the nation should worry less about another Tet and more about a revolt among its own forces.[47]

As central actors in these overlapping crises, soldiers and former soldiers took on new roles. In doing so, they intensified the questioning of military manhood already evident in debates over the draft and My Lai. A handful of veterans led the way by going public with their opposition to the war. Vietnam Veterans Against the War (VVAW), founded at an antiwar rally in 1967, and the Citizens Commission of Inquiry (CCI), another veterans' group, gained strength as the 1968 and 1969 veterans, who had lived through the worst of the war, arrived home. Others joined after encountering the ill-prepared and underfunded services of the Veterans Administration.[48]

In the spring of 1970, as newspapers continued to digest My Lai, CCI held underpublicized hearings, during which veterans spoke candidly of atrocities committed by American soldiers. "It is our crimes that are destroying our national unity," said one veteran. Mark Hatfield, the antiwar senator from Oregon, had their testimony read into the *Congressional Record*. The following Labor Day weekend, VVAW sponsored an antiwar march of two hundred veterans from Morristown, New Jersey, to Valley Forge State Park in Pennsylvania. Both events drew more skeptics than defenders. The Pentagon questioned whether the men were indeed veterans, and the American Legion and the Veterans of Foreign Wars expressed doubt that true soldiers would betray their country with such stark testimony. Many Vietnam veterans themselves were uncomfortable seeing their comrades siding with the antiwar movement. The sight of enlisted men openly and dramatically critical of the war surprised and dismayed most Americans.[49]

Though Calley remained the centerpiece of domestic debate over the war, antiwar veterans began to push into public view a new ideal soldier: the righteous confessor. VVAW and CCI organizers believed that if

Americans came face-to-face with soldiers' "crimes," expressed in the words of the soldiers themselves, they would reject the war. The private world of a soldier's conscience, revealed to all, would yield public evidence of American wrongdoing. "Help us to end the war before they turn your son into a butcher or a corpse," one VVAW flyer read. It was not lost on these veterans that Calley, then in military prison awaiting trial, had neither confessed to war crimes nor admitted that My Lai had been an atrocity.[50]

With righteous confession on their minds, antiwar vets looked for ways to demonstrate that Calley was the symptom of an immoral enterprise, not an exception in a legitimate war. (Most veterans, whatever their politics, had great sympathy for Calley.) In late January and early February 1971, CCI and VVAW joined forces to hold new national hearings. Al Hubbard, a black Air Force veteran, and other GI activists had scoured the country for witnesses, recruiting dozens of former soldiers into VVAW and collecting stories that shocked even the most experienced fighters among them. The Winter Soldier Investigations, as the hearings were called, featured ninety-nine veterans testifying before cameras and tape recorders in a modest two-story brick house in Detroit. Some adopted the fierce rhetoric and generational defiance of the New Left, but most stuck to the bare facts of their experiences. They spoke of civilians murdered, women and young girls raped, villages burned, livestock shot, crops destroyed, and civilians and soldiers tortured.[51]

Many accounts stressed the ritualized violence of unrestrained manhood called forth by the war's intimate brutality. "They stabbed her in both breasts," one vet said of a South Vietnamese woman. "They spread her eagle and shoved an E tool up her vagina." On top of these and countless other specific abuses, they spoke of the near-universal disdain among GIs for the Vietnamese. "We just didn't give a damn," Eugene Keys of the Twenty-fifth Infantry Division said.[52]

Winter Soldier attracted little more than a handful of short articles in prominent newspapers, so VVAW set its sights on Washington. The subsequent demonstrations, labeled Operation Dewey Canyon III, put antiwar veterans on American television screens. On April 19, 1971, vets began arriving on the Mall for what organizers called "a limited incursion into the country of Congress." Led by Gold Star Mothers, women who had lost sons in Vietnam, more than a thousand veterans marched to Arlington National Cemetery. They bore the emblems of both the military and the counterculture. Beards, long or bushy hair, and Afros signaled the unbound and unkempt manhood embraced by the counterculture. Fatigue jackets and shirts were torn or rolled up at the sleeves. Military-issue floppy bush hats were accompanied by headbands and beaded necklaces. They wore VVAW and peace buttons and T-shirts. Later in the weeklong protest they sang "Age of Aquarius" with the Broadway cast of *Hair.* They marched with crutches and in wheelchairs. They held hands and hugged. They cried. They paraded before the nation both the open wounds of a fallen manhood and the striking defiance of a new manhood reclaimed. In their comportment, in their dress, and in what they had come to do, the vets signaled their disaffection with a manhood of resolute toughness and grim tolerance of service and their embrace—partial in some cases, more complete in others—of a more emotional, expressive, and vulnerable alternative.

American culture had undergone prodigious change in a few short years, and the antiwar veterans were a measure of the distance the country had traveled. Most of these men had turned eighteen in 1966 or 1967, before the explosion of black, Chicano, and women's liberation, before the assassinations of Martin Luther King, Jr., and Robert Kennedy, before Stonewall and gay liberation and the massive antiwar demonstrations of 1968 and 1969, before the counterculture had hit its stride and stamped its androgynous, contrarian imprint on national life. On the other side of these events, in 1970 and 1971, the nation was a starkly different place. Some would have said worse, more coarse and angry; others would have said better, freer and less certain of old shibboleths. One of those shibboleths was exactly what the antiwar vets had come to Washington to bury: the Cold War military manhood on which they had been raised.

What followed the veterans' arrival was among the most colorful and unthinkable political spectacles ever staged in Washington. On April 20, vets performed guerrilla theater on the Capitol steps, dramatizing a search-and-destroy mission in which civilians were killed and villages destroyed. Improvised M-16s on their hips, vets ran down and "shot" women dressed as Vietnamese villagers. The next day, fifty of the vets attempted to turn themselves in for war crimes at the Pentagon (they were refused) as hundreds set up tents and prepared an encampment. American soldiers had not created this level of national attention in Washington since the Bonus Army, comprised of out-of-work World War I veterans, had camped on the Mall in the middle of the Great Depression.[53]

On April 22, Lt. John Kerry testified for two hours before the Senate

Foreign Relations Committee. Scion of a wealthy New England family, Kerry had served with distinction in the navy and been recruited to become a VVAW spokesman after activist veterans had seen him on *The Dick Cavett Show*. He gave VVAW a politically centrist face, especially important because congressional conservatives had accused the vets of being anti-American Communist sympathizers. His speech that day was an artful and reasoned explication of government deception and the impossible mission assigned to American soldiers. "How do you ask a man to be the last man to die for a mistake?" Kerry inquired. "Where are McNamara, Rostow, Bundy, Johnson, and so many others? Where are they now that we, the men whom they sent off to war, have returned?" The next day the veterans hurled away their medals.[54]

Coming a mere three weeks after the Calley verdict and the national outrage over his conviction, Dewey Canyon offered Americans a different vision of the grunt everyman: soldiers who admitted to crimes and renounced violence. Taking the baton from Joe Miles, the veterans broadened the notion of what the state owes a citizen: the right to dissent, the right not to be the last man to die for a mistake. VVAW membership soared to twenty thousand in the summer of 1971, and vets revived and moved to the center of the antiwar movement, which had been badly shaken by the Kent State and Jackson State killings the year before. Led by men such as the wheelchair-bound Ron Kovic and Bobby Muller, VVAW assumed a "we were there" moral leadership of the antiwar movement as it prepared for the 1972 campaign season.[55]

Meanwhile current soldiers pressed their case from within the military. Black and Chicano draftees brandished their militancy in challenging racism in the ranks. Other soldiers wrote caustic pieces for underground GI newspapers, which were widely distributed forums for unofficial, critical news of the war. Explicitly political actions such as these emerged alongside even more pervasive problems of discipline and insubordination, which were less politically oppositional than simply nonconformist and rebellious, the generational defiance of authority nurtured by the New Left and the counterculture. In addition to escaping through drugs and refusing assignments, soldiers assaulted officers or simply deserted. Between 1966 and 1971 the desertion rate quintupled and the rate of soldiers going AWOL tripled. Taken together, the political activity and disciplinary breakdown revealed an army in open revolt against the kind of war it was asked to fight.[56]

As early as 1966, when three army privates at Fort Hood filed suit against McNamara, charging that the war was "unjust, immoral, and illegal," small numbers of antiwar servicemen had made headlines. Miles and others like him became an inspiration, and GIs United Against the War in Vietnam grew into one of the largest of the antiwar organizations within the military. By 1970 more than a dozen antiwar GI groups claimed thousands of members in bases across the United States, Asia, and Europe. Working with civil libertarian lawyers, the GI movement developed a bill of GI Rights, which it defended in dozens of court cases. The movement's underground newspapers, with titles like *About Face* and *Up from the Bottom*, gathered together the percolating resentments among grunts; there were more than 150 such newspapers by 1973. The GI movement, like the veterans' movement, developed a gritty, working-class, occasionally multiracial character. Its activists embraced a tough-minded left-wing populism and antiauthoritarianism in which military brass and civilian politicians were universally disdained, the grunt everyman was celebrated, and patriotism derided as a sop to enlisted man cannon fodder.[57]

The emergence of the GI movement was shaped by influences that had an even broader effect on military culture in the late 1960s and early 1970s: black power, the Chicano movement, and the counterculture. Every war involving the United States in the twentieth century to that point had been an arena of racial contestation, but Vietnam coincided with the broadest, most sustained struggle for racial equality in American history. Racial nationalisms and a growing sensitivity to the Third World had radically shifted young African American and Chicano men's consciousness and forced a startling new awareness of American foreign policy. Many soldiers brought that new consciousness with them into the service, as Miles had, and others acquired it while there.[58]

The civilian, veteran, and GI antiwar movements and the civil rights, black power, and Chicano movements, taken together, had transformed the American soldier from an icon of democracy into an ambivalent symbol of neo-imperialism. The generational revolt against authority and inherited truths of all sorts interacted with a military infrastructure stretched to the breaking point, producing an unprecedented crisis. Armed services personnel from the length of the chain of command testified in the early 1970s that American combat troops, especially the army, were utterly without discipline and ineffective as a fighting force. Army Lt. Col. William Hauser's 1973 book *America's Army in Crisis* detailed the disaster from the inside, while a steady stream of books and articles, led by *The Washington Post's Army in Anguish*, chronicled it from the outside. Moreover, in the early seventies the press became filled with articles about the scarred, violent, and psychically damaged soldiers returning from Vietnam. They were drug-addicted, uncelebrated, and suffering from what psychologists and journalists began calling post-Vietnam syndrome (PVS), soon renamed posttraumatic stress disorder. Rarely in American history have so many soldiers so conspicuously and decisively, and on such a scale, evacuated their traditional roles and confounded the expectations of heroic and dutiful men as they did in Vietnam.[59]

•

As the withdrawal from Vietnam progressed through 1972 and 1973, debate over amnesty (and the fate of prisoners of war, taken up in a later chapter) replaced the debate over atrocities at the core of the war's meaning to Americans. Manhood remained the central pivot. The inevitable question—amnesty for whom?—was not nearly as simple as it seemed. Americans whom Nixon and journalists had labeled the "silent majority" or "Middle America" considered amnesty an offer of legal immunity to those who had "dodged" the draft and their duty to the nation. The evaders were imagined as middle-class white kids, children of privilege, whom one Nixon voter called "cowards and troublemakers." But as we have seen, the exiled antiwar draft resister was a small minority of the total number of young men who avoided the draft or ran afoul of Selective Service in the Vietnam decade. In one reasonable estimate, there were 210,000 men officially accused of draft violations and another 250,000 who had never registered at all, and overall most were working class and had remained in the United States. Almost half were nonwhite.[60]

Even these figures tell only part of the story. Between 300,000 and 600,000 additional men (exact figures were subject to intense debate) had received less than honorable discharges from the armed services. A less than honorable discharge was a stigma—bad papers, veterans called them—that barred veterans from all government jobs, disadvantaged them in the private-sector labor market, and denied them many VA benefits. Close observers of military justice found that the majority of less than honorable discharges were given to men whose actions, while insubordinate, reflected the chaos and unpopularity of the war. Moreover, bad

papers were unevenly distributed. Nearly *one-quarter* of African Americans were discharged less than honorably from the marines, and black
soldiers in all service branches earned a disproportionate share of bad
papers, reflecting the racial tensions between white (in many cases southern) officers and black grunts. For those who advocated the widest possible amnesty, dishonorable discharges deserved to be forgiven just as much
as draft avoidance or failure to register. All told, the number of those potentially eligible for amnesty stood at nearly a million.[61]

As the amnesty debate took shape in 1972, therefore, two crucial questions had to be answered: Who would be included? And what was meant
by the granting of amnesty? Mike Hendricks of the Montreal Council to
Aid War Resisters argued that "we cannot be forgiven for taking morally
correct stands against the immoral acts of our government." The former
Democratic senator from Alaska, and a vocal war critic, Ernest Gruening
sounded a related theme in congressional testimony. Calling draft resisters the "unsung heroes of this war," Gruening supported unconditional
amnesty for "those men who followed their consciences, who said, I will
not fight in an illegal and immoral war." Many of the war's critics went beyond Gruening, seeking amnesty for everyone from active conscientious
objectors to those who were negligent in registering for the draft. But for
hawks, any amnesty bill, even a limited one, represented an admission that
the war had been wrong. Such amnesty was therefore unconscionable.[62]

Few were as staunchly opposed to the possibility of amnesty as the
Republican senator James L. Buckley of New York, who called amnesty
"morally objectionable and historically unprecedented," and insisted that
draft evaders return to the United States and make their case in the
courts. Others, such as the former naval commander Lloyd Bucher, who
advocated amnesty for "objectors but not deserters," staked out compromise positions. For Nixon and his supporters in groups such as the VFW
and the American Legion, as well as for the tens of thousands of letter
writers who sent their opinions to the president, a citizen's duty was not to
judge the morality of war but to answer the nation's call of duty. Vice
President Agnew told a VFW audience that "these draft dodgers and deserters" should expect no mercy until "they recognize that it is they who
have erred and not the country."[63]

To antiwar groups, however, amnesty was as much about the unfairness of the draft as anything else. Universal amnesty advocates, such as
left-leaning congressional representatives Bella Abzug (D-NY) and Ron

Dellums (D-CA), along with Amex-Canada and other exile organizations, argued that "draft loopholes for the middle class" had given legal cover to hundreds of thousands of men who avoided service. If the selection process was rife with bias against the working class and people of color, what right did anyone have to persecute the same groups yet again while other, wealthier Americans used their class privilege to escape the dilemmas of the draft and Vietnam altogether?[64]

As fierce as the debate was in 1972 and 1973, by the mid-1970s, after the war's conclusion, polls suggested that Americans were increasingly willing to concede amnesty to men who had resisted the draft as a matter of conscience, though to few others. Between 1974 and 1975, Gerald Ford's Presidential Clemency Board granted clemency and alternative service to 21,000 men. The program was widely regarded as a failure, however, because only 27,000 of the potentially 350,000 eligible persons applied. President Carter granted amnesty to all draft resisters in the first year of his presidency and established a process for military deserters to avoid prosecution.[65]

Yet amnesty dogged Democratic politicians for the greater part of the 1970s. In 1972 Nixon allowed the then-unpopular issue to drown the liberal-left McGovern. Four years later, Carter's opponents cast the president's amnesty program as consistent with his allegedly soft foreign policy. As we shall see, the Democratic Party's openness after 1968 allowed VVAW and other antiwar and pro-amnesty groups to gain a foothold on the party's left, where they continued to loudly demand the broadest possible forgiveness of both resisters and soldiers. In the 1980s conservatives would decry such "permissiveness" and seize the mantle of the fighting military hero as one of their emblems.

In every way, Vietnam tore the connective tissue holding together soldiering and manhood, citizen and duty. As the war dragged on, a vocal and growing number of Americans believed that the heroes of Vietnam were not the obedient soldiers but the soldiers who insisted that a citizen's duty was not merely to serve and fight but also to refuse and resist. To others the resister was cowardly and unmanly, someone who violated centuries-old notions of civic responsibility and military propriety. Yet what of the atrocities? Who were these soldiers who killed children and shot women? And in the war's long wind-down, former soldiers reintegrated into an America where no victory parades awaited, where more than half a million had less-than-honorable discharges, and where so many veterans were psychically damaged. Whatever one's politics, the Vietnam soldier was unrecognizable to a nation steeped in the romance of victory in World War II and the righteousness of Cold War certainties.[66]

The alternative manhood that arose during the war made the Vietnam soldier a protean figure. Unlike any other U.S. war in the twentieth century, Vietnam elevated into the national political consciousness a multitude of contrary soldiers: the righteous confessor, the antiwar activist, the resister, the deserter, the murderer, the drug addict. Such figures were not new in an absolute sense, but in previous American wars the political narrative of national innocence had been powerful enough to push contrary soldiers to the margins. Not unlike the notion of breadwinning manhood, the responsibilities of the citizen soldier had been simply assumed. But Americans could no longer take this dutiful ideal for granted; in Vietnam, the contrary *became* the national narrative.

The Vietnam War thus produced a crisis in the political and cultural narrative of patriotism's alignment with manhood and its centrality to the mythology of the male breadwinner. Instead of coherence, what emerged was confusion over the larger question of rights and obligations in American life. Did working-class men fight while the middle class and rich remained safe? Did brave men fight while cowards deserted? Did noble men refuse to fight an immoral war, while others—Johnson, McNamara, Nixon—lied about the war and sent the nation's vulnerable youth to die? As the questions accumulated, the coherent manhood of the citizen soldier suffered a fatal fracture. More to the point, liberals lost control of the soldiering ideal as the fracture widened, and conservatives prepared to pick up the pieces to be reassembled in ensuing decades.

Popular commentators since the 1970s have often repeated the notion that Vietnam opened "wounds" in the nation that required time to heal, but this does not address the central political developments that emerged from the war. Of these, three stand above others for their contribution to broad transformations in national politics and military culture in the last quarter of the twentieth century. First, major parts of American society, the national political class, and the government, including the Defense Department and every branch of the armed services, emerged from Vietnam determined to reconstitute the national army and to remake the image of the soldier. Second, the fracturing of coherent wartime manhood laid the groundwork for conservative populists to claim the soldier, as they had done brilliantly in the Calley case, and its alignment of manhood and patriotism as a new weapon of political demagoguery. Third, the class politics of the war, in which American policy burdened its most economically vulnerable citizens with the bulk of wartime sacrifice, fed a politics of reactionary resentment against an educated, urban elite. Each of these developments would take decades to emerge fully. They would, nonetheless, both shape and limit the possibilities of American political discourse in ways that were not yet obvious in 1973.

3

HOMOSEXUAL TENDENCIES: GAY MEN AND SEXUAL CITIZENSHIP

The Cold War draft was fraught with anxiety for many American men, not least because it entailed an encounter with the military's sexual regime. When filling out the medical history form, draftees had to answer the question, Have you ever had or have you now "homosexual tendencies"? For a man who had such "tendencies" or had experienced sex with another man, to answer no was to lie under federal law, risking dishonorable discharge and even imprisonment if the lie was discovered. To answer yes meant immediate disqualification and compromised future private-sector employment: gay rejectees were officially deferred on medical grounds, grouped with alcoholics and drug addicts. Fortunate gay soldiers spent their service years officially closeted. Unlucky ones faced harassment, sometimes prison, less-than-honorable discharges, and permanent impairment in the job market.[1]

Alongside breadwinning and soldiering, heterosexuality was another taken-for-granted dimension of American manhood, an essential partner in a stable triumvirate. But even this bedrock notion was thrown into contentious dispute in the second half of the 1960s. What was known as the homophile movement pressed on the nation something startlingly new: the homosexual citizen, a rights-bearing member of a sexual minority denied equal protection of the laws. Gay men in the homophile movement questioned both heterosexuality and conventional manhood, upending the most indomitable taboo of modern American life; lesbians challenged similar, but distinct, sexual and gender ideologies. The language spoken by the homosexual citizen was a rights-based liberalism that drew on the rhetoric and spirit of the black freedom movement. Yet that citizen's pathway to liberation was distinct, for it bridged the divide between public and private, between rights and secrets.

To turn secrets into rights required a unique challenge to the notion of heterosexual manhood and the content of American citizenship. In conflicts over breadwinners and soldiers, the question was whether, and how, the circle of citizenship would grow more expansive to accommodate different, sometimes even counterintuitive elements. At issue was whether men behaved in ways that accorded with the myths of breadwinning and soldiering. So too with heterosexuality, but with a difference: gay men were not regarded as proper subjects and citizens from the beginning. Their challenge to the mythology of the proper American male citizen therefore was first and foremost inclusion within it.

Sexually discriminatory practices extended well beyond the military. Both custom and law forced homosexuality into the shadows in every province of American life. During the Cold War, a wave of repression amplified the legal restrictions inherited from earlier eras. Between 1948 and the early 1960s, homosexual purges stripped gay men and women of their jobs in Washington, D.C., and in state capitals across the country— government employees summarily dismissed because of their sexual difference. Insisting that they were protecting national security and the integrity of American ideals, gay- and red-baiting politicians launched this expulsion of public servants, a "lavender scare" that matched the more celebrated dismissals of suspected Communists. Antigay persecutions began in the State Department in the late 1940s and gained momentum under President Eisenhower's 1953 executive order declaring "sexual perversion" grounds for dismissal from any federal job. More than a thousand federal employees were dismissed over the next decade, while untold others sank deeper into public silence about their sexuality.[2]

The hardening of America's postwar "straight state" changed the life of Frank Kameny. A highly regarded Harvard-trained astronomer who had also compiled a distinguished record of military service, Kameny planned a career as a map surveyor in the years after World War II. Until, that is, he was fired from the Army Map Service in 1957 for being gay—a "deviate," in the idiom of the day. After four years spent filing petitions with the Civil Service Commission and drafting court pleadings to get his job back, Kameny was turned down by the Supreme Court in 1961. Unemployed, he then helped form, and was elected president of, the Washington Mattachine Society, named for one of the first gay political organizations founded a decade earlier. Between the spring and fall of 1965 Kameny, now a full-time homophile activist ("gay rights" had yet to emerge as a phrase, and "homophile" remained the name of choice), helped organize a series of public protests, most of them just a few blocks down Constitution Avenue from Congress and the Supreme Court.[3]

Agitating for rights was new in homophile circles. How was one to go public with sexual difference, defined by law and culture as a dark, terrible secret? Kameny answered in part by encouraging his fellow male activists to wear sensible coats and ties, and the women among them, conservative skirts and heels. Theirs was a demonstration of respectability as much as a call for rights. They held a small and little-noticed picket at the White House in April and a larger one at the end of May. A June picket at the Civil Service Commission was followed by demonstrations at the Pentagon and State Department and a final picket at the White House in October.[4]

Kameny was not alone in resisting the Cold War tide of homosexual persecution. By 1965 he was part of a growing, but still small and diffuse, network of homophile activists and organizations that publicly denounced the nation's consensus view of gay men and lesbians and sought to dismantle the legal restrictions preventing their full citizenship. The year of Washington Mattachine's pickets, there were active homophile groups in Washington, D.C., New York, Philadelphia, Miami, Chicago, Kansas City, San Francisco, Los Angeles, and a handful of smaller cities. Kameny, who urged homophile activists to seek "the complete integration of the homosexual—as a homosexual—into society at large," was part of a new generation of vocal and insistent, even militant, integrationists who revitalized the decade-old homophile movement in the first half of the 1960s.[5]

In the process, homophiles charted a preliminary course out of the postwar closet and into the public consciousness of the nation. In the quickly paced years from 1965 to 1968, arrayed against the country's major institutions—the state, churches, and the medical profession—homophile activists took up the deepest questions of what it meant to be men and women, what it meant to be sexual, and what these matters had to do with the rights and obligations of citizenship. Just as ideals of the American "breadwinner" and "soldier" began to crumble during this period, so did the ideal of a "heterosexual" nation. Less publicly conspicuous in the late 1960s than battles over either breadwinning or soldiering, in large part because of journalists' unsympathetic reporting, the homophile assault on heterosexuality was no less elemental to this era of upheaval.[6]

In the new homophile politics, private and public were inseparable. Homophiles demanded the right of privacy: the right not to have their lives policed, the right to be left alone. The dominant ideology of the movement, led largely by white gay men and lesbians, prior to 1968 emphasized this sexual privacy as an inviolable component of equal citizenship. If privacy and respectability constituted homophiles' overriding objectives, however, a minor chord in the movement was the call for sexual freedom and public rights. The Connecticut activist Foster Gunnison observed that "the danger of this phrase [in private]" is that acceptable heterosexual behavior—kissing in public, holding hands in the park—could "be classified as public indecency for the homosexual pair." Homophiles knew that the right to be gay, although rooted in notions of sexual privacy, increasingly required a quite public response *and* presence.[7]

Believed to be weak-willed, effeminate, emotional, secretive, prone to blackmail, and subversive of the nuclear family, gay men were not *real* men in the Cold War imagination. The homophile movement made the essential counterargument: a man who loves, and has sex with, other men is both a citizen and *a man*. In the heat of sixties social movement activism, however, even that inarguably profound challenge to the American social order came under assault, dividing homophile activists. Lesbians pounded the pavement and embodied homophile determination at every step, but they found women's concerns and priorities neglected by their male counterparts. Many lesbians came to see homophiles as the architects of a movement for men only. Whiteness too claimed a special place in gay politics, one essential to initial victories but almost immediately thereafter problematic. After the homosexual citizen broke into the nation's consciousness, this citizen would itself be subject to charges that it did not accommodate the full range of gender and sexual differences among Americans. So it would go for the social movements of the era. Positing inclusive new ideals proved more difficult than pointing to the shortcomings of existing ones. And yet the promise of an expanding liberal citizenship remained magnetic. Despite its shortcomings, it had shepherded virtually all the significant new rights and protections gained in the United States since the drafting of the Constitution. Gay men sought to step fully inside the circle of citizenship, and in making their case to do so further destabilized inherited assumptions about American manhood and the heterosexual breadwinner ideal.[8]

•

In 1964, the Florida Legislative Investigation Committee published a short booklet, entitled *Homosexuality and Citizenship in Florida*, that addressed the "quality of citizenship" in the state. The citizens on the minds of committee members were *straight* Floridians whose "health and moral well-being" were threatened by "homosexual activities." Part of southern resistance to the two *Brown* desegregation decisions, the so-called Johns Committee was convened to discredit the NAACP while ferreting out Communists and other disloyal Americans. The Johns Committee represented an increasingly common phenomenon in the South: opposition to desegregation evolved into opposition to alleged moral subversion of all sorts. Racial politics fed breadwinner politics. By 1964 the committee's mandate included "homosexual activities," and its report concluded that "homosexuals pose a problem demanding of serious attention by all concerned with sound citizenship."[9]

A response from homophile activists was not long in coming. "The Homosexual Citizen in the Great Society" was the theme of the 1965 meeting of the East Coast Homophile Organizations (ECHO) in New York. Now under the leadership of activists such as Kameny and a cohort of East Coasters that included Dick Leitsch and others from New York and Barbara Gittings and her partner, Kay Lahusen, among others, from Philadelphia, the organizations that met in September of that year addressed "the homosexual as a citizen and a social being, not a psychological subject." Two months earlier, on July 4, thirty-two gay men and seven lesbians had picketed at the site of the signing of the Declaration of Independence in Philadelphia, establishing what became known as the annual reminder, the major yearly demonstration for gay rights until Christopher Street Liberation Day was established in 1970. Homophiles seized on the term "citizen" and the symbolism of the Declaration not merely to prove themselves equal inheritors of American traditions. They aimed to shift an entire conceptual framework. Homosexuals were not objects of inquiry, victims of illness, or criminal deviants. They were not even *only* homosexuals. "I write as a homosexual American citizen," Kameny penned to Sargent Shriver in 1964, "with equal emphasis upon all three words."[10]

The sixties America in which Kameny found himself was suffused with ideals of manhood, alternately tough-minded and romantic, that brooked no involvement by women or homosexual men. The Kennedy men, with their touch football games and records of military and political heroism, embodied this manhood. Their New Left antagonists, street-fighting radicals well versed in political theory and striking the pose of angry young men, represented another variation. Figures as divergent as the the black power spokesmen H. Rap Brown and Eldridge Cleaver and the New Right conservatives William F. Buckley and Irving Kristol shared the obsession. So too did the politicians of all political stripes who so thoroughly dismissed the women's movement and barely recognized the homophile movement. Politics and social struggle for most of the decade had a distinctly masculine cast. Manhood was the sixties' cultural currency.[11]

To shy away from a fight was to be a "faggot" or, in the words of Joseph McCarthy a decade earlier, a "cock-sucker." Arthur Schlesinger, Jr., who coined the term "vital center" to describe Cold War American politics and who became the consummate Kennedy insider, cloaked the matter in only slightly more respectable language. Democracy, he had written in the late 1940s, was a "fighting faith" that required "new virility" and a banishing of "neurosis" from political life. By the late 1960s, however, gay men had joined the fray, insisting on a kind of equality that few straight people imagined possible or desirable. In opening a national conversation about sexual citizenship, the homophiles raised the possibility, however controversial, of expanding the rights revolution pioneered by African Americans to include "sexual" minorities.[12]

To be gay, lesbian, or otherwise sexually different in the United States in the 1960s was to possess a partial, compromised citizenship. Gay men and lesbians could be arrested and jailed on a variety of charges related to the display of alternative sexuality: lewd conduct, solicitation, vagrancy, and public nuisance headed the list. Sodomy was considered a serious crime, carrying prison sentences of up to twenty years, and for this reason legitimized the denial of other rights concerning employment, housing, public association, and speech. Few states outside Florida published official booklets on homosexuality, but state governments and urban police departments across the country investigated and harassed homosexuals throughout the first two postwar decades. Newspapers routinely published the names of men arrested in bars or outdoor cruising spots, ending careers and sometimes marriages, while psychiatrists commonly diagnosed gay men and lesbians as psychotic and subjected them to aversion therapy, including shock treatment. As late as 1968, homosexual acts remained a felony in every state except Illinois, New York, and New Jersey. Such measures were necessary, the *San Fernando Valley Citizen-News*, a Los Angeles newspaper, explained, because every homosexual "is a potential criminal and even killer." That attitudes like these were not marginal or rare was the first obstacle for homophiles.[13]

Most Americans believed that homosexuality was related not just to unconventional but to unnatural gender roles. The stereotypes of gay sexuality in postwar American culture veered between casting gay men as hyperfeminine and hypermasculine. Gay men were thought to have an incomplete, or "inverted," manhood. Weak, womanish, and laughably unmanly, they were convenient foils for heterosexual manhood and its breadwinning and soldiering prototypes. Or gay men were just the opposite, exhibiting too much of the wrong kind of manliness—sexual voraciousness. Lacking wives, they were culturally and legally ineligible to be breadwinners. Lacking manly resolve, they could not be soldiers. As sexual predators they threatened children. To be gay was to be a pariah, with virtually no exceptions.[14]

Homophiles understood that to claim their full rights as citizens, they would need to end forced secrecy. But in lifting sexuality out of the realm of secrets, they would make an equally powerful claim to privacy. In their pursuit of legal privacy and their rights as "homosexual American citizens," therefore, homophiles paradoxically had to make public what had always been in America imagined as private: sexuality itself. As gay men and women became more visible, declaring an end to their enforced double lives, they helped drive a larger political conversation about sexuality and rights. "What is most noteworthy about the pioneers of the movement," observed Clark Polak, president of the Homosexual Law Reform Society in Philadelphia, was their capacity to "keep alive the notion that the private sexual acts of consenting adults should not be considered criminal." The privacy they claimed was the privacy that most other Americans took for granted: straight citizens' sexual identities and lives were not "secret" in any meaningful sense, but they were certainly "private."[15]

Activists were therefore keenly sensitive to related legal contexts. The right to gather in public, for instance, one of the earliest demands of homophiles, was grounded in First Amendment association rights and not in

privacy. Legal disputes over gay bars and the mailing of homophile publications, dating to the 1950s, also hinged on the First Amendment. The
"right" to be gay from the beginning went beyond the right to sexual privacy. It was also about the right to gather in public; the right to speak and
publish about sexuality; the right to be free from arrest; the right to be free
from discrimination at work, at school, and in the military. The homophile
vision of equality required a certain kind of privacy, or "freedom from"
state policing, as well as a distinct kind of state protection, or "freedom to"
live as equal Americans. The sexual citizen they imagined—like the one
conceived by feminists in these same years, as we shall see—demanded to
be left alone by the state *and* simultaneously to be protected by it. It required the negative right of liberty and the positive right of equality.[16]

Extending either negative or positive rights to gay men and women
remained unimaginable in American law and politics in the mid-sixties.
In June 1965 the Supreme Court issued a modest but consequential decision in *Griswold* v. *Connecticut*. For the first time the justices interpreted
the Constitution to protect a "right of privacy," in a case concerning a
married couple's access to birth control. The Court's argument—that a
Connecticut law prohibiting contraception violated marital privacy—
prefigured the 1973 *Roe* v. *Wade* decision legalizing abortion. But *Griswold* had another lasting effect: it defined heterosexual marriage as the
domain of sexual privacy rights. Several months later, in October, at the
foot of the Statue of Liberty, President Johnson signed the Hart-Cellar Immigration Act, major new legislation widely praised for ending the nation's racially biased immigrant quota system. In a provision little noticed
outside homophile circles, however, the act simultaneously strengthened
a 1950s-era law making "sexual deviation" grounds for denying immigrants entry and for deporting those already in the United States. The
Supreme Court upheld the provision two years later.[17]

Organized homophile groups had first appeared in the early 1950s,
with the founding of the male-led Mattachine Society and the magazine
ONE in Los Angeles and the lesbian Daughters of Bilitis in San Francisco.
A handful of gay men and lesbians of that generation embraced rights
politics, and a few were left-wing radicals, but the dominant rhetorical
tone of the early movement was cautious and understated. Fears of exposure, arrest, and losing one's job kept militant voices in check. Prevailing
ideas about the sickness of homosexuality left many activists uncertain
how best to make their case in public, whether through sympathetic psy-

chiatrists and straight allies or by gay men and lesbians themselves. But the movement made a leap in 1964 and 1965. Inspired by the black freedom movement, the new militants defined homosexuals as a minority group—the "nation's largest minority group after the Negro," according to Kameny—and began to press their case through law reform, political pressure, and, though still less frequently, public protest in a language of rights liberalism.[18]

Against both the legal backdrop of *Griswold* and the first Washington Mattachine protests, one of the activists who flew to New York for the fall 1965 ECHO meeting was Bill Beardemphl. A talented chef in San Francisco, Beardemphl had helped found the Society for Individual Rights (SIR) with Jim Foster, who had been dishonorably discharged from the military. SIR was part of a seismic shift in gay politics in San Francisco in the early 1960s that also saw the creation of the Tavern Guild and the Council on Religion and the Homosexual (CRH). The San Francisco movement quickly matched the increasing visibility of East Coast homophiles, with a difference: while homophile organizations in New York, D.C., and Philadelphia had few members, San Francisco's movement was distinctly community based and membership oriented. Inspired by the westward gay migration that was transforming the city, homophiles in San Francisco engaged the broad gay community in municipal and state politics, and they also sponsored dances, drag balls, theater trips, bowling leagues, picnics and hikes, and other social events. SIR figured out how to bring together homophile activists and ordinary gay men—largely men—on the theory that the social fabric of gay life was bound up with and inseparable from the homophile political project of dignity and rights.[19]

An early advocate of gay power and not of mere tolerance or acceptance, not unlike emerging notions of black power, SIR was instrumental in transforming the notion of the gay political community into something tangible. Inspired by Beardemphl's belief that "the only things homosexuals will ever get is what they are strong enough to get," between 1964 and 1967 SIR added nearly one thousand members, becoming one of the largest homophile organizations in the country. Its frequent candidates nights brought city and state politicians before large gay audiences, creating a meaningful sense of gay community and allowing homophiles to press their representatives for legal reform directly. To bridge gay culture and politics, SIR distributed its magazine, *Vector*, in bars, circulated campaign literature in bathhouses, and established one of the first gay community centers in the nation. SIR pushed gay people further into local politics than many East Coast homophiles had done by imagining an incipient, but not yet named, "gay vote."[20]

Beardemphl, Larry Littlejohn, and other SIR activists consolidated ideas that had circulated among homophiles since the late 1950s into a homosexual bill of rights. A pathbreaking document, it demanded sexual privacy, elimination of solicitation laws, and nondiscrimination in hiring, military service, and immigration, along with a host of other legal reforms. That and SIR's other publications reached a national audience. The best known of these, called the pocket lawyer, was a document small enough to fit in the back pocket that explained what to do if one were arrested, including the crucial admonition "Admit to nothing, sign nothing, get counsel."[21]

Beardemphl joined Kameny, Gittings, and others in New York in 1965 in an effort to bring together West and East Coast homophile groups, along with midwestern and smaller southern contingents, under a national umbrella, the North American Conference of Homophile Organizations (NACHO). On the basis of the New York meeting, the first NACHO conference was held in February 1966 in Kansas City. There gay and lesbian homophiles adopted a version of the homosexual bill of rights and agreed on the first coordinated national protest: on Armed Forces Day, May 21, demonstrators in San Francisco, Los Angeles, New York, Chicago, and Washington, D.C., demanded the right of gay men and lesbians to serve openly in the military. It was a bold gesture. The military had been instrumental in the lavender scare, and the association of military service with both rights and duties, not to mention its centrality to patriotism, made Armed Forces Day an irresistible national coming-out for the movement.[22]

In the time between the first D.C. pickets in 1965 and the third annual meeting of NACHO in 1968, homophile activists created a distinct figure on the national political landscape: an American citizen defined as both a person and a sexual being. Minority status was based not on race, sex, ethnicity, nationality, or religion but on sexual or erotic identity. Many homophiles kept "sex" on the margins of the rights conversation in order to dispel the toxic stereotypes that had long haunted gay men and lesbians and to assume the partial cloak that respectability offered. But by defining homosexuals as a minority group, homophiles also challenged heterosexual norms, insisting that all Americans recognize an essential but long-ignored truth: citizens don't just have a sex; they *have* sex. Homophiles thus walked a fine line. They wanted sex in the conversation at the same time that they sought to keep it from becoming the primary issue. They wanted a citizenship based on equality with heterosexuals but remained ambivalent about how much to stress the *difference* of their sexuality.[23]

The intensity of postwar sexual panics and moral proscriptions against homosexuality in a nation stratified by class, gender, and race meant that the first to take gay rights public were otherwise the least vulnerable: middle-class white men. The resources, education, skills, public access, and professional status of homophile leaders were instrumental, perhaps even essential, to the articulation of what later became gay rights. But the movement's demands, as well as its notions of rights and community, stood in uncomfortable relation to more vulnerable gay people.[24]

Thus the new homosexual citizen was too often presumed to be a white man, an otherwise conventional American whose rights were based on sexual identity but whose status did not require delving into race, gender, or class matters. SIR's pocket lawyer and even its bill of rights pointed to police harassment, unequal law enforcement, and military service as the most salient gay issues. For many gay men, equal citizenship meant freedom from state surveillance of their sex lives, the negative right to be left alone. At the extreme end of this spectrum, being gay was about "lifestyle." But lesbians faced different obstacles and were subjected to a range of forces and disadvantages few gay men ever confronted. As women, and often as mothers, lesbians did not always find themselves reflected in the homosexual citizen conceived by the male-dominated homophile movement.[25]

The question of visibility, so central to the homophile movement, was additionally complicated by race. Gay cultures invoked two kinds of visibility. One was the gay world into which one "came out." The second, and more politicized, was the public world of family, friends, coworkers, and, optimally, society as whole. In both kinds of visibility, there existed a presumed "public" into which one moved: the limited, more welcoming gay public in the first instance and the discriminatory public of community and nation in the second. Race shaped each type of visibility in important ways. First, the idealized public square in the United States, the place where one has full rights and fully belongs, has always granted unequal access to members of nonwhite groups. For African Americans and other people of color, there was no neutral public in which race was not a factor.

Second, the homosexual citizen presumed that gay men were subject to harassment and discrimination solely because of their sexuality. This was a fraught assumption for people of color, who could never presume that race was not at work in their treatment. Forged in the largely middle-class world of white gay professionals, the homosexual citizen was both a remarkable new figure with enormous potential to remake sexual citizenship and win mainstream legal victories, and at the same time an incomplete, limited representative of gay experience and therefore a constraint.[26]

Though lamented by many, that limitation was also entirely predictable. The United States is too big, too diverse, too variegated a place, and too caught in the legacies of racial, class, and gender inequity, for any single notion of equality or freedom to capture the experiences and desires of all people. And sorting out possibilities and pitfalls was more than a game of identity politics. To have any chance of success in the United States, homophile politics required the social capital—access and influence—that respectability and whiteness conferred. Once leveraged, however, respectability and whiteness reproduce themselves and the privileges they convey. This was the dilemma of all postwar American rights movements on the liberal left, including sexual ones. Taking hold of public consciousness and mobilizing to secure equality from the margins was impossible without social capital. But every rights movement eventually had to confront its *own* margins or risk becoming simply another source of orthodoxy and silencing. Resolving the interplay of center and margin, especially in movements led primarily by middle-class men, was never easy and one of the stickiest dilemmas for political projects in the "rights" era.

•

For many gay men, cultivating respectability for public consumption was the equivalent of cultural suicide. To them, what gave gay life its vibrancy was precisely its ethic of men having fun with other men. Clark Polak, who published *Drum* magazine in Philadelphia, was of this thinking. Owner of a successful advertising company, Polak designed *Drum* to combine the style of gay male physique magazines, which featured muscled, bare-chested cover boys, with the news and opinion columns of more traditional homophile publications. "News for 'queers' and fiction for 'perverts,'" Polak promised, along with "photo essays for 'fairies' and laughs for 'faggots.'" With a circulation of fifteen thousand in 1968, *Drum* pledged to "put sex back into homosexuality." It worked. Polak reached more readers than all other homophile publications combined. *Vector* and *The Advocate* were less risqué than *Drum*, but they too combined a raunchy, celebratory vision of gay life with political journalism. Notices of drag balls, articles about the best "fag" beaches, warnings about "tearooms" (restrooms) to avoid, and full-page advertisements featuring naked men appeared alongside updates on gay rights legislation in the California Assembly and national news of the homophile movement.[27]

Drum and its brethren staked claims in territory considered treacherous by many homophiles—that of sexual freedom. In doing so, these publications attracted a wider readership than did the tamer homophile magazines, dramatically expanding the gay public sphere and gay politics in the second half of the 1960s. To equate respectability with cultural suicide was after all to make a bold claim for positive rights, including the right to be protected by the state when sexual identities were made public. To allow the public a glance at gay worlds, however, troubled homophile activists who saw respectability as a necessary shield and had spent years making inroads with it in place. Some believed that *Drum* and what it stood for would only invite public scorn and threaten the homophile rights project. A *Tangents* editorial in 1967 disparagingly referred to "those homosexuals who, with their bizarre costumes and shrill behavior, irresponsibly caricature and damage the image of the homosexual in the public mind."[28]

The ascendance of ideals of sexual freedom in homophile circles was part of a larger national transformation that had begun in the mid-1960s and accelerated after 1967: the rise of the counterculture. Too often characterized as a heterosexual phenomenon cultivated by hyperheterosexual hippies, the counterculture had shared origins that prominently included gay culture and gay figures, including, in the 1950s, a handful of the Beats. Rippling outward from bohemian urban enclaves such as North Beach and the Haight-Ashbury in San Francisco, Greenwich Village in New York, Hollywood and Silver Lake in Los Angeles, and a handful of college campuses, the counterculture was a shifting mélange of styles and attitudes, rather than a coherent ideology. The counterculture exhibited ironic detachment from, and open ridicule of, the "establishment," a term as ill defined as "hippie" and capacious enough to include "anyone over thirty." Unmoored from traditional hierarchies and institutions—church, the family, sexual propriety, the market—the counterculture promised liberation and was never far from chaos. In its brief flowering between

1967 and 1970—between the Summer of Love and the trio of disasters that were the Manson murders, the Rolling Stones' Altamont Concert, and Kent and Jackson State—the counterculture's infectious contrariness and romantic optimism laid the groundwork for dismantling the boundaries of gender and sexual conformities.

Nowhere were that contrariness and romantic optimism more in evidence than in Southern California's gay neighborhoods, on the northwestern edge of downtown Los Angeles. On a weekend afternoon in March 1968, a trail of signs along the main road in Griffith Park read, THIS WAY GIRLS. According to *The Advocate*, a crowd of "200 wild fairies" had gathered in the park and were "having a festive affair." "With limp wrists flying everywhere," the "delightfully outrageous queens" held the city's first gay-in. Presided over by a drag queen dressed "in broad-brimmed bonnet, Audrey Hepburn sunglasses, and semipsychedelic pantaloons" (who would not have met the dress code at Kameny's annual reminder), the event, along with *The Advocate*'s campy, tongue-in-cheek reportage, mocked heterosexual convention and homophile respectability alike.[29]

But the gay-in was nothing if not a political act. It called on gay men "to come out of the dark shadows of fear and paranoia and to establish themselves as free American citizens." *The Advocate* noted that the revelers were fighting "for their place in a hypocritical world which preaches, but seldom practices, equality for all." The kind of equality the gay men in Griffith Park celebrated—freedom for sexual expressiveness and gender transgression—still made many homophile activists nervous about obtaining public support for their program of privacy and legal reform. But to those who advocated personal freedom through sexual authenticity, the two were inseparable.[30]

Homophiles committed to sexual respectability were not alone in their disdain for the sort of gay culture on display in Griffith Park. Many ordinary gay men were as conservative in matters of gender presentation as their heterosexual counterparts. Gay culture and sexual liberation were not synonymous. "I don't like the exhibitionists any more than you do," one gay Chicagoan told a *Chicago Daily News* reporter in 1966. Antipathy toward "swishes," as effeminate gay men were often known, had been a part of gay life for decades, a function of gay men's policing of their own expressiveness. Whether "exhibitionists" were reviled for sustaining gay stereotypes in straight society or for their transgression of gender norms in gay society, patriarchal attitudes toward masculinity remained powerfully embedded in gay circles. In *Vector*'s "open forum" on drag in 1967, one respondent insisted that the vast majority of gay men "walk like men, talk like men, and dress like men."[31]

And what of sex itself? Homophiles, as Polak observed more than once, had stripped sex from the movement in the drive for respectability. Within the gay community, however, debates over sexual freedom only intensified. Bar culture and cruising celebrated sex but were prone to re-ducing gay life to what Rita Mae Brown called a "fuckathon." Beardem-phl blamed gay men for importing society's "warped concept of sex role-playing," which had "robbed many homosexuals of their person-hood." On the other hand, by the 1970s eroticism, role-playing, and "fuck-ing" held places of prominence in gay male culture, and many argued that they simply deserved the same privacy protections afforded hetero-sexuals. As a community constituted on the basis of sexual difference, gay men confronted a core question throughout this period: Could sexual freedom be the foundation for both personal and community authenticity?[32]

Homophiles by and large viewed the quest for rights and legal reform as the legitimate arena of politics. For a "middle class movement [that] sought respectability more than self-respect," in the words of gay activist Jim Kepner, rights politics for the moment trumped sexual politics. In a 1966 NACHO address, Kameny said that homophiles "are not fighting for sexual freedom." Yet demands for ever-wider gender and sexual noncon-formity had appeared from the start of homophile activism. The nature of the homophile movement—its reliance on respectable white men—meant that differences in gender expression, class, and race within the gay com-munity fell by the wayside in the consuming drive toward legal reform. Unsurprisingly, by the late 1960s a fundamental split was dividing gay politics. Respectability coexisted with simultaneous pressures toward sex-ual freedom. The leadership of the homophile movement saw the quest for legal equality as the preeminent political struggle, while a growing and unabashedly public smattering of gay groups and subcultures came to see the projection of gay identities into the public arena as a political and necessary act.[33]

And yet the choice between respectability and rights was too often proven a false one. An illustration of that truth occurred on a warm night in August 1968, in the Wilmington neighborhood of Los Angeles, in a bar called the Patch. Four men were harassing patrons of the well-known gay night spot. "God damn faggots! God damn faggots!" they yelled. A police car frightened away the "local punks," as *The Advocate* called the harass-ers. Complicating matters, two undercover LAPD vice cops in civilian clothing were already inside the Patch, socializing with the crowd. When they called five uniformed officers into the club and made two arrests, the Patch's manager, Lee Glaze, rushed to the stage. "It's not a crime to be in a gay bar," he told the crowd. "We're Americans too!" a young man exclaimed.[34]

Sensing the political import of the moment, Glaze urged his voluble, inebriated patrons to descend en masse on the police station. About twenty-five followed him to the Harbor Division of the LAPD shortly before 3:00 a.m. Provided with flowers by a Patch patron's florist shop, "they marched into the waiting room carrying bouquets of gladioli, mums, dai-sies, carnations, and roses." (*The Advocate* added, with a wink, "but no pansies.") Two hours later the crowd greeted the two who had been arrested, showering them with flowers, posing for photographs, and mugging in front of "Join the Los Angeles Police Department" posters. In a season of politi-cal assassinations, widening turmoil over the war in Vietnam, and escalat-ing violence between antiwar and black power advocates and police across the country, patrons of the Patch had brought a mellower "flower power" to a small corner of Los Angeles. The events in Wilmington were mild, and nonviolent, in comparison with the Stonewall riots in Greenwich Vil-lage ten months later. But they were evidence that for many gay men, the drive for privacy flew in the face of their most fervent beliefs.[35]

Footloose politics aside, the incident at the Patch revealed the cracks in homophile respectability. Now and again cops might chase away "the punks," but they were just as likely to arrest gay men in a bar. Opponents of respectability could reasonably point to the Patch and ask how privacy rights might have made a difference. "We're Americans too" was a far more urgent and compelling claim than the call to support reform through the nation's court system. The Patch was a gauntlet thrown down to signify a much larger coming fight, a fight on behalf of making a for-merly dark secret into the basis of personal identity, citizenship, and basic human rights.

•

Creating homosexual citizens meant disabusing the nation of the idea that homosexuality was an illness. If sodomy laws underwrote a sexual legal regime, the belief that homosexuality was a mental illness underlay broader perceptions of gay men and lesbians as unemployable, unreliable, and abnormal—a crucial buttress to heterosexual-male-breadwinner nuclear families. In 1969, capping off a series of major articles about homosexuality in the popular press, which catered to the public's lusty appetite for stories of dark and secret subcultures and taboo sexual encounters, *Time* asked, "Are homosexuals sick?" The question was, the august publication assured its readers, a "crucial issue."[36]

During the same years, a case winding its way through the judicial system confirmed that the entire homophile project faced the roadblock of illness. When Clive Michael Boutilier, a Canadian immigrant, applied for U.S. citizenship in 1963, he admitted with some embarrassment to an arrest years earlier on a sodomy charge. Since U.S. law prohibited the immigration of people with "psychopathic personalities," the Immigration and Naturalization Service (INS) argued for Boutilier's deportation on the ground that he was a "sexual deviate." The fate of Boutilier's naturalization application, which wended its way through lower courts before reaching the Supreme Court in 1967 (*Boutilier v. Immigration and Naturalization Service*) hinged on whether Congress had intended to include all homosexual aliens under the term "psychopathic personality." Boutilier's Supreme Court appeal, pursued with the assistance of the ACLU and the Homosexual Law Reform Society in Philadelphia (funded in part by Polak), was rejected in a 6–3 decision. The majority opinion declared that Congress had employed in its 1952 immigration legislation "a term of art intended to exclude homosexuals from entry into the United States." In part because of *Boutilier*, Congress clarified the language in the 1965 immigration act, using the term "sexual deviation" in place of "psychopathic personality." Boutilier, diagnosed as sick by American politicians, was deported.[37]

The American Medical Association (AMA) and the American Psychiatric Association (APA) considered homosexuality a mental disorder, a type of neurosis. The chief advocate of this position, Charles Socarides, was a practicing psychoanalyst and a professor at Columbia University. Calling homosexuality "a dread dysfunction, malignant in character, which has risen to epidemic proportions," Socarides was the public face of the homosexuality as pathology consensus. In a 1967 interview conducted by Mike Wallace on CBS television, Socarides called for "a national center for sexual rehabilitation" because however dread, the disease of homosexuality was "potentially curable."[38]

Notions of homosexuality as mental illness stoked fears of national weakness and criminality. In the lavender scare of the 1940s and 1950s, gay male sexuality had exemplified the subversion of Cold War norms of hearth and home. In postwar sex crime panics, it also stood for a "hard," predatory masculinity. In the psychiatric model, postwar psychiatrists and psychologists constructed the figure of the lonely, mentally disturbed, and gender-confused homosexual desperate for contact. Psychiatrists were careful not to claim that all homosexuals were dangerous or "potential killers," but in the popular imagination, fed by tabloid journalism and police department propaganda, all these characterizations blurred together.[39]

Police in particular drew on the officially sanctioned link between mental illness and criminality. Law enforcement departments across the country exhibited a harsh homophobia, and in the late 1960s and early 1970s concerns about gay male behavior played a not inconsequential role in the national law-and-order movement. Periodic efforts to "clean up" places such as Greenwich Village in New York or Hollywood Boulevard in Los Angeles were part of the ebb and flow of urban politics; visible morals campaigns always proved popular in a city's outlying suburban enclaves. Few departments were as hostile to gay men as the LAPD. Its 138-page 1972 booklet, *Victimless Crimes*, characterized homosexuality as "in every sense a psychological abnormality" associated with other "sexual aberrations." Many homosexuals, the report continued, "are prone to violence" and focus on minors as "the primary sex object."[40]

The psychiatric model of homosexuality came under assault in the 1960s from two groups: sympathetic physicians and homophiles. In 1967 Evelyn Hooker, a pioneer of social science research at UCLA, led a National Institute of Mental Health (NIMH) task force on the "issue." She was joined by the psychiatrists Judd Marmor and Jerome Frank and the legal scholars Morris Ploscowe and David Bazelon, among others. Their report, released in 1969, repudiated the orthodox view that homosexuality was pathological. Though the Nixon administration buried the report and fired Stanley Yoles, the director of the NIMH, physicians nonetheless continued to campaign for reform inside the profession. By 1971 there was a small but vocal group of gay psychiatrists and their allies agitating for the removal of homosexuality from the American Psychiatric Association's (APA) *Diagnostic and Statistical Manual of Mental Disorders* (DSM).[41]

Homophiles derided the psychiatric model over the course of the 1960s. In 1964 Kameny delivered a speech to the New York Mattachine

Society in which he insisted that the movement would succeed only by "taking a firm stand" against the illness diagnosis, exemplifying a new militancy. Joined by Barbara Gittings, Kay Lahusen, Larry Littlejohn, and Del Martin, Kameny insisted on complete overthrow of the psychiatric model. Between 1965 and the early 1970s, these and other gay and lesbian leaders challenged individual psychiatrists (including Socarides), sponsored panels at the meetings of NACHO and the Eastern Regional Conference of Homophile Organizations (ERCHO, which had replaced ECHO), and spoke before audiences of physicians and psychiatrists. By 1971 they had enough support within the APA to push for formal declassification in the *DSM*, which finally came in 1973.[42]

The successful challenge to the psychiatric model of homosexuality overturned postwar conceptions not just of sexuality but of gender and citizenship. Especially in the masculinity-obsessed fifties and early sixties, same-sex desire and "improper" gender behavior could be explained only by illness. If only illness could explain deviation from the opposite-sex nuclear family, then the "normalcy" of that family was bolstered. As in the pathologizing of black families in response to the Moynihan report, "sick" Americans were not fully entitled citizens; they were subjects of either pity or revulsion but not partners in an imagined future. Thus illness was a barrier to full rights. It blocked gay men and lesbians from inclusion in the "body politic" of the nation. Bringing the psychiatric model of homosexuality to an end was a prerequisite to the making of the homosexual citizen.[43]

•

As long as that model prevailed, gay men and women would remain in a state of social limbo, in between a "healthy" citizenry and a psychopathic other. As objects of diagnosis they could hardly be imagined as the rights-bearing social equals of heterosexuals. Their very presence in the public sphere was anathema to many conventional politicians, men such as Los Angeles city councilman Paul Lamport. Lamport stood before television news cameras in the spring of 1969 and held up a copy of *The Advocate*, the city's major gay newspaper, as though it were a smelly sock. He accused his opponent in the upcoming June city council election, Robert Stevenson, of "having homosexuals working for him in the campaign." Lamport, who represented Hollywood, Los Feliz, and Silver Lake, historically gay-friendly neighborhoods, vowed to drive *The Advocate* out of business. A major property owner, he supported urban renewal in Hollywood and had worked to banish the hippies, bikers, and flower children who congregated on the Sunset Strip. *The Advocate* feared that gay men were next and made Lamport's defeat a top priority.[44]

After a coordinated push by gay activists and *The Advocate*, Stevenson won the election. Lamport told the press: "I'm inclined to think that the final vote was the vote of about 3000 homosexuals who're probably pretty pleased today that they were able to defeat me." It was a sign of things to come. In the next five years, gay men and lesbians in Los Angeles helped elect half a dozen city officials, including city and district attorneys, city councillors, and a mayor, who supported sexual privacy and opposed gay harassment.[45]

A self-conscious and publicly acknowledged "gay vote" emerged in major cities across the country after 1968. In part, this was the natural evolution of the homophiles' push for equal rights. But the gay community's newfound political clout was also indebted to the work of *Drum*, *The Advocate*, *Vector*, Atlanta's *Great Speckled Bird*, and dozens of local publications in cities across the country that embraced gay culture and openly celebrated sexual liberation. They reached thousands and thousands of gay men and lesbians who never thought of attending a homophile meeting. The revelers in Griffith Park and the Patch were prescient: rights and sexual freedom were inseparable.[46]

The importance of such publications in mobilizing gay politics cannot be understated. In 1964 *Drum* published the voting records of House members on a bill to restrict Washington Mattachine's ability to fundraise. Polak used profits from the sales of *Drum* to fund the Homosexual Law Reform Society, and *Drum* editorials advocated political action. When a consenting adults bill was introduced in California in 1969—a result of SIR's lobbying efforts—*Vector* and *The Advocate* covered it extensively (the bill became law in 1975). During the 1969 city council race in Los Angeles, *The Advocate* published candidates' views on critical issues, following the trail blazed by *Vector* in 1965. The *Mattachine Midwest Newsletter*, Chicago's major homophile publication, followed local and state politics closely. More respectable homophile publications, such as the *New York Mattachine Newsletter*, *Homosexual Citizen* (Washington, D.C.), *Tangents* (Los Angeles), and the *Phoenix* (Kansas City), also were prominently featuring political news by the late sixties.[47]

Gay political power remained embryonic, especially nationally, but by 1970 gay communities seemed poised to fulfill the San Francisco Rev. Cecil Williams's 1964 exhortation that they "access the power structure." The most dramatic developments took place in California, where candidates' nights hosted by SIR in San Francisco were fast becoming a major stop on the campaign trail for liberal politicians. SIR worked to elect Alan Cranston U.S. senator in 1968, and in 1969 it printed ten thousand copies of its election guide to help elect Dianne Feinstein president of the San Francisco Board of Supervisors. Willie Brown was consistently reelected to the California Assembly in the late 1960s on the strength of the city's African American and gay votes, and he rewarded the latter by sponsoring the consenting adult sex bill in the legislature for six consecutive years. Noting the trend, *The Advocate* observed that gay men and lesbians in cities "with high concentrations of homosexuals" were seizing the "chances of influencing elections." Like other ethnic groups in American history, gay men and lesbians in the late sixties and early seventies developed an urban political presence that translated into rising influence in municipal government and state capitals.[48]

Despite some electoral successes in California, legal reform remained a daunting endeavor across the country. Passing consensual adult sex laws and removing sodomy statutes took decades in many states. Antidiscrimination laws and city ordinances represented even tougher challenges. Citizens or politicians who might be convinced to support the decriminalization of the intimate lives of gay men and lesbians still hesitated to approve measures *protecting* gay men and lesbians from discrimination. As we shall see, the years between 1972 and 1978 saw a major push for protective city ordinances across the country, from Ann Arbor to Miami, Boston to Los Angeles. San Francisco passed an early employment nondiscrimination ordinance in 1972 but did not approve a broader set of protections until 1978. From city to city, the battles were fierce and divisive, and repeal movements often followed in their wake.[49]

Results within the judicial system were even more mixed. In the 1965 case *Scott v. Macy*, the U.S. Court of Appeals ruled that the Civil Service Commission could not use vague terms such as "homosexual" and "homosexual conduct" to discharge employees—at least not without firm proof. The liberal judge overseeing the case, David Bazelon, began in the mid-sixties to chip away at the legal basis of the fifties' lavender scare. In 1969 his court ruled (in *Norton v. Macy*) that even if proof of homosexual conduct existed, civil service employees could not be fired unless "a reasonable connection" had been established between their private conduct and job performance.[50]

The *Scott* and *Norton* decisions encouraged activists, but additional victories were fleeting. When the Texas Supreme Court ruled that state's sodomy law unconstitutional in 1969, for instance, it specified that its opinion applied only to married heterosexual couples. At the national level, the U.S. Supreme Court remained firmly opposed to gay sexual privacy even as it expanded straight sexual rights under the two chief justices of the period, Earl Warren and Warren Burger. The High Court refused to hear cases challenging state sodomy laws, police entrapment, and bar raids and, in a case originating in Minnesota, declined to consider the constitutionality of a state's firing an employee for his sexuality and nothing else. The Homosexual Law Reform Society, SIR, state-level ACLU chapters, the national ACLU, and dozens of other local gay rights groups filed a tide of lawsuits against police departments, state and local governments, and public and private employers in the late sixties and early seventies. But without the Supreme Court's imprimatur, activists lacked the defining legal victory they so sorely needed.[51]

To unify the diffuse gay activist community, homophiles sought a stronger national organization. At the 1968 NACHO conference in Chicago, just weeks before the chaotic Democratic National Convention, delegates from homophile organizations across the country, now numbering in the dozens, adopted SIR's homosexual bill of rights and the motto "Gay is good," the latter indicative of a more aggressive, less "respectable" stance. But the agreement only hid deeper troubles on multiple fronts. Buoyed by the exuberant, youthful counterculture, Stephen Donaldson of Columbia University's Student Homophile League and other like-minded delegates pressed for an uncompromising embrace of sexual liberation. The Daughters of Bilitis (DOB) for their part favored a weak national organization because the male-dominated leadership in NACHO focused mostly on issues confronting gay men. And SIR and affiliated groups pushed for a protest-based strategy, to the chagrin of more cautious NACHO delegates. The various fractures raised two persistent questions in gay politics: Should NACHO, or any national organization for that matter, embrace sexual liberation? And could lesbians and gay men work together productively? The immediate answers seemed a resounding no when, following the conference, all the San Francisco–based organizations, including SIR and DOB, withdrew from NACHO.[52]

The political divisions brewing in NACHO reached a boil after a series of events in Greenwich Village. The Stonewall rebellion, in late June 1969, has long been seen as the starting point of the gay liberation movement and even the gay rights movement writ large. It passed through history into the founding mythology of "gay rights." In reality, it embodied all the contradictory impulses coursing through gay life in the sixties.

A gay bar on Christopher Street, the Stonewall Inn rested at the center of a complex web of relations among state authority, criminality, sex, race, and class. The mob operated the bar and paid the NYPD not to harass its patrons. Many of its regulars were working-class New Yorkers: African American, Puerto Rican, and white "ethnic" men and a handful of lesbians, who partied long into the night on watered-down dollar beers supplemented by various drugs available for purchase in the bar. Drag queens, transgender people, "scare queens," and unemployed gay youth, including hustlers, frequented the bar. The demographics of the patrons put Stonewall on the margins of the city's "respectable" gay culture.

During the 1969 mayoral campaign, which witnessed the liberal incumbent John Lindsay fending off a series of antigay, antiblack law-and-order candidates, the mob kickback system at the Stonewall Inn broke down. On the evening of June 27 the NYPD and the federal Bureau of Alcohol, Tobacco, and Firearms cooperated on an undercover operation at the bar. Searching for morals violations, plainclothes and undercover police officers unceremoniously took over the bar—"Police! We're taking the place"—and began checking IDs, frisking patrons, and separating out those to be arrested.

The raid, though conducted in a typical fashion, elicited an atypical response from the Stonewall's patrons. Transvestites and transgender people refused to go into the bathrooms to be examined: "Get your hands off me! Don't touch me!" they shouted. Lesbians, bullied and harassed by the police, screamed and cursed. When the action moved outside, and the police began putting patrons into the wagons and patrol cars, a large crowd, drawn by the uproar, gathered along Christopher Street. Drag queens already in the wagon yelled epithets at the police. Someone began slicing police car tires. Others threw coins. A Puerto Rican named Gino hurled a cobblestone. The crowd, animated by long-simmering resentments, became a mob, forcing the police back inside the bar.[53]

What followed was part riot, part rowdy performance, and part gay-in. As more reserved gay men and lesbians watched, the angry youths threw bottles, cans, coins, cobblestones, bricks, and eventually Molotov cocktails at the police. They smashed the Stonewall's front door with an uprooted parking meter. Eventually the fire department arrived and turned hoses on both the burning bar and the mob outside. A crowd of five or six hundred milled about in Christopher Park, many gawking at the young men, who sang "We are the Stonewall girls, we wear our hair in curls!" in a Rockette-style kick line.

Larger crowds gathered in front of the Stonewall the following evening, after news of the riot had spread through gay, New Left, and black power networks. A hundred cops faced a crowd estimated at two thousand. Advancing in flying wedges, the police contained the demonstrators, but it took nearly all night to disburse them through the narrow, angled streets of the Village. Though New York Mattachine activists arrived to disseminate their literature, the events at Stonewall were not the homophiles' fight. The spark had come from the least "respectable" gay men and lesbians: the gender-transgressive queens, the street kids, the butch lesbians, the working-class black and Puerto Rican barhoppers.

In the aftermath of the riot, later dubbed a rebellion by activists, an outpouring of support for sexual liberation from ordinary gay men and lesbians turned the homophile movement into a genuinely mass phenomenon. Hundreds of gay and lesbian organizations sprang up around the country in that watershed moment. But the distinctively working-class, gender-bending rioters would over time dissolve in the collective memory of Stonewall: the less respectable source of the riot was subsumed by later gay rights organizations, which remade Stonewall in their image.

While the rioters had not invented gay sexual liberation, the events at Stonewall offered a rejoinder to homophile respectability and asserted a new narrative of gay politics: ordinary people, sick of condescending authorities and secret lives, would lead a sexual revolution. The tone of the transformation was captured by *Esquire*, which reported in December 1969 on a community meeting in New York to discuss the riots in which Dick Leitsch, "in a staid brown suit," warned of the need to preserve the goodwill of the authorities. Rising to his feet, a young man defiantly interrupted: "We don't want acceptance! We want respect! Demand it!" If such respect would not soon be forthcoming, the young man offered words that by 1969 came rolling easily—perhaps too easily—off the tongues of youth inspired by the New Left and the counterculture: "Fuck them!" Stonewall was the first collective gay "fuck you," and it gave credibility, temporarily it would turn out, to liberationists.[54]

The decline of homophile respectability exemplified the generational rifts within every sixties movement. But was the ebbing of Kameny's politics evidence of the success of homophile activism, in that its victories, though minor, set the stage for later activism? Or had homophiles produced so little that greater militancy was necessary? The answer to both questions is yes. Homophiles brought an end to the lavender scare, demonstrated in the streets, fought in the nation's courts and legislatures, served notice to the medical profession that they would oppose every definition of homosexuality as a sickness, and made inroads into city politics in a handful of places. For all that, gay and lesbian Americans, and the larger collective of people who would in subsequent decades redefine and claim the term "queer," remained despised, feared, and misunderstood far more often than they were accepted, embraced, or celebrated.

As with the various women's movements, it is difficult if not impossible to separate gay activism in the second half of the sixties from the political space forced open by the black freedom movement. Black activists' calls for equality and new positive rights of protection from discrimination— alongside their deeper and more radical invocations of both a Christian and a humanist assault on white supremacy—profoundly shook the nation's legal traditions and cultural complacency. In making their case in the courts, in state legislatures, and on the streets, proponents of black freedom spurred other Americans to seek their own liberation and simultaneously showed them how to address the powerful institutions and cultures that prevented full recognition of their citizenship and humanity. This did not mean that the black freedom and gay movements would always find common ground, but it did mean that over time they would increasingly find themselves confronted by common opponents.

For many, the great hope embodied in the "homosexual citizen" was to create public legitimacy for an appeal for privacy. By decrying the hypocrisy of state regulation of private sexual lives, homophiles took the first steps toward broadening the circle of liberties—negative rights—to include the "sexual privacy" of nonheterosexuals. Simultaneously, the movement's steady minor chord, sexual freedom, pushed against liberalism's insistence of the sanctity of the line between public and private. By demanding that same-sex affection and erotic desire, projected into the world as components of personal identity, enjoy the protection of law, these homophiles did not merely add another democratic subject to the existing American catalog. They called for an entirely new, and heretofore nearly unimagined, sexual citizenship. That new citizenship had the potential to remake both the public sphere (through new positive rights to sexual expression, as well as to fair employment, housing, and the like on a par with heterosexuals) and the private sphere (through new kinds of families, transsexual reassignments, and bisexuality).

Many ordinary gay men and lesbians in the late sixties would not have endorsed, or wanted to talk about, such radical reorganizations. Respectability was too powerful, and too often necessary, an ambition. Sexual respectability conferred the privilege of sexual privacy. But the post-Stonewall sexual liberationists and a subsequent generation of gay activists would grasp the potential of the homosexual citizen to push for far broader and more transformative changes in American life. And yet as elements of the political liberal left, however haltingly and incompletely in these years, broadened the ideal of citizenship to accommodate sexual difference, the dedicated enemies of homosexuality would cling ever more definitively to a much narrower version of that ideal.

By the turning of the decade, then, by the time of Stonewall, the My Lai revelations, and the African American construction protests, all in 1969, American breadwinner ideology had come under assault. Men who otherwise had little in common with one another and were not part of a coordinated effort nonetheless challenged the heterosexual, white male breadwinner and his monopoly on representing the nation's citizens. Men abandoned traditional masculine roles, inhabited new ones, called into question received wisdom about manhood, and interrogated the proscribed racial and sexual identities of breadwinners in such a variety of ways and with such intensity that it was bound to produce a political crisis in the mythology of the family. And this is not even to consider the rising insurgency among women, which set forth the most thoroughgoing critique of both manhood and womanhood in the twentieth century, and to which we now turn.

PART 2

THE SUBJECTION OF WOMEN, 1964–1976

4

THE WORKING MOTHER HAS NO WIFE:
THE DILEMMAS OF MARKET AND MOTHERHOOD

Despite all the tumult and revolutionary rhetoric of the 1960s, the predicaments of men still received a disproportionate share of political attention. Meanwhile, women's subordinate status in law and the marketplace, the economic life of the nation, was casually regarded as natural, an organic consequence of their dependence on men that barely warranted comment. The nation's idealized notion of the nuclear family, on which male breadwinning, soldiering, and heterosexuality rested, was contingent on female domesticity. The incredulousness that greeted the inclusion of "sex" in Title VII of the Civil Rights Act symbolized the decade's assumptions about women's place in family and in society. But before the decade's end American women would ignite a social revolution in sex roles and gender norms more encompassing than anything their early-sixties critics imagined.

Half a century of enormous change has blurred public memory of the inequalities based on biological sex that made the 1960s so distinctly part of a different era. In most states married women could not retain their surnames and could not open bank accounts or apply for credit cards without their husbands' signatures. Men could sell or bequeath communal property without the consent of their wives. Employers routinely asked women about their marriages and childbearing plans, and married, pregnant, and older women could be fired without cause. Female flight attendants were required to quit in their early thirties, to make way for younger, presumably more sexually appealing women. Newspapers carried separate job listings for men and women. It was not illegal for male workers or managers to display pornography in the workplace or to touch female employees in sexually inappropriate ways. When combined with racial discrimination, these kinds of blatant but routine inequities made the occupational market even more perilous for women of color, who typically worked menial jobs and enjoyed the fewest protections.[1]

Women were the least remunerated, most exploited segment of the national workforce. On average, they earned roughly half of what men earned. The majority of blue- and pink-collar jobs available to women reinforced their status as servants and helpers and offered limited upward mobility: they cooked, cleaned, nursed, fetched, filed, typed, and performed rote assembly-line work. Meanwhile, professional jobs were so segregated by sex that in the mid-1960s only 3 percent of the nation's lawyers, 7 percent of its doctors, and 1 percent of its engineers and federal judges were women. A job market based on male breadwinning both undervalued and exploited women.[2]

The most ambitious and far-reaching assault on women's second-class economic status took place in the long decade after the Civil Rights Act was passed. Between 1964 and 1976 women in the United States engaged in campaigns to change how their citizenship and economic rights were configured, a burst of activism sometimes known as second-wave feminism. The black freedom movement, which provided women a model of how to take their case to the public and how to make their case before judges, was a crucial inspiration. But the internal conflicts that had unfolded in other of the era's rights movements were reprised in the new feminism. Seeking rights through available channels—the courts, the voting booth—did not unite all women, just as it did not unite African Americans and lesbians and gay men. For many middle-class, often white women, the problem, as famously described by Betty Friedan in *The Feminine Mystique*, was forced domesticity and the denial of access to market work. Talented women spent their best years as housewives and mothers, bereft "of a purpose that truly realizes their human abilities," in Friedan's words. For most working-class women, however, the problem was just as often the opposite: necessary market work and the denial of a purely domestic motherhood. To many working-class women, becoming a housewife was an *aspiration*.[3]

When Americans imagined men as breadwinners and soldiers, they imagined women as wives and mothers. (Both were imagined as heterosexual.) To change this dispensation, women had to make themselves visible and valued in new ways while also challenging political and cultural assumptions about manhood. They had to reveal the presumed "natural" order to be a social outcome, a chosen, not preordained, arrangement. But just as homophiles offered up a sexual citizen that fractured under the criticism that it was not inclusive enough, so too would the various versions of "woman" asserted by second-wave feminists be subjected to multiple recalculations. Women are both a coherent group, in the real sense of their biology, and disaggregated by the country's hierarchies of class, race, and sexuality. Their simultaneous sameness and difference, both from men and from one another, meant that any politics of women's rights had a built-in tendency to splinter.[4]

Despite the splintering, second-wave feminism rattled American patriarchy. It was the catalyst for the broadest questioning of inherited ideas about gender, sex, and sexuality in the long post–World War II period. Even the most moderate, "mainstream" feminists questioned core assumptions about men's privileges: from their access to the best jobs and educations to their control over reproduction and the home. And among radical feminists, nearly everything about women and men, even the sanctity of marriage and the nuclear family itself, was up for grabs. As a whole, the movement set before American society a basic proposition: a culture in which motherhood is a prerequisite for women to seek full citizenship or a measure of power is not a culture that regards women as fully human. While most women valued and desired motherhood, they did not wish to be punished for it.

The ideal of female domesticity against which most second-wave feminists arrayed themselves was a product of the ways market work and family work, and their cultural designations "public" and "private," had grown intertwined in the modern history of capitalism. Market work was remunerative labor; family work was unremunerated domestic labor. Since the early nineteenth century, the ideal of the breadwinner male supporting his dependent wife and children had shaped the market itself. Women's family work went uncompensated monetarily, yet their domestic reproductive labor, from childbirth to cooking and housekeeping, was central to the wage labor system of industrial capitalism. Employers came to believe that they were entitled to workers unburdened by family labor. It is not surprising that in an economy based on such assumptions women were paid far less than men because their wages theoretically did not support a family.[5]

In the wake of World War II, Americans invested the market's ideal worker with even greater cultural weight. Calls for domestic traditional-ism as reward for wartime sacrifice were bolstered by Cold War anticom-munism, which elevated the "normalcy" of the breadwinner nuclear family to the status of a national religion. But the country's anxious insis-tence on normalcy masked a rapidly changing reality. By the end of the 1960s, nearly half of all American women were drawing paychecks out-side their homes. The great irony is that the vast majority of them went to work precisely because they were not sustained by husbands or because their husbands' (or fathers') earnings were insufficient to support a family. Yet even as women poured into the workforce in ever-rising numbers, their labor was seen as inconsequential, as mere "women's work." The emphasis on male breadwinners and female dependents had long proved an inadequate mirror of the actual operations of the economy, but by the 1960s that inadequacy was verging on farce.

In this sense, women in the 1960s confronted not simply an unequal marketplace but the unresolved dilemmas of capitalism and the Western tradition of liberal democracy. Those dilemmas were many, but the most problematic had to do with the relationship between liberty and equality. Was the appropriate response to women's second-class economic status more liberty—that is, greater freedom to compete alongside men in the rambunctious marketplace? If so, was the society required to take any ad-ditional action to ensure women's equal chance in that market? As we have seen, the making of new citizens hinged on the issue of the govern-ment's role. Was the negative right to freedom sufficient or were positive rights necessary? The answer in the case of women, as for many other con-stituencies during this period, was the latter. As with African Americans and lesbians and gay men, the negative right of liberty without accompa-nying positive rights limited the scale of transformation that women could enact in these decades of social upheaval.[6]

Second-wave feminism advanced women's position in the marketplace, but winning support for motherhood proved elusive. Women emerged from the decade freer than they had ever been but more burdened with market and family work—what women's advocates had long called the double day. They were unable to secure government-supported child care, wage equity, and an end to poverty, elements many women's advocates believed were essential to supporting motherhood across the society. Point-ing out the flaws in existing arrangements proved easier than erecting new ones capable of winning political support and legal legitimacy.

The explanations for these failures reside in the interaction of three forces in American political and legal life. This chapter introduces that interaction, but large portions of the remainder of the book are devoted to fleshing it out fully. First is the strong bias toward liberty in American law and institutions. American legal traditions treat freedom from restrictions on individuals as more essential than entitlements to equality. Second is the market-oriented aims of many leading feminists, which were more easily accommodated by those legal traditions privileging liberty. The third force is the ferocious opposition to feminism among both powerful and ordinary Americans. Fueling the latter was the great and pervasive fear, which was both real and assiduously cultivated by opponents, that women would abandon motherhood in exchange for greater market opportunity.

•

The received popular history of second-wave feminism typically confuses its causes and effects. The women's movement of the late 1960s and early 1970s, the conventional logic has it, opened the job market to women, who then poured into the workforce. The truth is more complicated: women's prominence within the workforce in the early 1960s catalyzed the political rebirth of feminism. Women who wrestled with the competing demands of market work and family work—women for whom market work was never a choice—launched the feminist resurgence.

"Conventional Victorian attitudes limiting the role of the husband to patriarch and breadwinner, and wife to mother and homemaker persist," the Wisconsin Governor's Commission on the Status of Women observed in the mid-sixties. But for millions of American women these attitudes belied reality. Across the country in the postwar years married women and women with children engaged in market work to lift their families out of poverty, to enable teenagers to finish school, to compensate for unemployed or disabled spouses, to afford college tuition for children, their spouses, or themselves, to pay medical bills, to fulfill personal goals and ambitions. They engaged in market work for every conceivable reason, just as men did. Most rationales were directly related to family needs and took into account the labor still expected at home. For more and more women, "normalcy" in post–World War II America meant not a blissful life cleaning the hearth and raising children, but an endless cycle of duties at work and at home—the double day.[7]

Doris Thom's life was a succession of double days. Born in Janesville, Wisconsin, to German immigrants, Thom combined market work and family work her entire life. In 1938 she married a man who worked at the Rock River Woolen Mill and then at a nearby General Motors plant. Thom threw herself into jobs at the Parker Pen Company and Gilman Engineering, where she assembled landing gear for helicopters—until she was dismissed for becoming pregnant, a common occurrence in the 1950s. While her three children were young, Thom did seasonal work plucking turkeys and pelting mink hides, but within five years was working full-time at General Motors. "Economics" was the reason, Thom explained later. "You bet—we needed the money. We were like every young family. We wanted a home of our own." Thom worked the rest of her life at GM, fought to implement Title VII of the 1964 Civil Rights Act at the plant, and served on the Wisconsin Governor's Commission on the Status of Women in the 1970s. Thom was not lifted by her husband's wage alone into the middle class. Only the addition of her wage made that possible.[8]

The double day was more widespread in African American and Latino families, owing to the lesser job prospects for men in those families. For black women, domestic work in the homes of whites, unskilled industrial labor, and "back of the house" service work constituted the narrow range of available options, outside of teaching and a handful of professional occupations for the smaller, educated middle class. However narrow the options, the paid work of black women was essential because black men were much less likely than white men to earn a "family wage"—to say nothing of men's absence from the home altogether. Among Latina women too, racialized labor markets in the Southwest and in northern cities commodified their work at poverty level and ghettoized them in agricultural "stoop" and assembly-line labor and domestic work in Anglo homes. As black civil rights activists like Fannie Lou Hamer and Ella Baker and Latina advocates like Dolores Huerta and Francisca Flores knew, working-class women of color rarely received anything but the worst wages at the bottom of the labor market. By the late 1970s, black and Latina women represented 41 percent of women in poverty.[9]

Johnnie Tillmon knew that labor market. Born to black Arkansas sharecroppers in the 1920s, Tillmon grew up under the foot of Jim Crow. Married at an early age, she bore two children and spent fifteen years laundering clothes for whites and picking cotton. Better jobs for someone in her position did not exist. In 1959 Tillmon, now a single mother, joined her two brothers in Los Angeles. She found work ironing shirts in a laundry, where she labored until an illness forced her onto welfare. Tillmon then founded a welfare rights organization in her public housing project and eventually became a national leader in the welfare rights movement. As it had with Thom, the double day pushed Tillmon toward activism.[10]

Writing at the end of the sixties, the black feminist Frances Beal called the constraints faced by African American women like Tillmon double jeopardy. Each half of the double day required total commitment to a distinct role: worker, mother. Double jeopardy, however, was the specific inheritance of women of color, for whom those roles were determined by both gender and race, shunting them into segregated labor markets and subjecting them to the pernicious notion that their role was to serve whites and that their lives were less valuable than other women's. Beal called the dismal job prospects for black women since slavery "a severe cancer on the American labor scene."[11]

Beal's notion of doubleness was not only a claim of black women's "superexploitation." It was also a stab at the self-importance of black manhood. "Women are not resentful of the rise to power of Black men," she wrote. The central insult, rather, was for black men to step forward while asking black women to step back. Here lay a rarely spoken, but powerfully felt, tension in the economic lives of black women: Should they stress the historic denial of black *men's* access to breadwinner wages or their own "double" disadvantage?[12]

The so-called family wage could not resolve the tensions of the double day and double jeopardy. Asserted first in the fierce labor struggles of the late nineteenth century, the ideal family wage was compensation sufficient for a male breadwinner to support a wife and children. It was the basis of breadwinner liberalism and the class-based social contract of the New Deal beginning in the 1930s. But only professional and managerial occupations reliably provided it, while working-class men and women struggled. Among the latter, the family wage was more often an aspirational ideal than a real possibility. Buoyed by postwar economic growth, however, many of the nation's most powerful unions—the auto workers, steelworkers, electrical workers, and building trades—won significant wage increases in the 1940s and 1950s, along with health and retirement packages, which, cobbled together, approximated the family wage. That too was part of breadwinner liberalism.[13]

These gains, however, were not the sole catalyst for the dramatic expansion of the nation's postwar middle class. They helped, certainly, but by 1977 fewer than one-third of American households were composed of a male breadwinner, a full-time female homemaker, and at least one child. In actuality, the rising standard of living among Americans in the 1950s and 1960s in part resulted from women's paid labor—despite the sanctity of breadwinner mythology. The postwar expansion of the American middle class was made possible by women working double days.[14]

The single most dramatic development in the U.S. labor force between 1945 and 1970 was the increasing market presence of married women and women with children. By the early 1970s more than half of all women between the ages of eighteen and sixty-four engaged in market work, and women constituted nearly 40 percent of all paid workers. The share of the total labor force composed of men and single, childless women remained constant between 1945 and the early 1960s. But the share constituting working wives and mothers nearly doubled. By the late 1960s one in three married women worked for wages; among African American women, it was one in two. In 1970, 30 percent of women with children under the age of six engaged in market work, a dramatic rise from 1950, when the number stood at 12 percent. By 1974, 40 percent of all women with children between ages three and five were engaged in market work. This gradual resort to market labor by women was part of a decades-long trend, but the acceleration of that process in the 1960s was unmistakable.[15]

These numbers point to multiple developments, but three stand out above the others. First, many women had no choice but to work. In the early sixties, women headed one in ten American families. By the midpoint of the next decade, one in nine did. Most of these single mothers were poor. In 1974, half of all children in female-headed households lived below the poverty line; among African Americans, it was two-thirds. These numbers tell a story about the nearly life-or-death necessity of women's market work. "A woman with three kids—not twelve kids, mind you, just three kids—that woman earning the full minimum wage of $2.00 an hour is still stuck in poverty," Tillmon reminded the middle-class readers of *Ms.* magazine in 1972.[16]

Second, poor women were not alone in pursuing market work. Among married women, the highest labor force participation rates existed in families in which men's annual income fell between $3,000 and $7,000 ($19,300 and $45,700 in 2010 dollars). Because the poverty threshold for a family of four in the late 1960s hovered around $3,000, women's market work in this income range kept families out of destitution or lifted them into the lower middle class. Women's market work fed and clothed families, paid rent, and assured a minimum standard of living, or it allowed families to enjoy the much-celebrated essentials of middle-class consumption: helping to buy a house or a car, pay college tuition (the new gateway to the middle class), purchase new appliances, afford a second child without altering living standards, lower a spouse's retirement age, or support aging parents.[17]

Third, because of the limits imposed in the market by motherhood, a woman's paid work peaked statistically before she had a child, dipped in the time surrounding childbirth, and then slowly climbed again with advancing age. This stopping out of the labor force among women with young children dramatizes how family work constrained and disciplined market work. The demands of motherhood came with innumerable costs: loss of jobs, seniority, skills, and work networks and contacts, in addition to the loss of income. Many women willfully, even happily accepted such losses in exchange for the rewards of domesticity. But for women whose occupational advancement was compromised when they did, such trade-offs seemed further evidence of the market's pervasive assumptions about the "ideal" worker.

In the early sixties, as feminists began to press their demands for economic equality on state legislatures and Congress, they confronted a difficult choice. Should they emphasize women's right to the status of the "ideal" worker, a man unencumbered by family work? Or should they emphasize women's dual responsibilities, the double day, and reimagine the ideal worker as one who *does* have family work? And what of race? Would reformers' efforts to reimagine the ideal worker still presume a "color-blind" labor market, or should the long legacy of racial segregation be addressed as well? Each of these questions straddled the divide between negative and positive rights, between freedom and equality, and required Americans to choose the foundation on which they would build women's citizenship.

•

When women's advocates looked at the U.S. workplace in the 1960s, they saw legions of barriers to women's participation as the equals of men. Dismantling these barriers, one by one, was the difficult work ahead. Yet in fighting to acquire the same rights and market opportunities as men, women had to ensure that their differences were not erased in the process. Society valued motherhood, but under strict conditions in the home, apart from the market. Women thus confronted the challenge of reconfiguring both the market and the way society valued and organized motherhood.[18]

Labor feminists assumed that achieving equal standing in the labor market with men would produce profound inequalities because the market was not equipped to support women's family work. In the eyes of these trade unionists, so-called protective legislation, everything from shorter hours to mandatory breaks and maximum weight limits (for lifting), respected women's differences. But those same laws to "protect" women, enacted over the course of more than fifty years, could deny them shift assignments and overtime wages and perpetuate a double standard beneficial to male workers. "Most of the so-called protective legislation has really been to protect men's rights in better paying jobs," Representative Martha Griffiths (D-MI) said in 1964. Some laws, such as the nominal maternity leave and minimum wages on the lawbooks in a few states, guarded women's interests. But most laws did not, leaving women marginal and vulnerable in the name of protection.[19]

Middle-class white feminists since the 1920s, often known as equal rights feminists, had long averred that without formal equality with men in the marketplace, women would remain in low-paying, unsatisfying jobs. What became known as the Pauli Murray approach offered a way out of the stalemate between labor and equal rights feminist positions. Born in Baltimore, Murray was raised by her maternal grandparents in the middle-class black community of Durham, North Carolina. "I had in effect three mothers," she wrote in her autobiography: two aunts and her grandmother, who instilled in Murray personal ambition and a passion for fighting social injustice. "I cannot allow myself to be fragmented into Negro at one time, woman at another, or worker at another, I must find a unifying principle in all of these movements to which I can adhere," she wrote in 1967. A friend of Eleanor Roosevelt's, Murray was as deeply committed to women's equality as she was to racial justice. Appointed to the Committee on Political and Civil Rights attached to Kennedy's Commission on the Status of Women, she was instrumental in drafting the legal strategy employed by women's activists in the late sixties and seventies.[20]

Murray benefited from the advice and influence of a small but growing cohort of feminist attorneys, but her innovation was crucial. In a 1962 memo that remains a too-little-read document of sixties feminism, Murray proposed a jurisprudence for women based on an analogy to race. If the courts interpreted the Fourteenth Amendment to require racial equality, there remained no basis on which to exclude women from analogous protections, Murray argued. Sex and race were, in the framework she proposed, equivalent in a legal sense, if not in a historical one. Sex discrimination and race discrimination were not the same, but the legal redress for each was: application of the due process and equal protection clauses of the Fourteenth Amendment. In many respects, Murray's memo is the founding document of the legal efforts on behalf of women's equality.[21]

Murray argued that the law had to protect women both as equal to men *and* as different from them, especially their biological childbearing and historic responsibility for child care. In her view, women must be granted the liberty to compete for jobs in the marketplace while ensuring their equality in the workplace. This meant a shift "from a blanket conception of women's class attributes," she reasoned, "to the more realistic conception of their *functional* attributes, which vary widely." In Murray's view, women should not be treated as if they belonged to a single category, "woman," but as individual workers, whose attributes and needs varied. On the other hand, Murray recognized the way women had been systematically marginalized economically. The market's failure "to achieve full equality of opportunity based on individual merit," she claimed, justified "the intervention of the government" to protect women in "the assertion of their rights." Government could be a countervailing force in the market, not to advantage women but to ensure their equality. In Murray's memo, equality and difference feminism met and harmonized; it was the kernel of an equal rights strategy for women that preserved a legal basis for difference and sought to carefully balance negative and positive rights.[22]

The work of Murray and other women to conceptualize women's rights must be understood in the context of the black freedom movement. Three interrelated reasons underscore why. First, Murray had published a 1951 study based on months of fieldwork in the South, titled *States' Laws on Race and Color.* Her study of the language of Jim Crow laws informed her understanding of the discriminatory legal landscape for women. Second, and more broadly, since the early 1940s the various iterations of the black freedom movement had produced a new legal and political language of equality in the United States; it was a language of equal rights and human dignity that by the early 1960s was buttressed by arguably the largest popular protest movement in the nation's history. The overlapping movement for gender equality understandably borrowed both the language and élan of black freedom. Third, and inescapably, since the 1860s African American and women's rights had been entangled, and often set competitively against one another. This period was no different, and the question remained starkly familiar: to what extent were women's rights understood as *white* women's rights, and to what extent were African American rights understood as black *men's* rights?

After the passage of the 1964 Civil Rights Act, with the inclusion of "sex" in Title VII, women began to attack the provisions that held them back from certain jobs in the name of protection. Momentum came from two directions. Middle-class and professional women demanded full equality with men in the market. These women—such as the author and activist Betty Friedan, the journalist and academic Alice Ross, the professor of political science Kathryn Clarenbach, the professor of history Caroline Ware, the attorney Mary Eastwood, and the public relations executive Muriel Fox—were instrumental in asserting the equal rights framework to the American public and in the courts. A second agitation surged from below, as thousands upon thousands of women took it upon themselves to invoke Title VII in their workplaces. In the nation's factories, mills, offices, schools, and hospitals, working-class African Americans, whites, and Latinas pushed the newly created Equal Employment Opportunity Commission (EEOC) to take sex discrimination seriously. Less than two years after Johnson signed the Civil Rights Act, women had filed more than twenty-five hundred suits under Title VII.[23]

The Title VII filings gave birth to the National Organization for Women (NOW). Three EEOC staffers—Aileen Hernandez, Sonia Pressman, and Richard Graham—were sympathetic to women's complaints about workplace inequality, but their concerns were marginalized by the EEOC chairman Franklin D. Roosevelt, Jr., who had little interest in pursuing sex discrimination cases. Outraged by this attitude, Griffiths stood before her colleagues in the House of Representatives in June 1966 and asked: "What is this sickness that causes an official to ridicule the law he swore to uphold and enforce? Are such men qualified professionally to enforce Title VII?" Soon after, Friedan, Murray, and Clarenbach, among others, drafted a plan for NOW at the annual meeting of the state Commissions on the Status of Women. NOW was to emerge as an influential, but also contentious, voice for American women. Because its membership included both professional and working-class women, and because all sorts of women wanted a national organization to represent their perspective on the market, rights, and the meaning of equality, NOW was a fractious coalition from the outset. Moreover, its middle-class white leaders did not have existing ties to the largest and most influential social movement of the sixties, the one responsible for the EEOC's creation, black freedom. As NOW's organizers prepared to enter the national debate over rights, Murray worried that the women's movement "might develop into a head-on collision with an increasingly militant movement for 'Negro rights' as happened in the period immediately after the Civil War."[24]

For these reasons, Murray, present at NOW's conception, kept herself at arm's length from the new organization. After the first NOW conference in Washington, D.C., she explained her objections to Clarenbach, the organization's first chairwoman: "I saw no Catholic sisters, no women of ethnic minorities other than about five Negro women, and obviously no women who represent the poor." Murray's remarks underscored a tension over the scope and aims of the emerging women's movement. Conceived as an NAACP for women, NOW would never prove capable of uniting all women, just as the romantic "sisterhood" imagined by Robin Morgan and other young white women's liberationists in subsequent years would never fully compel black and Latina women, not to mention working-class white women.[25]

Specifically, Murray feared that NOW would become a narrow vehicle for professional women's interests and that the Equal Rights Amendment (ERA), which stood to benefit only women and which NOW had endorsed at its founding meeting, would distance efforts toward gender equity from the black freedom movement. The push for the ERA shunted to the sidelines the human rights approach that Murray favored. Her hope for a multiracial women's movement, anchored in human rights, was noble but also necessary. The racial analogy, for her, was not an analogy at all. For Murray, as for all women of color, gender could not be separated from race in their fight for equality.[26]

Meanwhile, largely without help and risking ridicule and the dismissiveness of male coworkers and bosses, women across the country undertook to democratize their workplaces, insisting that they deserved the same pay, opportunities, and rights as men. NOW led a handful of these campaigns, such as the effort to force *The New York Times* and other major newspapers to end the practice of separate help-wanted classifieds for men and women, and joined others, such as the fight to end the airline industry's practice of firing flight attendants ("stewardesses," as they were known at the time) when they reached a certain age.[27]

Title VII was the catalyst. A typical case was Velma Mengelkoch's. In the early 1960s Mengelkoch was hired by North American Aviation in Long Beach, California, as an electronics assembler. A single mother of three, Mengelkoch was a diligent and productive worker. But she chafed under the constraints that prevented her and her female coworkers from working more than eight hours a day, while men in the plant regularly worked overtime and earned the extra pay that went with it. "The laws are used to keep women down," Mengelkoch charged. She and two other women in the plant, also family breadwinners, filed suit under Title VII. It was one of the first such suits under the new law.[28]

The National Organization for Women believed Mengelkoch might be the case to test the logic of Murray's 1962 memo. They had reason to be hopeful. In 1966, Murray and Dorothy Kenyon had written briefs in *White v. Crook*, in which a federal district court for the first time tentatively applied Fourteenth Amendment protections to women (in a case involving jury selection). With that precedent in mind, the NOW lawyers Marguerite Rawalt and Evelyn Whitlow, with help from Murray and Hernandez, drafted an amicus brief on behalf of Mengelkoch. "It is becoming increasingly obvious," the NOW cofounder Hernandez told a California audience, "that the so-called 'state protective laws' are a serious barrier to working women." In a jurisdictional statement to the U.S. Supreme Court, Rawalt succinctly described the meaning of the case: "The right to earn a living is a fundamental right of all persons." *Mengelkoch v. Industrial Welfare Commission*, she stated, "should determine the extent to which the United States Constitution protects the rights of women as citizens under the law."[29]

By 1967, as *Mengelkoch* sat pending in federal court in Los Angeles, three distinct strategies had emerged to advance women's equality in the marketplace. *Mengelkoch* represented the first, which was the narrowest but the most promising: using Title VII to overturn workplace protective legislation. The second was Pauli Murray's Fourteenth Amendment approach: pushing the courts to use the equal protection clause to strike down all laws and practices that made distinctions based on sex in the same way they had used it to strike down laws making distinctions based on race. This approach meant the broadest possible protection for women because it would require not the abrogation of *all* laws making distinctions by sex, but only those that could be proven to materially harm women. The third strategy was to push for passage of the Equal Rights Amendment, which called for the sweeping elimination of all legal distinctions between men and women.[30]

Regarding the first strategy, at the beginning of the 1970s, it seemed that the EEOC was on the road to eliminating unfair protective laws from the books. Because NOW assisted with a *Mengelkoch* appeal, its attorneys decided to help two similar cases that challenged protective legislation, at Southern Bell Telephone and Telegraph and at Colgate-Palmolive. To the applause of women's advocates, between 1967 and 1971 all three cases were decided in favor of the plaintiffs. Title VII rejects, the judge in the Southern Bell case wrote, the "romantic paternalism" of protective laws and "vests individual women with the power to decide" whether to accept certain jobs. In 1971 another suit, brought against AT&T by women and African American and "Spanish-surnamed" men, resulted in one of the first large-scale race and sex affirmative action decrees in the country. In its report, EEOC attorneys had called AT&T "without doubt the largest oppressor of women workers in the United States." That an agency of the federal government had publicly labeled one of the largest corporations in the country an "oppressor of women" was stunning testimony to the distance women's advocates had traveled since 1964.[31]

Title VII litigation between 1966 and 1971 laid the groundwork for a much larger and more systematic assault on the inequities of the job market, the second strategy. By the end of the 1960s, NOW's Legal Defense and Education Fund, modeled after a similar structure in the NAACP, had made Title VII and Fourteenth Amendment suits a top priority. The Legal Defense and Education Fund was joined by another national organization, one that in time ranked among the most influential women's legal advocacy institutions in the country, the American Civil Liberties Union (ACLU) Women's Rights Project. Led by Ruth Bader Ginsburg, a top-of-her-class Harvard-trained lawyer, along with Pauli Murray, Eleanor Holmes Norton, and a new generation of feminist attorneys, the Women's Rights Project sought to make the "right to earn a living" a reality for women and in so doing dismantle the legal architecture supporting the male-breadwinner model of the national economy. Over the next three decades, the Women's Rights Project helped win protection from sexual harassment, helped outlaw firings of pregnant women, and played an instrumental role in achieving affirmative action and equal pay in many industries.[32]

Women's advocates pursued the third strategy, winning passage of the ERA, alongside the other two. Murray and other women of color were on balance less enthusiastic about the ERA, because it appeared to isolate gender as the principal axis of their disadvantage and seemed the biggest affront to black and Latino men. Yet women of all racial backgrounds rallied behind the ERA banner in the middle years of the seventies, after it became the target of a massive antifeminist backlash led by the conservative activist Phyllis Schlafly.

Despite notable progress, this era's feminism did not accumulate an unbroken string of successes. Two major stumbles stand out. First, the broadest expansion in women's market liberty in U.S. history occurred coincidentally with the decades-long process of deindustrialization and the rise of the service economy. This shift benefited educated women whose new freedoms allowed them to climb in a white-collar world organized around knowledge and service production. But it deepened existing occupational ghettos at the bottom of that white-collar world while creating new ones (such as in fast food and elder care), especially among the working class and poor, where women of color were disproportionately represented. The new service economy produced a small number of well-paying jobs that required education and training and a vast assemblage of unskilled jobs that paid little. Women's advocates hardly had the leverage to halt, or even slow, this shift—it was less their specific failure than the consequences of broad structural economic change. But it meant that in every decade between 1970 and 2010 someone would unknowingly echo the words of Elizabeth Duncan Koontz, the director of the U.S. Women's Bureau, who said in 1970 that despite all the EEOC lawsuits, "Women still occupy the majority of low-paying, routine, dead-end jobs."[33]

The second stumble centered on motherhood. Protective labor legislation, despite its paternalist pretensions, had almost never protected mothers from discrimination. In 1967 only two states provided maternity benefits, and no state guaranteed job security while a woman was on maternity leave. Subsidized child care existed in a handful of states for some poor women, and an organization called Head Start helped low-income families with children under the age of five. In total, however, these were meager, underfunded programs that failed to reach the vast majority of women. To "protect" women, six states prohibited employment before and after pregnancy without guaranteeing them a return to the positions they left. In sum, as women escalated their assault on the barriers and prejudices that kept them in "low-paying, routine, dead-end jobs," there remained virtually no public infrastructure to help reconcile market work and family work.[34]

The legal route to such reconciliation closed quickly. Women had begun challenging pregnancy discrimination from the moment Title VII took effect, seeking a range of rights, including the right not to be fired or demoted for pregnancy and the right to reasonable maternity leave. The question was, under Title VII, were these in fact "rights"? That is, were workplace rules that punished pregnancy acts of *sex* discrimination as forbidden by the Civil Rights Act? Women's advocates believed that there were few more insidious forms of workplace discrimination than the treatment of pregnant women. The EEOC concurred, issuing in 1972 new regulations under Title VII preventing many of the most flagrant practices. The Supreme Court, however, disagreed. In *Geduldig v. Aiello* (1974), six of the nine justices, reversing the district court, ruled that because those practices distinguished between pregnant women and nonpregnant men *and* women, they could not be construed as sex discrimination. Legal feminists marveled at the Court's twisted logic. Market liberty seemed to be for men only or for women who behaved, even biologically, like them.[35]

Four years after *Geduldig*, following considerable lobbying by women's advocates, Congress passed the Pregnancy Discrimination Act, which codified in law the EEOC's early-seventies rulings. The federal government would require employers to treat a woman's pregnancy with a minimum of regard. Yet the market's accommodation of motherhood remained partial at best, leaving women to navigate the relationship among pregnancy, childbirth, and market work largely on their own.

•

As Title VII grew more central to the women's movement's legal strategies, opponents of feminism began to find their footing. Advances in women's liberty in the marketplace, these opponents charged, would lead women to abandon motherhood. Only the accusation of lesbianism was a more powerful rhetorical weapon against feminism. To abandon motherhood was a sacrilege. It was to undermine the nation itself.

Conservatives were not alone in these fears. Dr. Benjamin Spock, the child-rearing guru and political liberal whose 1946 book *Baby and Child Care* had guided a generation of women through motherhood, evinced the tone and concerns of antifeminist critiques in a 1970 *Redbook* article. "The more radical feminists today insist that mothers have exactly as much right as fathers do to work full time outside the home," Spock wrote. But women's market work, he insisted, compromised their family work: "babies and young children have needs and rights too." Spock was certain that a woman could not be simultaneously a mother and a paid worker.[36]

Like Spock, enemies of feminism believed it to be unremittingly hostile to motherhood. Of course, the vast majority of women's advocates sought to reimagine motherhood, not to dismiss it. But because that reimagining required the undoing of so many conventions, feminists and other women's advocates found themselves critiquing motherhood while simultaneously defending it. They had to explain to Americans why conventional views of motherhood were intolerable while at the same time seeking massive legal and social changes to support their vision of it. They were confident that they knew what was wrong with the inherited conventions and mythologies surrounding being a mother, but coming up with alternatives that could gain wide public support proved exceedingly difficult.[37]

Their message was complex and nuanced because the debate it condensed was. Among the many views of motherhood articulated by women's advocates, four stand out. The first took shape on behalf of, and among, working-class women who had little choice but to try to balance market work and family work. When Kennedy's Commission on the Status of Women convened in 1961, Caroline Ware, the passionate New Dealer, complained that "many of the most conscientious and responsible mothers cannot adequately take care of their children because they do not have the facilities which the community should provide for that purpose." Motherhood, in Ware's view, was not just a private responsibility, enfolded entirely into the domestic world of women's family work. It required the support of public measures. The most necessary measure, then and now, was state-supported child care.[38]

Because tens of millions of women faced the double day, coalitions of workingwomen, including labor unions and other social welfare organizations, had pressed state legislators and the national government for child care since the New Deal. State child care advocacy networks were strongest in New York and California, where women's employment during World

War II had spurred the rapid growth of child care centers. By the early 1960s the National Committee for the Day Care of Children represented hundreds of local groups in Washington, D.C. Professional social workers and other educated professionals led the committee, but state and local organizations were typically headed by working-class women, whose lives were most affected by the absence of affordable child care. When their calls for government-supported child care in the early 1970s were denigrated by the political right as a monstrous socialist experiment that substituted the state for the nuclear family, these women were astonished. They wanted government child care precisely, as they saw it, because they so strongly valued their families.[39]

A second view of motherhood originated in the demands of professional women. Among a wide swath of the educated middle class, economic necessity, at least in the 1960s, had not yet called into question the male breadwinner. Rather, women's own ambitions had. Women were expected to choose between careers and motherhood; one was not supposed to have both. To enable women to pursue their ambitions in the market, while preserving the possibility of motherhood, middle-class liberal feminists reiterated the call for government-sponsored child care but added a distinct element. Guided by Friedan's *The Feminine Mystique*, which had punctured the bourgeois domestic fantasy in 1963, they demanded that men adapt to women's economic ambitions. When Friedan, Clarenbach, and others met in October 1966 to create NOW, alongside equal employment and educational opportunity, they endorsed "equal partnership between the sexes." In calling for the state to support motherhood, these feminists called for men to do their share as well.[40]

In this middle-class feminist vision, market work was fulfilling and family work was a coequal partnership. Marriage and motherhood were neither enemies nor institutions to be destroyed. Still, reform of both was in order. In a series of articles and speeches in 1971, Gloria Steinem gave full voice to this vision, to what she called "A New Egalitarian Lifestyle." Steinem, who in the early 1970s redefined white feminist chic with her long, straight hair and tinted eyeglasses, was the indispensable bridge between younger feminists just then entering the political scene and Friedan's and Pauli Murray's generation. No man, Steinem wrote, could consider himself "liberal, or radical, or even a conservative advocate of fair play, if his work depends on the unpaid or underpaid labor of women at home, or in the office." The first issue of Steinem's *Ms.* magazine, which appeared in July 1972, featured multiple articles on this theme, including "The Value of Housework: For Love or Money?," which calculated women's unpaid domestic labor, and "Marriage of Equals," about two married Stanford professors determined to create an egalitarian partnership.[41]

A third view of motherhood spoke to a large and varied group of women. For them, motherhood remained a sanctuary from the market itself; family work was *preferred* to market work. The former was rewarding, life affirming, identity sustaining. The latter was harsh, repressive, capricious, a world endured by men so that women did not have to. In 1966 the New York writer and editor (and mother of five) Patricia Coffin published a rejoinder to Friedan to make this point. Friedan, Coffin claimed, had deluded women about market work. Creative? Satisfying? How many *men* have such luxuries in their jobs? The market offered only prickly bosses, stultifying labor, and ruthless politicking. To add insult to injury, "The career woman has no wife to come home to." Leave the soul-crushing market to men and feather the nest, Coffin told women. "You are a gender apart, and lucky to have a man to lean on." This remained a not uncommon, and not dismissable, article of faith among ordinary Americans. Feminism's opponents in particular would encourage similar views and place them at the center of the pro-family movement in the second half of the seventies.[42]

Coffin's critique of "career women" and their ambitions was not an exclusively conservative one. Versions of it appeared in the otherwise staunchly left-wing welfare rights movement. In 1966, the Congress of Racial Equality (CORE) activist George Wiley and the welfare rights advocates Beulah Sanders from New York, Johnnie Tillmon from Los Angeles, and Etta Horn from Washington, D.C., created the National Welfare Rights Organization (NWRO). Calling for higher welfare benefits and an end to government violations of women's privacy, the NWRO turned the shame of the "undeserving poor" into a rights-based critique of a stingy state and a discriminatory economy. Valorizing women's responsibilities as mothers, NWRO activists accused state and federal governments of sabotaging poor families by pushing unskilled women into dead-end jobs, an even more thankless prospect than the "career" track savaged by Coffin. Wiley organized a Mothers' March on Washington in August 1967; protesters carried MOTHER POWER signs and took issue with welfare's new work requirements. Wiley told lawmakers that poor women "should not be in the labor force, because they have other important responsibilities at home, to take care of their families."[43]

The needs of the women represented by NWRO were indeed underserved by the market freedom sought by equal rights feminists. For many working-class and poor women, marriage to a gainfully employed man still represented one of the best economic options available to them. It meant economic security for those—and not just women on public assistance—who otherwise faced raising children alone on low-paying dead-end jobs. For many women, motherhood remained not just one choice among many but an indispensable identity. Risking it, and the honorifics that accompanied it, in a quixotic quest for economic liberty seemed naive. The differing political objectives of middle-class, working-class, and poor women reflected the reality of different life opportunities. Those differences complicated alliances. For instance, when Martha Griffiths's name began circulating among feminists in the early 1970s as a possible Supreme Court nominee, Beulah Sanders warned her liberal "sisters" that NWRO would withhold its support because "Griffiths has been terrible on welfare issues . . . having advocated some of [the] worst forced work provisions."[44]

A fourth view of motherhood during the late sixties and early seventies, one articulated by what became known as women's liberationists, stood at a tangent to the other three. Between 1968 and 1970 these liberationists, galvanized by the male chauvinism of the New Left and black power and inspired by an explosion of radical feminist writing, set fire to the debate over women's place in American society. The term "liberation," borrowed from black power, suggested a total transformation of women's position in society, rather than integration within existing social and market arrangements. Building on a series of conferences and caucuses within the Student Nonviolent Coordinating Committee (SNCC), Students for a Democratic Society (SDS), and other New Left and black freedom groups, women's liberationists burst onto the national stage in 1968.[45]

Blunt about the inequities of marriage and family life, they shared the sentiments of the African American feminist Toni Cade. "I think most women have pondered, those who have the heart to ponder at all, the oppressive nature of pregnancy, the tyranny of the child burden, the stupidity of male-female divisions, the obscene nature of employment discrimination," Cade wrote. Women such as Cade were in no mood to temporize. A generation younger than many of the founders of NOW, and nearly two generations removed from the women who had served on Kennedy's Commission on the Status of Women, they brought the urgency and ardor of a revolutionary age to the debate over motherhood and the American family. But they also followed in the footsteps of those other women because Cade and others like her took the rhetoric of earlier critiques of women's citizenship to their logical end point. Once labor feminists and the women in NOW had opened womanhood to question, in an era of accelerating social deconstruction the complete unraveling of that ideal could be held at bay only so long.[46]

Women's liberation was a massive, but loose and ideologically diverse, movement. One of its core animating ideas, taken from radical feminism, was that motherhood and family were political and even coercive notions posing as "natural" arrangements. Among the radical feminists' articles of faith was that men's historic control of women's bodies and the breadwinning ideal kept women in a state of dependency. Unlike their more moderate feminist counterparts, they refused to think in terms of public and private life. Instead, fired by the refrain "The personal is political," they contended that patriarchy depended on the public-private divide to exploit women's labor, control their sexuality, and harness their reproductive capacity. Real freedom for women, they argued again and again, went beyond the freedom to work any job in the nation. It had to be based on the right to think beyond inherited ideals of motherhood, family, and domesticity because these were mandated conventions even if it appeared that one "chose" them.[47]

Kate Millett and Shulamith Firestone offered liberationists their most influential touchstone texts. Millett's *Sexual Politics* (1969) named the source of women's oppression—"patriarchy"—and viewed relations between men and women through the lens of power. She assailed romantic love ("a means of emotional manipulation which the male is free to exploit"), called for an end to monogamous marriage and the family ("patriarchy's chief institution"), and proposed a sexual revolution that would "bring the institution of patriarchy to an end." Firestone, in *The Dialectic of Sex* (1970), posited that heterosexuality itself was grounded in oppressive conventions of the nuclear family. For her, "the tyranny of their reproductive biology" and women's entrapment in the nuclear family placed them in a cultural straitjacket. Following Millett and Firestone, a torrent of radical feminist critiques of the nuclear, or "bourgeois," family flooded the pages of women's movement publications.[48]

Millett, Firestone, and the manifestos inspired by them defined the radical edge of women's liberation. In grasping the full implications of collapsing the boundary between public and private, they empowered women to speak honestly about sex and power in new ways. Radical feminists encouraged women to recognize that what they had been taught to believe was "private" and personal was in fact political and invested with public ramifications. Disabused of society's expectations of their roles, women could see that traditional domesticity was, at best, their inescapable fate and, at worst, a coercive "system" that would forever constrain their humanity. Despite sharing aspects of this way of thinking, African American and Latina liberationists questioned the idealized "sisterhood" implicit in much of the first blush of women's liberation writing, advancing in its place a Third World critique that viewed patriarchy through the lens of race and the colonialism of a specifically Western or Euro-American patriarchy. Sometimes wide-eyed, always utopian, women's liberationists, radical feminists, and Third World feminists inspired millions of women to rethink their subservient role vis-à-vis men.[49]

Most Americans, then as now, were not radicals, and those surging into the women's liberation movement in the early 1970s were no exception. Most participants blended liberal and radical positions and never dismissed motherhood out of hand. Many, for that matter, were already mothers or gave birth to children after they joined the movement. Radical feminism gave them the language and reasoning to call into question, rather than condemn, received notions of motherhood that resigned women to dependency on men. As one young women's liberationist put it, "I don't put down the care of children. I just put down the fixated relationship that the mother has, the never-ending association, her urge that the child be something so that *she* can be something."[50]

For all their good intentions, political passion, and bold intellectual forays, women's liberationists drew the ire of ordinary working-class women, who resented the implication that domestic work was synonymous with subjugation. Even as the rhetoric of radical feminism grew more urgent and forceful in the early seventies, for many women the marketplace, not the home—the "public," not the "private"—remained the principal site of their subjugation, at least as they saw it. Furthermore, most black and

Latina women knew someone in their family who labored, or had labored, in the homes of whites. To see those same middle-class women likening marriage and housework to "slavery" and labeling men oppressors, as was common, could seem at best evidence of an unexamined hypocrisy. At worst it was raw racial privilege.[51]

The differing positions on motherhood in feminist circles each suffered from a sort of group-wide solipsism. Middle-class liberal feminists' emphasis on full market equality for women produced, despite official rhetoric, an often weak commitment to government-supported child care and class-based social justice (this was especially evident in local NOW branches). Radical feminists theorized themselves into an impasse. Absent the complete eradication of patriarchy, every woman's "choice" was either collaboration with oppressors or evidence of a wrongheaded belief that patriarchy was escapable: "every fuck is a rape," the lesbian feminist Sharon Deevey memorably wrote in 1975. Welfare rights advocates often spoke as if the state could solve all the inequities of capitalism and repair impoverished communities. Each set of blinders is understandable and was not fatal. But they were indicative of the larger class- and race-based splits preventing the emergence of a unified women's movement that could systematically rethink motherhood as a precondition for full female citizenship.[52]

•

In the midst of the debate about motherhood and family, Myra Wolfgang, a Detroit trade unionist, gave voice to one of the core dilemmas of women's economic citizenship. "The working mother has no 'wife' to care for her children," she told a Senate subcommittee in 1970. Wolfgang, unlike Patricia Coffin, raised the issue not to skewer career women but to defend all female workers. She had spent most of her life organizing women who labored at the bottom of the economy: waitresses, maids, and laundry workers. Without child care legislation "to enable women to work outside the home," she insisted, "the expressed desire for equal rights is an empty promise and a myth."[53]

American women, divided by class and separated by distinct experiences of race, never shared a single vision of motherhood and its relationship to market work. Nevertheless, a majority agreed that in the realm of child care there remained a "desperate need for more facilities for the children of working mothers," as a *Chicago Tribune* columnist put it in 1967. This desperation was as widely shared as any single issue among women's organizations in the late 1960s: from the Mississippi Delta, where Marian Wright Edelman fought recalcitrant white supremacists to establish child care centers for poor women, to Los Angeles's suburban San Fernando Valley, where pink-collar women struggled with how to care for their kids while they worked. Across the country, the problem was the same: in 1964 less than one-third of women with children under the age of six had access to child care. "Childbearing still has an honored place in our culture," Letty Cottin Pogrebin wrote in the *Ladies' Home Journal* in 1972, "*except* in the labor market."[54]

The nation remained conflicted, however, over how to address this "desperate need." Viewing it as a social, rather than an individual, problem meant recognizing that the family wage was a myth and that tens of millions of Americans depended on women's market work. Viewing it as a question of rights, as part of women's democratic citizenship, raised an even more far-reaching implication: that the relationship among the market, the family, and the state might require reimagining.

Rights that in many European political systems developed as universal, rather than employment-based, entitlements—old-age pensions, unemployment insurance, and health care, to name the most significant—have been in the United States closely tied to market work. Earning power has determined social welfare rights. This "economic citizenship," as some historians have called it, was established by the New Deal and postwar amendments to the Social Security Act and was viewed from the beginning as the province of men. As a result, women's relationship to the American state, their social citizenship, has been defined largely through their roles as wives and mothers. By engaging in market labor, women increasingly gained access to the social citizenship entitled to citizen workers, but because of their lower earning power and the constraints of their family work, their social benefits lagged behind men's.[55]

In the logic of American political life in this era, from Johnson's Great Society through Nixon's New Federalism, child care was not taken to be a universal social policy for all women, a new addition to the social contract. It was, rather, a limited program for poor women that aimed to "reduce dependency" by requiring welfare recipients to earn a paycheck. Far from being a positive right of all women, government-supported child care was imagined as a mechanism to *shrink* social rights: child care would facilitate poor women's transition from dependents to workers. Few women's activists argued that the indigent did not need child care, but the connection between poverty and child care in the minds of policy makers undercut the larger demand among women from all classes. Poor women and women on public assistance required child care, to be certain, but so did other women.

By 1971 the push for a more comprehensive national child care policy had reached Congress. Democratic senator Walter Mondale of Minnesota and Democratic representative John Brademas of Indiana introduced bills that jointly became the Comprehensive Child Development Act (CCDA), which represented the most substantial attempt in the nation's history to make child care a near-universal part of the nation's social welfare system. The bill redefined the social contract itself. Behind the legislation stood a trio of influential feminists in Congress: Patsy Mink (D-HI), Shirley Chisholm (D-NY), and Bella Abzug (D-NY). Organized labor, especially such female-dominated unions as clothing and garment workers and communications workers, added their full support and lobbying resources, and a massive child care movement, led by dozens of groups, including the National Council of Negro Women, NWRO, and NOW, took to the streets and picked up their phones. Government-supported child care, Chisholm told her colleagues on the House floor, is "what the oft-heard phrase 'reordering our national priorities' is all about."[56]

The CCDA's chances looked good. The coalition behind it was sizable, if divided by the aforementioned economic and racial disparities. Public support for state-sponsored child care consistently ran at more than 50 percent. The success and popularity of Head Start had introduced an additional element, a focus on children. Since the early 1960s experts had been arguing for the benefits of early childhood education—along with good nutrition, physical exercise, play, and peer group socialization—in child "development." Marian Wright Edelman, in particular, in her work with the Poor People's Campaign and the Washington Research Project (which founded the Children's Defense Fund), had come to see child development as essential to combating poverty. Wright Edelman told the Senate Committee on Labor and Public Welfare that the "more than 12 million working mothers in this country" needed "access to comprehensive developmental child care services" and that child development would help create "a new generation of self-sustaining American citizens."[57]

Fundamentally, the CCDA was an attempt among progressive political forces to tie together the New Deal, the black freedom and Chicano movements, the Great Society, and the women's movement. This merging of social contract politics with feminist politics laid a core question before the nation: Could the social welfare liberalism of the Roosevelt coalition be married to racial justice and the rights-based liberalism of the Great Society? And could such a fusion establish a new social citizenship for women that reduced the discriminatory effects of motherhood? In pushing the private life of the home into public view and into the realm of law, the CCDA aspired to expand the circle of positive democratic rights. In establishing a new element of the social contract, the "right" to child care affirmed that democratic citizenship was not based on the supposedly universal characteristics of men. It was quietly revolutionary.

As it moved through committees, the bill became entangled in the very issues its advocates had hoped to avoid. The minimum annual income to qualify for free child care had initially been set high in the legislation, at $6,960, a figure that would have extended benefits to the lower middle class. Nixon's Health, Education, and Welfare (HEW) head, Elliot Richardson, however, charged with curtailing Great Society programs, made it clear that the administration would not support the high number (it was eventually reduced to $4,320). A second point involved control of the new program. Child care advocates, led by Wright Edelman and Evelyn Moore of the Black Child Development Institute, believed that child care centers should be operated at the local level. They hoped to bypass recalcitrant state officials, especially in the South. Richardson, Nixon administration officials, and southern politicians, on the other hand, wanted nothing that resembled the War on Poverty's focus on empowering communities, instead favoring state-run programs. Ultimately, the two sides struck a compromise: "sponsoring units" with populations of one hundred thousand or higher were eligible, making states and large cities the principal administrators.[58]

Anxiety over changing racial and gender norms underlay these compromises. Southern politicians knew that local control would mean racially integrated child care centers and black-controlled institutions. Such a direct assault on their ongoing project of massive resistance to, or careful finessing of, the *Brown* decision and desegregation could not be sanctioned. Northern governors and mayors—their own political wounds from War on Poverty–inspired community coalitions still fresh—favored city-level administration, to take funding out of the hands of potentially oppositional neighborhood groups. Conservative religious activists and emerging anti-feminists worried less about "race mixing" and community control than about what "child development" meant for the family. The bill's fiercest critics viewed Wright Edelman's notion of child development as a socialist or even "Soviet" program to replace the family with government-run child rearing. The compromises made in passing the CCDA thus revealed the prevalent fears that freeing women from some of the burdens of family work represented a dangerous threat to the social order and that community-controlled institutions undermined white dominance in the South and urban political machines in the North. The CCDA was among the first post-Moynihan national issues to galvanize disparate conservative constituencies in defense of an idealized family.

Yet in a testament to the regnant power of liberalism as a political force and the growing influence of the women's movement, the bill passed. The bill Congress sent to Nixon in December 1971, approved with narrow majorities, nevertheless promised the broadest commitment to state-sponsored child care in the nation's history. It included a sliding-scale payment system that would have made child care far more affordable for the nation's poor and middle class alike. It came closer than any previous legislation to recognizing child care as part of women's economic citizenship. But the conservative opposition it aroused saw only the invasive hand of the state and a feminist-inspired attack on the privacy of the family and on motherhood itself.

Nixon's consideration of the CCDA marked one of the first moments when the still-diffuse populist right came together to express its indignation over a perceived threat to the family. Kevin Phillips—next to Pat Buchanan, the most reliable idea man behind Nixon's "New Majority"—had urged the president to support state-sponsored child care. "Welfare mothers are hardly likely to vote for him," Phillips conceded, "but working mothers, a *huge* slice of the electorate, are extremely reachable on the subject of day care" (Phillips's "working mothers" were presumably white). Buchanan and others with close ties to the emerging populist right, however, pushed Nixon for a veto. The internal debates within Nixon's circle were heavily influenced by anti-CCDA diatribes in the conservative press— attacks led by the conservative columnist James Kilpatrick and the conservative newspaper *Human Events*—as well as the tide of letters arriving at the White House castigating the bill as an assault on traditional motherhood and a discredited form of liberal social engineering.[59]

After a conspicuous delay, Nixon vetoed the bill. Calling it "the most radical piece of legislation to emerge from the Ninety-second Congress," he claimed that it called forth "communal approaches to child rearing over the family-centered approach." The bill would, he said decisively, destroy "parental authority and parental involvement with children . . . when social attitudes and a conscience are formed and religious and moral principles are first inculcated." Nixon had played the symbolic "bad mother" card (a crucial precursor to the "welfare queen" stereotype that was to derail useful debate in the years to come). While women on welfare could qualify for some subsidized child care, and child tax credits were added in subsequent years, on balance, women and families were left to their own devices and to the private market to care for children while parents worked.[60]

Between Nixon's veto of the CCDA in 1971 and the Supreme Court's 1976 decision in *Craig v. Boren*, American women won greater market liberty, in a legal sense, than they had ever enjoyed before. In establishing the "intermediate scrutiny" test for laws that discriminated by sex, the court in *Craig* did not adopt the same standard it employed for race ("strict scrutiny"), but nonetheless laid the groundwork for the elimination of most employment and other economic laws that distinguished between women and men. In the 1970s and 1980s, wielding Title VII of the 1964 Civil Rights Act and Title IX of the 1972 Education Amendments, feminist attorneys broke down gender barriers in the professional world and transformed higher education, including law and medical schools. These gains remade the American labor market in subsequent decades in ways that would have astonished the women Kennedy had appointed to the Commission on the Status of Women in 1961.[61]

A measure of positive rights was won as well. Additional legislation later in the decade, especially the 1978 Pregnancy Discrimination Act, alongside federal and state affirmative action programs, and the creation of sexual harassment law in the second half of the 1970s, made the American workplace far more hospitable to women than it had been at the beginning of the 1960s. A revolution of sorts had taken seed, and its urgent transformation of American life would continue in subsequent decades.

But that transformation remains incomplete. Liberty won out over equality. Women were set free to compete with men in the market, but little was done to transform that market to accommodate the unchanging necessity of women's family work. The ideal "citizen worker" remained a childless adult—a distinct improvement over a childless man, but still a long way from what many women's advocates believed necessary. Not only did the double day not disappear, but by many accounts it became even more burdensome. And even less was done to assist working-class women from all racial backgrounds. Measured in strictly economic terms, among full-time workers the gender wage gap closed from fifty-seven cents (for every dollar men earned) in 1969 to eighty cents by 2009. That overall gain hid much lower figures in heavily female sectors, such as services (seventy-two cents), and the fact that many women continued to work part-time. Meanwhile, 6.5 percent of all workingwomen remained below the poverty line (excluding the unemployed and those on welfare), a figure that was more than 12 percent among African American and Latina women.[62]

Thus those best positioned to take advantage of whatever Title VII, the Fourteenth Amendment, and Title IX could do were middle-class white women. That fact was the result of existing class and racial privilege, to be certain, but it was also the result of the distinct ways that domesticity and the market—and the rigid cultural expectations of each—had divided different groups of women over more than two centuries. Addressing and alleviating those divisions, one imagines, would (and will) take generations of effort. That project had barely begun in the 1970s. As workingwomen have declared in lawsuits from *EEOC v. Sears*, first filed in 1973, to *Dukes v. Wal-Mart*, first filed in 2000, "choice" may be appealing in theory but has proven elusive for most women in the marketplace.[63]

Many second-wave feminists struggled to resolve the ways the market divided women; many others could have joined the struggle but did not. Yet for all the divisions among women's advocates in these years, feminism's greater challenge was the opposition it mobilized. Opponents of feminism, more than differences among women, proved to be the greater barrier to women's equality. As charges leveled against the women's movement grew sharper and more insistent in the early 1970s, opponents cast feminism as a radical program that would wreck womanhood and ruin motherhood. Voices on the conservative right led that opposition, but a broader political cross section of Americans, including many liberals, were uncomfortable with, if not definitively opposed to, feminism's call for a reorganization of gender and sexual conventions.

Those on the right could proclaim that feminists had wrecked womanhood, but by historical standards feminists were modernizing it, moving it into line with broad economic and cultural shifts that had been under way for decades. The divide between the public world of the market and the private world of the home had long ago collapsed for most workingwomen. By the late 1970s it was fast collapsing for the remaining others. At the end of that decade, most American women knew they would spend the vast majority of their adult lives working for wages or salary. Economic change, capitalism's relentless evolution, had made certain of that. Feminists and women's advocates made mistakes, but their efforts to transform womanhood represented a fundamentally adaptive, not destructive, project. Additional adaptive steps—creating positive entitlements to certain rights, such as child care or universal maternity leave—were possible, but the American legal and political system refused them. The historical irony is that in resisting the reorganization of gender and sexual norms in the name of an idealized womanhood, feminism's opponents made being a woman in American society more difficult.

5

BODIES ON TRIAL:
THE POLITICS OF REPRODUCTION

In their pursuit of liberty and equality in the marketplace, women's advocates challenged conventional views of motherhood and the divide between public and private life in America. The women's movement exposed the male-breadwinner model of the economy as a fiction, and women from all social ranks fought for new economic arrangements and cultural norms. In many respects they succeeded; in some they failed. Women gained new freedoms in the marketplace, but feminists did not fully resolve the dilemmas of motherhood or win political support for new initiatives to support it. Nor did they harmonize the interests of different groups of women. A similar story accounts for the successes and failures women met when they challenged, at the same time and with equal commitment, another dimension of American life that many considered not just deleterious but cruel and repugnant: their lack of control over their own bodies.

In the late sixties and seventies, women's advocates cast the female body as a site of political struggle, the place where the intimate and personal became the legal and public, where the personal became the political. In doing so, they put forward reproductive rights as a bedrock of female citizenship. Abortion and forced sterilization emerged as the key issues. Across the country in the early 1960s, state laws prohibited virtually any form of abortion, turning hundreds of thousands of ordinary women each year into criminals, and dozens of states coerced women into sterilization procedures. In response, feminists from all walks of life demanded an expansive bodily integrity for women, which included access to abortion but also freedom from sexual violence and forced sterilization and control over their own health and sexual identities. They sought to define what it meant to be a full citizen not in an abstract sense but what it meant to be a woman with a *body*, with biology and dignity alongside freedom, and in that basic sense what women's citizenship itself meant.

Before any progress could be made, women's advocates had to bring the personal and private world of reproduction into the public realm. Nothing evidences the secrecy of abortion in the United States better than the hundreds of letters that arrived at Patricia "Pat" Maginnis's San Francisco apartment each year in the late sixties. Written by women from all walks and all stages of life, they were composed when most abortions were illegal. Virtually all the writers were concerned with one thing: the safest and most discreet way to end a pregnancy. "I'm 42 years old, the sole support and mother of 3 children; thus I'm practically desperate at the thought of pregnancy at this point in life," one wrote. Another hinted at the horrors that could attend the predicament of an unwanted pregnancy: "Last week I tried to do it myself with some pointed objects but nothing happened. I'm desperate and will do anything." Similarly desperate women reached out to Leontyne Hunt at the *Chicago Defender*, the city's leading African American newspaper. Hunt, a Planned Parenthood employee and author of the column "Keep Your Family the Right Size," dispensed advice about matters sexual and reproductive. "I am 43 years old and have three children," a Mrs. J.R. wrote, "but now I am getting married again to a man who is 52 [who] says we don't have to worry about birth control because he's too old to make babies . . . Is he right?" A panicked Mrs. R.M. confessed that "I have seven children . . . Now I am pregnant again and just worried sick . . . Please tell me where I can go to get an abortion."[1]

To break open the world of private secrets in which abortion dwelled and make it a public domain of rights required women's advocates to adopt two parallel strategies. First, they had to wrestle the debate over reproduction away from the male physicians, clergy, and population control activists who dominated public discussions of abortion for much of the 1960s. Not until late in the decade did women's advocates have the numbers and the political leverage to do that successfully. Second, they had to craft cultural and legal arguments that would sway male-dominated legislatures and courts. The National Association for the Repeal of Abortion Laws (NARAL) and NOW, the two largest reproductive rights advocacy organizations, eventually settled on "choice," what they and others called a woman's right to choose an abortion.[2]

In addition to advocating choice, feminists, like homophiles, had to redefine "privacy." They had to make abortion public and political in order to protect it as a woman's private decision. Choice and privacy emerged as critical concepts in the space of seven years, 1967 to 1973, between passage of the first state abortion reform laws and the Supreme Court's decision in *Roe v. Wade*. As a tide of women massed behind demands for "reproductive rights," liberal activists, justices, and politicians sought to organize such rights under the framework of privacy, a legal domain increasingly recognized by the Supreme Court after 1965. Privacy, it seemed to many, was one of the privileges of being an American citizen and was a liberty shared by men and women alike. However, as a negative right—the right "to be let alone"—access to privacy as a component of citizenship varied sharply by income and race (as well as sexuality). As a result, the possibilities of privacy promised to protect some groups of women, while the dilemmas of privacy promised to leave others vulnerable.[3]

Those dilemmas, just like the ones that confronted women in their pursuit of market liberty, derived from class and racial inequalities in American society. In the broadest terms, most reproductive rights advocates embraced individualism for women, a nearly radical concept in the 1960s. Every woman has the right "to determine her own biological destiny," wrote Bella Abzug, the Manhattan congresswoman and fierce defender of reproductive freedom. Yet that freedom meant little to vast numbers of working-class and poor women, for whom abortion procedures were too expensive (or forbidden in public hospitals and under public health insurance), and the indignity of forced sterilization was all too real. For them, in reproductive matters, as in the marketplace, freedom was insufficient without various positive rights to make that freedom meaningful. Thus for the radical feminists who defended the poor and for feminists of color, "privacy" was too weak a protection for so fundamental a right. They called for "abortion on demand," the availability of an abortion at no cost for any woman, whenever and wherever she required it, as part of a larger women-controlled health system. Anything less was "compulsory pregnancy" and, as one women's liberation essay put it, subjugation "by the male medical establishment."[4]

What all this meant for womanhood, and particularly motherhood, as it was understood in the postwar United States remains central to the story. Over the first two-thirds of the twentieth century, family planning and the use of birth control grew increasingly acceptable for women; they did not offend "good" motherhood. For millions of Americans, however, that acceptability stopped short of abortion. Family planning remained rooted in the private domain of *family* and domesticity. But abortion and reproductive rights suggested a more radical liberation of women, an individualism that posited women as prior to, even outside, the family. For many Americans, this was an unacceptable breach of how they understood womanhood. Because abortion undermined their understanding of motherhood and family and constituted the taking of a "life," for them it could never be the basis for women's equality. Indeed, as this chapter introduces and subsequent chapters explore in greater detail, they found such an idea as deeply offensive and absurd as other women found strict abortion laws and constraints on women's reproductive freedom.[5]

•

The legal concept that would ultimately be invoked to secure abortion rights for women, privacy, was a compromise, the product of an emerging women-centered movement searching for a foothold and an American judiciary grasping for an underlying constitutional rationale to cautiously extend women's liberties. From 1959 to 1969 abortion activists disagreed among themselves over how to argue for reproductive rights in state legislatures and the courts. The most basic division was between those who advocated reform of existing laws and those who sought repeal of all such laws. Those years deserve close scrutiny because the notion that a right to an abortion might be protected constitutionally by "privacy" had only a handful of advocates before 1969. This decade, characterized by an increasingly urgent debate about what abortion meant—to individual women, to the social order, to physicians and hospitals, under the law, and in the proscriptions of religion—is crucial to understanding how women's advocates settled on privacy.[6]

Two episodes from that period illustrate the shifting political terrain. In 1962 George McLain, president of the National League of Senior Citizens, testified before an all-male committee of the California Assembly considering reform of the state's century-old abortion law. "A woman should have the right to determine whether or not she wishes to be a mother," he told the committee, a notion that dated to the voluntary motherhood movement of the early twentieth century. He scanned the room for Eleanor York, his wife, seated in the audience, who had "done the research on my presentation today." His dependence on his wife's intellectual labor, while he sat at the microphone, was telling. The most intimate and personal decisions confronting women about their bodies were debated in the public sphere largely by men.[7]

Seven years later, in 1969, Betty Friedan delivered a passionate speech in a packed ballroom at the First National Conference on Abortion Laws in Chicago. There is "no full human dignity and personhood possible for women until we demand the control over our own bodies," she insisted. Her audience was sympathetic but unprepared for such directness. Those in attendance were accustomed to male doctors and religious leaders, men like McLain, delivering sober appeals to moral conscience and championing cautious reform of existing abortion laws rather than their repeal. Something palpable changed between McLain's testimony and Friedan's speech: women across the country began to seize the microphone, community by community, state by state. Their voices were to carry the abortion debate beyond the cautious reform proposals of the early 1960s and focus it on repeal. Few developments are more emblematic of the extraordinary transformations wrought by sixties feminism than the shift from male to female authority in the abortion debate.[8]

There was widespread agreement in much of the psychiatric, medical, and liberal religious communities in the early 1960s that the nation's abortion laws were broken. Outlawed in every state, safe, legal abortions could be obtained only in the instance of life-threatening danger to the pregnant woman. As a result, each year hundreds of thousands of women— some estimates suggest a million—sought illegal abortions outside the medical establishment. Thousands died or suffered permanent injury. These numbers represented an increase from previous decades, and though there was no single cause behind the climbing figures, an important factor was women's growing participation in the workplace. As women's market work increased, and as education became increasingly central to women's employment chances, so did the cost to them, and their families, of each individual child.[9]

Access to abortion procedures had not always been so limited. In the 1930s, law enforcement officials in major American cities had permitted select hospitals, physicians, and clinics to perform extralegal abortions. This imperfect, ad hoc system did not guarantee universal access, but it functioned on the realist premise that abortions were a fact of life. Between the 1930s and the 1950s, however, city and state governments, spurred by the growing public awareness of the ubiquity of abortions and the subse-

quent moral agitation, all but eliminated this option. Alongside the lavender scare and other wartime and Cold War efforts to guard domestic
normalcy, the mid-century resurgence of a hallowed, and anxious, vision
of motherhood drove abortion underground.[10]

Physicians, psychiatrists, and public health professionals, mostly male,
were among the first to respond to the restrictive legal environment. In
1959 the American Law Institute (ALI) recommended a model abortion
law that legalized pregnancy terminations to protect the woman's health,
in the case of rape, and when the fetus was deformed—so-called therapeutic abortions. Deferring to public opinion and with feminism at its
nadir, however, the ALI embraced the view that sex outside marriage
was immoral, choosing not to frame its law in the language of women's
rights. The ALI model became the basis for the abortion law reform
movement, which took shape in the early 1960s, and was endorsed by
prominent physicians, particularly those associated with Planned Parenthood of America, such as New York's Alan Guttmacher, who became
the organization's president, and Mary Steichen Calderone, its medical
director.[11]

In the early 1960s, a small number of activists began to insist that
women's voices assume a larger place in the abortion debate. Women
such as Maginnis, the underground Chicago women's abortion collective
known as Jane, and Rev. Howard Moody's Clergy Consultation Service
on Abortion in New York City asserted the primacy of women's experience
in considerations of abortion. They stressed the harsh reality of illegal
"abortion mills" and the dreaded "back alley abortion." They emphasized
women's anguished search for safe abortions. Others, especially social workers and clergy who worked with poor women, pointed to the class bias of
contemporary abortion restrictions. The safer solutions, including expensive trips to legal clinics in Japan, Mexico, or Sweden, were viable only for
wealthy Americans. Neither argument was doctrinaire, however. Women's
advocates combined aspects of each in eclectic ways as they searched for a
language that captured women's experiences and the social consequences
of restrictive abortion laws.[12]

Far too often those consequences were emotional and physical agony.
Maginnis and Moody knew the stories by heart. In a typical one, "Susan,"
from Tallahassee, Florida, traveled to New York City in the mid-1960s to
seek the help of a friend to obtain an abortion. Furtive phone calls led
to a midnight visit to a New Jersey doctor. After checking to ensure that

"Susan" was pregnant ("Sometimes policewomen try to trap me," he said), the doctor told them that "I can set up an operating room in twelve minutes in a hotel room." After a nervous nighttime car ride, a terrifying procedure in a hotel, and an eight-hundred-dollar payment (more than four thousand dollars in 2010), the pregnancy was terminated. Unable to access such underground networks or to afford to pay, other women turned to homemade remedies—inserting objects (usually coat hangers or knitting needles) into the vaginal canal, flushing the uterus with soap, chemicals, or Coca-Cola, and ingesting a variety of chemical compounds (such as camphor gum, quinine, and turpentine). Illegal abortions were unfortunately common. In New York City one study of low-income women found that as many as one in ten had attempted a self-induced abortion, and more than one-third knew someone who had. In 1962, sixteen hundred women were admitted to Harlem Hospital for incomplete abortions. A pastor and abortion counselor in Chicago estimated that "in Cook County hospital, in Chicago, 4,000 women each year are treated for complications resulting from botched abortions . . ."[13]

The fact that this life-and-death urgency did not yet drive the abortion debate was a source of endless frustration to those who worked directly with women struggling with unwanted pregnancies. Instead, reformers continued to embrace a wide range of rationales for changing abortion law. Paul Ehrlich's 1968 book *The Population Bomb*, which advocated abortion as "a highly effective weapon in the armory of population control," influenced the founders of an organization called Zero Population Growth, which made "freely available" abortions a central aim of their agitation. Ehrlich's book sold hundreds of thousands of copies in its first year in print and decisively influenced a 1970 American Friends Service Committee's (AFSC) study titled *Who Shall Live?* Bemoaning the population pressures exacerbated by the illegality of abortion, *Who Shall Live?* observed, almost as an aside, that abortion laws "invade marital privacy." The AFSC endorsed abortion law repeal, going beyond mere "reform" of existing laws, but its focus on population control over privacy concerns typified the eclecticism among abortion rights activists in those years.[14]

Privacy entered the rhetoric of repeal advocates through the Supreme Court's 1965 decision in *Griswold v. Connecticut*, in which the Court held that state laws preventing the distribution of birth control to married couples violated "marital privacy," a concept that protected, the majority wrote, "the sacred precincts of the marital bedroom." A breakthrough in birth control politics, *Griswold* was nonetheless a limited one, bestowing privacy rights only on married heterosexual couples. Harriet Pilpel, a member of the President's Commission on the Status of Women under President Kennedy and one of the architects of the legal strategy in the *Griswold* case, envisioned a more far-reaching ruling. She published her vision in *Harper's*. "A strong argument can be made that when a woman is denied the right to terminate a pregnancy which threatens her well-being or that of her family," she reasoned, "[it] jeopardizes her life and liberty in violation of the Fourteenth Amendment." She saw in the concept of marital privacy the promise of individual privacy. And drawing on the work of psychiatrists and psychologists who reported on the personal trauma caused by unwanted pregnancies, she interpreted "well-being" to include psychological and economic health.[15]

But why privacy, as opposed to some other legal framework? The answer requires a brief detour into legal history. As the Court had articulated it in *Griswold*, privacy was the classic negative right. Subsequent decisions that relied on *Griswold* consistently grounded privacy in women's "liberty" to make choices about their lives. In doing so, justices typically cited the due process clause of the Fourteenth Amendment and Ninth Amendment rights "retained" by the people. But just as there had been when "liberty" assumed a central place in women's access to the job market, there were substantial drawbacks in a similar approach to reproductive rights. Judges could have also invoked, but manifestly and repeatedly refused to do so, the Fourteenth Amendment's equal protection clause, which requires a law to treat all citizens equally. An equal protection argument for reproductive rights, as it was later articulated in early-seventies feminist legal circles, had two dimensions. First, it asserted women's right to control their bodies as a foundation of their basic sexual and economic equality with men. Second, it demanded that *all* women, regardless of economic circumstances, benefit from abortion reform or repeal. Negative liberty, the equal protection argument went, could not guarantee equality. Only positive rights could.[16]

An equal protection argument was not constitutionally available to women until 1976, however. The Warren Court had not identified women as a suspect or protected class under the provisions of the Fourteenth Amendment, as it had African Americans and other nonwhite citizens. Not until a series of cases bookended by *Reed v. Reed* (1971) and *Craig v. Boren* (1976) did equal protection become available to women. By then, however, the judicial logic of privacy outlined in *Griswold* had become the de facto basis for pursuing abortion rights in the courts; few other rationales were ever recognized by judges. Equal protection in reproductive rights cases was also limited by the *San Antonio Independent School District v. Rodriguez* decision in 1973 (the same year as *Roe v. Wade*), in which the new Burger Court ruled that the range of protected classes of citizens did not include the poor. That decision marked a conservative turn in equality law with broad implications for the future of reproductive rights in the United States, virtually ensuring that access to abortion would continue to vary with economic class. With equality law effectively dismissed by the legal establishment, abortion rights advocates leaned heavily on the liberty argument available under due process.[17]

Pilpel had not been alone in seeing privacy as an avenue for judicial invalidation of abortion laws. The journalist-activist Lawrence "Larry" Lader, author of the groundbreaking 1966 book *Abortion*; attorneys in the ACLU (after 1972 the ACLU Women's Rights Project); and a third-year law student at New York University, Roy Lucas, who was to write a key law review article on privacy in 1968, all had begun elaborating the concept of privacy in 1965 and 1966. Without a decisive Supreme Court ruling on behalf of women as a protected class, legal minds in the late 1960s believed that when it came to intimate life and the family, privacy was the soundest basis on which to overturn abortion laws.[18]

As abortion activists plotted their legal challenges, contending legislative approaches emerged. One sought the reform of existing state law, based on the ALI model (abortion to protect women's health), while the other focused on the repeal of abortion statutes altogether (complete legalization). The two approaches had advanced furthest in California, New York, Illinois, Hawaii, and Michigan, although activists in a handful of other states, especially Colorado, Iowa, and New Jersey, were not far behind. Legal reform efforts were typically advanced by professionals, mostly male doctors and clergy, and middle-class women, usually employed in health care. Repeal efforts, by contrast, were led by a more eclectic group of college-age volunteers, radicalized women volunteering their time, social workers who worked closely with those seeking abortions, and, increasingly, feminist attorneys. Reform advocates focused on the physical and emotional harm to women and children, the threat of population growth, and the problem of underground markets in abortions. Repeal activists shared some of these concerns, especially the physical and emotional trauma to women, but they spoke in an incipient language of women's rights that grew increasingly self-assured over the second half of the 1960s.[19]

The experience of abortion activists in California sheds light on the tension between reform and repeal movements as well as on the growing opposition to *any* change in abortion law. The failure of ALI-style reform bills in the state assembly between 1963 and 1965 led a sympathetic group of physicians, clergy, and professionals to form the California Committee for Therapeutic Abortion (CCTA). Its speakers suffused the state, addressing more than three hundred meetings in a ten-month period in 1966. They lobbied legislators, published a newsletter, and drew more than two dozen statewide organizations into a big-tent coalition. Just over a year later, in June 1967, the assembly passed the Beilenson bill, based on the ALI model, which Governor Ronald Reagan signed. Beilenson, like most such state laws, created state boards to oversee abortion decisions and monitor the number performed by individual hospitals. Though less restrictive than previous abortion laws, it nonetheless fell far short of broad access.[20]

As the CCTA was leading the drive for reform, Pat Maginnis launched a repeal campaign. She founded the Society for Humane Abortion Laws in 1965 and, along with a small group of like-minded activists, traveled across the state, teaching women how to perform abortions on themselves and doing radio interviews, all while running an abortion referral service out of her home. She personally referred thousands of women to physicians and clinics in half a dozen countries, as well as to underground abortion clinics in the United States. She fervently believed that reform was a dead end, and her frequent arrests testified to her unwavering commitment. Reform still left far too many women treated as criminals for actions she believed to be a right. "The most gross invasion of privacy," Maginnis said after she had been arrested for distributing literature on abortion, "is the use of police surveillance to control what should be a private matter between a woman and her physician."[21]

Reform and repeal advocates disagreed over how much freedom women should have in reproductive matters, but their opponents fought all proposed changes to abortion law with equal passion. In California, as across the nation in the 1960s, the principal opponent of both reform and repeal was the Catholic Church. The U.S. church had emerged from the Second Vatican Council (1962–1965) divided into a liberalizing laity and a hidebound leadership. A 1966 statewide poll in California revealed that half of all Catholics disagreed with the church's teachings on abortion, at the same time that leading bishops were calling for a "murder in the womb" campaign against any changes to the law. Labeling the cautious ALI-style bill an "infant slaughter law," California's Catholic leadership spoke of the "slaughter of innocents" and fought liberalization at every turn. Catholic antiabortion activists published photos of unborn fetuses, labeled abortion "infanticide," and likened it to the eugenic practices of fascist Germany. After the passage of the Beilenson bill, California's experience became the national experience and set the tone of the abortion debate for decades to come. While reformers and repeal advocates saw abortion in terms of public health and rights, opponents framed the issue in terms of human life, the "sacred" life of the fetus. They spoke past, rather than to, one another.[22]

As additional states held hearings and considered reform legislation similar to California's between 1967 and 1969, it became increasingly clear to repeal advocates that a woman's right to control her own body was not driving the conversation. Three moments of public activism in 1969, however, reoriented abortion politics around women's voices and bodies. In February, the Redstockings, one of the first women's liberation collectives, founded in New York City by Kathie Sarachild, Shulamith Firestone, and other young radical feminists, attended hearings on a proposed abortion reform law in Albany, New York. Fourteen men and one woman were scheduled to address the committee, and the lone woman was a Catholic nun. After sitting quietly through several speakers, Sarachild leaped to her feet and bellowed, "Now let's hear from the real experts!" Others joined her, shouting, "Repeal the abortion law, instead of wasting time talking about these stupid reforms!" For the first time a state legislature was forced to engage directly with the women's liberation movement. No longer content to see women sitting in the back of the room while men cautiously debated issues central to women's experience, the Redstockings, along with NOW members picketing outside, declared women the "only experts" on abortion the assembly needed to consult.[23]

The second moment took place the same week, when more than a dozen organizations and 350 individuals met in Chicago to convene the First National Conference on Abortion Laws: Modification or Repeal? It was in front of this audience that Friedan demanded "control over our own bodies." In the same speech she echoed the Redstockings' Albany refrain: "I am no expert on abortion, but I am the only expert there needs to be now . . ." Organized by the physician and feminist Lonny Myers, a tireless advocate for the legalization of abortion, the Chicago convention led to the creation of the National Association for the Repeal of Abortion Laws (NARAL). Myers and Ed Keemer, an African American physician who had been jailed for performing abortions in the 1950s, assumed the reins of NARAL, which quickly drew into its orbit a national network of feminist activists, such as Maginnis, Carol Greitzer, Shirley Chisholm, Lucinda Cisler, Lana Clark Phelan, and Lee Gidding (who was to become executive director). Within a few years NARAL's board of directors would be dominated by feminists, who ensured that women's reproductive rights remained at the center of the national debate over abortion.[24]

The third development followed quickly on the heels of the other two. In March 1969, at a church in Washington Square, on the edge of Greenwich Village in New York City, twelve women "rapped" about their own abortions before an audience in excess of three hundred. The first abortion speakout, as it became known, represented the emerging women's liberation call to reveal the personal to be political. Sponsored by the Redstockings, the speakout had a straightforward aim: to push the most deeply private matters of being a woman into the public arena and thereby to expose the grip of patriarchy on women's lives. Reclaiming their bodies, for the radicals at the speakout, meant more than reproductive choice. It meant reclaiming female sexual desire and sexual freedom, which was impossible so long as women bore responsibility for unwanted pregnancies yet could not abort them. "The laws are not made in terms of a woman," one woman said at the speakout. Moreover, women were imagined as owing their reproductive capacity to society, another observed. Women are thought of as having "a debt. We have no debt."[25]

Thus was 1969 the turning-point year in the national debate over abortion. The energy of that year—indeed, of just its first three months— was the product of forces unleashed by the emergence of women's liberation. Between 1969 and 1971 women threw their support behind their local NOW branches, NARAL, and scores of local and state-level organizations devoted to abortion law repeal. Others eschewed such traditional advocacy and founded women's collectives, liberation "cells," and all manner of women-only groups based on the principles of participatory democracy and women's self-determination. Both inspired by and deeply disgusted with the sixties New Left, women turned their backs on its cult of masculinity.[26]

In thousands upon thousands of consciousness-raising groups, in women's centers, in living rooms, and in other formal and informal settings, women began to rethink feminism. Now, as never before, sex—the act, its politics, its outcomes, its cruelties, its joys—mattered. For many women, this new feminism was a reaction to what Robin Morgan called "the counterfeit male-dominated Left," the antiwar and civil rights men who condescended to or dismissed women's issues while taking women's labor for granted and assuming their bodies to be sexually available. For Michele Walker, a founding member of the National Black Feminist Organization (NBFO), it took "three years to understand that the countless speeches that began 'the black man . . .' did not include me." Morgan and Walker were joined by Gloria Steinem, Frances Beal, Kathie Sarachild, Flo Kennedy, and perhaps two or three dozen other prominent writers and organizers, who emerged as spokeswomen for the diffuse women's liberation and Third World feminist movements.[27]

Even more than sex, the body moved to the center of women's politics. Women's liberationists recognized that what they had been taught to think of as personal and private was in fact social and political—not unlike homophile activists and their eventual successors in the gay liberation and gay rights movements. Bodies might be individual, but their treatment by society, medicine, the media, and other male-dominated institutions constituted a *collective* political problem for women. This newfound understanding, coupled with an ethic of togetherness, produced a surge of activism and institution-building nearly on par with the black freedom movement. Their energy and their numbers, as much as any other single force, changed the context in which Americans discussed abortion.[28]

"Women's liberation played an important part in the passage of this bill," New York Governor Nelson Rockefeller declared when he signed the nation's most liberal abortion law in April 1970. Albert Blumenthal, a Democrat from Manhattan, and Constance Cook, a Republican from Ithaca, led the legislative fight for abortion reform in New York State, but as Rockefeller and other leaders of the liberal wing of the Republican Party recognized, absent the lobbying, demonstrations, and publicity generated by the women's movement, especially abortion rights activists and organizations from New York City, Syracuse, Buffalo, and Ithaca, their efforts would have met with defeat.[29]

The notion of reproductive rights enjoyed a spectacular ascent in the nation's consciousness in the last years of the sixties. In 1965 abortion had been a taboo subject, rarely discussed in public. Five years later millions of women viewed restrictive abortion laws as an obstacle to their full citizenship to the same degree as workplace discrimination. During this period of activism and reform, four states—New York, Hawaii, Washington and Alaska—eliminated nearly all restrictions on abortion within the first trimester. Other states, notably California, Colorado, New Mexico, Georgia, and Oregon, passed ALI-style reform laws, and ten other states passed some kind of reform bill. Though these results fell far short of what most activists believed necessary, in historical perspective the transformation in both law and public opinion had been swift.[30]

The successes of abortion activists at the state level were a direct result of their ability to build powerful coalitions composed of women's groups, liberal clergy, and medical professionals. These groups united around the notion of choice. Calling abortion a woman's private choice, however, is not the same thing as grounding the right to make that choice on the *legal* concept of privacy. NARAL and other women's advocates asserted the "inalienable right" of every woman, as Shirley Chisholm said at NARAL's inaugural press conference, "to choose whether or not she will bear children." However, the constitutional doctrine of privacy did not then, and does not today, secure anything close to the inalienability Chisholm desired. Because it is a negative right—"to be let alone"—privacy does not ensure that any woman who needs or desires an abortion will be able to have one. Attorneys forged ahead with the privacy argument regardless, because it remained the most powerful legal tool at their disposal. In September 1969 the California Supreme Court ruled, in *People v. Belous*, that the language of the state's prereform abortion law was unconstitutionally vague and that "a 'right of privacy' or 'liberty'" included a woman's "fundamental right to choose whether to bear children." Two years later, in *United States v. Vuitch*, the U.S. District Court for Washington, D.C., cited "a woman's liberty and right of privacy" as the linchpin of reproductive rights.[31]

"Privacy" was thus a compromise between women's emerging struggle for self-determination and a jurisprudence set in motion by *Griswold*. The concept had multiple advantages. Among religious Americans, it suggested an individual conscience wrestling with a complex and difficult moral decision. Motherhood as the responsible choice of an individual woman resonated with broader, liberalizing shifts in American attitudes toward consensual sex—at least heterosexual sex. Nonetheless, privacy and choice, with their undeniable commonsense appeal, made the fight for abortion rights a fight for individual freedom. And as with the fight for workplace rights, conceiving of access to abortion as a "negative" right to individual liberty meant that social inequalities would as often as not determine the quality of the liberty afforded by privacy. And, like employment law, abortion law was left vulnerable to erosion by its opponents and subsequent Supreme Court decisions.[32]

•

Reproductive rights were not simply a question of the freedom to have an abortion. There was also the question of justice. When it came to abortion, reproductive choice could mean little to women of limited financial means if they could not *pay* for an abortion. Compounding the issue was that the unwanted child of an impoverished mother, many argued, would in many cases create a greater burden on society than the unwanted child of a middle-class woman. Such children trapped women and families deeper in poverty, turned unwanted offspring to delinquent behavior, and limited women's contributions to society. Moreover, because large numbers of women who could not afford abortions would seek to end unwanted pregnancies regardless, unsafe abortions would still physically and psychically harm women. Poor women risked facing these indignities and burdens even under a "choice" framework for abortion.[33]

For poor women in America, reproductive rights carried other implications as well. For hundreds of thousands, if not millions, of working-class African American, Puerto Rican, Mexican American, and white women, compulsory sterilization and other constraints on childbearing were as real a possibility in the 1960s and 1970s as unwanted pregnancies. To these women, reproductive liberty meant the right to have a pregnancy as much as the right to terminate one. As late as 1971 half the states in the nation still legally authorized, and in some cases mandated, the sterilization of convicted criminals, the mentally ill, and certain categories of welfare recipients. The origin of the term "reproductive rights" in fact comes from radical feminists' recognition that "abortion rights" could not account for all of the reproductive dilemmas facing American women.[34]

For African American women, the quest for reproductive self-determination was entangled in the legacy of slavery and the contemporary fact of racism. Slaveowners had profited from their slaves bearing children (who were, of course, not uncommonly the result of the sexual violation of slave women by their owners). After emancipation, however, when the economic logic of humans as property lost its purchase, black childbirth was stigmatized by southern whites. Profligate "breeders," in this view, were a drain on society. In the twentieth century, large, impoverished black families faced additional scrutiny from state welfare departments. White middle-class Americans had long evinced discomfort with large working-class families, regardless of race, but reserved particular scorn for fecundity among the black poor. In their fight to secure control over their own bodies, then, black women had to navigate sexual, racial, and class politics all at once.[35]

Nowhere were these politics more entangled than in the South. Opposed to the federal welfare entitlement program, Aid to Dependent Children (which became Aid to Families with Dependent Children), since its inception during the New Deal, populist southern politicians denigrated the black welfare recipient as unfit for motherhood. In their harsh rhetoric, which drew on the classic American idea of the "undeserving poor," she was an immoral "chiseler" who manipulated the naive goodwill of the white public. Georgia governor Herman Talmadge's promise to "put an end to illegitimate baby-having business" in his state represented a common election-year theme. Generally, such promises meant a purging of the welfare rolls, often just in time to make poor women available for cotton-picking season. Moreover, in the years since the *Brown* decision, segregationists such as Talmadge, Mississippi senator James O. Eastland, and North Carolina governor Luther Hodges had used the alleged immorality of the black poor as an argument against school desegregation. The rising tide of profligate black welfare recipients threatened white culture, they claimed. And, like desegregation itself, this tide was a product of an overreaching federal state.[36]

What went unmentioned by southern politicians, even by demagogues such as Talmadge, was the practice of forced sterilization. African American women, along with Mexican American and Puerto Rican women, often found themselves at the mercy of doctors in public hospitals who surgically sterilized them without permission—typically just after their having given birth or in the course of another surgical procedure. By 1970 an estimated one-third of women in Puerto Rico and hundreds of thousands of African American and Mexican American women across the United States had been sterilized. Sterilization of black women was such a common practice in the South that it became known colloquially as a

Mississippi appendectomy. The practice and the attitudes behind it were not limited to the South, however. In post-Moynihan America, more and more whites agreed with the conservative columnists Robert Novak and Rowland Evans's claim that "the American problem of population explosion is centered in illegitimate Negro births in the slums of the great Northern cities."[37]

The racial dimensions of sterilization and population control were really nothing new, though. Since their origins in the late nineteenth century, the birth control and population control movements had been closely linked with eugenics and white supremacy. As a result, African Americans in the sixties were as suspicious as their forebears at even liberal attempts to assist black mothers. In the summer of 1965 Leontyne Hunt received a pointed letter for her column "Keep Your Family the Right Size." "My neighbor insists that the real purpose of the Planned Parenthood Association is to reduce the number of Negroes," the letter explained. "My neighbor thinks I'm betraying my race." Hunt, herself African American, assured her readers that this was not the case: "at least 50 of our Chicago Planned Parenthood staff of 95 are Negroes—and NOT Uncle Toms!" Planned Parenthood divorced itself from such distasteful associations in the postwar decades, but many state welfare programs continued to practice coercive sterilization.[38]

The history of forced or coerced sterilization was revealed in full by the 1973 case of two African American sisters, Minnie and Mary Alice Relf, aged fourteen and twelve. Without their parents' informed consent, they had been surgically sterilized in an Alabama hospital. With the assistance of the Southern Poverty Law Center and the National Welfare Rights Organization (NWRO), the Relfs filed suit against the U.S. Department of Health, Education, and Welfare (HEW), which funded sterilization in state clinics and hospitals. The district court discovered that tens of thousands of poor people had been sterilized annually since the 1950s under federally sponsored programs. The "consent" many had given often meant little. Illiterate patients, including the Relfs' mother, were in many cases not informed of the meaning of the agreements they signed. The Relf case forced the HEW to revise its family planning programs. Yet more than twenty-five states still permitted the sterilization of minors and the mentally disabled, while state agencies—like the North Carolina State Eugenics Board—continued to walk the hazy line between voluntary and coercive birth control. Along with the 1972 revelations about the Tuskegee syphilis trials, the Relf case came to symbolize disregard for black bodies among white Americans.[39]

Leading black nationalists had been denouncing birth control and abortion as white plots well before the Relf case. In the second half of the sixties, black nationalists declared procreation a revolutionary imperative. They condemned birth control and insisted that "sisters" populate the new black nation, a notion backed by the Newark Black Power Conference in the summer of 1967 and supported by nationalists from Huey Newton to Amiri Baraka. In their critique of birth control and their romanticizing of black women's fertility, nationalists celebrated a new black manhood, one based on a refusal—with the help of black women's wombs—to do the bidding of whites. The black sociologist Robert Staples's long response to the Moynihan report celebrated the "role of the black woman in the black liberation struggle . . . From her womb have come the revolutionary warriors of our time."[40]

In decrying family planning as a genocidal conspiracy of whites, however, male nationalists ignored the widespread demand for reproductive self-determination voiced by women in their own communities. That demand was evident in the testimony of scores of African American health experts, social workers, and civil rights leaders, who spoke publicly on behalf of black women's reproductive rights. A broad swath of black activists— from the Urban League director Whitney Young and the NWRO head George Wiley to the New York congresswoman Shirley Chisholm and the National Alliance of Black Feminists executive director Brenda Eichelberger—combined a critique of the white population control movement with a demand for reproductive freedom for black women. In one of the first ever discussions of abortion on the floor of the U.S. Congress, in December 1969, Chisholm called for "all of those family planning services available to the middle-class, rich, and white, [to] be made available and accessible to the poor, black and brown." Chisholm made clear that the "genocide argument," as Michigan's African American Secretary of State Richard Austin called it, did not serve the needs of black women. Though nationalist men had seized the initial rhetorical ground on birth control and set the tone for debate, African American women and their allies soon shifted the terms of debate to focus on a black revolution that included female self-determination.[41]

Black feminism was born in the midst of this hail of competing liberationist ideals. African American feminists found themselves caught between black men's politicized manhood, ordinary black women's increasingly urgent demands for control of their reproductive lives, and white feminists' presumption that their version of liberation was universal. "Black women have the right and the responsibility to determine when it is [in] the interest of the struggle to have children or not to have them," wrote Frances Beal, one of the earliest black women's liberationists to call for abortion rights. She added that a black woman must also determine "when it is *her* own best interests to have children." Even though they did not entirely trust the white women's liberation movement, black feminists—from liberals such as Dorothy Height, president of the National Council of Negro Women, to more radical activists such as Flo Kennedy, Linda La Rue, and Barbara Smith (the latter two of the liberationist Combahee River Collective)—were unapologetically in favor of reproductive rights. Chisholm said simply that the black nationalist anti-birth-control position was "male rhetoric for male ears."[42]

Mexican American and Puerto Rican communities divided along similar lines. Male Chicano activists of both liberal and nationalist persuasions resisted Planned Parenthood–led efforts to bring birth control to ordinary Mexican American women and their families. César Chávez and the United Farm Workers considered "family planning a form of Anglo racism," believing its aim was smaller, and thus socially and politically weaker, Chicano families. (In California the *Madrigal v. Quilligan* trial in 1978 eventually exposed, as the Relf case had done for African Americans, the coercive sterilization practices to which Chicanas were routinely subjected.) Drawing heavily on the teachings of the Catholic Church and a romanticized Aztlan past, Chicano nationalists considered large families part of the nationalist project of community liberation. Chicana feminists, like their African American counterparts, challenged nationalist men by seeking to reorient their community's politics around women's as well as men's needs. Chicana activists such as Anna Nieto Gómez, a major organizer of Chicana caucuses across the country, along with a younger generation of Chicana college students in organizations such as MEChA (Nacional Movimiento Estudiantil Chicano de Aztlán), led the way. Birth control, child care, and abortion rights headed the list of demands in the early 1970s, alongside equal employment and an end to Anglo racism. "Abortion is a fact of life," wrote Francisca Flores, a founder of the Comisión Femenil Mexicana (CFM), the major Chicana feminist organization in California. Abortion is "a personal decision. The woman must be allowed to make it without legal restrictions."[43]

All these arguments over reproductive rights took place in the inescapable shadow of the 1965 Moynihan report. The report highlighted the fundamental contradiction at the heart of the white-led mainstream effort to secure reproductive freedom on the basis of privacy. How could urgent calls for welfare policies explicitly designed to stabilize "the Negro family structure" coexist with a legal focus on privacy regarding sex, marriage, and other issues of morality? It may have seemed that whiteness, at least middle-class variants, was itself a form of protective privacy. In the white middle-class imagination, the state kept women from their reproductive freedom. Liberty, rendered as privacy, was the answer. Free from state intervention, women would be able to govern their own lives. For the poor, however, the law and state had to be a vehicle for, not just the grantor of, reproductive rights. Ending government regulation of the body and securing personal liberty would not benefit those whose chief access to medical care was through the state itself—through public hospitals or government assistance—or whose economic safety net might be conditional on various invasions of personal privacy.[44]

When considered as an exposition of breadwinner liberalism, however, the Moynihan report reveals much more than the dilemmas facing reproductive rights advocates. It reveals the very heart of the transformation of American politics during the late sixties. The Moynihan report and the successive summers of violent urban uprisings between 1965 and 1968 came at a crucial turning point in the politics of liberalism. During these years feminists, gay rights advocates, and the counterculture pushed liberals to embrace a politics of privacy. Just as sexual privacy was becoming a central feature of sixties liberalism, the Moynihan thesis and its defenders, which included notable liberals, insisted on precisely the opposite: that black family life was not only a legitimate arena, but an absolutely necessary arena, of national governmental action and intervention. Neither position was greeted with much sympathy by those who had once been at the center of breadwinner liberalism, working-class whites.

More than just about anything else, then, the politics of privacy divided liberals, illuminating three distinct arenas of the era's radical and liberal activism: those fighting for gender, sexual, and reproductive freedoms; those fighting against the continued oppression of the lower classes and racial minorities; and those defending the fragile gains that breadwinner liberalism had afforded their communities since the 1930s. The divides among these constituencies would determine the strengths and more often the weaknesses of American liberalism for decades.

•

In the three years before the 1970 New York abortion law, the women's liberation movement had made access to safe abortion a cornerstone of women's rights, and women of color claimed a voice in the debate. Concrete gains were made, and not just in New York. The movement represented a broad cross section of the American public, a diverse collection of combatants and dreamers: radical lesbians, black and Puerto Rican liberationists, female college students, progressive clergy, liberal feminists, and many others. The capaciousness of their project was also its strength. Americans from vastly different economic and social backgrounds could agree that abortion—at least in the first trimester (a time frame derived from medical practice and the academic medical literature)—ought to be both legal and accessible.[45]

But any narrative of triumph, even one cognizant of the role of class and race in dividing women, must take into account the forces of opposition that abortion activists confronted. Right-to-life committees—and in New York a Right to Life political party—had formed in nearly every state, and their efforts slowed the progress of repeal. Millions of Americans believed, or came to believe, that abortion was an immoral act that defied religious doctrine and human compassion. Less organized initially than the abortion reform and repeal movements, by 1970 the Catholic Church and a small handful of evangelical Protestant ministers had begun to coordinate the disparate foes of abortion.

Leading these efforts was Father James McHugh of Long Island, New York, director of the U.S. Catholic Conference's Family Life Division, who in 1967 laid the groundwork for what within a year was known as the right-to-life movement. In 1970 antiabortion activists held the first meeting of the National Right to Life Committee (NRLC), which emerged as the leading voice of the antiabortion position and whose state affiliates had grown so quickly that a full list ran a dozen pages by 1971. In addition to the NRLC, groups such as the National Commission on Human Life, Reproduction and Rhythm, the Human Life Foundation, Birthright,

Voice of the Unborn, and the U.S. Coalition for Life, among dozens of others, actively worked against reform and repeal in state legislatures and the courts. A collection of combatants and idealists as eclectic and committed as the reproductive rights side, the antiabortion movement emerged quickly and purposefully.[46]

The growing strength of the counteroffensive became evident between 1971 and 1972, when efforts to liberalize existing abortion laws were defeated in thirteen states. A useful example is Michigan. There, Proposal B, a referendum to legalize physician-performed abortions in the first twenty weeks of pregnancy, enjoyed 59 percent support statewide a month before the vote. After a two-week media campaign by the Catholic group Voice of the Unborn, 60 percent of voters cast ballots against it. Meanwhile, in New York, the Right to Life Party and the Right to Life Committee (RLC) undertook one of the most aggressive antiabortion campaigns in the country. The party won enough "pro-life" seats in Albany and convinced enough incumbents of the rightness of its cause to repeal the liberal legislation Rockefeller had signed into law just a year earlier. Only the governor's veto, delivered after a bitter and vitriolic battle, preserved the reform. By 1972 there was a nationwide antiabortion movement, composed of volunteers, financed by the Catholic Church, and organized largely at the state level, that was capable of fighting the women's movement in legislatures, in courts, and in the streets.[47]

Right-to-life groups' great and lasting innovation was to call abortion murder. As a result, the passion and rhetoric surrounding the abortion debate matched the passion and rhetoric surrounding black power and Vietnam. In a typical instance, antiabortion protesters in Los Angeles marched outside Avalon Memorial Hospital in the spring of 1972 with placards depicting the mutilated bodies of aborted fetuses. The hospital's assistant medical director told the *Los Angeles Times* that women seeking abortions had to endure enough emotional turmoil without "putting a sign in front of their face about baby killing." Abortion opponents employed tactics that many among their number accused feminists of employing first, extreme intimidating rhetoric above all.[48]

Rockefeller's fate after his support for abortion law reform in 1970 indicated the rising power of the right-to-life activism and the related careening fortunes of liberal politics. The national leader of liberal Republicans and a presidential candidate in 1960, 1964, and 1968, Rockefeller found himself marginalized within the party over the course of the seventies. By the time of Ronald Reagan's landslide 1984 reelection, most "Rockefeller Republicans" had been either driven from the party or sidelined in a shrinking minority. Between 1972 and 1984, a politician's stance on abortion was elevated to a test of party purity. Antiabortion Democrats were to share Rockefeller's fate.[49]

Even though women's advocates struggled to win legislative victories in the early seventies, public opinion increasingly supported liberalization. A 1971 Opinion Research Corporation poll found that 60 percent of Americans believed that abortion ought to be legal even if the mother's life was not in danger, and 50 percent believed abortion was a matter best kept between a couple and its doctor. Between December 1969 and June 1972, according to Gallup polls, the percentage of Americans who favored allowing a woman to end a pregnancy within the first three months increased from 40 to 64, a strong indication that the efforts of the women's movement were reaping rewards in Americans' beliefs, if not in their legislatures. Harris surveys put the percentage lower, at 52, but revealed a similar increase over the same two years. Every poll found Catholics the least receptive to legalization, but not by the margins one might expect given the church hierarchy's fierce opposition to abortion. The 1972 Gallup poll found for the first time that the majority of Catholics—56 percent— supported abortion rights.[50]

As abortion law repeal failed in state after state in the first years of the 1970s, fueling the hopes of right-to-life activists, more than opinion polls kept their reproductive rights counterparts optimistic. So did progress in the courts. In fact, alongside Rockefeller's line-in-the-sand veto in 1971, legal breakthroughs were the chief inspiration for reproductive rights advocates in these years of fierce tug-of-war and escalating rhetoric. In the spring of 1970, the U.S. District Court in Wisconsin deemed that state's abortion statute unconstitutional in a far-reaching and definitive decision (*Babbitz v. McCann*). Roy Lucas, whose 1968 article on the right of privacy in the *North Carolina Law Review* had become the legal movement's touchstone, won a decision against New Jersey's abortion law in early 1972, shortly after courts had overthrown statutes in Illinois, Vermont, and Florida. Suits were planned or in progress in nearly a dozen other states. Attorneys with the ACLU, NARAL, the National Emergency Civil Liberties Committee (NECLC), and state-level civil liberties organizations were optimistic that because the nation's judicial system had embraced the principle of right of privacy, the only logical outcome was abortion legalization.[51]

In October 1972, when the U.S. Supreme Court heard arguments in the cases of *Roe v. Wade* and *Doe v. Bolton*, abortion politics had arrived at a complex juncture. The repeal movement was stalled in state legislatures, even as public opinion increasingly supported the legalization of abortion. To unfreeze the impasse, Bella Abzug proposed a federal Abortion Rights Act, which fell flat in a Congress reluctant to take a stand and anticipating further court decisions. In New York, where abortion had been legal for nearly two years, abortion rights supporters remained mired in legal battles to force public hospitals and clinics to provide abortions. Meanwhile, three-judge federal panels had rejected cases against abortion statutes in five states, even as panels in other states affirmed privacy as a solid constitutional protection of reproductive decisions. And the Catholic Church increasingly asserted itself as the nation's conscience on matters of human life, even as studies confirmed that Catholic women were no less likely than non-Catholics to seek abortions. It was a muddle, waiting for a clarifying event.[52]

All sides, then, were understandably anxious to hear how the Court would decide *Roe*, a case that had originated in Texas in March 1970. Jane Roe was Norma McCorvey, an unemployed former carnival employee from Dallas. Her case was supported by the Dallas Committee for the Study of Abortion and a women's liberation collective from Austin. She was represented by Sarah Weddington, a twenty-six-year-old feminist attorney from small-town West Texas and the daughter of a Methodist minister. (In 1967, a pregnant Weddington, facing a dearth of options, had had an abortion performed in Mexico.) A month after Weddington and another lawyer named Linda Coffee filed suit on McCorvey's behalf against Dallas County district attorney Henry Wade, attorneys and activists with Georgia Citizens for Hospital Abortions filed *Doe v. Bolton* in an Atlanta court on behalf of a woman named Sandra Bensing. Both cases claimed violations of a constitutional "right of privacy or liberty in matters relating to marriage, family, and sex," and both eventually found their way to the U.S. Supreme Court's docket in 1972.[53]

More than forty amici curiae—friend of the court briefs—from organizations, individuals, and legal teams across the country were filed in support of *Roe* and *Doe*. Lucas filed one that ran more than one hundred pages. Harriet Pilpel, writing on behalf of Planned Parenthood, found it "difficult to imagine a more drastic restriction on privacy or on the fundamental freedom to control one's body and one's life [than] compulsory pregnancy." Many of the briefs went beyond matters of personal liberty and privacy to the matter of bodily integrity. Representing a group of physicians and feminist attorneys, Carol Ryan wrote: "The freedom to be master of her own body, and thus her own fate, is as fundamental a right as a woman can possess."[54]

The Supreme Court issued its *Roe* and *Doe* decisions together in a single opinion in January 1973. Once a taboo, abortion was now a right, albeit a heavily circumscribed one. The 7–2 majorities in both cases extended the jurisprudential logic of privacy by a considerable margin. But they also placed the right to an abortion on the fault line between negative and positive rights. Justice Harry Blackmun, writing for the majority, asserted plainly that "the right of personal privacy includes the abortion decision." However, the Court found "important state interests in regulation" that it believed should take hold after the first trimester, including "health, medical standards, and prenatal life." Antiabortion activists in subsequent years seized on the phrase "important state interests" to reduce the circumstances under which abortions were legal. Blackmun insisted, furthermore, that *Roe* did not establish "an unlimited right to do with one's body as one pleases." Chief Justice Warren Burger concurred: *Roe* did not mean "abortion on demand." Even as the women's movement celebrated a historic decision and a massive improvement over the patchwork of state laws, its adherents saw the limitations of *Roe* from the start.[55]

The two dissenting justices, joined by antiabortion forces across the country, cast *Roe* as jurisprudentially hollow and an unmitigated judicial blunder. Justices Byron White and William Rehnquist took the right-to-life position in their curt rebuttal. The Court "simply fashions and announces a new constitutional right," White charged, that values "the whim or caprice of the putative mother more than the life or potential life of the fetus." If the majority's embrace of the feminist language of reproductive freedom was noticeably partial, the minority's embrace of the right-to-life language was nearly absolute. Antiabortion activists in 1971 and 1972 began denigrating abortion as the "whim" of irresponsible women who preferred "lifestyle" over "life." This and similar accusations were to acquire a sharper edge over the course of the seventies.[56]

Despite being greeted by feminists as a triumph, if short of total victory, and by right-to-life advocates as a calamity, *Roe* and *Doe* did not fundamentally transform the abortion debate. Both sides had been pursuing legal remedies for years, and both still are to this day (abortion law has been in continuous litigation somewhere in the United States since the 1960s). *Roe* and *Doe* merely intensified the debate. "The Supreme Court has done anything but 'settle' the abortion issue," declared the New York senator and abortion rights foe James Buckley.[57]

Enforcement of the *Roe* and *Doe* decisions was another matter entirely, one in which antiabortion activists and sentiments were for a time the clear winners. Many states chose to ignore the decisions. In the summer of 1973 NARAL and the ACLU had to sue ten states to force tax-supported hospitals to provide abortions. According to NARAL's Larry Lader, "the Court decision has been stalled and rendered virtually inoperable in most states by the refusal of the public hospitals to comply." Legislators and other public officials opposed to abortion rights sought court orders to limit the kinds of institutions that could perform abortion procedures; reproductive rights advocates claimed that preventing doctors from performing abortions in their offices could cut availability by as much as 50 percent. Just ten days after *Roe* the state medical commission in Virginia ruled that no public municipal hospital in the state could perform abortions. Other states followed suit. Moreover, across the country Catholic hospitals, among the most important in providing health services to the poor, refused to perform abortions.[58]

To say, as one participant in the 1969 Greenwich Village abortion speak-out had, that women "had no debt" was to declare women unequivocally the equals of men. It was to say that their full citizenship rested not on motherhood—the "debt" owed being children—but on the same freedoms that men enjoyed. In the two-hundred-year history of liberal democracy this was a revolutionary claim. *Roe* did not inaugurate or end that revolution, but it did mark a point of transition for women's activism in the United States. In the eight years between *Griswold* and *Roe*, grassroots activists, legal theorists, feminists, and women's advocates successfully forced the nation's judicial and political establishment to grant women the right to control their reproductive lives. They swayed the public too. Mid-seventies polls showed that a majority of Americans supported *Roe*. Alan Guttmacher, who began the sixties a cautious supporter of ALI-style reform, was a feminist by decade's end: "abortion on demand is the only civilized way to handle the problem," he declared.[59]

And yet privacy, the basis of just about every legal success for reproductive rights, produced a cleaved citizenship. Positive rights do not usually follow the codification of negative rights. Once a woman's liberty to seek an abortion was established, opponents endeavored to constrain and circumscribe that right by preventing the government from funding entitlements that protected it. To leave a negative right unprotected, or to withhold the resources without which the right is inaccessible, is to make it a matter of market forces. Feminists and other women's advocates were to discern this reality soon enough. So would the New Right, which in time yoked its antiabortion politics to the larger goals of privatization, federalism, deregulation, and the dismantling of the domestic welfare state. New Right activists would see to it that tax dollars did not support abortion. Thus did the dilemmas of liberal "rights," the inequities of capitalism, and the legacies of the public-private divide, to say nothing of a determined opposition, constrain the women's movement's quest for bodily integrity and forestall the extent of transformation it could produce.[60]

6

AMERICAN SAPPHO: THE LESBIAN POLITICAL IMAGINATION

"It was a terrifying thing to be told one's whole life that one's destiny is to be attached to a man and yet to feel nothing for men," recalled Susan Madden Johnson. Lesbians had little standing in America's patriarchal society. Their sexual independence of men made them doubly vulnerable to accusations that they violated acceptable womanhood and to economic marginalization absent male breadwinners. "Her sexual preference places her at the rock bottom in society's eyes," Sidney Abbott and Barbara Love wrote in their 1972 book *Sappho Was a Right-On Woman*. Yet precisely because they found themselves at the "rock bottom," and because they wrestled with the inseparable dilemmas of personal authenticity and political subjectivity, lesbians' outsider status afforded them a view of American society few others had. In the late sixties and early seventies they questioned the conventions governing heterosexuality and womanhood as thoughtfully and vehemently as any group in national life.[1]

For lesbians, the homosexual citizen imagined by mid-1960s homophiles was a legal necessity. But too often this citizen did not fully capture their life experiences or their political visions. As was the case in the larger homophile movement, lesbian politics encompassed many often contending viewpoints and approaches, from respectability to sexual radicalism. As women working within the confines of a homophile movement led and largely defined by men, however, lesbians were asked to compromise in ways that, for many, were no longer tolerable by the second half of the decade. Between 1965 and 1970, unifying mantras such as "We are citizens!" gave way in favor of more thoroughgoing and radical critiques of patriarchy and sexism—in *gay* as well as straight society. Calls for inclusion as homosexual citizens alongside gay men in the liberal project of winning new rights yielded to uniquely lesbian versions of women's liberation. Third World lesbians added racism and the legacies of colonialism to the catalog of forces that shaped women's sexual status. By the early 1970s lesbian feminism had become a vibrant political philosophy, one distinct from any of its forebears or contemporary analogues.[2]

Lesbian political thought developed two indispensable insights in these years. First, lesbian activists declared that the basis of homophobia is sexism. "Dyke" and "faggot" are different kinds of slurs, the Radicalesbians wrote in 1970, but they share a common origin: "the contempt in which women—or those who play a female role—are held." Second, they posited that heterosexuality is a coercive institution posing as a natural one. Much as radical feminists, among whom lesbians were numerous and essential, put forward the notion that compulsory motherhood constrained women, lesbians made the same claim about heterosexuality. They went beyond the liberal model of individual rights in search of an authentic female self and a reordered society outside of, they romantically imagined, patriarchy. And much like other groups caught in and responsible for the maelstrom of post-1964 activism, they found their beliefs both liberating and limiting. Like no other group, though, lesbians faced daunting challenges in their efforts to amass influence and win rights while simultaneously pushing against the allowable boundaries of gender and sexuality in the American imagination.[3]

Nowhere were those challenges more in evidence than in lesbians' encounters with the many versions of feminism that had proliferated by the end of the sixties. Lesbians fought side by side with women from all walks of life in every stage of the women's movement. But throughout, *lesbianism*—as an identity, a way of loving, a political philosophy, a state of being—occupied a volatile space in feminist politics. Charges of "man-hating dyke" and accusations of being antifamily became the most consistently deployed rhetorical weapon against every version of feminism. Buffeted from all sides, the forces and compromises that shaped individual lesbian identities and collective politics were never simple. Yet they allowed gay women to look at American society "from the rock bottom" and, in so doing, to articulate some of the era's most audacious claims about citizenship and the political meanings of affection and sexual desire.[4]

•

As they were for the larger homophile movement, the years 1964 and 1965 were a crossroads for lesbian activists. Founded in San Francisco in 1955 by white women committed to uplift and respectability, the Daughters of Bilitis (DOB), the chief vehicle of lesbian politics, was long preoccupied with "the problems of lesbians." Its mission—"education of the variant," facilitating "her adjustment to society," and "participation in research projects"—struck many a decade later as unforgivingly apologetic. Inspired by the black freedom movement and early second-wave feminists, by 1965 lesbian homophiles had begun to embrace a rights-based legislative strategy. They had also linked arms with male homophiles to build the organizations and nurture the gay public sphere that pushed guardedly at the limitations of respectability and refused the notion that lesbians and gay men had to adapt to a hostile society. Alongside gay men, lesbians led the charge against society's regime of heterosexuality.[5]

However, this shift from accommodation to activism affected lesbians differently from gay men. Same-sex affection and everything that came with it in postwar America—their diagnosis as "deviates," their vulnerability to persecution and firing, and their lack of basic rights—made lesbians and gay men natural allies. No less than male homophiles, lesbians confronted the dilemma of how to combine respectability and militancy. Yet their gender and what it meant for two women to love each other, as opposed to two men, added a complication to their political aims. Were they lesbians in the homophile movement or women in a men's movement?

All social movements in American history have been identity-based to one degree or another; seeing oneself in the collective is a precondition for participation. Lesbians asked not *whether* identity could be the basis for their politics, but *which* identity. Should they seek inclusion in American life as women, as gay, or as citizens with privacy? All three? Who would be logical partners in such a struggle? Lesbian activists were central to the homophile movement from the beginning, but the gay public sphere fostered by *Drum, The Advocate, Vector,* and their analogues was dominated by and preoccupied with men. Moreover, many gay men had little interest in defending lesbians as women. So long as lesbian objectives remained synonymous with gay men's—discrediting the psychiatric model of homosexuality, for instance, or ending police harassment— alliances were possible, even necessary. But when lesbians turned to abortion, job inequality, and child care, many gay men lost interest. Like straight men, many gay men took for granted the centrality and naturalness of their concerns. Lesbians thus labored on two fronts. First, they attempted to forge a militant yet still "respectable" demand for homophile rights. And second, they endeavored to clarify an acceptable relationship to gay men that did not subsume their interests as women.[6]

The quest for the right mixture of respectability and militancy began in earnest in the mid-sixties, in San Francisco and in East Coast cities. In 1964, DOB members Del Martin, Phyllis Lyon, and Cleo Glenn joined gay men in a venture with progressive Methodist ministers Ted McIlvenna and Cecil Williams of San Francisco's Glide Memorial Church. The resulting Council on Religion and the Homosexual (CRH), the first gay-straight-church alliance in the country, worked with the city's police department and mayor's office to reduce harassment of lesbians and gay men. Back east in 1963, the New York DOB helped found the East Coast Homophile Organizations (ECHO), the first meeting of which was held just days after the August March on Washington for Jobs and Freedom. In Philadelphia the Homosexual Law Reform Society began its advocacy in the courts, and the inaugural annual reminder picket at Independence Hall, in which Barbara Gittings, Kay Lahusen, Marge McCann, and four other lesbians participated, took place in July 1965 (Washington Mattachine's pickets had also begun in 1965). This new generation of lesbian activists evinced a militancy still partially hidden by the well-pressed skirts of respectability. But the institutions they created signaled their growing desire to go beyond the cautious incrementalism of the early homophile movement.[7]

Barbara Gittings and Florence Jaffy lived on opposite coasts. Gittings shared with her partner, Kay Lahusen, an apartment near Rittenhouse Square in Philadelphia and then a house in West Philadelphia. There, between 1963 and 1966, Gittings edited *The Ladder*, the lesbian monthly published by the DOB. Jaffy lived in San Francisco and taught economics at the College of San Mateo. For much of the 1960s she was the DOB's national research director. Despite their shared commitment to the Daughters, Gittings and Jaffy did not see eye to eye. Gittings, who was known to have dressed as a young man to hitch rides with truckers from Philadelphia to New York in the 1950s, had grown weary by 1964 of "mousing around with heterosexual society." Impatient with the DOB, and viewing the black freedom movement as a model for lesbians, Gittings longed for action. She wrote Jaffy in July 1964 to say that she and Lahusen "no longer buy the 'integration into society' and 'adjustment to society' bits." In reply, Jaffy defended her own political sensibility. "I strongly favor 'integration,'" she wrote, "but this means a sense of some things *held in common with the rest of humanity*; it does *not* mean acceptance of society's stigma." Jaffy preferred to demonstrate to the American public the "normalcy" of lesbians before pressing for rights. Gittings represented the future, but in 1964 Jaffy's approach obtained among most lesbian activists.[8]

Sorting out their relationship to the gay men in the homophile movement proved similarly vexing and divisive for lesbian activists. In August 1966, just a few months after Betty Friedan, Kathryn Clarenbach, and other liberal feminists founded the National Organization for Women (NOW), lesbian homophiles met in San Francisco and planned their own feminist insurgence. Dubbed "ten days in August," the DOB convention was coordinated with the National Planning Conference of Homophile Organizations (the forerunner of NACHO) as a showcase for the West Coast homophile movement. Members of CRH, the Society for Individual Rights (SIR), and the Tavern Guild joined the DOB and homophile activists from across the country. The *San Francisco Chronicle* even ventured the headline SAN FRANCISCO GREETS DAUGHTERS, and local radio and television stations covered the convention, the highlight of which was a speech by a nurse from New York, and the new DOB president, named Shirley Willer.[9]

Willer stood before her sisters and gave voice to the inchoate sentiments of lesbian activists. "The problems of the male homosexual and the female homosexual differ considerably," she said plainly. "Lesbian interest is more closely linked with the women's civil rights movement than the homosexual civil liberties movement . . . There has been little evidence that the male homosexual has any intention of making common cause with us." Willer well knew that many in the hall, including the women who had helped found the CRH, were partners in productive alliances with gay men. Willer was not against such alliances in theory, but she warned that in practice lesbians allied with gay men would remain junior partners and would have to work, first and foremost, on men's issues: "police harassment, unequal law enforcement, legal proscription of sexual practices . . . wash-room sex acts and transsexual attire."[10]

Willer laid out a lesbian agenda that shifted focus away from the sexual "civil liberties" predominant among male homophiles. "Few women are subject to police harassment," Willer noted. "The problems of importance to the lesbian are job security, career advancement, and family relationships." As women, lesbians rarely earned the family wage to which men had claim and could not fall back on male providers; economic class mattered fundamentally to them. Moreover, many lesbians in the 1960s generation were in straight marriages and risked losing their children if they came out, while others wished to adopt children. As a consequence, equal employment, divorce and adoption law, and economic independence were all more central to lesbians than was sexual privacy. Willer was unfair to those male homophiles whose politics went beyond the quest for sexual privacy, but she captured the essence of the lesbian predicament and pointed the way forward for lesbian politics. Concluding her address, Willer called on gay men "to be as concerned about women's civil rights as male homosexuals' civil liberties." She stepped down to a robust ovation.[11]

The Ladder soon echoed Willer. Barbara Grier, a lifelong iconoclast from Kansas City and an important midwestern DOB anchor, supported Willer's feminism. "The enormous prejudice" that affects lesbians, Grier wrote (under the pseudonym Dorothy Lyle), "she faces each day because, first and foremost, she is a woman." A succession of contributors followed Willer's and Grier's lead. They included Stella Rush, a writer for ONE magazine since the early 1950s (pseudonym Sten Russell). Rush was a former Rosie the Riveter at Firestone Tire and Rubber in wartime Los Angeles and a close confidante and observer of L.A.'s male homophiles. By 1967 she and her partner Helen Sandoz found themselves gravitating toward feminism. Rush wrote in The Ladder that after thirteen years "listening to men's opinions of what it is to be a woman, with little or no chance to answer . . . most of us, if not actually all of us, have grown at least temporarily testy on the matter."[12]

The phrase "temporarily testy" exemplified The Ladder's respectable discourse but also perhaps represented a tacit admission that breaking from male homophiles was a risky move. As the feminist tide swept over lesbian activists in 1966 and 1967, two obstacles appeared. First, it was not clear in those years that out lesbians would be welcomed into the emerging women's movement. There were already signs that sexuality would not figure in NOW's politics. Second, activists such as Gittings, Lahusen, Martin, Glenn, and even Willer (and her partner, Marion Glass) had forged close and productive ties with gay men. Lesbians thus faced the prospect of having no voice in the women's movement and losing their voice in the homophile movement.

Race, unsurprisingly, further shaped lesbian political strategy. Lesbian politics followed the same pattern as other liberal-left movements, the pattern that was to frustrate so-called identity politics for generations. Conscious first and foremost of being marginalized because of their gender and sexuality, white lesbians in the middle 1960s invested less time examining their racial privilege. The black freedom movement had inspired lesbian homophiles to assert that they too were a coherent minority denigrated and denied rights by the majority. And the black power movement's emphasis on community pride and self-determination, as well as its rejection of the politics of assimilation, had inspired white lesbians to argue that society's prejudice, not homosexuality, was the problem. The irony, with lesbians as with feminists and male homophiles, was that they drew on the ideas and methods of black freedom at the expense of people of color in their midst. African American, Chicana, Puerto Rican, and other lesbians of color too often found "lesbian" an insufficient foundation of either identity or politics.[13]

The life of Puerto Rican–born New Yorker Juanita Ramos (pseudonym for Juanita Díaz-Cotto) is illustrative. Attracted to women all her life, Ramos had few role models in her immigrant Catholic neighborhood in 1950s Brooklyn. Influenced by the few acquaintances who knew anything of lesbian subcultures, Ramos adopted a butch persona in her late teens. After returning to Puerto Rico in the early 1970s, she read Albert Memmi's *The Colonizer and the Colonized* and devoted herself to Puerto Rican nationalism. But in the estimation of the male-dominated Puerto Rican left, she, as a lesbian, was "sick." Back in New York, Ramos found the women's liberation movement, while now openly supportive of lesbians, dominated by middle-class white women who could not comprehend her experience. For Ramos—a Puerto Rican, a woman, and a lesbian—the varieties of sixties and seventies left activism were not various enough.[14]

Ramos's story gets to the nub of the dilemmas facing insurgent rights-based social movements in this era, which were motivated by the country's limited vision of full citizenship. To redress historical inequality and to make political headway, a range of Americans out of necessity coalesced around identities—black, homophile, female. However, once the notion of a universal democratic subject, a universal "American," was fractured, it was a complicated matter to reassemble. The liberal and radical movements that challenged the idea of a universal American were inherently circumscribing, not all-inclusive. The risk of their strategy was that the dominant group within each constituency—whether whites or heterosexuals or men—would simply assert a new presumed universalism: "woman" or "homosexual." Male homophiles could argue that the heterosexual vision of the American citizen marginalized gay men, while Willer could argue that the male homophile vision of the American citizen marginalized lesbians, and Ramos could argue that Willer's lesbian citizen did not account for her experiences of race and colonialism.

What they all had in common was a desire to expand the circle of democratic inclusion. What divided them were the complicated legacies of privilege and power embedded in every iteration of "citizen" since the French Revolution. These were legacies not of their making, and their strategies for addressing them time and again came up against challenges of diversity and inclusion that their opponents rarely had to face.[15]

In the headwind of these dilemmas, Willer was a visionary but also a pragmatist. She facilitated the opening of local DOB branches across the country and, intent on helping the emerging national homophile organization, brought the DOB to the first NACHO conference. But she could not prevent the DOB's relationship to the mainline homophile groups on both coasts from fraying. Nor could she quell internal dissension within the Daughters. In Philadelphia lesbians dissolved the local DOB and founded the Homophile Action League in 1968. Many in New York were ready to do the same. By 1968 rapid change and grand thinking had overtaken cautiousness, and an ever-growing number of lesbian activists were pulled toward radicalism. The question was no longer if the movement would change, but the extent of the change itself.[16]

•

Whatever political strategy lesbians decided to pursue, they, like male homophiles, confronted a roadblock that extended in all directions: sickness, the psychiatric model of homosexuality. On a December day in 1963, Gittings opened her mail to find a terse, accusatory letter from a Columbia University psychology professor, Albert Ellis. Ellis claimed that his views had been presented with "an unusual number of mistakes" at the ECHO conference earlier that month. He did not think homosexuals were "psychopaths," he wrote. Rather, "homosexuals are properly to be diagnosed as borderline *psychotic* or outrightly psychotic." Such was the tenor and focus of the debate in the psychiatric and academic community in the 1960s. Homosexuals were sick. Only the kind of sickness was in doubt.[17]

Mid-sixties psychiatry swept up male and female homosexuals together as deviant. As with gay men, lesbians were subject to a combination of officially sanctioned science and popular prejudices loosely validated by that science. But lesbianism was considered distinct from male homosexuality, as a specific and deleterious psychiatric condition outside the bounds of proper womanhood and femininity. Lesbians evincing a masculine gender presentation so confounded postwar expectations of womanhood, and so thoroughly flummoxed conventional notions of femininity, that little other than mental illness seemed a likely explanation. Equally confounding for postwar Americans was the "femme": unmarried and often childless but indisputably feminine. The mothers of lesbians, the prominent psychoanalyst Irving Bieber wrote, did "not encourage such typical female pursuits as cooking and homemaking . . . few, if any, ballerinas, are homosexual." Mid-century psychiatric treatises like Bieber's were riddled with distant fathers and hyperprotective mothers and, ironically, their opposites, as explanations for sexual difference in offspring.[18]

The lesbian activist Martha Shelley was particularly adept at pointing out the absurdities in this psychiatric model of homosexuality. In 1968, in response to ideas like Bieber's, which exerted considerable cultural power, she observed that "most of my straight friends had possessive mothers, puritanical upbringings, competitive or absent fathers, seductive mothers, etc." Why were they not gay? Shelley asked. Her insights went further, striking at the heart of psychiatry's theories of sex and self. How, if society disdained homosexuality and the state rendered homosexual acts illegal, could homosexuals *not* feel guilt and confusion? How could they not, in other words, appear psychologically damaged? "To suggest that homosexuality is a disease because it involves guilt feelings, confusion about one's sexuality, and other psychological problems is again a sophistry," Shelley wrote. Psychiatry told lesbians and gay men that they were sick and then used their feelings of guilt and confusion about that "fact" to diagnose them as sick.[19]

In spite of its questionable logic, the psychiatric model of lesbianism obtained in sixties America. In its persecution of lesbian teachers in the late 1950s and early 1960s, the Florida Legislative Investigation Committee settled any potential confusion over what should be done with those arrested: "mandatory psychiatric examination prior to sentencing" and "provision for outpatient psychiatric treatment." In 1964 Edward Sagarin (a closeted psychiatrist writing under the pseudonym Donald Webster Cory) published *The Lesbian in America*. It was a follow-up to his 1951 book *The Homosexual in America*, in which Sagarin made the seemingly contradictory argument that homosexuals were mentally disturbed yet should fight for their rights as minorities. He went to great lengths to dispel the myth that lesbians represented the psychological equivalent of men trapped in women's bodies, while feeding others, including that lesbian identity was defined entirely by sexual desire. Ellis wrote a flattering introduction for Sagarin, assuring his readers that while "homosexuals and lesbians are severely disturbed persons," they have the capacity "of becoming less disturbed and of overcoming their sexual deviation." That same year, the New York Academy of Medicine's Public Health Committee released a report on homosexuality underscoring the conclusions of Sagarin, Ellis, and another Columbia professor and a bulwark of the psychiatric model of sexual difference, Charles Socarides: "the homosexual is an emotionally disturbed individual."[20]

Notions of lesbians as sick and gender confused fed a larger suspicion of women's associational culture. Close female friendships and densely populated female professional and educational networks had long been conventionally accepted. Indeed, they were creatures of, and embedded in, the idealized separate private and public spheres women and men were expected to inhabit. Lurking never far beneath the surface of these socially acceptable forms of female interaction, however, was anxiety that such all-female worlds could be subversive of heterosexuality. The policing of women's friendships for signs of sexual content grew increasingly institutionalized over the course of the twentieth century among teachers, women in the military, and students in colleges and universities, as authorities worried that ordinary female networks could nourish, harbor, and conceal "deviant," unwomanly sexual desire.[21]

Sagarin's book on lesbians and the Academy of Medicine report prompted Gittings to stage a debate in *The Ladder* between Frank Kameny and Florence Jaffy. Like Kameny, Gittings was committed to the complete defeat of the psychiatric model, what she called "the lucrative sickness concept" because it sold books like Sagarin's. Kameny, Gittings, and like-minded homophiles believed that rights and freedom were a matter of politics and humanism, not science. To validate psychiatrists and other researchers as "experts" was to forfeit strategic ground and the movement's existential ballast. Writing in the May 1965 issue of *The Ladder*, Kameny was typically direct: "We cannot declare our equality . . . from a position of sickness." Jaffy, in contrast, believed that research by experts would in time normalize homosexuality for the straight public, and writing as Florence Conrad, she replied two issues later to Kameny's "broadside attack on research." "You are dealing with a hostile, uninformed, and prejudiced public," Jaffy reminded Kameny. Only the weight of science, confirming the normalcy of homosexual desire, she insisted, could convince a deeply skeptical public. "I would ask where the Negro civil rights movement would be today . . . if research into racial differences had not long ago supported the Negro's claim to equality of treatment?"[22]

Jaffy's position, however, was losing credibility among lesbian activists, many of whom were in open revolt against the psychiatric establishment by 1970. That year, in alliance with gay men, lesbian activists—Gittings, Martin, and Lilli Vincenz, the editor of *Homosexual Citizen*, in particular—launched an uncompromising assault on psychiatric "sophistry," with Martin telling American Psychiatric Association (APA) members that psychiatry was "the most dangerous enemy of homosexuals in contemporary society." Activists attended the 1970 APA conference and during a session on "aversion therapy," leaped from their seats and began shouting at the assembled psychiatrists. In the ruckus, Dr. Leo Alexander, one of the presenters, physically handled a protester, "Judy X," and later called her "a paranoid fool and a stupid bitch." Over the next three years, Vincenz, Martin, Gittings, Kameny, Larry Littlejohn, and other militant activists, including some from the newly formed Gay Activists Alliance (GAA), stormed APA sessions; infiltrated others, posing as psychiatrists and researchers; recruited gay psychiatrists and other allies from within the APA ranks; and disrupted the smooth functioning of the APA until homosexuality was officially "delisted" from its *Diagnostic and Statistical Manual of Mental Disorders (DSM)* in 1973.[23]

As those battles raged, the authors of *Sappho Was a Right-On Woman* observed in 1972: "The Lesbian is one of the least known members of our culture . . . Less is known about her—and less accurately—than about the Newfoundland dog." Reforming psychiatry was one thing. Confronting prejudices about lesbians in the popular imagination was another. And here the "sickness concept" blended with sexism to create a potent and specific form of homophobia. "Man-hating dyke" was such a common phrase by the early 1970s that women's liberationists and feminists, straight and gay, heard it repeatedly. Lesbians' central challenge to the social order was their independence of men and their challenge to conventional womanhood and motherhood. Their "sickness" was thus synonymous in the popular imagination with the rejection of two of America's most powerful mythologies and a subversion of how the country defined itself, the family, and its national priorities.

•

Like its male counterpart, lesbian homophile respectability posited the middle class as guardians of upright behavior and as the appropriate agent of political bargaining. As we have seen, laying claim to an existing position of political legitimacy was often crucial to advancing claims to greater liberties and rights. But it was also immediately limiting. Lesbianism thrived in subcultures, but it required a public face to be influential. Presenting a respectable face, by asserting that lesbians were much like straight women, save for their object of desire, was increasingly effective. But it was a strategy that argued for lesbians' inclusion in existing freedoms, not the protection of unique and heretofore unrecognized rights. As lesbians emerged as distinct political actors, in both the homophile and women's movements, putting on the necessary public face was always fraught with equal parts reward and risk.

Politicized lesbians represented a small minority of all gay women in the 1960s. The vast majority lived apolitical lives in the conventional sense. But every lesbian had to manage her identity, and that was another kind of politics. Knowing where one was "safe," where one could and could not admit to being "in the life," which mask to adopt or identity to project in a particular situation: these were the requirements of psychic and often economic survival. Dubbed the "invisible sorority" in 1967 by the *Philadelphia Magazine*, lesbian culture was never a single set of practices or expectations and never fully "invisible." Same-sex desire and the resulting social marginalization produced both a forbidding closet and the possibility of a deeply felt sorority.

Joan worked for the federal government in Washington, D.C. "It put a tremendous, tremendous burden on us," she told an interviewer. "You always had to be guarded." For Joan and her lesbian friends and colleagues in the early 1960s, work was not a safe space. "You had so much to lose." Home was safer. She frequented house parties in and around Washington to meet other lesbians, to feel authentic. Another Washingtonian, Deb Morris, remembered rent parties, and Char Ank recalled "a lot of home socializing." Apartment buildings provided a certain anonymity but also curious neighbors. Detached houses offered some privacy, but caution remained essential. Still, lesbians describe parties from the 1950s and 1960s as festive, sometimes nearly public events. African American lesbian house parties in Buffalo and Detroit lasted entire weekends in some cases, with guests, including gay men and friendly straights, leaving briefly on Sundays to attend church, returning afterward.[24]

Managing the mask of heterosexuality at work, in front of family, and in church required a parallel management of information about oneself. Shielding same-sex relationships meant ceaselessly assessing to whom one could safely reveal one's sexuality. Joan Nestle, who traveled from New York to Selma in 1965 for the civil rights march to Montgomery, recalled "the secret I carried, my queerness." As a white volunteer living with religiously conservative African American hosts, she "feared I would not have been taken into this home if my lesbian self had stood in the church with me." Among lesbian activists, especially writers, anonymity was essential, and pseudonyms were common. Cleo Glenn, the African American lesbian activist in San Francisco, became Cleo Bonner. Lilli Vincenz became Lily Hansen, Kay Lahusen became Kay Tobin, Eva Friend became Eva Freund, Marion Glass became Meredith Grey, Stella Rush became Sten Russell, Florence Jaffy was Florence Conrad. Barbara Grier wrote under a variety of pseudonyms, including Gene Damon and Dorothy Lyle.[25]

The politics of concealing one's true identity, which lesbians came to take for granted, extended to the politics of community and nation. The secrets the closet demanded and the silences it enforced, what Nestle called "the weight of my disguise" and most deemed simply a "mask," left profound psychological scars, alienated people from the basic institutions of society, including family, religion, and schools, and denied people essential human rights and equality before the law.[26]

Lesbian subcultures could not change all that. But the lives lesbians created allowed them to see themselves belonging not to a despised and sick community but to one another and to a larger human community. Whether in house parties, potlucks, softball leagues, bars, cocktail lounges, rooming houses, friendship networks, coffeehouses, or college clubs and dorms, lesbian women created safe spaces where same-sex attraction was normalized and, first cautiously and in later years raucously, celebrated. Making subcultures out of difference—whatever that difference may be— is ultimately a process of making individuals indispensable to the collective: first the small collective of insiders but then, finally, to the crowd of modern life, to the public, and ultimately to the law itself.[27]

Bars assumed an oversize importance in certain lesbian subcultures, especially among blue- and pink-collar women. Most working-class lesbians did not have access to the kind of spacious houses that conferred privacy; they lived with other women, with family, or in small apartments. Bars became oases of same-sex camaraderie. "It was a together place. We could get out there and dance. We could communicate with each other," an African American lesbian recalled of a bar in Detroit. In the fifties and early sixties, the working-class lesbian bar—in cities as different as Buffalo, Omaha, Memphis, and San Francisco—became the hub of butch-femme culture, an elaborate, even ritualistic expression of temperamental and erotic identities. Derided by a subsequent generation of lesbian feminists as mimicking of heterosexual (and sexist) norms, butch-femme culture nevertheless anchored lesbian identity in stable and predictable roles that made survival in the precarious 1950s and 1960s possible.[28]

Butch-femme lesbians appropriated heterosexual gender presentation. Butches wore working-class men's attire, jeans and T-shirts, and cut their hair short; they evinced a toughness, physicality, and aggressive sexuality associated with masculinity. Femmes wore makeup, sported long hair, wore blouses and sometimes skirts, and assumed the more passive posture of traditional womanhood. "I used to love to buy her silk nightgowns," Julia Perez remembered of her femme girlfriend. "I loved to see her in those little numbers!" Kathleen Saadat, an African American lesbian from Missouri, remembered that in the bars "the first question I got was 'You butch or femme?' You didn't want to be called a pancake, somebody who flips over." Audre Lorde recalled coming of age in New York as "part of the 'freaky' bunch of lesbians who weren't into role-playing." Her butch-femme sisters, black and white, laughingly disparaged her lack of a distinct role with the term "AC/DC."[29]

Because of its emphasis on gender conformity, the working-class lesbian culture of the 1950s and 1960s could seem just as ruthless and unforgiving as the heterosexual world. "I was freaked out because I went to a lesbian bar to get away from men," one woman told the authors of *Sappho Was a Right-On Woman*. Once there she found herself "relating to women

just as I was relating to men." Yet Nestle has insisted on a more complicated understanding of the butch-femme dynamic, one that its critics
missed. In ways utterly unavailable in mainstream society, it offered a way
for some lesbians to inhabit a masculine identity without denying their
femaleness and for others to inhabit femininity outside the gaze of men.
"The words which seem so one-dimensional now stood for complex emotional exchanges," she wrote in the early 1980s. To Nestle, butch-femme
couples were transgressive and made closeted lesbians anxious because
"they made lesbians culturally visible." In retrospect, butch-femme was
less regressive than incipient: it anticipated the move from the closet into
public view.[30]

And while the majority of lesbians did not participate in butch-femme
bar culture, the masculine-feminine dynamic was in some ways inescapable. Wherever women stood in relation to the closet, virtually everyone,
including other lesbians, read their gender presentation and their bodies
in terms of the dominant culture's understanding of "male" and "female."
As a dichotomous model of sex and power comprehensible within the
conventional gender and sexual paradigms of the era, butch-femme reflected what most people took for granted as a universal form of desire:
some women (feminine) remained objects of desire, while others (masculine) pursued them. Butch-femme seemed to posit the safest framework of
same-sex intimacy. But at the same time, of course, this "conventional"
way of loving flagrantly transgressed acceptable boundaries because men
were not part of the sexual equation. The butch-femme dynamic thus
prepared the way for more radical forms of gender and sexual difference.[31]

Race too was inescapably read onto lesbian bodies. Of Anglo and Mexican American background, Cherríe Moraga came of age in the 1970s
among lesbian, feminist, and New Left circles in California. In her startling book of poetry and stories *Loving in the War Years*, Moraga recounts
that growing up as a light-skinned Chicana, she absorbed the values and
assumptions of whiteness without fully understanding the privileges enjoyed by her Anglo classmates and lovers. "It was whiteness . . . and safety.
Old lovers carried their whiteness like freedom / and breath / and light,"
she wrote. The African American Loretta Mears remembered being "the
token dark woman" at Chicago Lesbian Liberation (CLL) meetings. While
working on *Lavender Woman*, the CLL's publication, she found herself
navigating, with great frustration, through "the self-hate that many dark
people have" while "being a standard bearer" as a black woman among

"the white and Jewish lesbians." Pat Lichty-Uribe, a biracial Chicana like Moraga, recalled that people in the "lesbian and gay movement . . . said racist things to me because they did not know I was Chicana."[32]

Class distinctions were felt especially acutely in lesbian life. In an economy structured around male breadwinners, lesbians faced a dual disadvantage. As women confined largely to the bottom of professional and blue- and pink-collar occupational tracks, they had to work harder to make less. And no male provider waited to enfold them in marriage and a family economy. Moreover, a femme identity could be an index of class as much as personal preference because classically feminine "skirt-wearing" women were far more accepted than their butch sisters in white-collar and professional worlds, where they could "pass" as straight. Back in 1955 the DOB had committed to elevating "readers above the bar-clinging level," symbolizing its worry that psychically damaged lesbians would turn to alcohol. But that commitment also represented a middle-class critique of working-class sexual frankness. Such sexual frankness, insisted Doris Lunden in the late 1970s, arose because "the lower-class lesbian doesn't have much 'respectability' to lose." Having less "respectability to lose" was a double-edged sword. For some, it made the closet even more essential, to protect what little status was available. For others, especially working-class butch lesbians, it made the closet purely hypothetical, its protections largely unavailable to them from the start.[33]

Invisibility meant group powerlessness. Only by making subcultures visible—what later gay activists called coming out—could lesbians lay claim to full citizenship. Yet striving for full citizenship in a patriarchal world hostile to lesbianism was less important to many women than striving toward their vision of a "lesbian nation." As with black freedom and any of the other proliferating identity-based political projects of this era, the tension between participating in the common social order and separating from it never disappeared. There was always the promise that one could do both, but for many lesbians at the dawn of the 1970s it remained just that: a promise, nothing more.

•

It was the "bar-clinging" lesbians derided by their self-consciously respectable sisters who helped light the flame of rebellion that soon became an international symbol of gay liberation. The June night in 1969 when gender-transgressive lesbians, alongside working-class gay men and transgender bar hoppers, stormed police barricades and burned the Stonewall Inn bar in Greenwich Village was a transcendent moment for lesbians just as it was for gay men. Lesbian bargoers were central players in the two-day riot. Martha Shelley, who was soon to pen the manifesto "Gay Is Good," began to plan a march with New York Mattachine. Within days, Shelley, Marty Robinson, and a handful of others had founded the Gay Liberation Front (GLF), a left-affiliated organization that soon spread to dozens of cities. The more revolutionary phase of sixties gay and lesbian activism had been under way for a year, but Stonewall was its coming-out party.[34]

In time Stonewall attained symbolic import in lesbian cosmology, but its cathartic pleasures and rebellious spirit did not hold sway over lesbian political consciousness in 1969: women's liberation did. The women's movement, not the newly radicalized gay movement, captured the imagination of most lesbians and gave wing to their political aspirations. From the feminist salons of New York to local NOW branches and consciousness-raising groups across the country, lesbianism—as identity, practice, and theory—became ever more intertwined with the women's movement in all its class and racial configurations.[35]

Lesbian feminism, by politicizing women's attachments to one another (whether those attachments were erotic or simply emotional), imagined a world beyond patriarchy. The most radical lesbian feminists endeavored to create a world entirely without men; they wished neither to join men in public life nor to reform them in private life. While the majority of lesbians and straight women never desired such a world, lesbian feminism nonetheless inspired a new generation of American feminists, gay and straight, to take women's sexual freedom seriously. In earlier eras, bonding among women had been domesticated as part of their family responsibilities and exclusion from the male-dominated public sphere. Lesbianism had thrived in women's separate sphere, yet the politicized lesbianism of the late sixties and early seventies marked a change from earlier periods: such bonding was linked not to domesticity but to a political project of women's equality. As Moraga put it, "sex has always been part of the question of freedom, the freedom to want passionately." In a feminist context, Moraga's notion was part of the recovery of female same-sex attraction and love, but it was also a statement of purpose. The feminist movement was about women's freedom in every possible respect, including sexual.[36]

Even though in this sense lesbian politics embodied the highest goals of the women's movement, straight feminists panicked over the damage an antilesbian backlash might do to feminism's fragile legitimacy in the larger culture. Straight women's own homophobia, and that of society at large, accounted for this fear. "When a woman showed up at a feminist meeting and announced that she was a lesbian, many women avoided her," Shelley wrote in an early lesbian manifesto. "Others told her to keep her mouth shut." Betty Friedan uttered her notorious warning about the perils of the "lesbian menace" in 1969, and the prominent liberal feminist from Wisconsin and NOW cofounder Kathryn Clarenbach wrote to Del Martin that it would constitute "a disastrous blunder" for the organization to support women's sexual freedom. Black and Latina feminists felt extraordinary pressure to shore up their heterosexual credentials as well. If the first charge against black and Latina feminism by their male compatriots was that it was a white (or gringo) project, the second was that it was a lesbian one.[37]

Nineteen seventy was the watershed year for lesbians in the feminist movement. It began with convulsive disputes over lesbianism on the national NOW board and in the New York branch. In May, Radicalesbians, the first new lesbian-only organization on the East Coast since the founding of the DOB in 1955, published "The Woman-Identified Woman" and distributed it at the Second Congress to Unite Women. Because lesbianism embodied "the primacy of women relating to women, of women creating a new consciousness of and with each other," the manifesto read, lesbians were at "the heart of women's liberation." Kate Millett's *Sexual Politics*, which called for a revolution against patriarchy, appeared simultaneously and catapulted her onto the cover of *Time*. That anchor of middlebrow American consensus initially praised Millett's book but in a subsequent issue claimed that her lesbianism "cast doubt on her theories" because it would "reinforce the view of those skeptics who routinely dismiss all liberationists as lesbians." Meanwhile, on the fiftieth anniversary of suffrage, hundreds of thousands of women across the country—straight, gay, bisexual, and transgender—participated in the largest women's march in the nation's history.[38]

At the Congress to Unite Women in May, Karla Jay and a handful of

other New Yorkers, including Rita Mae Brown and Michela Griffo, prepared a rejoinder to Friedan. They spent hours silk-screening purple
T-shirts with the words "Lavender Menace," and when the conference
convened, Jay and her compatriots, camouflaging their shirts, stood on
the floor of the auditorium at Intermediate School 70 in Manhattan with
three hundred other feminists. At a prearranged signal, Griffo cut the
lights, and Jay and others took positions on the stage and among the crowd.
The lights were restored, and seventeen lesbians in their purple T-shirts
screamed, chanted, and held up signs reading SUPERDYKE LOVES YOU!
and TAKE A LESBIAN TO LUNCH! It was the kind of high-concept activism
typical of New York. But the message was clear: lesbians would not be
driven out of the women's movement. They were there to stay.[39]

Nothing announced the presence of lesbians in the women's movement and in American life like the manifestos that began to appear in
1970. Carl Whitman's "A Gay Manifesto," which endorsed lesbian liberation, Martha Shelley's "Gay Is Good," the Radicalesbians' "Woman-
Identified Woman," Anne Koedt's "The Myth of the Vaginal Orgasm,"
Alice Malloy's "Gay Women's Liberation," and Rita Mae Brown's "Coitus
Interruptus" all made the case for the virtues of lesbianism. Like so much
else from these years of rhetorical bombast and ideological experimentation, these works were intemperate in their attacks on the existing order.
"What is so terrible about two women loving each other?" Brown asked in
"Coitus Interruptus." "To the insecure male, this is the supreme offense,
the most outrageous blasphemy committed against the sacred scrotum."
The Gay Women's Liberation collective, in "A Kiss on the Mouth," added
that "a woman who makes love to another woman can rest assured that
she is not being 'screwed.'" Lesbian feminist writers rooted out every vestige
of patriarchy. Sacred scrotums, getting screwed, oppressors of women, and
other relics of patriarchy were out, as in the space of a single year lesbians
announced their presence in American life like a boxer's punch to the jaw.[40]

Among the documents that captured the spirit of 1970 was Del Martin's essay "If That's All There Is," which looked back on the place of
women within the homophile movement and glanced forward to the
emerging lesbian feminism. With regard to the former, Martin was blunt
and unsparing. The homophile movement was led "by hollow men of
self-proclaimed privilege. They neither speak for us nor to us." Borrowing
from Robin Morgan's "Goodbye to All That," a fierce condemnation of the
male New Left that had appeared only months earlier, Martin said her

goodbyes: "[to] the defense of wash room sex and pornographic movies . . . to the biased male point of view . . . to the gay bars that discriminate against women . . . to the male homophile community." Martin's essay marked the end point of her personal political odyssey: from the respectable homophile uplift of the 1950s, to the flowering of a united gay and lesbian activism in the mid-1960s, to the advent of lesbian feminism in the 1970s. Temperamentally, she was not as radical as Brown, Shelley, and Nestle, nor did she share the sensibility of Nancy Tucker, for that matter, who followed Martin with the even more provocative essay "Fuck You Brothers, or, Yet Another Woman Leaves the Gay Liberation Movement." Martin, born in 1921, was generationally an old head in a young movement, and she was always more apt to stress her femaleness over her lesbianism. This distinguished her from lesbian activists such as Gittings, who remained committed first and foremost to homophile and gay politics. Nonetheless, Martin's age and experience made her uncompromising declaration—"I have no brothers in the homophile movement"—all the more damning.[41]

But did Martin have sisters in the women's movement? Friedan, the woman widely considered the mother of the sixties-era white women's movement, along with other NOW veterans, saw lesbians as a threat to their political hopes. In 1971 Friedan told reporters that for feminists' enemies, "the best tactic is to divide women's energies on an issue just like this one—lesbianism." Rather than confront the "issue," however, Friedan and other feminist leaders tried to bury it. In doing so, they revealed more than activist tactics. They revealed their discomfort with women openly loving other women. Friedan remained both personally and publicly dismissive of lesbianism until a tentative, and incomplete, rapprochement in the mid-1970s. All this resistance existed despite the reality that lesbians were integral to feminist politics. "I am reasonably certain that the women's movement in general is going to have to acknowledge us or lose many of its stronger workers," Barbara Grier warned the NOW national office.[42]

Friedan, along with the NOW vice president for public relations Lucy Komisar, relentlessly accused lesbians of threatening to "take over" NOW, especially its New York branch. In 1970 and 1971 personal disputes and strained working relationships revealed the depth of the homophobia among the organization's leadership, as several NOW staff members were asked to resign ("purged," as lesbian activists put it). Straight feminists from younger generations rose to defend lesbians and lesbianism. In

December 1970, Gloria Steinem, Ti-Grace Atkinson, Flo Kennedy, Susan Brownmiller, and more than a dozen other prominent feminists held a press conference in New York to announce their emphatic support for lesbians. Then, nine months later, at the annual NOW conference in Los Angeles, the incoming president Aileen Hernandez, the Caribbean American veteran of the EEOC, called lesbian baiting "sexual McCarthyism" and threw her support behind freeing "all our sisters from the shackles of a society which insists on viewing us in terms of sex." The conference attendees passed a resolution acknowledging lesbians as a legitimate constituency of the women's movement and complete sexual freedom as a proper aim of feminism.[43]

Though the gradual and official acceptance of lesbians by the women's movement in the early seventies was important, lesbians also took their own path toward political relevance. A public lesbian community began to emerge across the country that was both separate from and merged with the larger women's movement. Lesbians founded consciousness-raising groups, housing collectives, and child care centers. They created poetry magazines and a music festival, established women's health clinics, and breathed life into local NOW branches and radical feminist organizations alike. By 1972, Radicalesbians and the Lesbian Feminists (who broke from the New York DOB) had been joined by The Furies Collective in Washington, D.C., the Lavender Ladies in Chicago, Michigan's State-wide Lesbian Political Action Collective, Seattle's Gay Women's Alliance, the Atlanta Lesbian Feminist Alliance, Gay Women's Liberation in Berkeley, California, and Lesbian Feminists in Los Angeles as the most visible lesbian feminist organizations in the country. Dozens more had sprung up in college towns, rural areas in New England, and the West. The lesbian press circulated the era's many manifestos, reaching women in western Massachusetts, southern Oregon, Iowa City, Atlanta, San Francisco, and places in between—a colorful, kaleidoscopic lesbian political community.[44]

To fully escape male power, many radical lesbians and straight radical feminists in the early seventies transformed daily life itself by creating a world with no place for men. The collectives, communes, rooming houses, coffee shops, and small businesses they founded were all-female spaces, where women circulated writings, developed and debated ideas, and fashioned identities in opposition to, and, so the hope went, completely independent of, the dominant culture. As Wendy Cadden put it in a poem, "we are the ones who must write / the stories and articles / that describe us." Like the all-female spaces of the broader white women's liberation and Third World women's liberation movements, of which lesbians were always an integral part, these lesbian spaces depended on a horizontal, rather than vertical, notion of knowledge and culture: women talking to women. Thinking through politics at the "rock bottom," in Abbott and Love's memorable phrase, meant forging new knowledge from the shared experience—"the personal"—of women themselves.[45]

Bold theorizing was not limited to writing and discussion but became for some women lived tenets. Along with separatism came a new political subject in American life, what Yolanda Retter has called the "catalyzed" lesbian. Unlike "lifelong" lesbians, women whose same-sex attraction had always been present, catalyzed lesbians made a conscious decision to love women. "I cut my hair as a symbolic cut with my past, and because I wanted to look like a 'real' lesbian," one such catalyzed lesbian wrote. "I gave up my privileges to become a dyke." "Woman-identified lesbianism is, then, more than a sexual preference," The Furies wrote in 1972; "it is a political choice." Such a choice depended on decentering sex and defining lesbianism, as Del Martin and Phyllis Lyon did in *Lesbian/Woman*, as "the expression of a way of feeling, of loving, of responding to other people." In short, "it is a way of life, encompassing the structure of her whole personality," as well as the most adamant rejection of heterosexuality and all that came with it.[46]

As essential as this kind of radicalism was to the fullest vision of feminism, it had its critics. The most radical lesbian and straight feminists preoccupied themselves with theorizing at the expense of concrete political gains. The simple gesture of valuing lesbian lives and experiences—of seeing the world from the standpoint of lesbians—was a "revolutionary act" in and of itself, of course. If women lived in a "male supremacist shit-pile," as one Berkeley writer put it, lesbians seemed uniquely positioned to think society's way out from under the excrement. And yet the escalation of radical and separatist rhetoric alienated many ordinary lesbians, often those at the bottom of America's class and racial hierarchies. As Zulma Rivera warned, evincing a sentiment shared by many of her sisters, "Quite simply, the lesbian feminist movement will not help Puerto Rican women get better jobs, better education, and positions of power in the community."[47]

Whatever its shortcomings, however, lesbian feminism advanced two ideas that profoundly shaped the women's movement in the early 1970s.

The first was that the root of all homophobia, whether directed at lesbians or gay men, is sexism. Following the publication of "The Woman-Identified Woman," a host of lesbian intellectuals and activists, including Moraga, Rita Mae Brown, and Adrienne Rich, built on that premise to explain how patriarchy and sexism had created a culture in which man as sexual agent and woman as sexual object depended on devaluing the feminine. "At the root of this sexist culture is intense woman hatred," Brown wrote in 1970. "It will take men much longer to see this, to discover that sexism is political, than it will for women," she predicted.[48]

The second idea was that erotic desire, sensuality, and emotional attachment did not necessarily have to involve men. Lesbian feminists drew on a long tradition of female homosociality in American life, but they fashioned their own late twentieth-century response to a heterosexual, male-dominated world. Lesbian feminists' all-female world was not a testament to women's weakness, frailty, or lack of fitness for the public sphere, but to their opposite. They made an explicit and public decision to reject patriarchy. This did not mean that lesbian feminists were united in their attitudes toward sex. Nearly all agreed that women loving other women was essential to lesbianism, but the agreement ended there; while some lesbians insisted that sex and even erotic attraction were irrelevant and that lesbianism was a political choice, others saw sex as essential. The creation of a loving female framework, whether explicitly erotic or not, nonetheless seemed to promise new possibilities, both for personal interaction and for political action. If patriarchy depended on the labor of women and their subordination to men in the heterosexual nuclear family, lesbians endeavored to make a place for themselves, and to a lesser extent for all women, outside that system of "exploitation."[49]

In both ideas, race continued to exert its power to differentiate and privilege. Women such as Anita Cornwell, Flo Kennedy, Barbara Smith, and Moraga were among the most visible lesbians of color whose high-profile activity shaped both gay and women's liberation movements. However, as Juanita Ramos's story reveals, lesbians of color too often remained orphans within the liberal and left sexual activism of the sixties and seventies. Smith, a black lesbian, remembered feeling caught between "clueless white people" and "being rejected by my black brothers and sisters." Carmen Vázquez, a Puerto Rican lesbian who moved from New York to San Francisco in 1975, remembered attending a meeting of the Gay and Lesbian Latino Alliance and finding herself repulsed by "these guys . . . sitting around just ribald with, like *maricón*, and jokes and laughing . . . I was overwhelmed with rage . . . you know you're talking in front of a lesbian," she wanted to shout at her oblivious "brothers." Finding themselves constantly in between white feminism, gay men of all backgrounds, and the civil rights and nationalist movements brewing within their own communities, lesbians of color wore the mantle of outsider in these years.[50]

From the middle of the seventies forward, lesbian feminism continued its productive yet contentious relationship with the women's movement. Women still debated whether lesbianism was a choice or biologically determined. Related debates over bisexuality and eventually transgender persons would come to preoccupy lesbians in the late 1970s and throughout the 1980s. But in the larger conflicts that shaped national political culture in the 1970s, these would remain secondary. Instead, the original question—what place would and should lesbians have in American feminism?—remained at the center of the most visible and contentious disputes in the women's movement. And this question became more pressing as the incipient opposition to feminism and lesbianism gathered strength.

In October 1971, in a telling letter from the St. Louis NOW branch to Wilma Heide, the local president bemoaned the ongoing tension over lesbianism. "We are slowly building a trust relationship with some of our gay sisters in St. Louis," she wrote. "We want to be able to work with them on issues that are of importance to all of us." Unfortunately, a recent *Newsweek* piece, "Militant Homosexuals," had recycled Friedan's dismissal of lesbians from 1969 and 1970 and "put a real strain on that relationship . . . and has caused anger and disillusionment among our gay sisters." Friedan and other straight feminists evinced a persistent homophobia, but conservatives would in subsequent years take up the most vitriolic antilesbian rhetoric and make it a wedge to divide women and discredit feminism. It was a strategy that would haunt the women's movement during the debates over the Equal Rights Amendment between 1973 and the early 1980s.[51]

Because lesbians stood at the intersection of multiple identities long marginalized in American public life—woman, homosexual, black, Latina, and beyond—they brought into sharp relief the dilemmas not only of the women's movement but of liberalism considered as a philosophy of governance, a way of organizing the polity. The civil rights project for sexual minorities, to which large numbers of lesbians, like gay men, remained committed, conceived of lesbians as a coherent group. But as identities proliferated—as bisexuality, transgender, and gender presentation emerged as newly politicized realities, and as lesbians of color developed the notion of standpoint feminism—the coherence of a single lesbian sisterhood dissolved. By extending the frontier of identity further beyond the white heterosexual male breadwinner than virtually any other Americans, lesbians entered uncharted territory with few guides or signposts.

Yet as the sameness, and thus the solidarity, of all lesbians were revealed to be an illusion, new strengths emerged. The multiple lesbian identities that began to proliferate in the 1970s challenged the middle-class gay and lesbian notion that sexuality was primarily a personal quest synonymous with lifestyle. Rather, it was political.

There were few historical precedents for the lesbian feminism of the sixties and seventies, and instead of a single authenticity, lesbians fashioned rich and diverse political and cultural communities. They fashioned the messy but dense political world that a politics of identity compels. This was transformative. Lesbian activists could not resolve all the problems of an incomplete democratic citizenship, but they established their own sexual politics in the heart of the American democratic project and refused to budge. In *Loving in the War Years*, Cherríe Moraga's book of poetry and memoir, she remembered "lovin on the run . . . in collisions." She meant that affection and love are political and that for far too many women they happened "on the run," outside social convention. But she added that such love was both "female and *un*compromising," urging her readers to see the collisions not tragically but joyfully.[52]

PART 3

THE PERMISSIVE SOCIETY, 1968–1980

7

WILD BEFORE THE FIRE: THE SEXUAL POLITICS OF AN EROTIC REVOLUTION

In his inimitable portrait of 1968, *Nixon Agonistes*, Garry Wills observed that for the counterculture, "screwing in the grass had become a political act." For Chicago police officers walking the beat during the Democratic National Convention, however, the affront was not "*the fact* that kids were screwing in the parks," which was nothing new. Rather, it was "that they *proclaimed* that they were doing so; said they *should* do so." An insurgent sexual paradigm was upending the social order not because it represented new practices but because it had ushered in new values. Secrets were becoming public, pride was replacing shame, and pleasure was emerging from the shadows and into the sunshine. And yet, as Wills instantly recognized, many Americans saw "screwing in the parks," and the freedoms it announced, as signaling the ascendance of a "permissive society."[1]

As the project of reconceiving women and men as citizens with new rights and liberties advanced in the late 1960s and early 1970s, the individual model of pleasure on which heterosexual sexual freedom was based threatened long-standing institutional and moral constraints. Since the 1920s Americans had grown increasingly comfortable with heterosexual sexual pleasure, which was understood to be a healthy component of personal happiness and successful marriage. But the shifting erotic terrain of the late 1960s and early 1970s pushed far past marital contentment. As it did so, many Americans came to believe that the distance between sexual freedom and total sexual license was negligible. Slippage from one to the other led to unhappy results: the loss of parental control of children, erosion of social codes defining "good" and "bad" girls, debasement of women, and even prostitution, rape, and sexual "deviance" (homosexuality). At the same time, many people worried that market relations and commerce, rather than moral codes and proscriptions, would determine sexual values, further eroding the foundations of the nuclear family.[2]

But it was not just conservative moral reformers who opposed this shift in American sexual mores. Feminists joined them, though for very different reasons. Both groups found the so-called, and much ballyhooed, sexual revolution wanting. While conservatives sought to restore sex to its traditional confines, especially its place at the center of heterosexual marriage, feminists pushed for new liberties and sought new protections in an effort to yoke sexual freedom to the larger project of women's self-determination and full citizenship. Both groups began the seventies harboring serious misgivings about what Lawrence Lipton called "the Erotic Revolution . . . [the] new morality." Behind these misgivings lay two questions: What role should government play in the regulation of sexual knowledge and who ought to set the terms of sex itself—men or women?

Because the new morality upended existing institutions and constraints, answering the first question required rethinking the state's relationship to its newly sexualized citizens. Religious Americans and moral reformers of all sorts believed that the state should support conventional notions of family, based on religious morality. As they believed it had traditionally and rightfully done, the state should censor sexually obscene material and leave sex education to parents, restoring the positive right of citizens to construct a moral universe absent the corrosive effects of "smut." Feminists, by contrast, saw "family and religion" as synonymous with patriarchy. They regarded the state as a potential protector from sexual violence but also as a dangerous source of censorship and sexual repression. Neither group trusted the market, where libertine sexual entrepreneurs, in the model of pornographers Hugh Hefner, Al Goldstein, and Gerard Damiano, pushed male sexual fantasy and voyeurism to unprecedented levels in the mid-1970s.

Answering the second question required a specific effort from women in particular. They had to consider anew the divide between pleasure and peril, between freedom and danger. Different women would disagree over exactly how that divide ought to be negotiated, but most believed that any effort had to begin with women's consent. Yet even the seemingly straightforward concept of consent proved murky because so much of what constituted the new morality was transmitted through media and was governed only by the logic of the market. As the new sexual ethic suffused virtually every arena of American life—the schoolroom, workplace, corner movie palace, college campus, and, of course, the bedroom—it became increasingly urgent for the society as a whole, and for women especially, to decide what was permissible and what was not. Nothing short of women's full citizenship, their capacity to participate in the social order on an equal basis with men, stood in the balance.

•

"Girls can say 'yes,'" Helen Gurley Brown instructed her readers in 1962's *Sex and the Single Girl*. "Reconsider the idea that sex without marriage is dirty," she urged, and enjoy "unadulterated, cliff-hanging sex." Brown, an editor at *Cosmopolitan*, cast herself in the role of the urbane everygirl who would usher the educated single Manhattan woman toward personal fulfillment. Professional success would not come, she cautioned, in the boss's bedroom, as many in the secretarial pool believed, but through hard work, intelligence, and political savvy—through the boardroom. But what would that success buy? More attention from men and "cliff-hanging sex," including dalliances with a "potpourri" of married men. At once titillating and empowering, Brown's vision encouraged women to turn the tables and use men "in a perfectly nice way just as they use you." But her clever reversal dodged the central question of sixties sexual liberation. Would the tables really turn? Or had she applied a thin patina of female empowerment to what was and remained a man's game?[3]

From the opening pages of Brown's *Sex and the Single Girl* to the 1968 antiwar poster that read, "Girls say yes to boys who say no," sixties sexual pop affirmed the erotic availability of women. Availability cut many ways. It could empower women, offering an escape from the restrictions of "bourgeois marriage" and the moral double standard that suffocated women's erotic desire. Too often, however, "yes" disposed of bourgeois marriage without providing a satisfying alternative. "If man and wife in a suburban split-level was a symbol of all that was wrong with plastic, bourgeois America," the feminist Susan Brownmiller wrote, "'man and chick' in a Lower East Side tenement flat was hardly the new order [women] had dreamed of." The setting and culture may have changed, but the sexual dynamic remained in many respects the same. For far too many men, "yes" had eliminated even the pretense that women's sexual point of view mattered.[4]

In 1970 the feminist writer Robin Morgan, then living in Brown's single-girl paradise, offered an indirect but powerful rejoinder to the *Cosmo* editor. During the half decade after the appearance of Brown's treatise, Morgan labored in what she eventually dismissed as the "counterfeit male-dominated left." In "Goodbye to All That," a defining manifesto of seventies feminism, Morgan denounced the "theory of free sexuality but practice of sex on demand." She reeled off a litany of male sins: "the token 'pussy power' and 'clit militancy' articles"; the "'Instant Pussy' aerosol-can poster"; a male colleague's list "of people in the Women's Movement he has fucked." Morgan turned Brown's world on its head. Hard work, intelligence, and political savvy had earned women exactly nothing—only the right to be "fucked," to become erotic trophies for countercultural men who, like their corporate brethren, ran the show. Brown and Morgan agreed that in the sixties and going forward, girls say yes. The question that separated them was whether "yes" emanated authentically from women or was simply a capitulation to male fantasy and desire.[5]

When women's point of view *was* contemplated by men, at least in the first blush of the heady new sexual climate of the mid-1960s, commentators reached for trite clichés. Alexander King, an editor at *Life* who was a generation older than the women who increasingly filled the low-level white-collar ranks of publishing and advertising, was horrified by "women sitting like district attorneys, to see what the man can or cannot perform." If Freudians had fretted over the "frigid" suburban housewife of the 1950s, the sexually in-charge single girl of the 1960s evoked equally disparaging reactions among the male-dominated commentary class. Not all were as caustic as Philip Wylie, the pop psychologist who in 1963 warned men of the "career women [who] use their sexuality in the manner of the Sirens." But in post–*Sex and the Single Girl* America, it was not difficult for men to exchange their dread of the undersexed wife at home for fear of the oversexed striver at work. Both calibrations, and their obliviousness of actual female sexuality, were precisely what feminists and women's rights advocates protested.[6]

Thus, as sexual freedom became more and more closely linked with the era's smashing of inherited conventions, feminists looked with disdain at their father's generation of groping "sexists" and with distrust at their own "liberated" brothers-in-arms in the black freedom and antiwar movements. Violette Lindbeck lamented women's leaving the New Left "because [their] chief role was to serve as a sex pool for the [male] leaders." Judith Brown, the southern civil rights activist and coauthor of the 1968 manifesto "Toward a Female Liberation Movement," condemned men's "sexual privilege" and "unwarranted domination," which seemed the clearest outcomes of sexual liberation. For these women—Wills's kids in the park notwithstanding—sexual liberation remained a promise unfulfilled, compromised by the ignorance and obstinacy of men.[7]

African American feminist Toni Cade shared the sentiments of Lindbeck and Brown but saw sexual liberation through a distinct lens. She wondered what good could come of women's sexual freedom when "other aspects of her social roles remain the same." Sexual objectification was certainly *one* problem, but one among many. "Life required many things of her," Toni Morrison wrote of black women, "and it is difficult to be regarded as a sex object when the burden of field and fire is on your shoulders." To Mary Ann Weathers, by contrast, "field and fire" were part of the equation because sexual objectification had always been embedded in black women's subordinate social roles, dating to their sexual vulnerability as slaves. She was joined by the Chicana feminist Elizabeth Martínez, who rued that her sisters were "working 16 hours a day" but were still "viewed as a sexual object rather than a human being." The question that would divide women in the late sixties and early seventies was not so much whether women of different racial and class backgrounds resented their sexual objectification—most plainly did—as the extent to which they prioritized that particular aspect of sexism over others and how, or even whether, they saw their sexuality linked to inequities produced by class and race.[8]

Despite the many meanings of "yes," it was inescapably the flashpoint of sexual transformation as the sixties became the seventies, at least among heterosexual women. "Yes" became an essential first step in destroying the cultural double standard that celebrated men's sexual adventurism and punished the same adventurism in women. And because women bore the weightiest consequence of sex, pregnancy, "yes" also conveyed the power to shape sexual encounters on their own terms. It was linked to the larger aim of securing a place for women in the social order on an equal footing with men. The knife edge between sexual freedom and sexual exploitation, between pleasure and peril, was hardly new in the 1960s. Women had walked that precipice for most of the twentieth century, since the birth of the "modern" woman herself. But the collective urgency to define the terms of sexual freedom *was* new.[9]

Yet who helped create a world in which "girls say yes"? Pop culture protofeminists such as Brown, of course, and her imitators. Liberal, radical, lesbian, and Third World feminists had their say, as we'll see. Structural changes to the social and biological context of sex mattered too. The birth control pill, introduced in 1960, and gradually liberalizing abortion laws together promised to liberate women from certain biological imperatives. But rendering something possible and making something so are different things. Outside of prominent feminist writers, among the myriad forces that authored the new sexual ethic four constituencies stand out: ordinary women themselves, sex scientists and commentators, sex entrepreneurs, and the counterculture.

Ordinary women were the most important constituency pushing for a new sexual ethic. College and university women, in particular, took on crucial roles in changing sexual values and practices, as they democratized higher education in unprecedented numbers and simultaneously recast middle-class sexual morality in these decades. Inspired by feminism and the broader demand for freedom and equality in all sixties social movements, students stressed female empowerment and shared pleasure between partners. Student publications such as *Elephants and Butterflies . . . and Contraception* at the University of North Carolina, *Birth Control, Abortion, and V.D.: A Guide for the B.U. Student* at Boston University, and *Sex and the Yale Student,* among dozens of others, reimagined the pleasurable possibilities of "yes" for the young white middle-class woman. Many of course did not see themselves as pioneers of social change. "It's not a revolution just because you sleep with some guy," a female California college student told the *Los Angeles Times* in 1966. "I just feel I am expressing myself the way I feel at that moment in the most natural way." Whatever the intent, however, sixties and seventies college students blazed the path to a new sexual order.[10]

On and off campus, women built institutions and forged new understandings to advance and protect their sexual self-determination. Planned Parenthood enjoyed a renaissance, as a new generation of women sought to make sexual and reproductive knowledge as broadly accessible as possible. The National Welfare Rights Organization (NWRO) fought to ensure that poor women's sexual choices did not imperil their welfare benefits. And the tidal wave of institution-building recounted in Chapter 5 established women's centers and clinics, rape crisis centers, student organizations, and, eventually, a robust assemblage of articles, manifestos, testimonials, and books, all devoted to encouraging women to act on their sexual desire in healthy ways and to protect them from sexual abuse. And this is not even to begin to account for the millions of women who, day after day, braved the "sexual politics" of forging mutuality in their individual relationships with men.[11]

A second group, sex scientists and their popular interpreters, advanced "yes" through bestselling books. In 1966, as the number of American women taking the birth control pill Enovid passed six million, William Masters and Virginia Johnson published *Human Sexual Response*. The two sexologists had measured more than ten thousand orgasms, female and male, in their laboratory at Washington University in the decade between 1954 and 1964. They took Alfred Kinsey's scientific detachment to new levels of technical sophistication to comprehend the physiology of intercourse, but their dense, turgid prose prevented the birth of a page-turning sensation. No matter, as middlebrow writers made Masters and Johnson's ideas accessible to a curious, prurient American public. Dr. David Reuben's notoriously awful *Everything You Always Wanted to Know About Sex* appeared in 1969, as did L. R. O'Connor's *The Photographic Manual of Sexual Intercourse*. The next year, *The Sensuous Man* (1970) by "M" and Joan Garrity's *The Sensuous Woman* (1970) appeared. Xaviera Hollander published *The Happy Hooker: My Own Story* in 1971—the same year Reuben followed *Everything* with *Any Woman Can!*—and the next year Alex Comfort published *The Joy of Sex*, a bestseller regarded as essential middle-class "reading" for much of the first half of the seventies (it sold 3.8 million copies in the first two years). The deluge of guidebooks based on the work of Masters and Johnson, rightly criticized by feminists as patronizing and weighed down by clichés, assured its audience that sex between consenting adults, married or not, could be mutually pleasurable, healthy, and even spiritual.[12]

Masters and Johnson made the cover of national newsmagazines, and their interpreters gave the impression of a true sexual revolution. But lesser-known sex researchers were less convinced. Plenty of them noted measurable shifts in sexual attitudes, especially among women, but usually on a narrow range of issues. Opposition to "premarital coitus," for instance, declined considerably between 1958 and 1968 among women, while remaining roughly constant, though lower, among men. A major National Opinion Research Center survey in the middle 1970s confirmed that attitudes had grown more permissive *only* regarding "premarital heterosexual relations." Attitudes toward homosexuality and extramarital sex remained "distinctly restrictive." Such studies suggested that Americans were enjoying less a sexual revolution than an evolution of sexual attitudes from earlier eras.[13]

It was in the spirit of that acknowledgment that the feminist Shere Hite undertook a major survey of women's attitudes toward their own sexuality between 1972 and 1975. Bemoaning the lack of recognition that "female sexuality might have a complex nature of its own," Hite sought a forthright understanding of women's bodies and sex lives to correct both male-focused sex researchers and the middlebrow how-to books. She recorded hundreds of women talking honestly about sex, masturbation, and lesbianism, among other topics. Her methods remained controversial because middle-class feminists in New York and California were overrepresented among her interviewees, but the resulting book sold millions and brought the concept of woman-centered sexual knowledge and practice to a mass audience.[14]

Sex entrepreneurs, the third constituency involved in the creation of "yes," took the opposite approach to female sexuality. They ignored it. In the hands of pornographers, sex became the province of male gratification, what Barbara Ehrenreich called the "flight from commitment," the psychic vacation from domesticity men took into sexual fantasy. This attitude was pioneered for a mainstream audience by Hugh Hefner's *Playboy*, which first appeared in the fifties and assumed on every page that women said only yes, and which engaged in a visual trick in the mid-1960s. "What sort of man reads *Playboy*?" it asked. Its answer was *you*, the (male) reader, and in the handsome man pictured on the beach surrounded by beautiful women men should thus see themselves. Larry Flynt of *Hustler* and Al Goldstein of *Screw* surged past Hefner's sixties-era bachelor beach bums and jazz aficionados and in the early seventies declared their right to traffic in whatever base form of sexual exploitation they desired. "Our stock in trade is raw, flailing sex," Goldstein proclaimed. He added, proudly, that "*Screw* is so vile and ugly in its unrelenting efforts to achieve sexual candor that I've been arrested ten times . . ." Pornographic magazines and films, not to mention topless bars and emerging sex districts—neighborhoods with concentrations of pornography and prostitution—in countless cities, made it clear that to some Americans, "yes" was the foundation of a sound, if perhaps disreputable, business plan.[15]

The difference between sex entrepreneurs and the counterculture, the fourth constituency, was not as great as it seemed. If Hefner's assault on what he deemed "sexual puritanism" created the sexually liberated bachelor hipster as an antidote to postwar domesticity, the counterculture conducted an equally snarky assault on the supposed puritanical repressiveness of the "straight" majority. It was in large part based on the idea that sexual freedom was authentic, expressive, and *real*, the antithesis of plastic America and its male breadwinners and nuclear families. On the pages and in the new "singles ads" of alternative newspapers such as *The Village Voice, Rat*, the *Los Angeles Free Press*, the *San Francisco Guardian*, the *Berkeley Barb*, the NOLA *Express* in New Orleans, the *Fifth Estate* in Detroit, and Atlanta's *Great Speckled Bird*, this sensibility predominated. The vast alternative press was instrumental in crafting a unique countercultural sexual idiom from New York to California.

That countercultural idiom embraced a wide swath of sexual politics. The *L.A. Free Press*, one of the first alternative newspapers to emerge in the sixties—*The Village Voice* had been founded in 1955—attacked the hypocrisy of a culture that eroticized warfare ("soft-core pornography," its writers called the nation's nuclear missiles) and recorded southern whites saying "nigger" while censoring pictures of sexual intercourse on obscenity grounds. *Free Press* reporters chronicled and condemned the L.A. Police Department's assaults on flower children gatherings in Griffith Park, where both topless women and marijuana were in evidence, and closely followed the city's abortion rights movement. But then the *Free Press* celebrated anything that threatened middle-class culture, including the novels of Henry Miller and the pornographic films at the Show Time West theater; the latter's advertisements, boasting "Hollywood's Spread Beaver Stars," were common in the *Free Press*. Moreover, by the late 1960s, its pages were stuffed with erotic photographs and sketches of naked women. Like other alternative newspapers, the *Free Press* was frank about sex but did not always differentiate between disdain for establishment hypocrisy and Hefner-like celebrations of "yes" as basic male prerogative.[16]

In the decade between Brown's *Sex and the Single Girl* and Comfort's *The Joy of Sex*, heterosexual Americans from vastly different points of view and with distinctly different interests embraced a new sexual ethic. They invested in "yes" for wildly different reasons. For some, sexual freedom meant nude beaches, forthrightness about sex and bodies, and a rejection of "bourgeois marriage." For others, it simply meant enjoying premarital sex, sans guilt, on the way toward traditional marriage. For the readers of Comfort's *Joy*, it meant, or at least promised, the discovery of "hot" sex within the confines of marriage. For still others, it meant simply money. As with all forms of liberation in this era, as the rules went out with the old morality, new guidelines emerged slowly, and experimentation was the refuge of the unsure.

•

Most Americans believed that greater sexual freedom did not automatically profit the social order. But how to minimize the costs of the new sexual ethic while securing its benefits remained in dispute. In a 1965 sermon in Cheswick, Pennsylvania, the Reverend Richard K. Kennedy told his parishioners that "the Church controls the expression of the sex drive through its insistence on monogamy, the marriage of one man to one woman . . . Discipline is necessary to fulfillment." Many religious activists believed that by releasing sex from its confinement within the heterosexual nuclear family, sexual freedom augured a radical and dangerous moral reorientation. Americans of religious faith—among Catholics, Protestants, and Jews alike—matched the advance of the new sexual ethic step by step with sermons, editorials, manifestos, and even their own guidebooks. As they did so, many among them identified yet another force behind that new ethic, one they considered ill suited to the task: government.[17]

The advancing "sexual revolution" had dissolved the discipline even otherwise liberal-minded religious leaders believed necessary to stabilize marriage and ensure personal happiness. Loosed from marriage, the Baptist seminarian Joe E. Trull warned, sex had become "king of our American society." For Trull and others of like mind, this was sexual anarchy. People encountered new freedoms but lacked older guideposts. They had been set loose in what the social diagnostician Vance Packard called, in a book by the same title, a "sexual wilderness." The antidote, for Trull, was a Christian "counterattack" to restore "the meaning and purpose of sexuality."[18]

In the late 1960s Christian readers had access to their own alternative library to counter the Masters and Johnson–inspired how-to books. A short list would have included Norman Vincent Peale's *Sin, Sex, and Self-Control* (1965), John Wynn's *Sex, Family, and Society in Theological Focus* (1966), the five-part Concordia Sex Education series that included *Parents Guide to Christian Conversations About Sex* (1967), John and Mary Ryan's *Love and Sexuality: A Christian Approach* (1967), and *Sexuality and Moral Responsibility* (1968) by Robert O'Neil and Michael Donovan, among a host of others. Indeed, it is notable that all were published prior to the avalanche of secular sex books. Most emphasized that, as a Methodist seminarian wrote in 1968, "sexuality is an endowment from God."[19]

These efforts were part of liberal Protestantism's postwar project of modernizing and liberalizing its faith. Protestant theologians, inspired by the existentialist Paul Tillich and led by ministers within the National Council of Churches, the nation's principal liberal-minded ecumenical Christian association, sought not a purer faith but a more relevant one. Some Catholic leaders after the Second Vatican Council (1962–1965) wanted the same thing. When Pope Paul VI condemned "artificial" contraception as "evil" and a sin, more than six hundred Catholic clergy registered their objection in a formal declaration. Liberal-minded Protestants and Catholics broadly embraced a realistic, modern view of sex, and they spent the sixties adapting to, not fighting, the new sexual ethic.[20]

This liberal Christian sexual ethic was opposed by fundamentalist Protestants and conservative Catholics. Between 1968 and 1970 these constituencies made themselves heard loud and clear in a nationwide controversy over the place of sex education in public schools. Back in 1960 the White House Conference on Children and Youth had recommended that "education for family life, including sex education," be included in public school curricula, and in 1965, Dr. Mary Calderone, the medical director of Planned Parenthood, founded the Sex Information and Education Council of the United States (SIECUS) in order to make that recommendation a reality. Her efforts were supported by Rev. William Genne of the National Council of Churches and a handful of physicians, including the Chicago abortion rights advocate Dr. Lonny Myers, liberal Protestant ministers, and education professionals. Calderone was the most conspicuous proponent of sex education in the country, but she was no radical, telling *Playboy* that sex was "an exciting gift from God." In 1968 and 1969 SIECUS joined the National Council on Family Relations (NCFR) and the American Social Health Association (ASHA) to formulate sex-ed guidelines for local school boards.[21]

Conservative religious leaders, by contrast, favored purity over relevancy and decried sex education. Leading the opposition were the John Birch Society's MOTOREDE (Movement to Restore Decency) committees and Christian Crusade, an anti-Communist, fundamentalist Protestant ministry based in Tulsa, Oklahoma, that broadcast on hundreds of radio and television stations in the Plains states and the South. Christian Crusade's education director, Gordon Drake, published *Is the Schoolhouse the*

Place to Teach Raw Sex? (1968) and *SIECUS, Corrupter of Youth* (1969). More than three hundred local citizen action groups—with names such as MOMS (Mothers Organized for Moral Stability) and PURE (Parents United for Responsible Education)—took the fight directly to school board meetings and state legislatures. Opponents of sex education were adamant that it encouraged premarital sex, that it was obscene and therefore an inappropriate educational subject, and that—at least in the minds of white southerners—it encouraged interracial sex. Others worried that homosexuality would be insufficiently condemned in these programs. The most frequent complaint, however, was that sex education intruded on the family's moral responsibilities and rights, that public school sex education was a government invasion of the private family sphere.[22]

Thus well before the rise of conservative and fundamentalist Christian churches as a national political force, a phenomenon of the late 1970s and early 1980s, antiliberalizing and antigovernment moral conservatives announced their presence on the American political landscape in the sex education fight. With prayer and Bible reading already excluded from public schools by the Supreme Court in the early sixties, sex education seemed to them yet another example of government's "secular religion." Not unlike the hard hats who could not understand how their employment kept others from working, and not unlike the right-to-life activists who could not conceive of abortion as anything other than murder, the anti-sex-education activists viewed the family, not the government, as the natural site of morality, ethics, and responsibility.[23]

Parent-led firestorms over sex education burned hottest in California, where cities and school districts across the state became explosive battlegrounds in 1969. SIECUS estimated that two-thirds of the anti-sex-education groups in the country (that is, more than two hundred) were based in the state. Outraged parents in Sacramento, San Luis Obispo, Redwood City, and San Mateo sued school administrators and trustees. In Anaheim, the Citizens Committee of California, a still-active Goldwater for President group, attacked the school district's four-year-old program and attempted to unseat three pro-sex-education board members. San Mateo's Citizens for Parental Rights fought sex education all the way to the U.S. Supreme Court and convinced Governor Reagan to appoint something called the Moral Guidelines Committee, whose open-ended mandate was to develop a moral code for *all* state activities.[24]

With the State Board of Education ordering an investigation of sex education programs, competing bills fought for allies in the state legislature. The outcome of these at times raw and vicious conflicts left sex education largely in local district hands. New state board guidelines endorsed sex education ("a necessary part of local educational programs") but urged that it be offered "only on a voluntary basis," that it "place strong emphasis on the harmful effects of premarital sex," and that SIECUS materials be deemed "inappropriate." Moreover, faced with massive lobbying by groups like the John Birch Society, the legislature passed a law requiring parental permission for students to receive sex education. Predictably, despite the compromise, neither side was satisfied and each believed it had lost. But sex education advocates were particularly despondent. One said simply, "It looks like rational sex education is done for in California."[25]

Despite the intensity of fights like those in California, most Americans who participated in the 1969 sex education battles hewed to a middle ground. They sought not an absolute ban on sex education but a commonsense balancing of church, home, and school as sources of sexual knowledge and moral instruction. A 1969 Gallup poll found that seven out of ten of Americans favored some sort of sex education in public schools, and local observers reported reasonable and informed debate in many communities. But vocal New Right and conservative Christian forces, led by the Birchers, overwhelmed the middle ground. Their capacity to stir controversy, garner newspaper headlines, and turn out huge constituencies at school board meetings drove the conversation. Not unlike the left-wing movements they decried, these conservatives discovered that a lot of noise goes a long way.[26]

The sex education wars of 1969, which periodically reignited in local skirmishes across the country in subsequent decades, occurred at the same moment that feminists and women's advocates were formulating their own position on sexual knowledge. They shared SIECUS's conviction that sex education should be a component of public school education. As they saw it, women's sexual freedom was impossible if sexual knowledge was strictly monitored and controlled by parents—or by men, the medical profession, whomever. At the same time, they stressed that sex education was meaningless, regardless of its institutional source, absent a woman-centered perspective. Radical feminists went further still. By 1970 a growing number of feminist writers had extended their critique of patriarchy into a new theory of female pleasure and sexual liberation. Woman-centered sexual knowledge *and* pleasure, in their view, were truly revolutionary.[27]

For women's liberationists and radical feminists, knowledge of one's body was instrumental to achieving sexual pleasure. The New York radical feminist Anne Koedt's essay "The Myth of the Vaginal Orgasm," reprinted hundreds of times, put the work of Alfred Kinsey and Masters and Johnson to new ends, refuting the myth that female orgasms were centered in the vagina. Koedt also drew on the work of Dr. Mary Jane Sherfey, a psychoanalyst who argued that "frigidity," a diagnosis commonly applied to women by physicians and psychiatrists in the 1950s and 1960s, was simply due "to the absence of frequent, prolonged coitus." In *Women in Sexist Society*, the liberationist Alix Kates Shulman offered a common-sense revision of Kinsey, Masters and Johnson, Koedt, and Sherfey. "Women know from personal experience that there is only one kind of orgasm," she insisted. "It is a sexual orgasm." The "personal experience" of which Shulman wrote was the floor on which everything else rested: What do women know about their bodies and how might that knowledge best be exchanged among women and between generations?[28]

Calls to reclaim female sexual knowledge from a male-centered sexual culture received their most democratic popularization in *Our Bodies, Ourselves*, the brainchild of the Boston Women's Health Book Collective. Conceived by a dozen women during a consciousness-raising session at a women's liberation conference in 1969, *Our Bodies* first circulated in 1970, like so much of the thinking in these years, as an amateur mimeograph. Early versions instructed women in a broad array of anatomical and health-related issues, including childbearing, menstruation, cancer, aging, and sex and sexuality. Similar efforts were under way on the opposite coast, at the Women's Self-Help Clinic in Los Angeles, which was to spawn other feminist women's health centers across the country. Judy Wenning, president of the New York City branch of NOW, said at the opening session of the 1973 Women's Sexuality Conference: "There is probably nothing in life as difficult as to make some kind of statement about sexuality, intimacy, caring, closeness, and love." Wenning might have added that for heterosexual women to take ownership of sex and to place female knowledge and pleasure at the center of sexual exchange was far more revolutionary than *Playboy*'s centerfolds, Hefner's philosophical musings about American sexual puritanism, and even SIECUS's sex-ed classes.[29]

•

Both the SIECUS- and feminist-inspired debates over sexual knowledge took place in an era of explosive growth in commercial pornography. Whatever school-based sex education might look like, the sexual revolution grew relentlessly embedded in the marketplace, where Americans had to discern the line between private sexual pleasure and public sexual excess. The search for that demarcation led many to question whether the male-driven market in pornography, which had soared to half a billion dollars by 1969, ought to shape the nation's sexual values. Beginning in the late 1950s, free speech arguments consistently triumphed in the "porn wars," and the courts allowed pornography to behave like any other commodity in the market. Pornography's sudden pervasiveness made the quest for new guidelines, to say nothing of a restoration of "traditional" sexual values, all the more difficult.[30]

First Amendment arguments did not sit well with both antipornography conservatives and a considerable number of left-leaning feminists. The former blamed the liberal state for unleashing the pornographic flood. As with abortion, conservatives saw the withdrawal of state regulation, ironically, as an insidious state *intervention* in private morality; they saw not the negative freedom "to be let alone" but the positive right of pornographers to invade the domestic sphere of private morality. For feminists, the issues were more complex. Pornographic images objectified women in the most blatant way, blurring into rape fantasies. Most feminists, though, were loath to endorse censorship, which seemed an even more sinister form of female sexual repression. But in the second half of the 1970s feminists launched an antipornography movement, partly in response to the 1976 release of *Snuff*, a film of unrepentant sexual violence. By the end of that decade pornography's extensive reach had produced no simple standoff between civil libertarians and puritanical moralizers, but a maze of political alignments that reflected the complexity of the new sexual terrain.[31]

Civil libertarians had pushed against obscenity censorship in the 1940s and 1950s until, in *Roth v. United States*, the Supreme Court nearly toppled it in 1957. Ruling that material that dealt "with sex in a manner appealing to prurient interests" was not protected speech, the Court added that definitions of "prurient interest" varied and that obscenity meant material "utterly without redeeming social importance." The test of "social importance" proved murky and led to judges in subsequent cases watching hours of pornographic films, ruling on the visible areolae of topless female dancers, and commenting in detail on the plot lines of erotic novels.

By the second half of the 1960s, successful prosecutions of pornographers were rare, particularly in large metropolitan areas, because defense lawyers became expert at interpreting "social importance" as broadly as possible. Yet as pornographers and the owners of topless bars and strip clubs extended their reach into neighborhoods and especially downtown commercial districts, more and more local governments sued to stop them. The result was clogged state court systems. So state legislatures began to liberalize obscenity laws to free up the courts and conform to *Roth*.[32]

Finding the courts unhelpful, antipornography activists, led by Protestant ministers and Catholic priests, broadened their attack on what the novelist and critic George P. Elliott called "erotic nihilists who would like to destroy every sort of social and moral law." In a typical instance, in the San Fernando Valley of Los Angeles—an epicenter of the antipornography movement—the West Valley Citizens Committee for Decent Literature and the Representative Committee for Moral Betterment led campaigns against magazine stands that sold erotic books and magazines. A Valley newspaper complained that "the U.S. Supreme Court clips [prosecutors'] wings and lifts bans on objectionable magazines." Such moral condemnations and attacks on government perfidy were representative of the antipornography movement across the country. Like the campaigns against abortion rights and sex education, the conservative drive against pornography was grounded in a belief that the state had become a moral arbiter, displacing the traditional institutions of church and family.[33]

Antipornography activists sought to counter the argument, increasingly prevalent among civil libertarians, that sexually explicit material was "victimless." Pornography was not merely offensive, they claimed; it was dangerous. Pornography encouraged "young people to turn sexual passions into a species of hobby," Jo Regan, a Los Angeles activist, explained. It led to out-of-wedlock pregnancies, abortions, and the erosion of sexual discipline on which family stability was based. Regan argued that men "enslaved by disgusting literature or sex urges" were responsible for "the greatest individual crimes." She and like-minded activists worried about rape, which many antipornography activists (not unlike many feminists) believed originated in pornographic fantasies, the spread of venereal disease, and an increase in marital infidelity. Their opponents portrayed antipornography activists as prudish Puritans or out-of-date Victorians. But the concerns of antipornography activists flowed logically from a worldview in which the discipline of church and family established a moral economy of restraint and "decency." In their view, the market and the state had usurped the role of these legitimate moral arbiters.[34]

As with the conflict over sex education, California was a major arena of dispute over pornography. The state had "the worst obscene literature problems in America," according to the *Los Angeles Times*. In 1966 Los Angeles deputy district attorney Harry Wood and county supervisor Warren Dorn sponsored Proposition 16, known as the CLEAN initiative. Dorn called California the "smut capital" of the nation, and gubernatorial candidate Ronald Reagan invoked John F. Kennedy's "missile gap" in telling Republican Party activists that "a morality and decency gap" had opened in the state capital. Proposition 16 would prevent judges from overturning obscenity convictions if there was "reasonable" disagreement over the offensiveness of the content. A month before the election, polls showed that a majority of voters supported the initiative, no doubt in part because of Reagan's law-and-order campaign against student radicalism at the University of California in Berkeley. But as the November election approached, local district attorneys and major newspapers, including the conservative *Times*, began campaigning against it, claiming that it could lead to bans of Shakespeare and the Bible. The eventual failure of CLEAN strengthened moral reformers' sense that they confronted a political system in bed with sexual libertinism.[35]

National antipornography activists closely watched Proposition 16. Among them were Charles Keating and Morton Hill. Keating, a Cincinnati lawyer and real estate mogul, had founded Citizens for Decent Literature in 1958. In 1964 he financed the antipornography film *Perversion for Profit*, which chronicled the nation's vast production and marketing of sexually explicit literature and film. The Citizens for Decent Literature executive director Raymond Gauer toured the country, showing *Perversion* and another film, *The Pornographic Conspiracy*, to local antismut organizations, churches, and Republican Party clubs. Hill, a Jesuit priest in New York City, had founded Morality in the Media in 1962 and led a series of campaigns against "indecent literature" in the first half of the decade. Keating and Hill, along with hundreds of local activists—ordinary citizens such as Jo Regan—were not the simple-minded moralizers envisioned in the diatribes of Hugh Hefner who sought a return to pre-turn-of-the-century censorship. But neither did they trust the market's version of the sexual revolution, which, they insisted, encouraged sexual desire outside the discipline of marriage, corrupted children, and turned men away from hearth and home.[36]

Keating and Hill played starring roles in a national showdown over pornography that shot the issue from the back pages of newspapers to the heart of American politics. Awakened by the grassroots antipornography movement, President Lyndon Johnson and Congress together created the President's Commission on Obscenity and Pornography in 1967 "to determine whether such materials are harmful to the public." Appointed to the commission, Keating and Hill found themselves, along with Winfrey Link, a conservative physician from Tennessee, nearly alone in their vehement opposition to the pornographic flood. After three years of hearings and data gathering, the commission produced a report, to considerable national surprise, calling for the repeal of all federal, state, and local laws prohibiting the showing and selling of pornography. "Public opinion," the commission concluded, supported "the view that adults should be legally able to read or see explicit sexual materials if they wish to do so." The state, the report reasoned, was a poor arbiter, and citizens deserved the greatest possible freedom to make consumer decisions. Moral conservatives, needless to say, were stunned.[37]

When the report was released in 1970, long after Johnson had retreated to his Texas ranch, President Nixon labeled it "morally bankrupt" and directed the Department of Justice to ignore it. Keating, Hill, and Link, the three dissenting members of the commission, penned lengthy repudiations of what they called a "Magna Charta [sic] for the pornographer." The Reverend Billy Graham called the report "one of the worst and most diabolical ever made by a presidential commission." As letters condemning the report from ordinary Americans piled up in the commission's office, a stinging editorial in William F. Buckley's National Review accused the commission of recommending "a re-education of sexual attitudes so massive that only the Federal Government can do it," while warning that "government is fast establishing authority in the area of family life." The report was so politically toxic that the Senate voted 60–5 to reject and censure it, with southern Democrats declaring their unreserved opposition. Conservatives had identified—and identified themselves with—a potent issue, one that combined anxiety about moral decay with fear of a usurping federal state.[38]

Making no mention of homosexuality, the presidential commission assumed that "an acceptance of sex" meant acceptance of heterosexual sex, making the report's conclusions a mixed bag for the emerging gay movement. Both common parlance and legal practice in the postwar decades held that homosexuality was itself, ipso facto, obscene. Any representation of gay or lesbian eroticism, including men holding hands or women kissing, was subject to legal jeopardy under obscenity and lewdness statutes. In 1954 a U.S. circuit court ruled that the political and literary magazine ONE, published in Los Angeles by gay activists and artists, was obscene and could be banned from the U.S. mail. ONE and its attorneys persevered, and in 1958 the U.S. Supreme Court (in ONE v. Olesen) overturned the decision and ruled that the magazine was not subject to obscenity law simply for content that discussed homosexuality. Nonetheless, local judges and district attorneys continued throughout the 1960s and 1970s to consider representations of homosexuality, whatever their nature, to be obscene. This treatment of gay and lesbian sensuality overlapped with the legal regime that emerged in most local jurisdictions in the late 1960s in which homosexuality as an "identity" was legal, but homosexual "acts," including their presentation in literature, were not.[39]

Two years after the pornography commission's report the film Deep Throat appeared on movie screens across the country, bringing so-called hard-core pornography to a mainstream audience. Legal challenges in dozens of cities increased its sensationalist allure, and the upscale ticket buyers in Times Square made it, The New York Times wrote, "the most popular hard-core sex film ever to play here." New York City police seized the film in the fall of 1972, and a ten-day trial produced more than one thousand pages of testimony, which constituted a referendum on the commercial sexual revolution. To considerable surprise, given that the film had withstood obscenity challenges in more than seventy cities, the New York criminal court judge Joel J. Tyler ruled that Deep Throat was "indisputably and irredeemably" obscene, "a Sodom and Gomorrah gone wild before the fire." If the New York trial was a referendum, however, the decision across the country remained split. Deep Throat continued to show in major cities and was in and out of the courts for years, as were two subsequent releases, Behind the Green Door (1972) and The Devil and Miss Jones (1973).[40]

In the wake of the commission's report and the release of Deep Throat, conservatives' claim that "smut" incited rape did not lead to an immediate alliance with feminists. Betty Friedan, Kate Millett, the National Organization for Women, and most women's advocates opposed court-imposed sanctions on pornography. After all, these women reasoned, if moral reformers had their way, the recently published *Our Bodies, Ourselves* would be banned as "obscene." Moreover, the report's recommendation that the nation undertake a "massive education effort" aimed at achieving "an acceptance of sex as a normal and natural part of life" supported their efforts to gain greater control over their bodies and sexual lives. While pornography forced feminists of all ideological persuasions to confront a serious dilemma, women's activists in the early seventies refused to join the antipornography chorus, seeing in its moralizing tone a potential threat to their own sexual liberation.[41]

This reluctance was short-lived. In 1974 the high-profile radical feminists Robin Morgan and Andrea Dworkin condemned pornography outright and inspired women to resist its growing place in American culture. Morgan's indelibly memorable phrase "Pornography is the theory, rape is the practice" was the basis for her claim that rape, as "male fantasy," provided men a model of violence and domination that extended to all aspects of their interactions with women. Dworkin's *Woman Hating* took on not just "the literary pornography of our forebears" but the counterculture's belief that pornography was a taboo-busting, convention-overturning genre. When it comes to pornography, Dworkin wrote, "there is no 'counter' to the culture . . ."[42]

The power of Morgan and Dworkin's critique motivated women in New York and California to begin formal organizing against pornography. In Los Angeles in 1976, Julia London and other members of the local NOW branch formed Women Against Violence Against Women (WAVAW), and in the same year Women Against Violence in Pornography and Media (WAVPM) was founded in San Francisco. They immediately began protesting the film *Snuff*, which portrayed a woman's rape and evisceration. In 1978 Dworkin and Morgan helped found Women Against Pornography in New York, and a signal of antipornography's new importance to mainstream feminism was the endorsement of Gloria Steinem, Adrienne Rich, Shere Hite, Susan Brownmiller, and Karla Jay, among the most recognizable feminists in the country. By the early 1980s, antipornography feminists had built a robust movement that even sought, in a handful of cities, local ordinances banning pornography as a form of sex discrimination. At this farthest edge of feminist action, the courts budged little, however, holding First Amendment speech rights superior to any claim by women of discrimination.[43]

Few issues confounded women's advocates quite like the relationship of pornography to women's sexual citizenship. Even the apparent consensus of the late 1970s in time came undone. Groups of radical lesbians, affirming fluid gender and sexual roles, opposed the antipornography movement's insistence that rape was pornography's only script. Women's pleasure was just as central, they claimed. In the 1980s they were joined by straight feminists who saw pornographic fantasy as playful rather than violent and censorship as a slippery slope toward the broader repression of sexuality. Antipornography feminists had to address these critics while also confronting their growing discomfort, on the opposite political flank, with conservative moral reformers as allies. The latter were reenergized by Ronald Reagan's election to the presidency in 1980. Reagan's Commission on Pornography, run by Attorney General Edwin Meese, held hearings in six cities in 1985 and 1986 and raised anew the question of tighter government censorship. The so-called sex wars of the 1980s reignited the core seventies tension between women's sexual freedom and commercial exploitation, between pleasure and peril, but did little to slow the saturation of American society with pornographic images of women.[44]

•

In the decade of the 1970s, heterosexual Americans invested in "yes." (Their lesbian and gay counterparts did too, the subject of the next chapter.) Many enjoyed the widespread availability of pornography, while many others, religious and conservative Americans above all, attempted to censor pornography in an effort to protect their visions of family and society. The general legislative and legal emphasis on negative rights—the freedom to do and buy as one pleased—produced a conservative reaction that decried the ways government now seemed to define American morality. And feminists moved from an acceptance of pornography to the condemnation of it. Through all of this, "yes" remained the period's defining ideal. But if "girls [women] can say yes," from what relative position of power and choice did they do so? From what position of consent? As the new sexual ethic pushed sexual politics out the bedroom door and into nearly every corner of American life, feminists and women's advocates insisted that if new rules were to emerge from the transition, they ought to protect women from the more pernicious aspects of the sexual revolution.

If female self-determination and the consent it implied meant anything, they surely meant freedom from sexual assault. Nothing defined the "peril" in the ever-present tension between pleasure and peril, and discounted women's consent, like rape. An act of violence with the power to humiliate, injure, and impregnate its victims, rape could also produce a corrosive and deadening sense of guilt and shame. Blaming women for rape was part of a timeworn worldview that deemed women temptresses— their skirts too alluringly short, their manners too provocative, their pasts promiscuous. The inherent violence of sexual assault was too often belittled by men as nothing more than a schoolboy's prank, a lover's impulse, or the deranged lust of a deviant. The notion that women "wanted it," "asked for it," or secretly "liked it" shaped male and in some cases female responses to rape. Feminist Susan Griffin famously called it "the all-American crime," alleging that it was the most frequently committed but most widely ignored crime in the country. Few Americans in the 1960s would have denied that rape was criminal. But equally few would have recognized it as an issue of women's equality with men. By the early 1970s, however, white women's liberationists and black and Latina feminists made sexual assault as central to the women's movement as reproductive rights.[45]

Helen Rawson was raped by a man she met at a play reading. Filled with both disgust and shame, she blamed herself. As recounted in Diane Russell's 1975 compilation of women's rape stories *The Politics of Rape*, a trip to the local police station discouraged her from filing charges. Did she want her sexual history discussed at trial? Did she want to be portrayed as having encouraged her attacker? Did she wish to be accused of exaggerating "rough lovemaking" into a claim of rape? Not worth it, Helen decided. Having had "someone deceive me, brutalize me, rape me," she buried her fury and later admitted tellingly that "the bulk of the anger was directed at myself." No single woman's experience with sexual assault is representative, but Russell's stories gave human voice to the raw statistics that antirape activists increasingly carried with them to meetings with legislators, law enforcement officials, and journalists.[46]

Even by themselves, those statistics told a compelling story. Between 1966 and 1975 reported rapes tripled in the United States, a stunning rise only partially attributable to the increased reporting encouraged by the women's movement. Still, most experts estimated that between 70 and 90 percent of all rapes were never reported to the police. A Seattle study revealed another dimension of the problem: fewer than half the rapes reported in that city were committed by strangers. Most victims knew their assailants. Research in Philadelphia showed that rape was also overwhelmingly an intraracial crime; sensational cases aside, white men tended to rape white women, black men black women. Rape was consistent with a segregated America. And the reality remained that nationwide less than 10 percent of rape prosecutions resulted in convictions. Antirape activists thus faced a profound dilemma: how to account for a crime punishable in most states by twenty years or more in prison but treated with cavalier indifference by local police and criminal courts, utterly misunderstood in the wider culture, and rarely successfully prosecuted? "All too often," a study of rape in Prince George's County, Maryland, noted, "the rape victim is treated at best as an object, a piece of evidence, and at worst, as a criminal."[47]

Histories of the antirape movement typically begin with the first rape speakout, sponsored by the New York Radical Feminists in 1971, where white women, for the first time outside the intimate space of consciousness-raising groups, talked openly about the experience of sexual assault. The speakout led to the New York Radical Feminists' Rape Conference and the founding of New York Women Against Rape. An electric charge that ignited the nationwide rape awareness movement, the speakout inspired the formation of dozens of antirape groups across the country. Women in countless consciousness-raising groups, NOW branches, lesbian organizations, and radical feminist cells began to break the silence about the trauma and guilt of sexual assault.[48]

After 1972, ordinary women took up the fight against rape with remarkable swiftness and muscle. The first rape crisis centers were established in Seattle, Berkeley, and Washington, D.C., that year, followed quickly by centers in Ann Arbor, Philadelphia, and New York. By the end of the 1970s there were more than four hundred rape crisis centers in the United States. Groups such as Berkeley Bay Area Women Against Rape, the D.C. Rape Crisis Center, Women Against Rape in Chicago, Seattle Rape Relief, and dozens of others, many drawing on the youthful energy and organizing resources of college-age women, emerged as vocal advocates of law reform, women's self-defense, and an empowered vision of female sexuality. Within a few years of its founding in 1972, for instance, Seattle Rape Relief offered a rape hotline, crisis counseling, legal advocacy, and programs with local hospitals, law enforcement, and schools. Susan Brownmiller, a member of the New York Radical Feminists and the author of one of the most powerful books on rape, *Against Our Will*, admitted that before writing the book, she had long thought of rape as "a sex crime, a product of a diseased, deranged mind," and believed that the women's movement "had nothing in common with rape victims." That view was impossible by 1975.[49]

Antirape activism had a different history among African American women because rape was embedded in racial as much as sexual politics. It had been woven into the fabric of American racial narratives and was inescapably part of the history of white supremacy. Since the turn of the century, the black rapist mythology had rationalized the terror of white rule in the South. Hundreds of years of white men's sexual exploitation of black women meanwhile remained an unspoken subject. Because rape, women's subordination, and racial terror were inseparably linked, the arena of sexual assault proved to be one of the most challenging for feminists of all racial backgrounds in the 1970s.[50]

Because of this history, black women experienced the "all-American crime" as a component of both male supremacy and white supremacy. Beginning in the 1950s, African American women in the black freedom movement had begun to grow more aggressive in pursuing legal action in rape cases in which the perpetrator was white. In 1959, twelve years before the first white-led rape speakout, more than a thousand African American women on the campus of Florida A&M University protested the rape of Betty Jean Owens by four white men. Ella Baker, Rosa Parks, and other black freedom activists increasingly called attention to sexual assault in the civil rights era. And Fannie Lou Hamer, who rose to national prominence during the 1964 Freedom Summer in Mississippi, made clear, in sentiment if not in words, that "the personal is political" when she spoke about her own and her grandmother's sexual abuse at the hands of whites and connected that abuse to white supremacy.[51]

Black women's political encounters with rape in the postwar decades left them facing painful ironies. In politicizing rape first as an *inter*racial crime of white supremacy, they found that *intra*racial sexual assault, at the hands of men in their own communities, received far less attention. Forced to defend themselves against white attackers and black men against false white accusations, black women found that their sexual abuse at the hands of black men was seldom discussed as a *political* issue. Black feminists were to change that, but doing so took time and courage. During the seventies well-known writers such as Angela Davis, Michele Wallace, and

Frances Beal, and less heralded women working in local communities, women such as Brenda Eichelberger in Chicago and Nkenge Toure in Washington, D.C., made sexual assault, as well as other forms of sexual and domestic abuse, a core concern in the larger project of asserting black women's value in American society.[52]

Though at times only dimly aware of black women's thinking about rape, white women's liberationists likewise cast rape as a fundamental women's issue. To them, rape was not a specific problem for some women but a universal problem for all; it was not an isolated "carnal" event but an embodiment of the constant threat of violence that underlay male social power. For radicals like Brownmiller, Russell, and Catharine MacKinnon, rape represented the perverse combination of pleasure and violence (and pleasure *in* violence) that was elemental to patriarchy. Women's groups used rape awareness to highlight broader questions about the ways their bodies were subjected to male gaze and power: from comments on the street and groping at work to sexual pressure from husbands or boyfriends. Rape was no marginal crime committed by the deranged or desperate, but the presumed right of friends and neighbors, husbands and boyfriends, of ordinary men. It was, in the words of Barbara Mehrhof and Pamela Kearon, "the most perfect of political crimes . . . communicated to the male population as an act of freedom and strength."[53]

As with abortion, the attention brought to rape by women's liberationists led to calls for legal reform. Rape law in the majority of U.S. states in the 1960s exposed female victims to a process nearly as frightening and psychically violent as the attack itself. Local police departments and hospitals were ill equipped, both practically and temperamentally, to address the physical and psychological needs of rape victims. They had no rape or trauma counselors, no specifically trained police officers, no medical procedures for obtaining evidence or for testing women for pregnancy and venereal disease. Some hospitals refused entirely to treat rape victims; sexual assault victims were known to take expensive cab rides in a desperate search for hospitals where they could be treated. If they filed criminal charges, women faced enormous, often humiliating hurdles. Most courts required "corroboration" of the assault, and in every state a woman's full sexual history could be used by the defense. Finally, judges issued stringent "cautionary instructions" to the jury—that rape was an easy charge to make, was difficult to prove, and required more careful scrutiny than other cases—that presumed, in the words of one California reformer, "the rape victim was lying because she was a woman." In sum, health care institutions gave little comfort to the victims of sexual assault, and the justice system offered little hope of successful prosecution.[54]

Yet as swiftly as it had transformed the abortion debate, the women's movement reconfigured political discussions of rape. In 1972 and 1973, a fast-growing network of activists, women's legal theorists, and sympathetic elected officials in Washington, D.C., New York City, Seattle, and various California cities began drafting rape statutes to replace existing state laws. NOW established a Task Force on Rape, with Mary Ann Largen its director. Largen had herself been the victim of an attempted rape several years earlier. The disregard of doctors and law enforcement officials she encountered had propelled her into the antirape movement in Prince George's County, Maryland, and Washington, D.C. She had joined the D.C. Rape Crisis Center, worked rape hotlines, and engineered some of the first efforts to change the legal definition of sexual assault, from a "carnal" act to a violent one. Once in charge of NOW's task force, she began working closely with Maryland senator Charles Mathias, a political ally who introduced a bill in 1973, drafted with Largen's assistance, to create the National Center for the Prevention and Control of Rape. Two years and one presidential veto later the center was established, its mission to support and coordinate research and law reform at the state level.[55]

With one eye on Congress, Largen turned to the individual states, where she began working with local NOW rape task forces. Antirape movements, driven by young women entering the movement for the first time and by established activists with resources and political connections, had advanced quickly in California, Michigan, Iowa, New York, and Washington State. In California the northern and southern regional branches of NOW, working with Largen in the national office, forged a broad coalition of women's organizations and law enforcement officials to press for two major new rape laws in 1974. The legislation's sponsor, the state senator Alan Robbins from Los Angeles, attributed passage of the bills to the women's organizations that "had worked tirelessly" to change public attitudes. A New York law passed the same year. It "breezed through the legislature," according to one antirape activist, "and the legislators gave all the credit to the women's movement." Iowa, Michigan, and Florida followed with similar laws in 1974. In three years, between 1971 and 1974, the

women's movement, now well organized at the state level, starting virtually from scratch, produced broad changes in law and public attitude.[56]

The focus on rape law reform, however, was not universally hailed
among feminists and women-centered activists. Many radical and African
American feminists worried that the antirape movement had edged too
close to an alliance with law-and-order conservatism. The D.C.-based
Feminist Alliance Against Rape, for instance, charged that "encouraging
women to prosecute a rape" would only "reinforce the legitimacy of the
criminal justice system," a system that, the group added, "convicts primarily poor and non-white men." As they watched some of the most vehement
antirape groups escalate their rhetoric—calling for castration for rapists,
for instance, or insisting that only a .38-caliber pistol was sufficient protection from men on the prowl—more temperate feminists wondered if the
"woman as victim" paradigm was stoking a culture of fear, contributing to
the crime panics and racial backlash on which conservatives capitalized
in the early 1970s. Confronting such charges in 1972, Brownmiller was
defiant: "O.K., so it's a law and order position. We never said we were for
anarchy."[57]

The law-and-order dilemma was nonetheless real. Studies consistently
showed rape to be a predominantly intraracial crime, but sensationalized
cases continued to replay the racialized rape narrative entrenched in
American history. Calls for "law and order" had become a hallmark of
conservative politics in the early 1970s, and white feminists risked being
drawn into assuming that reactionary position. Observing the racial and
sexual dynamics in Washington, D.C., the sociologist Nathan Hare complained that "the black woman is getting raped while the white woman is
doing the screaming." Hare accused white feminists of using a "rape
scare," which played on that racial narrative, to advance their political
project. White feminists were not always willing or able to disentangle
their antirape activism from a right-leaning law-and-order politics favoring long prison terms and tough public rhetoric. Their racial blinders
were sometimes quite real. The difference between Brownmiller and
Hare was another instance of the paradox of the era: the politics of identity, which were necessary to achieve greater freedoms and protections,
reflected and sometimes reinforced existing racial inequities and thus
prevented the emergence of a single reform movement.[58]

Next to the rapist, Brownmiller wrote in *The Village Voice* in 1971, stood "the gooser . . . the ogler, the lip-smacker, the animal-noise maker, and the verbal abuser." Brownmiller's sliding scale of sexual assault was prompted by an encounter in Greenwich Village. While "handing out some leaflets for the Radical Feminist Conference on Rape" and distracted by a conversation with her female companion, Brownmiller was "goosed" (groped) by a man. Recalling similar encounters in her past, Brownmiller observed that her postpubescent life had been "a long and systematic continuum of humiliation." On the street, unwanted sexual advances and touching, alongside hostile sexual commentary, jokes, and whistles, constituted an unpredictable form of assault from which there was little protection save individual chutzpah. It was this *culture* of sexual assault and humiliation that was the larger target of antirape activists.[59]

The workplace was perhaps the preeminent bastion of this culture, outside of pornographic magazines and films. In fact, the workplace was often the place where pornography, sexual coercion, and even rape intersected. Almost nothing was more common to all women than the experience of some form of unwanted sexual attention at work. In 1976 more than 80 percent of nine thousand *Redbook* readers reported such experiences. What many men sloughed off as harmless "passes," "jokes," or requests for a date, women, usually in subordinate positions, encountered as serious barriers to their equal standing at work. "If your boss patted you on the bottom, you traditionally giggled and batted your eyelashes," one feminist activist admitted. This reality would begin to change as women, rooting their complaints in the principle of consent, took the offensive against what they termed sexual harassment alongside their efforts against pornography and rape.[60]

Building on late-1960s campaigns against sexism in specific industries, in a long and demanding legal fight between 1971 and 1986, feminist activists, attorneys, and the EEOC director under President Carter, Eleanor Holmes Norton, created American sexual harassment law. As with rape, hundreds of local groups worked through the courts and in state legislatures, which, combined with federal action, changed the legal landscape. No simple summary can do justice to the complex, variegated, long-term struggle to make all American workplaces safe for and welcoming to women, to rid them of the vestiges of jokes, gropes, slaps, pinches, lures, and stares, not to mention actual pornography itself and brazen demands for sexual favors. But the key, as with so much of the reconstruction of women's citizenship in these years, was Title VII of the Civil Rights Act and its prohibition of employment discrimination based on sex in addition to race. Backed by legal theory developed by feminist attorneys such as MacKinnon, Norton threw the weight of the EEOC behind a revamping of workplace equality law. Sexual harassment, EEOC guidelines specified after 1977, was a violation of women's rights as workers under the Civil Rights Act. And though it still took a decade, to the surprise of many, the Supreme Court agreed (*Meritor Savings Bank v. Vinson* in 1986).[61]

Women's advocates in the sixties and seventies made their version of "yes" a viable one, embedding it in American culture and law. For women's advocates during the continuous sex wars of these decades, the route out of Packard's "sexual wilderness" was straightforward: cultural recognition and legal protection of women's consent. Winning that recognition and protection represented a triumph. Along with other gains made by women's advocates—sex education, women-focused health care (including women's clinics), rape counseling, and reproductive rights—defining "yes" as a source of empowerment helped create a new place for women in democratic society, even if that place was, as we have seen time and again, more accessible to middle-class white women than others. For a time, the self-regarding misogyny of American culture was placed on the defensive and what emerged were new legal protections for women and a broad set of institutions supporting their sexual self-determination.

But as transformative as it was, consent ran up against limits as well. Those limits were especially evident in three critical arenas. The first was the market, the site of a frenetic production and consumption of pornography that would grow only more pervasive and elaborate over the coming decades. Feminists argued vehemently among themselves about whether pornographic treatments of women were oppressive, but it would be difficult to dispute the ways in which the intensified sexual objectification of women in American consumer culture writ large—whether or not technically "pornography"—abetted the cultural decline of feminism in subsequent decades. The second was rape law reform. The antirape movement, including the "Take Back the Night" campaigns, which began in the late 1970s and accelerated in the 1980s, produced a host of new laws, practices, and protections. The result was definitively better than what had stood before. But even these epochal reforms did not fully alter the legal and personal jeopardy that women who filed rape charges confronted and the "he said/she said" morass into which they too often tumbled.

The final limit invites a return to where the chapter began: "screwing in the grass." Conservative moral reformers did not downplay women's consent—particularly in the face of pornography and sexual violence—but they saw sexual freedom through a distinct lens. If it fell to the women's movement to articulate new cultural and legal guidelines, the conservative right would take up the capacious language of restoration. Its purveyors sought not an accommodation to, or a harnessing of, the new sexual ethic but a restoration of conventional norms and institutions: female sexual "innocence," church- and family-centered sexual instruction, censorship, heterosexuality. They agreed with Boris Sokoloff, whose 1971 screed *The Permissive Society* bemoaned the erosion of social, and especially sexual, order. Whether women consented to "screwing in the grass" was less important to these Americans than that such things were happening at all.

8

A PROCESS OF COMING OUT: FROM LIBERATION TO GAY POLITICS

On an evening in late November 1970, Dick Cavett was noticeably ill at ease on his own television show. As he welcomed to the stage Marty Robinson, Arthur Evans, and Dick Leitsch of the newly formed Gay Activists Alliance (GAA), Cavett attempted an awkward, sexually suggestive introduction, accompanied by campy music. But the joke was on Cavett. Wearing a T-shirt bearing the Greek letter *lambda*, the organization's chosen symbol, Robinson had not come to indulge in snickers and double entendres. He told Cavett that "heterosexuals live in this society without any scorn—they live openly, their affection is idolized in movies, theater." "Homosexuals" wanted the same thing. During a forty-minute interview, the three gay men laid out for a nonplussed Cavett (he later said to the audience: "I don't know what we can learn from this exactly . . .") the cultural and political agenda of the emerging gay movement. "Gay people . . . have a process of 'coming out,' that is, coming out sexually," Evans explained. "We've extended that to the political field."[1]

To Cavett and his late-night audience, his guests were exotic strangers. Their exoticism was, to the men from GAA, precisely the problem and what "coming out" was meant to address. Lesbians and gay men, along with bisexual and transgender people, were to begin coming out in ever greater numbers in the 1970s, transforming the homophile movement into a richer, broader, and more visible national presence, symbolized for gay men and lesbians by the new emphasis on the term "gay" itself. "Until we have power, we'll never be free," Evans told Cavett, hinting that however revolutionary "coming out" might seem, behind it lay an age-old struggle for political leverage in a diverse and contentious polity.[2]

But what was "power" and how was it best seized? Since the early 1960s, homophile politics had been shaped like a Venn diagram. One circle encompassed revolutionary sexual values. It included everything from radical lesbian feminism to tamer forms of sexual freedom; the animating desire was to forever change American culture. A second circle encompassed the struggle for rights. It included the Gay Activists Alliance, Society for Individual Rights (SIR), Daughters of Bilitis, and the Mattachine Society among many others; gay rights legislation, legal action, and liberal pluralism were its hallmarks. The circles overlapped, as in any Venn diagram, and the two tendencies shared a great deal in common. But they were not the same thing. Between 1968 and 1974 the size of the two circles relative to each other switched. Suddenly, for a brief but extraordinary period, the "revolutionary" circle expanded and took up a larger part of the rights-oriented circle than it had ever done during the homophile era.

The sine qua non of the new moment was, as Robinson explained to Cavett, *coming out*. To come out, to be out, to leave the closet was an existential and a political act. It meant claiming one's most authentic self and at the same time dealing a blow to the social order's persecution of consensual sexual choices and unconventional love. "'Gay Liberation' means much more than legislation of legal protection against discrimination," a New Jersey man wrote in 1974. "To me, it means the establishment of a community of gay people . . . among whom I can develop real relationships with genuine human content." To advance the revolution in both sexual values and rights that the homophiles had started, post-1968 gay activists, under the mantle of liberation, set forth a compelling project based on pride, power, sexual freedom, and the moral legitimacy of same-sex love. Gay is not just acceptable, they insisted. Gay is *good*. Far more than the Stonewall uprising or any other single event, this idea marked the boundary between the homophile politics of the 1960s and what many called the liberationist politics of the early 1970s.[3]

As lesbian and gay activists rode the crest of coming out, gay politics followed a distinct arc between 1968 and 1978. As the decade turned, liberationists threw open the closet door and trumpeted an erotic revolution they hoped would end homophobia and sexism, place the nation's puritanical sexual past in eclipse, and win legal rights for lesbians, gay men, and bisexuals, if not yet fully for other sexual and gender nonconformists. By the mid-1970s the most radical of those dreams had begun to wane, but they left in their wake a much larger national activist base than the homophiles had ever enjoyed. In the courts, in the streets, and in the voting booth, lesbian and gay people had leveraged their increasing visibility in the form of a liberal rights-oriented movement that achieved notable, if partial, progress by the end of the decade.[4]

However, gay visibility and the handful of small victories the movement won in these years awakened a fiery, often vicious backlash. Casting sexual difference as the enemy of a moral nation and corrosive of its social order, the opponents of the gay movement struck back with determined force in the second half of the decade. The gay movement posited a new citizen, one with rights protecting it from discrimination based on sexuality, and its opponents countered by asserting the rights of an idealized nuclear family. As courageous and pioneering as the homophiles of the 1960s had been, they had not wrought fundamental changes in public attitudes toward sexual difference. The homophobia of the 1970s was in fact less restrained than in earlier eras. It was, in a sense, *out* and unapologetic as well. The whisper campaigns and firings of the lavender scare era had wreaked havoc on thousands of lives; now opponents of gay rights traded whispers and innuendo for rallies, press conferences, modern political campaigns, legislation, and, on the whole, a far more caustic and influential antigay public discourse.[5]

Thus did the 1970s represent a familiar pattern in gay politics, but in a new, more urgent and divisive context. Proliferating identities and politics within lesbian and gay circles produced internal movement fault lines, while external foes mounted challenges to progress on every front. New opportunities for gaining influence and leverage, especially in big-city politics, emerged alongside an opposition determined to roll back each and every gain.

As calls for reclaiming authentic selfhood grew louder, and as coming out became both a personal and political act, gay people still had to face down a hostile homophobic world largely on their own terms. Regardless of the political slogan of the moment, ordinary women and men went about the difficult process of coming out to families, friends, spouses, lovers, children, ministers, employers, and the like—or not. They did so largely on unfavorable ground. For every story of understanding parents and friends or a gracious pastor or a supportive employer or spouse, there is a matching story of abandonment and rejection. Indeed, the urgency of gay liberation, not unlike the urgency of black power, derived from the desperate necessity of doing everything possible to make individual lives better and to call into being a world of honesty and authenticity rather than lies, veilings, and silence.

•

The central tenet of the gay liberation politics of 1968–1974—that sexual identity was the basis for personal authenticity and collective politics—opened a vast terrain of possibilities, not just for reimagining the American citizen but for reimagining personhood itself. After the tumult of the late sixties, including Stonewall, the meanings of liberation proliferated because its philosophical foundation was self-determination and its animating principle was, as Philadelphia's Homophile Action League put it, "confrontation." The notion that politics consisted of unifying a fractured self drew on the sentiments of the Students for a Democratic Society's Port Huron Statement, from 1962, which advocated seeking "a meaning in life that is personally authentic [that] unites the fragmented parts of personal history."[6]

"Come out!" the liberationists urged, and make our difference collectively powerful. Indicative of the new mood was Karla Jay's declaration that "our self-love and our love for our gay sisters and brothers [are] the core of our revolution." And so for a time a thousand revolutions bloomed. For many lesbians, liberation meant reimagining sexuality as *sensuality*, an escape from the tyranny of the orgasm. For others, it signaled the opposite: the freedom to celebrate the female orgasm without the presence of men. For many gay men, liberation meant an uninhibited indulgence in sex. For others, liberation revealed homophobia as the cousin of other forms of inequity, including racism and the economic disparities on which capitalism rested. Transgender people, then known as transexuals, seized on the spirit of liberation to press their own claims of authenticity on society, on the medical profession, and on lesbians and gay men, many of whom preferred to keep them at arm's length. To still others, liberation meant simply a more militant public stance in pursuit of the concrete legal objectives identified by homophiles in the mid-1960s. In the garden of a thousand blooms, liberation implied both a specific radical politics and a broader, more free-flowing impulse to live authentically and overturn convention.[7]

After Stonewall, however, calls for political unity reigned, and a movement was reborn. Gay liberation coalesced swiftly after the riot. The Gay Liberation Front (GLF) of New York, formed within days of Stonewall, published the first issue of *Come Out!* in November 1969, and by the following summer the organization had spread to dozens of cities. In July 1970 marches commemorating the first anniversary of Stonewall filled the streets of New York, Chicago, Los Angeles, and San Francisco, and "gay pride" (known then as gay freedom day and other names) was born. Activists protested at major newspapers (many of which still refused to use the words "homosexual" and "gay" in print), television stations, and city halls and statehouses. By 1971 virtually every major newsmagazine had run a feature on what *Newsweek* called "the militant homosexual."[8]

In its earliest post-Stonewall iteration, liberation was synonymous with the GLF and its explicitly left-wing and often socialist politics. Radical liberationists such as Allen Young from New York, Phil Saperia from Boston, and Morris Kight from Los Angeles pressed the North America Conference of Homophile Organizations (NACHO) to oppose the war in Vietnam, endorse black power, and commit to a broad critique of capitalism. These veterans of the New Left hoped that sexual politics could be folded into, and perhaps even lead, a revived American left. Despite calls for unity, moderates found this marriage of the socialist left and the homophile movement unsatisfying and accused liberationists of "using the argot of the extremists on the left," which would "only alienate those homosexuals whom we need to help us achieve our goals." Radicals replied in kind, accusing NACHO of focusing on law reform while ignoring larger issues of sexism, racism, and class inequality. GLF activists were not wrong, but neither were they efficacious. Like much of the fraying far left in the early 1970s, they too often devolved into a caricature of angry militants shouting down anything "reformist." Their social critiques were noteworthy, sometimes even stirring. The irony was, however, that too many GLF groups, particularly in New York and California, soon became little more than debating societies devoting their time to determining the best way to create a "revolutionary situation" in American society—a situation that never came close to existing in any meaningful sense.[9]

As both longtime homophile activists and a younger generation fired by the spirit of liberation grew disenchanted with left-wing rhetoric, they pushed the GLF to the margins of lesbian and gay political culture. Jim Owles, Robinson, Evans, and a handful of mostly gay men founded the GAA in the spring of 1970 on the principle of civil disobedience and as an alternative to both the radical GLF and the slow-moving Mattachine Society. The GAA immediately turned to practical matters, recruiting Democratic Party allies like Bella Abzug to push the New York City Council to consider Intro 475, a gay rights ordinance. Robinson stunned the otherwise liberal council member and women's advocate Carol Greitzer when he shouted at a meeting of the Village Independent Democrats, "Listen, Carol, baby, you're antihomosexual, antihomosexual!" Activists in Chicago and Los Angeles followed suit, forming GAA groups or like-minded organizations and pressing for city council action. Across the country activists sought to fashion a "liberationist" politics disentangled from the splintering radical American left.[10]

There were costs to the GLF's eclipse, however, because it was one of the few male-dominated organizations that would sustain a critique of gay male sexism and one of the few white-dominated organizations that would raise awareness of how class and race shaped the lives of gay men and women. Also lost was the chance that lesbian feminists would remain in large numbers in organizations with gay men. The GLF was idealist but sectarian, and it could not survive either the narrowness of identity politics or the urgency with which lesbians and gay men desired a measure of real political power and the protection of basic rights.

The liberationist turn produced more than a welter of new organizations. It unleashed the kinds of protests, though on a smaller scale, that had characterized the black freedom movement between 1960 and 1965. A catalog of such protests would fill a volume, but a small sample from 1970 and 1971 illustrates the arc of events. In January 1970 the Reverend Troy Perry, founder of the gay and lesbian Metropolitan Community Church (MCC), led 250 marchers to the California state building in Los Angeles. That July Perry and seven activists staged a ten-day fast to urge passage of a consensual sex bill in the legislature, and Perry performed a lesbian wedding that he hoped would become a test case for marriage equality. In Massachusetts and Minneapolis gay activists stunned politicians by appearing en masse to testify before the legislature and state human rights commissions. New York GAA members "zapped"—a zap was a surprise, rambunctious protest by a small number of activists—nearly a dozen politicians, including Mayor John Lindsay, along with news outlets and local New York television stations. A summer Gay-In in Griffith Park in Los Angeles drew 500 revelers who watched Morris Kight perform "mateship" ceremonies, while body painters worked the margins of lewdness statutes under the watchful eyes of the LAPD.[11]

In the winter and spring of 1971 alone lesbians and gay men in New Orleans picketed city hall for six straight days; New York GAA led three thousand marchers in Albany demanding a consensual sex bill; Jack Baker, an out gay law student, was elected president of the forty-three-thousand-student association at the University of Minnesota; three thousand lesbians and gay men marched together (under the banner OUT NOW!) in an antiwar demonstration in San Francisco; in Washington, D.C., Frank Kameny and fifty GAA members from New York invaded the American Psychiatric Association annual meeting and commandeered the microphone to make speeches denouncing the APA's stand on homosexuality. Meanwhile, forty activists held a scream-in in the office of a Los Angeles psychiatrist; two hundred lesbians and gay men, chanting "Gay power," demonstrated at LAPD headquarters; kiss-ins and gay-ins were held across the country; GLF branches formed in nearly a dozen college towns, including Lawrence, Kansas, and Columbia, Missouri, in the heart of the Bible Belt; Kameny campaigned for Congress; and consensual sex bills passed in Connecticut, Colorado, Idaho, and Oregon. The gay movement was *out*.[12]

The generational and attitudinal shift among lesbian and gay people between 1968 and 1974 forged a new narrative of the gay movement: ordinary Americans, sick of condescending authorities and secret lives, would lead a revolution in sexual values and demand new rights. Any hoped-for revolution depended on gay visibility and rested on full membership in civil and political life. The sexual privacy demands, which had dominated homophile politics, remained, but there was no question that even those demands more than ever required a public gay presence.[13]

•

In spite of calls for gay unity and female sisterhood, lesbians began the decade of the 1970s uncomfortably caught between the disregard and even misogyny of gay men and the homophobia of straight women. In her 1970 article "If That's All There Is," Del Martin told gay men that she was "pregnant with rage at your blindness and your deafness." Leaving male homophiles and liberationists behind, Martin turned to the one place she believed lesbians could find "acceptance, equality, love, and friendship": the women's movement. In contrast, Rita Mae Brown, a founding member of The Furies, a lesbian feminist collective in Washington, D.C., called for lesbians to "get out of the straight women's movement" because it was inhospitable to same-sex affection and could not "accept Lesbianism as a political issue."[14]

Lesbians spent a great deal of time contemplating their in-betweenness as they sought to define a place for themselves in the nation's increasingly divisive sexual politics. Radical lesbian feminists, such as Brown, thought of their sexuality not simply as an authentic identity but also as a blow against patriarchy. If, as Jill Johnston claimed in *Lesbian Nation*, "The sexual satisfaction of the woman independently of the man is the *sine qua non* of the feminist revolution," then lesbians stood in the vanguard. As "male identified," heterosexuality was by definition counterrevolutionary. Among some lesbian and straight radicals, this notion expanded into a proscriptive definition of feminism *as* lesbianism. Only women who rejected men sexually were true feminists. "Every fuck is a rape," wrote The Furies' Sharon Deevey.[15]

For American lesbian politics, the years in between Martin's farewell essay and the International Women's Year (IWY) conference in 1977 constituted an extraordinary period of endeavors in multiple directions. Lesbian collectives sprouted up across the country, and an underground lesbian press thrived, publishing poetry, short stories, manifestos, photography, artwork, and erotica. Lesbians helped found a women's music festival, women-only communes, women's health clinics, and rape crisis centers. A travelogue composed by Birdie MacLennan that survives in the Sophia Smith Archives at Smith College documents how together, these circulars, places, and events formed a national women's network, a lesbian highway whose travelers felt "a sense of strength, power, and autonomy with other wimmin." By mid-decade lesbians had created a world of their own—a world largely, if not exclusively, without men. From major cities to college towns, from neighborhoods to farms, lesbian travelers could leapfrog the country, touching down in welcoming women-only spaces. Earlier lesbian subcultures enjoyed versions of such solidarity, but the wide lesbian universe that opened up in the 1970s had few historical parallels.[16]

The advent of the lesbian highway did not, however, guarantee a unified lesbian politics. Radical lesbian feminists cast sexuality as purely a social creation and insisted that women's sexuality was political first and erotic second. For some, as powerful as this notion seemed, it led into an ideological cul-de-sac. If lesbianism was the essence of feminism, a new orthodoxy was a short step away. Lesbianism as "the rage of all women condensed to the point of explosion," the Radicalesbians' 1970 declaration, was a brilliant manifesto formulated to bring sexual outsiders to the center of a new political project. But it came dangerously close to a litmus test of feminist purity: every fuck a rape and only lesbianism a true subversion of patriarchy. And plenty of longtime lesbian activists bristled at the notion that lesbianism constituted primarily a political identity and that its essence was rebellion. The homophile stalwarts Barbara Gittings and Kay Tobin, who were never especially oriented toward feminism, criticized the Radicalesbians for advancing a "pointless prescription" irrelevant to the lives of ordinary lesbians. Rage and rebellion "aren't the central stuff of lesbian experience," they wrote, and the vast majority of lesbians simply wanted to be around other women "in the legitimate pursuit of friendship and love."[17]

But like the GLF, radical lesbian feminists revealed a great deal about sexual, and indeed social, freedom that their more moderate counterparts did not. Radical lesbian politics showed how what Adrienne Rich later called "compulsory heterosexuality" constrained women's self-determination. They exposed how accusations of lesbianism disciplined all women, in the same way that "fag" could be used as a weapon to question any man's loyalty, seriousness, or personhood. And in fact, the most politically damaging uses of "lesbian" in the 1970s came from the pens of conservative women and men, such as antifeminists Phyllis Schlafly and Sam Ervin. But private shaming, often among otherwise liberal-minded people, was no less damaging. In 1970 one lesbian recalled a conversation with a close straight friend at a college reunion. When she said the words "I'm homosexual," her companion was visibly shocked and affirmed that only silence on the subject would preserve their friendship. For some, even "acceptance" was condescending. "Your friendly smile of acceptance," Martha Shelley wrote to her straight feminist sisters, "from the safe position of heterosexuality—isn't enough."[18]

The effort to locate a new authenticity on which both individual identity and a movement could be based pushed the most vocal lesbian activists toward separatism between 1971 and 1974. The Furies, Radicalesbians, *The Lesbian Tide*, *off our backs*, and *Better Homes and Dykes* collectives, and dozens of smaller groups around the country embraced a radical critique of patriarchy and heterosexuality and encouraged as complete a disengagement from male society as possible. The relationship of their thinking to ordinary lesbians thus entered a complex terrain because people had real, not theoretical, lives. Was the ethical imperative of moving from women's autonomy to self-imposed exile practically helpful? And was the only choice between exile or collaboration with patriarchy? Could the "lesbian nation" and its highway be simultaneously separate from and part of the public life of the larger nation? Whatever the hotly debated answers to these questions, the lesbian feminist version of coming out was not a call to be "let in" to mainstream American culture.[19]

White lesbian authenticity, as ever, came up against the lives of a diverse range of real women. The long shadow of the Moynihan report, alongside black power's insistence on the heterosexual nuclear family as a necessary buttress to the movement, meant black lesbians had little room to maneuver. Moreover, the strong multigenerational ties among black women and their often collective responsibility for child rearing rendered political, and especially separatist, lesbianism a threat to the internal architecture of black communities; separatism could be celebrated by white lesbians in ways that proved intrinsically difficult for many lesbians of color. Audre Lorde, Barbara Smith, and Cheryl Clarke began articulating these dilemmas in the early 1970s, even as they broke politically with black nationalism—Clarke derided the mythological "'tug-o'-war' for the black penis." Chicana and Puerto Rican lesbians, for their part, confronted concepts of *la familia*, which were shaped by Catholicism and notions of machismo, alongside the nationalist rhetoric of the Chicano and Puerto Rican movements. In the case of Chicanos, nation and *la familia* were virtually synonymous. A *maricón* ("fag") or a *marimacha* ("dyke") stood outside not just straight society but the political project of Mexican American community empowerment itself.[20]

At the outer edge of differentiating identities, lesbians confronted an equally challenging question: transsexuality. A handful of transsexual organizations, led largely by male-to-female transsexuals, had come into existence since 1970; they included Street Transvestite Action Revolutionaries, founded by Sylvia Rivera, a veteran of the Stonewall riot, and Transexual Action Organization in Los Angeles [*sic*]. The Los Angeles Gay Community Services Center offered some of the earliest transsexual counseling. Yet the sexual status of male-to-female transsexuals was much contested in lesbian circles. As lesbian feminism and separatism reached their historical crest, some lesbians resented male-to-female transsexuals' (in time, "transgender") pressing for inclusion in lesbian and feminist organizations. In 1973, for instance, the transsexual folk singer Beth Elliott was banned (along with all transsexuals) from the San Francisco Daughters of Bilitis by a close, divisive vote. To some, Elliott was a man and therefore had no place in feminist meetings, whereas to others, judging "the sexuality of another sister," as one lesbian put it during the Elliott imbroglio, was hypocritical and a betrayal of the "openness" of feminism.[21]

Like straight feminists, lesbians thus engaged the politics of authenticity on multiple levels in the first half of the 1970s. Variations of lesbian politics all rested on one or more of three main propositions, however. First, sexuality was a social construction. If sexuality was not natural, its plasticity could be a source of self-determination and therefore personal and political strength. The second proposition posited not exactly the reverse but a parallel, alternative reasoning: lesbianism was natural and biological, an expression not of politics but of authentic personhood. In this sense, coming out did not mean smashing patriarchy but revealing and releasing one's real self. The third proposition revolved around womanhood. Was there, many lesbians asked, an essentially female form of love? Butch-femme culture had raised the question of whether feminine and masculine were essential or mutable forms, but many lesbians in the 1970s, often joined by straight feminists, insisted that women's love was more nurturing, encompassing, and compassionate than men's, which tended to be more sexual, self-interested, and fickle. Regardless of the ways individual groups of lesbians conceived of themselves in the seventies, they stood on the shoulders of the female homophiles and earlier challenges to entrenched cultural ideals of sex and womanhood.[22]

Yet whether a political choice or biological destiny, a blow against patriarchy or the heart's dearest desire, lesbianism inhabited a political world of citizens, nations, and laws. Feminist thinking and debate could happen in a vacuum; living could not. New initiatives, whether rape crisis centers, the creation of families and the raising of children, or simply going to work required at every turn new rights, new concepts of the citizen. Lesbian feminism had to be bent toward the world in order to do work within it. And as more and more ordinary lesbians made their feminist ideals do that work, the core questions became different. How could they recast the relationship between the private, intimate world and the legal, public one? How could they secure the negative and positive rights that would make their lives truly their own?[23]

•

In the 1970s lesbians quietly but with determination began to reinvent the American family. They did so by bringing their own lives and sexuality into the courts, putting both on trial in a nearly literal sense. When Martha Shelley claimed in "Notes of a Radical Lesbian" that for gay women "the rewards of child raising are denied her," she misunderstood one of the core concerns of ordinary lesbians. Again and again, among both lesbian activists and those who never joined an organization, motherhood emerged as a powerful desire and a site of struggle over citizenship and the meaning of family.[24]

Coming out might promise long-term personal and societal transformation, but for mothers it often carried enormous short-term risk. Because so many lesbians in the 1970s were in straight marriages and had borne children, the matter of child custody in divorce proceedings faced increasing scrutiny as the decade of "out" progressed. These proceedings began to rewrite family law, and lesbian motherhood became a de facto project of gay rights.

In the late 1960s, appellate courts in a handful of states had begun to rule that homosexuality was not proof of "unfitness" for motherhood. But local family court judges had wide discretion in determining fitness, and many continued to regard lesbianism as anathema to proper mothering. Legal observers estimated that lesbian women in the mid-1970s had only a 50 percent chance of gaining custody of children if their sexuality was revealed. And when custody was awarded, judges often placed restrictive conditions on the mother(s). In the 1972 case of Sandy Schuster and Maddy Isaacson, a Washington State judge awarded each woman custody of her children, from separate previous marriages, but forbade the couple from living together. In another much-publicized 1972 case, a lesbian from San Jose, California, won custody of her children but could not live with her female partner and was allowed to be with her only during the day when the children were in school. This was a regulation of private lives that had never appeared on the homophiles' list of grievances.[25]

No struggle better illustrates the combination of negative and positive

rights required for full citizenship than the long fight over lesbian motherhood. Legal advocates for lesbian mothers asserted the three core claims
of the gay movement: guaranteed privacy of adult consensual sex, protection from discriminatory treatment, and, perhaps most important, ethical
and legal recognition of same-sex relationships. In case after case before
judges, it became clear that women had to have both the liberty of sexual
privacy and the positive right of state recognition of child custody. Yet
ironically, given the debunking of conventional motherhood by feminists
in the decade, to win in court, lesbians and their advocates often had to
argue that lesbians embodied "traditional" notions of both womanhood
and motherhood.[26]

As custody battles gained notoriety in lesbian circles, women formed
support groups and organizations to provide legal assistance. One of the
first emerged from the 1971 Gay Women's West Coast Conference in Los
Angeles. The Lesbian Mothers Union, led by the tireless Del Martin,
began working with San Francisco's Family Service Agency to broaden
approaches to family. A major stumbling block for lesbians seeking child
custody was the assumption among family court judges that lesbianism
was immoral and therefore created an unhealthy climate for children. To
counter such assumptions, the Lesbian Mothers Union arranged expert
witnesses to testify on behalf of lesbian mothers, advocated research studies to document the positive family environment created by lesbians, and
demanded that the Family Service Agency "cooperate with lesbian mothers to educate the public, including mental health and legal professionals." Within a few years of the founding of the Lesbian Mothers Union,
nearly a dozen lesbian mothers' organizations had emerged across the
country. The Seattle-based Lesbian Mothers National Defense Fund
(LMNDF) published a newsletter, *Mom's Apple Pie*, and in the early
1980s the Lesbian Rights Project in San Francisco produced the *Lesbian
Litigation Manual* to assist women through the intricacies of divorce and
custody proceedings.[27]

Operating on a shoestring, these organizations provided critical assistance to individual women, but American jurisprudence was slow in ac-
commodating lesbian mothers as a group. Few men sued for custody of
children, but they often threatened to sue in order to improve the terms of
a divorce settlement. Judges generally favored the mother if a custody dispute actually came before the court, but biological motherhood alone was
insufficient to win these cases. Judges placed on trial motherhood itself, as

a set of skills and as a reservoir of emotional sustenance and moral rectitude. This was treacherous terrain for all women, regardless of their sexuality. For instance, employment could be regarded as compromising maternal responsibilities, even when it was financially necessary. And all women's private lives were heavily scrutinized for "immoral" behavior. Lesbian mothers shared these vulnerabilities in court with straight mothers. But their added burden of having to defend their sexuality as compatible with motherhood made lesbian custody disputes even more difficult and complicated.[28]

A typical case was that of Mary Jo Risher, a Dallas contractor and interior decorator. When she divorced her husband in 1971, her lesbianism remained unknown to the father and the court, and she was awarded custody of her two boys. Two years later she met Ann Foreman, a lesbian mother of a young girl, and they established a household. In 1974 Mary Jo's eighteen-year-old son left home, "ashamed" of his mother, he claimed. When the biological father sued for custody of the younger son, Richard, who wished to remain with his mother, Mary Jo found herself in court, before a jury—rare in custody cases, which were generally heard by a judge.[29]

Mary Jo's fitness for motherhood was understood, in the courtroom, solely through her sexuality. Having remarried, her ex-husband told jurors that his new wife "could be there to attend to [Richard's] needs twenty-four hours a day . . . There would be a father and mother image that he could model himself after." "Modeling" emerged as central to the arguments of both sides, each attempting to answer the question: Would Mary Jo raise her children to be gay? As a result, stereotypes dominated the proceedings and determined the outcome of the case. One of Mary Jo's own witnesses testified that Ann's daughter "espouses a traditional feminine role" and that Richard "wants to be a policeman," proof that lesbianism could be contained, the children "unaffected." A court-appointed psychologist, on the other hand, condemned Mary Jo's parenting skills because "as a lesbian" she should have been "more sensitive" when Richard wore unisex clothing in public. The ex-husband's lawyer closed the case by appealing that Richard not become "a guinea pig for someone else's social experiment." In the end, evidence that the father had once broken Mary Jo's nose and had a drunk driving record did not stop the jury from awarding him custody.[30]

Lesbian mothers' organizations vowed to educate judges and juries, but often the very experts brought to testify on lesbians' behalf espoused pernicious assumptions about sexuality. In a 1974 Ohio case, testifying in support of a lesbian mother's custody, a UCLA psychiatrist who had interviewed the mother assured the judge that "only an occasional hug or kiss" would be exchanged between the two lesbian partners in front of the child, "nothing of a graphic sexual nature." Moreover, he explained, the mother "had made special efforts to insulate Martha [the child] from exposure to a large number of homosexual groups . . ." Surely the psychiatrist was merely anticipating what he assumed were the judge's own beliefs about homosexuality, because no one in lesbian circles was arguing for the right to engage in "graphic" sex in front of children. But in such cases lesbians and their allies found themselves defending an old-fashioned view of womanhood as nearly sexless. This was the apparent price of custody.[31]

The heterosexual bias of judges and the slow evolution of state case law were predictable, if frustrating, obstacles to lesbians' broadening of the cultural and legal notion of family. That the arguments of lesbians and their advocates in that context would bend toward conventional respectability is understandable. Nothing less than the integrity of women's families, their ability to be mothers, was at stake. The evolution of these cases over the course of the 1970s made striking down the psychiatric model of homosexuality even more critical because judges in child custody cases placed great weight on psychiatric testimony. The work of these mothers—and their supporters in advocacy organizations, the American Civil Liberties Union (ACLU), the National Lawyers Guild, and other groups—was unglamorous and often harsh. Cases dragged on for years. It was rough-and-tumble politics by other means, but it slowly (for some, far too slowly) broadened the horizon of possibility for untold numbers of women.[32]

Lesbians had begun to change family law, but lesbian political culture was rife with debates about motherhood. As lesbian separatism gained momentum in the mid-1970s, a handful of prominent radical lesbian feminists dismissed the possibility that women could raise nonsexist male children and even rejected child-raising altogether as a relic of patriarchy. Concerned about antimale attitudes within the lesbian community and with the bias family court judges had shown against lesbians with male children, the LMNDF published *Male Children: A Lesbian Mother Perspective* in 1974 to reassure and assist lesbians with sons. Suspicion of male children was by no means universal in lesbian communities, but neither was it easily dismissed, especially in the heady days of lesbian separatist ascendancy. Despite the presence of lesbian mothers' support groups, many women engaged in custody battles felt isolated from the lesbian political community, whose commitments often lay elsewhere.[33]

Two closely followed custody cases in the second half of the 1970s illustrate the continuing dilemmas of lesbian mothers as well as their progress in changing family law. Jeanne Jullion lived in the San Francisco Bay Area with her Italian husband (they had met during a college year abroad). When she came out as a lesbian and the couple divorced, Jullion coparented with her ex-husband for a time but eventually lost custody of both her sons when he sued, claiming that her sexuality made her an unfit mother. Several appeals later Jullion won custody of her younger son, only to have both children kidnapped and held by her ex-husband in Italy. She was eventually reunited with them, but her long struggle exemplified the jeopardy in which lesbian mothers continued to reside. A similar custody narrative unfolded in Michigan. Margareth Miller, like Jullion, had come out as a lesbian and divorced her husband in 1972. Four years later he sued for custody of their two children. Miller's battle to keep her son and daughter lasted three years, ending only in 1979, when the Michigan Supreme Court ruled in her favor. That a state supreme court had felt compelled to reverse multiple lower court decisions, and to proclaim definitively that a parent's "sexual status" alone was not ground for denying custody, gave lesbian mothers, at the close of an extraordinary decade, some reason for optimism.[34]

By the end of that decade, the legal landscape of lesbian motherhood was improving but still hazardous. A handful of states had passed new divorce and adoption laws, easing the path to state-recognized parenthood for both lesbian mothers and gay fathers. And the Miller decision in Michigan was indicative of a progressive impulse among judges in states such as California, Illinois, New York, Washington, Maine, Vermont, and several others. Yet in the context of variable state law and judicial discretion, many lesbians continued to take the closet with them into divorce proceedings. Despite these evident limitations, lesbian mothers in the 1970s had begun the process of broadening the legal and political definitions of both "mother" and "family" in American life. In this context, "coming out" *did* mean "let me in"—to one of the most hallowed institutions of national life. Whether the unradical desire for motherhood became a radical one when claimed by two women (or parenthood by two men) was to remain an open question in lesbian and gay circles.[35]

•

In the early seventies lesbian and gay activists began to fashion a decidedly liberal movement out of the embers of post-Stonewall radicalism. In the American traditions of voluntarism and liberal pluralism, this movement blended street protest and old-fashioned politics. The trappings were familiar, but the course was unique. As lesbians and gay men organized at the municipal, state, and national levels, their pathway through the nation's sexual politics remained uncharted, their guidebooks only provisionally sketched by the homophiles of the 1960s. Coming out remained the organizing principle of the movement and one of the most powerful social movement concepts of the 1970s. But in the street fight for full citizenship in the American political system, abstract critiques of heterosexuality yielded to the realpolitik of coalition-building and vote-counting.

The notion that gay people formed a distinct minority group with shared political interests had to be invented. Indeed, this was the implicit project of the 1960s homophiles. After he became district leader of the Greenwich Village Independent Democrats by ousting the Tammany machine in 1964, for instance, Ed Koch called for a campaign to rid the Village of "bums, degenerates, and homosexuals." When Hendrik Ruitenbeek, a Village resident and editor of *The Problem of Homosexuality in Modern Society*, confronted him, Koch protested that it had never occurred to him to consider homosexuals a political constituency. Nor did this occur to John Lindsay when gay votes helped elect him mayor of New York in 1966. "Italians do it; Jews do it; Catholics do it; Blacks do it," wrote Nancy Tucker, a lesbian activist who worked on Frank Kameny's 1971 congressional campaign; why not lesbians and gay men? Making certain that politicians like Koch and Lindsay and their counterparts in Los Angeles, San Francisco, Chicago, and other major cities understood the power of the gay vote represented the first step.[36]

Like most social movements before it, the gay movement of the 1970s had two gazes. One it turned outward to the nation, where it cast appeals for equality in the language of rights liberalism. The other it turned inward, to address unresolved and contentious issues, including the closet (how out could the movement be and still win political influence?); the class politics of elite white male organizations relative to the larger, more variegated lesbian and gay communities; the ongoing tensions between lesbians and gay men; and the brewing conflict over transsexuality. Both the public and the internal terrain remained treacherous in this decade, as the struggle for gay rights became entangled in Americans' most treasured notions of the political subject, the neighborhood, and the family.

Gay movements in the nation's most prominent major cities followed a similar trajectory over the course of the decade: from despised or ignored outsiders ("bums, degenerates, and homosexuals") to an organized and savvy, if not always politically successful, acknowledged political constituency. New York's GAA was quickest to the punch on the East Coast. In 1971, Jim Owles, Marty Robinson, and Bruce Voeller pressed the liberal Greenwich Village city councilwoman Carol Greitzer to sponsor Intro 475, an ordinance banning discrimination in employment, public accommodation, and housing, which was modeled on the 1964 Civil Rights Act. Intro 475 was handily defeated in its first few years before the council, but GAA protests and signature gathering placed gay rights permanently on the city's political agenda. On the West Coast, San Francisco's SIR had pioneered candidates' nights and the homosexual bill of rights in the 1960s and by the early 1970s was occupying such a prominent place in city politics that the local GAA complained of a "SIR–Tavern Guild political machine." By 1971 SIR had helped elect city supervisors, including Dianne Feinstein, a staunch SIR ally; the powerful Democratic whip in the state assembly, Willie Brown; the city supervisor and then state senator George Moscone; and the U.S. congressman Phil Burton. Indeed, by 1971 SIR's Jim Foster was already an "insider" within the liberal wing of the San Francisco, and California, Democratic Party. San Francisco's annual "police vs. gays" softball game, an institution by the mid-1970s, may have been unique among major American cities, but it stood for the movement's mainstream arrival.[37]

A related trajectory prevailed in Los Angeles. After The Advocate and gay activists defeated a homophobic city councilman from Hollywood in 1969, post-Stonewall gay liberationists focused energy away from electoral politics. They established the Gay Community Services Center, which became one of the nation's largest, and lesbian feminists pursued a variety of community-centered projects. But in 1973 gay activists launched a major political gambit on behalf of the liberal coalition that elected Tom Bradley the city's first African American mayor; along the way, they secured a gay-friendly city attorney and three pro-gay city council members. Within a few years the gay Stonewall Democratic Club had become the largest Democratic organization in Los Angeles County, and the Municipal Elections Committee (MECLA), under the leadership of gay men, had become one of the city's most influential political groups. By the end of the decade, these organizations, like SIR in San Francisco, looked at politics from the inside out, their endorsements necessary for any serious liberal candidate for posts from county commissioner and sheriff to mayor, state senate, and Congress.[38]

San Francisco and Los Angeles represented rare cases of gay political successes early in the decade, yet they forecast and provided the blueprints for other cities down the road. In particular, both San Francisco and Los Angeles gay politics featured alliances with African Americans that became a hallmark of liberal urban political coalitions in the late 1970s and throughout the 1980s. This was not limited to high-profile mayors, such as Bradley, Harold Washington in Chicago, or, in the 1990s, Willie Brown in San Francisco, but included city councillors and state legislators as well. These alliances could be tenuous and fraught, but as the two most reliably liberal voting blocs in most major American cities, the gay and black communities needed each other politically. Plenty of African Americans resented gay claims to the "civil rights" mantle, not to mention the access that wealthy white gay men had to politicians. But the realities of urban coalition-building and their constituencies' collective interest in expanding individual liberties and protections brought a gay–African American alliance into being in half a dozen of the nation's largest cities soon after their first appearances in San Francisco and Los Angeles.[39]

This kind of coalition-building was not easy, however. When the decade began, the vast majority of local officials across the country were at best ignorant of lesbian and gay issues and at worst openly hostile to them. With a handful of exceptions, most big-city police departments remained deeply homophobic and continued to harass gay businesses and venues and make petty arrests. Following one such raid in 1976, Ed Davis, the notoriously combative and homophobic Los Angeles police chief, told reporters that he refused to "turn Los Angeles over to the gays." After his election in L.A., Mayor Bradley kept back channels open to gay leaders while soft-pedaling his support in public. In New York City, Greitzer, an avowed feminist, told GAA that she "didn't relate to the homosexual cause." In New York, Philadelphia, and Chicago, among many other cities, local politicians from heavily Catholic neighborhoods were reliably hostile to gay issues. Big-city politicians grew incrementally more comfortable with the gay community during the decade, but a certain circumspection and respectability were often the price of gay political influence.[40]

Despite evident tensions, by the end of the decade gay politics was a vibrant part of big-city life. A dozen major American cities had one or more gay political clubs, more than twenty cities and four counties had passed some form of gay rights legislation (though in many cases these were limited to municipal employment), and gay neighborhoods had emerged as among the most reliably liberal Democratic in the country. The extraordinary migration of gay men—and, though to a lesser extent, lesbians—to urban gay epicenters, like San Francisco's Castro and Mission, Los Angeles's Silver Lake and West Hollywood, New York's West Village, Boston's South End, and Chicago's New Town (later Boystown), in the 1970s had made "gay neighborhood" more than an underground term. In a decade of white ethnic revival, lesbians and gay men had taken their place, albeit a still precarious one, as an "ethnic" group of sorts in the bruising give-and-take of urban politics.[41]

Votes are one way to account for the rising influence of gay political clubs in major cities. Class and race are another. Most gay political organizations were led by middle-class white men, who had greater resources and more political connections than most lesbians and other gay men—and, crucially, sought limited rather than expansive rights. The Seattle Dorian Group admitted that it "was never set up to be a participatory organization. It is a vehicle for bringing the middle class in touch with public officials." San Francisco, however, as it did in other arenas, offered a paradigmatic instance. SIR's Jim Foster, backed financially by the attorney David Goodstein, created the California Committee for Sexual Law Reform and the Whitman-Radclyffe Foundation in 1972. Both became embroiled in controversy in early 1973, when Los Angeles activists Morris Kight, director of the Gay Community Services Center, and Jeanne Cordova, of *The Lesbian Tide* collective, attacked Foster, Goodstein, and the foundation as "a small cabal of elitists" whose fund-raising among wealthy lesbians and gay men (many of them closeted) insulated them from ordinary homosexuals.[42]

Goodstein, who called liberationists' "very tired 1960s rhetoric" distasteful and ineffectual, stirred more controversy when he purchased *The*

Advocate in 1974. The following year he called an invitation-only meeting of gay leaders to plan a national campaign for a federal gay rights bill. Calling on the movement to suppress "gay spoilers," Goodstein asked the delegates to devise ways "of keeping them off the broadcast media . . . keeping them away from legislators or at least neutralizing them." Invited delegates themselves, who included Barbara Gittings, Frank Kameny, Jim Owles, Bruce Voeller, and Jean O'Leary, dismissed Goodstein's attempt to control militants while endorsing his vision of a national fund-raising and lobbying campaign. "Dear brother, you bought *The Advocate*, not the movement!" wrote one critic. Nonetheless, Goodstein's post-gay-liberation political strategy, based on money, focused lobbying, and a "respectable" bourgeois image, remained an influential, if not dominant, one in gay circles.[43]

Debates about Goodstein's approach proved immediately relevant because gains in urban politics led to more influence at state and national levels. The Democratic Party is a case in point. In California, San Francisco's Alice B. Toklas Democratic Club and Los Angeles's Stonewall Democratic Club placed activists (including Foster from San Francisco and Kight from Los Angeles) in key positions on the California Democratic Council (CDC), the most important liberal-left Democratic organization in the largest state in the country. In 1976 the CDC recommended to the national party a fifteen-point statement on lesbian and gay equality more far-reaching than anything before it. Yet wary of repeating the party's 1972's presidential election disaster (recounted in Chapter 9), the platform committee at that summer's Democratic National Convention defeated every gay rights plank, at the behest of the presidential nominee Jimmy Carter's top aide, Stuart Eizenstat. Still, lesbian and gay delegates and activists, many from California and New York, were a much stronger presence than they had been in 1972. The Gay Rights Support Caucus convinced more than six hundred delegates to sign a petition endorsing most of the CDC's statement.[44]

Some years before, in 1973, former New York GAA stalwarts Voeller, Gittings, Kameny, Martin Duberman, Ron Gold, and Howard Brown had launched the National Gay Task Force (NGTF), hoping to transcend the localism of existing gay organizations and fulfill the dream of many lesbian and gay activists since the early days of NACHO. "Gay liberation has become a 9–5 job," Gold quipped. Two years later Jean O'Leary, who had earlier left GAA to found Lesbian Feminist Liberation, joined the

NGTF as legislative director and national coordinator. With Voeller and O'Leary as codirectors, the NGTF emerged in the middle of the decade as a central clearinghouse and lobbying organization, on behalf of an estimated 850 local groups. Charlotte Bunch and Barbara Love joined the board, and Ginny Vida was hired as media director, making lesbians and lesbian feminism more central to the NGTF than they had been to any previous national gay organization.[45]

The rise of the NGTF embodied the evolution of gay liberation into a traditional liberal rights project. Working closely with the ACLU and the Lambda Legal Defense and Education Fund, also founded in New York in 1973, the NGTF assisted in court cases around the country, lobbied Congress for a national gay rights bill, and joined in the planning, begun in 1973, for a march on Washington. Like its models and predecessors the NAACP and NOW, the NGTF also monitored the national media for evidence of homophobia and worked with corporations and other businesses to improve gay equality in the job market and workplace. This was politics as small, incremental steps and equal parts public education and glad-handing. It was about changing hearts and minds along with laws. At the 1976 Democratic National Convention, O'Leary admitted that "we've gotten a lot of people familiarized with the issue . . . The victories that we've had have just not been visible, that's all." O'Leary measured her political time horizon in years, even decades, a "reformist" project that still rankled many radicals. Because the NGTF's emergence coincided with a mid-decade decline in gay radicalism, many lesbians and gay men still worried that traditional interest-group politics would not realize, and perhaps even eclipse, the broader revolution in sexual values they sought.[46]

The appearance and success of openly gay political candidates in cities across the country vindicated to many the incrementalism of the NGTF and its desire to work within the political system. In 1974 in Ann Arbor, Michigan, Kathy Kozachenko became the first out gay person elected to public office in the United States. Her predecessor in the seat, Nancy Wechsler, had come out as a lesbian during her term. The same year Elaine Noble, a lesbian from Boston and the moderator of *Gay Way Radio* on a local public radio station, won a hard-fought campaign for the Massachusetts State House. Modeling her efforts on successful African American politicians then emerging across the country, Noble did not hide her lesbian identity (as they did not deny their racial identity), but she focused on housing, education, and conditions for the elderly, the pressing concerns of her South End district constituents. Noble's patron in the clubby world of Massachusetts politics was Barney Frank, then a closeted member of the statehouse (and a future out member of the U.S. Congress). In Minnesota, state senator Allen Spear, elected in 1972, came out of the closet, and two years later the former GAA member Jim Owles ran for the New York City Council.[47]

•

Another openly gay politician was Harvey Milk, the owner of Castro Camera in one of San Francisco's blue-collar-turned-countercultural neighborhoods. When Milk announced that he was running for city supervisor in 1975, he reminded his gay supporters that "it is the tremendous straight vote which makes the real decisions." Milk had moved to San Francisco from New York in 1972, and this was his second campaign for supervisor. Like Noble, Milk understood that while gay civil rights remained a crucial objective for him, his political message needed to reach beyond what a supporter called "one of many minorities we voters expect you to represent." By the mid-1970s, as lesbians and gay men increasingly took their case to city councils and state legislatures, "the tremendous straight vote" came into ever sharper relief.[48]

This vote proved to be divided and fickle and in many places reactionary. *The Advocate* optimistically called 1975 "a year to remember," when "gay rights progress shifted and expanded." But it was also a year in which the contours of a new struggle emerged. Fourteen cities passed gay civil rights ordinances, and five states, including California, reformed their sexual criminal codes that year, with major newspapers, including traditionally conservative ones such as *The Wall Street Journal* and the *Los Angeles Times*, lending support for the first time. But no gay rights bill mustered enough votes in any state legislature, and the introduction of such bills in Oregon, California, New York, Connecticut, Colorado, Massachusetts, and four other states awakened fierce opposition. In Pennsylvania, Governor Milton Shapp barred gay discrimination in state hiring but then watched legislators introduce no fewer than seven antigay bills, most with broad popular support. Louisiana passed a measure banning same-sex marriage, while Arizona nearly did. Georgia amended its sodomy statute specifically to include women. As gay rights opponents found their footing, each gay movement victory seemed to be matched by a defeat and occurred against the backdrop of two years of rising antigay violence. Suspected arson fires had burned several Metropolitan Community Churches across the country (including the founding church in Los Angeles), the GAA office in New York, and a gay bar in New Orleans, where more than twenty people died in 1973.[49]

An extraordinary sequence of events in California between 1975 and 1978 illustrates how the gay movement and its gathering opponents and the specter of violence collided in the second half of the decade. In 1975 the California legislature passed a consensual adult sex law. The bill had been sponsored by two state legislators from San Francisco, George Moscone and Willie Brown, and endorsed by SIR and the Alice B. Toklas Memorial Democratic Club (known as Alice), both of which were under Jim Foster's leadership. Governor Jerry Brown kept his promise to sign the bill into law, a promise made at SIR's request during his 1974 campaign.[50]

Seven days after Governor Brown signed the bill, a group called the Coalition of Christian Citizens announced a referendum campaign to repeal the new law. Religious response to the Moscone-Brown law revealed an emerging schism among California Christians, one that mirrored a national split. Progressive Anglicans, Methodists, Presbyterians, Lutherans, and Baptists (and a handful of Catholics) had begun to reconsider their stance toward both private sexual behavior and lesbian and gay people themselves. Influenced by the National Council of Churches, leaders in these and other denominations endorsed the Moscone-Brown law. Conservative church leaders, however, some from these same denominations, supported the recall efforts of the Coalition of Christian Citizens, led by a Sacramento newspaper promoter and a Southern California evangelical Nazarene. Working through a network of Bible bookstores, most of them in Southern California, the coalition garnered media attention but did not gather sufficient signatures to place a recall measure on the statewide ballot, despite two efforts, in 1975 and 1976.[51]

The California law and its survival in the face of determined opposition were major victories, but the gay rights movement soon after suffered a grievous defeat. In Florida a conservative Christian activist and singer had a different approach to undoing gay protections. She emphasized not abstract rights but the direct threat these protections posed to the family. Anita Bryant, a nationally known television personality, launched a campaign to overturn Dade County's (Miami's) 1977 antidiscrimination ordinance, which banned discrimination against gay people in housing,

employment, and public accommodation. She founded Save Our Children from Homosexuality (later shortened to Save Our Children), and for
six months Bryant, her husband, Bob Green, and the popular former
baseball player and manager Alvin Dark turned Miami and Dade County
into the epicenter of the fight over gay rights; it was the first such fight to
become a national story. Network television covered Bryant's campaign,
as did national weekly magazines and major newspapers. Activists and
celebrities from across the country traveled to southern Florida in the first
week of June to deliver passionate appeals both for and against the repeal
effort. In the end Bryant emerged battered (she lost a television program
and her Florida Citrus Commission contract because of the publicity and
endured the indignity of a pie in the face) but victorious. Dade County
voters repealed the ordinance.[52]

Television ads played an important role in swaying Dade County residents. A typical spot played footage of the gay freedom day march in San
Francisco as an announcer intoned that those who turned "San Francisco
into a hotbed of homosexuality want to do the same thing to Dade County."
Bombarded with images of bare-chested men and drag queens, viewers
were exhorted to protect their children's innocence. Similarly, Bryant
shrewdly declared that the new law would require the hiring of "homosexual" teachers (ignoring the fact that despite the purges of the 1960s,
lesbian and gay teachers currently worked in the county). Under siege and
threatened by the menace of homosexuality, the family needed state protection. "Do what you want in the privacy of your own home," one man
told gay rights activists. "Don't tell me I gotta accept it in mine."[53]

Among those who traveled to Miami in the summer of 1977 to support Bryant was the conservative Republican California state senator John
Briggs, from Fullerton. Impressed with Bryant's campaign, which turned
the question from a civil rights issue into a Christian crusade to rescue
families, Briggs, who had his eye on the governorship, returned to California and devised a ballot proposition to ban gay teachers from the public
schools. He followed Bryant's successful formula and placed children at
the center of his campaign. He decried the teaching of "alternative lifestyles," frequently citing a San Francisco "lifestyle class" that taught "about
homosexuality as an alternative to family life," even though the San Francisco Board of Education repeatedly denied that such a class existed. By
the summer of 1978, with the assistance of wealthy right-wing supporters, such as Carl Karcher, owner of Carl's Jr. burger chain, Briggs had

collected enough signatures to place the measure on the November 1978 ballot as Proposition 6.[54]

He soon found himself facing off against Harvey Milk in San Francisco. Brash and headstrong, Milk had entered the San Francisco political scene in 1973 as a novice, campaigning for city supervisor as a countercultural gay man, complete with a "hippie" ponytail, vaguely interested in government reform and fired by little-guy populism. Before deciding to run, Milk had consulted with Foster and Goodstein, who were then building support in the California Democratic Party for the consensual sex law. Foster kept Milk at arm's length, however; the newcomer had not paid his political dues. It was typical Foster-Goodstein hardball politics, but underneath their dismissal of Milk lurked their distaste for the counterculture and their fear that Milk would damage the image of respectable gay politics.[55]

Foster and Goodstein were not the only San Francisco operators Milk managed to offend. He lost races in 1973 and 1975, but his strong showing—he finished tenth out of thirty candidates in citywide voting in 1973 and in 1975 missed a seat by just one position (the top six vote getters won supervisorial seats)—nonetheless marked him as a formidable community leader. In 1975 George Moscone won the mayoral election, with considerable gay support. Moscone subsequently appointed Milk San Francisco's first "gay commissioner," a liaison between the city and the gay community. The following year, however, the ambitious and iconoclastic Milk announced that he would run for the state assembly against a Moscone ally. "If he runs," Moscone said, "he'll set the record for the shortest commissioner in history, and I'm not talking about his size." Milk stayed the course, and Moscone dismissed him as promised. That had the unintended effect of rallying both gay and straight community leaders, save Foster and Goodstein, behind Milk and his charge that San Francisco was on the verge of replicating Chicago's insular political machine. The iconoclast lost, but his rising status in the city's gay community had been confirmed.[56]

Dade County and other troubling events meanwhile had begun to rouse San Francisco's gay community. On the night of June 7, 1977, following the vote in Miami, five thousand gay men and women marched to Union Square, chanting, "We're gay and we're proud" and "Out of the bars, into the streets!" A week later Briggs called a press conference at San Francisco City Hall to announce his measure banning gay teachers. "San

Francisco is the fountainhead of all homosexual activity in the country," he told gathered reporters. "It is in captured-nation status." Between seventy-five and one hundred gay activists shouted at Briggs, and the confrontation eventually devolved into a shoving match. Just a week later, on the night of June 22, tragedy struck. A gay man named Robert Hillsborough was assaulted and stabbed fifteen times in the face and chest by four attackers, who shouted, "Faggot, faggot" and "Here's one for Anita!" Mayor Moscone called Briggs a "demagogue" who will "have to live with his conscience" in the wake of the murder. In July a stunned, angry, and awakened gay community staged the largest, most militant gay freedom parade in the city's history.[57]

Milk's campaign for city supervisor in the fall of 1977 was inescapably embedded in these events. His campaign this time was unique and poignant because of its timing and because of his inimitable style. He had elbowed his way past the gay old guard into the city's politics, forging critical alliances with Teamsters in the city's robust and not terribly gay-friendly labor community. He believed that straight liberals would not reliably take up gay concerns without plenty of gay muscle and noise. He combined the conservative instincts of the petit bourgeois businessman (he had supported Goldwater in 1964) with the countercultural sensibility and populist resentments of the early-seventies left. And he was aided by a crucial reform adopted in 1976 that replaced the citywide ballot with balloting by districts. This made it even more possible for a gay candidate to win in District 5, encompassing the Castro and Eureka Valley neighborhoods, into which gay men had been pouring for nearly a decade. On election day he defeated a number of gay candidates, including an Alice-backed one. With one arm around his boyfriend, Milk was inaugurated on the steps of city hall in January 1978.[58]

He immediately turned to two pressing matters: winning a gay rights ordinance in San Francisco and defeating Briggs's statewide initiative. Working with longtime gay allies Moscone and Dianne Feinstein, who was then president of the Board of Supervisors, Milk convinced the board to pass one of the strongest city ordinances protecting lesbians and gay men in the country. In a 10–1 vote, on a council with several conservatives, the lone holdout was a former police officer named Dan White, who represented a blue-collar district of mostly white, conventional nuclear families.

Milk then turned to Briggs. Though the state's liberal establishment stood against Proposition 6, Milk and other gay activists worried that liberal leaders did not comprehend the gravity of the threat. Lesbians and gay men went door to door across the state, speaking directly to voters, and Milk made confronting Briggs a personal mission, debating him in numerous forums and attending his rallies as the face of the "No on 6" campaign. Polls taken in the spring and summer showed Proposition 6 passing easily, but by October the numbers revealed a slim majority in opposition. In November voters defeated it by more than a million votes, 58 percent to 42 percent. Milk and the "No on 6" campaign had made a difference ("Come out, come out! wherever you are!" was one of its slogans), but so had the opposition of the conservative stalwarts Ronald Reagan and Howard Jarvis.[59]

The defeat of Briggs heartened the gay movement, but it came on the heels of three losses, all influenced by Anita Bryant, that in retrospect were more predictive of the coming political standoff. After her victory in Miami, Bryant and her husband took their message on the road. In the spring of 1978 in St. Paul, Minnesota, Wichita, Kansas, and Eugene, Oregon, this message took hold. Voters were told that gay rights implied "special privileges" that "ordinary" Americans did not have. Gay "behavior is not a civil right," claimed an Oregon radio spot. The St. Paul movement declared that gay rights violated "the basic right of parents and families," most notably the right to "protect their children." The result was that voters in all three cities overwhelmingly (four to one in Wichita) repealed "gay rights" from their cities' protections of its residents. ST. PAUL VOTERS KILL GAY RIGHTS, read one headline.[60]

"Kill" proved to be a tragic choice of words. Six months later, on November 27, 1978, just weeks after helping defeat the Briggs initiative, Harvey Milk and George Moscone were assassinated by Dan White in San Francisco City Hall. In his account of Milk's life and politics, *The Mayor of Castro Street*, the journalist Randy Shilts, a reporter for *The Advocate*, writes of Milk's telling his lover that White was "a real closet case." Whatever the truth about White's sexuality may have been, it is tempting to read his internal torment and depression, his resentment of Milk and Moscone, his opposition to gay rights, and his later suicide as a parable of the possibilities and hope of outness and the emotional and kinetic violence of the closet. That reading is a possible and compelling one. But another version would prove just as compelling: as the closet swung open, it became

Black power militants such as H. Rap Brown asserted a conspicuous masculinity in the late 1960s, a complex response to decades of white belittling of black men and to the violence visited on black communities in these years. (Associated Press)

The National Welfare Rights Organization, led largely by African American women, defended traditional motherhood and called for the expansion of government assistance to the poor. (Associated Press)

The war in Vietnam became a battleground over manhood. Americans fought over who served, who did not, and how soldiers comported themselves, as questions of patriotic manly duty. (Associated Press)

In abortion debates prior to 1969, Americans heard largely from men, like the physicians and the priest pictured here with Eunice (Kennedy) Shriver. Feminists seized the abortion conversation in the 1970s and made reproductive rights a cornerstone of women's liberation. (Associated Press)

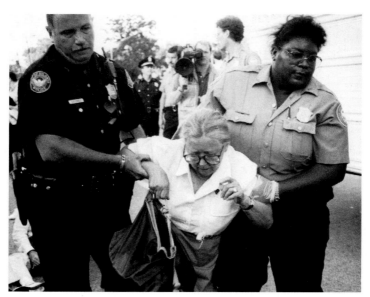

By the late 1980s, the anti-abortion movement had momentum and a new militancy. Operation Rescue activists used civil disobedience protest tactics to draw public attention to their cause. (Schlesinger Library, Radcliffe Institute for Advanced Study, Harvard University, Cambridge, Massachusetts)

Once reviled, misunderstood, and closeted, lesbians and gay men made themselves central to debates over citizenship in the 1970s and 1980s. Among the San Francisco lesbian activists pictured here, two went on to become judges, one became a city supervisor, and one became the city's police commissioner.
(Greg Day)

Betty Friedan, the most prominent liberal feminist of the 1960s, called lesbians a "lavender menace" and said they were unwelcome in the women's movement.
(Bettmann/Corbis)

Del Martin and other lesbians defied Friedan and became some of the women's movement's most ardent activists and supporters. (GLBT Historical Society, San Francisco)

The white, working-class "hard hat" emerged as a symbol of patriotic, hetero-sexual, breadwinning manhood in the early 1970s. Once a liberal icon, he was fast becoming a conservative one. (The Estate of Garry Winogrand, courtesy Fraenkel Gallery, San Francisco)

In 1972, Democratic presidential nominee George McGovern helped open his party to new gender and sexual politics, making it difficult to court hard-hat voters. (Associated Press)

Shirley Chisholm pushed the Dem-ocratic Party to embrace African Americans and Latinos, women and feminists, and lesbians and gay men. (Associated Press)

In the 1970s, lesbian feminists questioned whether the presumption of heterosexuality was healthy for society. (Associated Press)

Black feminists such as Angela Davis and other feminists of color questioned whether by "women" American society meant "white women." (Bettmann/Corbis)

Opponents of the Equal Rights Amendment, led by Phyllis Schlafly, protesting in front of the White House in 1977. Schlafly helped write traditional womanhood into the conservative iconography of the New Right. (Associated Press)

Gay activist Harvey Milk, who became a San Francisco city supervisor in 1977, helped fight the first wave of antigay backlash in California, which originated in Anita Bryant's Save Our Children campaign in Miami, Florida. (Harvey Milk Archives—Scott Smith Collection, The James C. Hormel Gay and Lesbian Center, San Francisco Public Library)

In that same decade, lesbian mothers remade family law by battling in court for custody of their children, helping to redefine family itself. (Cathy Cade Photographs Collection, The James C. Hormel Gay and Lesbian Center, San Francisco Public Library)

Two men kissing in front of New York City's St. Patrick's Cathedral during a march sponsored by the gay activist groups ACT UP and Queer Nation in 1990.
(Associated Press)

During the 1980 presidential campaign, the Reverend Jerry Falwell, pictured here with Phyllis Schlafly, held I Love America rallies across the country. Falwell and others on the New Right resurrected the patriotic, heterosexual breadwinner and made him a conservative emblem. (Associated Press)

clear to many lesbians and gay men that only the violence of others could close it.[61]

Bryant's Dade County campaign and her invocation of the language of family established the model for future battles over gay rights. The prime lesson the opponents of gay rights took from Dade County, Wichita, St. Paul, Eugene, and even Briggs was that a calibrated argument about gay "special" rights or privileges, alongside a defense of parental and family rights, promised political traction, if not always victory. As that argument came into focus, a truism of rights politics emerged with equal clarity. Whether in the black freedom movement, feminism, or the gay movement, the limitation of rights as a framework of citizenship was straightforward: for every announced or demanded right there was a countervailing right claimed by opponents. Yet the implications of Bryant's campaign went beyond gay rights. In a decade when defining the family came to seem an urgent necessity, Mike Thompson, who had served as communications director for Save Our Children, urged the Republican Party to make Bryant's antigay crusade part of its national identity and to "position itself as the party of the family." Thompson sensed something tangible and reproducible in Dade County, as well as a grander political strategy.[62]

Gay liberationists had opened the 1970s by announcing their belief that one kind of love cannot be better than another and that the rights and protections offered by their nation ought to reflect this truth. By the end of the decade, lesbians and gay men were on the defensive. That defensiveness had long been endemic to gay life and politics, but two decades of visibility, organizing, and institution-building had created an opposition prepared to push back against any victory, no matter how small. Visibility produced liberation and backlash in equal measure. Who pushed back and how and who listened would prove important. Thus the questions for the coming decades were clear. Would sexual difference retain its power to stir fear and therefore remain politically volatile or would it be woven into the larger fabric of a modern citizen subject? And had lesbians and gay men built the political institutions with the muscle to accomplish the latter?[63]

9

NO STEELWORKERS AND NO PLUMBERS: LIBERALISM IN TROUBLE

In the history of postwar national elections, 1972 stands in the consider-able shadow of 1968, when the Democratic Party devoured itself on na-tional television over the war in Vietnam and watched its segregationist wing bolt into obstructionism. But clear away the smoke and tear gas, and 1972 provides a more clarifying snapshot of a nation in transition. The social movements of the previous decade had drawn Americans from the political margins into era-defining battles over the nature of citizen-ship and the withheld promise of equality. The leading wedge of those efforts, the African American freedom movement, had forced an end to disfranchisement and cracked open the old order of the Democratic Party—a crack widened to a breach in 1968 by the antiwar movement. Other floods then came rushing in. In 1972 the women's movement, joined by the gay and lesbian and welfare rights movements, led a revolt from below against the party's power structure. Gender, sex, and sexual-ity, subtexts in 1968, had joined black freedom as the most impor-tant issues confronting a party and an ideology—liberalism—coming undone.

Nineteen seventy-two proved to be the moment when the political instability precipitated by efforts to reimagine gender, sexuality, and fam-ily became transparent and inescapable. Struggles to expand the circle of full citizenship since 1964 were grounded in claims that the subject of American democracy was malleable: "breadwinner," "soldier," "hetero-sexual," "woman," and so forth were not fixed natural categories but were open to reinvention. This claim was galvanizing and empowering. Ameri-cans from all walks of life rushed to proclaim new versions to replace the old. But multiple imaginings are by definition less politically efficacious than a single, conventional understanding of gender or sexuality or family. This had been apparent all along but became unavoidable in 1972, when the patriotic, heterosexual-male-breadwinner nuclear family fractured as a political ideal and put in jeopardy the fortunes of one of the nation's major political parties.

The Democratic Party appeared ripe for transformation because of political realignments already under way. The black freedom movement and the Vietnam War had discredited the Cold War liberalism of bureaucratic labor unions, the hidebound parochialism of urban political machines, and the segregationist "way of life" defended by the southern congressional delegation. They had discredited, that is, the three principal sources of Democratic power: unions, big cities, and the solid South. With the traditional power brokers on the back foot, women and sexual minorities pushed for no less than a new gender and sexual order. They saw the 1972 convention as the culmination of party reform that dated to 1964, when the Mississippi Freedom Democratic Party had tried unsuccessfully to unseat the segregationist Mississippi regulars.

In between the two conventions, between 1964 and 1972, the black freedom struggle had arced through a dizzying set of transformations. Having pushed for and won the Civil Rights and Voting Rights acts and made their cause central to President Johnson's Great Society by 1965, African Americans then endured a disheartening combination of success and setback. Northern Democrats saw black voters as essential, white student radicals saw black power as the vanguard of revolution, and both civil rights and black power had inspired all the subsequent movements for gender and sexual equity and self-determination. Yet the riots between 1965 and 1968 had discredited the movement in the eyes of many whites, those same northern Democrats had to secure black votes while holding on to their restless white "ethnic" constituencies, and the War on Poverty had succeeded only in stirring greater white backlash, both North and South. The black freedom movement had been the essential beacon of party reform for a decade, yet by 1972 its national profile had been weakened, and it increasingly shared the Democratic Party stage with other once-outsider groups.

Calls for reform, accelerated by the disastrous 1968 convention in Chicago, had made it possible for the party to become noticeably heterogeneous and younger. In 1971, after two years of hearings, the Democrats had adopted the McGovern-Fraser Commission recommendations to increase the number of women, African Americans and Latinos, and young people (under age thirty) selected as delegates to the national convention. To critics such as the columnist Max Lerner of the *New York Post*, it was "quota democracy," but to the surging left wing of the party, it was a much-needed correction to a broken system. The new rules now assured them, and the wide variety of social movements they represented, a seat at the formerly exclusive Democratic table.[1]

But imposing their will on the party proved difficult because of determined opposition within party ranks and because there was no consensus on what the updated Democrats should look like. The result was that over four days in July, the 1972 Democratic National Convention descended nearly into incoherence. Shirley Chisholm and Coretta Scott King shared the podium with segregationists. Welfare rights activists, who advocated a guaranteed national income, mixed on the floor with "hard hat" trade union leaders, whose constituency deplored welfare. Gloria Steinem, whose preview issue of *Ms.* had hit the newsstands in January with its abortion rights petition, mixed with Catholic delegates deeply opposed to abortion rights. On the convention's second night, George Wallace, triumphant in a wheelchair following an assassination attempt, delivered a bruising populist oration aimed at the white working class, while Jesse Jackson and the black caucus, along with amnesty and peace advocates, collectively held their breath. Still, a changing of the guard had taken place. Following the convention, the AFL-CIO president George Meany summed things up starkly: "We listened to the Gay Lib people . . . We heard from the abortionists. But there were no steelworkers, no pipefitters, and worst of all, no plumbers."[2]

McGovern lost spectacularly in November. His failure resonated among the Democratic old guard for decades (and even young idealists at the time, such as Bill Clinton, carried the memory with them throughout their political careers). But McGovern's futility was ultimately less important than the emerging divisions within the party and the nation. Feminism and gay and lesbian rights, following black freedom and economic justice, had come to stay in the Democratic Party. But instead of a new consensus—instead of a replacement for breadwinner liberalism—there was uncertainty and animus.

•

In early July 1972, Fannie Lou Hamer left Mississippi for Miami. She had been named to the National Women's Political Caucus (NWPC) and had been elected a delegate to the Democratic National Convention, pledged to the presidential candidate Shirley Chisholm. After narrowly losing a race for a seat in the Mississippi State Senate in 1971, and anxious about her fragile health, she was determined to make her third Democratic convention. Meanwhile, Jim Foster boarded a plane in San Francisco to make the cross-country trip to Miami, his first national convention. A founding member of the Society for Individual Rights (SIR) and coauthor of the homosexual bill of rights, Foster had helped found the Alice B. Toklas Gay Democratic Club in San Francisco earlier that year. He was a delegate pledged to George McGovern. Carol Greitzer too was on her way to Miami as a McGovern delegate. A member of the New York City Council from Greenwich Village, Greitzer was the president of the National Association for the Repeal of Abortion Laws (NARAL) and a liberal reformer who, along with Ed Koch, had founded the Village Independent Democrats in the early 1960s to challenge Tammany Hall.[3]

Hamer, Foster, and Greitzer were not ordinary convention delegates, spirited by thoughts of a long week of cigars and whiskey toasts in the Florida sunshine. They came to Miami to change the Democratic Party. Indeed, they and hundreds of delegates like them dreamed even bigger. They wanted to change American democracy and in doing so to change American life.

The previous summer had been a tense one for women's rights activists. New York's pioneering abortion law had come under assault in the state assembly, and right-to-life committees had massed popular opposition to liberalization in other states. Reproductive rights activists had begun to worry that the tide had turned against them; only the Supreme Court's decision to hear *Roe v. Wade* and *Doe v. Bolton* gave them hope. The Equal Rights Amendment (ERA) had passed in the House of Representatives by an overwhelming margin, but the conservative North Carolina Democrat Sam Ervin had blocked its progress in the Senate. Even as the women's movement extended its influence deep into American life, women's advocates recognized that the 1972 Democratic convention represented a potential turning point. The future of the movement—and, as they saw it, the future of American women—would depend in large part on their ability to cast their concerns as coincident with the concerns of other Democratic Party constituencies.[4]

Despite the media's insistent focus on "women's libbers," the movement was far richer and more complex than most Americans realized. Variety and invention remained its strength. Yet it also meant that outside of a handful of issues, agreement over priorities proved elusive, and as evidenced by the antiabortion stance of the otherwise feminist Women's Equity Action League, even the seeming cornerstone of reproductive rights was not universally endorsed. This raised a question, as much strategic as philosophical, that this movement of movements, like every feminist insurgence in American history, could no longer avoid with the convention on the horizon: Did the concept "woman" unite actual women?

More than three hundred women had gathered in Washington, D.C., in July 1971 to found the NWPC and to try, implicitly, to answer this question in the affirmative. Led by Bella Abzug, Chisholm, Betty Friedan, and Steinem, the NWPC set a broad women's rights agenda for governmental action, but its immediate goals were to win 50 percent of the delegate seats at the 1972 Democratic Convention and to secure women's rights planks in the party platform. "This is the year of women's liberation," Steinem declared, while Chisholm warned potential opponents within the party: "Women have the political power to turn out of office every politician who does not support equal rights."[5]

Steinem had by that time become the bridge between younger liberationists and Friedan's and Pauli Murray's generation of liberal feminists. Her speaking tours with Flo Kennedy were an attempt, if a sometimes superficial one, to forge a true multiracial feminism. She played a similar role in the NWPC. To dispel the notion that women were too different to close ranks in a single movement, Steinem stressed what they had in common: "a systematic exclusion from the responsible positions in the political parties and in governmental offices and politics."[6]

Dependent on middle-class white feminists, who eased institutional and media access, the NWPC nonetheless established a national board that reflected its vision of a united women's rights constituency. The board included Hamer, Myrlie Evers (who had moved to California after the assassination of her husband, Medgar, and run for Congress in 1970), Beulah Sanders of NWRO, Dorothy Height and Vivian Carter Mason, both longtime activists in the National Council of Negro Women, and LaDonna Harris, an Indian rights activist from Oklahoma. Hoping to inspire a generation of women "to unite against sexism, racism, institutional violence, and poverty," the NWPC had begun to craft a broadly inclusive rhetoric of the women's movement.[7]

Still, division persisted and caveats were necessary, evidenced by the existence of the NWPC's Black Caucus, which praised the organization's "principled positions on issues that concern us" but countered that "these have not been the issues to which the organization has committed its resources." The caucus called for white women to fight just as passionately against "budgetary cuts in social services" as for reproductive rights. Hamer put it succinctly: "if the women's movement is to be successful, it must recognize the broad variety of women and the breadth and range of their interests."[8]

Despite white women's weak cross-racial consciousness, Latina and African American women still made themselves central to any "new" Democratic Party. After a massive 1971 conference, convened by Elma Barrera of the Magnolia Park YWCA in Houston, Chicanas developed a strong presence within the NWPC, led by Rhea Mojica Hammer (who was to be elected NWPC vice president in 1973). Among African American women, the Third World Women's Alliance and the Black Women's Alliance had grown substantially since 1968, though their politics were still more radical and social than electoral. But in 1972 three African American women launched campaigns for congressional seats: Barbara Jordan from the newly created Eighteenth Congressional District in downtown Houston; Yvonne Brathwaite Burke from Los Angeles; and Cardiss Collins from Georgia. Each played a prominent role in Miami.[9]

Virtually everyone in the women's movement celebrated the "breadth and range" of women's interests, but as the movement gathered steam, priorities were made. In particular, NARAL and the NWPC gambled that abortion could stand as "the crucial feminist issue." That gamble, of course, risked alienating Catholics, a core Democratic constituency in the industrial Northeast and Midwest and increasingly in the heavily Latino Southwest. And the gamble would meet with success only if millions of women (and men) came to appreciate the centrality of female reproductive freedom to women's equal place with men in society. After all, the politics of sex and reproduction had not been the feminist politics of the early sixties, which had focused on workplace and economic equality. It was Steinem's generation, those who named "sexism" and called for women's sexual liberation and self-determination, that had posited reproductive rights as the foundation for all other women's rights and liberties. Now, many argued, it was time to combine the economic and sexual feminist arguments. "Power in the kitchen and power in the bedroom are no substitutes for, or shortcuts to, political power," said Greitzer.[10]

Like the NWPC, gay and lesbian activists saw the Democratic convention as the place to announce their political ambitions. By 1972 gay rights and gay liberation had largely eclipsed the old homophile movement. Splits between lesbians and gay men and the movement's racial myopia persisted, as did divisions between sexual liberationists and civil rights reformers. Nonetheless, post-Stonewall organizing, fired by ideologies of gay liberation, had begun to forge an unprecedented political consciousness among the nation's sexual minority communities. The gay movement now represented significant political constituencies in San Francisco, Los Angeles, New York, Minneapolis/St. Paul, Miami, Philadelphia, Chicago, Dallas, Washington, D.C., and Boston. And in three states—California, New York, and Minnesota—gay activists were a major presence in the state Democratic Party. The effort to integrate a liberal gay civil rights agenda into the party's mainstream had not quieted the internal disagreements over sexual freedom, feminism, transgender issues, and the closet. But civil rights demands at least set forth a minimal program most could agree was a necessary foundation.[11]

National unity had eluded gay rights advocates since the dissolution of NACHO in 1969. The 1972 election seemed to offer an opportunity to create this unity anew. In February the New York Gay Activist Alliance and the Chicago Gay Alliance sponsored an invitation-only meeting of delegates from nearly eighty gay rights organizations nationwide. Frank Kameny, still a respected intellectual leader in the movement, was on hand, as was Jim Foster, representing the Alice B. Toklas Democratic Club in San Francisco. Fewer than 10 percent of the delegates, however, were women; Del Martin's account of the movement's male-dominated leadership seemed all too confirmed. Calling themselves the National Coalition of Gay Organizations (NCGO), the delegates drafted a platform based on the homosexual bill of rights first developed by SIR in San Francisco in 1964. Attendees also planned to seek delegate slots at the convention. Foster was elected as a McGovern delegate from California, and a lesbian folk singer from Buffalo named Madeline Davis was recruited by the local Mattachine Society to run as a McGovern delegate. She won and, like Foster, headed for Miami in July.[12]

For those activists who were able to look beyond their immediate battles, a broader question loomed: Did all this myriad foment constitute a new politics? The two major forces that had challenged the party's old guard in 1968, the black freedom and antiwar movements, remained the heavyweights of the liberal left. But those movements, for all their power, had lost some dynamism by 1972. Moreover, neither the black freedom movement nor antiwar activists had yet fully embraced the politics of gender and sexual equality that were so important to large numbers of the delegates heading to Miami. And, to be fair, neither had the advocates of gender and sexual equality always shown themselves to be partisans of the black freedom cause. As the various roads to the convention converged, the new politics envisioned by various social movements were only slightly better prepared than the party's (and the nation's) center and right to embrace the claims of new citizenship that had erupted with such force in the previous eight years.[13]

•

As women's and gay rights activists prepared to take their case to the Democratic Convention, Jaquie Davison too was on the road. Davison had founded Happiness of Womanhood (HOW) and the League of Housewives (LOH) in her living room in Kingman, Arizona. By the middle of 1972 her organizations claimed three thousand members in forty-seven states. "As real women, we want to defend our homes," Davison told reporters, adding that her members "want to be loved and protected by our men." The previous summer Davison had spoken at an anti-ERA "Satin Pillow" rally in Los Angeles, where she and NOW activists exchanged hostile gibes.[14]

Davison's "Satin Pillow" tour appealed to the sentiments of what Richard Nixon had famously called the silent majority. Nixon had meant Americans who "silently" supported his war policies, but the press quickly grasped the concept's broader implications. *Time*'s January 1970 issue proclaimed "Middle Americans" the "Men and Women of the Year." "Discovered first by politicians and the press," *Time* explained, "their silent but newly felt presence" stands in defense of "a system of values that they see assaulted and mocked everywhere." Davison broke the silence. As she toured the country between the summer of 1971 and the fall of 1972, she

cataloged for each audience a list of liberal offenses: pornography, sex education, women's liberation, abortion, the Child Care Development Act,
and the ERA. Her proudly defiant blond bouffant stood in sharp contrast
with the Steinem-inspired straight hair worn by so many young white
feminists and the "naturals" popular among black liberationist women.
Inclined to produce photos of her six children for reporters, Davison was the
first in a long line of antifeminist populists to denounce feminism's alleged
assault on the family.[15]

Davison was no Democrat, but she did not frame her speeches in
terms of party politics. This was not unusual. In the early seventies the
emerging contest over gender, sexuality, and family had not yet come to
define the contest between political parties. It remained a war within each
party. Nelson Rockefeller, the Republican governor of New York, had
signed the nation's most liberal abortion law in 1970. A year later he vetoed its repeal, which made him only the nation's most conspicuous Republican supporter of abortion reform; senators Jacob Javits of New York,
Lowell Weicker of Connecticut, and Robert Packwood of Oregon were
among the many others. Meanwhile, the Democratic Party would campaign in 1972 with a vice presidential nominee, Sargent Shriver, who was
opposed to abortion rights and whose wife, Eunice (Kennedy) Shriver,
had actively campaigned against abortion liberalization. And when the
Republicans met in Miami a month after the Democrats, their platform
included an unconditional endorsement of the ERA and other progressive
stands on women's issues (though they sidestepped abortion rights). Thus
what would later be called values politics had not yet solidified into the
partisan rancor that was to mark the politics of the 1980s and 1990s. Nineteen seventy-two proved to be the year that set the terms of political debate
for decades to come.[16]

If the hard edge of partisan rancor had yet to be forged in 1972, it was
not for lack of trying by Spiro Agnew. He had spent nearly two years, from
February 1969 through the November 1970 midterm elections, wooing
the silent majority with talk of "traditional American values." Agnew
matched the escalating rhetoric of the various social movements, condemning the "glib, activist element who would tell us that our values are
lies." Calling for a "positive polarization" in American politics and grasping the national bully pulpit like few vice presidents before or since,
Agnew castigated the traditional enemies of the American anti-intellectual
tradition: the elite, the media, and professors. Those enemies, in Agnew's

worldview, had given credence to excessive black demands for racial justice and were now embracing the equally excessive, and permissive, demands of women. Salvation was clear. To reform a "degenerating democracy" in which the mob would "dominate the affairs of government," the nation had to rediscover "discipline and authority in the home."[17]

Agnew left a decidedly unpleasant trail through national politics, but he was prescient. Like Nixon, he understood that in the face of the complex challenges to conventional understandings of gender, sexuality, and family, appeals to a patriotic and heterosexual breadwinner nuclear family were politically expedient. Tectonic political plates were in motion, as what had been a liberal project—breadwinner liberalism's patriotic, heterosexual nuclear family—was fast becoming a conservative one, absent the government social insurance that had defined the New Deal and Great Society. As the political project of two Democratic Party generations, breadwinner liberalism, came undone, what remained for conservatives to claim was the symbolism of family. That would, so they hoped, consign social welfare programs to history's dustbin.

Davison's politics were related to but distinct from Agnew's unfocused outrage at "elites" and the "activist element." She, like Phyllis Schlafly, who founded STOP ERA in the spring of 1972, was first and foremost an antifeminist. Davison took up the mantle of moral outrage at sexual liberalism that had taken root among conservative and religious Americans since the mid-fifties. The Warren Court's liberalization of obscenity laws in *Roth v. United States* (1957) and its prohibition of prayer in schools in a series of cases in the early 1960s inspired calls for a moral counterrevolution. So too did sex education, which had emerged as a national issue in the second half of the 1960s. Already convinced that pornography and sex education represented government-imposed sexual values—a breach of the private sphere of the family—moral reformers were a ready constituency for antifeminism. As we shall see, moral conservatives increasingly embraced Davison and Schlafly's notion that pornography, sex education, abortion, the ERA, gay and lesbian rights, and feminism writ large were less distinct issues than a single revolution in which the state sought to displace the family as the nation's moral arbiter.[18]

For antifeminists, as for feminists, abortion was the most pressing issue. Many early-seventies conservative activists had come of political age opposing abortion liberalization in the 1960s at the state level. They had the powerful Catholic Church on their side. "Traditional Catholics simply do not accept that abortion is a simple matter to be left between a woman and her doctor," a Texas priest explained. Between 1962 and 1969, before abortion rights had been firmly anchored in women's rights and the women's movement, leaders of the Catholic hierarchy had emphasized abortion's sinfulness. For the state to license killing as a form of "birth control" was more than the desecration of life: it represented the ultimate invasion of the family's privacy. Unwanted pregnancy constituted the natural break on sexual permissiveness, and to permit abortion was to reverse this natural, and to many divine, logic. It was to stand against the family and its natural disciplinary order. Between 1969 and 1972, when abortion rights became central to women's rights, Catholics began to attack "women's lib" and the politicians they believed catered to it. The same Texas priest was repulsed by "a candidate [McGovern] who is trying to keep his votes with the Women's Lib group, and at the same time regain his strength among Roman Catholics."[19]

Antiabortion Catholic leaders chided feminists for believing that women desired "liberation" from the family. Monsignor James T. McHugh of the U.S. Catholic Conference called family "the perduring social agency where the individual person is born and nurtured and comes to a knowledge of individual personality and social responsibility." Few in the women's movement would likely have disagreed with that sentiment, but they would have reached an entirely different conclusion from its premise. Antiabortion activists and feminists argued past each other on distinct conceptual planes. Where the women's movement insisted that individual women existed prior to the family, Catholic leaders, many millions of their parishioners, and large numbers of conservative Protestants conceived of women as embedded in, and not prior to, the "perduring social agency." For antiabortion activists, society made individuals who they are, not the other way around.[20]

Prominent among antiabortion Catholics were what national opinion makers in the early 1970s increasingly referred to as "ethnics." Kevin Phillips had first identified ethnics—working-class, second- and third-generation Irish, Italians, Poles, and other people of Central and Eastern European origin—in his 1969 manifesto *The Emerging Republican Majority*, Nixon's alleged campaign playbook. Ben Wattenberg and Richard Scammon followed a year later with *The Real Majority*, in which they famously warned Democrats to pay attention to "what is bothering that lady in Dayton." That "lady" was a suburban Catholic housewife married to a blue-collar worker who almost surely opposed affirmative action and sympathized with those who bloodied the antiwar marchers on Wall Street in 1970. Ethnics represented an electorally volatile group; they were the very people who were the focus of breadwinner liberalism between the 1930s and the early 1960s. Without their votes, the theories of Phillips, Wattenberg, and Scammon went, neither party could assemble a governing majority.[21]

Writing in the contentious weeks before the 1972 Democratic and Republican national conventions, Monsignor Geno Baroni, director of the National Center for Urban Ethnic Affairs, called such ethnics "unmeltable Americans" and declared that "the Catholic vote is up for grabs." In addition to opposing abortion, according to Baroni, these voters distrusted black civil rights, despised the counterculture, and anxiously sensed their own downward mobility. In reality, ethnics were a more diverse ensemble than Phillips, Wattenberg, Scammon, and the journalists who echoed them allowed—plenty would never have voted for a Republican presidential candidate. Nonetheless, there was a great deal of truth to Patrick Buchanan's assessment of the Democratic Party later that fall. The blue-collar, lower-middle-class ethnics and white southerners "who gave FDR those great landslides" had come to distrust, Buchanan believed, the "intellectual aristocracy and liberal elite who now set the course of their party."[22]

Worries about ethnics abounded in the months leading up to the Democratic National Convention. For Democratic Party leaders, those worries overlapped with a broader concern over the fate of what Hubert Humphrey called "the great broad middle of our party." Voters of the "broad middle" had since the 1930s and 1940s been managed—mobilized—by powerful trade unions in states such as Michigan, Illinois, Pennsylvania, and California and by powerful urban political machines in major cities such as Chicago, Philadelphia, Boston, Cleveland, Milwaukee, San Francisco, and St. Louis, as well as smaller ones such as Dayton, Toledo, and Providence. In the South, various "rings," machines, state party organizations, paternalist networks, and demagogues, all relying on black disfranchisement, had maintained the Democratic Party's hold on the region. Because it relied on unions, patronage networks, city contracts, political clubs, and small-town city halls to get people to vote for its candidates, and because these institutions were connected to the home, the workplace, and the neighborhood, the party relied on conventional racial, family, and sexual values to give it stability. Gender equity, women's liberation, sexual freedom, abortion, and gay rights—to say nothing of black rights and economic justice—questioned the patriarchal order of family, community, and faith and thus threatened the party's architecture and even its very viability.[23]

Democratic Party regulars—local elected officials, congressional representatives and senators, trade unionists, and state conventions—believed that the party in 1972 was in no position to further test the patience of its "broad middle." It was not simply that the issues offended them; it was that new constituencies threatened to introduce new calculations that could remake the whole system by which the electorate was managed. Social movement activists disagreed. Believing that the party ought to extend the civil rights revolution it had boldly endorsed in 1964 and 1965, they saw the 1972 convention as an opportunity to remake the Democratic Party, as the immigrant working class had done in the 1930s, only this time with African Americans, women, gay men and lesbians, Chicanos, and young people at the center. What took shape at the Democratic convention that year was not structured by calculated emotional politics or the contrived "family-values" disputes of later decades. It was a real crisis of political orthodoxy. That crisis resulted from the deeply felt belief on the part of some that a new racial, gender, and sexual politics was essential and an equally deep fear on the part of others that such a politics threatened social chaos and the political marginalization of the Democratic Party.

•

In June, with the Democratic convention a few weeks away, Hubert Humphrey sent a stern warning to George McGovern. "Radical elements" supporting McGovern had trounced traditional Democratic forces with "overzealous tactics" at many state conventions, Humphrey charged. In Humphrey's home state of Minnesota, for instance, McGovern supporters had pushed the Democratic Farmer-Labor Party to endorse unconditional amnesty for draft violators and sexual freedom for gay men and lesbians (alongside marijuana legalization). "These proposals are abhorrent to the mass of Democratic voters," Humphrey continued. "And if they are jammed into our national platform, we could have mass voter defection to Mr. Nixon." Humphrey, the party's centrist standard-bearer and ally of labor and big-city party bosses, worried that the Democrats were risking everything by moving far to the left of the majority of the country. He urged McGovern to restrain his "zealots" and to hew to the political middle.[24]

Other party regulars shared Humphrey's grave concern; they included George Meany, president of the AFL-CIO; Richard J. Daley, the mayor of Chicago and backroom architect of Democratic politics since the late 1950s; and Hale Boggs, the House majority leader from Louisiana. Meany threatened to sit out the presidential election, withholding labor's official endorsement in the general election should McGovern be nominated. Daley was entangled in a legal dispute over his slate of convention delegates, and Boggs fretted that only forty-one House members had been selected as delegates, compared with eighty-five in 1968 (U.S. senators who were delegates dropped from forty in 1968 to seventeen). All three worried that if party regulars could not tame the social movement activists, or if defeating insurgents required fierce clashes in front of television cameras, there would be a Nixon landslide in November. To them, McGovern had to be denied the nomination if the Democratic Party was to survive.[25]

McGovern came to the convention leading in the delegate count, the chief beneficiary of reforms he himself had championed as chair of the Commission on Party Structure and Delegate Selection. He had supported "Guidelines A-1 and A-2," which required state parties to "eliminate all vestiges of past discrimination by affirmative steps to encourage representation on the national convention delegation." Three categories of representation were specified: African Americans (and "Spanish-speaking" in some states), women, and youth. The Minnesota congressman Donald Fraser took over the chair's duties in 1971, but the reforms were forever linked with McGovern, who announced on the Senate floor that "the 1972 Democratic Convention will be the most open political convention in American history." In the primaries in the spring of 1972, he emerged as the candidate of the party's left wing, particularly the antiwar New Left, and in one of the most unlikely political ascensions of the postwar period, steadily overtook centrists Humphrey and Edmund Muskie, as well as center-right candidates Henry Jackson and George Wallace.[26]

McGovern was not the only beneficiary of party reform. Chisholm announced her own candidacy for president in January with an eye on the new rules. Most state conventions would now assign delegates in proportion to vote totals—rather than on a winner-take-all basis—so Chisholm believed that despite her lack of national recognition, she could come to Miami with enough delegates to influence critical debates. "Shirley's candidacy is not symbolic," her campaign literature declared. She would come to Miami "as a candidate whose interests must be contended with." The NWPC, NARAL, NWRO, and gay rights activists too benefited from the reforms. The NWPC held dozens of state conventions in advance of party caucuses and primaries in order to recruit potential delegates and to draft a women's rights platform. NARAL and NWRO each had delegates at the convention and hoped to win support for reproductive rights and a national minimum income, respectively, in the Democratic platform. In Chicago 13 percent of the delegates had been women; in Miami nearly 40 percent were, remarkably close to the NWPC's goal. And the National Coalition of Gay Organizations sent two delegates (Foster and Davis) and planned to make a strong push for gay rights. In short, the delegate selection reforms did exactly what they were designed to do. They displaced many of the powerful white men who ran the Democratic Party and opened the convention to women and racial and sexual minorities.[27]

When the convention opened on July 10 at the Miami Beach Convention Center, three core issues stood unresolved. First, would state delegations that violated the McGovern reforms, refusing to observe the quotas, be seated? Second, who would be the presidential nominee, McGovern or a candidate drafted by the massing stop McGovern forces? Third, would the delegates affirm the party platform drafted in late June by McGovern supporters or amend it to include three controversial excluded items: reproductive rights, gay rights, and a guaranteed national income?

The Washington Post characterized the Democratic Party in Miami as "bathed in sunshine but still searching for its soul." It did most of that searching, in an age before conventions were scripted for television, in the dark hours of the morning. The gavel would not fall on the first night of the convention until nearly 5:00 a.m. McGovern would not deliver his acceptance speech on the final night until 3:00 a.m. The *Great Speckled Bird*, Atlanta's countercultural newspaper, called it "the Woodstock of 1972 . . . a high-energy, electronic, kaleidoscopic freakout." Hunter S. Thompson, on the other hand, missing Abbie Hoffman and his 1968 Yippie conspirators, observed soberly: "What happened in Miami was too serious for the kind of random indulgence that Gonzo journalism needs." The dread that lingered among Democratic regulars over the convention's four long days was of the nail-biting, slow-burn sort not easily subject to Thompson's comic amplification.[28]

The convention's first order of business was the issue of challenged delegations. None was more in the spotlight than the one from Illinois. Daley had refused to meet the conditions of the McGovern-Fraser reforms, instead handpicking a slate of fifty-nine delegates (including himself) that won election as "uncommitted," meaning they would come to the convention prepared to back any candidate who stood a chance of beating McGovern. Immediately after the Illinois primary in March, however, a coalition of independent Chicago Democrats, including Anna Langford, the first African American woman elected to the Chicago City Council, and Jesse Jackson, head of Operation PUSH, challenged the "Daley 59." Daley was defiant in his public utterances. "I understand they want a certain percentage of women, a certain percentage of blacks, and a certain percentage of Spanish speaking," he told the press. But "where are the rights of the people to elect who they want as delegates?"[29]

Given his long association with Chicago's ruthless machine politics, the moral high ground Daley sought proved slippery. His delegation lost every appeal, including one before the credentials committee and in dramatic floor vote on the first day of the convention. Embittered, he refused even to come to the convention. Instead, he watched the events on television, frozen out of a process in which he had been a power broker, some even said president maker, for two decades. Mike Royko, Chicago's legendary political journalist, wrote a column angrily addressing the insurgent Democrats: "Your reforms have disenfranchised Chicago's white ethnic Democrats, which is a strange reform."[30]

Other observers saw in Daley's fall more than the fate of a single power broker. They wondered if the Democratic Party could *evolve* into a progressive coalition that joined the New Deal to the era's social movements, or would the old framework have to be blown up and the pieces reassembled? It was hardly an idle question. The McGovern-Fraser reforms, McGovern's own candidacy, the silencing of Daley, and the rising prominence of reproductive rights and gay rights, alongside the ongoing struggle by African Americans for influence in the party, suggested that the old order might simply be shoved aside in one immense push. For some, this was political folly, and they saw in the 1972 delegates not a romantic populism representing a true "people's" movement but a misguided radical takeover whose inevitable result would be a massive split in the party and a retreat into the political wilderness. "Roosevelt's handiwork has pretty surely been undone," mused Joseph Alsop, the famously acerbic columnist and forty-year veteran of Democratic politics.[31]

Activists pressed on, fired less by the rough-and-tumble realities of winning national elections than by the democratic principles of fairness and equality. The credentials committee, chaired by Patricia Harris, former dean of the Howard University Law School and a rising figure on the party's liberal left, heard more than forty challenges to state delegations. The entire South Carolina delegation was challenged (it contained 7 women out of 32 total delegates), as were the delegations from four congressional districts in southern Illinois (2 women out of 26 delegates). In all, the credentials committee sat 114 additional delegates in more than a dozen states in an attempt to balance the totals with respect to women, African Americans, and youth. To the party's left, this process was true to the McGovern-Fraser reforms and just recompense for generations of exclusion; to party regulars, it was a transparent "quota system" and a barely concealed McGovern power grab. Whatever the intent behind the delegation challenges, Democrats were taking sides against one another.[32]

McGovern, though he was the candidate of idealists, was a protean political maneuverer. He proved both more shrewd as a parliamentarian than his opponents expected and less committed to the new politics of gender and sexuality than some of his most ardent supporters hoped. McGovern had first acquired a following in 1969, when he became chair of the commission on party reform that informally bore his name. He was the party's antiwar conscience, inheriting Robert Kennedy's and Eugene McCarthy's followings after 1968; he and Senator Mark Hatfield from Oregon had introduced a Senate amendment calling for immediate, complete withdrawal from Vietnam. As for his relationship to the black freedom movement, his voting record on civil rights was strong, but he lacked close ties with the principal leaders and organizations that had carried that movement forward for more than a decade. McGovern ran in the primaries from this position on the party's antiwar left and then gradually tacked toward the center in the weeks leading up to and including the Miami convention. Though he secured the nomination, McGovern ended up in no-man's-land. His views on abortion, welfare, gay rights, and amnesty proved too radical for the national electorate, but to the social movement left he was not radical enough.[33]

More than any other male politician of national standing, however, McGovern had seemed to comprehend the stunning rise of the women's movement after 1968 and, if much more tactically, grasped the increasing electoral power of gay men and lesbians, especially in California and New

York. As chair of the reform commission, in appearances before women's groups, and in numerous speeches on the Senate floor, McGovern identified himself with the women's movement, particularly its economic objectives. His temporizing on abortion was usually forgiven because virtually every other politician in the party waffled as well. NWPC branches across the country worked diligently for him in state primaries. With respect to gay rights, Jim Foster drafted, and McGovern's office released, a seven-point platform that included major liberal movement demands, including broad employment and housing rights, reform of discriminatory immigration laws, and a reversal of all dishonorable military discharges given for "homosexual tendencies." Announced in March, just ahead of the California primary, Foster's efforts helped boost McGovern's profile in the politically active gay communities in San Francisco and Los Angeles.[34]

On the eve of the convention, however, McGovern submitted to political reality. His supporters on the platform committee, led by Bella Abzug, helped draft before the convention in late June what the *Los Angeles Times* called a "mostly moderate" platform. It contained predictable swipes at Nixon, a call for withdrawal from Vietnam, proposals to raise corporate taxes, and a vague statement about the "right to be different." George Wallace's planks against busing and opposing withdrawal from Vietnam were rejected, but so were, with McGovern's approval, planks supporting reproductive rights, gay rights, and a guaranteed national income. "If the Democratic party falls into the hands of any narrow, ideological elite," McGovern explained as the platform committee was performing its work, "if it focuses its concern on matters of interest to only a handful of the privileged, or if it neglects the day-to-day concerns of the many, then the long and scrupulously planned 'emerging Republican majority' may well be upon us." Indeed, McGovern had identified the core political challenge for those who would displace breadwinner liberalism: What would take its place? From the perspective of the twenty-first century, the 1972 Democratic platform looks decidedly left-leaning on economic issues and the welfare state, but to the party's social movement activists, it seemed like a grand centrist compromise.[35]

At the convention itself, McGovern continued to hedge, on abortion in particular. At a meeting of the National Women's Political Caucus organized by Friedan and Abzug on the first day of the convention, he failed to impress the more than seven hundred female delegates who attended. When introduced as the architect of the reforms that secured 40 percent of the delegate slots for women, McGovern quipped that he "really couldn't take credit" for all the women at the convention. That credit "would have to go to Adam." Full-throated hisses and boos greeted the strange remark, and McGovern stammered to recover. As he moved into his familiar antiwar stump speech, women shouted, "What about abortion?" and "What about women's issues?"[36]

Shirley Chisholm's reception by the same group of women was just the opposite. A ten-minute ovation followed her introduction, accompanied by delirious shouts of "We want Chisholm!" She walked to the podium not just as a founder of the NWPC but as one of the five most important female members of the House of Representatives. Along with Martha Griffiths and Edith Green, who had held their seats since 1954, Chisholm joined Patsy Mink (Hawaii) and Bella Abzug (New York), who were elected in 1964 and 1970 respectively, as powerful progressive voices for women in the halls of Congress. These women had drafted or been crucial sponsors of legislation dealing with child care, child development, welfare, women and Social Security, and women in federal employment, as well as Title IX (concerned with gender equity in public education) and the Equal Rights Amendment. The heroine's reception in Miami was a counterpoint to the more modest enthusiasm Chisholm had generated in the primaries. Running on her American Express card and funds from small speaking fees and fund-raisers, Chisholm competed in twelve states and amassed twenty-eight delegates, generating enormous excitement among feminists, if not among a wider public.[37]

Chisholm came to Miami as the embodiment of the promise, and the unfulfilled ambitions, of the women's movement. She was a former day care center director, and her feminist politics were born among some of the poorest women in the nation. She saw firsthand how the lack of child care, the absence of reproductive freedom, and the dead-end pink-collar occupational ghetto trapped poor women in cycles of poverty and dependence. First in the New York Assembly (1965–1969) and then in Congress (1969–1973), she sought legislative remedies for these bald economic inequities. For multiple reasons, including her race and that of her constituents, she was less likely to declare "marriage is slavery," or to decry the bourgeois family than she was to seek laws that would secure equal economic and educational opportunities for women. "Racism and anti-feminism are two of the prime traditions in this country," she wrote in 1970. Despite, or perhaps because of, her willingness to critique white feminism, she won allies in Friedan and Steinem, both of whom ran in the Democratic primary as Chisholm delegates (both lost).[38]

Chisholm, part of a still minuscule feminist presence in American politics, ran to make her constituency heard. She saw that even left-leaning politicians like McGovern had "no understanding of how women are victimized and oppressed by prevailing attitudes . . . They appear to be concerned . . . but just as an instrument to help them retain political power." Chisholm was equally cynical about black politics. Though she was a founding member of the Congressional Black Caucus in 1969, she experienced many black leaders to be as sexist as their white counterparts. Neither black activists nor politicians, including the prominent figures Amiri Baraka and Jesse Jackson, were encouraging when she first explored entering the presidential race. In part this was a result of the perception that Chisholm was insufficiently nationalist, owing to her inborn independence, her strong following among white women, and possibly her Caribbean heritage as well. She was also seen by black leaders such as Jackson as a threat to their hope for a united bloc of black delegates at the convention. At the 1972 National Black Political Convention in Gary, Indiana, in March, Jackson, Baraka, Richard Hatcher, and other black leaders had composed a new platform for the black freedom movement, and they had high hopes for its reception in Miami.[39]

Her cynicism begat pragmatism. Chisholm's convention strategy was not unlike George Wallace's, though they came from opposite ends of the party. Like Wallace, she knew the nomination would go to an establishment figure. But she hoped that a vigorous campaign could rouse the party's left and leave her with power at the convention and a platform from which to shape a Democratic agenda. Neither hope was realized, as she won too few delegates to bargain with party insiders. Her role at the convention was largely symbolic.

If Chisholm was pragmatic, McGovern proved to be ruthless in pursuit of the nomination. Determined to maximize their power at the convention, California Democrats had rebuffed the McGovern-Fraser reform requiring delegates to be assigned in proportion to votes, keeping instead a winner-take-all format. The credentials committee then stripped McGovern, who had won California, of the state's 151 delegates. In a move equal parts ironic and coldly calculating, McGovern challenged the ruling of the committee, supporting California's violation of the progressive reform that bore his name. The challenge succeeded, and California's delegates, and the nomination, went to McGovern. His nomination was a victory for the party's social movement left. But the disingenuous manner in which he secured it became yet one more indication that the left's urgent idealism would struggle to prevail over the usual political exigencies. To the party's center and right—to Daley, Meany, and Boggs—McGovern's win in Miami seemed only to presage disaster.

•

With three days of the convention remaining, Democrats devoted themselves to finalizing their party platform in advance of McGovern's presidential campaign. McGovern and his allies were determined to ensure that none of the controversial "minority planks" would be approved lest they damage Democratic prospects in the fall election. Such planks had been rejected by the platform committee prior to the convention but had enough support to warrant putting them to a full convention vote. There were a total of thirteen, and three of the most controversial were the direct result of the gender and sexual politics of activist party delegates: guaranteed annual income, reproductive rights, and gay rights. And when the Vietnam Veterans Against the War brought their report in favor of unconditional amnesty to the convention, they raised a fourth matter central to the previous decade of gender politics: military manhood.

The minority plank calling for a $6,500 guaranteed annual income represented a more robust version of the Family Assistance Plan (FAP) defeated in Congress the previous year. It called for the federal government to supplement any family's income that fell below the designated level. McGovern had been temporizing since the spring on social welfare policy. He had started out advocating tax increases and a guaranteed annual income, which were broad redistributive policies favored by the party's left. But these proved enormously unpopular on the campaign trail during the primaries, and by the convention McGovern had backtracked. Still, the guaranteed income measure had enough support to be put to a floor vote on day two.

Frankie Mae Jeter and Beulah Sanders of NWRO stepped to the podium to speak in favor of the report. Declaring that "welfare recipients are blamed . . . for the financial crisis facing our states, and for the failure of the entire welfare system," Sanders pointed out that "we did not build the ghetto that we live in." She proposed a vast reordering of national priorities, including reductions in military expenditures, closing tax loop-holes for the wealthy, and full employment. Absent from the convention, though no doubt skeptical that significant new welfare proposals would gain political traction, was Daniel Moynihan, who had been furious with NWRO for opposing Nixon's FAP proposal a year earlier. A less promi-nent welfare skeptic than Moynihan, a self-declared "family farmer from Wisconsin," followed Sanders to the podium and bemoaned that "$6,500 is more than many farmers and rural workers make working full time all year." His final message, however, was pragmatic, not sentimental: he urged delegates to reject the report so as not "to produce strain on these people who support our ticket in 1972." The report failed by a margin of two to one.[40]

The political distance between Moynihan in 1965 and Sanders in 1972 is symbolic of the Democratic Party's struggles in this era. The par-ty's center remained committed, like Moynihan in 1965, to a breadwinner liberalism that combined modest social welfare programs (Social Secu-rity, unemployment insurance, minimum wage, job training, and the like), support for organized labor, and antidiscrimination laws to protect women and nonwhites. That centrist Democratic position encountered two major problems between 1965 and 1972. First, it was increasingly under heavy assault from right-wing forces outside the party and was beginning to lose its political traction in the national electorate. Second, it was also under heavy assault from inside the party, from people like Sanders on the left, who believed that centrist breadwinner liberals were not aggressive enough in their response to women's poverty and to the broader economic legacies of racial segregation. Breadwinner liberalism was increasingly decried on the right as undermining individual responsibility and on the left as insufficient in scope and commitment.

Abortion was next. The Abzug-led platform committee had crafted the most extensive pro–women's rights party platform in American his-tory, with calls for an ERA, strong antidiscrimination and equal pay mea-sures, and the appointment of women to the highest levels of government. Despite vigorous lobbying by NARAL and the NWPC, however, repro-ductive rights were not mentioned. The committee deemed the issue too politically toxic. Abortion was, however, permitted to go to a convention floor vote as a minority plank. McGovern, like virtually every politician in 1972, wanted to stay as far away from abortion as possible because taking a stand on one side or the other was so politically risky. Moreover, *Roe v.*

Wade was scheduled for reargument in October, to allow the new Nixon appointees William Rehnquist and Lewis Powell to be present, so it also seemed prudent to wait for the Court's verdict. On the eve of the convention, when Agnew charged McGovern with supporting legalized abortion, the presumptive Democratic nominee had given this noncommittal response: "I am for leaving it up to the states."[41]

Despite the fact that reform efforts had been under way at the state level since the early 1960s, abortion was a relatively recent arrival as a national issue. Some politicians, most notably Nelson Rockefeller in New York, had been forced to take sides, but most national political figures dodged the issue as best they could. Led by Abzug, Steinem, Chisholm, Eleanor Holmes Norton, and dozens of other feminists, women on the floor of the convention were determined to change that.[42]

For anyone who had been following the reproductive rights debate since the late 1960s, little that was said at the Democratic convention was new. The surprise was that such a debate was taking place at a major party convention at all. Frances "Sissy" Farenthold, a state legislator from Texas who later finished second to Missouri Senator Thomas Eagleton for the vice presidential nomination, objected to "government control of the reproductive lives of individual citizens" and claimed the party had an obligation to endorse the "fundamental right" of individual reproductive control. The one innovation by Farenthold and other female delegates was to go beyond the national question of women's rights as U.S. citizens by situating reproduction in a framework of universal "human rights." By avoiding a more radical language derived from the women's liberation movement, Farenthold and Norton, who also spoke, tempered their message for centrist appeal but simultaneously elevated it to a higher plane of justice. On balance, however, their speeches hewed to the "privacy" line of reasoning that had proved so effective in the courts.[43]

A true surprise came next. Violating a promise made by McGovern aides, a right-to-life delegate, Eugene Walsh from Missouri, was allowed to address the convention. Steinem and Abzug fumed as Walsh spoke of the "slaughter of the most innocent . . . whose right to live is not mentioned in the minority report." Tears streaming down her face, Steinem searched the convention floor and found Gary Hart, McGovern's campaign manager, among the throngs of delegates and berated him: "You promised you would not take the low road, you bastards." A second shock followed. Shirley MacLaine, one of the women's movement's celebrity allies, came to the podium next and delivered an odd and rambling speech about "working together" and voting "your own conscience" in which she appeared to oppose the report without precisely saying so. A photographer later captured an irate Abzug pointing her finger at MacLaine as she accused the actress of taking part in a McGovern plot to defeat the report. A long and tense floor vote produced a tally of 1,101.37 for and 1,572.80 against (delegations were allowed to vote in fractions). Reproductive rights supporters were despondent.[44]

From a political point of view, McGovern's temporizing on abortion reaped few rewards. Despite his dogged efforts to keep the issue off the party's platform and his belated selection of the Catholic Sargent Shriver for his vice presidential running mate after Eagleton's withdrawal, many Americans nonetheless identified McGovern with abortion rights. "I'm a native New Yorker . . . I am a Catholic who still goes to Mass," wrote one disgruntled Democrat to Shriver. "I was heavily involved in John F. Kennedy's presidential campaign [and] I may vote for Richard Nixon in November . . . I consider abortion murder." Meanwhile, others found McGovern's backtracking insulting. "Quite frankly, the main reason I supported you was your stand on women's rights," wrote one Floridian to the candidate after the convention. "Could you please let me know where you stand *now*?" McGovern had alienated women's rights supporters without gaining a compensatory political advantage.[45]

Like the floor debate on abortion, consideration of the gay rights report descended into turmoil. In March, ahead of the California primary, Jim Foster had led the drafting of a full gay rights statement that was approved and released by McGovern's Northern California and New York campaign offices. The campaign booklet handed out at the convention, *McGovern: The Man and His Beliefs*, specified "homosexuals" in a long list of Americans for whom "Liberty and Justice" should be guaranteed. But yet again McGovern caved to what he perceived to be political necessity. Having kept an official gay rights plank out of the platform drafted just before the convention, he pushed debate over the gay rights minority plank to the last possible moment, just after the rancorous abortion debate (which turned out to be 4:30 a.m.). That's when, in succession, Foster, Madeline Davis, and a McGovern delegate from Ohio named Kathleen Wilch stepped to the podium.[46]

The minority report brought by Foster and Davis stopped far short of the changes gay men and lesbians had been calling for since 1964. It

stopped short as well of the demands that emerged from the National Coalition of Gay Organizations (NCGO) Convention in Chicago earlier
that year. The report was cautious and understated, and its affirmation of
liberty in "lifestyle" was little more than a placeholder for the movement's
real demands. Nevertheless, the delegates grasped the euphemism, and if
not, Foster and Davis made it plain. "We do not come to you pleading for
your understanding," Foster told the convention. "We come to you affirming our pride in our lifestyles." Right before 5:00 a.m. Davis followed
Foster to the podium. "We are coming out of our closets and onto the
convention floor," she announced. "We must to speak to the basic civil
rights of all human beings." The speeches of Foster and Davis were
unprecedented in American political history: the "homosexual citizen"
had openly addressed a national party. The hopefulness of the moment
was dashed, however, when Wilch reached the microphone next. Claiming that the minority plank committed the party to "repeal of all laws involving the protection of children from sexual approaches by adults" and
those "related to prostitution, pandering, and pimping," Wilch invoked all
the stereotypes about gay men as predators and homosexuality as akin to
criminality. The report was defeated by a resounding chorus of noes.[47]

That was not the end of things. The day after her convention speech,
Wilch issued a strange retraction. In a press release, she claimed that "the
speech was prepared for me by a lawyer on the staff of the platform committee" and that "I was not aware that the speech would imply that homosexuals are child molesters." Furious, the NCGO charged the McGovern
staff with manipulating Wilch (his staff had also physically restrained gay
activists from attempting to hand out leaflets containing McGovern's own
pro–gay rights statements). Ten days after the convention, McGovern's
press secretary publicly repudiated *all* of McGovern's earlier pronounce-
ments about gay rights. However, when Gay Activist Alliance (GAA)
members occupied McGovern's New York office and chained themselves
to a telephone console, another press agent declared McGovern's *support*
for gay rights on New York television stations. "They've given good statements to the New York stations," the GAA state chairman John Howard
said, "but not to the people of Arkansas who couldn't get here today."
McGovern wanted the gay vote in New York and California without of-
fending the sensibilities of "the people of Arkansas" and other states where
gay rights were deplored.[48]

On the final night of the convention, well before McGovern delivered his early-morning acceptance speech, antiwar activists presented not a minority plank but a resolution that raised the politically volatile issue of amnesty. Antiwar Democrats were among McGovern's most steadfast supporters, and McGovern had endorsed general amnesty for draft evaders the previous year. The official party platform drafted before the convention called more modestly for "amnesty, on an appropriate basis," at the war's end. But just prior to the convention, Nixon's Justice Department had detained twenty-one leaders of the Vietnam Veterans Against the War (VVAW), who had been scheduled to speak to the Democratic delegates. It was widely interpreted as an effort by the president to keep amnesty advocates off television. Edwin Selby, a VVAW member, addressed the Democratic convention in lieu of his comrades and introduced a resolution condemning the Justice Department. Patricia Simon, a Gold Star mother, followed him and quoted a Vietnamese poet, Ngo Vinh Long, an act that demonstrated a change since 1968, when the war movement had been battered in the streets outside the convention hall. Determined yet again to please both sides of the party, however, McGovern's staff arranged for the mayor of Talladega, Alabama, John B. McKinney, to take the stage next. To scattered applause and a chorus of boos, McKinney declared: "If we let these people [draft dodgers] come home from Sweden, I hope the boat sinks, because they are not Americans."[49]

McKinney's assumption that men who abrogated their duties as citizen soldiers were not real Americans was widely shared. In the home stretch of the presidential race, McGovern was shaking hands with workers at the Western Electric Company plant in Columbus, Ohio—he often donned hard hats for photo ops in these appearances. In a pointed encounter while glad-handing, McGovern was confronted by a man who demanded, "How come you want amnesty for traitors?" "I'm not for traitors," McGovern countered, rattled by the worker's directness. "Well, the people that left this country won't fight for Vietnam and for America," the man continued. McGovern defended himself against charges of "surrendering" and allowing "traitors" to return from overseas with amnesty. The man was unconvinced. He planned to vote for Nixon and saw little he liked in McGovern's reasoning. The politics of military manhood, like the politics of welfare, abortion, and gay rights, proved nearly impossible for McGovern to finesse.[50]

The polarizing debate over those issues gave witness to a party coming apart. To hold the fractious Democratic coalition together, McGovern needed George Meany's plumbers, steelworkers, and pipe fitters, not to mention northern Catholics and Bible Belt southerners. He needed the gay vote in San Francisco and the Christian vote in Arkansas. He needed the African American vote in Harlem and the white ethnic vote in Queens. He needed the help of urban machines like Daley's in Chicago. Nineteen seventy-two was different from past elections in which a left-wing candidate had to run from the center in the general election because the issues that framed it, especially those of gender, sexuality, and race, were so passionately felt on both sides and therefore brooked little compromise. McGovern had to fold the sixties social movement left into the New Deal order without losing the electoral constituency of the latter. The black freedom battles of the 1960s had already prompted an exodus from the party of white southerners and suburbanites across the nation. Welfare, abortion, gay rights, and amnesty placed McGovern in an even more untenable position, securing his defeat in the general election and further weakening the Democratic coalition that had dominated American politics since the Great Depression.

In the wake of the convention, McGovern's opponents, not just Republican, eagerly derided the Democratic nominee as left-wing, permissive, and soft. The anti-McGovern forces at the convention had been "working-class and traditional Democrats" and were, according to one of Sargent Shriver's aides, "deeply worried that McGovern is slightly radical and anti-American." Just as the party's social movement insurgents exulted at the liberatory possibilities of a new gender and sexual order, the party's stalwarts, not unlike many on the incipient New Right, saw a world tearing at the seams. Yet it is possible to overstate the electoral realignment that occurred during the 1972 election. Despite the AFL-CIO president George Meany's famous refusal to endorse McGovern and the lack of enthusiasm for the Democratic candidate among most heavy industry and construction unions (the hard hats), the "labor vote" did not abandon the party of the New Deal in nearly the numbers Nixon strategists had hoped. Moreover, despite McGovern's drubbing Congress remained firmly in Democratic hands, and the party even gained seats. For all the attacks on breadwinner liberalism from the social movement left, conservatives had yet to devise either the rhetorical or the institutional might to assert an alternative. The more permanent changes were still to come.[51]

Nonetheless, 1972 was a fulcrum of political and ideological realignment. In this realignment, race, gender, and sexuality worked together in complex ways. The Democratic Party's embrace of the Civil Rights Act in 1964 and the Voting Rights Act in 1965 alone would have produced at minimum a partisan realignment in the white South. But the question of racial equality rarely stood by itself in political contest. As crucial as it was to restructuring American life in these decades, the struggle over racial equality cannot by itself account for the ways that breadwinner liberalism came unglued or for the ways that a right-wing vision of breadwinning nuclear families moved to the center of conservative politics after the 1970s. Only by considering the politics of gender, sex, and sexuality in tandem with—and just as often embedded in—the politics of race can we understand how breadwinner liberalism over the two decades after 1972 became breadwinner conservatism. For some whites, racial animosity fueled their breadwinner politics—in debates over affirmative action ("the best man for the job"), crime, and welfare. For others, struggles over gender, sex, and family were enough to propel them rightward.

Nineteen seventy-two reveals that an outer edge of political possibility had been reached. The heady sense of optimism in the social movement push to expand the nation's circle of equal citizenship had run into the reality of political efficacy. For all the challenges to the breadwinner ideal—the white patriotic, heterosexual male at the head of the nuclear family with which the book began—it remained a powerful political myth. And no one, least of all anyone in the American political class, had come close to devising an alternative that could sway the nation. If the left had forced the Democratic Party to revise or even abandon the myth in 1972 and, in doing so, to rethink breadwinner liberalism, activists on the right had not, despite Nixon's considerable efforts, taken the myth and made it their own. The postconvention headline in *The Advocate* read GAYS VS. STEELWORKERS, a playful but insightful summation of the previous four years of political combat. Any rendering of the new gender and sexual politics of the 1970s as hard hats versus black power militants, antiwar protesters, women, or gay men and lesbians remained far too simplistic. But in that single headline, *The Advocate* described the outlines of the nation's emerging political culture.[52]

10

A STRANGE BUT RIGHTEOUS POWER: THE BREADWINNER CONSERVATISM OF FORGOTTEN AMERICANS

A year before the 1972 presidential election, John Schmitz, a member of the John Birch Society and a well-known Republican congressman from Orange County, California, warned his colleagues in the House of Representatives of a looming new threat, the Comprehensive Child Development Act, a bill to provide near-universal child care to American families. Schmitz predicted "destruction of the basic family unit" if the bill passed. Other opponents were no less hyperbolic. Senator James Buckley (R-NY) insisted that the legislation would "destroy parental authority and the institution of the family." Congressman John Rarick (D-LA) said it insulted motherhood and augured the "death of God." Furious congressional debate over the bill, on behalf of which feminists and welfare rights activists had campaigned passionately, was followed by a popular uproar that prompted President Nixon's veto.[1]

Opposition to the Child Development Act had little to do with children. It was, rather, a response to feminism. The fiery rhetoric of Schmitz and his colleagues marked a defining moment in a new antifeminist politics; the child care debate preceded *Roe v. Wade* by a year and a half and the Equal Rights Amendment controversy by two. Just as Moynihan had claimed in 1965 that the gravest threat to the African American family was black culture's alleged pathology and welfare dependency, so did many conservatives claim in the early 1970s that the gravest threat to *all* families was feminism. They charged feminists with appropriating the state to reengineer the family. Opposition to feminism had resonated in Congress since at least the Title VII debate in 1964, but 1971 marked the debut of a more determined and strident antifeminism, forcing the president, despite the presence of advisers favorably disposed to the bill within his administration, to issue a ringing denunciation in his veto message.

To Schmitz and those of like mind, women's liberation had bullied its way onto the historical stage to lead an assault on the nuclear family. As they saw it, women's liberationists—rendered derisively as "women's libbers"—denied differences between men and women and sought an impossible and anyway undesirable equality between the sexes. Worse, they placed the state above the nuclear family and its natural division of labor, which dictated that men labor in the market and women in the home. Even though most feminists, of all sorts, articulated their abiding support for motherhood and the family in these years and insisted that such things as government-supported child care, reproductive rights, and equal employment were not *anti*family, their opponents remained incredulous and grew louder as the decade wore on.

The child care debate resounded all the more because of its timing. The Winter Soldier investigations had taken place the previous January and February, William Calley had been convicted of the My Lai murders in late March, and the Dewey Canyon III demonstrations by Vietnam Veterans Against the War had filled the Washington Mall in April. Meanwhile, Congress continued to chew over H.R. 1, the Nixon administration's Family Assistance Plan (FAP), which had stirred so much contestation over male breadwinning and federal welfare policy. It was an extraordinary year, 1971. Politicians, activists, and ordinary Americans considered anew what it meant to be a man and a woman in America, what it meant to head a family, and what any of that meant for the role the government should play in the private life of the nation's citizens. From the conservative vantage, the state, yoked to feminism and "rights" liberalism broadly, threatened to supplant the family as the moral center of American life.

Child care opponents, who accused feminists of seeking to destroy womanhood and the family, were in many, if not most, cases the same people who accused antiwar activists and liberals of undermining American manhood—by seeking amnesty for draft violators and by elevating the welfare recipient above the self-reliant breadwinner. Indeed, it became more and more evident after 1971 that African Americans and other non-whites, women, and gay men and lesbians had common political opponents. Those opponents joined together to forge a compelling narrative of crisis, in which the powerful forces unleashed by the new rights liberalism threatened the very existence of "traditional" womanhood, manhood, and family. This was conservatism of both a traditionalist and a reactionary bent. It was traditionalist in that it decried the erosion of allegedly natural values and hierarchies. It was reactionary in that it sought to undo what its proponents claimed government had wrought in the name of a dangerous leftist creed.

As the 1972 presidential campaign demonstrated, the patriotic, heterosexual male breadwinner, the liberal ideal driving expansions of the welfare state in the early 1960s under Kennedy and Johnson, just as it had during the New Deal and World War II under Franklin Roosevelt, was fast losing its coherence. Little about the ideal itself had actually changed, however. Both liberal and conservative versions valorized patriotism, the nuclear family, and male breadwinning. What was new (or resurgent) was the usefulness of the ideal for conservatives, who would deploy its potent myths not to expand the welfare state but to constrain it. Owing in large part to the splits in the Democratic Party brought about by the failure of liberal politics to account for the demands of African Americans, women, and lesbians and gay men, liberals had lost control of their own ideology. Conservative Republican politicians, including Schmitz, Buckley, and Nixon, stepped into the breach with varying degrees of political opportunism and earnestness. In the early seventies most liberals still subscribed to the heterosexual breadwinner ideal, but the reality was unavoidable: breadwinner liberalism was rapidly becoming breadwinner conservatism.

Among those stepping forward to shape the conservative narrative was George Gilder, an obscure silver-spoon, liberal Rockefeller Republican soured by his encounter with late-sixties radicalism. In 1971 he penned an uncompromising defense of Nixon's child care veto. Shortly thereafter he declared himself, on William F. Buckley's television show *Firing Line*, to be "America's number-one antifeminist." In 1973 he continued down this path by publishing *Sexual Suicide*, an attack on feminists for inciting "revolution and reaction, while undermining the most important source of stability in civilized society—the female role in the family." Gilder's conversion from genteel liberal to conservative polemicist evidences the vehemence underlying the reactions to feminism. For many Americans in the seventies, family and the place of women in society were so sacred that questioning them produced a prodigious political backlash, on a scale nearly equivalent to the backlash against the black freedom movement.[2]

Like Buckley, however, Gilder was more comfortable in the intellectual salons of New York and Cambridge than in the living rooms of ordinary

Americans. Though both men wielded influence, breadwinner conservatism was above all a populist politics. It represented not policy but, like
populisms of earlier eras, a diffuse sensibility widely shared among Americans of all religions, Americans of no religion, and Americans of either
partisan persuasion. It was the dramatic emergence of a populist combination of antifeminism and patriotic traditionalism, both understood racially as white, that allowed a new generation of conservative political
entrepreneurs to connect with an inchoate, but deeply felt, quest for order
and certainty in the nation at large. Not yet identified with a single political party, the result, breadwinner conservatism, emerged in debates over
abortion, the ERA, and Vietnam in the first half of the seventies. It was
not yet clear in the early seventies, but came into focus in the 1980s, that
breadwinner conservatism would give the nation's political right the coherent populist message that it had lacked since the New Deal. That message, joined to free-market, antistatist fundamentalism, would prove a
powerful lever in tilting national politics rightward.[3]

What most sharply divided Americans in these years were distinct
worldviews. The feminists and other liberal and left-leaning activists of the
1970s believed in the liberating potential of social analysis. Alongside the
politics of personal experience—the "personal is political"—such analysis
laid bare how people lived and the forces that shaped their lives. New
freedoms and better ways of organizing society would be the result. Individuals existed prior to, and thus could remake, society. Even if those activists held to an ideology, it was an ideology based on sociology. Their
opponents disagreed fundamentally with this premise. For them, the family, gender roles, and the nation were not subject to sociological contextu-
alization and relativism. They were, rather, fixed immutably within a
natural order that cemented obligations between the individual and society and conferred knowable destinies on women and men alike. To subject that order to sociology was to undermine community and ultimately
the self. Society existed prior to, and thus constituted, individuals. Conservatives sought not an analysis of power but an affirmation of tradition.

Thus breadwinner conservatism was a true ideology, impervious to
reason and nuance. For its adherents, this was precisely its value. It anchored them. In dismantling breadwinner liberalism as an insufficiently
broad foundation for civic rights and full citizenship, feminists and other
liberal-left advocates ended up provoking something far more contrary to
their worldview.[4]

•

In the popular imagination, women's liberationists took karate classes, hated men, and demanded the reinvention of the American family. Their opposites celebrated motherhood, welcomed the support and protection of men, and found in "traditional" femininity personal fulfillment and psychic satisfaction. This version of things was exaggerated, but it reflected genuine truths at the opposing radical edges. Many feminist activists were angry, frustrated, and animated. Many asserted that the bourgeois family was a site of oppression. And for that matter, many antifeminist women baked pies and declared themselves members of the weaker sex.

Between 1968 and 1970 Robin Morgan, Gloria Steinem, Shulamith Firestone, Kate Millett, and Germaine Greer rose to prominence as the apostles of white women's liberation, what many called the new feminism. Touchstones from among their writings—the "class oppression of women" (Firestone), the "castelike status of the female within patriarchy" (Millett), and "the female . . . as a sexual object for the use and appreciation of other sexual beings, men" (Greer)—defined the influential and uncompromising new language of women's liberation, especially its insistence that female equality required a thorough recognition, and transformation, of "sexual politics." At that outer edge, their thinking went beyond calls for "rights" to calls for an end to patriarchy. Radicals went beyond broadening the definitions of "woman" and "family" to replace them with something utterly new, something that many ordinary Americans struggled to envision.[5]

Morgan, Steinem, Firestone, and Millett lived and wrote in New York (Greer in London), the hothouse of women's liberation. By the time that movement had reached its zenith in the early 1970s, however, women across the country had been fashioning an opposing worldview for a decade. In 1963, the same year that Betty Friedan published *The Feminine Mystique*, Helen B. Andelin, a California housewife, produced a homemade copy of a book that she titled *Fascinating Womanhood*. Like Friedan's treatise, Andelin's began with the premise that "never before in history" have women been so "disillusioned, disappointed, and unhappy in marriage." Yet unlike Friedan's, Andelin's prescription was for women to submit happily to domesticity and patriarchy, to become "the ideal woman . . . the kind a man wants." The book ultimately sold more than two million copies, and Andelin used it as the basis for "Fascinating

Womanhood" classes, which by the early 1970s boasted eleven thousand trained teachers and four hundred thousand graduates.[6]

In Miami an evangelical Christian named Marabel Morgan wrote a similar book several years later, titled *The Total Woman*. Like Andelin's, Morgan's was initially a dog-eared mimeograph, urged on other women by someone who felt personally compelled to counter the heresies of feminism. And like Andelin, she taught a class based on her writing. When *The Total Woman* was published commercially in 1973, it became the year's bestseller. It ultimately sold more than four million copies. *The Secret Power of Femininity*, written by the Mormon couple Maurine and Elbert Startup, followed. The Startups taught "Femininity Forums" in the Los Angeles area through their American Family and Femininity Institute. Just as women's liberation depended on the circulation of low-cost mimeographed journals and manifestos, conservative writers depended, at least at first, on their own invention and hustle. And while their books might not figure in histories of the sixties and seventies in the way that Brown's *Sex and the Single Girl*, Friedan's *The Feminine Mystique*, and Millett's *Sexual Politics* do, they spoke to a restive and growing constituency. The pedagogic aspect of their endeavors, though similar in some ways to feminists' consciousness-raising groups, was largely their own invention.[7]

Fascinating Womanhood, The Total Woman, and *The Secret Power of Femininity* invoked the moral authority of Christianity. *The Total Woman*, for instance, insisted that the road to "peace, pardon, purpose, and power" was "to plug yourself into the One, the Only One [God]." Taking the Bible's lead, these books praised patriarchy. Men were natural leaders and protectors, women gifted emotional givers. Though domesticity was not without its challenges, women could strengthen their marriages and find happiness in submission to male desire. *The Total Woman* proposed the "four As" for dealing with husbands: "accept, admire, adapt, appreciate." *Fascinating Womanhood* taught that "submissiveness will bring a strange but righteous power over your man." Sex roles were biblically ordained and inscribed in "the fundamental unit in our society—the family." All the authors believed that disruption of the domestic order and its natural hierarchies was the source of women's unhappiness.[8]

Their books appealed not just to Christian Americans but to many working-class women without strong religious beliefs. As educational and professional opportunities gradually increased for middle-class women over the course of the decade, domestic labor—Friedan's "comfortable concentration camp"—lost much of its appeal in those quarters. Women of all classes still wished to be wives and mothers, but for many middle-class women domestic labor was no longer their only fate. However, for working-class—blue- and pink-collar—women, the life of the hearth retained some of its appeal, compared with their options in the labor market. Homemaking could still be validating and identity-sustaining in a way that cleaning other people's homes and offices, typing memos and answering phones, or working in factories might not. For many middle-class women, women's liberation could resolve the disconnect between their occupational ambitions and the cultural expectations of womanhood. For less advantaged women, however, women's liberation promised alienation from domesticity and family without compensatory options in the labor market. Understandably, for many working-class women, *Fascinating Womanhood* made for more compelling reading than *The Feminine Mystique*.[9]

The majority of American women who had a stake in such arguments of course occupied the vast middle ground between women's liberationists and their conservative opponents. In 1969 a trio of professional New York women in that middle declared that "the lamb chop is mightier than the karate chop" and proclaimed themselves the Pussycat League. Self-identified feminists, they nonetheless rejected what they called "militant" feminism in favor of "being sweet, soft, and smelling good and using our attributes to persuade, not force, men to work for women's rights." Jeannie Sakol, Joan Elbaum, and Lucianne Goldberg—a writer, a lawyer, and a former congressional lobbyist—identified "man-hating" as the militants' gravest mistake. In 1971 Sakol and Goldberg published *Purr, Baby, Purr,* a manifesto exhorting women to become "cuddly, gentle persuaders of women's liberation." While Sakol, the leading voice of the group, affirmed such "desirable objectives as equal pay for women, day care centers for working mothers, child guidance centers and abortion reform," she insisted that women must "use our femininity rather than deny it."[10]

Midge Decter, a midwestern-born writer and the managing editor of *Harper's*, carved out another distinct territory between women's liberationists and contented housewives. Like her husband, the neoconservative writer and critic Norman Podhoretz, she castigated all liberal-left activists as unrepresentative of the majority of Americans. But she reserved special venom for women's liberationists. In two popular books in the early 1970s, she accused them of leading women astray and falling prey to the romantic radicalism of the New Left and black power. In her 1972 *The New*

Chastity and Other Arguments Against Women's Liberation she charged that because women's liberationists were "attempting to change the basic structure of human society by making the roles of men and women indistinguishable," the movement was nothing less than "an expression of [women's] deep hatred for themselves."[11]

Decter advanced her own theory of female crisis. In her view, women's liberation was less a yearning for new freedoms than a response to "an inability to manage the rights and freedoms women already have." The key was, as with nearly all antifeminist arguments, difference. Women and men had distinct capacities and instincts as well as different desires and ambitions. To deny those distinctions and differences, in Decter's view, was both intellectually dishonest and psychically perilous. Feminism had been born out of the already reshaped sex roles of modern life, but as women's liberationists improvised in the new conditions, she concluded, their anxiety led them to overreact. Marriage, for instance, "is an institution maintained and protected by women, for the sake of and at the behest of women, and in accordance with their deepest wishes." Women were foolish to seek its revision.[12]

The authors of *Fascinating Womanhood* and *The Total Woman* would not likely have agreed with the members of the Pussycat League and Decter about abortion, child care, and women's economic equality. But they shared a belief that femininity and subservience conferred on women a distinct power, one they were loath to relinquish. Women's power flowed from their difference from men. This was a widely held belief among countless Americans. However, by the mid-seventies a tonal shift was becoming evident in antifeminist politics. The hard edge already present in Decter's 1972 book increasingly defined how opponents spoke about women's liberation. In battles over abortion and the ERA, these opponents, whom we encounter below, saw feminism's sexual politics as not just new but deeply threatening, even evil. They saw them as an indictment of their values and worldview by people they believed did not fundamentally understand them. As a consequence, antifeminists' own view of womanhood hardened into fixed and rigid terms that were not just traditional but ordained and implacable.

•

As the demands of feminists grew more insistent and their massing chorus of critics grew louder, opposition to abortion became one of the unifying positions of antifeminism. By the mid-1970s the antiabortion political movement comprised hundreds of national, state, and local organizations, a funding base in the Catholic Church, and a growing legion of dedicated activists among ordinary Catholics and, as the decade wore on, fundamentalist and evangelical Protestants. The fight they brought to supporters of reproductive rights in the 1970s rattled the nation like few other controversies in the second half of the twentieth century. Only the black freedom struggle was more deeply felt and raised greater passions on all sides.

As we have seen, prior to 1972 abortion politics were largely confined to state legislatures, courts, and referenda. This period saw ordinary women and men drawn out of life's routines into the political arena for the first time in their lives by a deep sense of abortion's moral evil. Ellen McCormack, a New York homemaker who was to run for the Democratic presidential nomination on a right-to-life platform in 1976, told *Newsday* that prior to becoming involved in antiabortion activities in the early 1970s "I was a very contented housewife, happy with my family." But, she continued, "the feminist movement had become the darling of the media and they were pressuring the legislatures around the country to legalize abortions. And they were winning." Though dependent on the funding and organizational support of the Catholic Church, the right-to-life movement drew its strength from coffee klatches and discussion groups—not unlike the women's movement itself.[13]

For the greater part of the 1960s, however, the right-to-life movement was not synonymous with antifeminism. It was, rather, dedicated to saving the life of the unborn fetus. The language of "life" was so ubiquitous that to hear from one group is to convey the message of all. The Missouri Citizens for Life (MCL) declared that free will for women ends "once conception has occurred." Beyond that point "the child thus created has an unalienable right to life which cannot be ignored . . ." Just as the period between *Griswold v. Connecticut* in 1965 and New York's pioneering abortion law in 1970 had seen the emergence of a woman-centered political and legal argument for abortion reform, so too did it see the emergence of a fetus-centered, rights-based argument opposing such reform. Abortion's foes cited the Fourteenth Amendment's clause barring states from depriving individuals of "life, liberty, or property" without legal due process. Thus, early in debates over abortion, opponents of reform asserted that the legal right to life took precedence over the right of individual liberty ("privacy") the courts had begun cautiously to apply to women.[14]

As the abortion debate unfolded in the states in the years leading up to *Roe*, it divided Catholics and fundamentalist Protestants from mainline Protestants and most Jews. During hearings on New York's abortion law in 1969, in a typical instance of this cleaving, the mainline Protestant New York Council of Churches endorsed total repeal, while the Catholic Church opposed even moderate reform. The American Protestant Hospital Association, by unanimous vote of two thousand delegates at its 1970 convention, sanctioned abortions if they did not conflict with the religious views of the woman or her physician. Its resolution emphasized that "the integrity of the family unit and the institution of marriage is jeopardized, if not destroyed, by unwanted children."[15]

Still, most mainline Protestants were uneasy about abortion. The African American sociologist and minister C. Eric Lincoln despaired that "laissez-faire abortion" was "one more example of the retreat from responsibility which seems characteristic of the times." Many religious Americans sought a middle ground because they did not take abortion lightly or wish to see it practiced with greater regularity, but admitted nonetheless to a certain ethical ambivalence about what "life" meant and how one ought to weigh the interests of women, along with men and families, against those of the fetus. In the face of that uncertainty, they saw individual moral conscience as the appropriate basis for the decision. Charles Bayer, a Disciples of Christ pastor and an abortion counselor in Chicago, confessed that, despite his ambivalence about abortion, "the final judge is the woman."[16]

In contrast, within the Catholic Church and among many lay Catholics and most fundamentalist Protestants, individual conscience was regarded as a fragile foundation of social order. It was the first step toward promiscuity. The threat of unwanted pregnancies, in this view, acted as a deterrent to individual sexual misconduct; abortion removed the natural restraints on sexual freedom. Among religious right-to-life advocates, sex, pregnancy, and childbirth were organically connected through motherhood to the divinely sanctioned nuclear family. To allow women's individual conscience to take precedence over those relationships was to invite moral chaos. Lonny Myers, president of the National Association for the Repeal of Abortion Laws (NARAL), told the Illinois Family Study Commission in 1969 that two of the most frequent arguments she encountered from legislators reluctant to change abortion laws were "fear of promoting promiscuity" and "anxiety about the sexual emancipation of women."[17]

Their belief in the sanctity of motherhood and their wariness of female sexual freedom gave right-to-life advocates reason to develop an antifeminist argument against abortion. To posit reproduction as exclusively a woman's choice, linked to her "personhood and dignity," they felt, was to sever the obligations of motherhood and the distinctively feminine virtue of self-sacrifice and responsibility for children. These qualities and burdens were not imposed upon women by patriarchy; they were natural, and women should take great pride in them. Moreover, for millions of women, motherhood remained one of the few identities that allowed them any measure of authority, whether in society or the family. Protecting the life of the unborn fetus remained activists' core argument, but bracing it was a reluctance to see women's sexual liberty as a positive social force. To permit "abortion on demand" was to risk losing the very essence of motherhood, to set women adrift in a sea of moral ambiguity without the safe harbor of a distinct and valorized womanhood. This view was as deeply felt as the attachment to "life" in the worldview of antiabortion activists. Thus, among those opposed to abortion, what had begun as a fetus-centered argument became an increasingly antifeminist one.[18]

For all these reasons, right-to-life advocates saw "state-sanctioned" abortion as an intrusion by government into the private sphere of the family. Legalized abortion, not its restriction, represented government overreach. This notion emerged between the 1969 New York state abortion hearings and the *Roe* arguments in 1972, the same period during which feminists themselves made abortion a core issue in their movement.

When the abortion debate went national with *Roe* and *Doe*, right-to-life forces were prepared. The National Conference of Catholic Bishops declared the first week of October, just before the opening arguments, "Respect Life Week." Attendees Cardinal Terence Cooke of New York and Cardinal Patrick O'Boyle of Washington, D.C., singled out government for blame, focusing on the Presidential Commission on Population Growth and the Future's 1972 report, which had just recommended further liberalization of birth control and abortion laws. O'Boyle told a Washington audience of six thousand supporters at the National Shrine of the Immaculate Conception that all Catholics should oppose "the trends in our society that are attempting to bring motherhood into disrepute." Across the country priests read letters from the National Conference to their parishioners and distributed a thirty-two-page "Respect Life Week" booklet. Right-to-life parades were held in hundreds of locales.[19]

In the closing months of 1972, in the calm before the announcement of the justices' decision in *Roe*, the conservative-leaning, evangelical *Christianity Today* affirmed "that public and legislative opinion is running against acceptance of abortion . . ." There were reasons for such confidence. Despite the passage of liberal abortion laws in New York, Hawaii, and Alaska in 1970, similar efforts had been defeated in nearly a dozen states in the subsequent two years. Right to Life committees operated in more than thirty states, and were joined by a multitude of other state-level groups, such as Voices of the Unborn, Society for Human Life, and United for Life. In addition to the National Right to Life Committee, two other nationwide organizations, Americans United for Life and the U.S. Coalition for Life, had emerged. *Christianity Today* overstated popular opposition to abortion liberalization—polls showed a majority of Americans consistently favored it—but was not wrong in pointing out that a welter of new state laws had not materialized and a rapidly expanding national opposition movement had.[20]

To this movement, the January 22 decision in *Roe* was cataclysmic. Catholic bishops and leaders of Right to Life and Human Life spoke of a "tragedy" and compared the ruling with the *Dred Scott* decision, "which held that a black man or woman is less than human." Cardinal John Cody, chair of the Committee for Pro-Life Affairs of the National Conference of Catholic Bishops, urged followers to use "all means possible" to oppose the decision, a statement that inadvertently echoed the declaration of "massive resistance" following the *Brown v. Board of Education* decision that had rendered racial segregation unconstitutional a generation earlier.[21]

The massive resistance to *Roe* took shape in two approaches. First, antiabortion forces sought passage in Congress of a "human life amendment" to the Constitution, one that would overturn *Roe* and prevent the federal government and the states from making most abortions legal. Second, they sought to render abortion entirely a negative right—that is, entirely "private"—by eliminating all public funding for clinics, hospitals, or programs that provided or in many cases even discussed abortion. This required state-level initiatives and suits to block public funding and enjoin institutions and individual physicians from performing abortions as well as a massive national legislative push. In both approaches, "life" emerged as the legal argument; if the fetus was a person, it had Fourteenth Amendment protections. The moral argument rested on the same notion but included as well the argument that abortion violated the family and subverted womanhood.

Antiabortion senators and representatives introduced the first human life amendments in Congress in 1973. Over the next decade more than three hundred variations were drafted, though only one, in 1983, made it out of committee to a floor vote. But the hearings held on the amendments, especially those that took place between 1974 and 1976, provided a forum for the arguments that were cleaving the nation in two. In 1974, the executive director of the National Right to Life Committee, Ray White, said that any human life amendment had to be "designed to afford the constitutional protection of the Fifth and Fourteenth amendments to the U.S. Constitution to all human beings." ("Deprived of life" also appears in the Fifth Amendment, though in a less directly relevant context.) Mildred Jefferson, chair of the NRTLC board of directors, added a secondary constitutional argument that would in time carry enormous emotional weight within the antiabortion movement: "Man, the father of the child, was reduced to the level of subcitizen with no defined rights . . ."[22]

None of the human life amendments made it out of the Senate Subcommitee on Constitutional Amendments in the 1970s. The subcommittee's chair, Birch Bayh, a liberal Democrat from Indiana and a steadfast ally of the women's movement, stalled and delayed the amendments for years, making him a hero to feminists and a villain to right-to-life activists. The right-wing columnist John D. Lofton called Bayh's behavior "disgusting and disingenuous" and charged him with a failure of moral leadership. Bayh's firm stance made him an early political target of the antiabortion movement, likely costing him votes against Jimmy Carter in the 1976 presidential primaries. He was defeated for reelection to the Senate in 1980 by Dan Quayle, a "family-values" candidate who embraced the new conservative antifeminism.[23]

In the same 1974 hearings, abortion foes also seized on the limited nature of *Roe*, which did not give women an absolute right to an abortion. Senator Jesse Helms (R-NC), one of Congress's staunchest foes of abortion and women's rights, said simply: "U.S. Government funds should not be used to pay for or promote abortions." Randy Engel, national director of the United States Coalition for Life, echoed Helms, telling senators that Congress "has permitted an anti-life philosophy and anti-life programs and policies to become matters of *national policy*, promoted and supported by tax dollars." Helms and Engel, and the growing right-to-life constituencies they represented, sought a complete reversal of *Roe* and a return to prereform abortion laws in the states. But while they pursued that ultimate objective, in the near term they sought to sever all federal funding for abortion provision, including Title X of the 1970 Public Health Service Act, which provided federal money for family planning, much of which went to Planned Parenthood clinics.[24]

Without sufficient congressional support for a human life amendment, right-to-life forces invested their hopes in this severing of government funding of abortions. In state after state they sought court injunctions against publicly funded abortions. By the summer of 1973, NARAL and the ACLU Women's Rights Project had filed suit in New York, Massachusetts, Texas, New Jersey, Ohio, and half a dozen other states—which together accounted for more than half the national population—against public hospitals that refused to perform abortions. In 1975 Henry Hyde (R-IL), along with Representative Robert Bauman (R-MD) and Senator Dewey Bartlett (R-OK), introduced resolutions prohibiting the use of Medicaid funds to perform abortions. What became known as the Hyde Amendment thus represented the national version of a tactic that had been employed at the state level since at least 1970, when New York's reformed abortion law first went into effect.[25]

The adoption of the Hyde Amendment in 1977 marked a significant political and rhetorical victory for right-to-life activists. On the political side, abortion opponents had won a ban on the approximately 30 percent of American abortions paid for with federal Medicaid funds; activists claimed the law stopped five hundred thousand abortions annually. Though it came under repeated challenge in federal courts, the amendment ultimately received the Supreme Court's blessing in 1980 and has remained a cornerstone of federal policy ever since. Rhetorically, Hyde signaled the triumph of the language of the antiabortion movement. In an ABC news report in 1977, Barbara Walters said the question was simply "Should the government pay for abortions?" Stripped of moral complexity and a full analysis of women's rights, this bare-bones language played to the American polity's increasing suspicion of government-supported social programs, especially those that involved questions of sex, sexuality, and reproduction.[26]

The post-*Roe* political debate exposed the fault lines in American political thought and legal practice between public and private, and thus between negative liberties and positive rights. Feminists and antifeminists disagreed about which aspects of family and reproduction should be subject to government regulation and support. For feminists, the positive right of access to abortion, in the form of a public subsidy like Medicare, ensured that the reproductive rights of millions of women were *meaningful*; absent state support, many women's "right to privacy" was hollow. Antiabortion conservatives wished to ban abortion altogether, but absent that, they would leave it a negative right, subject to one's "private" capacity to find and pay for an abortion. Thus did Americans' profound disagreement over the rights and obligations of women as citizens lay the groundwork in the 1970s for the private system of abortion provision that has persisted to this day.[27]

Antiabortion arguments in the early 1970s, however, were not all born of a reflexive mistrust of feminism. In the pages of the nation's newspapers and religious journals, the transcripts of congressional hearings, and the speeches and comments of opinion makers and ordinary citizens alike, there existed reasoned and morally complex defenses of fetal life. Moreover, organizations such as Feminists for Life and the National Women's Equity Action League combined a woman-centered politics with opposition to abortion. Feminists for Life, for instance, issued a fifteen-point program that combined a call for "equal opportunity and equal protection of the laws regardless of sex" and "a strong, flexible family structure" with opposition to abortion. The self-declared Catholic feminist Sidney Callahan called support for abortion a "sell-out of feminist values," even "male oriented" because it defined "control [as] killing." On balance, reproductive rights were a signal element of most definitions of feminism, but there was a vocal minority of women that begged to disagree.[28]

Despite the presence of nuanced voices, it is impossible to ignore the reality that antiabortion politics fueled antifeminism. Writing in *The New Republic*, the Catholic M. J. Sobran held that the abortion rights position was "a tentacle of those secularist and anti-traditional creeds that are usually grouped together under the (inadequate) heading 'liberalism.'" By privileging individual freedom, Sobran bemoaned, feminist abortion proponents denied "that a healthy society . . . must be based on the perception that sex is essentially procreative, with its proper locus in a loving family." The otherwise left-leaning antiwar activist Charles E. Fager, also a Catholic, complained that "militant feminists" had, in their haste to defend the liberties of individual women, too often insisted "that the act [abortion] is of no moral weight whatever." What Fager rightly sensed was the urgency women's activists had begun to feel: that, as Bella Abzug said, the "agonizing problems of millions of women" were being discounted and the opinions of the majority of women ignored. It had not taken long for the grip of rhetorical stalemate over abortion to take hold, with little sign that the two sides even spoke the same language.[29]

•

If the rise of the reproductive rights movement encouraged abortion opponents to articulate their beliefs about women, motherhood, and the family with insistent clarity, the debate over the Equal Rights Amendment (ERA) had the same effect. Senator Sam Ervin (D-NC), a man steeped in southern resistance to federal power and civil rights who professed to adhere to a code of chivalry, complained to his colleagues when the ERA was reported out of the Senate Judiciary Committee in 1970 that the "militant women who back this amendment [sought] to make men and women exactly alike." Four years later, with the ERA stalled in state legislatures, Maurine Startup, now California chairwoman of STOP ERA, warned that the amendment would "contribute to the breakdown of the American home and family." For Ervin and Startup, the ERA represented the central fallacy of women's liberation: a blurring of sex roles and a denigration of mothers and wives. A self-proclaimed "country lawyer," Ervin spoke of the amendment's threat to "rob women" of the legal protections "to which they are justly entitled on account of their roles in life."[30]

First introduced in 1923, the Equal Rights Amendment had long divided women's advocates, splitting those who favored full legal equality from those who sought workplace protections for women. That divide was finally bridged with passage of the amendment in the House in 1971 and the Senate in 1972. In an economical twenty-three words, the amendment forbade states and the federal government from abridging equality on the basis of sex. Within the first year twenty-two states had ratified the amendment; they were joined by eight others by the end of 1973. Full ratification (thirty-eight states) seemed assured. However, led by Phyllis Schlafly and her organization STOP ERA, opponents quickly and permanently reversed the momentum. Only three additional states ratified in 1974, and Tennessee rescinded its ratification the same year. The ERA then went down in defeat in sixteen out of seventeen state legislatures, four other states rescinded their previous approvals, and only one additional state, Indiana, approved the amendment before the ratification period—extended by Congress to 1982—came to an end.[31]

Following its defeat, ERA proponents spent a decade debating the causes of the unexpected turnaround. Many argued that Schlafly and other opponents had lied to the public and to legislators about the amendment's potential effects, distracting them with facetious concerns about unisex toilets and women in military combat. Others suggested that because the courts increasingly interpreted the Equal Pay Act, Title VII of the 1964 Civil Rights Act, and the Fourteenth Amendment as invalidating laws that distinguished unfairly between men and women, the ERA no longer seemed an urgent national priority. Still others came to believe that after 1974, wishing for the divisive issue to disappear, many state legislatures, dominated by men, voted against the controversy aroused by the amendment and not the amendment itself. Most succinct and compelling, however, is the account that stresses the framing of the issue: after 1974 the ERA was increasingly associated not with abstract equality, which polls showed Americans strongly favored, but with concrete changes in the lives of women and men. The eclipse of support for the ERA corresponded to charges that it would erode sex roles, make men and women the same, and undermine the family. It was defeated, in short, by antifeminism and breadwinner conservatism.[32]

No one did more to cement this interpretation of the ERA in the public's mind than Phyllis Schlafly. An archconservative Catholic whose 1964 defense of Barry Goldwater, *A Choice Not an Echo*, remained a right-wing classic, she stood on the shoulders of Jaquie Davison, Marabel Morgan, and Maurine Startup. Schlafly advanced their arguments through an extraordinary work ethic and a disciplined, media-savvy message. She converted the anticommunism of her early-sixties activism into an antifeminism that connected with millions of women and men. Much of Schlafly's success was based on the realization that she could defeat the ERA by positioning herself against the most unpopular and widely diffused version of feminism: the army-pantsed, man-hating image of the militant feminist. In a 1973 interview she asserted that all women's liberationists "hate men and children." Because she presented an unnuanced narrative of polar opposites competing for the hearts and minds of Americans, she became a fixture in print and on television. Schlafly's genius lay not in creating an anti-ERA politics but rather in helping shape existing traditionalist sentiments about women and family into a sharply focused antifeminist political movement.[33]

With equal parts biting wit and relentless determination, Schlafly threw herself into the anti-ERA cause as passionately as she had her earlier crusades against Communist sympathizers and in support of the conservative Taft-Goldwater wing of the Republican Party. In 1972 she founded STOP ERA and converted her monthly newsletter, *The Phyllis Schlafly Report*, into its principal mouthpiece. One of her first dispatches, entitled "The Right to Be a Woman," posed the question "What about the rights of a woman who doesn't want to be treated like a man?" In an artfully simple line, Schlafly captured and condensed the anxieties that feminist challenges to breadwinner liberalism and demands for sexual and reproductive freedom had called forth. Was this the meaning of women's equality? To lose the support of husbands, in both marriage and divorce? To face the market unprotected? To unmoor oneself from the family to compete, economically and sexually, in society as a lone individual? "Surely the right to be a woman should be as sacred as the right to be a man," Schlafly wrote.[34]

Schlafly, along with Ervin, anchored the anti-ERA forces. In articles, editorials, speeches, television appearances, individual discussions with elected officials, and her many debates with feminists, she developed a two-part political strategy. First, she endeavored to neutralize the liberal feminist argument—what she called the position of "business and professional women"—by pointing out to state legislators that she supported efforts to ensure workplace equality through Title VII. "We support you in your efforts to eliminate all injustices and we believe this can be done through the Civil Rights Act," she said. Second, she kept the image of the "totally radical" women's liberationists "who hate men, marriage, and children" front and center. Using Decter's *The New Chastity* and Gilder's *Sexual Suicide* as her textbooks on women's liberation, for her legal arguments Schlafly drew on a 1971 *Yale Law Journal* article that advanced an extreme reading of the amendment. She made frightening claims that women would be dragged into military combat, denied child support in divorce cases, forced into unisex bathrooms, and saddled with all of the burdens, labors, and financial responsibilities of men.[35]

Ervin brought this approach to Congress. In 1972, he read into the *Congressional Record* the *Yale Law Journal* article on which Schlafly based her claims. The ERA would, its authors asserted, make "sex" a prohibited legal classification and thus invalidate all but a tiny handful of laws, institutions, and practices that distinguished between men and women. Ervin's "report," as one Indianan called it, was widely circulated by anti-ERA activists in the states where battles over ratification were most intense, including Indiana, Illinois, Nevada, North Carolina, and across the Deep South between 1973 and 1977. Ervin's reputation as a moderate southerner with a national profile—he had been instrumental in censuring Joseph McCarthy in 1954 and had chaired the Senate Watergate Committee in 1974—lent his objections to the ERA credence.[36]

ERA ratification in individual states was not defeated by Ervin's and Schlafly's notoriety but by thousands of activists and volunteers. They created or joined organizations such as Florida's NEVER (No Equality via Equal Rights), New York's Wakeup (which defeated a state-level ERA in 1975) and WUNDER (Women United to Defend Equal Rights), Jaquie Davison's Happiness of Womanhood, Mississippians for God, Family, and Country, the Texas-based Women Who Want to Be Women (WWWW), the Catholic Daughters of America, and dozens of state STOP ERA chapters. In Illinois and New York they baked bread and pies in 1973 and 1974, hand-carrying the fresh goods to state legislators with notes reading "My heart and hands went into this dough. For the sake of the family, please say no." These activists spoke glowingly of womanhood and motherhood, but many of them also learned the rough-and-tumble art of lobbying in state legislatures and the increasingly essential trade of public relations. They were instrumental in defeating the ERA, and their work between 1973 and 1977 created the institutional architecture for one wing of what became known later in the decade as the pro-family movement. They were forging the broad popular appeal that conservatives had mostly lacked in the postwar decades.[37]

Schlafly, Ervin, and state-level activists relied on rhetoric more than reason, but they made enough plausible arguments to persuade anxious legislators. Taking advantage of the amendment's unknown effects—the courts, after all, would have to interpret what it meant—the anti-ERA forces claimed that the measure would create no new advantages for women while stripping them of needed protections. An ERA would not raise women's pay, they argued. It would, however, make women who chose to be homemakers ineligible for their husbands' Social Security benefits; similarly, divorced women could no longer look forward to child support. Legal experts legitimately disagreed over the likelihood of these outcomes, but anti-ERA activists spoke of them as inevitable. In their most implausible but frightening claim, many ERA opponents argued that the amendment would force homemakers into the market to find jobs, a casualty of the ERA's ironclad insistence that men and women be equal in every respect.

Whatever their merits, all these arguments gained traction because so many Americans, whatever their political allegiances, knew firsthand that the market disadvantaged women. The breadwinner ideal still obtained in many families and communities, and married women were among the most consistent and vocal anti-ERA activists. For them, gender role differences were not only natural but economically beneficial. Women cared for children and the home, and in exchange they were spared the ravages of the market by supportive men who shouldered that burden. In a line of reasoning voiced often by Schlafly herself, married women among the anti-ERA forces argued that their economic dependence on men was a *privilege*. The ratification of the ERA would mean the end of their advantages and the ascendancy of an elusive and unobtainable, not to mention undesirable, "equality." Indeed, in the nightmare scenario the ERA might even give new rights to men.

Anti-ERA activism not only stopped the amendment in its tracks but also marked the public debut of an unapologetically fundamentalist Christian antifeminism. Americans had been joining evangelical churches in the 1960s and early 1970s in a revival of historic proportions. This swiftly growing constituency was committed to conventional gender roles, and it turned to the Bible to solve the problems of modern society. The evangelical chair of the Illinois Eagle Forum and one of antifeminism's stalwarts in the 1970s, Rosemary Thomson, wrote that in the "Judeo-Christian faith, the husband is provider and protector of his wife and children." Citing chapter and verse—1 Corinthians 11:3, 1 Timothy 5:8, Proverbs 31:10–31—she spelled out the ERA's tragic consequences for women, for the family, and for the nation. Constitutional equality for women would "undermine the Biblical role of the authority and responsibility God originally intended for men, beginning with Adam, in the marriage relationship." In formulations like Thomson's, which were especially prevalent in the ERA debates in Bible Belt states, the certainty of biblical injunctions cast both men and women as victims of feminism's latest gambit. As we shall see, antifeminism would find its most fervent adherents in a very particular version of fundamentalist Christianity. Indeed, before male preachers made religious fundamentalism a political instrument in the late

1970s in organizations such as the Moral Majority, antifeminist women like Thomson went public with a political version of Christian faith.[38]

As the tide of anti-ERA sentiment gathered strength, determined feminists attempted to thwart its momentum. In particular, Karen DeCrow and Eleanor "Ellie" Smeal, NOW's fourth and fifth presidents respectively, made passage of the amendment their personal missions. In more than fifty one-on-one debates with Schlafly between 1974 and 1977, DeCrow did her best to debunk the notion that women were privileged and that the ERA would render them more vulnerable to exploitation. In her estimation, the opposite was true. She pointed out that divorced women were often disadvantaged because their years of labor as homemakers could not be assigned a dollar value, whereas a man's salary and wealth could. In the second half of the 1970s DeCrow and Smeal oversaw the "59 Cents" campaign, which stressed the ERA's potential to mandate "equal pay for equal work" and so named because women earned fifty-nine cents for every dollar a man earned for most of the decade.[39]

The economic appeals of the "59 Cents" campaign, though, were overshadowed by four concerns raised by anti-ERA activists. According to its foes, the amendment would eliminate female bathrooms, mandate women's military combat, invalidate any law limiting abortion procedures, and allow lesbians and gay men to marry and to adopt children. The problem posed by these claims to pro-ERA forces was simple: many feminists and women's liberationists wanted gay marriage and adoption, argued that if military combat service was required of men, women ought to perform it as well, and hoped that the ERA would lead to stronger reproductive freedom. In short, they agreed with their opponents. Because DeCrow and Smeal were not the heads of a single movement but spokeswomen for one branch of a sprawling multitude of women's movements, they could not control everything about the pro-ERA message. Thus, in spite of the efforts of DeCrow and Smeal to situate the ERA debate in economic reality, the pro-ERA message often seemed uncomfortably like the caricature painted by opponents: a vast rearrangement of gender roles and sexual norms that reconceived womanhood and the family as many Americans understood it.[40]

•

Schlafly's success in deflating enthusiasm for the ERA depended on recasting the feminist principle of equality as a threat to the conservative principle of conventional womanhood. It rested on the argument that a shared, commonsense understanding of gender roles was under assault from a radical minority that would use the power of the state to reengineer the family. Schlafly's antifeminism was one component of an emerging breadwinner conservatism. As that breadwinner conservatism emerged fully over the course of the 1970s, its tenets minimized women's economic role in American life and valorized the white male breadwinner and his impatience with, if not resentments against, government, people of color, and the counterculture. It brought together in political matrimony Schlafly's contented housewives and the Nixonian hard hats.[41]

As we have seen, the hard hat rose to prominence in the spring and summer of 1970. The previous year, white construction workers had mobilized in Chicago and Pittsburgh against African American demands for access to construction jobs and the Nixon administration's affirmative action Philadelphia Plan. Several months later they sent an equally muscular message. Following the shootings at Kent State on May 4, antiwar protesters had gathered at the corner of Wall and Broad streets in Manhattan's financial district. On a subsequent day of protests, May 8, 1970, as the young antiwar marchers chanted, "Peace now!," more than three hundred hard hats turned Wall Street into a "bloody melee," beating protesters with lead pipes and crowbars, while chanting, "All the way, U.S.A.!" "These hippies are getting what they deserve," said one construction worker. Over the course of a four-hour rampage that left seventy people injured, hard hats, as journalists dubbed them, cheered on by Wall Street employees and police officers, made flag-waving patriotism the province of a tough blue-collar manliness.[42]

The hard hat rioters gave President Nixon a timely gift. Having already absorbed the arguments of both Pete Hamill's "The Revolt of the White Lower Middle Class" and Kevin Phillips's *The Emerging Republican Majority*, Nixon had grown confident that he could turn blue-collar male resentment to his political advantage. In April 1970 he received from the Department of Labor a paper entitled "The Problem of the Blue-Collar Worker," which spelled out how these "forgotten people—those for whom the government and the society have limited, if any, direct concern and little visible action"—could be converted into Nixon voters.[43]

"The President was very happy with our demonstrations in New York City," Peter J. Brennan, president of the New York Building Trades Council, said later that month, "and asked if we had plans for similar actions elsewhere." Indeed, throughout May construction workers, longshore-men, and other blue-collar workers continued to march in New York, wearing hard hats and carrying American flags. That these workers hailed largely from the longtime politically conservative unions in the building trades did not dampen the message. Their season of anger culminated in a pro-Nixon rally of one hundred thousand at the end of the month. The day after the final rally, Brennan, a guest of the Oval Office, presented Nixon with an actual hard hat, emblazoned with "Commander-in-Chief," as "a symbol of our support for our fighting men." Marches in St. Louis, Miami, New Brunswick, New Jersey, and Baltimore followed in the summer and fall. In October Vice President Agnew stirred the populist embers, bemoaning "elitism" and declaring that in "a choice between the high hat and the hard hat, the American people come down on the side of the hard hat every time."[44]

In what many viewed as an increasingly permissive society, hard hats—disciplined, patriotic, and manly—represented an antidote. Between May and September they converted the complexities of domestic police violence, the invasion of Cambodia, and U.S. foreign policy writ large into a contest between two types of men: cowards and heroes. "The hard hats have seen everything they believe in torn down," opined the *Los Angeles Times*. The hard hat demonstrations of the spring and summer of 1970 were broadcast to a nation as weary of antiwar protests as it was of the war, inaugurating a lasting political narrative of the Vietnam War not as a bipartisan foreign policy failure but as a struggle between two countervailing types of men. This struggle soon became the primary way Americans thought about the war, overtaking subtler and knottier questions of the war's purpose and cost. That it did so was one of the victories of breadwinner conservatism.[45]

The highest levels of American opinion making were not immune to this version of the war. On a CBS evening news broadcast the night of the pro-Nixon march, the respected editorialist Eric Sevareid offered a poignant commentary on the ideals of manhood at stake. The spectacle of "a hundred thousand men who work with their hands and minds, not with their books and minds" struck Sevareid as "a different kind of class conflict." It was not "between workers and ownership this time. This is town versus gown with a vengeance . . ." Class was not material, about who made $6.50 an hour versus $9.00. It was cultural, a felt sense of a stable, knowable world called into question, attacked, even vilified. "They were

men reacting not only out of the instinct of patriotism, however oversim-
plified, but in defense of their sense of personal worth, that is, their work
in life," Sevareid concluded.[46]

Sevareid rightly grasped the deep cultural and political anxieties of
many Americans about how civil rights, feminism, and the war had recast
American manhood. With a handful of exceptions, however, white blue-
collar workers sought to become neither symbols of bigotry and resistance
nor avatars of bootstrap self-reliance and heroic everymanness. Their elevation to either status was a function of the national press corps' demand
for story lines and Nixon's calculated tactics. This would continue to be so,
as over the next two decades elite political managers became ever more
practiced at conjuring such cultural conflict for tactical political advantage. And yet underneath the story lines and tactics one can see Americans of all sorts grappling with questions as a known world ripped apart.
In particular, anxiety about how the tenets of manhood would stand up
under assault was a palpable and understandable feature of this period for
many millions of Americans.

Hard hats were not solely responsible for bringing these anxieties to
light. Only a week before hard hats attacked antiwar protesters in New
York, Mrs. Bruce G. Johnson, the Kansas wife of a career army infantry
officer missing in Vietnam, sat before a House congressional committee.
"Our middle child, Bryan, is our sensitive child," she told legislators. A
recent dream had particularly disturbed him. "The Vietcong were beating Daddy but I saved him and we ran away," the child reported. Appealing to Congress to make the status of prisoners of war (POWs) and others
missing in action (MIAs) a priority in negotiations with the North Vietnamese, Johnson then said: "How great a burden would be lifted from
our children if they could believe and be assured that their fathers were
not being treated cruelly." Her testimony was part of a coordinated effort
in the early 1970s—called the "Go Public" campaign—by the National
League of Families of American Prisoners and Missing in Southeast Asia
to dramatize the plight of American POWs.[47]

Between 1969 and 1972, the league, along with Congress and the
White House, went to great lengths to transform the POW into the public
face of the war. Secretary of Defense Melvin Laird first introduced the issue of POWs in May 1969, just after the public revelations of the My Lai
massacre. In November there was a National Day of Prayer for U.S. Prisoners of War in Vietnam, and the following May, Kansas senator Robert

Dole hosted more than a thousand POW-MIA family members in a much-publicized "day of tribute." There were multiple sets of hearings in both the House and the Senate, and the league sponsored a nationwide advertising campaign to win the "hearts and minds" of the American public. By 1971 Nixon and Republican members of Congress had made the release of POWs a condition of American withdrawal from South Vietnam. In the wake of My Lai, the invasion of Cambodia, the student rebellions of the spring of 1970, and the emergence of Winter Soldier and the Vietnam Veterans Against the War, Nixon had seized on a populist issue to transform the war into a noble cause, calling on Americans to support the war in order to fulfill their obligation to "good fighting men" who had sacrificed for their wives, their children, and the nation.[48]

In February 1973 the highly orchestrated Operation Homecoming campaign welcomed released POWs back to the United States. Between February and March, 587 POWs returned home, amid an outpouring of national emotion. The cover of *Time* magazine featured a photo of children holding a WELCOME HOME DADDY! sign. Huge crowds greeted the men on the tarmac at Travis Air Force Base in California and other military outposts across the country. *U.S. News & World Report* observed that "the only good thing" to have emerged from the war was the POWs' courage. Nixon hosted the largest dinner party in White House history, attended by John Wayne, for POWs and their families in late May. There Nixon justified the brutal 1973 Christmas bombings of North Vietnam: if we "hadn't done it, you wouldn't be here tonight." For five months following the January signing of the Paris Peace Accords, the POWs offered the Nixon administration a unifying image of manly endurance, heroic sacrifice, and family reunification around which the country could unite. As these men returned home, they reinforced the sanctity of home itself; they were walking avatars of breadwinner conservatism.[49]

Critics were quick to point out that Nixon had "manipulated" the nation's "hunger for heroes," as a Yale researcher who studied veterans said. Pete Hamill, writing for the *New York Post*, elicited great criticism when he reminded readers that the POWs had "committed unlawful acts" by bombing an enemy in an undeclared war. And even as Nixon feted a few hundred POWs, he presided over a Veterans Administration that was woefully unprepared to meet the needs of the hundreds of thousands of noncelebrity vets returning home. One mother complained to Congresswoman Bella Abzug that "the average GI who was not taken prisoner is not mentioned at all" while "celebrations and ovations [are] bestowed on the POWs."[50]

Just as troubling was that because the POW campaign overlooked and marginalized "the average GI," it masked the class realities of combat and whitened the war in the American imagination. Nearly 20 percent of the Americans who died in Vietnam were African American and Latino, but greater than 99 percent of the POWs were white and Anglo. Most prisoners were pilots, and most pilots were college-educated white men. Paul Ruiz, writing in *La Raza*, contrasted the "emotionalism around the POW" and the "POW as a great national hero" with Chicano infantrymen who were mere "cannon fodder."[51]

Narratives of POWs as husbands and fathers, and their families as victims of a callous enemy, proved difficult to counter. Nonetheless, opponents of the war attempted to fashion a counternarrative. If Nixon positioned the POWs as symbols of national healing, the Senate antiwar stalwart Ted Kennedy (D-MA) wished to do the same for draft evaders and others who ran afoul of military justice during the war. Kennedy called hearings in the spring of 1972 in order to present the counternarrative to the public. During the hearings, a former marine testified that "the one group of men who said 'no' to that war . . . are also victims." A year later a group of families joined together to form the Families of Resisters for Amnesty (FORA). Compared with the 587 POWs, FORA countered, "nearly one million people" including "tens of thousands of resisters in exile or underground," had participated "in one form of resistance or another," and their families too had been irrevocably damaged. In congressional hearings, television appearances, and advertising campaigns between 1973 and 1975, amnesty supporters from FORA, Amex-Canada, the National Council for Universal and Unconditional Amnesty (NCUUA), and other groups praised the courage and moral vision of resisters and their families, so that they, and not POWs, might represent the war in the national imagination.[52]

But over time the POW narrative proved decisive in the struggle to define the war's meaning. Schlafly, demonstrating her full command of populist symbolism, called the POWs "just average American guys" who "put their lives on the line for the United States." Like William Calley, another "average guy," POW-MIAs emerged from the war as symbolic heroes of the right. The POWs joined Calley to stand for a politically useful narrative through which Americans could imagine themselves as victims of the war in Vietnam and to reclaim righteous innocence amid military defeat. A *VFW* magazine article, entitled "I'll Die If I Must," made this explicit. Placing words into the mouth of a POW, the author wrote: "I am an American fighting man. I will go where I must go. Fight when I must fight. Die if I must, but I will never betray my God, my country, my President, my fellow countrymen or fellow fighting men."[53]

The domestic politics of Vietnam turned "fighting" and "loyalty" into populist codes for "class." If Vietnam was a "class war," as James Fallows later wrote, its battlefields extended across the Pacific, from Inchon to the induction lines at home, where class determined who lived and who died. In his 1971 collaboration with the photographer Jon Erikson *The Middle Americans: Proud and Uncertain*, the ethicist Robert Coles touched on this reality. Describing a blue-collar nuclear family struggling with their son's death in Vietnam, Coles asked: "How are they to make sense of their son's sacrifice?" To them, their son is "a hero in a war others decry . . . rich liberals don't by and large lose their sons in war." As did many ordinary Americans, Coles raised this as an abiding question that could not yield to the easy platitudes of politicians. But that did not mean politicians would not try.[54]

Drawing on those sentiments, George Wallace spent much of the late sixties and early seventies shaping the inchoate resentments of blue-collar Americans into a forceful populist discourse of us versus them. During his 1968 campaign for the presidency on the American Independent Party ticket, one of his repeated laugh lines on the stump involved pointing out the anti-Wallace protesters who inevitably gathered at his rallies. These "hippies," as Wallace called any young leftists, were all too eager to shout expletives, he would tell his supporters from the podium. Then, pausing for effect with the crowd on his side, Wallace would offer them "another four-letter word: W-O-R-K." Inevitably, the crowd roared with laughter, and Wallace had drawn the emotionally felt class line that divided patriotic Americans from unpatriotic ones. "Plain working people," as everyone from *The New York Times* to Coles himself called them, had little time for protest and no stomach for sympathizing with the nation's declared external enemies. They *worked* for a living. They shouldered the burdens of the market to support Schlafly's ideal homemakers. They shouldered the burdens of war instead of college students, who protested in the streets.[55]

Wallace's class politics were pure southern demagoguery. He did not appeal to much of the suburbanizing middle-class electorate of the late

1960s and 1970s. But he did not intend to. Wallace spoke to the economically squeezed white blue-collar neighborhoods of Baltimore, Milwaukee, Detroit, and Cleveland and to the small towns of the upper Midwest, Northeast, and South. He cast these blue-collar worlds as male. People there valued hard work and professed a no-nonsense acceptance that life was a chore and forging one's place in it was difficult. "The steelworker, the paper worker, the rubber worker, the small businessman, the cab drivers," Wallace intoned, "are getting tired of the intellectual morons in Washington and in the liberal newspaper offices and the federal judiciary telling them when to get up in the morning."[56]

Wallace's brand of southern populism was to have great staying power in the national political culture. It was a politics of the "little guy," who does his best to be a breadwinner and live up to the obligations of manhood, while others—hippies, feminists, welfare recipients, intellectuals—do no real work and use the state for experiments in social engineering. In his 1976 autobiography, *Stand Up for America*, Wallace recalled a poor tenant farmer from his childhood "who had virtually nothing [but] was ready to stand up for his country." Now, Wallace said of his own day, those "who have everything under the sun . . . are doing their best to destroy our democratic system." Such resentments did not yet have a wide array of organizations and institutions on the right to focus them into clear political goals from below, so they remained in the early seventies subject to Wallace-style demagoguery from above.[57]

The manhood-inflected populist resentments exploited by Wallace—imitated by Agnew, sometimes mouthed by Nixon, and codified by the Nixon aide Pat Buchanan—aimed unsubtly at what was by 1971 emerging as the weak underbelly of the liberal coalition: white men. For the thinkers and politicians most committed to reviving liberalism in the early 1970s, finding an equally manhood-inflected alternative to Wallace's populism was the political holy grail. Those who tried were men like Jack Newfield, the New Left journalist, and Jeff Greenfield, a former speechwriter for Robert Kennedy. Their 1972 book *A Populist Manifesto* bowed to conservatives' charge that the country had abandoned "those human values the ethnic workingman prizes most: family, hard work, pride, loyalty, endurance."[58]

Newfield and Greenfield, along with a handful of politicians who campaigned as "new populists" in the early 1970s, instinctively returned to the male-breadwinner nuclear family as the organizing conceit of politics.

The latter were men such as Daniel Gaby, who ran for a U.S. Senate seat in New York, and "Howlin" Henry Howell, who ran unsuccessfully for governor of Virginia. All of them believed that answering the Wallace-Agnew-Buchanan version of American populism from the left was essential. But their alternative to breadwinner conservatism was to simply ante up on the breadwinner liberalism of the early sixties. Their versions of economic unfairness did not include unequal pay for women, sex segregation in employment, reproductive rights, or any of the other issues women's advocates had been raising since at least 1964. They had little but recycled rhetoric from the 1930s.

That they did not raise these issues or consider them embedded in "class" is understandable, given their backgrounds and the history recounted in earlier chapters. But it points to the continuing power of breadwinner liberalism and the reluctance of even many liberals in the political class to fully grapple with the complex changes roiling American society. Moreover, if appeals to male household heads was to be liberals' only purchase on a critique of economic unfairness and corporate power, they were in trouble. The battles brewing between Davison, Startup, and Schlafly, on one hand, and Steinem, Friedan, and Chisholm, on the other, were revealing that liberals would increasingly have a difficult time regaining purchase on the male-breadwinner mythology even if they could somehow "outman" the conservative populists. Womanhood too was at stake, and the left-wing populists seemed barely to recognize that.

In the first half of the 1970s, the politics of antifeminism and breadwinner conservatism stopped the ERA, helped energize a massive post-*Roe* anti-abortion movement, and successfully painted the left and liberals as anti-family and unpatriotic. Nixon's child care veto in 1971, Schlafly's STOP ERA campaign, and Operation Homecoming in 1973 all signaled the shifting terrain of American politics. On that terrain, two overlapping but distinct contests that were to remain at the core of the country's politics for the next three decades had taken shape. One was a legal and legislative contest, over the role that gender, sex, and sexuality would play in the rights and liberties of the nation's citizens. The other was a question of political mythology. It was a contest to determine how the complex nitty-gritty issues of ordinary life and the disparate beliefs and emotions of millions of people would be represented in a political mythology that appeared self-evident and worthy of public defense and was, ultimately, capable of winning elections and defining national priorities.

To feminists and others on the liberal left, the new conservative populism was sentiment and ideology posing as common sense. Schlafly and other antifeminists countered that being a woman was not the weary grind feminists invoked. Rather, it was to occupy a safe space at the heart of a family, protected from the market, supported by men, and enclosed in a stable moral order. Whether most women and men actually lived in such a world is a different question; indeed, most did not. But political messages that invoked and praised such a world were compelling and persuasive. The power of antifeminism and breadwinner conservatism in the first half of the 1970s was not that they described an actual world but that they buttressed a belief system: they were not sociology but ideology.

As feminists and their allies assaulted and demolished the assumptions of breadwinner liberalism, its conservative variant would prove durable. Conservative resistance to the idea that the lives of Americans deserved close study and nuanced prescriptions offered an appealing alternative to the liberal left's efforts to reconceive women, men, and families on a new footing. Indeed, many Americans found the narrative of nation and family contained within the emerging conservative populist politics reassuring and even instinctive. In the second half of the 1970s populist versions of antifeminism and breadwinner conservatism would acquire ever-larger numbers of adherents and political spokespersons. This would in time include a religious insurgency of historical proportions, which would be one of the leading edges of the revival of the political fortunes of the American right.

PART 4

FAMILY VALUES, 1973–2011

11

THE PRICE OF LIBERTY: ANTIFEMINISM AND THE CRISIS OF THE FAMILY

On the 1976 presidential campaign trail, Democratic nominee Jimmy Carter worried aloud about the American family. "I find people deeply concerned about the loss of stability and the loss of values in their lives," he explained in one of his most earnest speeches. "The root of the problem is the steady erosion and weakening of our families." Carter's prescriptions to stop "the breakdown of the American family" aimed at a tenuous middle ground: in between the feminist and antifeminist movements. He called for national day care, tax policies to help working families, and investment in education, and at the same time he expressed distress over rising divorce and "illegitimacy" rates, juvenile crime, and venereal disease. The question was whether such a middle ground existed, because in American politics "feminism" and "family" had been pushed into unmistakable tension.[1]

The "breakdown of the American family" was a protean political notion, one easily cast into rhetorical boilerplate appealing to one partisan audience or another. In the 1976 campaign President Ford called for tax policies to preserve "the family home, the family farm, and the family business," while Ronald Reagan, running against Ford for the Republican nomination, used the word "family" seventeen times in a nationally televised speech in which he praised "the world of the family and the neighborhood and the America we love." It was all too much for *The Wall Street Journal*'s James Gannon, who accused the candidates of "overworking" the family issue and dressing in new garb late-sixties populist appeals to "the fearful, frustrated middle-class."[2]

"Family" had quite suddenly and powerfully joined communism and civil rights as the battlegrounds on which conservatives would wage war against liberalism. In the late 1960s and the first half of the 1970s a variety of conservatives, many Catholics among them, had come to view the family as under assault by a "new morality," whose advance guard included the sexual revolution, abortion, government-supported child care, and women's equality. In the second half of the 1970s, conservative activists, many of them now evangelical Protestants, began to consolidate the disparate antifeminist constituencies into what they called a pro-family movement. In the conservative mind, feminism, like socialism, communism, trade unionism, and the black freedom movement before it, would wield the power of the authoritarian state against individual liberty and moral certainty.[3]

As this conservative pro-family movement gained traction in the late 1970s, breadwinner liberalism was coming further undone. Real wages stagnated, inflation reached double digits, trade unions were on the back foot, the war on poverty was a memory, and more families than at any point since World War II depended on two or more incomes. None of the decade's three presidents—Nixon, Ford, and Carter—could fully halt the slide, and the political class as a whole pursued policies that led the nation closer to abandoning its commitments to government economic regulation, wage support, and the social contract. The breadwinner economy was always as much myth as reality, but the global economic restructuring that began in the 1970s and continued in subsequent decades drove it nearly out of existence altogether and gave fresh momentum to those who called for a freer market and fewer social welfare provisions. As a result, little was done to arrest the process of privatizing the costs of economic restructuring onto individual families.

As breadwinner liberalism began to lose its remaining traction in the second half of the 1970s, determining who would define the politics of "family" in the national discourse became all the more crucial. To assert their own definition, feminists and women's advocates consolidated more than a decade of demands at two national events: the 1977 International Women's Year (IWY) Conference and the 1980 White House Conference on Families. They affirmed the liberties and positive rights women had already won; called for an expansion of liberties and rights to lesbians and gay men, the elderly, and children; and promoted policies feminists believed supported individual women and strengthened the economic and emotional stability of families. They sought a broad expansion of the social

contract. Yet as left-wing and liberal women advanced their most comprehensive vision of full citizenship to date, "family" was becoming ever
more the province of a revived political right. Conservative family politics,
combined with national economic drift and frightening inflation, derailed
feminists' efforts to replace breadwinner liberalism's definition of the family while preserving the government-guaranteed social welfare that came
with it.

This was so because the family, the foundation of New Deal and
Great Society state expansion, was fast becoming a conceit of conservative
state contraction. Feminists and their allies wanted an expanded gender
and sexual citizenship under the liberal banner of economic security. To
compete with that vision, conservatives put forth a family facing not economic hardship but moral assault. They sought not to assist families economically but to protect them from moral danger. Led by the indefatigable
antifeminist activists Phyllis Schlafly and Rosemary Thomson, and joined
by Catholic priests, evangelical ministers, John Birch Society activists,
right-to-life organizers, and moral traditionalists of every sort, they sutured
together the disparate rhetoric of family decline circulating in the larger
culture into a focused attack on feminism and the modern American
state. By the end of the seventies, though they still had limited political
power and did not yet have their hand on the levers of public policy, antifeminists determined the cast of the national discourse over the family.

•

Nineteen seventy-five was a disappointing year for advocates of women's
equality. The Equal Rights Amendment was defeated in close votes in
North Carolina and Florida; in the latter, state senator Lew Brantley proclaimed passing the amendment akin to "repealing the law of gravity." In
New York, epicenter of the national women's movement, a state-level ERA
went down to defeat. After a hard-fought campaign, the national ERA remained mired in stalemate in the Illinois legislature. Having led the anti-
ERA opposition in Illinois, Schlafly, the nation's most visible opponent of
feminism, was then appointed to that state's Commission on the Status of
Women.[4]

The United Nations International Women's Year (IWY) conference
in Mexico City that same year provided some hope. Hundreds of women
from the United States, and thousands from around the world, attended.

Some returned inspired. Others returned distressed by the tensions between women from the developed north and women from the developing global south. Optimism prevailed, and the American head of the National Commission on the Observance of the IWY, the feminist Republican Jill Ruckelshaus, along with Democratic New York congresswoman Bella Abzug, convinced Congress in the post–Mexico City afterglow to authorize five million dollars for a U.S. conference to be held in 1977. "The heart of all this," Hawaii congresswoman Patsy Mink told her House colleagues, "is that we simply want for the first time in the history of this country an opportunity for women to meet."[5]

That goal was achieved at the massive IWY National Women's Conference in Houston in November 1977. More than two thousand delegates, chosen in state-level conventions, and nearly twenty thousand people in all attended, including celebrities such as Billie Jean King, activist icons such as Coretta Scott King and Betty Friedan, and a bipartisan trio of First Ladies: Lady Bird Johnson, Betty Ford, and Rosalynn Carter. Conference delegates approved a twenty-six-point National Plan of Action that called for ratification of the ERA, women's reproductive rights, government-supported child care, and gay and lesbian rights, alongside nearly two dozen additional items. Like 1963's *American Women*, the report of President Kennedy's Commission on the Status of Women, the Plan of Action was formally presented to President Carter in 1978 with the expectation that it would become the framework for new laws and public policies. The IWY plan represented the high point of efforts to replace breadwinner liberalism's definition of the family while extending the social contract to new Americans.[6]

Rather than mark the birth of that project, however, the IWY only intensified the divisive struggle over women's equality and allowed feminism's opponents to tighten their grip on the political rhetoric of family. Fighting over the IWY lasted two years, from December 1975 until November 1977, and continued both inside the Carter administration and between feminists and the president for the remainder of his term. Liberal Democrats in Congress turned some of the plan's points into legislation, but Carter's chilly reaction to the IWY denied the plan's supporters the national bully pulpit they needed. Conservatives took advantage of liberal infighting to refine their argument that feminists sought greater government authority over American family life. The long imbroglio underscored that while the "crisis of the family" was often an empty populist mantra, the question of who registered in the national consciousness as pro-family mattered a great deal.[7]

Schlafly opposed the IWY from its inception and decried the conference's five-million-dollar government subsidy (a small but symbolic sum) as part of her intensifying campaign to discredit feminism and the liberal state. Schlafly charged that "big money and tough tactics" were behind what she derisively called "Bella Abzug's Boondoggle" and "A Front for Radicals and Lesbians." "We all know the record of the women's libbers in using taxpayer money to lobby for the ERA . . . and to promote the narrow radical view of women," Schlafly wrote to her supporters. Those arguments won a hearing in federal court when the Illinois STOP ERA chairwoman Harriet Mulqueeny filed suit against the IWY commission, charging violation of federal lobbying law, but the judges unanimously ruled that STOP ERA did not have standing to claim injury and dismissed the suit.[8]

It was a mere tactical defeat. In the second half of the seventies, Schlafly conceived a political strategy for the New Right that was to be taken up by political and religious activists in subsequent decades. She grafted the antiliberalism of her 1964 classic, *A Choice Not an Echo*, onto the conservative, populist views of gender, sex, and family that had emerged with such force after 1970. She spread her message through STOP ERA (which became Eagle Forum) and her growing national network of conservative activists. Richard Nixon, George Wallace, the neoconservative intellectuals, and countless other political figures and opinion makers on the seventies' right shared and articulated similar views. But Schlafly understood better than anyone how to link feminism and the state and to make a war on one synonymous with a war on the other. HOW THE LIBS AND THE FEDS PLAN TO SPEND YOUR MONEY, read the headline of *The Phyllis Schlafly Report* in May 1976.[9]

Schlafly portrayed the broad legislative agenda of feminists and other women's advocates as both antifamily and a burden on beleaguered taxpayers. This was the basis of her opposition to government-supported child care. Direct subsidies for child care—as proposed in the Brademas-Mondale bill, a version of the 1971 Comprehensive Child Development Act that remained alive in the mid-1970s—Schlafly told readers of the *Report*, would transfer "your rights as parents of your own children into the hands of HEW bureaucrats." Even the child care tax credit passed as part of the Tax Act of 1975 did not satisfy her. It would "subsidize the careers of working couples who can hardly be described as 'poor.'" Echoing Schlafly, the Texas Pro-Family, Pro-Life Coalition warned that "Big Sister government" under feminist control would "not only increase federal involvement in our private lives but escalate taxes and inflation." Schlafly and those inspired by her made both economic and cultural arguments in their indictment of feminism as an elitist project of middle-class women that would destabilize the family and increase the power of the interventionist state.[10]

Among Schlafly's many followers, male breadwinning was so taken for granted that feminism, not economic necessity, they claimed, was driving women into the workforce. However compelling they might be, such arguments did not take into account the actual relationship between women's paid labor and the family economy of a majority of Americans. Millions of wives and mothers had worked for wages for decades; their labor had lifted families into the expanding postwar middle class. Though many Americans still believed in the breadwinner "family wage," fewer and fewer of them had access to that luxury after the early seventies. Between 1973 and the early 1990s every major income group except the top 10 percent saw their real earnings either remain the same or decline. Over this period the typical male worker saw a 10 percent drop in real wages. To keep their families from falling behind, women joined the workforce in even greater numbers. Between 1950 and 1994 the proportion of women aged twenty-five to fifty-four working for pay increased from 37 to 75 percent. Much of that increase occurred in the 1970s. From nearly the top of the income ladder to the bottom, Americans were fast becoming dependent on the multiple-income household.[11]

Ideological challenges to breadwinner liberalism in the 1960s by the welfare rights movement, feminists, lesbians, and women of color had chipped away at its shortcomings, if not the spirit of its social contract. After 1973, stagnation and unemployment nearly demolished it. A 1978 report of the National Commission on Employment and Unemployment Statistics gave official imprimatur to what women's rights advocates had been saying for some time: the heterosexual male breadwinner–headed family was no more. "Changing family patterns," the report concluded, had broken down "the relationship between individual earnings and household income." Most families had multiple earners. Half of all poor households had *no* earners. "There are full-time career workers among men, women, mothers, youths, and those over 65." In the dry language of social science, the report's authors documented a kaleidoscopic workforce and an infinitely complex landscape of family economies. Anyone could be in the labor market, regardless of sex, age, and marital or parental status.[12]

Sidestepping this reality, Schlafly and her allies accused feminists of celebrating women who performed market work while denigrating women who labored in the home. Rosemary Thomson, an Illinois antifeminist and author of *The Price of Liberty*, who was to colead the national fight against the IWY, worried that "even Christian mothers are being lured into full-time employment outside the home—distracting them from the nurture of their own children." Though Thomson identified a real feminist vulnerability—the women's movement's ambivalence about domesticity and its emphasis on professional careers—her suggestion that the massive female workforce of the postwar decades had been "lured" by feminism into the job market defied observable economic reality. Whereas in the sixties breadwinner liberals had been blind to the increasing presence of women in the workforce, in the seventies breadwinner conservatives were the culprits. They acknowledged the trend, to be sure, yet chose to understand it ideologically, as a result of feminism, rather than sociologically, as a result of economic change. That analysis led not to proposals to assist women in managing the double day but to the launching of a jeremiad against feminism.[13]

After failing to halt federal funding of the IWY, Schlafly and Thomson created the IWY Citizens' Review Committee (CRC) to ensure that conservative viewpoints received fair hearing at the state conventions that would elect delegates to Houston. Led by Thomson, the CRC discovered that feminists in the Labor Department, where IWY planning originated, had prepared a slate of "core" resolutions for state conventions that included support for reproductive rights and the ERA. (Feminists had indeed monopolized IWY planning.) Relentlessly working Schlafly's network, which included dozens upon dozens of state and local antifeminist and right-to-life organizations, Thomson did the hands-on, day-to-day work of crafting the anti-IWY movement, which emerged with greatest strength in the Bible Belt, the southern Midwest, and western states such as Utah and California.

With NOW, NARAL, and hundreds of feminist groups on one side and Thomson, Schlafly, Eagle Forum, and the antifeminist movement on the other, the pre-Houston state conventions became contentious, often malicious battlegrounds over what it meant to be "pro-family." In early 1976

Schlafly called on her supporters to replace the feminist IWY agenda with a "pro-family, pro-homemaker, pro-morality, pro-life image." At the Illinois state convention in June, more than five hundred anti-ERA activists marched out of the hall singing "God Bless America" when delegates voted to endorse the amendment. At the California state convention in Los Angeles, the local CRC protested outside the University of Southern California auditorium where the meeting was held and charged the "backers of the Equal Rights Amendment and abortion on demand" with controlling the proceedings. New York's CRC joined with right-to-life activists to propose anti-ERA and other "pro-family" resolutions for the state convention. When none of those resolutions appeared on the agenda at the convention itself, CRC representatives denounced the strong-arm tactics of the IWY organizers. From New York to California, feminists insisted that they had simply mobilized larger numbers of women than their opponents. Those opponents countered, not entirely incorrectly, that feminists had manipulated the process, freezing conservative viewpoints out of conference planning.[14]

All of the deeply felt differences over women's rights and family were on display at the Mississippi IWY convention. On one side stood representatives of the state's black freedom and women's movements, led by Dr. Jessie B. Mosley, an officer in the National Council of Negro Women. On the other side, conservative women organized themselves under the banner of Mississippians for God, Family, and Country, led by Eddie Myrtle Moore, an Eagle Forum activist, and Dallas Higgins, the wife of the Mississippi Grand Dragon of the United Klans of America (KKK). As in a handful of other states, conservative Mississippi women were able to elect a sizable number of delegates, to win approval of a resolution condemning gay rights, and to defeat the ERA and child care resolutions. Nevertheless, upon heading to Houston with the Mississippi delegation, Moore blasted the "extremely small, extremely loud minority" of women she charged with dominating IWY planning and alleged they were "ruining the Christian-based fiber on which everything worthwhile in this country is based."[15]

The rise of Mississippians for God, Family, and Country illustrates a broader political reorientation in southern, especially Deep South, states in the second half of the 1970s. Antifeminism and breadwinner conservatism had joined and occasionally seemed to replace white supremacy as the foundation of the region's conservative politics. Southern patriarchy and its regime of sexual surveillance, especially its prohibition of sexual contact between black men and white women, had long been intertwined with white supremacy. However, the shift from explicit white supremacy—what Lee Atwater called the politics of "nigger, nigger, nigger"—to the new politics of the family did not go unnoticed by both passionate and neutral observers. "Even if they say they are for God, country, and family, they're the same group of people that have always oppressed black people," said Unita Blackwell, a former Student Nonviolent Coordinating Committee and Mississippi Freedom Democratic Party activist. The longtime *New Orleans Times-Picayune* political reporter Bill Minor marveled at the "new form of militant conservatism [that had] emerged to replace the old-time anti-black militancy of the White Citizens' Council and the Ku Klux Klan." For Minor, Mississippi's conservatives had broadened their platform from opposition to the "black man" to opposition to "liberalism in any form."[16]

There remained a good deal of texture and complexity to southern conservatism in this era. The rising politics of the pro-family movement was neither a front for nor fully a replacement of white resistance to black freedom. Religious convictions about God's ordained family structure and appropriate sexual behavior were anchors of stability for many millions of people who felt deeply and sincerely the tug of what they called Christian values. Yet it is also true that the South's traditional hostility to federal power and the spirit of liberalism provided a ready-made framework for its decisive rejection of the women's movement and gay and lesbian rights in this era. So too did the white South's long tradition of protecting white womanhood from threats both sexual and racial. Charges of sexual deviancy, which had been used against black and white civil rights activists in the 1960s, retained their considerable power. Robert Shelton, the Alabama-based Klan Imperial Wizard, drawing on this tradition, called the women's movement a home for "all the misfits of society, including self-admitted lesbians."[17]

A final point stands out in the historical sweep of the second half of the twentieth century. Looking at a map of states that ratified the ERA, NOW's Karen DeCrow was struck by the virtually "solid South" standing in opposition; if Tennessee's rescission of its earlier pro-ERA vote is included, of the former Confederate states, only Texas ratified the amendment. "They may call it the new South, but as far as I'm concerned they still vote like the old South. These are the same states that voted to keep slavery," DeCrow remarked. A combination of religious conservatism, historical resistance to federal power, and the legacy of a white paternalist and seg-regationist order spelled defeat for the amendment in the South. Anti-feminism and breadwinner conservatism knew no regional boundaries, but a significant number of conservative activists, ministers, congrega-tions, and politicians, much of the movement that would declare "family values" as its anthem, came from the South.[18]

In a valiant attempt to head off a major clash in Houston, the chil-dren's advocate and feminist Eleanor McGovern (wife of Senator George McGovern) proposed a summit meeting of women's organizations in the weeks just before the November conference. "It is becoming apparent that a great rift is occurring between women in this country," she said. McGovern had watched as a handful of other state conventions had fol-lowed Mississippi's example and rejected the feminist IWY agenda. Conser-vatives in Alabama, Missouri, Oklahoma, Ohio, Nebraska, and Utah—states with influential conservative Baptist, Pentecostal, and Mormon churches— rejected the ERA, gay rights, and child care resolutions. (Significant con-servative opposition arose in Hawaii, Montana, Kansas, and Indiana as well.) McGovern gloomily concluded that "women are prepared to verbally attack women, to disparage each other and to polarize against one another." Neither side was in a mood to compromise, however, and the summit idea fizzled. Upbeat that women's rights advocates had claimed the vast majority of delegates, IWY organizers headed to the Sam Houston Coliseum, while Schlafly, Thomson, and thousands of conservative activists began prepa-rations for a counterrally to be held simultaneously in the Houston Astro-dome complex.[19]

State controversies had not been limited to clashes between feminists and antifeminists. One California activist described her state's feminist delegation as "far from united." In the nation's fastest-growing multiracial state, African American and Chicana women, in particular, continued to sense white women's disregard. Less than three weeks before the Houston convention, the Chicana caucus walked out en masse from a meeting of the California IWY delegation to protest their marginalization. In Illinois the National Alliance of Black Feminists (NABF) held a major conference on the eve of Houston called "A Meeting of the Minds: A National Con-ference for, by and About Black Women." Intended both as a supplement to and a comment on Houston and as an internal conversation among black women, the conference addressed health care, education, religion, and other issues through the lens of double jeopardy. Lesbians in several state delegations too had an uneasy relationship with the straight majority. That such divisions persisted remains unsurprising. Born in the crucible of the rights and identity politics of the late 1960s and early 1970s, not to mention the shadow of racism and homophobia, the women's movement was still struggling to forge a unifying notion of womanhood.[20]

Despite that ongoing struggle, the Houston conference produced, over four days, powerful personal experiences and a compendium of feminist demands. *Redbook* described the conference as a "long weekend on an island of women." *Time* called it "some kind of watershed in their [women's] own history and in that of the nation," and one European observer considered it "a kind of constitutional convention for American women." Women of every age, class, and American racial and ethnic group were present in the Coliseum, many having stood in line for hours to get tickets. "ERA Yes" buttons were distributed by the hundreds. Lesbians carried "We Are Everywhere" balloons. "Viva la Mujer," "Human Rights Begins at Home," and "I Own My Own Body, but I Share," and dozens of other slogans adorned buttons, T-shirts, and placards. Coretta Scott King led the crowd in a rousing rendition of "We Shall Overcome." Signs reading PRO-PLAN IS PRO-FAMILY signaled the delegates' frustration that their efforts were cast by opponents as antifamily. Throughout, Abzug kept the proceedings lively and moving with her characteristic passion and New York bluster. With her signature hat waving, she had run through the streets of Houston herself, helping relay a torch that had been carried from Seneca Falls, New York, site of the first women's rights convention in U.S. history. "Some of us run for office," Abzug told the delegates, "but all of us here run for equality, and we never run for cover."[21]

In the National Plan of Action, delegates summed up more than a decade of feminist political work. Liberal feminist demands for economic equality were well represented among the twenty-six resolutions, but so were concerns about older women, homemakers, women in prison, and women who were victims of sexual violence and domestic abuse. Led by Maxine Waters, the congresswoman from Los Angeles, Carmen Delgado Votaw, the Puerto Rican–born civil rights and feminist activist, and Dorothy Height, the longtime president of the National Council of Negro Women, women of color drafted a powerful resolution on minority women. The resolutions affirming gay rights and reproductive rights (which included opposition to the Hyde Amendment and forced sterilization) stirred controversy and provoked ardent speeches against them, but both passed easily in the end. Above all, the delegates clamored for immediate ratification of the ERA, the goal that had eluded feminists for five years.[22]

Across town at the Astrodome, fifteen thousand women at the counter-IWY conference, sponsored by the Pro-Family Coalition, declared their meeting the "Pro-Family Rally" and produced their own catchy slogans: "IWY, International Witches Year," "E.R.A. Is a Turkey," and "God Made Adam and Eve, not Adam and Steve," among others. "Mommy, when I grow up can I be a lesbian?" read one of the Pro-Family flyers that doubled as a newspaper ad meant to shock and offend. Delegates represented a variety of pro-life, religious, and conservative organizations. They listened to speeches valorizing the "traditional" roles of wife and mother (this included a rousing address by Schlafly, who was under armed guard because of the extraordinary tension and publicity), sang spirituals and patriotic songs, and engaged in group prayer. Some of the attendees had just come from protesting outside the IWY conference.[23]

At a press conference on the IWY's second day, Abzug, visibly agitated, said: "No one has a monopoly on the family." It had become clear that this was precisely what was at stake: who could control "family" as a political term and, through it, some sort of national purpose. "It is completely apparent now that the women's lib movement means government-financed abortions, government-supported day care and lesbians teaching in our schools," Schlafly said in a derisive summation of the IWY.[24]

Her invocation of lesbianism was part of the antifeminist worldview: only women who stood outside the heterosexual nuclear family could desire the kind of female empowerment embodied in the IWY. It was also an example of what Pauli Murray had identified a decade earlier as the tactic of "humiliation" employed against the women's movement. Yet plenty of pro-IWY delegates were also anxious about lesbianism. Lesbian rights had been the most controversial and contested issue at the state conventions. The longtime feminist strategist Catherine East led moderates' opposition to the lesbian resolution, while Jean O'Leary of the National Gay Task Force and the IWY Lesbian Caucus tirelessly worked the state delegations to convince ambivalent feminists that lesbian rights were essential to a broad women's agenda. The affirmative vote for the lesbian resolution became possible only when Friedan herself stepped to the podium and endorsed the measure (she said, in an understatement, that "I have had trouble with this issue"). It passed by acclamation, and hundreds of pink and yellow balloons reading "We Are Everywhere" flooded the hall as supporters of the lesbian resolution danced joyfully. Women from the Mississippi delegation, holding signs reading KEEP THEM IN THE CLOSET, bowed their heads in prayer.[25]

The elation of that moment would not last. In March 1978 Abzug and other members of the IWY commission delivered *The Spirit of Houston*, the official IWY conference report, to an ambivalent President Carter. His long record of outspoken opposition to abortion and his Southern Baptist traditionalism did not give Abzug, Gloria Steinem, or the NOW president Eleanor Smeal confidence that he would make the report's recommendations a priority in his policy goals. He appointed Abzug, whom he deeply disliked, and Delgado Votaw cochairs of a National Advisory Committee for Women. Yet his strong personal sense that "family" was a moral issue distinct from women's rights, and his administration's ongoing plan to hold a National Conference on the Family, a major campaign pledge, led him to keep the committee at arm's length. Distrust prevailed on both sides. Feminists began to suspect that they had been welcomed inside the administration only to cool them off. Carter embarrassed the committee by turning a major strategy session into a fifteen-minute photo op, and the committee returned the favor when it issued a press release critical of his handling of inflation. Shortly thereafter Carter fired Abzug, and half the committee (twenty women) resigned in protest. The president's relations with feminists became so chilly that many women's advocates campaigned against him in 1980.[26]

Houston was a peculiar moment in the political history of liberal feminism and the larger project of reconceiving American women as citizens. Even as thousands of women, from all racial and class backgrounds, gathered to forge a national agenda, an aggregation of a decade's worth of activism, feminism was losing its political traction. It was not feminists' analysis of American society that fell short. Rather, their inability, in the face of a largely unsympathetic press, ambivalent liberal politicians such as Carter, and massing opposition, to manage the political narrative of the "crisis of the family" led to their marginalization. Like the president, many Americans saw women's equality and family stability as distinct, even unrelated concerns. At the IWY, feminists had endeavored to show how they were related. But too few Americans were convinced.[27]

This was the paradox of late-seventies American feminism. Stagnating wages, inflation, and the necessity of two or more incomes had begun to sap more families than ever, leaving women with less time at home and more hours of paid work. Yet in *The Price of Liberty*, a representative compendium of antifeminist positions, Thomson crafted a narrative of national decline with little attention paid to that reality. While feminism "lures" women into the workforce, "education professionals" become replacement parents, filling children's heads with "humanist" nonsense. This version of the American economy may have appealed to ordinary men and women with real economic grievances for whom feminism seemed a distant ideology of the already privileged. But it could hardly have spoken to the actual economic realities of most Americans. *The Spirit of Houston* and *The Price of Liberty* offered Americans two distinct analyses of the present and two incompatible visions of the future.[28]

•

Among the twenty-six resolutions enthusiastically approved by delegates to the National Women's Conference was one calling for a "policy of full employment so that all women who are able and willing to work may do so." No economic issue preoccupied American liberals in the mid-1970s quite like full employment. Feminists at the IWY conference joined the Congressional Black Caucus, the AFL-CIO, and leading liberal politicians such as George McGovern and Hubert Humphrey in the shared belief that a national commitment to full employment would remedy the country's economic ills and open opportunities for Americans otherwise doomed to the margins of the job market. As the long postwar economic expansion ground to a halt and millions of people faced unemployment and endured record inflation between 1973 and 1982, families struggled to adjust. More jobs, women's rights advocates believed, would advance the cause of women's economic citizenship, so they joined the liberal push for a full employment bill.[29]

Raw numbers from the period tell an uncomplicated story. Most American families depended on women's domestic and paid labor. Among married opposite-sex couples—surveys of same-sex households were rarely done—wives in the labor force accounted for an average of 26 percent of family income in the decade. Among wives who worked full-time and year-round, their median contribution was 38 percent. Overall, 56 percent of all women under the age of fifty-five in the labor force were married, and in 1978, 70 percent of all women in the workforce had children under the age of eighteen. Women headed half of all families in poverty, and such households represented one-seventh of all American families by 1978. An emerging trend in the immediate postwar decades had continued on its upward trajectory through the late 1970s. The American economy was not organized around male breadwinners.[30]

The numbers tell two different stories of American life in these decades. First, most American families were running in place: in blue-collar and pink-collar families, women had to work for wages just to sustain their families' standard of living. Studies in the second half of the 1970s showed that at middle and lower incomes, women's paid work enabled families only to barely keep pace with inflation; they had little opportunity to better their economic status. Moreover, the number of single women raising children nearly doubled between 1965 and 1990. Women's paid labor was making up for the falling earning power or the absence of men in American households. With declining male blue-collar employment and rising divorce rates, women's work at these income levels did not catapult them ahead; it kept them, if they were lucky, from falling behind.[31]

Second, a growing class divide was becoming starkly evident among women. In aggregate, women's average real income grew during the 1970s and 1980s as a result of the opening of professional and skilled jobs to educated baby boomer women. During these decades, universities and their professional schools, provoked both by lawsuits based on Title VII and Title IX of the 1972 Education Amendments and by a changing cultural climate, admitted more women (or admitted them for the first time). Beneficiaries of the legal and legislative push for equality in both educational institutions and the market, women pursued careers and salaries unthinkable to their mothers' generation. As more and more opposite-sex dual-career professional couples took advantage of these opportunities for women, they laid the foundation of the new urban-suburban professional class (yuppies) of the 1980s and 1990s. The economic world of women began to take the shape of a pyramid. At the top there was an increasing number of jobs available to those with higher education and advanced degrees. In the middle was the traditional range of jobs, mostly in health care and teaching, that had once been the ceiling for women's aspirations. Most women of course still labored at the broad base of the pyramid, in a vast array of service sector and light industrial jobs. Despite the remarkable changes, there remained clearly defined characteristics of most women's market labor: service sector, caregiving, assisting, or serving, and low paid.[32]

At the same time, blue-collar men were losing ground. Between 1960 and 2000, sectors they traditionally dominated—manufacturing, construction, transportation, and agriculture/forestry—went from employing nearly half of all workers in the country to employing less than 30 percent. Meanwhile, sectors that employed large numbers of both pink- and white-collar women—education, health care, retail, finance, hotel and food service, and finance and insurance—experienced the opposite trajectory, surging from roughly one-third of total employment to well over half. These trend lines, heading in opposite directions, spoke volumes about where the country was headed. Moreover, the service sectors that enjoyed the most robust growth in these decades were the ones that featured a large wage gap between the knowledge workers at the top and the menial workers at the bottom. Women were becoming more responsible for filling the jobs the economy created, but most of those jobs came with lower wages and fewer benefits than those the economy had once created for men.[33]

Underneath the numbers was an American economy more chaotic and jittery than at any time since the 1930s. Unemployment had climbed steadily by 1974 to just under 6 percent, which was hardly an unprecedented figure in the postwar years but, when combined with rising inflation, was enough to put a unique burden on ordinary wage earners. Unemployment then jumped to 8.5 percent in 1975 and spent the rest of the 1970s between 6 and 7 percent before leaping to 10 percent in the recession of the early 1980s. Many major urban areas fared terribly. In the second half of the 1970s and the first two years of the 1980s, unemployment in many American cities, including New York, San Francisco, Los Angeles, Detroit, and Buffalo, rarely dipped below 10 percent. Despite notable economic fluctuations, such a prolonged employment slump had not occurred in decades. Inflation hovered around 4 to 5 percent in the early 1970s, jumped to 11 percent in 1975, dipped back down to just under 6 percent in 1976, and then spiraled upward again to more than 13 percent by 1980. The infamous "stagflation" of these years confounded both economists and politicians, whose confidence in Keynesian tinkering was repeatedly undermined.[34]

In the face of economic crisis and political disarray in the middle years of the decade, many liberals called for a federal full employment law. Its advocates saw the proposal as a solution to multiple problems and as a way to unite a splintered liberal coalition. For African American politicians and the AFL-CIO, for instance, full employment promised a truce over the fight for jobs. In major cities, unemployment in the construction trades had surged to between 25 and 50 percent in the worst years of the 1973–1976 stagnation. In that context, affirmative action compounded white anxiety that black workers were taking "white" jobs. Bayard Rustin had proposed full employment as a salve for interracial conflict as early as 1970. Similar concerns drew many feminists into full employment advocacy. "Jobs for all" had the added benefit of echoing President Truman's Fair Deal and the unfinished business of the Employment Act of 1946, one of mid-century liberalism's most notable achievements.[35]

Congressional Democrats, still in the flush of their post-Watergate triumph in the 1974 midterm elections, hoped to use a full employment bill to highlight President Ford's economic failures and catapult a Democrat into the White House in 1976. Hubert Humphrey (D-MN) in the Senate and Augustus Hawkins (D-CA) in the House sponsored a bill similar to the Human Security Plan that McGovern had championed in 1970. The Humphrey-Hawkins bill would pledge the president to work with state governors to keep unemployment below 3 percent. Targets would be met largely through traditional Keynesian fiscal and monetary strategies, but when necessary, the bill gave the president authority to create jobs "through reservoirs of federally operated employment projects and private nonprofit employment projects . . ." Democrats believed that even absent its passage, the bill would resonate with a public facing double-digit unemployment and Ford's unpromising economic policies, including his much-maligned WIN ("Whip Inflation Now") campaign.[36]

The full employment battle set up like a traditional left-right economic debate. Democrats hoped that Humphrey-Hawkins would revive the Keynesian formula many believed was the centerpiece of the remarkable sixties expansion but that had proven unable to counteract the unemployment-inflation combination of the mid-1970s. Republicans, flummoxed by stagflation themselves, increasingly looked to their right wing for fresh ideas. The latter included healthy doses of deregulation, tax cuts, and welfare state belt tightening, a formula that was not yet Republican orthodoxy but that had gained substantial traction since 1964. The conservative senator Robert Taft, Jr. (R-OH), for instance, favored tax cuts, which would allegedly yield "new factories which go on producing and hiring for years."[37]

Debate over full employment, however, revealed that neither conservatives nor most liberals had yet abandoned the male-breadwinner model of the economy. Indeed, in the summer of 1973, less than three years before the full employment hearings, Congress's Joint Economic Committee held multiple sessions on the "economic problems of women." Some of the hearings were so poorly attended that Aileen Hernandez, NOW cofounder and former EEOC attorney, opened her remarks by pointing to empty committee chairs and remarking that it was "unfortunate that the men are not present . . ." Hernandez offered a ten-point proposal that called for dramatic new steps to combat employment discrimination against women prior to any consideration of full employment (which was the proposal's last point). Politicians and commentators largely ignored the issues raised by Hernandez, however, and working drafts of the Humphrey-Hawkins bill did not consider welfare recipients, part-time workers, and other categories dominated by women. Worse, one version of the bill contained a clause that imposed restrictions based on "the number of employed persons in a household." As the Northwestern economist Robert Eisner observed, this would "almost certainly [. . .] discriminate against the employment of women."[38]

Some liberals still hoped to rebuild an old political coalition around full employment. After McGovern's decisive defeat in 1972 and the accompanying criticism of his welfare proposals, many liberals backed away from efforts to broaden welfare benefits. The political costs of increased subsidizing of poor families seemed too much to bear. Full employment appeared to be a less perilous approach and had the added benefit of constructing a bridge between white and black working-class voters. Indeed, one historian has suggested that full employment liberalism emphasized "male breadwinning as a bond across racial divisions." Understandably, some African Americans and white liberals continued to see the employment crisis among black men as a more pressing problem than sex discrimination. After all, black male unemployment seemed to drive families apart and condemn whole communities to economic marginalization. But the emphasis on male breadwinning repeated the mistakes of the 1960s, privileging a mythical male provider over the pressing realities facing millions of workingwomen.[39]

Nevertheless, women's advocates threw their support behind a revised Humphrey-Hawkins bill. Coretta Scott King, who cochaired the Full Employment Action Council, supported the bill in principle but urged the Senate to eliminate criteria regarding the "number of employed persons in a household." NOW too supported the legislation but argued that the 3 percent target "must be specifically defined as a goal for *each* worker group," lest women's unemployment rate be allowed to drift higher than men's. The final bill, called the Full Employment and Balanced Growth Act, which President Carter signed into law in 1978, replaced the household workers criteria with a slightly less discriminatory household income threshold but did not include targeted quotas for different subgroups of workers. In the end, the act was little more than a symbolic liberal victory. Carter and each subsequent president ignored most of its provisions.[40]

Instead of committing the nation to full employment, Carter and congressional liberals took the first halting steps toward what became known as neoliberalism, a politics of deregulated markets and reduced domestic social welfare spending. The term itself denoted not the welfare liberalism of the New Deal and Great Society, but a "new" form of traditional, free-market liberal ideas—the "classic" liberalism of Adam Smith, updated by Friedrich Hayek and Milton Friedman. What California Governor Jerry Brown famously called "the era of limits" hamstrung late-seventies liberals. Forced to choose between fighting unemployment or spiraling inflation, Carter and mainstream liberals largely chose the latter, a decision opposed by the Democratic Party's left, led by Ted Kennedy (D-MA). Sustaining New Deal and Great Society programs would have required an expansionary budget (and taxes), something Democrats believed would worsen inflation and hurt the president and the party politically. Carter's budgets, his confrontation with unions over wage increases, and his support for a variety of deregulatory proposals together helped move the Democratic Party's economic policies toward the political center. Feminist hopes for an expanding economic citizenship for women had run into a massive economic downturn and a reluctant liberal establishment.[41]

More than a decade of social-movement activism since the Great Society failed to secure government-supported benefits to offset the capitalist restructuring of the American economy. Feminists and women's advocates achieved a handful of legislative changes that made women's participation in market work more equal and humane and their economic citizenship more fully recognized. But in the face of the failure to secure government-supported child care, the stagnation (and then decline) of the minimum wage, deindustrialization, and the ongoing shift to a service economy and away from manufacturing, the legislative changes look less impressive. The gender and sexual "revolution" of the sixties and seventies had begun to redefine the citizen subject without meaningfully shielding it from large-scale economic change. New liberties and freedoms, negative rights, had been gained far faster than positive rights entitling Americans to protection and assistance. New freedoms had been won, but the social contract was fraying.

•

Every valence of the American family—economic, emotional, and social—was shifting. As an economic unit, families were adjusting to deindustrialization, the rise of a service-knowledge economy, the flattening of real wages, and the feminization of poverty. Emotionally, marriage had become more fragile, its bonds more fleeting and less durable. By the 1980s, first opposite-sex marriages were no longer the principal institution through which over a lifetime people experienced sex or raised children, and 40 percent of all Americans born in the 1970s would at some point in their lives live with a single parent. Marriage endured and remained much sought after, but it did so as one component of a much more complex and varied landscape of American families.[42]

Nothing during the seventies seemed to bolster conservative laments about the breakdown of the family quite like the rising divorce rate. It had been steadily climbing since the 1920s, but it spiked in the late 1970s and early 1980s. Indeed, the lower divorce rates of the decade and a half after World War II were aberrations in the century's trends, and by 1980, 50 percent of all marriages ended in divorce. Another shift became apparent as well. Until the 1970s, divorced people, especially women, tended to remarry at very high rates. Remarriage rates had begun to fall in the 1960s, however, and continued to do so through the end of the century. By 2000 half of all divorced women had not remarried (or even lived with a partner) within five years.[43]

Conservative activists looked at the increasing fragility of marriage and connected it to the rise of women's movement activism. Antifeminists typically blamed the rising divorce rate on the women's movement's support for no-fault divorce laws. Less partisan observers, however, noted several facts. Divorce rates had begun to rise when most states adopted no-fault rules, but the majority of states had adopted a de facto no-fault practice between the late 1950s and the mid-1960s, well before the rise of feminist activism on the issue. Moreover, according to most statistics, men, as often as women, initiated divorce proceedings.[44]

Despite conservative laments, most Americans did not view the rising divorce rate as a natural consequence of feminism. Many mainline Protestants and progressive Catholics in particular saw the decline of marriage as part of a larger decline in social and communitarian values. In their view, rampant individualism had made marriage disposable, a lifestyle choice subject to whim rather than a bedrock social institution buttressed by the community. An alternative interpretation was provided by the Christian academic sociologist John Scanzoni, who wrote that marriage had simply "changed to accommodate individual rather than traditional interests," adding that rather than bemoan the changes, Christians ought to "raise aspirations aimed at new family traditions." Still other Americans saw the rising divorce rate as regrettable but acceptable and as a sign of a new frankness about human relationships and of a greater willingness to end unsuccessful marriages. Bob Frishman, writing about families for the liberal group People for the American Way, argued: "Dissatisfaction with a specific spouse, not disillusionment with marriage, is almost always the cause of divorce." Society is better off, Frishman insisted, "when people are free to unmake bad marriages and remake better ones." Divorce was not desirable, in this view, but it remained preferable to forcing people to live with unhappy or destructive relationships.[45]

As families grew more complex, a single model for how to construct them became more elusive. Two opposing views of the family arose in response. One came from feminists, who put forward the notion of choice. Drained by the brutal war over women's rights in the first half of the decade, and faced with continuing right-wing charges that feminists hated men and the family, liberal feminist leaders such as Steinem, Abzug, and Smeal fashioned a politics they believed capable of surviving in a hostile world: choice feminism. They incorporated selected elements of radical, lesbian, and Third World feminism into a liberal framework while distancing themselves from militant critiques of the "bourgeois family." (The IWY represented one of the first steps in this project.) Their central claim was deceptively simple: women ought to be free to choose the content of their lives. Marriage and motherhood were choices. Women could choose to have careers or to become homemakers, or they could combine market work and family work in creative ways. Even sexuality, whatever its biological basis, had to be understood as a choice, rooted as it was in women's right to control their own bodies.[46]

Choice feminism demanded a specific kind of privacy alongside a particular set of public supports. Choice feminists asserted that marriage, reproduction, sexuality, and family structure were choices. Whom one married (or loved), when, and under what conditions one engaged in sex, and how, when, and under what conditions women had children were decisions made in the private world of individual choice. From this perspective, laws restricting divorce, regulating abortion, and prohibiting certain sexual acts (or sexualities) all were invasions of the private sphere by an unwelcome state. This was the privacy, the negative right of freedom, that feminists and lesbians and gay men had claimed since the early 1960s.

Realization of the full possibilities of choice, however, required positive rights and certain kinds of state intervention. Choice was meaningless for many women if the state did not assist in child care, provide access to abortion for poor women, and level the economic playing field by attacking sex discrimination (and sexual harassment) in employment. From Title VII in 1964 through the Pregnancy Discrimination Act in 1978, women's rights legislation, in the choice view, represented an essential recasting of both the public world of work and the private world of sex, in the process liberating women into full citizenship. In more left-leaning formulations, the state would also guarantee full employment, attack poverty, and guarantee affirmative action.[47]

These positions, so necessary in the eyes of women's rights advocates, opened them to accusations that they trusted the state more than parents, that they would empower government bureaucrats over families, and that they valued individual liberty more than social stability. To be certain, "family" was fashioned into a simplistic antifeminist rhetorical trope. Yet feminists themselves could not avoid their own complex debate about how best to achieve the kinds of families they envisioned, how best to balance a forthright individualism with women's social embeddedness in families. "Choice" represented a center-left attempt to build the most capacious feminist umbrella possible and thereby to draw as many Americans under it as possible. Its middle-class bias and emphasis on liberty and individualism were evident, but all political versions of "choice" except the most bourgeois-professional came anchored to a set of state-guaranteed rights. That had been the lesson of more than a century of feminist agitation in the United States: women's equality, like the equality of other citizens long marginal in the polity, required an assertive state.[48]

The other view of the family came from pro-family conservatives, who held the opposing interpretation of privacy and public responsibility.

To them, privacy protected the rights of parents to shape the moral content of family life. Privacy was the barrier that stood between Christian families and the secular world. Legal abortion, lax obscenity and pornography laws, the Equal Rights Amendment, government-supported child care, and gay and lesbian rights represented radical invasions of this private world of morality. Through such measures the secular state imposed unwelcome, even loathsome, values and practices on families and violated the rights of parents. The outlines of this broad position came into focus at the 1977 National Parents' Rights Conference in Chicago, which issued "Organizing Paper Number 1," proclaiming the pressing need to "reestablish the family as the basic unit of society, venerated, respected . . ." Doing so required recognition that "parents are a primary resource for the formulation and execution of public and private institutional policy affecting families and family life."[49]

Broadly, the two opposing sides believed that the ordering of private lives was the public's business. But they offered two radically different definitions of family and its connection to national political life. Feminists' aim was less to *order* private lives than to support women and men in choosing the kind of order their private lives would have. Late in the decade NOW defined a family as "two or more persons who share resources, share responsibility for decisions, share values and goals, and have a commitment to one another over time . . . [it] is this network of sharing and commitments that most accurately describes the family unit, regardless of blood, legal ties, adoption, or marriage." The conservative pro-family movement believed this approach relied too much on individual choice and "rights" and not enough on moral discipline and traditional social and sexual hierarchies. In their view, the feminist, or broadly humanist, approach had produced catastrophic divorce and abortion rates, moral laxity, and an unhealthy environment for children. In contrast with the feminist-endorsed family, Connie Marshner, a leading antifeminist who edited the *Family Protection Report* and chaired the National Pro-Family Coalition, countered that a family should be defined as "Persons related by blood, heterosexual marriage, or adoption." The feminist definition of "family" was humanist and sociological. The conservative pro-family definition was archetypal and prescriptive.[50]

The public was unsure which version it favored. Opinion polls consistently showed that a majority supported women's equality yet feared concrete changes in family life, such as shifting gender roles in the household and rising divorce rates. When Americans were asked if they supported the Equal Rights Amendment, 67 percent of those surveyed in 1977 said they did. But when researchers asked additional questions about women's roles, two-thirds of the respondents expressed "conservative" attitudes, including that women should not hold jobs when unemployment was high and their husbands could support them. On the other hand, even as Americans professed a strong belief in "traditional" families, they went about creating an enormous variety of "nontraditional" ones—single parent, divorced, lesbian, gay, and transgender, straight couples with no children, single households, etc. By the end of the 1970s, households composed of heterosexual, male-breadwinner nuclear families with children represented less than one-third of all families in the country.[51]

In the long view, the family that antifeminists endorsed in the 1970s looks like the historical anomaly. Ideologically and demographically, that family was largely a creation of the period between the 1920s and the 1960s. In prior decades, multigenerational families and multiple strategies of organizing the family economy were far more common than male-breadwinner nuclear families. In the middle decades of the twentieth century economic conditions and government social policy made possible a dramatic expansion of the middle class and with it middle-class norms of nuclear family organization (though as we have seen, that expansion depended a great deal on women's market work). By the late 1960s, however, those norms had already begun to shift under a variety of social and cultural pressures, and economic conditions had begun to erode the single-earner family. Indeed, in virtually every family-related demographic category, including divorce rates, age at marriage, and number of children per family, the 1950s and 1960s stand out as historical exceptions to long-term trends. Still, the ideal breadwinner nuclear family remained a powerful *aspirational* concept into the seventies, a reality pro-family advocates were to seize with both hands.

•

Conservatives were hardly alone in their professed concern for the family, however. A vast network of liberal policy and advocacy organizations, including feminist, women- and child-centered groups, progressive churches and religious organizations, social work professionals and academics, teachers, physicians, psychiatrists, and psychologists, the National Gay Task

Force, and African American– and Chicana-led organizations, among many others, all professed belief in preserving and protecting the family. Between 1977 and 1980, President Carter's White House Conference on Families (WHCF) offered this network an opportunity to become more visible to elected officials in Washington and to shape a national policy agenda for the American family.

As a candidate in 1976, Carter had made the promise to host such a conference. He hoped that doing so would win him votes. McGovern's 1972 campaign had revealed the Democratic Party's "Catholic problem" (52 percent of Catholics had voted for Richard Nixon), while the Roe decision and the IWY and ERA controversies had made "family" a central issue on the political right. Child care, women's rights, and discriminatory tax policy meanwhile had made "family" an issue on the left. Something family related thus seemed a sure winner for a politician seeking a safe middle ground. The Arizona Democratic activist Ted Kratzet sent the Carter aide Stuart Eizenstat a report calling "the family and the community the two sleeping issues of the '76 campaign." Carter, the first evangelical Christian with a legitimate shot at the presidency, hoped that "family," a "soft" issue in political parlance, would entice Catholics back to the party, speak to both feminists and antifeminists alike, and attract a substantial portion of the nearly one-third of Americans who were born-again Christians.[52]

However, as with the IWY, Carter's middle ground disappeared in no time. The WHCF conference would be divided yet again between two opposing constituencies. On the liberal left was the flourishing pro-feminist family movement, which boasted substantial support in a Congress dominated by Democrats. Joint House and Senate WHCF hearings in 1978 under the control of the liberals Ted Kennedy, John Brademas, Alan Cranston, and Harrison "Pete" Williams brought leading proponents of this movement to the Capitol; they included representatives from the Carnegie Council on Children, the Black Child Development Institute, the National Conference on Hispanic Families, the National Council of Jewish Women, and the National Council of Churches. Conservative pro-family forces made up the second constituency. Though they lacked the same number of congressional allies in the late seventies, conservatives wielded enough media and political clout to temper liberal ambitions. For instance, WHCF's executive director, John Carr, told journalists that the conference would not be a referendum on the ERA or homosexuality. Abortion too was off the agenda. "After ten years, we can make no meaningful contribution to that debate," Carr said. Nevertheless, the stakes registered high to both sides. "People are angry, nervous, and scared," Ann Rohlen, the Illinois conference organizer, said on the eve of that state's planning meeting. Nothing about family and government by 1978 was without that combination of anger and nerves.[53]

In an effort to salvage some sliver of middle ground, liberals inside and outside the White House steered the conference toward the economic problems of overburdened families and away from the more contentious issues of reproduction and sexuality. An elaborate series of state-level hearings and conventions preceded three national meetings, which together constituted the conference, held in Los Angeles, Minneapolis, and Baltimore in the summer of 1980. More than one hundred thousand people were ultimately involved in these events. At the state hearings, the need for government action to help the poor emerged as the top issue. "Eleven million children live in poverty," the Columbia University social policy professor Sheila Kamerman told an audience of WHCF planners. The Alliance for Black Social Welfare added: "The fact that 53 percent of our nation's Black families are poor must be given high priority by the National Advisory Committee." The Baltimore session prioritized the "economic pressures" American families faced and set forth thirty-six recommendations for government, private business, and nongovernmental organizations (NGOs) to assist and support those families.[54]

Despite liberals' efforts, reprising their IWY conference attacks, leading pro-family conservatives charged that the WHCF was a radical project of feminists and lesbians. The *Moral Majority Report*, published by the Baptist minister Jerry Falwell's recently organized Moral Majority, called it the antifamily conference. "To accept the pre-determined recommendations [of the conference] would be to drive more nails into the federally funded coffin of the American family," proclaimed Janie Triggs, a pro-family delegate from Nevada who attended the Los Angeles conference. To protest the WHCF, Paul Weyrich's Free Congress Foundation sponsored two major pro-family conferences, one in Long Beach and one in Washington, D.C., in the summer of 1980. The many thousands who attended each conference witnessed the biggest demonstration of conservative pro-family politics yet. Well-known conservatives such as Jerry Falwell, Jesse Helms, and Phyllis Schlafly spoke, alongside lesser-known but increasingly important figures such as wife and husband Beverly and Tim

LaHaye and James Dobson, founder of Focus on the Family. All denounced the Carter administration for having sided with feminists and for "wooing the homosexual vote."[55]

The WHCF imbroglio revealed that there was no longer political middle ground—if there ever had been—on feminism, gay rights, and the family. Americans themselves certainly disagreed on key issues, especially abortion and gay rights, but the ideological and rhetorical gap between political activists had become a yawning chasm. And by 1980 that gap had become far more partisan than it had been only a decade earlier: *Roe*, the IWY, the late-1970s gay rights controversies, and now the WHCF had forced politicians of both parties to take a stand on specific issues. This had the effect of pushing the parties farther apart on questions of gender, sex, and family. Believing he could use the WHCF to broaden his appeal to multiple constituencies, Carter had not yet succumbed to that reality. Instead, he provoked a hornet's nest. His staffers, led by Joseph Califano, delayed the conference for many years, changed its structure, and ultimately decided not to have any of the national meetings in Washington, D.C. By 1980, the president distanced himself from the conference altogether. Carter's middle road went nowhere.

The WHCF reports from the three conference sites, delivered to Carter just before the 1980 election, represented a tempered liberal viewpoint. They included a call for government at all levels to craft policies with (largely heterosexual) families in mind—to, for instance, eliminate tax and Social Security policies that disadvantaged married couples. Reflecting the priority given to economic issues, other recommendations called for full employment and better tax incentives for homeownership, enforcement of antidiscrimination laws in employment and housing, affirmative action, and a range of new policies to assist handicapped citizens. Despite planners' efforts, conference attendees debated the ERA and often discussed abortion as well. Still, of the thirty-four recommendations adopted by all three national conferences, only support for the ERA and increased government funding of child care—approved by three-quarters and two-thirds of delegates respectively—stirred the kinds of passions that had been on display in Houston in 1977.[56]

The WHCF report and the IWY's National Plan of Action together embodied a new liberal vision of the American citizen—racial minorities, women, and lesbians and gay men now included—and the changing American family. The vision's authors had not thrown out the heterosexual-male-breadwinner model of the social contract entirely, but together the two documents sketched the social and political possibilities for a broader array of citizens and families than either the New Deal or the Great Society had imagined. Liberalism had traveled a great distance since 1935, the year of the Social Security Act, and even since 1965, the year of Lyndon Johnson's Great Society legislative flurry and Moynihan's report on the black family. The politics of identity, which had flourished on the left since 1965, had been divisive. Yet the divisiveness had not prevented a subset of liberals, working across racial, class, and sexual identity boundaries, from endeavoring to update and reimagine the nation's social contract and in doing so to preserve the liberal accomplishments of the past while putting them to work for a new generation of citizens and families.

Right-wing critics preferred to protect families, not support them. They saw an American family under moral siege, not a family under increasing economic strain. Their remedy was not greater economic and social assistance but greater restriction of sexual, reproductive, and familial life. Led by Richard Viguerie's Free Congress Foundation and Connie Marshner's National Pro-Family Coalition, along with a burgeoning network of pro-family organizations and religious leaders, conservatives conceived the Family Protection Act, which was introduced in the Senate in 1979 by Paul Laxalt (R-NV). An omnibus bill with little chance of passage, it proposed denying federal funds for sex education, school desegregation, and legal services in cases involving abortion and divorce, as well as banning federal support for any form of gay rights, and it called for the establishment of a Family Protection Administration. Largely symbolic in 1979, the bill survived in more limited legislative proposals in years to come.[57]

On the heels of the FPA, in a provocative 1980 article entitled "Blueprint for Destroying the Family," the longtime New Right theoretician Paul Weyrich charged the feminist Gloria Steinem with developing "advance plans . . . to destroy the family as we know it, and redistribute power and wealth." To prevent such a dire outcome, Weyrich insisted, "those who believe in traditional values" had best mobilize behind Ronald Reagan. Weyrich had been roused by the final issue of *Ms.* in 1979, in which Steinem praised the "massive consciousness-raising" that had broken "the conspiracy of silence on the depth of sex-based inequities" in that decade. Much remained to be done, according to Steinem, who urged her readers to fight for "a redistribution of power in families, a revolution in the way children are raised, and by whom, flexible work schedules outside the home, recognition of work done by women (and men) in the home . . ." Emblazoned in the Weyrich-Steinem contretemps was confirmation of the arrival of a new political order.[58]

By historical standards, the model of family set forth by feminists, lesbians and gay men, and others on the broad liberal left was adaptive and sociological. The model set forth by conservatives was archetypal and ideological. In the day-to-day lives of Americans, adaptive families were fast becoming the norm. Indeed, the proliferation of different kinds of families had a sociological momentum that would prove difficult to arrest. But the archetypal family—the white, heterosexual-male-breadwinner nuclear one, the one fewer and fewer Americans experienced as the principal family form—was winning the rhetorical war to set the terms of political debate. This may simply be because archetypes work better than sociology as the material of symbolic politics. Yet it also meant that so long as the archetypal family organized political contest, those pushing hardest to assist and empower multiple kinds of families would remain at a distinct disadvantage.

During the preparations for the WHCF, a broad Gallup survey of American attitudes toward family revealed a paradox. Eighty percent of Americans considered family the "most" or "one of the most" important elements of their lives. A majority of the country supported changes in tax, welfare, and housing policies to help families. Large majorities supported sex education. A reasonable majority supported some form of government assistance to poor families and tax credits for a whole range of support systems, including child care. It was far from the robust state-guaranteed social contract that many on the liberal left desired, and full lesbian and gay rights were still noticeably absent, but neither was the public's attitude fundamentally antigovernment. On the other hand, when Gallup asked Americans which institutions ought to be the "main factor" in strengthening families, "government laws and policies" barely registered. Private sources of support, including family traditions, religion, and counseling were far and away the favored choices. Feminists, lesbians and gay men, and others on the American liberal left knew that negative liberties and positive rights, for individuals and families, could be guaranteed only by the state. But Americans on the whole associated family life with private, not public, concerns. In the coming years, conservatives would take advantage of this important subtlety in public opinion.[59]

In the first half of the 1970s, feminists and women-centered activists had achieved unprecedented influence in American politics. The passage of the ERA by overwhelming congressional majorities in 1972 is only the most notable example. Congress in 1971 passed comprehensive child care legislation, which ran afoul of Nixon's veto, crafted Title IX of the 1972 Education Amendments Act, and ushered into law countless other provisions expanding women's liberties and, to a lesser extent, positive rights. The Supreme Court decided *Roe v. Wade* in 1973 largely on terms favored by women's advocates and between 1971 and 1976 developed the "intermediate" constitutionality test, which assured women near absolute legal equality with men. None of these developments went as far as most women's advocates believed necessary, but together they represented a burst of legislative and legal victories that were thought to be impossible or unlikely a mere handful of years earlier. The second half of the 1970s tells a different story: of the erosion of this political capacity and a steady decline in the power of women's advocates to define a national agenda and to set the terms of political debate. In subsequent decades, the consequences of that erosion and decline would come into ever sharper focus. The market's absorption of women as "citizen workers" had a relentless momentum. But the backlash against feminism, against women's collective cultural and political voice, had its own unforgiving momentum as well.

12

GO YE INTO ALL THE WORLD: GOD, FAMILY, AND COUNTRY IN THE FOURTH GREAT AWAKENING

Ordinary Sunday-afternoon routines changed for tens of thousands of residents of metropolitan Chicago and Miami in the fall of 1978. At one o'clock in the afternoon, after returning from their local church services, they could now tune in to the Reverend D. James Kennedy's *Coral Ridge Hour,* an evangelical broadcast devoted to "sharing the gospel of Jesus Christ." Kennedy, who subscribed to the evangelical injunction "Go ye into all the world," headed Coral Ridge Ministries, located in a crabgrass suburb just north of Fort Lauderdale, Florida. The *Coral Ridge Hour* had joined a crowded television lineup that by the late 1970s included more than a dozen Christian ministries broadcasting around the nation and the globe.[1]

Kennedy was the prototypical seventies Christian entrepreneur, and the fortunes of his church followed an increasingly familiar arc. Under his watch, Coral Ridge Presbyterian Church grew from a congregation of a few dozen in the early 1960s to several thousand a decade and a half later. In 1967 Kennedy created Evangelical Explosion, a training program for aspiring proselytizers of the gospel; a radio program followed in 1974. Eventually Kennedy left the Presbyterian Church in the United States for the more conservative Presbyterian Church in America, a signal of his disaffection from the moderate tone of mainline, often ecumenical American Protestantism. By the 1980s Coral Ridge was producing prime-time television specials with titles such as *Pornography: An American Tragedy* and *Abortion: A Reflection of Life.* When he founded the Center for Reclaiming Christ in 1996, with offices in Fort Lauderdale and Washington, D.C., Kennedy's fundamentalist evangelical empire touched the lives of millions of people in the United States and more than fifty countries. And he was just one preacher among many.[2]

This new generation of conservative evangelical Christian ministers changed the face of American religion. Following in the footsteps of Billy Graham, whose crusades in the 1940s and 1950s had made him the nation's most prominent postwar Protestant preacher, these men—Oral Roberts in Oklahoma, Jerry Falwell and Pat Robertson in Virginia, California's Robert Schuller, Tim LaHaye, and Louis Sheldon, the Texas minister James Robison, North Carolina's Jim Bakker, Mississippi's Donald Wildmon, and Georgia's Charles Stanley, among dozens of others—remade evangelicalism for a new age. Seeking nothing short of national renewal, evangelicals built Protestant churches at a furious pace, turning the United States into the most religious society in the developed world. Mainline denominations lost membership after 1965, while Southern Baptist, Pentecostal, Church of Christ, Mormon, Seventh-Day Adventist, Assemblies of God, Missouri Lutheran Synod, and other conservative, largely evangelical churches surged. By the late eighties a third of Americans belonged to evangelical churches. As in earlier Great Awakenings, evangelical ministers in the 1970s and 1980s spoke to, and for, a society troubled by the perception of moral decline and the sinking status of middling Americans.[3]

They changed the face of not just American religion but of the nation's politics as well. Many among this generation of ministers created nation- and worldwide television and radio networks and crusaded and published on an equally far-reaching scale. They founded research and advocacy institutes that brought their ministries into public policy debates. And not a few of them set up political organizations, local and national, to mobilize "Christian voters" at election time. Prior to the 1970s evangelicals had eschewed politics, believing it to be an earthly concern irrelevant to saving individual souls. That changed in the seventies, as these Christian leaders grew convinced that *only* political activism could save both souls and the country. "All the moral issues that matter today are in the political arena," Falwell said in 1980. "There's no way to fight these battles except in that arena."[4]

Kennedy, Falwell, Robison, and the other ministers built politically on the populist edifice erected by George Wallace, Phyllis Schlafly, and other like-minded antifeminists and breadwinner conservatives. They tapped into a similar moral outrage but couched their message in a righteous absolutism new to American politics. Their churches gave conservatives an institutional presence in every congressional, state legislative, and school district in the country. Along with right-to-life groups, the new evangelical Christian political organizations in time became the right wing's institutional base. By 1994 half of all evangelicals identified as "conservative," and nearly another third as "moderate"; only 16 percent self-identified as "liberal." After watching the role of the new conservative evangelicals in the 1980 election, George McGovern observed: "Their zealotry, self-righteousness and vindictiveness . . . connote something radically different from the authentic conservatism of, say, Robert Taft or Senator Goldwater."[5]

No account of the New Right's investment in the politics of breadwinner conservatism is thus comprehensible without first understanding the ascendancy of evangelicals in the 1970s and 1980s. Fused from disparate constituencies and conservative sensibilities, including anticommunism, free-market individualism, and moral traditionalism, the New Right of the seventies needed something to hold it together. Conservative evangelicalism would ultimately place the greatest resources, organizing potential, and political muscle behind a vision of the conventional heterosexual breadwinner nuclear family, making it the glue to an insurgent conservative movement. In doing so, evangelicals fused the growing conservative attacks on government regulation with people's emotional attachment to family and religion. For these Christian activists, the family was a demarcated private space, where parental discipline and moral instruction held sway. But it was also the elemental social and emotional unit of American life and thus an institution of enormous public consequence. The family was even coterminal with the nation itself.

The two-party American political system produces large, unwieldy, and internally contradictory partisan coalitions. In a diverse nation of more than three hundred million people (by 2010) this fact is structurally inescapable. The religious right's pro-family movement provided an ideological cement that joined the economically disinherited—rural and small-town working-class whites in the South and Midwest—with the affluent bourgeoisie of the ultramodern Sun Belt metropolitan fringe and the middling blue-collar suburbanites of the aging Northeastern industrial belt. Pro-family advocates spoke in the allegedly colorblind language of family sanctity and renewal, crafting a capacious political mythology for a post-feminist and post-civil-rights era. Forging that electoral alliance was a critical element of the New Right's success and one of the signal accomplishments of the conservative ministers, activists, and acolytes between the late 1970s and the early 1990s.[6]

For millions of Americans drawn to its creed, evangelicalism had a great deal to offer. To be "born again" meant to have a second chance at life. The born again righted foundering marriages, got sober, or committed themselves anew to a positive life. Evangelical churches provided marriage and drug counseling and ran soup kitchens. The ideal evangelical family and community offered stability, certainty, and neighborliness in a nation devoted to liberty and the vagaries of the market. The actual American families drawn to evangelicalism and its evocation of "God, family, and country" may not have lived the perfectly ordered lives proscribed by preachers, but they found great solace in messages of moral certainty, unambiguous sexual and familial relationships, and divine forgiveness. These things anchored their convictions and validated their hopes. What they feared was a descent into the moral ambiguity of a new gender and sexual order, which displaced men from the center of economic production and public life and weakened women's moral authority within the family and in society at large.[7]

The religious and community role of evangelical churches in these decades was not so different from the role of churches in any era. But the *political* role of these churches was distinctly of its time. Their dynamic growth and the increasingly public commitments of ministers in these years were rooted in a belief that Christian morality should shape public policy. The New Deal welfare state and the Great Society's "rights" liberalism had extended government into the realm of families, sex, and sexuality in countless ways between the 1930s and the 1970s. For many committed Christians, the state had usurped private morality. Government had become a competitor in the American marketplace of ideas. Religious-right activists fought back. As they did so, they claimed that secularism was itself a state-supported religion. "Who's going to lock up that unbridled, excessive, uncontrolled federal government?" James Robison intoned from his pulpit in a fiery speech urging his flock to vote for conservative Republicans in 1980. Robison knew who: God and his righteous army.[8]

•

William F. Buckley, despite being a wealthy Catholic, exemplified the growing concern of American Christians of all sorts over the direction of the nation in his 1951 *God and Man at Yale*. Stateism and atheism, Buckley wrote, had replaced virtue and individualism as core values in Yale's curriculum. Buckley identified a postwar dilemma that resonated among conservative Catholics and mainline Protestants as well as evangelicals, both moderate and fundamentalist. Where did the future of Christianity lie in an increasingly bureaucratic world defined by the secular liberalism of the welfare state?[9]

Evangelical Protestants in particular worried that secular principles had spread farther and faster at mid-century than Christian values. In the early postwar years evangelical leaders had responded with a combative anticommunism that helped attract new followers after decades of slow or nonexistent growth. They were not alone. Virtually all American faiths enjoyed a resurgence in the late 1940s and early 1950s, with the threat of nuclear annihilation looming. But the evangelical message was especially compelling. Its conservative moral outlook and emphasis on God's punishment of the wicked gave evangelical churches a leg up in a suburbanizing nation deeply anxious about rapid change at home and threats abroad. At his massive 1949 revival in Los Angeles, Billy Graham told his followers that their city had been targeted for an atomic attack because it was a "city of wickedness . . . known around the world because of its sin, crime, and immorality."[10]

Evangelicals' quest to provide "The Christian Answer to Communism," as a 1961 pamphlet put it, aligned them early on with Cold War conservatives. Graham was unrelenting in his condemnation of communism, as was "Fighting Bob" Shuler, whose Los Angeles church, Trinity Methodist, was a hotbed of Cold War conservatism. Carl McIntire, a fundamentalist preacher in suburban New Jersey, used his popular radio program *The Twentieth Century Reformation Hour* to rail against communism and socialized medicine. Evangelicals kept a close eye on local school boards and city councils, monitoring the teaching of social studies, for instance (they worried about students being exposed to "world government"), and the implementation of sex education programs. Believing themselves to be spiritually obligated to oppose "godless communism," evangelicals found new purpose in the decades after World War II.[11]

Christian fears of an intrusive secular state were realized in a series of Supreme Court decisions in the early 1960s. The Warren Court, increasingly devoted to expanding civil liberties after its landmark *Brown v. Board of Education* decisions in 1954 and 1955, turned in the sixties to the question of religious worship in public schools. In *Engel v. Vitale* (1962) the Court ruled that public school prayer represented an unconstitutional violation of the separation of church and state. In *Abington School District v. Schempp* (1963) the justices went further: Bible reading in school was unconstitutional too. (Later decisions by the Burger Court protecting the teaching of evolution and forbidding states to display the Ten Commandments on school property sustained this line of reasoning.) Already inclined to see the modern American state as hostile to religion, evangelicals viewed the *Engel* and *Abington* decisions as a direct assault on Christianity.[12]

The forces of secularism struck another blow in 1970, when the Internal Revenue Service denied tax exemption to private religious schools that practiced racial discrimination. After the *Brown* decisions, it became common practice for southern white communities facing court-mandated desegregation to establish white-only private religious academies. Between 1970 and 1980 alone the number of Christian schools in the United States doubled, largely, though not exclusively, as a response to court pressure to implement *Brown*. By the mid-1980s more than 2.5 million students were attending some eighteen thousand Christian schools, many of them fundamentalist evangelical and most in the South. These academies incorporated religious instruction into their curricula, but their primary purpose, as the Department of Justice, the U.S. Civil Rights Commission, the IRS, and other federal agencies argued, was to resist desegregation. While there were many Christian schools, North and South, that did not originate in this racial scheme, nearly all felt the financial sting of the IRS ruling. Bob Jones University, the nondenominational evangelical university in Greenville, South Carolina, spent more than a decade unsuccessfully fighting the ruling, and evangelicals nationwide found common cause in opposing what they saw as incontrovertible evidence of the state's hostility to Christianity.[13]

By the early 1970s religious Americans saw in these and other developments an analogue to communism in the West: secular humanism. For many evangelical Christians and not a few conservative Catholics, the values of secular humanism—economic collectivism, faith in technology and science, and robust welfare state liberalism—were distinguishable from communism in degree but not in kind. Francis Schaeffer, an evangelical theologian, was most responsible for introducing this idea into American Christian thought in a series of books and films in the early and mid-1970s. Secular humanism was America's "state religion" taught in the public schools. The classroom had replaced the church house as the place of moral instruction. Indeed, since World War II, only abortion has proven to be a more heartfelt issue among conservative Christians than the "secular values" taught in public schools.[14]

In this context conservative, fundamentalist variants of evangelicalism began to flourish following a period of relative dormancy. Between the 1920s and the 1940s fundamentalism, as a particular strain of Protestant thought, had been defeated within most mainline Protestant denominations by liberal-minded ministers who sought to modernize the Bible. Even moderate evangelicals moved in this direction, founding the National Association of Evangelicals (NAE) in 1942 to represent a more flexible and adaptive view of the proselytizing impulse. Fundamentalist voices grew muted but never disappeared and were kept alive by devoted ministers and a small number of Bible colleges. Fundamentalists largely held to the doctrine of premillennialism, a belief that Christ's "second coming" would inaugurate a one-thousand-year reign of the Kingdom of God on earth, and they cast the Bible as the literal Word of God. Until that reign of Christ, however, secular society would remain irredeemable; politics was largely irrelevant. Doctrinal debates flourished within the evangelical world, but not until the 1960s did the conservative, fundamentalist strain again find its footing.[15]

Evangelical churches, and especially fundamentalist ones, enjoyed spectacular growth after 1960. Led by the Southern Baptist Convention, the membership of which tripled from five million in 1940 to more than eighteen million by the 1990s, evangelicals (and Pentecostals and charismatics) drew tens of millions of Americans into their churches and denominations. Growth was steady in the 1960s and then spiked in the 1970s and 1980s, when the Assemblies of God grew by an astounding 300 percent. As early as 1971, the Southern Baptist Convention, the Lutheran Church–Missouri Synod, and the Church of Christ combined had nearly sixteen million members, 8 percent of the entire American population. Most churches were southern or midwestern and prospered in rural areas and the burgeoning suburbs ringing midsize and large cities. Noting these trends, Newsweek declared 1976 "The Year of the Evangelical," and that November the nation made Jimmy Carter the nation's first evangelical president. In a national Gallup poll, 34 percent of Americans answered yes when asked, "Would you describe yourself as a 'born again' or evangelical Christian?" By the 1980s, of the 400,000 churches in the

United States, 110,000 were evangelical and fundamentalist, and an estimated twenty to thirty million Americans attended them regularly. It was a stunning ascent.[16]

Much of this astonishing growth came through the creative use of television. Graham had pounded the pavement and sweated for hours in front of ecstatic live audiences to reach converts. But a new generation of preachers brought religious conversion directly into Americans' living rooms. These so-called televangelists erected huge media empires on a foundation of small donations from millions of avid viewers, advertising revenue, and regular tithing. Most started on the radio, where they patiently built an audience before making the leap to television. Jerry Falwell's *Old-Time Gospel Hour*, Robert Schuller's *Hour of Power*, James Robison's *James Robison: A Man with a Message*, Pat Robertson's *700 Club*, and Jim and Tammy Bakker's *PTL (Praise the Lord) Club* were the leading pioneers in this televised race for American souls, but another dozen, including Oral Roberts, Jimmy Swaggart, Richard Hogue, Charles Stanley, and D. James Kennedy, soon followed them onto the airwaves. Together they made the 1970s and 1980s the era of Christian broadcasting. Viewership statistics were subject to frequent exaggeration, but in 1979 Falwell, Robertson, and Robison alone appeared on 540 local television stations nationwide and commanded a weekly audience of more than twenty million.[17]

Televangelists inspired among believers an emotional sense of a community of righteous but beleaguered Christians. The secular world was wicked and made no place for the Christian faith, these ministers told their audiences. "The Supreme Court has trampled our schools, religious liberties, and our method of government in an egregious fashion," Pat Robertson explained in a 1986 interview. "The government has become public enemy number one, far, far too often," Robison told his congregation. In that hostile environment a loving and forgiving God welcomed believing Christians into a world of moral clarity, fixed principles, and a knowable afterlife. Televangelists cultivated among their viewers a stirring mixture of righteous collective anger at the secular world, the promise of moral certainty, and the possibility of personal salvation and forgiveness of one's transgressions. It was a winning combination.[18]

Televangelists re-created the psychic melodrama and emotional stagecraft of the tent crusade in their studio churches. In a typical Jimmy Swaggart telecast from 1985, the broadcast opens with a visual montage of the ministry's vast global scope as the announcer boasts against soaring music

of Swaggart's "worldwide crusades . . . Bible schools in many countries . . ."
Swaggart is on the road, at a crusade in Milwaukee. When the minister
appears at the podium, Bible clutched in hand, an American flag flies on a
massive projection screen behind him, and Swaggart warns his audience:
"In the last twenty years, the United States has suffered an invasion . . .
Satan is laying a diabolical plot to destroy the citadel of democracy in the
world." He lashes out at alleged critics, forecasts further national decline,
and rails against "You newsmen, you hypocrites! Why don't you write
about abortion?" Tie loosened, Swaggart gains momentum, as the crowd
cheers and applauds at each invocation of worldly treachery and hypocrisy. "The state has no right, sir, to force atheism, secular humanism, ma-
terialism, socialism, Communism, down the throats of our children!"[19]

"God, family, and country" had a hold on the Christian imagination
in the fifties but acquired its central place in conservative Christian politics in the late sixties and seventies, when feminism and antiwar radicalism prompted evangelicals to invest "family" and "country" with firm new
meanings. In 1974 a prominent Mormon leader named Ezra Taft Benson
penned *God, Family, Country: Our Three Great Loyalties*, a wide-ranging
primer on the centrality of free-market capitalism, individual liberty,
and conventional gender roles. (Mormons were conservative Christians,
though not officially part of the evangelical community.) Less an analyti-
cal treatise than a compendium of emotional appeals, *God, Family, Country* saw no contradiction between liberty and the admonition that "the
father is the presiding authority in the home . . . the mother is the help-
mate, the counselor." Indeed, while the license liberty grants in matters of
sex is kept in check by the moral authority of parents and the home, the
license liberty grants in the market is celebrated, even sanctified. Benson's
work was an early indication that religious conservatives had no difficulty
reconciling strict moral codes with unregulated capitalism.[20]

"God, family, and country" was a slogan that gestured at an ideology.
"Country" evoked the taken-for-granted Christian founding of the nation,
which evangelicals traced to a number of elements: the line in the Declaration of Independence that reads "endowed by our Creator with certain
inalienable rights"; the many references to prayer by "founding fathers";
and the first U.S. Congress's directive to George Washington to proclaim
"a day of public thanksgiving and prayer" that would celebrate "the many
favors of Almighty God." Jerry Falwell wrote in *Listen America!*: "I believe
God has blessed this nation because in its early days she sought to honor

God and the Bible . . ." Christianity, evangelicals insisted, had decisively influenced the Bill of Rights, whose separation of church and state ensured freedom *to* worship, not freedom *from* worship. Indeed, among many fundamentalists, the United States was an earthly instrument of God's will. Any threat to the nation was an attack on Christianity itself.[21]

"Family" embodied a set of concerns at once embedded in and distinct from "God" and "country." Biblical teachings, evangelicals insisted, made the family, rather than the individual, the irreducible unit of social organization. Families were governed by a patriarchal father (in God's image) whose role as breadwinner and disciplinarian was balanced by the nurturing and spiritual figure of the mother. Gender roles were ordained and fixed and not subject to human reimagining. "There are those in high places who would radically alter the structure of the American family in the name of social progress," warned the Evangelical Welfare Agency in a typical complaint. Abortion, homosexuality, and feminist demands for equality symbolized the fallacy of secular attempts to alter the family's divine structure. "A married woman's responsibility—especially one who has little children—is first and foremost to be a homemaker, NOT to be a breadwinner," Paul Kroll wrote in *Plain Truth*, an evangelical magazine founded by the Radio Church of God head Herbert W. Armstrong.[22]

One of the remarkable and often misunderstood dimensions of the religious right was the role it set for women. By collapsing politics and family life—by insisting that family morality had to be protected by public policy—the pro-family movement legitimized women's activism. Male ministers may have been the most visible representatives of evangelical politics, but much of the movement's work was performed by women, such as Rosemary Thomson, the anti-ERA activist; Marabel Morgan, the author of *The Total Woman* and teacher of classes by the same name; Connie Marshner, chair of the National Pro-Family Coalition; Jo Ann Gasper, editor of *The Right Woman*; and Beverly LaHaye, a prominent Orange County evangelical activist and minister's wife. Not unlike female-led movements throughout American history, the religious right appealed to many women precisely because it extended women's "traditional" moral authority over family and home into the public sphere.

Quite apart from their beliefs regarding the sins of abortion, feminism, and homosexuality, evangelicals were deeply sensitive to the daily challenges faced by real families. A spate of books and conferences in the mid-1960s and 1970s confirmed that evangelical writers, ministers, and church activists were committed to assisting Christian families and helping marriages survive. Unsurprisingly, many saw irreligion as a core problem. A 1964 volume penned by Southern Baptist authors, entitled *The Church Looks at Family Life*, suggested that to save a troubled home, "Christianity must pervade all our relationships, and especially . . . marriage." Evangelicals promised the fallen Christian that a renewed commitment to God would revitalize marriage. Between 1965 and 1975, evangelical authors published more than three dozen books to guide both the saved and the unsaved toward a biblical family life. Organizers of the 1975 Continental Congress on the Family promised that when "the family is on trial . . . [w]e face an unprecedented opportunity to express the excellence of Christian family life and to be God's instrument of healing for our generation."[23]

In the second half of the 1970s, conservative evangelicals created a furor over the state of the American family without precedent in the twentieth century. From the end of World War II through the early 1960s evangelicals burnished their anticommunism and anticollectivism, built their churches, and focused on saving souls. Between the early 1960s and the early 1970s, as the libidinal politics of the sexual revolution and rising divorce rates emerged prominently in American life, evangelicals developed a family-centered call for moral regeneration. Between 1973 and 1980, however—in the era of the ERA, *Roe v. Wade*, and gay rights— evangelicals, led by right-wing fundamentalists, raised the specter of family breakdown as national ruination. Family dissolution was no longer just a distinct ill subject to Christian remedy. The nation itself needed the same remedy, on a much larger scale. Evangelicals had found their greatest purpose: saving family and nation.

No one embodied this calling quite like the fiery Southern Baptist preacher James Robison, from Pasadena, Texas. Robison built a prominent television ministry in the sprawling Houston suburbs, the James Robison Evangelistic Association. Like D. James Kennedy's church in Coral Ridge, Florida, Robert Schuller's in Garden Grove, California, Pat Robertson's in Virginia Beach, Virginia, Charles Stanley's outside Atlanta, Georgia, and hundreds upon hundreds of smaller churches, Robison's was filled with Sun Belt suburbanites, middling bourgeois Americans inclined toward traditionalism and conditioned to distrust government. With his television broadcast flourishing, in 1979 and 1980 he published three books, *God's Blueprint for Homes That Last*, *Attack on the Family*, and

Save America to Save the World, which warned of great national calamity if Americans did not reconstruct their lives *and* politics in a biblical vocabulary.[24]

Robison's books illustrate the late-seventies political turn of fundamentalist evangelical ministers. First, there is the overwhelming threat: those who seek "to destroy marriage and the family because . . . they sincerely believe these institutions are outmoded" or, worse, "those who are out to destroy these institutions because they want to destroy America." Echoing Schlafly's criticism of feminism, Robison writes that the core problem facing the American family was not economic restructuring but feminist forces "turning women against their roles as housewives and pushing them into the job market . . ." As for men, their roles too have been devalued and diminished by "enemies of the home." An "offensive against the father" has rendered men unable to take up their traditional responsibility for disciplining children, for instance. The "enemies" Robison cites are a mixed lot but dominated by a recognizable handful: feminists, lesbians and gay men, psychologists, and the Supreme Court.[25]

In contrast, the families favored by God are governed by great love, uncompromising discipline, unambiguous gender roles, and literal biblical Scripture. The husband "is the head of the wife," and "the wife is subject to the husband," Robison writes in *God's Blueprint for Homes That Last.* Men rule, but they also incur obligations: to love their wives absolutely ("All other ties are to be severed"), to support and sacrifice for the family, and to devote emotional energy to their wives. "The husband is the one who undergirds, supports, and keeps the home together." For their part, women, "the ladies, the wives, the mothers," are submissive, though short of becoming "slaves." When a woman steps out of the submissive role, she is "immediately debased . . . trying to fill the role that only a man can fill."[26]

Enemies of the Christian family were everywhere. In his autobiography, *Thank God, I'm Free,* Robison tells an illustrative story. In early 1979 he spoke on his television program against homosexuality. His Dallas affiliate promptly canceled his show and invited a gay rights organization to respond on air. "I had been forced off the air," Robison explains, in violation of "freedom of speech, the right to preach." He reached out for counsel among the national Christian community, which had been, he explained, "polarized" by the "crisis." Robertson, Falwell, and J. Harold Smith, the Tennessee-based Southern Baptist whose *Radio Bible Hour* reached millions in the heart of the Bible Belt, came to Robison's aid, with a Freedom

Rally in Dallas. Howard Phillips, the national director of The Conservative Caucus, reminded the twelve thousand cheering acolytes who attended that "the authors of the Declaration of Independence said that we are endowed by our *Creator* with certain inalienable rights . . ."[27]

Phillips's presence at the rally was no accident. That year the Conservative Caucus, a nonreligious New Right organization, claimed three hundred thousand members and 250 congressional district chairs. Phillips liked to claim that within seventy-two hours he could deliver twenty-five thousand letters to Washington, D.C., on any one of a dozen issues. Positioning himself as the glue that held the increasingly sprawling New Right coalition together, Phillips—Jewish by birth but born again by choice—assiduously cultivated fundamentalist ministers and their constituencies. In 1978 readers of the *Conservative Digest* voted him the most admired conservative after Ronald Reagan. Phillips, alongside Paul Weyrich, Richard Viguerie, Edward McAteer, and other first-generation architects of the New Right's political strategy, saw the televangelists and their flock as a crucial part of the conservative coalition in the making, "God's army" marching to the polls.[28]

•

In Robison's *Save America to Save the World*, published in advance of the 1980 presidential election, the Texan gave his followers explicit instructions: pray, vote, speak out, get involved. Fundamentalists had in earlier decades shunned all worldly activities, politics sometimes above all. Now political action was not just religiously sanctioned but necessary for the betterment of the world. "Christians have an invincible weapon to wield against the oppression of either dictatorship or permissiveness," he wrote. It is, simply, "the genuine absolutes emanating from the throne of God."[29]

Fundamentalists such as Robison forged the religious right in the decade between the national midterm elections of 1978 and the presidential election of 1988. Fundamentalist Protestants, alongside smaller numbers of conservative Catholics and moderate evangelicals (and a handful of conservative Jews), made conservative religion a new political force. At its core stood ministers and their churches. But this movement also included policy institutes, political action committees, fund-raising and direct mail organizations, publishing networks, hundreds of state and local groups, and dozens of national umbrella political organizations. Jerry Falwell's

Moral Majority, which dominated journalists' accounts of New Right alliances with evangelicals in the 1980s, played an instrumental role in mobilizing Christian voters, but the turn to politics occurred across a wide swath of the evangelical world.[30]

Before Falwell, Robison, and other fundamentalist evangelicals stumped for Ronald Reagan in 1980, there was William "Bill" Bright. Bright had founded Campus Crusade for Christ in 1952 and turned it into a worldwide organization with five thousand staff members in more than eighty countries. The ambitious Bright was determined to "bring Christ back into government," and in advance of the 1976 national election he began laying the foundation to achieve that goal. He founded Third Century Publishers in 1974 to produce political literature for Christian organizations and in the same year opened the Christian Embassy in Washington, D.C., officially "nonpolitical" but unofficially one of the first lobbying organizations of the religious right. Along with the conservative Arizona congressman John Conlan and a handful of wealthy donors, Bright assumed control of the financially troubled Christian Freedom Foundation and turned it into a political vehicle to "bring the United States back to God by the end of 1976." Bright endorsed Ronald Reagan in the Republican primary that year and hosted a prayer breakfast for a thousand delegates during the Republican National Convention at which Pat Boone proclaimed, "God is working in the political process here." Though he cringed at the election of a Democrat to the presidency, he was at least heartened that Americans elected their first born-again chief executive, the Southern Baptist Jimmy Carter.[31]

Carter's southern roots and his appeal in the Bible Belt helped him against a weak Gerald Ford and a Republican Party hobbled by the Watergate scandal, but the Georgian thoroughly disappointed conservative evangelicals during his presidency. He refused to support the Human Life Amendment, pushed in the Senate by the emerging New Right standard-bearer Jesse Helms (R-NC) and in the House by the passionately antiabortion (and Catholic) Illinois representative Henry Hyde (R-IL). Carter also supported in 1979 the creation of the federal Department of Education, which conservatives loathed because it promised even greater secular influence in the nation's schoolrooms. For these and other disservices, many evangelicals decried Carter as a "secularist" in evangelical clothing and redoubled their efforts to build a movement capable of influencing politics and public policy more decisively.[32]

To this end the Baptist minister Robert Grant created Christian Voice and, along with the Orange County writer and publisher David Balsiger, developed the "Biblical Scoreboard" for presidential and congressional elections. First used in the midterm congressional elections of 1978, the scoreboards rated candidates in categories such as "faith and morality," as well as on specific issues: "Abortion/Pro-Life," "ERA/Pro-Family," "Homosexuality/Lesbianism," "Pornography," and "Parental Rights/Child Rights." Printed as a magazine, the scoreboard offered Christian voters easy candidate-to-candidate comparisons. Sprinkled with scriptural references (on abortion, Exodus 20:13, Deuteronomy 5:17, Jeremiah 1:5, etc.) and quotations from the candidates (Jimmy Carter: "I think abortion's wrong. [But] I don't think government ought to do anything to end abortion"), the scoreboards became one of the most widely distributed right-wing political publications of the 1980s; the half million mailed in 1980 grew to one and a half million in 1988. These scoreboards and their many imitators, such as the Family Values Voting Index, embodied the religious right's aggressive effort to reshape the nation's political culture, election by election.[33]

Conservative Christians founded a number of additional political organizations in advance of the 1980 election. Edward McAteer, a retired sales manager for Colgate-Palmolive, established the Religious Roundtable. McAteer, who had a salesman's sensibility, said frankly that the "biggest part of this market [Christian voters] is the evangelical community . . ." He recruited prominent ministers, priests, and a handful of rabbis to the roundtable, which quickly became the movement's most important bridge among evangelical Protestants, Catholics, and conservative Jews. Within a few years McAteer ranked among the most important behind-the-scenes conservative activists in Washington. Aiming at a more local scale of political action, in the middle of her campaign against the White House Conference on Families, Beverly LaHaye created Concerned Women of America (CWA). Not unlike Schlafly's Eagle Forum, CWA focused on organizing small groups of women at the grassroots, "consciousness-raising" efforts of a sort designed to cultivate conservative strength in local neighborhoods, suburbs, and small towns. Also in 1979, Jerry Falwell, at the urging and with the considerable assistance of Paul Weyrich, established the Moral Majority. We're "enforcing God's law in the voting booth," Falwell said.[34]

These new organizations maintained ties with key figures in the secular New Right. Among the most important were Weyrich, Phillips, and

Viguerie. Weyrich, a Goldwater acolyte, was founder and director of the Committee for the Survival of Free Congress (also known as the Free Congress Foundation) and cofounder of the Heritage Foundation. Phillips, who had headed the Office of Economic Opportunity (OEO) under President Nixon, chaired the Conservative Caucus. Viguerie, a former executive secretary of Young Americans for Freedom (YAF) and veteran of the Goldwater movement, founded *Conservative Digest* in 1975 and maintained one of the most effective right-wing direct mail fund-raising organizations in the country. Weyrich and Viguerie were Catholic, and Phillips was born again, but the organization each ran was nominally secular and maintained close connections to the broader right-wing institutional landscape, especially think tanks such as the American Enterprise, Cato, Hoover, and Manhattan institutes and the Heritage Foundation and political organizations such as the American Conservative Union and the National Conservative Political Action Committee.[35]

Alongside the political institutions of the emerging religious right, three notable research and advocacy organizations emerged in these same years. Each coalesced around a pro-family message, and each in time grew closer to the core of right-wing activism. In 1977 the child psychologist and evangelical James Dobson founded Focus on the Family in Arcadia, California. Four years later he created the Family Research Council, which became one of the religious right's most important sources of policy ideas regarding families, sex, and sexuality. In Mississippi, the Methodist minister Donald Wildmon founded the National Federation for Decency in 1977, which became the American Family Association; by 1992 it had 640 local chapters and six-million-dollar annual fund-raising tallies. Finally, in 1980, the conservative Presbyterian minister Louis P. Sheldon founded the Traditional Values Coalition in Orange County, California.[36]

These organizations did more than just consolidate the pro-family message. They became a formidable political rival to the institutional foundations of liberalism. In an era when local Democratic Party organizations were generally more robust than the Republican equivalent, when labor unions gave the Democrats a ready source of volunteers, and when feminists and lesbians and gay men had begun to forge their own local and national organizations, the religious right constructed the architecture of a conservative competitor. Within a decade the ability of New Right conservatives to launch letter-writing campaigns, produce volunteers, organize protest rallies, and do the work of grassroots politics in both state and congressional districts had begun to equal and would soon surpass that of liberals. Moreover, by the mid-1980s, even as religious-right influence varied from election cycle to election cycle and from state to state, organizations such as the Family Research Council and American Family Association were a consistent presence in Washington, enabling the pro-family movement to demand a seat at every policy table and to have a voice in every conversation and debate. In the early seventies conservatives did not have an institutional base for articulating and defending breadwinner conservatism and antifeminism. By 1980 they did.

The institutions of the religious right advanced a broad conservative agenda but devoted the lion's share of their resources to matters of gender, sex, and family. McAteer's Religious Roundtable took up issues of foreign policy and adopted the emerging economic orthodoxy of the late 1970s New Right: deregulation and low taxes. Falwell campaigned loudly against the SALT II Treaty with the Soviet Union. The tax status of Christian schools was another issue close to the hearts of conservative evangelicals, as was Carter's allegedly weak foreign policy. On balance, however, these organizations foregrounded abortion, homosexuality, pornography, feminism, and family breakdown. "Abortion is now the leading cause of death in America," the evangelical *Christianity Today* told its readers in 1976. Balsiger's "Biblical Scoreboard" made abortion its number one issue in 1978 and 1980, followed closely by the ERA and homosexuality.[37]

Its size set the religious right apart from previous American religious movements. Falwell announced the formation of the Moral Majority on a telecast of *The Old-Time Gospel Hour,* before an audience of no less than a million. Televangelists famously inflated their viewership numbers— Falwell claimed 20 million viewers, as did Jim Bakker of the *PTL Club*— but Nielsen ratings suggested a smaller, though still considerable, home viewership: in 1980, 2 million each for Oral Roberts and Rex Humbard, a bit more than 1.5 million for Jimmy Swaggart, 1.2 for Falwell, and just over 500,000 for Bakker. (These were per-show figures. Many broadcasted daily or several times a week.) Nielsen estimated the total televangelist audience in 1980 at 20 million, or roughly 8 percent of Americans. Falwell and the televangelists had perfected one model of fund-raising: small, individual donations from viewers. Viguerie and Weyrich perfected another: the direct mail. Television ministries and direct mail became instrumental in stoking moral outrage among ordinary Americans and directing that outrage toward conservative causes and policies.[38]

Meanwhile, wealthy elites lined up to add their own hefty contributions. Men such as Joseph Coors, John M. Olin, Richard Mellon Scaife, James O'Keefe, and Walter Knott helped finance the American Enterprise Institute and other early conservative think tanks. By the early 1980s the religious right controlled well-financed political organizations, an officially nonpolitical but closely allied television empire, a vast publishing (and eventually filmmaking) apparatus, and a sympathetic conservative magazine, Conservative Digest, that carried their message to a larger national audience, both secular and religious. This joining of wealth and the Bible, money and the Word, small donations and corporate gifts, would be the key to coming New Right political successes.

Despite its prominence over the airwaves and in national politics, the religious right was predominantly a Sun Belt phenomenon. Its metropolitan centers of power stretched from Fairfax County, Virginia, southward along the eastern seaboard to Broward County, Florida, home of Kennedy's Coral Ridge Ministries. Pat Robertson's ministries called Virginia Beach, Virginia, home, while Jerry Falwell's operations dominated the small town of Lynchburg, Virginia, and suburban Charlotte was home for many years to Jim Bakker's Praise the Lord (PTL) ministries as well as to Ross Rhoads's conservative Calvary Presbyterian Church. Charles Stanley's First Baptist Church in suburban Atlanta had eight thousand members, and Stanley's media outreach included his Stand Up America cassette tapes, a satellite television broadcast, and books such as Is There a Man in the House? Westward, Jimmy Swaggart's ministries were based in Baton Rouge, Robison's church and television studios in metropolitan Houston, and W. A. Criswell's First Baptist Church—the largest in the world—was in Dallas. On the West Coast, Southern California was the power center: Los Angeles, Orange, and San Diego counties were home to dozens of fundamentalist churches and organizations, the latter including Christian Voice, Focus on the Family, and the Traditional Values Coalition.[39]

This sweeping arc from Fairfax County to Orange County had a parallel arc just to its north. It followed the Appalachian Mountains and Ohio River Valley from small-town Pennsylvania southwestward through the southern regions of Ohio, Indiana, and Illinois into the heart of the Missouri Bible Belt and through Oklahoma (where Oral Roberts University was founded in 1963) and Kansas into Mormon-dominated Utah. In small and medium-size towns and in the booming metropolitan suburbs along both these southern and northern arcs lay the vast majority of evan-

gelical and fundamentalist churches in the country and the major institutional homes of the religious right.

The southern religious right was not a cover for racial backlash, but its
rise cannot be entirely divorced from the political rupture caused by the
black freedom movement. When the latter erupted in the region in the
1950s, led with prophetic Christian moral passion by black ministers, far
too many white churches stood on the sidelines. Indeed, many lent their
names and prestige to the Christian academies through which white southerners avoided the consequences of desegregation. As the old southern
order collapsed under the twin pressures of black protest and federal law,
and as the rhetoric of black ministers eliminated the possibility of a biblical defense of racial segregation, stabilizing the gender and sexual order
assumed greater importance among white southern fundamentalists.

Because so much of the white South was abandoning the Democratic
Party as a result of its embrace of black rights, it can be difficult to disaggre-
gate racial from religious factors. However, given the prominent place of
anti-busing and anti-affirmative-action positions in religious-right rhetoric—
and in the 1979 Family Protection Act, for instance—Protestantism's historical role as a champion of the southern moral and racial order, and the
close association in the worldviews of many southern fundamentalists of
feminism, homosexuality, and black equality, neither is it without reason
to see southern white enthusiasm for the religious right as part of a broad
rejection of the rights revolution forged in the postwar decades. Since
1954, southern opponents of school desegregation had slowly but percep-
tibly turned toward a rhetoric of family morality and breadwinner responsibility in their defenses of racial segregation. Breadwinner conservatism
thus largely replaced, or incorporated in subtle ways, white supremacy as
the public face of southern conservatism after the 1970s.[40]

This fact made the religious right largely anathema to African American Protestants, despite black evangelicals' own social conservatism. The
revivalist and prophetic traditions within much of African American Protestant religious practice had prioritized group resistance to white supremacy since the days of slavery. Those same traditions, including some of the
most expressive evangelicalism in the American canon, held to a gender
and sexual orthodoxy not entirely unlike that preached by many white
churches, especially regarding abortion and homosexuality. Many African American Christians retained quite conservative views of gender and
sex in this era, but the more powerful current of opposition to racism,

maintenance of group solidarity, and commitment to a rights-protecting state precluded anything like a wholesale political embrace of the pro-family movement.[41]

•

The religious right did not have a strong voice in Congress in the seventies. Following President Nixon's resignation in August 1974 and midterm elections the subsequent November, liberal Democrats dominated both houses through the remainder of the decade. Indeed, even prior to that year, Congress had passed landmark feminist-inspired liberal legislation, including the 1971 child care bill, Title IX, and the Equal Rights Amendment. National lawmaking in the mid-seventies was not wholly a project of social democracy, but on balance Congress leaned moderately toward the left side of the political spectrum. A handful of allies of the religious right—especially the conservative senators Paul Laxalt (R-NV), Orrin Hatch (R-UT), and Jesse Helms (R-NC) and a handful of right-wing congressmen, including Henry Hyde (R-IL), Larry McDonald (D-GA), and Bob Dornan (R-CA)—had emerged in Congress prior to 1978, but evangelical activists could rightly claim that their political interests were marginalized in the nation's highest lawmaking body.[42]

Assailing liberalism from the margins, however, suited the New Right, whose narrative of victimization at the hands of liberal political culture was part of its core message. Viguerie's *Conservative Digest* demonstrated the political usefulness of marginalization. The plucky *Digest* had in 1975 joined the *National Review* as the New Right's journals of record. But Viguerie's publication—grittier and less high-minded than Buckley's— was more willing than Buckley's to champion the emerging religious right and its pro-family politics. It gave a column to JoAnn Gasper, publisher of the antifeminist journal *The Right Woman*, and regularly reported enthusiastically on campaigns against the ERA, gay rights, abortion, pornography and feminism. As the far right's fund-raiser-in-chief Viguerie used the *Digest* to catalog the movement's leading figures and its new faces, welcoming "born-again Christians [as] a new political force." In advance of the 1980 election he published *The New Right: We're Ready to Lead* and declared, "We've already taken control of the conservative movement, and conservatives have taken control of the Republican Party. The remaining thing is to see if we can take control of the country."[43]

Reagan had been the favorite presidential candidate of Viguerie and the far right since 1976 (if not since 1964). But Americans confronted an odd, if not ironic, choice in the 1980 presidential election. The Democratic Party nominated the nation's sitting president, Jimmy Carter, a self-declared born-again Christian and devout Southern Baptist. Another born-again Christian, John Anderson, a member of the First Evangelical Free Church, ran as an independent after faring poorly in the Republican primaries. Neither Carter nor Anderson, despite their deep Christian faith and evangelical identities, supported an explicit mixing of religion and politics. "I reject the concept of a 'moral majority' as it applies to contemporary American politics," Anderson said a month in advance of the election. In contrast, the Republican Party nominated Ronald Reagan, a man of no obvious religious convictions for the greater part of his life who was a nominal member, and infrequent attendee, of a Presbyterian church in Bel Air, California. Americans chose the least religious of the three candidates in an election that was nonetheless widely hailed as a decisive victory for conservative Christians. Carter's unpopularity, the Iranian hostage crisis, and the disastrous economic stagflation would likely have produced a Republican victory in the absence of the ministerial mobilization. But the Moral Majority's voter registration drive, the countless endorsements Reagan received from fundamentalist ministers and religious-right organizations, and their grassroots work on his behalf gave them ample reason to lay claim to being decisive.[44]

However, Reagan had not even taken office before prominent secular-minded New Right spokespeople began urging him to ignore the "moralistic claims" of the fundamentalists. Both William Safire and George Will penned prominent admonitions to the religious right in late 1980. Mark Hatfield, a liberal Republican senator from Oregon, despite being a born-again Baptist himself, condemned the religious right. "They're not basically Republicans as such," Hatfield said of the new movement's members. "They're looking for an instrumentality by which they can advance their cause. So it's a takeover . . ." The preceding spring a "Washington for Jesus" rally on the National Mall, in which more than two hundred thousand people listened to speakers condemn homosexuality and the ERA and call for the reinstatement of the draft, had shaken the secular Washington establishment, which was unaccustomed to the arresting sight of ecstatic religious believers demonstrating for biblical righteousness. And in the months leading up to and following the election, Falwell's near-ubiquitous media presence and his exaggerated claims about the Moral Majority's political influence had produced a minor panic in the national press.[45]

The prominence of Christian foot soldiers on election day did not yet mean that the religious right had arrived as a political heavyweight. Falwell was adamant that the Moral Majority had secured Reagan's victory in 1980, and Robison, Swaggart, LaHaye, and other ministers, as well as Phyllis Schlafly, advanced similar claims of their electoral sway. There is reason to believe there was at least some truth in their assertions. The scholar of American religion and politics Albert J. Menendez estimated that Carter lost a majority of counties with high Southern Baptist, Lutheran, and Catholic populations, a reversal of his 1976 fortunes. Evangelical bluster and electoral might were not matched by concrete political results, however. Once in office, Reagan, who had endorsed public school prayer, bemoaned the state of American abortion law, and roused moral reformers with his denunciations of pornography, sexual immorality, and family decline, did not prioritize the broad religious-right agenda of family renewal. When the Reagan special assistant Morton Blackwell urged Falwell in 1982 to accept "incremental" gains on Christian issues, the Moral Majority leader shot back that he expected more "with one of our 'own' in the White House." Incremental, he added bitingly, "would be something one could hope for with a liberal Democratic administration." In the president's first two years in office, his advisers fielded a steady stream of mail from religious-right, and especially right-to-life, leaders deploring Reagan's inaction, or his "incremental" efforts, on their behalf.[46]

Toward the end of Reagan's first term, the Baptist seminarian Bruce Shelley worried in the pages of *Christianity Today* that the "visibility of evangelicals . . . has not translated into significant social impact." Viguerie complained that "the GOP has behaved as if conservative Christians and Jews could be bought off with rhetoric." Meanwhile, leading New Right ideologues, as well as prominent centrist Republicans such as George H. W. Bush, Robert Dole, and Howard Baker, continued to caution against allowing evangelicals influence over administration policy and Republican Party ideology. The moderate senator Lowell Weicker (R-CT), like Packwood a dying breed of Rockefeller Republican, formed a Senate "gang of six" in an attempt to block religious-right input on the party's 1984 platform. Weicker cautioned against the GOP's becoming known as "God's own party."[47]

Thus the Reagan coalition was nearly as sprawling and fractious as the New Deal coalition of the postwar decades. Reagan had to mollify fundamentalists without seeming to empower the "American Ayatollahs." Viguerie believed that the president was "genuinely interested" in moral issues, such as pornography, abortion, and school prayer, but that his advisers cared about them "only as political gimmicks." Back-and-forth accusations between the religious right and secularists in the Reagan coalition were to become a hallmark of the conservative revolution, a fixture of the necessary political give-and-take required to keep any characteristically unwieldy American governing majority intact. Worried that religious leaders had become anxious about his commitment to them, in advance of the 1984 election Reagan gave major speeches to the National Religious Broadcasters and the National Association of Evangelicals, proposed a constitutional amendment permitting prayer in public schools, and affirmed his support for tuition tax credits, which assisted parents who sent their children to religious or parochial schools.[48]

•

The steady rise of the religious right in the national imagination camouflaged a furious war taking place within American Christianity. The pages of *Sojourners*, the magazine of liberal evangelical opinion, and of *Christian Century*, the magazine of mainline Protestantism, were filled in the early 1980s with editorials questioning this new, and in the view of many, radical mixing of faith and politics. Billy Graham, whom the mainstream press treated as the nation's evangelical conscience, wondered dismissively if "the Moral Majority would represent more than 10 percent of the evangelicals in America." News outlets, from nightly network news and big-city dailies to weekly newsmagazines, carried a steady stream of articles, filled with quotations from moderate religious leaders anxious to speak against the new crusaders, evincing a deep skepticism about blurring the boundary between the private world of belief and the public world of politics.[49]

Even before the 1980s, the rise of antifeminism and pro-family moral traditionalism had divided Christians. The influential Christian feminists Letha Dawson Scanzoni, Nancy Hardesty, and Rosemary Radford Ruether challenged both mainline and evangelical churches to take women's liberation seriously. Scanzoni's articles in the evangelical magazine *Eternity* questioned the church's male hierarchy and advocated "equal partnership" in Christian marriages. She and Hardesty in 1974 penned the

influential *All We're Meant to Be: A Biblical Approach to Women's Libera-*
tion, which quickly became the standard text for evangelical feminists and
has remained in print since. Scanzoni and Hardesty urged that women
"be freed from gender-role stereotypes and traditions" and that Christian
families be founded on the basis of "a marriage of equal partners."
Ruether meanwhile advocated a "liberation theology" that blended ancient
goddess worship with a Bible-centered attention to all oppressed people.
By the late 1970s, a small but vocal evangelical women's movement was
pushing for the ordination of female ministers, arguing against the blanket condemnation of divorce, forging a middle ground on abortion, and
generally advocating for a transformation of evangelical practice to accord
with women's full equality.[50]

In the mid-1970s, these women's rights advocates helped bring into
being a larger progressive movement within American evangelicalism.
The kernel for such a movement was the magazine *The Post-American* (it
soon became *Sojourners*), which was founded in 1971 by a group of Trinity Evangelical Divinity School seminarians outside Chicago. They conceived the magazine as a forum for socially engaged Christian opinion
and journalism. In 1973 forty evangelical leaders met in Chicago and issued the Declaration of the Evangelicals for Social Action, a call for
Christians to fight poverty, racism, and sexism known as the Chicago
Declaration. "We acknowledge that we have encouraged men to prideful
domination and women to irresponsible passivity," the declaration read.
An Evangelical Women's Caucus convened at the Chicago meeting and
in 1975 sponsored a national conference called Women in Transition,
which became the first in a series of conferences dedicated to progressive Christian womanhood. Supportive of the civil rights movement, the
Equal Rights Amendment, and reproductive rights, progressive evangelicals invoked the Bible just as their conservative counterparts did but drew
very different conclusions from its passages.[51]

The quest to restore traditional "family values," and condemnation of
homosexuality in particular, came closest to uniting Christians in the
1970s and 1980s. Throughout the former decade mainline Protestant denominations typically sided with biblical injunctions against "immoral"
lesbians and gay men. Even the most progressive Baptist organization,
the American Baptist Convention, claimed that lesbians and gay men
intended to "change the moral climate of our country to suit their own
extreme permissiveness." With Billy Graham presiding, the National Asso-

ciation of Evangelists condemned homosexuals at its national convention the same year. In 1975, after years of lobbying by lesbian and gay church groups, the liberal National Council of Churches passed a resolution upholding nondiscrimination based on "affectional or sexual preference," but the same year it denied membership to Troy Perry's largely gay Metropolitan Community Church, a ban that continues to this day. All seven of the historically African American Protestant denominations, including the African Methodist Episcopal (AME) Church and the National Baptist Convention, condemned homosexuality as "an abomination." Mainline and moderate evangelical churches officially opposed homosexuality, though with less vitriol than conservative evangelical, and especially fundamentalist, churches, to which homosexuality represented, after abortion, the gravest threat to the American family and the nation's moral fiber.[52]

The apparent consensus on homosexuality, however, could not hide the stirrings of a doctrinal and practical debate over lesbian and gay Americans within Christian circles. A few voices on the Christian left pushed for unequivocal acceptance of lesbian and gay sexualities and people. Ralph Blair, a psychotherapist and committed Christian, in 1972 penned *An Evangelical Look at Homosexuality*, in which he called on evangelicals to "abandon unbiblical crusades against homosexuality." The Methodist seminarian and professor of biblical interpretation Walter Wink argued in 1979 that the Bible "knows only a love ethic," which it brings to bear on "whatever sexual practices are dominant in any given country, or culture or period." Scanzoni partnered with another evangelical feminist, Virginia Ramey Mollenkott, to advocate for a "homosexual Christian ethic" in the 1978 *Is the Homosexual My Neighbor?* (Mollenkott, along with *All We're Meant to Be* coauthor Hardesty, came out as lesbians in this period.) Pushed by gay and lesbian groups within their ministries, the United Church of Christ, United Methodists, Episcopalians, and Presbyterians began debating the ordination of homosexual ministers in the mid-1970s. Three of the most influential gay-friendly Christian projects appeared at this time in California: the Glide Memorial Methodist Church's Council on Religion and the Homosexual (CRH); Troy Perry's Metropolitan Christian Church (MCC) in Los Angeles (which had grown to more than 250 congregations in nearly two dozen countries by 2010); and, also in Los Angeles, Carl Bean's African American Unity Fellowship Church, which ministered primarily to the African American lesbian and gay community.[53]

None of these efforts halted the rise of the fundamentalist version of biblical righteousness and its inflexible vision of family values, however. No struggle better illustrates this fact than the fight for control of the Southern Baptist Convention (SBC) in the 1980s. Despite the prominence of Southern Baptists in the religious right (men such as Robison, Stanley, and McAteer), the SBC itself held to the proud Baptist traditions of individual church autonomy and respect for civil liberties. For decades the fundamentalist versus modern controversy that had split many other American congregations had been kept at bay in the SBC by what one historian has called a "grand compromise." Beginning in the late 1960s, however, fundamentalists, led by W. A. Criswell, pastor of a massive Dallas church, asserted greater and greater influence and in the early 1980s moved decisively to gain control of SBC agencies and its seminaries, the gateways to individual church pastorships.[54]

Fundamentalists cited doctrinal differences over "inerrancy" as the source of their mobilization, but few involved in the dispute doubted that shifts in southern, and American, culture lay at the heart of the struggle. Criswell and his allies charged that SBC seminaries taught modern, historical readings of the Bible, rather than emphasizing Scripture as the "inerrant" and infallible Word of God. Only a return to inerrancy could save the convention. One Criswell ally was the influential editor of *Christianity Today*, Harold Lindsell, who wrote two books—*The Battle for the Bible* (1976) and *The Bible in Balance* (1979)—that egged on, and gave ammunition to, the right-wing radicals. Moderate Baptist leaders, however, recognized that the inerrancy controversy was a symbol of fundamentalists' deeper concern with abortion, feminism, and homosexuality and perhaps even a sign of their anxiety about the erosion of white supremacy. "Undoubtedly, history will record that the controversy was not really about the Bible," wrote the Baptist scholar Leon McBeth. William Finlator, the liberal minister of Pullen Memorial Church in Raleigh, North Carolina, was among those who led the fight against the fundamentalist takeover. Baptists were historically "civil libertarians," Finlator emphasized, but the fundamentalists had decided that "unless you are against gay rights, unless you are against abortion, unless you are against obscenity . . . you're not a Christian." The Baptist seminarian and ethics professor Paul Simmons used even stronger words. Comparing fundamentalism with McCarthyism, Simmons called it "a power-crazed authoritarianism, a win-at-any-cost ethic and a total disregard for personal values and religious freedom . . ."[55]

By the late 1980s what observers called the conservative takeover of the Southern Baptist Convention was nearing completion. Among the first and most prominent casualties were women. Based on the "submission God requires," a campaign by fundamentalists against the ordination of female ministers was successful in 1984. Reproductive rights too suffered in the Baptist turn to conservatism. Throughout the 1970s, guided by moderates, the SBC had staked out a flexible position that recognized the spiritual validity of pro-choice positions. By the middle of the 1980s, however, fundamentalists had replaced this moderation with one of the most rigid and unyielding antiabortion statements issued by an American religious group. Across the country, SBC moderates had been silenced, many liberal Southern Baptist churches were simply expelled from the convention, and a new orthodoxy reigned.[56]

Two decades of scholarly debate have not yielded a consensus about the exact composition and influence of the religious right. Was it a noisy but ineffectual sideshow in the boisterous and increasingly television-driven political marketplace? A rearguard action against ineluctable progress toward modern readings of the Bible and definitions of gender, sexuality, and family? Snapshots of the religious right at any given moment would reveal elements of both characterizations. But its broader influence and power, over two political generations, is undeniable. Antifeminism and breadwinner conservatism would not have achieved the political leverage and longevity they did without the formidable institutional resources of conservative Christianity. Equally important, the pro-family moral traditionalism of the religious right forged cross-class political alliances among otherwise starkly different Americans, particularly in the Sun Belt, the Midwest, and the Catholic Northeast. And this traditionalism displaced complex structural questions of racial equality and racial injustice—involving crime and the penal system, welfare, and affirmative action, for instance—into a putatively race-neutral world of "family values."

By the end of the 1970s, the organizing mythology of the liberal Great Society family had undergone a decade and a half of challenges from the left. All the political fights required to widen the inclusiveness of the myth since 1964—to accommodate democratic citizens with the new liberties and positive rights recounted in the first half of the book—had strained and splintered the myth's political purchase, its capacity to act as a legitimating symbol of liberal-left commitment. A variety of individuals and constituencies arose and campaigned to reclaim the "traditional," patriotic, heterosexual-male-breadwinner family and its political possibilities in the 1970s. No constituency did this more effectively than the religious right.

Of perhaps even greater long-term importance, the SBC battle stood for broader trends in American political life: activists driven to radical, absolutist positions and the casting of one's political opponents not as fellow citizens engaged in spirited debate but as traitors, heretics, and pariahs, based on the conviction that compromise is defeat and empathy for fellow human beings a fall from moral righteousness. Not everyone on the religious right anchored themselves to inflexible and severe biblical reasoning. But enough did. Enough of them spoke and wrote from positions of great influence, and enough of them were willing to protest, demonstrate, organize, and destabilize (as the left had done in an earlier generation). Dissenting voices from within and from outside evangelical Christianity could not stop the religious right from changing the nature of American politics and political language and from pushing the nation's ideology and its electoral process rightward.

13

ANCIENT ROOTS:
THE REAGAN REVOLUTION'S GENDER
AND SEXUAL POLITICS

Uniting behind Ronald Reagan, the religious right joined conservatives of all stripes and voters weary of liberalism's alleged moral permissiveness and economic failures in a broad Republican coalition between 1980 and 1988. With an ally in the presidency, the religious right and the pro-family right, which were nearly, though not entirely, synonymous, launched an ambitious agenda for government. In response, feminists, lesbians and gay men, and liberals of all stripes mobilized to defend the incomplete gains of previous decades. The resulting showdown widened political divisions over gender, sexuality, and family to a gulf and intensified the rhetorical warfare between right and left. The Republican Party marginalized feminists within its ranks, and right-to-life advocates abandoned the Democratic Party, as gender and sexual politics grew ever more determinative of political alignments in the nation at large.

As the liberal left had begun to realize and the Reagan coalition came to understand, political movements in American life are by nature disappointments in waiting. The aspirations that collect millions of people under an ideological banner are always imperfectly realized in the compromises and trade-offs that shape government policy under a two-party, federalist, divided system of governance. In this regard, the forces massing on the American right in the late 1970s were like countless insurgencies before them, including those on the left. The gushy nostalgia among conservatives for Reagan in the twenty-first century has obscured the reality of that era's conservatism, which met success and failure in equal measure. Amid the ordinary catalog of political victories and defeats, what stands out about conservatism in the 1980s, however, particularly among religious right and pro-family activists, is how central a narrative of defeat and be-trayal became to the movement itself.[1]

Thus the key story of the Reagan revolution is of the relationship be-tween success and failure. Four overlapping developments exemplify that relationship. First, pro-family activists within the New Right successfully merged antifeminism and breadwinner conservatism with antigovern-ment, free-market conservatism. Despite notable political tensions among Reagan's tax cutters, budget watchers, and Cold Warriors and so-called values conservatives, it is remarkable how thoroughly these groups came together in ideological harmony. Indeed, the pro-family politics of the Reagan coalition represented a crucial axis of the neoliberal transforma-tion in the United States that began in the 1970s and continued through the turn of the century—"neoliberal" meaning economic deregulation in the spirit of the "liberal," or free-market, principles developed in the eigh-teenth century.

Second, and despite this success, the conservatives' family agenda suf-fered notable defeats. Congressional liberals defended women's rights, re-sisted the homophobic hysteria that accompanied the HIV/AIDS crisis, and saved critical government programs, such as Title X funding for sex education and family planning. When conservative pragmatists, includ-ing Reagan himself, moved slowly or cautiously on many issues, espe-cially abortion, religious and pro-family activists believed they had been betrayed. This produced notable tension in the coalition and led to a radicalization of disappointed far-right religious conservatives. They felt themselves victims of their chosen representatives, and their narrative of vic-timization at the hands of the left became, in some cases, a narrative of victimization at the hands of the secular right. By the end of the decade those radicalized conservatives had to choose between embracing the poli-tics of the possible and demanding policies in line with their absolutist principles. Like the radical left of the late 1960s, the radical moralist right of the 1980s saw the very choice itself as a sign of defeat.

A third development took place not among the grassroots but among conservative political operatives such as Paul Weyrich, Richard Viguerie, Pat Buchanan, and Lee Atwater. They and a handful of influential voices among a growing class of political "consultants" increasingly came to view issues such as abortion and gay rights as instruments of electoral power and not necessarily important to governance. They cared some-what less about shepherding a counterrevolution in government policy on gender, sexuality, and family than about taking advantage of voters' anxiety about moral decline for partisan political advantage. This strategy depended entirely on mobilizing the narrative of victimization. No matter how hard they worked, conservatives claimed, their objectives were stymied by liberal intransigence, a biased media, or betrayal at the hands of their own.

Finally, whatever the failures and compromises of their legislative agenda, the New Right achieved the objective of insurgencies everywhere: it changed the terms of debate and placed its opponents on the defensive. Feminists and other women's advocates, lesbians and gay men, civil rights activists, and other liberals found themselves on the back foot for long periods after the 1980 election. They had to defend not just the legal and legislative gains of the previous two decades, which for lesbians and gay men were largely at the state and local level, but the "rights" framework in which those gains were embedded. The Reagan coalition transformed the debate about the content of American citizenship from one about rights to one about government provision. The issue became not who deserved equal citizenship but what the government would provide and support. Once reframed that way, rights, which imply state obligation, increasingly yielded to free-market orthodoxy.

Ronald Reagan was a tax cutter, a free-market deregulator, and a Cold War martial nationalist. He was not a moral traditionalist. He may have promised to "clean up the mess in Berkeley" in his 1966 gubernatorial campaign, but he signed California's liberal abortion law in 1967 and opposed the antigay Briggs initiative in 1978. However, when the religious right and the pro-family movement transformed the Republican platform between 1976 and 1980 by eliminating support for the ERA, positioning the party as defender of "family values" (a phrase inserted into the Republican platform for the first time in 1976), and calling for a constitutional amendment to restore the "right to life" of the unborn, the chameleonlike Reagan changed his colors. What was poorly understood at the time, but became clearer over subsequent decades, is that the religious and moral conservatives who became so crucial to Republican fortunes in the 1980s and beyond incorporated their demands for greater moral discipline and "traditional" families into the free-market, low-tax, and states' rights conservatism of the Reagan coalition with relative ease.

•

Defined too often by journalists and social scientists as a "single-issue" movement, antiabortion was always embedded in the larger universe of values articulated by pro-family activists. Right-to-life stands as one of the most influential political movements of the postwar decades. This was so in part because activists in that cause condensed all the disparate critiques of a "permissive society" into a focused campaign around a morally compelling issue. But it was also true in an electoral sense. Antiabortion may have been more than a single-issue movement, but large numbers of American voters in and after the 1970s began to see abortion as a litmus test of political principles. That fact made antiabortion activists even more critical to the emerging conservative coalition.

The sober-faced CBS News reporter Roger Mudd, whose résumé included hosting network coverage of the 1963 March on Washington, filed a series of reports on abortion in 1978. "There may be no more emotional issue in American life today than abortion," Mudd explained in one as footage rolled of antiabortion protesters writing down the license plate numbers of women visiting an abortion clinic. "Something new is happening: the targeting of women after they've had abortions." In another report, Mudd interviewed right-to-life Iowans who had just helped to defeat Democratic senator Dick Clark in one of the nation's first congressional elections to turn largely on this issue. "Abortion could be the most volatile single political issue in the country today," Mudd observed with dry foreboding, "and the right-to-lifers the most powerful single-issue bloc."[2]

Mudd had it partly right. Abortion was consistently one of the most emotional issues in American politics. But it was not so in the larger life of the nation. Time and again in the late 1970s and early 1980s polls confirmed that a majority of Americans hewed to the center on women's reproductive rights. Public surveys taken in 1981 and 1982, for instance, revealed that fewer than one-third of Americans believed that abortion should be illegal, and 57 percent answered yes when asked if an abortion ought to be available to women who wished to have one. Most Americans considered an unwanted pregnancy to be a deeply personal matter that, within the first three to four months of conception, ought to be resolved solely by a woman and her closest confidants. Politically, however, abortion remained a divisive, emotional, and explosive issue because both feminist activists and their conservative counterparts saw women's reproduction as central to the values and public policies in which each believed. For feminists, access to abortion was the foundation of women's sexual and economic, even existential independence. For right-to-life activists, abortion under any circumstances was murder and an affront to their vision of motherhood and ordered family life.[3]

Until the early 1980s, however, the enormous chasm between feminist and right-to-life positions did not map precisely onto partisan alignment. Not a few conservative Democrats, especially in heavily Catholic northeastern states and in the South, opposed abortion rights. Many progressive Republicans, most notably New York power brokers Nelson Rockefeller and Senator Jacob Javits, Senator Lowell Weicker in Connecticut, and Senator Robert "Bob" Packwood in Oregon, supported women's choice. The sea change occurred between 1978 and 1984, when right-to-life Democratic and pro-choice Republican politicians were almost entirely purged from their parties. Activists in NARAL and NOW and in various right-to-life organizations, including the heavyweight National Right to Life Committee, launched determined campaigns to elect politicians who agreed with them and to defeat those who did not. Activists on both sides saw these as critical years, as battles over the Hyde and Human Life amendments intensified in Congress. Overall, however, the right-to-life movement made the most substantial and unmistakable political gains.

A signal event in the right-to-life counteroffensive was Ellen McCormack's presidential campaign in 1976, the first presidential election since *Roe*. Like so many of the women who became antiabortion activists in the 1970s, McCormack, a Catholic housewife from Merrick, Long Island, was a political novice animated by a powerful belief that abortion was a great moral evil. In 1970, when Governor Rockefeller signed the nation's most liberal abortion law, she and other self-declared homemakers from New Deal Democratic families in the Long Island suburbs formed the New York Right to Life Party. Between 1970 and 1976 McCormack and her allies—a true grassroots army of women—forged one of the most influential antiabortion, antifeminist political movements in the country. Determined to force the issue into national politics, she campaigned for the Democratic nomination for president in 1976 on a right-to-life platform. "We know you're there and we know you believe in the traditional values, as Ellen does," her campaign literature assured voters. Competing in eighteen states, McCormack won an average of 3 to 5 percent of the primary vote, enough to convince many right-to-life activists that antiabortion voters represented a tangible political constituency among Democrats.[4]

McCormack's campaign was not the only development in the 1976 presidential race that worried supporters of reproductive rights. Feminists' principal allies among contenders for the Democratic nomination, Indiana senator Birch Bayh and California governor Jerry Brown, could not stop the political ascent of Jimmy Carter, who did not hide his opposition to abortion or his discomfort with outspoken feminists. McCormack's campaign demonstrated that there were Democratic voters ready to embrace an emphatic opponent of *Roe*, and Carter's rise demonstrated that plenty of Democratic voters were willing to overlook a politician's tepid endorsement of abortion rights. Both developments clarified the new post-*Roe* political landscape for Democratic feminists; they were in for a fight.[5]

That McCormack was a Democrat from the Catholic-heavy first-generation Long Island suburbs was indicative of the ongoing political and ideological realignment. New Deal liberalism had underwritten the ascent of blue-collar Catholic families like hers from Brooklyn walkup apartments to Nassau County ranch homes, from renting in the crowded city to homeownership in the spacious suburbs. But the rights liberalism embodied by feminism seemed to those same families more like a moral threat than a lift up. Since the publication of Kevin Phillips's *The Emerging Republican Majority* in 1969, political observers had taken bets on when, not if, the Democratic coalition would succumb to the backlash against civil rights, crime, and welfare. Abortion was the latest, and possibly the most crucial, piece in the jigsaw puzzle of realignment. In the 1980 election McCormack and her female compatriots switched parties and put the full weight of their political movement behind the antiabortion Republican Alfonse D'Amato, who won and joined his party colleagues in a new Republican Senate majority elected alongside right-to-life Ronald Reagan.[6]

Though McCormack's run for the Democratic presidential nomination in 1976 had been largely symbolic, right-to-life political strategists across the country intended to win, not to merely make their voices heard. They took advantage of the logic of American elections. The 50 percent plus one rule for deciding political races in the United States—commonly called first past the post—creates unique opportunities for vocal minorities. With an evenly divided electorate, elections are frequently decided by the shift of just 3 to 5 percent (or less) of voters. Insurgent political movements need not convince 51 percent of voters. They must sway (or frighten) only enough people whose convictions are not fixed to create a 51 percent majority. By 1980 one antiabortion organization could boast that "state after state had organized anti-abort [*sic*] constituencies that could produce a solid 3–5% of the vote . . ." The same national polls in which a majority of Americans endorsed abortion rights also revealed that one-third of voters were willing to support a candidate who favored banning abortion—the soft underbelly of the nation's pro-choice majority. Right-to-life strategists could amass political influence, candidate by candidate and election by election, even in the face of a pro-*Roe* national consensus.[7]

Right-to-life activists took the Democratic candidate McCormack's 3 to 5 percent tactic and made it their own, to the ultimate benefit of Republicans. One of the movement's first targets was the pro-choice Democratic Iowa senator Dick Clark. In a particularly telling moment in his 1978 reelection campaign, right-to-life forces took over a Clark rally during which Ted Kennedy was scheduled to appear. Clark's supporters could barely be heard over the chants of "Kennedy, Clark, antilife!" from the huge pro-life contingent. Clark's opponent, Republican Roger Jepsen, won, putting wind at the back of the right-to-life movement heading toward the 1980 election.[8]

That year the National Pro-Life Political Action Committee (NPLPAC) and the Life Amendment Political Action Committee (LAPAC) made McCormack's 3 to 5 percent a national strategy in seeking a right-to-life majority in Congress. Both groups focused on dozens of key congressional races, what LAPAC called the dirty dozen of pro-choice members of Congress. They mobilized passionate local volunteers and generated enormous publicity around the "single issue" of abortion. They worked alongside another major conservative political action committee that had emerged in the right-wing buildup to the 1980 election, the National Conservative Political Action Committee. By insisting that candidates no longer dodge abortion or finesse their stand on it, LAPAC and NPLPAC launched a decade-long effort to make antiabortion a litmus test of conservative political credentials.[9]

In 1980 the two national groups were instrumental in helping defeat some of the nation's leading Senate liberals, including George McGovern (D-SD), Birch Bayh (D-IN), and Frank Church (D-ID). Bayh in particular suffered mightily from the withering attacks of religious and pro-family conservatives; antiabortion forces suffused churches throughout the state on the last Sunday before the election, carrying their message that Bayh was the Senate's leading proponent of abortion. Watching the 1980 campaign unfold, the Americans United for Life activist Mike

Budde opined that "the right-wing types may be on the cutting edge of an entirely new synthesis" in bringing together opposition to abortion with traditional right-wing economic conservatism. McCormack's campaign in 1976, Jepsen's victory in 1978, and the defeat of key liberals in 1980 had proved to Republicans that antiabortion activists were dedicated, vocal, and more than capable of helping to swing elections.[10]

Right-to-life rhetoric vaulted between two narratives. In one, abortion was part of a lifestyle chosen by women who wished to remain unburdened by child rearing. "When a woman decides to abort her baby out of *convenience*," said Peter Gemma, executive director of NPLPAC, it "goes against the traditional religious, medical and ethical values of this nation." Gemma and others thought of abortion as a consequence of sexual promiscuity and liberal sex education and thus part of a larger breakdown of sexual morality and family discipline. But primarily it was a feminist project that denigrated motherhood and elevated "lifestyle" above "life." In a second narrative, opponents cast abortion as an unconscionable act of brutal violence and murder, a "slaughter of innocents" comparable to the Holocaust. Photos of aborted fetuses, with their tiny mangled limbs and their skulls crushed, figured prominently in the imaginations and on the placards of activists. In both narratives feminists were not seen in the tradition of Americans seeking legitimate rights but as moral ciphers with no rightful claim on public goodwill.[11]

The political successes of the antiabortion movement between 1976 and 1980 stunned feminists and women's advocates, placing them on the defensive. Internal memos and reports within NOW and NARAL from these years betray a growing frustration that what a NOW report called "reactionary forces" were thwarting the nation's poll-verified pro-choice majority. The "vocal and visible [antiabortion] minority," a NOW letter contended, "command neither the votes nor the support of the general public." However, NOW activists were well aware of NPLPAC's and LAPAC's electoral strategy, mobilizing what the report called "their hardcore vote— the 3–5% of the electorate that are adamantly opposed to reproductive rights." The "3–5 percent" principle from the McCormack campaign had become institutionalized even in the reproductive rights camp. Feminists and their allies bristled at the corrosive "baby killer" charge, and so they responded in a language they believed the country at large embraced: privacy and choice. They endeavored to match the antiabortion forces with their own grassroots campaign—letters to congresspeople, lobbying on

Capitol Hill and in state legislatures, door-to-door "neighborhood calls" to speak with voters, and other outreach efforts—on top of ongoing legal battles to protect *Roe* in the courts.[12]

In the summer and fall of 1980, right-to-life leaders believed things had turned decisively in their favor. In June, the Supreme Court ruled (5–4) that the Hyde Amendment, which banned federal Medicare payments for abortions, was constitutional (the Helms Amendment had banned direct U.S. funding of abortions overseas since 1973). Right-to-life activists celebrated. "It is a victory for congress and for the people," the National Right to Life Committee chair Dr. John Willke proclaimed. Then, in November, Americans elected a right-to-life president and sent a Republican majority to the Senate, including a dozen new right-to-life voices, ousting McGovern, Bayh, Church, Javits, and other key abortion rights supporters, such as Warren Magnuson (D-WA) and John Culver (D-IA).[13]

Most commentators saw the rightward electoral shift in 1980 as a result of the poor economy and Carter's controversial foreign policy, not an upwelling of right-to-life sentiment. Exit polls suggested too that anxiety about inflation and disaffection with Carter dominated voters' concerns. But NPLPAC, LAPAC, and their allies believed, in all likelihood quite rightly, that they had been instrumental in many congressional and Senate races. Given the disastrous state of the economy and the volatile situation in the Middle East, it was difficult for antiabortion activists to prove that their issue had been decisive. Nonetheless, NPLPAC and LAPAC had made their presence felt—McGovern in particular decried the tactics of right-to-life activists, which put him constantly on the defensive—and established a basic pattern in American politics that continues to this day: no conservative candidate could risk *not* seeking a right-to-life endorsement. Antiabortion activists now possessed a sufficiently robust institutional presence to create a powerful claim that they made an electoral difference.[14]

Reagan had revived the Nixonian formula of 1972, capturing all of the New Deal coalition's onetime strongholds in the South and in the northern blue-collar industrial belt from Massachusetts to Wisconsin. But the single-minded focus on Reagan among both historians and opinion makers has obscured the extraordinary grassroots political work that antiabortion forces invested in key races—and continued to invest in subsequent elections through the early 1990s. By the mid-1980s more than fifty antiabortion political action committees were spending tens of millions of dollars each election cycle in state and national campaigns and mustering battalions of volunteer activists willing to make enormous sacrifices to end abortion. The Democratic and Republican parties became divided on abortion in the eighties not as an inevitable outgrowth of party ideology but because determined organizations such as NRTLC, LAPAC, and NPLPAC remade American politics from the bottom up.[15]

The tide had not completely turned, however. After helping elect the first Republican Senate since 1953, a movement dedicated to an absolute proposition—abortion is murder—became acquainted with the realities of political compromise. In one of the great political showdowns of the Ninety-sixth Congress (1981–1982), Bob Packwood led a monthlong filibuster to prevent Jesse Helms's antiabortion bill from coming to a floor vote. An eleventh-hour intervention by Reagan himself, who proclaimed "this national tragedy of abortion on demand must end," could not save the Helms bill, which would have defined "life" as beginning at conception, thus conferring legal personhood on a fetus. While the Senate's pro-choice liberals, backed by NOW and NARAL, held firm, the right-to-life forces were themselves divided. Helms led a faction that favored direct legislative action to end abortion provision, and Orrin Hatch led another that preferred a constitutional amendment to overturn *Roe*. That tactical split, combined with the influence of the still-powerful pro-choice forces, made the Ninety-sixth Congress a deeply disappointing one for antiabortion activists. They achieved none of their major objectives and had to settle for a handful of antiabortion riders on appropriations bills. "How did a congressional session of which so much was expected produce so little?" wondered Senator Thomas Eagleton, the antiabortion Democrat from Missouri.[16]

If Congress proved disappointing, the Reagan administration simply confounded right-to-life activists. The president's rhetorical support was unwavering: he gave numerous antiabortion speeches, appointed right-to-life leaders to his administration, declared support for a Human Life Amendment, and published a long ghostwritten article, "Abortion and the Conscience of a Nation," in *The Human Life Review* on the tenth anniversary of *Roe*. But Reagan watched the polls and chose not to leap too far ahead of public opinion. His support for the Helms and Hatch bills and other right-to-life Senate initiatives was calibrated not to disrupt his economic agenda on Capitol Hill. And when the first chance to appoint a Supreme Court justice arrived quickly in 1981, he seized the opportunity to name the court's first woman, Sandra Day O'Connor, ignoring vocal right-to-life opposition. As an Arizona state senator in 1970, O'Connor had voted to repeal Arizona's abortion law, which had permanently disqualified her from the bench in the minds of right-to-life activists.[17]

Nonetheless, by the end of Reagan's first term there was no question the nation's reproductive politics had shifted to the right. Right-to-life forces could still not win a major legislative victory in Congress, and the Hatch-Eagleton Human Life Amendment, the first and only antiabortion constitutional amendment to reach a floor vote, fell eighteen votes short of the required two-thirds majority in 1983. Yet the bill's arrival on the Senate floor represented the rising influence of the right-to-life agenda in national political life. Outside of the national legislature, right-to-life organizations met real success in their efforts to eliminate all federal support for abortion procedures. At the 1984 International Conference on Population in Mexico City, Alan Keyes, an assistant secretary of state, announced the global gag rule, which became known as the Mexico City Policy—the policy of denying U.S. government funding to any overseas birth control or family planning programs that counseled about, provided, or encouraged abortion. Alongside the Helms and Hyde amendments, the Mexico City Policy significantly narrowed women's access to safe abortions around the world.[18]

The ascendancy of right-to-life rhetoric and politics threw the class politics of abortion into relief. In both the United States and abroad, those most affected by Helms, Hyde, and Mexico City were primarily working-class and poor women. The dissenting justices in the Supreme Court's decision on Hyde saw this clearly. Thurgood Marshall, stalwart of sixties rights liberalism, wrote of the decision's "devastating impact on the lives and health of poor women." William Brennan flatly penned that it "deprives the indigent woman of her freedom to choose." Henry Hyde himself said in 1977: "I certainly would like to prevent, if I could legally, anybody having an abortion, a rich woman, a middle-class woman, or a poor woman. Unfortunately, the only vehicle available is the . . . Medicaid bill." Working-class and poor women in developing nations, whose very life chances and ability to provide basic necessities to their families depended on their reproductive choice, were the victims of the Mexico City Policy, while in the aftermath of Hyde and each successful attack on *Roe* at the state level, an American woman's right to an abortion depended more than ever on her ability to pay for it. *Roe* survived but with it a calculation feminists had never intended: choice requires money.[19]

The political cost to the women's movement was grave. Abortion politics in the late 1970s and early 1980s forced women's rights organizations with the deepest pockets and the broadest bases of support, such as NOW and NARAL, into a defensive posture. Enormous human and institutional resources were invested in defending *Roe* and fighting the Hyde and Human Life amendments. The case that upheld Hyde (*Harris v. McRae*), for instance, evolved out of a four-year struggle by New York feminists to preserve abortion access for poor women in that state. Moreover, because Hyde covered only federal Medicaid funds, there were prolonged, multiyear battles in every state legislature over the use of state funds (by the 1990s virtually every state was following Hyde), as well as attempts to force public hospitals to provide abortions. Burdened with defending reproductive rights in Congress, state legislatures, and the courts, much of the energy of the women's movement after 1980 was siphoned into reactive rather than proactive campaigns.[20]

As right-to-life forces became central to the conservative movement, a striking polarity of failure and success followed them. Their presence in American politics produced few major national legislative triumphs. Indeed, they would assemble their legislative defeats into a narrative of loss and victimization that would fuel further radicalization, fund-raising, and protest. And yet, without question, they changed the national debate by shifting political discussion away from women's rights to fetal life and taxpayer provision of abortion. They institutionalized the Helms and Hyde amendments and made the Mexico City gag rule de rigueur for Republican presidents. And in an increasing number of states they secured passage of ever-stricter laws regulating access to abortion. Most broadly, all these efforts required that they work politically on behalf of conservative politicians and causes, making antiabortion activists and voters critical to the New Right coalition.

•

The religious right and the pro-family movement felt it could not rely on the Reagan administration to act on its agenda unless the political costs were minimal. Reagan's domestic priorities included passing the Economic Recovery Tax Act, his promised tax cuts, and accelerating the process of economic deregulation begun under President Carter. All this did not mean, however, that there was no room for family-issue conservatives to maneuver in the new Washington. As they did so, these activists left a distinct legacy: they achieved hard-won incremental victories instead of headline-making triumphs, and yet by the end of the 1980s had created a dense Washington-based network of organizations and activists dedicated to the surveillance of government policy.

The outlines of this network appeared at the dawn of the decade. In the heat of the 1980 presidential race, Richard Viguerie's *Conservative Digest* proudly presented "The Pro-Family Movement" to its readers in a ten-page spread. Complete with minibiographies of dozens of prominent conservatives—from congressional representatives to evangelicals and "anti-pornography" and "antihomosexual" leaders—the feature was a coming-out party. Viguerie's editors even unself-consciously drafted the kind of a diagram beloved of conspiracy theorists on the left, one depicting "The Pro-Family Network," with arrows indicating connections among "umbrella groups," "pro-life," "anti-gay rights," "evangelicals," and ultimately the "Washington Connection." The latter was anchored by Howard Phillips of the Conservative Caucus, Robert Billings, executive director of the Moral Majority, Connie Marshner, editor of the *Family Protection Report*, and the ubiquitous Paul Weyrich. Here, Viguerie intended to say, is the future of American conservatism.[21]

To make their priorities clear to the political class, family-issue conservatives revived the Family Protection Act (FPA) in the first months of Reagan's presidency. Senator Roger Jepsen, just two years removed from his victory in Iowa, introduced the omnibus conservative bill that would bar federal funding of all forms of abortion counseling; strengthen parental rights in a wide range of matters; prohibit Legal Aid attorneys from taking cases involving divorce, homosexuality, and abortion; eliminate most federal education programs; and deny federal funding to organizations "advocating homosexuality as a lifestyle" or denigrating "the role of women as it has historically been understood." The bill also contained a number of tax credits for families with children and for those caring for older adults in their own homes. In one mighty blow, the bill's authors sought to sever all ties between the national government and behavior they considered immoral or antifamily while simultaneously using the state's taxing power to promote what they considered traditional family forms.[22]

The bill fared miserably in Congress, never reaching the floor of either house. Its tone of moral outrage elicited derision from the national press. Reagan staffers offered symbolic support but little else. Many of its provisions nonetheless eventually found their way into national policy. In particular, two basic propositions survived the firestorm of criticism: divorcing the federal government from abortion provision and tax credits for families with children. The first survived because of the enormous pressure brought to bear by the right-to-life movement, and the second survived because it represented a political middle ground between the liberal proponents of government-supported child care and the conservative pro-family movement.[23]

Alongside the revival of the FPA, in the first years of the Reagan presidency conservatives launched a strategy, years in the making, that they called "defund the left." Speaking at the first Grassroots Pro-Life Conference, "Unity '81," Howard Phillips, the chief architect of "defund the left," explained "how to defund the antilife, antifamily organizations and programs" of the federal government. Phillips, like Phyllis Schlafly before him, contended that since the Great Society much of the liberal left had been supported by the federal government—especially through vehicles such as Legal Aid, which funded activist attorneys, and Title X of the 1970 Public Health Service Act, which funded local family planning clinics. Tax dollars supported not just the institutions but the left-wing activists who ran them, the argument went. The day after Reagan took office, Lyn Nofziger, Reagan's longtime aide and adviser, called a meeting with the New Right stalwarts Viguerie, Terry Dolan (of the National Conservative Political Action Committee), and Phillips at which the latter laid the philosophical groundwork for the "defund the left" campaign. PRESIDENT'S MOVE TO DE-FUND THE LEFT IMPORTANT PART OF HIS ECONOMIC PLAN, read the headline in Viguerie's *Conservative Digest*. Reagan's "block grant" program, which identified more than forty federal programs whose funding and control would be returned to the state and local level, became the broadest "defund the left" initiative.[24]

Conventional interpretations of the post-1970s conservative coalition too often claim that so-called cultural or "values" conservatives stood in tension with fiscal conservatives. In some specific instances, the alliance was fragile and not altogether natural. But in far more cases, the budget-cutting, anti-welfare-state fiscal conservatives found natural allies in the religious right and the pro-family movement. The latter wished to see the ax fall on all the federal grants and programs, established by the liberal Congresses of 1965 to 1975, that eased access to abortion, promoted family planning and sex education, empowered welfare recipients, and interfered with parental authority. Indeed, because Social Security and Medicare, which, alongside the Pentagon, accounted for the great bulk of federal spending, remained politically off-limits, Reagan-era budget cuts fell hardest on small, modestly funded social programs that mostly assisted the poor, including millions of poor women.[25]

Of all the "defund the left" targets, nothing raised conservative hackles quite like Title X of the 1970 Public Health Services Act. Judie Brown, president of the American Life Lobby, one of the largest right-to-life organizations in the country, made the elimination of Title X her personal mission. She was joined by the Heritage Foundation, the Conservative Caucus, and Senators Helms and Hatch. Opposing them was an equally formidable coalition consisting of the Planned Parenthood Federation of America, the American Civil Liberties Union, a handful of Health and Human Services (HHS) civil service administrators, and liberal stalwarts in the House and Senate.[26]

Opponents of Title X considered its principal beneficiary, Planned Parenthood Federation of America (PPFA), to be a left-wing organization undeserving of federal funding; it received between thirty and forty million dollars annually through HHS appropriations. Planned Parenthood's counseling of teenagers, Brown said, served no purpose "except to create a lot of promiscuity" and encouraged what the Heritage Foundation called "anti-parent attitudes among adolescents." Reagan HHS appointees imposed new, stricter rules on Planned Parenthood, including mandatory parental notification for minors given contraceptives (the so-called squeal rule). Many of the new rules survived legal challenge, but parental notification was thrown out by a circuit court in 1983.[27]

It was PPFA's abortion provision, however, that most provoked Brown and her allies. Planned Parenthood performed tens of thousands of abortions annually in clinics across the country, in addition to providing abortion counseling. According to the letter of the law, funding for abortions could not come from federal sources. But in practice, since each PPFA clinic was responsible for its own budget, it proved impossible to track what money went where. Brown, Phillips, and the anti–Title X coalition argued, not incorrectly, that this constituted a direct taxpayer subsidy of a practice they considered abhorrent.[28]

The campaign against Title X raged throughout Reagan's two terms in office. His administration annually sought to include Title X in its block grant program (grants to states), thus enabling conservatives at the state level to impose restrictions on family planning clinics. Congress saved it each time. Hatch and Helms introduced bills in the mid-1980s to prevent Title X clinics from performing abortions (Hatch) and to eliminate Title X funding altogether (Helms). Each time, again, Congress preserved the program. In 1987, to circumvent the congressional blockade, Jo Ann Gasper, publisher of *The Right Woman* and an active antifeminist, used her position as a deputy assistant in HHS to refuse federal grants to two Planned Parenthood clinics. Since agency staff were not authorized to set broad policy, she was fired—a casualty, antiabortion activists insisted, of a deeply compromised federal bureaucracy. Finally, pressed by a right-to-life movement that had grown increasingly militant, HHS and the Justice Department drafted a rule requiring the complete physical and financial separation of clinics that performed abortions from family planning clinics and prohibited the latter from counseling for or advocating abortion. A divided Supreme Court upheld the rules, 5–4, in *Rust v. Sullivan* (1991).[29]

The efforts of the religious and pro-family movements worked to make rights in American society subject to the market rather than supported by the state. The Catholic legal scholar Douglas W. Kmiec touched on the stakes involved in this transformation by derisively claiming that feminists and others on the left believed that "fundamental rights are just not worth having unless they are federally bankrolled." The liberal-left insurgencies since 1964 had of course presumed that a right not supported by government was fragile, if not meaningless. In every significant arena, from the rights of African Americans and other racial minorities to the rights of women and lesbian, gay, bisexual, and transgender people, negative rights of liberty alone were insufficient. Lyndon Johnson's Great Society had perceived and acted on this reality; its liberal architects simply had not envisioned the breadth of inclusion that later insurgents would demand. Thus a measure of the political and ideological realignment that had taken place by the early 1980s was the degree to which Kmiec's words increasingly resonated among Americans.[30]

In 1986 Reagan's Working Group on the Family, headed by Undersecretary of Education Gary Bauer, merged free-market and family-centered conservatism, creating a right-wing politics for a new age. Under the auspices of Reagan's Domestic Policy Council, headed by Attorney General Edwin Meese, Bauer assembled a critical mass of the administration's conservative appointees, including Clarence Thomas, then chairman of the EEOC, William Kristol, who was part of William Bennett's

brain trust at the Department of Education, Jo Ann Gasper, the antifeminist and dedicated right-to-life activist and columnist then at HHS, and
Dorcas Hardy, an HHS staffer and advocate of the privatization of Social
Security. The Working Group combined the religious right's antifeminism
and breadwinner conservatism and tax-cutting state retrenchment in its
final report, entitled *The Family: Preserving America's Future.* The report
showed how right-wing pro-family principles could be applied to public
policy in an age of neoliberal restructuring and welfare state dismantling.[31]

Drawing on two decades of conservative disdain for the Great Society, feminism, and the sexual revolution, the report advanced two core
claims: that the welfare state had been bad for families and that a re-
vamped tax policy—especially lower taxes and the strategic use of tax
credits—ought to be the principal means to "preserve and protect the
American family." The "rights of the family are anterior, and superior, to
those of the state," the report contended. Since "every totalitarian movement of the twentieth century has tried to destroy the family," Americans
were rightly suspicious of social welfare policies such as payments to poor
mothers or government-supported child care. In their place, *The Family*
recommended a host of tax credits (for couples with children, for instance), market-oriented programs (such as housing vouchers for the
poor), the transfer of surviving welfare programs to state legislatures, and
a dismantling of federal programs that promoted any form of what they
considered sexual immorality (including homosexuality and teenage
sex). Bauer's group sought a fundamental reorientation of government
policy regarding issues of sex, sexuality, and the family, and the report's
conclusion—"the tax cuts of 1981 and the tax reform of 1986 are major
victories for the American family"—made plain that this would involve a
shrinking of the domestic responsibilities of the national state. As in the
antiabortion push of 1981–1983, the greatest success of "defund the left"
was to shift the terms of debate away from rights onto the terrain of government provision.[32]

•

In the worldview of the religious right and the pro-family movement, the
appearance of acquired immune deficiency syndrome (AIDS) in the early
1980s confirmed the narrative of American life they had advanced for
more than a decade. Indeed, one could draw a straight line in conservative

thought from George Gilder's 1973 *Sexual Suicide* to the 1983 *Human Events* headline, AIDS EPIDEMIC: THE PRICE OF PROMISCUITY. To conservatives, sexual immorality and a general undisciplined profligacy had spread a relentless and deadly disease; sin and sexual permissiveness were being punished. Meanwhile, they believed that liberals were so concerned with the rights of gay men and other potential HIV/AIDS victims that they prevented the government from responding effectively—by quarantining all homosexuals, for instance, or requiring the testing of all gay men, two proposals the Reagan White House considered. The obsession with individual rights among liberals therefore endangered children and threatened an innocent population; liberalism had once again taken the side of liberty, license, and permissiveness over discipline and responsibility. When Pat Buchanan opined of AIDS in 1983 that "the sexual revolution has begun to devour its own children," he echoed more than a decade of conservative warning that sexual indiscipline, especially homosexuality and sex outside marriage, would produce social chaos.[33]

The men in national life who articulated this narrative of the AIDS crisis were not obscure or marginal. They were members of Congress and the Reagan administration, heads of think tanks and policy institutes, and prominent religious leaders: Senator Helms, Representatives Newt Gingrich (R-GA), William Dannemeyer (R-CA), and Robert Dornan (R-CA), the ministers Jerry Falwell and Pat Robertson, the Republican strategists Weyrich, Atwater, and Buchanan, the Focus on the Family founder James Dobson, and Secretary of Education Bennett and his deputy, Bauer, among many others. For these New Right captains, the AIDS epidemic was a national medical emergency and a moral crisis but also an opportunity to discredit the entirety of the liberal worldview they associated with the Great Society and the equal rights movements of the 1960s and 1970s.[34]

This was underscored in a 1984 *American Spectator* article, entitled "Gay Times and Diseases," by Buchanan, the conservative political strategist and Nixon-era holdover who was to become Reagan's White House communications director in 1985, and J. Gordon Muir, a physician. Buchanan and Muir took a politically instrumentalist view of AIDS: "Gay rights promises to become for the eighties what bussing and abortion were to the seventies, the social issue that sunders the Democratic coalition." In the context of an HIV/AIDS epidemic emanating from "New York and San Francisco, the Sodom and Gomorrah of the sexual revolution," gay rights had acquired a new toxicity that, in their view, would further erode liberals' political standing. For emphasis, the article was subtitled "Whom the Democrats Would Embrace, They May Be Infected By." Echoing the same theme, Weyrich, the founder of the Heritage Foundation and the Committee for the Survival of a Free Congress whose influence in 1980s Washington was unmatched, called AIDS "the hidden issue that can re-frame the 1986 election."[35]

New Right political tactics were not the only controlling factors in the national response to the crisis, however. Medical professionals and scientists, gay, lesbian, and human rights activists, and a majority of American politicians forged a remarkable consensus by the end of the 1980s. They argued that HIV/AIDS was a global epidemic requiring a multivalent political, educational, and epidemiological response, not moral condemnation. They left several critical issues unresolved—especially the class and racial dimensions of infection, detection, and treatment—but their ideas were essential to future efforts to combat the epidemic. First, though, they had to push the loud and determined voices of the far right to the margins of debate. Although those voices did not eventually prevail, they paralyzed the Reagan administration for years and contributed to a massive burst of antigay hysteria in American culture, which included some of the most mean-spirited and poisonous examples of homophobic defamation in the second half of the twentieth century. Conservative obstructionism crippled nearly the entire first decade of public health response to the epidemic.[36]

That battle between different interpretations of the epidemic raged with such ferocity in part because the identification of AIDS in 1981 and the subsequent explosion of the epidemic raised unresolved issues of visibility, sexuality, and respectability. Here was a disease, spread largely (though not exclusively) by sexual contact and in the early years found most prominently among a population whose privacy and citizenship were already partial and in question (75 percent of U.S. AIDS cases in the decade were gay men). In the gay rights era to become visible, to "come out of the closet," was to claim sexual difference but also to assert common humanity. "Out of the closet" was the only place human rights could be secured. The HIV/AIDS epidemic complicated visibility by resurrecting older prejudices about gay bodies as diseased and unhealthy. To come out for many men with HIV and/or AIDS was to reveal oneself as both gay and diseased. Among a public still rife with antigay prejudice, this confirmed popular

notions of nonheterosexual sex as wrong and unnatural. Even its early official name, "gay-related immune deficiency," suggested a link between
homosexual behavior and danger, if not public disorder.[37]

For the first generation of AIDS activists, those who began to respond
immediately in 1981 and 1982, there were two massive challenges. One
involved fostering a conversation among gay men, and ultimately the
larger sexually active society, about responsible (what was later called safe)
sex that did not smack of internalized homophobia. Gay men had to ask
themselves: Was *any* discussion of responsible sex by nature homophobic?
Would the price of fighting HIV/AIDS be the hard-won sexual liberation
of the previous decade? A second challenge involved crafting a public
discourse about the disease—in the media, the halls of Congress, and the
medical and scientific research community—that addressed rampant societal homophobia and the loud condemnations coming from the religious
right.[38]

These challenges were further complicated by the lack of legal protections for gay rights. By the mid-1980s more than a dozen states had
decriminalized sodomy, and more than two dozen cities had gay rights
ordinances. Still, few states legally protected gay rights, and no law at the
national level shielded gay men, lesbians, and transgender people from
discrimination in jobs, housing, or health care. And in what became an
increasingly common and fraught scenario, gay men were only in rare
cases legally empowered to make complex end-of-life decisions for termi-
nally ill lovers and life partners. The HIV/AIDS epidemic spread within a
legal regime in which only heterosexual sex and sexual identity enjoyed
constitutional protection.

With respect to the first challenge, between 1981 and 1983 gay men
engaged in a wide-ranging debate about their sexual practices. It was not
wide-ranging enough, however, for Larry Kramer, who cofounded Gay
Men's Health Crisis (GMHC) in New York to respond to AIDS in 1982.
In a 1983 article reprinted dozens of times around the country, "1,112 and
Counting," Kramer pilloried the gay press for ignoring the epidemic and
castigated gay men "who moan that giving up sex until this blows over is
worse than death." "Get your stupid heads out of the sand, you turkeys!"
he demanded. Kramer had reason to chastise some gay men for their initial attitude toward the epidemic, but the conversation he implored them
to have was in fact already well under way. In New York, San Francisco,
Los Angeles, and Boston the gay press in 1982 and 1983 had initiated a

dialogue about sex, disease, gay identity, and politics that evolved and deepened with time. That dialogue replayed the debates about respectability and liberation that had dominated the gay press in the late 1960s and early 1970s, with a new urgency. When the San Francisco–based AIDS Behavioral Research Project interviewed more than a thousand Bay Area gay men in 1983, for instance, it found that AIDS had changed sexual practices little and that 69 percent of men with more than three sexual partners in the month before the interview agreed with the statement "It is hard to change my sexual behavior because being gay means doing what I want sexually." For men such as Kramer, such findings amplified the urgency of the moment.[39]

In the long run, the most influential campaign (and new language) to emerge from the focus on sexual practice in the early 1980s was "safe sex." Jim Geary, head of the Shanti Project in San Francisco and among those who helped lead the way, opined that AIDS was a problem "not because we have multiple sexual partners. It's because we don't take the necessary precautions in having sex." Originating in a range of institutions on both coasts, such as the New York Coalition for Sexual Responsibility and the San Francisco AIDS Foundation (SFAF) in that city, some safe sex campaigns stressed the erotic possibilities of "safe" practices, while others stressed "informed consent," testing, and education. At their heart, though, the arguments for safe sex that evolved out of the heated debates of the early 1980s avoided moral condemnation, celebrated sex, and encouraged men to see preventative practices as both erotically charged and socially responsible.[40]

With respect to the second challenge, the public campaign to fight both AIDS and homophobia called for a more concerted government and scientific response to the crisis. "This is a political issue dealing with the whole medical and governmental establishment," the lesbian AIDS activist Cindy Patton wrote in 1983. Antigay discrimination suddenly had a threatening new power: it placed men's very lives at risk. Henry Waxman, chair of the House Subcommittee on Health and the Environment and an early ally of AIDS activists who demanded more resources from the Reagan administration for the Centers for Disease Control and the Department of Health and Human Services, did not mince words in 1982: "There is no doubt in my mind that if the same disease had appeared among Americans of Norwegian descent or among tennis players, rather than among gay males, the responses of both the government and the medical community would be different." In 1983 GMHC, SFAF, and dozens of smaller AIDS social service and political organizations were joined by the National Association of People with AIDS (PWA) in a bottom-up campaign to change the country's approach to the crisis. Founded at a meeting in Denver, the PWA issued what became known as the Denver Principles, which included the principle that people with HIV/AIDS ought to play a role in AIDS policy. Overall, the grassroots response to the epidemic was robust (if underfunded), and by 1987 there were more than three hundred local AIDS organizations.[41]

For President Reagan and his staff, political calculations dueled with epidemiological considerations to shape executive branch policy. Within the administration, Bennett, Bauer, and Carl Anderson, a Catholic attorney in the Office of Public Liaison, pressured Reagan to treat the epidemic in terms of moral questions of personal responsibility, the rights of parents, and the sanctity of heterosexual marriage. Outside the administration, a wide range of figures, most prominently Gingrich, Buchanan, Weyrich, Dannemeyer, Helms, Falwell, and Dornan, joined this chorus. Reagan Surgeon General C. Everett Koop and a handful of staffers from the departments of Health and Human Services and Justice countered this view. And after 1987 the head of the newly created Presidential Commission on the HIV Epidemic, Adm. James Watkins, did so as well.[42]

By the mid-1980s, AIDS public policy debate in both the administration and Congress divided between two basic propositions. Liberals, joined by Koop and Health and Human Services Secretary Otis Bowen, argued for a massive safe-sex public education campaign, government-supported access to confidential, voluntary HIV testing, antidiscrimination protections for those carrying HIV, and greater funding for a variety of AIDS-related health and education services. Koop's support was especially notable inasmuch as Reagan had appointed him because of his opposition to abortion and his evangelical Presbyterian convictions. Alternately, conservatives Dannemeyer, Helms, Bennett, and Bauer argued for mandatory testing of at-risk populations, reporting of the names of all HIV-positive individuals to public health authorities, and abstinence-oriented sex education. Each side in essence saw HIV/AIDS as it saw the world. Public health and rights dominated the liberal view; sexual discipline and public order dominated the conservative view. A compromise between the two sides proved difficult to orchestrate between 1984 and 1987. Congress gradually increased federal AIDS-related research funding in these years, nearing a half billion dollars annually, but it was still a quarter of what the National Academy of Sciences believed necessary. And more important, no comprehensive HIV/AIDS public health campaign emerged from Washington until the final year of the Reagan administration, seven years after the discovery of the virus.[43]

As the epidemic's death toll climbed and official Washington remained paralyzed, a different kind of political battle raged to define the disease's meaning. As gay men debated the past and future of their sexual practices, *The New Republic* editor and syndicated columnist Mort Kondracke worried that "some conservatives are about to use the disease to spread panic and hatred against the gay rights movement." The silence of President Reagan, who was not himself temperamentally antigay, allowed conservative voices to grow more confident between 1984 and 1987. The HIV/AIDS files in the Reagan Library show that a steady stream of explicit and increasingly more defamatory and ugly antigay material from far-right sources circulated among presidential staffers in these years. The historian ought to be careful to attribute any particular administration action to such material, but its ubiquitous presence in the archive suggests how vicious one segment of the New Right had become and how determined it was to use every possible point of leverage to tout its superior sexual values.[44]

Against this background, 1986 and 1987 proved to be both tragic and decisive years in the unfolding epidemic. The Supreme Court announced in June 1986 its decision in *Bowers v. Hardwick*, proclaiming that "proscriptions against [homosexuality] have ancient roots." Justice Byron White's majority opinion (5–4) upholding a Georgia sodomy law sent a dire message to gay and lesbian communities across the country. Even if the HIV/AIDS epidemic had not been a national emergency and even if religious conservatives had not been stoking societal anxieties about sexual difference, *Bowers* would have been dismal news for gay and lesbian activists. At the height of the HIV/AIDS panic, it was a devastating blow. To counter the plaintiff's claim that sexual privacy was rooted in American traditions of "ordered liberty," White and his colleagues went beyond constitutional doctrine. They selectively reached into history, citing sodomy prohibitions from the era of the English Reformation to establish the "ancient roots" of injunctions against same-sex relations. The Court's reasoning was echoed in a letter to *The New York Times* by Noach Dear, a New

York city councilman: "Homosexuality is not protected by the basic law of our land. Homosexuality is indeed, 'different' . . ." Only the passionate dissenting opinion by Justices Blackmun, Brennan, Marshall, and Stevens offered hope that *Bowers* had not fully shut the door on extensions of sexual privacy.[45]

Close on the heels of *Bowers*, in October 1986, the surgeon general released a major report on HIV/AIDS. Despite his religious convictions, Koop stuck to the science and resisted the right-wing position of Bennett and Bauer. The report recommended educating all Americans about the epidemic, including young children, in a manner befitting a national public health emergency. Koop had consulted with numerous HIV/AIDS advocacy organizations, including the National Coalition of Black Lesbians and Gays, and his report was one of the first government documents to address racism's role in shaping the crisis. Compassionate and respectful of the communities hit hardest by the epidemic, Koop's report, in calling for a massive national conversation about HIV/AIDS and a systematic public health response, swam against the tide of the administration of which he was a part.[46]

Though calculated to be a reasoned, centrist document, the report was swallowed in a tide of conservative denunciation and ridicule, and Koop with it. The surgeon general heard of his alleged capitulation to sexual liberalism from New Right stalwarts such as Phyllis Schlafly and from far-right organizations such as the Family Research Institute, which titled one of its own reports "Homosexuality: Our Number One Public Health Problem" and suggested that AIDS was more welcome in public schools than prayer. Criticized for advocating condom use and for employing the terms "penis" and "vagina," Koop tried to maintain a sense of humor. "I didn't know what else to call them," he later quipped. It didn't help. Koop reported receiving "a tremendous amount of hate mail" from fundamentalist Christians.[47]

The surgeon general's report infuriated gay rights advocates and AIDS activists too. They criticized Koop's caution and moderation, symbolized by his embrace of "monogamous relationships," his underreporting of AIDS cases, and his failure to demand increased federal funding of AIDS research. In gay activist circles the report was called everything from "overrated" to "meaningless," and the executive director of the National Gay and Lesbian Task Force (NGLTF) said the report proved that "they still haven't come to terms with the magnitude of AIDS."[48]

Meanwhile, the insistence in medical, public health, and progressive activist circles for a comprehensive national HIV/AIDS policy grew more pronounced. A major 1986 National Academy of Sciences report called for quadrupling federal investment in AIDS research and education, warning of a "catastrophe" absent concerted national action. Scientists at the Centers for Disease Control and the World Health Organization, the American Foundation for AIDS Research, health professionals in HHS, Americans for a Sound AIDS/HIV Policy, and hundreds of AIDS advocacy groups, labor unions, churches, and educational organizations joined the chorus. Sympathetic mainstream journalists joined too and grew more openly critical of the administration. Loretta McLaughlin of *The Boston Globe* accused Reagan of having "played politics" with AIDS and condemned Falwell and the "preachers of political extremes" for terrifying the public. This growing but loose coalition was called into public action in the fall of 1986, when the right-wing libertarian Lyndon LaRouche sponsored a California ballot initiative calling for quarantining HIV carriers and AIDS sufferers. Galvanized liberals helped defeat the measure and signaled that there was emerging and widespread support for a rights-based public health response to the crisis.[49]

Following a year that saw Reagan propose cuts in AIDS funding, the *Bowers* decision, the Koop report, and the LaRouche initiative in California, liberal-left forces began to mount a national response. In early 1987 Larry Kramer and a small group of New York gay activists, who had launched the Silence = Death campaign a year earlier, founded ACT UP (AIDS Coalition to Unleash Power), an organization devoted to militant street protest and political action. PWA filed a discrimination suit against Reagan, and then, in October, after a year of planning, between a quarter and half a million Americans participated in a massive March on Washington, the largest demonstration in the capital since the Vietnam War. The march's theme, "For Love and for Life, We're Not Going Back," united religious, labor, feminist, and social justice organizations. Jesse Jackson, César Chávez, and NOW president Eleanor Smeal made speeches, and march organizers announced a broad agenda of gay rights legislation, reproductive freedom, and legal recognition of same-sex relationships, among other demands. All told, in 1987 HIV/AIDS activists and their allies seized the public platform from conservatives and defined the meaning of the epidemic and the necessary response in their own terms.[50]

Inspired by the internal conversation among gay men about the epidemic, gay activists created two institutions that redefined AIDS for the nation. Together they articulated with renewed militancy a double message about gay people in American life: difference and sameness, sexual diversity in a common human family. One was ACT UP, which grew quickly into a multifaceted guerrilla protest organization that orchestrated militant confrontation and creative street theater. In its uncompromising assertion of *outness*, its irrepressible insistence on a public gay presence, and its core message about the life-threatening danger of homophobia, ACT UP represented the boldest gay political voice since the liberation era of the early 1970s. A second institution was the Names Project AIDS Memorial Quilt, which was unfurled for the first time at the October March on Washington. The brainchild of Cleve Jones, founder of the San Francisco AIDS Project, the quilt was a stunning invention: at once a memorial, a political statement about gay humanity, a site of mourning, and the reappropriation of an iconographic domestic American tradition, quilting. The AIDS Quilt vaulted to worldwide fame within a few years, growing to more than forty thousand panels and touring the nation and the world; in 1989 it was nominated for the Nobel Peace Prize.

In time, ACT UP, the AIDS Quilt, and the safe sex campaign would define the essential cultural politics of HIV/AIDS activism. Gay men were victims, of both an epidemic disease and homophobia, but they were not *defined* by their victimization. They were gay and different—and proud and defiant. But they simultaneously shared in a common humanity, a communal impulse toward health and happiness that stitched them into the fabric of an expansive human family. These claims had been made before, but the AIDS epidemic lent them a new and specific urgency.[51]

Yet the chasing of homophobia from national life remained agonizingly slow. The AIDS crisis revived opposition to the "special rights" gay men (and others) allegedly sought. Helms and Dannemeyer claimed that antidiscrimination protections for HIV/AIDS victims (protection from getting fired, for instance, or thrown out of housing) was merely the vanguard of a broader gay and lesbian agenda. Moreover, as much as ACT UP, the Quilt, and the March on Washington made gay men the face of AIDS, politicians and journalists—and much of America—remained more comfortable with straight victims. During Senate hearings in 1987 on an omnibus AIDS bill, the first witnesses to testify were Louise and Cliff Ray, Florida parents of three HIV-positive boys. (They were hemophiliacs who had received blood transfusions.) Louise and Cliff told the assembled senators that their family had been "threatened, harassed, and discriminated against," and few present seemed to grasp the irony of this claim, coming as it did from a middle-class straight white couple. Television and print media coverage in the late 1980s regularly gave special attention to sensational cases of HIV-positive children and the threat to the blood supply. These were legitimate concerns, but ones that marginalized the higher rates of HIV/AIDS in gay men, intravenous drug users, and people of color.[52]

Moreover, the absence of presidential leadership and the silence of the national political class permitted the consolidation of what can only be called a poisonous homophobia. To be certain, its most aggressive purveyors were on the far right. Groups such as Alert Citizens of Texas, which published "The Gay Plague" in 1983, and individuals such as the Virginia publisher P. A. Brown, who produced the "AIDS Is Looking for You" booklet with illustrator Dick Hafer, whose "Homosexual Deathstyle" was popular among fundamentalist Christians, represented the most visible homophobia. We miss a great deal about American society in the 1980s, however, if we imagine that this homophobia was exclusive to the margins of the right. The American Legislative Exchange Council (ALEC) was an organization founded in 1973 by Weyrich and Henry Hyde whose board of directors included senators and congresspeople and whose ambition was to draft conservative "model legislation" for state legislatures. Its mid-1980s report on homosexuality embraced all the major tenets of right-wing homophobia, including the notion that the "homosexualization of society" would legalize pedophilia and protect predatory teachers. Gay rights had been funded by the federal government, the report insisted, and states should be prepared to defend themselves against the "special rights" sought by homosexuals. By the late 1980s, ALEC was one of the most influential mainstream conservative nonprofit organizations in the country.[53]

Ronald Reagan delivered his first speech about AIDS in 1987, six years after the disease had been identified. That year, under pressure from ACT UP (which protested at the White House in May) as well as from a bipartisan group of senators, Reagan appointed the Presidential Commission on AIDS (known as the Watkins Commission). The commission's 1988 report praised the gay community's efforts to combat the disease at the local level and called for broad antidiscrimination legislation to protect HIV/AIDS victims as well as massive funding for research, education, and local organizations. Despite the report's official government imprimatur, conservative resistance to a comprehensive HIV/AIDS policy remained prominent and in some cases in control in official circles. Koop began to speak openly about how the administration had muzzled him; Helms and other far-right members of Congress insisted that no federal dollars be spent on sex education; HIV/AIDS status had been made a basis for denying immigration to the United States; and a firestorm of criticism erupted on the right in 1988, when the Centers for Disease Control prepared a forthright educational booklet on HIV/AIDS to be mailed to every household in the country. As the epidemic's death toll surged toward one hundred thousand by decade's end, the machinery of the American state remained nearly frozen.[54]

The challenge of making homophobia central to the national conversation about HIV/AIDS revealed the complicated ways sex and sexuality remained embedded in the contested ideas of citizenship that marked the last third of the twentieth century. AIDS activists had to fight tooth and nail to break the silence imposed by homophobia and forge a space in national life for gay men just to speak on their own behalf. Fighting the epidemic required securing the positive rights gay men and lesbians had been calling for since 1964—protection from discrimination especially. It also required disentangling homosexuality, once again, from disease—this time not a psychiatric disorder but a contagious and fatal immune disorder. In that context, the urgency of winning positive rights that protected sexual difference, among which, in time, marriage would gain increasing prominence, was greater than ever. The nation remained more deeply divided than ever, however, over whether an American citizen was entitled to such protections and positive rights.

Yet many HIV/AIDS and social justice activists complained, not without reason, that making gay white men the public face of the epidemic enforced its own kind of silence. By the late 1980s the rapid spread of AIDS among African Americans, Haitians, and other people of color, as well as among female sex workers (not to mention the international epidemic, whose victims are largely in the global south and largely heterosexual), ensured that the majority of HIV/AIDS sufferers were poor, nonwhite, and politically powerless. As this book has shown across multiple scales and struggles, every politics of identity potentially silences another. The HIV/AIDS political battles have been arduous for the gay and lesbian community, but that community's rise to leadership in the U.S. struggle to define the public health response to the epidemic has created additional political challenges both within and outside gay and lesbian circles. Antigay crusades continued to constrain the official government response to HIV/AIDS beyond the 1980s, but so did the equally pervasive social invisibility of poor people of color.[55]

•

Even as a new conservative political tone seemed triumphant in the "morning in America" Washington of the mid-1980s, religious-right activists worried about their waning influence during Reagan's second term. "If it is 'morning in America,' it is a morning bleak and gray. The dawn proved false," wrote William Lind, the longtime Cold War anti-Communist and Washington insider. In 1987 *Christianity Today* bemoaned the movement's "lost momentum." "The sun is setting on the Reagan years," wrote the Baptist Charles Colson, "and on the hopes of once-euphoric evangelicals as well." Their "hopes" had run into the realities of give-and-take American politics. Religious-right leaders thus faced a choice: accept the compromises of the legislative process or radicalize the movement and demand even greater purity of principle.[56]

Many conservatives chose the latter. Their disappointment with Reagan, their own chosen candidate, bordered on outrage. Nowhere was this more evident than among the most passionate foes of abortion, who took to the streets to solve a problem they believed politicians would not. The Methodist and religious-right champion Donald Wildmon noted that if Abraham Lincoln had been "pro-choice" on slavery, black people would still be in bondage. To antiabortion activists of such mind, moral values have to be imposed if they are correct: there could be no compromise, no truck with political pragmatism.[57]

Between 1979 and 1984 right-to-life activists inspired by this radical posture of moral certainty had begun to protest at clinics and hospitals. None was more committed than Chicago's Joe Scheidler. A former Benedictine monk and a dapper dresser who sported a fedora at protests and rallies, Scheidler was, in the estimation of his supporters, a "warrior," the "father of pro-life activism," and (according to Pat Buchanan) the "Green Beret" of the right-to-life movement. His Chicago-based Pro-Life Action League initiated small protests at Chicago-area clinics in 1979, when such tactics were still considered too extreme by much of the right-to-life movement. Scheidler's "truth squads" drew on the example of left-wing sixties activists, using civil disobedience to get his organization and its message into the newspapers.[58]

In 1984, as far-right disillusionment with the Reagan administration intensified, radical right-to-life forces surged past Scheidler's civil disobedience. They turned to clinic bombings, arson, and gunfire. That year alone there were more than thirty violent incidents, largely in the South and Southwest. Two clinics in Virginia and Maryland were firebombed in February; two separate arson attempts targeted a clinic in Everett, Washington, in March and April; Molotov cocktails were hurled into several clinics in Texas in August and September; and bombings struck clinics in Washington, D.C., Georgia, and Florida in the fall and winter. Gunfire too made a frightening appearance. In April 1984, in a representative instance, the Ladies First Medical Group in Pembroke Pines, Florida, in the Miami metropolitan area, was shot up in the middle of the night with a nine-millimeter machine gun. In most cases the perpetrators remained unknown and were never apprehended. But virtually all the attacks targeted clinics where there had been extensive picketing and protesting by right-to-life activists.[59]

In this increasingly tense context, one of the many young conservative Christian activists inspired by Scheidler, an Elm Bible College graduate from upstate New York named Randall Terry, refocused the clinic protest movement. With Scheidler's assistance, Terry founded Operation Rescue in 1988. His goal was not just to stop abortions but "to rescue the nation." "America still deserves the righteous wrath of almighty God," Terry was to write. From 1988 to 1991 Operation Rescue stood on the front lines of the antiabortion movement. In 1988 a sequence of demonstrations, including in Philadelphia, where seven hundred activists were arrested, and in New York City, where nine hundred were arrested, concluded in Atlanta, site of the Democratic National Convention. In the "Siege of Atlanta," twelve hundred activists, including Terry, were arrested, and the movement received continuous national press coverage. A serious student of civil disobedience, Terry understood that producing "tension in the nation and pressure on the politicians" was a legitimate objective of protest. Not unlike the antiwar movement in the late 1960s, antiabortion activists had launched their own "days of rage."[60]

Other conservative strategists plotted a less rageful way forward. With great fanfare in 1987, Weyrich and the Free Congress Foundation announced the publication of *Cultural Conservatism*. Written by Lind and the Catholic William Marshner, husband of the antifeminist activist Connie Marshner, *Cultural Conservatism* represented an attempt to correct what Weyrich called "certain shortcomings" of the religious and pro-family right while still chastising Reagan for his failings. The way forward, the book stressed, was a cultural renewal that would address the "moral vacuum" at the center of post-sixties American life. Weyrich, no political neophyte, sought a tactical middle ground. He criticized Reagan, saying that "nothing this president has done . . . could not be wiped away by a single Democratic president working with solid liberal majorities . . ." But he also called on conservatives to contain their "hatred of government" in order to create a sustainable political coalition capable of producing lasting change.[61]

Though seeming opposites, Weyrich's tactical rethinking and the religious and pro-family right's "days of rage" laid the groundwork for the founding of the Christian Coalition and the presidential primary campaign of Pat Robertson in 1988. Robertson was a product of the certainty on the far right that Reagan had failed, but he was equally a product of Weyrich's call for the religious and pro-family right to embed themselves permanently in the Republican Party. Founder of the Christian Broadcasting Network, Robertson had pledged in 1987 to run for the Republican nomination if three million Americans would sign a petition asking him to do so (they did). Supporters of the Christian Coalition saw Robertson as the religious and pro-family antidote to the Republican standard-bearers Vice President George H. W. Bush and Senator Bob Dole of Kansas. If Reagan had been a disappointment, conservative Christians would elect one of their own. Unlike the Moral Majority, which was fading in political importance, the Christian Coalition aimed to constitute real capacity and leverage at the state level, with the aim of capturing state party organizations. It did so in Michigan in 1987, to the shock of that state's entire political class. Declaring that "as president of the United States, I am free to serve God as my conscience dictates," Robertson ran on a campaign of moral reawakening and the "family values" that had become the religious and pro-family right's anthem. He won only four states and 5 percent of Republican votes, but his presence helped conservative Christians write their agenda ever deeper into the Republican platform.[62]

Robertson's bid for the Republican presidential nomination represented the closing of one era and the opening of another. On one side of that divide, the religious and pro-family right had spent a decade institution-building, forging the political capacity to join the Reagan coalition and shape its tone and agenda. Robertson's campaign, along with the Operation Rescue protests in New York, Atlanta, and Wichita, were tacit admissions that for all that work, the ordinary realities of political give-and-take had prevented the religious and pro-family right from achieving its ultimate objectives. Developments during the decade regarding abortion and HIV/AIDS demonstrated that an increasing number of conservatives were determined to advance an ever-narrower, nearly absolutist definition of family and sexual morality. In the peculiar logic of political movements, the right's defeats encouraged an internal narrative of victimization, which in turn amplified the call to action among the conservative grassroots.

What conservative self-assessments missed, historical perspective makes clear. During the years of the Reagan presidency the religious and pro-family right realized two massive accomplishments. First, it shifted the political debate about American citizenship away from rights toward government provision—what government ought to *provide*. Whether it was access to abortion and sex education or to research and potentially lifesaving AIDS drugs, the right used family politics both to challenge women's and lesbian and gay rights and to oppose the taxpayer provisions and legislation that would render any such rights actual and meaningful (it did the same for the rights of racial minorities). Second, it recast liberalism for large numbers of Americans as a moral threat rather than as a lift up. In place of the liberal left's expanded citizenship, capacious definition of family, and belief in government assistance, the right posited a moral family that required government protection. This shift in American politics is not attributable to one piece of legislation, one court decision, or one protest. Just as the left changed American politics in the sixties and early seventies through years of organizing, petition, and agitation, so the religious and pro-family right did something similar in the eighties. As a result, by decade's end, liberals of all sorts, to say nothing of radicals, found themselves forced into a defensive posture on unfavorable terrain.

EPILOGUE: NEOLIBERALISM AND THE MAKING OF THE CULTURE WAR

In the nineties and beyond, conservatives anchored their political fortunes to two key propositions. Both dated to the presidency of Richard Nixon but did not become the twin bases of Republican politics until the late 1980s. One was that liberalism had precipitated a revolution in gender, sexuality, and the family that had damaged the nation. The second was that government based on regulatory and social welfare principles impeded the "natural" functioning of the market and was responsible for any economic downturn or sluggish growth. Only by reconstituting the moral center of national life around the heterosexual-male-breadwinner nuclear family and by freeing markets from regulation and lowering taxes could conservatives save America.

What is often lost in accounts of this particular kind of conservatism is that the first proposition paved the way for the second. The conservative notion of family values fundamentally changed the frame of debate about rights, public policy, and citizenship and contributed to a wholesale rightward realignment of national politics. Thus breadwinner conservatism legitimated the transition to a neoliberal ethos in American life; heterosexual male breadwinners, as conservatives saw them, were not dependent on the state for either welfare or rights. The result was a political culture for a new age, one defined by the resurgence of laissez-faire market principles, a diminished welfare state, and a citizen whose nominal "freedom" was in no need of measures to protect that freedom. In this realignment of American democracy, late-nineteenth-century notions of citizen and government had replaced mid-twentieth-century ones.

On the flip side of conservative success lies the fate of liberal politics since the sixties. There were two major projects of the liberal left from the Great Society through the rise of the Reagan coalition. One was broadening the social contract to include both new rights and new citizens. This involved struggles for government-supported child care, reproductive rights, antipoverty measures, and workplace rights for African Americans and other people of color, women, and lesbians and gay men, among other objectives. The second project was freedom and opportunity based on identity. The two projects overlapped, and many on the liberal left saw them as indistinguishable.

Both these projects were incompletely realized, but identity politics were more successful than social contract politics. As this book has argued, positive rights proved difficult to win. And even those that were won—reproductive rights, sexual harassment protections, affirmative action—weakened over time in the face of determined conservative opposition. Social contract politics required broad new expansions of state action on behalf of a new generation of Americans, something akin to the New Deal. This was not forthcoming. Meanwhile, American capitalism proved far more adaptable to identity politics than had been predicted in the 1960s and 1970s. New groups—African Americans, women, lesbians, gay men, Latinos—have been welcomed into the consumer and labor marketplace to compete with dollars and talent. This is not to diminish ongoing identity-based discrimination, but rather to note that for educated middle-class Americans racial, gender, and sexual identities were less of a barrier to economic competition in the 1990s and 2000s than they had been in the 1960s.

The outcome was a neoliberal political culture with newfound opportunities to compete as "free" citizens for heretofore marginalized groups. Yet as American democracy became more nominally inclusive, it simultaneously grew stingier and less forgiving. Conservative family-values politics were instrumental in forging this outcome. This was so not because family values distracted voters from their economic interests but because conservatives successfully argued that family values could flourish only with a weak government that absented itself from both the market and the "private" domain of family morality. (It must be remembered that abortion, pornography, women's rights, and the like were understood as government *invasions* of private morality.) In a world where individuals rise by their merits, the market follows its "natural" and "most efficient" course, and families are protected from the moral harm caused by new gender and sexual values, there is no room for a broad social contract that socializes common goods and economic costs.

To understand how this outcome was possible, one can do worse than consider a simple line from a report that Richard Nixon received from the Department of Labor in 1970. The report spelled out how America's "forgotten people—those for whom the government and the society have limited, if any, direct concern and little visible action"—could be converted into Nixon voters. The memo identified a process well under way: many Americans increasingly saw government as benefiting primarily racial minorities, the poor, women, lesbians, and gay men. All one had to do to nudge political transformation further along, the report concluded, was to encourage this view among white male breadwinners and their families. Over the course of the succeeding two decades conservatives made good on this idea. They convinced enough Americans that government was an irresponsible force that promoted abortion, supported (broken) families on welfare, advocated absolute equality between women and men, and rewarded racial minorities at the expense of hardworking white breadwinners to discredit the social contract and remake the nation's politics.[1]

The final battles in that decades-long struggle were staged in the culture war that engulfed the nation between the early 1990s and the early 2000s. Though liberals and others on the broad left won tactical victories here and there, the war in total advanced the larger neoliberal project of state retrenchment and privatization. By the end of the 1980s, at the dawn of the culture war, breadwinner liberalism was a spent force politically. The story of the last decade of the twentieth century and the first decade of the twenty-first is thus twofold. On one hand, it is the story of the largely unsuccessful attempts by the liberal left to reconstitute a political mythology to replace breadwinner liberalism, and on the other it is the story of how breadwinner conservatism was worked ever deeper into the fabric of national social policy and dominant conceptions of the national polity itself.

•

Between 1988 and 1994, between Pat Robertson's presidential primary campaign and the 1994 national midterm elections, when the Republican Party captured a majority of the House of Representatives with its pledged Contract with America, the "rage" on the American right grew in both size and volume. That rage led to more than the institutionalization of conservative views of gender, sex, sexuality, and family in think tanks, policy organizations, political action committees, lobbying groups, and religious alliances. It fixed a worldview and a habit of mind as one corner-stone of the Republican Party. The issue had thus become a tactical one. The question was not whether the Republican Party was committed to breadwinner conservatism, which it unquestionably was. The question was the role extreme versions of family values ought to play in any given election cycle. Ideologically, the issue was settled. Tactically, it was not.

In the twenty-first century, memorializers cast Ronald Reagan as an inspiration to conservatives. Their tribute contained more than a little imagined history. In the half-dozen years following his presidency, the most prominent American conservatives, particularly those on the reli-gious right, expressed considerable disappointment with the so-called Reagan Revolution. They were less inspired by Reagan than furious with him. What *Time* magazine called the "thunder on the right" in 1984 had become a full-scale hurricane by the early 1990s. Originating in Reagan's first term, the right-wing discontent gained momentum in the abortion wars and the AIDS crisis and consolidated during the presidency of George H. W. Bush, a moderate with no particular affinity for conserva-tive evangelicals or facility in the language of family values.

The longtime conservative strategist Pat Buchanan rode this wave of discontent during his campaign for the Republican presidential nomi-nation in the 1992 primaries. Though he was unsuccessful in unseating the incumbent Bush, his jeremiadlike address at the 1992 Republican National Convention in Houston resounded through conservatism and American politics writ large. Buchanan claimed that a "cultural war" had engulfed the nation. A Democratic administration, he warned, would bring homosexuality, feminism, abortion on demand, godlessness, and a draft dodger (Bill Clinton, the Democratic nominee) into the heart of American government. Intemperate and indignant, he signaled the ar-rival of a new and unyielding righteousness in mainstream American politics. For the second presidential election in a row, a candidate claim-ing to speak for absolute religious values and to command a constituency of religious followers occupied the very center of the nation's politics.[2]

The worldview revealed in Buchanan's speech posited a never-ending "war" over American "values." In this war, because it was fought over moral absolutes rather than the content of a shared citizenship, any action or rhetoric was justified and any compromise was a betrayal. Despite the fact that many establishment Republicans found this worldview off-putting, Buchanan garnered almost three million Republican primary votes to just over nine million for Bush. Many Republican critics subsequently blamed Bush's 1992 presidential loss on Buchanan and rushed to distance the party from his intemperance. Yet more than his fellow cultural warrior Pat Robertson, Buchanan discovered that he had the power to influence conservative debate, even if he would not be president. The number of Americans who shared his worldview, or at least voted for it, was growing.[3]

The power of the constituency Buchanan represented was confirmed in the Bush administration's response to the major abortion-related Supreme Court decisions of the period. In *Webster v. Reproductive Health Services* (1989) and *Planned Parenthood v. Casey* (1992), prominent religious-right voices insisted upon, and Justices William Rehnquist (chief justice), Antonin Scalia, Clarence Thomas, and Byron White vociferously advocated, overturning *Roe*. And in *Casey*, the Bush administration filed a brief pushing to overturn the 1973 decision. The moderate Bush, who had a history of cautious support for abortion rights, thought it prudent to appease his family-values critics. Though in both cases the justices lacked the five votes necessary to overturn *Roe*, each represented a dramatic narrowing of the accessibility of abortion and thus a substantial victory for antiabortion activists. However, in the internal narrative of the religious right a limited victory was regarded as a defeat, fueling even greater passion about the moral turpitude of the nation's laws.[4]

Antigay state ballot measures in 1992 in Oregon and Colorado revealed the power, as well as the limits, of the culture war political formula. In Oregon the far-right Oregon Citizens Alliance (OCA) placed before voters a measure that would have defined homosexuality as "abnormal, wrong, unnatural, and perverse," while denying all protections to lesbian and gay people. Echoing Buchanan's speech just a few months before, Lon Mabon, head of the OCA, told his followers that "these are the first units of the cultural war meeting on a political battlefield." While Oregon voters turned down Mabon's measure, the less rhetorically extreme Colorado measure passed. This law, backed by supporters decrying "special privileges," forbade local protections in housing and employment for lesbians and gay men. In the difference between the Oregon and Colorado measures, the right found its calibrated route to political success, even if

404 ALL IN THE FAMILY

the surprise Supreme Court decision in *Romer v. Evans* (1996) declared the Colorado measure unconstitutional.[5]

Colorado and Oregon were part of conservative religious activists' renewed attention to local organizing between 1992 and 1994, following the disappointment of Bush's presidency and the Moral Majority's overwhelming focus on Washington, D.C. In Oregon, despite the statewide defeat in 1992, the OCA won more than two dozen antigay measures at the municipal and county levels and established a strong presence throughout the state, outside of metropolitan Portland. In Oklahoma conservative evangelicals helped Republicans sweep Democrats out of power in the 1994 elections; five of the state's seven congressional representatives (they enjoyed a seven-to-one advantage over Democrats) had strong ties to the religious right. In South Carolina a born-again Southern Baptist, with fervent support among the state's Pentecostal and charismatic activists, won the governorship. In Louisiana conservative evangelicals controlled a third of the Republican Party's state committee, and in California religious-right activists were victorious in eleven of thirteen targeted state assembly races. The religious right found local success in Texas, Alaska, Georgia, and Florida as well. In all, the Christian Coalition and other religious-right and pro-family groups made 1994 the year of evangelical political resurgence.[6]

By that year, the far right's rhetoric of cultural warfare had become institutionalized by Republican Party strategists and opinion makers, while tactical infighting over how to calibrate that rhetoric continued. In 1992, owing to Buchanan's challenge of President Bush in the primaries and the increasing power of evangelical activists, the Republican Party platform had embraced a wholesale conservative family-values ideology. "If I didn't know any better, I would assume the platform was written by the religious right," said Martin Mawyer, president of the Christian Action Network. However, in the wake of the party's presidential loss in 1992, strategists led by Newt Gingrich proposed the Contract with America, which was composed of conservative economic orthodoxy more than family-values demands. As a result, evangelical disappointment with the Republican promises of 1994 was palpable. "There are many of us who think that America's deepest problems are not economic in orientation, they are laden with the debate over values," said James A. Smith of the Southern Baptist Christian Life Commission. In the spring of 1995 Ralph Reed, director of the Christian Coalition from 1989 to 1997, introduced his organization's own Contract with the American Family to "strengthen families and restore common sense values."[7]

Tactical adjustments from year to year or campaign to campaign, however, did little to change the basic conservative dynamic at work in these years. There is no doubt that many Republicans remained uncomfortable with the moral absolutism and jeremiad of the religious right. Following the 1992 election, the Oregon Republican Party chair Craig L. Berkman lashed out. "We have to get the party back from the mean-spirited, intolerant people who want to interject big government into people's personal lives." Nevertheless, a substantial portion of far-right family-values conservatives believed they were fighting such a war. And that was enough to make a political difference, even if they could not always convince party captains to foreground their concerns.[8]

To many conservatives, their rhetoric and determination had risen justifiably. They had to match what they saw as the extreme demands of feminists, lesbians and gay men, and others on the liberal left. Their rhetoric and successful political insurgency set the stage for a new political era. With liberals on the defensive, centrist Democrats in the 1990s grew more aggressive in their efforts to find a politically defensible middle ground—a "vital center" for a new age—that could enable them to win elections and fend off the right's rage. The very fact that so many Democrats searched with such determination for a vital center on gender, sex, and family is an indication of the very success of breadwinner conservatism over the previous decades.

●

A too-narrow focus on the evangelical and pro-family right, however, misses many of the crucial transformations of the Reagan and post-Reagan periods. One was the rehabilitation of military manhood after Vietnam, a project that was at once distinct from the culture war and of a piece with the broader family-values-driven politics of neoliberal retrenchment and moral regeneration. Every narrative of the war, liberal and conservative and otherwise, imagined a rift in American life that could be mended only by remaking manhood, patriotism, and nationalism. Many different institutions and constituencies—the Reagan administration, the national press and electronic media, Vietnam veteran activists, and the Pentagon—argued about how those qualities were best remade. Two episodes illustrate the contentious process of repairing the rift and reimagining manhood: the construction of the Vietnam Memorial and the Iran-contra hearings.[9]

Jan C. Scruggs conceived of the Vietnam Memorial in 1979 as a populist gesture, a "people's memorial." An infantryman who was wounded in Vietnam in 1970 and saw nearly half his company killed or injured, Scruggs proposed a memorial entirely funded by small, private contributions from individual Americans. The grassroots project would "help Vietnam veterans psychologically to feel that their sacrifices were appreciated," Scruggs said. He and a handful of other veterans founded the Vietnam Veterans Memorial Fund in 1979 and by 1980 had secured a congressional resolution (with President Carter's signature) and a site on the Washington Mall. Following a national competition, in May 1981 a committee of veterans, landscape architects, and appointed officials selected a design by an unknown Yale University architecture student named Maya Lin.[10]

Lin's proposal for a low-slung black granite wall sparingly adorned only with the names of American soldiers killed in the war (those missing in action were added later) stirred immediate opposition. Congressman Henry Hyde and two dozen Republican lawmakers formally complained that the memorial made "political statement of shame and dishonor" and perpetuated "national humiliation." James H. Webb, a Vietnam veteran and future senator from Virginia, complained that it would become a "wailing wall" for antiwar protesters. Secretary of the Interior James Watt refused to allow the groundbreaking of the memorial to commence absent additions: a statue of soldiers and an American flag. Scruggs and Lin thus found themselves at the center of yet another "war over the war," as the *Los Angeles Times* put it, opposed by a vocal group of veterans, who called it a black ditch, and most conservatives. The monument's supporters persevered, and with the help of key allies, including General Westmoreland, who supported the design, oversaw the construction of the memorial largely as Lin had envisioned it.[11]

When the memorial was unveiled in the late fall of 1982, it quickly became the touchstone for a national narrative of reconciliation and loss. Lin's monument, much as she had imagined, evoked in those who stood before it a visceral and deeply emotional, but simultaneously ambivalent, response. "You have to touch it. There's something about touching it," one veteran said, describing what in time became the memorial's archetypal scene: veterans and their families running their fingers over the monument's engraved names, feeling the grooves of carved stone, using paper and other materials to etch take-home prints of the names of the fallen. In the first few days following the unveiling, more than 150,000 Vietnam veterans and hundreds of thousands of friends and family members came to Washington, D.C., to visit the memorial. One marine said on seeing the memorial that "I cried for the men who had been there, for their families, for the country . . ."[12]

In offering a solemn space in which male bonding and effusive crying were made to stand for collective suffering and redemption, the memorial gave Americans a potent symbol of the war's meaning. In this narrative the war's real victims were American men or, indeed, American manhood itself. The unity in "healing," however compelling, in time proved difficult to sustain within the larger culture. National reconciliation in the fire of men's pain remained, but it was increasingly isolated to the memorial itself. It had no longer reach.[13]

President Reagan played a minimal role in the memorial's development, but once it was unveiled he adroitly yoked it to his administration's larger vision of a robust national defense and expanded Pentagon. Even though many veterans saw the memorial as evidence of public thanks for a thankless and perhaps even unjust war, Reagan drew the opposite conclusion. The monument helped Americans see "how much we were led astray at that time. We are beginning to appreciate that they were fighting for a just cause." On the day of the monument's unveiling, leaving the National Cathedral, where names of Americans who had died in Vietnam were read aloud, Reagan remarked that "the names that are being read are of men who died for freedom just as surely as any man who ever fought for this country."[14]

The resurrection of military manhood, both real and symbolic, was a crucial aspect of national life in the 1980s. Reagan's revival of Cold War rhetoric after nearly a decade of détente and his administration's undertaking of proxy conflicts in the developing world were coded in the language of manly determination. This was both for public consumption, as Reagan sent budget requests to Congress amounting to a 60 percent increase over Carter's, and for internal consumption in the armed services themselves, which were still recovering from the early-seventies "army in anguish." Reagan's defense team, including the president's longtime associate and political ally Caspar Weinberger, former CIA deputy director Frank Carlucci, and the neoconservative Richard Perle, saw rebuilding both military capability *and* morale as essential to their aims for a more aggressive U.S. posture on the world stage.[15]

Critical to that larger strategy was a new military recruitment paradigm, which first appeared in the second half of the 1970s but did not truly take off until the 1980s. The new paradigm emphasized the financial and educational opportunities military service offered. With promises of money for college and training in technical skills, the "Be All You Can Be" campaign, which launched in December 1980, barely two months after Reagan's election, cast the military as one more option in a free-market wage labor system. The all-volunteer army privatized the human costs of the nation's new foreign policy, ensuring that wars would not demand large-scale sacrifice across the society (and would not, as a result, produce much large-scale opposition). Even as women were recruited into the post-Vietnam armed services in record numbers, seeking the same economic opportunities as men, the image of the military remained decidedly male, as the near-constant presence of "Be All You Can Be" television advertisements in the 1980s attests.[16]

With "Be All You Can Be" images of strapping American soldiers providing the background anthem for the Pentagon's resurgence, Iran-contra revived the Vietnam debates and cast them in new terms. Subverting left-wing revolutions in Latin America had assumed new importance under President Reagan's national defense team. When the revolutionary government of Nicaragua became a target of U.S. destabilization efforts, Congress outlawed U.S. funding of any counterrevolutionary activities in that country. When it was discovered in late 1986 that Reagan officials had circumvented the law by channeling money to the Nicaraguan contras from arms sales to Iran, Democrats in Congress undertook a massive investigation. Meanwhile, the national press reveled in a fresh political scandal with spy game intrigue and a list of prominent officials caught red-handed. At the center of the drama stood the forty-three-year-old marine and Vietnam veteran accused of masterminding the plan, Oliver North.[17]

A strange but telling episode in the long Iran-contra drama occurred in May 1987, during Senate hearings. Concluding his testimony, Robert W. Owen, a former staffer in Dan Quayle's Senate office, asked to be allowed to read a poem. Its provenance was vague (Owen said only, "It is a poem that was written"), but its meaning, and the work it was meant to do in the hearings, were clear. Nicaraguans lived in "darkness and despair" but were heartened to learn "that on this troubled earth there still walk men like Ollie North." North had displayed "bravery in [his] youth" and "patriotism throughout [his] life." But still, his "enemies are more clever and treacherous than ours"—a reference to the Democratic legislators determined to find him in violation of the law. Owen concluded by saying, "I love Ollie North like a brother." And now he had been betrayed by the very country he had dutifully defended.[18]

In the conservative imagination, North was another William Calley. The former Reagan national security adviser Robert McFarlane called North "a very solid, determined, energetic, devoted officer." He added that as "a veteran of an experience in Vietnam," North knew "how worth it it was" to oppose tyranny. The air force general Richard Secord called both North and John Poindexter (a member of the National Security Council) "dedicated and honest men" who simply tried "diligently and conscientiously to carry out the policies of the president . . ." In the wake of the scandal, however, these men were "betrayed, abandoned, and left to defend ourselves [sic]." Time and again, North's defenders struck the same chord. He was an aggressive, dedicated marine, full of patriotism, who observed the requisite manly code of military service: unquestioning loyalty; tough-minded attention to duty; heroism in the face of an unyielding enemy. Like Calley, he merely carried out orders, and like Calley, he was now "abandoned" to defend himself, a scapegoat at the bottom of the chain of command.[19]

Unlike the ne'er-do-well Calley, however, North fully embodied a forthright military manhood. Starched and upright, he was the star of the Iran-contra hearings, broadcast for weeks on live national television in the spring of 1987. His face appeared on countless magazine covers, and his fate was the subject of constant speculation among journalists and opinion makers. When North was convicted on three felony counts in a 1988 criminal trial, no less than Jerry Falwell took up his cause, raising money and gathering signatures for a pardon. In a narrative nearly identical to Calley's elevation as a populist hero a generation earlier—only this time with a star from central casting—North became a potent right-wing symbol of patriotism and militarism.

Reagan-era Cold War militarism required the nation to craft a new story of manhood, patriotism, and war that once again allowed Americans to claim innocence in the extension of liberty and righteousness in the defense of home. This effort envisioned more than a return to the optimistic post–World War II but pre-Vietnam notions of American fighting men. It meant defeating bad memories. When at the conclusion of the 1991 Gulf War President George H. W. Bush declared, "By God, we've kicked the Vietnam syndrome once and for all," he summarized what the national press corps and a generation of Reagan-era defense advisers had been saying, publicly, about the war's potential for creating American military manhood anew.[20]

By the early 1990s, soldiering manhood and patriotic certainty had become conservative political touchstones. The domestic wounds of Vietnam had been symbolically contained in the Lin memorial and then "defeated" in Iraq. It was left to liberals to navigate the new terrain. Some proved more able to than others. Though he had used school and connections to avoid the Vietnam-era draft and then protested against the Vietnam War, Bill Clinton nonetheless proved adept at defusing the issue. John Kerry did not fare as well. Kerry had volunteered for service in Vietnam and had served valorously; after his return to the United States, he had joined the Vietnam Veterans Against the War and delivered some of the most artful antiwar speeches of the early 1970s. When supporters of the incumbent president George W. Bush financed a vicious campaign against him as the Democratic presidential nominee in 2004, Kerry had no answer. Swift Boat Veterans for Truth spent millions of dollars on television ads accusing him of lying about his military record for political gain. The ads were blatantly false, but they successfully played on suspicions that Kerry was insufficiently patriotic and confirmed that patriotism and military manhood had been restored to the pantheon of conservative myths.[21]

A line drawn from the "Be All You Can Be" recruitment campaign through the Vietnam Memorial, Oliver North, and Bill Clinton to John Kerry would mark two critical post-Vietnam developments. The first was a renewal of the mythology of heterosexual military manhood. That mythology was *politically* deployed primarily to delegitimize American liberals, to place their views on the defensive, and to structure the terms of debate about American foreign policy. From Calley to North to Swift Boat, military manhood remained a crucial symbolic weapon in the conservative political arsenal. To criticize American military adventurism was to risk being accused of not "supporting the troops" and of being insufficiently manly or unpatriotic. The second development had to do with the private and public dimensions of the new armed services. In the era of the draft, military service had been socialized across male society; the burden was shared and seen as a citizen's public duty. In the era of the volunteer army, service was less about national duty than about individuals making the most of opportunity in a world of private choices. The human costs of war were privatized—only volunteers, largely working class, died—and made a question of choice, a question of the market. But the financial costs were socialized across the middle of society and made a question of patriotism and duty. This new arrangement, whether intentionally or not, was perfectly engineered for a neoliberal age. It permitted American leaders, and in particular the president (regardless of party), to treat the military as a privatized army supported by public funds.[22]

•

On April 5, 1992, more than half a million people marched in Washington, D.C., in support of abortion rights. Staged in advance of arguments made in *Planned Parenthood v. Casey*, which were to be heard late in the month, the March for Women's Lives was one of the largest single political gatherings in American history. Declaring, "We will not go back!" speakers from across the political landscape of the liberal left, led by the National Organization for Women's Patricia Ireland, defended women's reproductive freedom in total. Three years later, surrounded by congressional Republicans, Ralph Reed presented to journalists his organization's Contract with the American Family, calling for, among other items, new federal limits on abortion.[23]

The political space separating Ireland and Reed was no greater than the space between feminists and their antiabortion opponents in the 1970s. What had changed between 1973 and 1992 was the institutional and political leverage of conservatives. What had changed was the political culture, and its center of gravity, in which the conflict between people like Ireland and Reed took place.

In that new political culture in the mid-1990s Democratic President Bill Clinton proposed a set of centrist initiatives that recalibrated the politics of the family. This was Clinton's "triangulation" (a term coined in the 1996 presidential race by the political consultant Dick Morris) between the liberal left and the conservative right. With women's, civil rights, HIV/AIDS, lesbian and gay, and social welfare activists defining the liberal left and family-values and low-tax and free-market conservatives defining the right, the Democratic Leadership Council (DLC), of which Clinton was a product, sought to steer a moderate, "middle" course. However, in "triangulating" between the political position occupied by people like Ireland

and the position occupied by people like Reed, out of perceived political necessity Clinton, the DLC, and other liberals helped further cement the rightward, neoliberal shift in the nation's politics and public policy.

The new president had carefully calculated his policy proposals and language to strike a middle ground. This calibration was evident, for instance, in his repeated assertion that abortion ought to be "safe, legal, and rare" and in his market-oriented health care proposals. His abortion language won praise in a private letter from Edward Dobson, the pastor of the conservative evangelical Calvary Church in Grand Rapids, Michigan. Dobson, a former Moral Majority board member, congratulated the president on "articulating Christian values along with compassion and understanding." Dobson was especially pleased that Clinton had spoken "in favor of life over abortion." Clinton was the most visible, but hardly the only, liberal politician who sought to regain rhetorical purchase on the mythologies of family in the 1990s.[24]

In the era of triangulation, gay rights suffered. The year before Clinton took office congressional liberals had introduced bills to repeal the ban on lesbians and gay men from serving openly in the military. Clinton sided with them after his election but ran into a solid wall of resistance among the officer corps and congressional conservatives. Claiming that "unit cohesion is the bottom line here," Senator Sam Nunn (D-GA), chair of the Senate Armed Services Committee, opined that the presence of openly gay servicemen and servicewomen "gives a great deal of discomfort to an awful lot of people who are heterosexual." The compromise, the "don't ask, don't tell, don't pursue" policy, was a centrist political bargain but a policy failure. Every year after 1993, the Servicemembers Legal Defense Network, dedicated to assisting military personnel dismissed because of their sexuality, produced a report showing that the policy had stopped neither harassment nor dismissals of lesbian and gay soldiers.[25]

Meanwhile, the HIV/AIDS epidemic grew more deadly and more complex in the mid-1990s, and though government policy grew incrementally more aggressive, it failed to keep pace with the disease. The 1990 Americans with Disabilities Act and the Ryan White Comprehensive AIDS Resources Emergency Act gave antidiscrimination protection to HIV carriers and AIDS victims and increased federal expenditures. But by 1994, AIDS deaths in the United States had surged to nearly twenty-five thousand annually. Moreover, AIDS had spread well beyond gay communities and in the first half of the 1990s had begun to ravage African

American communities in rapidly increasing numbers; by the second half of the decade nearly *half* of all new individuals in the United States infected with HIV were African Americans. In this context, President Clinton's careful political calibration, combined with the post-1995 conservative Congresses, led to yearly and agonizing political battles over funding. The end result was that the nation never developed more than a piecemeal AIDS policy that did not match the severity, spread, and human toll of the epidemic, especially among the poor.[26]

"Don't ask, don't tell" and HIV/AIDS revealed that while liberals could marshal a national conversation about important issues, conservatives could relatively easily block any full-scale liberal policy initiatives. By contrast, a bipartisan consensus converged around marriage. In 1996 the Hawaii Supreme Court ruled in *Baehr v. Miike* that barring same-sex marriage violated the equal protection clause of the Fourteenth Amendment. Fearing that the ruling would launch a judicial revolution or at the very least force other states to recognize same-sex marriages from Hawaii, congressional conservatives, led by Georgia Representative Bob Barr, introduced the Defense of Marriage Act (DOMA). It passed easily, with many Democrats joining the Republican majority, and Clinton signed it into law in September 1996. The law allowed individual states to refuse to recognize marriages performed in other states (ending a long-standing interstate reciprocity) and prohibited the federal government from recognizing same-sex marriage. Polls showed that 85 percent of Americans supported equal job rights for lesbians and gay men, but 60 percent opposed legal same-sex marriage.

Conservatives also used their new majorities to enact welfare reform. They did so against a backdrop of renewed vilification of African American families and the repoliticization of "welfare dependency." This vilification took many forms, such as the famous portrait painted by Reagan in 1976 of the "welfare queen" who collected government checks and drove a Cadillac. By the late 1980s the welfare queen had become a stock character of media-driven politics. Simultaneously, black men found themselves vilified as criminals. Increasingly strict, but biased, drug laws at both state and federal levels overlapped with the emergence of a crack cocaine epidemic. The two produced stunningly disproportionate incarceration rates for blacks and whites and the emergence of the most punitive carceral state on the globe. By 2000, 1 out of every 20 African American men over the age of eighteen was in federal or state prison (among whites the rate was 1 in 180). The combination of extreme vilification of black men as criminals and black women as welfare dependent once more cast the black family itself as undeserving of national attention. Indeed, the partisan consensus on both welfare reform and the drug war symbolized the rightward shift of the national political center since the 1970s.[27]

Welfare reform had been stymied since the Family Assistance Plan had sunk in 1970. The 1994 election broke the quarter century deadlock. Republican congressional majorities gave conservatives the opportunity to write bills, but the Clinton administration had been developing its own, DLC-inflected reform agenda since his 1992 campaign promise to "end welfare as we know it." Complex negotiations in 1996 produced the legislation that eliminated federal Aid to Families with Dependent Children, a New Deal–era program, and replaced it with a system of time-limited benefits for poor women who worked in the private market. Setting the policy particulars aside, what stands out about welfare reform is the effort of Clinton and other Democrats to reclaim the breadwinner mythology against which welfare had been positioned. Clinton staffers were told that welfare reform was about "work and responsibility" and "a paycheck, not a welfare check," and that a principal component of the reform was penalties for "deadbeat dads" who refused to pay child support. There was no room for a war on poverty in Clinton's triangulation.[28]

In his 1996 State of the Union address, Clinton claimed that "the era of big government is over." He soon received a sharp memo from Benjamin Barber, one of his outside advisers. Barber hoped the president did not mean "the end of all democratic responsibility for public goods." Barber, like many Americans politically to the left of the DLC, worried that this was precisely the direction the country was headed. Over the previous two decades, encompassing presidents and Congresses of both parties, evidence of this direction had accumulated. Reproductive rights had been curtailed and privatized. Market-driven empowerment zones had replaced the War on Poverty. Welfare had been dismantled. Marriage and its multitudinous attendant benefits had been narrowed. Conservative judges took a skeptical attitude toward class-action lawsuits, one of the principal ways "rights" are protected by the state. Indeed, the era of large-scale government programs to socialize (democratize) the costs of capitalism and the price of public goods was evidently over. What remained for liberals was tinkering: the Family Medical Leave Act (1993) was perhaps the Clinton era's signal liberal legislative achievement, but it was small-bore compared with liberal ambitions during the previous sixty years.[29]

•

In a pointed gibe at liberals in the fall of 1987, Paul Weyrich accused them of failing to stand behind their best chance in the 1988 presidential race, Gary Hart, the former senator from Colorado and George McGovern's campaign manager in 1972. Journalists had revealed Hart's extramarital affair. "The very liberals who invented a 'right to privacy' to justify abortion and homosexuality," Weyrich wrote, were "quick to decide that in matters of personal morality Gary Hart had no right of privacy." Weyrich's framing of the scandal illustrates the confused, torturous ways that sex, privacy, and politics had become entangled by the 1980s. Weyrich misrepresented the connections many feminists and lesbian and gay activists would have drawn between sexual and reproductive "privacy" and secret adulterous behavior, but his very confusion and misrepresentation were endemic to the larger culture in these years. Between the late 1980s and the present day a complex and deleterious culture of sexual scandal arose within American politics and national life.[30]

Scandals, sexual and otherwise, have long been part of the tactics and stagecraft of political conflict, as the powerful and ambitious seek any means to discredit rivals and climb. However, there are distinct features of the post-1987 sexual scandal culture in American politics that make it uniquely emblematic of the struggles over gender, sexuality, and full citizenship that originated in the sixties.

The 1991 case of Anita Hill and her testimony in the Senate confirmation hearings for Supreme Court justice nominee Clarence Thomas provides one of the best examples. In the simplest terms, two story lines were put forward to compete in the national imagination. One was advanced by Thomas and his conservative defenders. From humble, utterly disadvantaged beginnings in Georgia, the African American Thomas had made himself into a successful, respectable breadwinner. Even the fact that affirmative action helped him make the leap from College of the Holy Cross to Yale Law School could be yoked to a conservative narrative because Thomas had turned against affirmative action. And his tenure as a Reagan appointee at the Equal Employment Opportunity Commission

(EEOC) was devoted to radically slowing down the agency's efforts to bring racial minorities and women into fuller participation in national economic life. This was a tale of bootstrap black male breadwinning and respectability, divorced from both state intervention in the market and the legacies of allegedly ill-conceived sixties programs.[31]

Hill put forward a different narrative. Hers focused on the sexual harassment and humiliation she had repeatedly endured while working under Thomas at the EEOC from 1982 to 1983. This was not a story of respectable male breadwinning, but of the sexual vulnerability of women in the American workplace. Thomas's defenders used Hill's silence to indict her: If this was so traumatizing, why had she said nothing before now? Hill's feminist defenders countered that this was precisely the point: silence about sexual harassment is the price women pay for competing alongside men as "equals" in the marketplace; Hill had had to keep quiet if she wanted to rise. But Hill's story also invoked a positive rights-granting state. Thomas was not charged with any offense, civil or criminal, but Hill's testimony and her use of the term "sexual harassment" explicitly referenced the legal right of women to be free of such workplace abuse and the state's obligation to protect them from it. Indeed, the very agency that Thomas had directed was charged with overseeing sexual harassment complaints from across the country. Hill's was a narrative born of, on the one hand, second-wave feminism's efforts to expose the sexual politics that lie, "in private," behind the cloak of respectability and, on the other, to win for women a combination of marketplace liberties and positive entitlement to equal protection in the enjoyment of those liberties.[32]

When she appeared before the Senate Judiciary Committee, however, the all-male panel of legislators pilloried Hill. Committee members, led by Republicans John Danforth (MO), Arlen Specter (PA), and Alan Simpson (WY), put forward additional narratives of gender, sex, and race to diminish Hill and discredit her story. Her status as unmarried was suspect, and her sexuality was questioned. She was a pawn of radical feminists (and possibly a lesbian), a sex-obsessed liar, or a vindictive spinster angry that her sexual desire for Thomas had gone unreturned. It was even implied by some of Thomas's defenders that Hill was an incompetent product of affirmative action. Collectively, the senators betrayed how little they knew about sexual harassment as a phenomenon and about the considerable body of sexual harassment law that had accumulated by 1991.

Indeed, in front of a television audience in the tens of millions, they reversed the terms of "public" and "private" put forward in Hill's narrative. Hill's private life was suddenly on trial. She no longer had the benefit of privacy; the senators implied that every detail of her personal life was open to question and dissection. The public space that feminists had devoted a quarter century to carving out for women to speak about sexual humiliation collapsed around Hill.[33]

Thus, on the one hand, the Thomas-Hill scandal provided a forum for a national conversation about sexual harassment; despite the belligerence of the Judiciary Committee, this conversation was at times honest and efficacious for advancing the cause of workplace equality. On the other hand, though, the scandal had proved the mythic power of the respectable male-breadwinner citizen subject, updated in Thomas's case by a racial narrative of bootstrap self-invention; when he was nominated by President George H. W. Bush, Thomas said, referencing his own rise, "In my view, only in America could this have been possible." He appealed to that story line throughout the saga. Hill's testimony had destroyed "what it has taken me forty-three years to build," he insisted. "It is drowning my life, my career and my integrity, and you can't give it back to me."[34]

A distinct set of narratives about public-private and the democratic citizen competed seven years later, in the scandal involving President Bill Clinton and the White House intern Monica Lewinsky. Their private, consensual sexual liaisons became public knowledge through a series of bizarre and complicated events following Clinton's January 1998 deposition in a sexual harassment suit brought by Paula Jones. Jones had pursued the case against Clinton for four years, charging him with propositioning and sexually harassing her in 1991, when he was the governor of Arkansas and she was a state employee. That case was ultimately dismissed, but Clinton's deposition testimony required him to reveal other nonmarital sexual relationships. In a direct question about Lewinsky, Clinton lied, denying that a sexual relationship had taken place. The lie was soon leaked, and in subsequent weeks and months it was revealed that on numerous occasions between the autumn of 1995 and the spring of 1997, the president had engaged in sexual conduct with Lewinsky in the White House.[35]

Clinton's subsequent impeachment by the House of Representatives raised constitutional and political questions. The scandal had quickly been put in the service of—indeed, had likely emerged out of—efforts by a rapaciously anti-Clinton wing of the Republican Party to fatally damage the president, if not cause his removal. But the episode took on a different meaning for the generation of feminists who had forged the second wave in the 1960s and 1970s. There could seem no clearer instance of patriarchy's double standard than a powerful married man's sexual dalliance with a young woman who worked for him. Yet prominent feminists, from Gloria Steinem to Katha Pollitt, defended Clinton (Barbara Ehrenreich called it "The week feminists got laryngitis"). Then the young feminists Amelia Richards and Jennifer Baumgardner published a defense of Lewinsky in *The Nation*, summarizing much of the multigenerational response, in which they defended "the right to be sexually active without the presumption that we were used or duped." No means no and yes means yes. Here was one version of choice feminism: the right to make decisions (however poor or unwise) of one's own volition. And yet observers could not help wondering if in this extreme version of choice a critical vantage of the power of patriarchy had been lost.[36]

The lessons of Anita Hill and Monica Lewinsky seemingly ran counter to each other. Hill revealed the extent to which women are subjected to sexually hostile environments by their coworkers and superiors. But that message was soundly defeated in the public circus that followed. Lewinsky, by contrast, was a sexual free agent who pursued the charismatic Clinton for a series of consensual private encounters. Yet Clinton paid a terrible political price, Lewinsky a terrible personal and professional one. The choice seemed to be between women as victims (Hill) and women as empowered (Lewinsky). What makes them part of a single story is how each episode obscured an underlying reality: women in Hill's position require state protection of their right to workplace equality, and women in Lewinsky's position require state recognition of their right to conduct private consensual sex lives.

A unique subset of sexual scandals involved conservative evangelicals and other conservative politicians being outed as gay. The most celebrated recent case was that of Ted Haggard, who was the pastor of the New Life Church in Colorado Springs, one of the seats of the family-values movement. Haggard was not known for outspoken opposition to gay rights, though he did preach against homosexuality. But a succession of conservative public figures and politicians who had vocally opposed or consistently voted against gay rights were outed in various ways between the late 1980s and the 2000s. They included, among others, Terry Dolan, cofounder of the National Conservative Political Action Committee, who died of AIDS in 1986; Arthur Finkelstein, a conservative political consultant who worked for Jesse Helms; Ed Schrock, a Virginia congressman opposed to gay rights; Paul Crouch, president of Trinity Broadcasting Network, the largest Christian television network; David Dreier, a California congressman; and Larry Craig, an Idaho senator. Critics of the outings, particularly in Craig's case, because he was arrested for solicitation, claimed that discussions of private consensual sexual behavior had no place in the public square. Supporters have countered that such outing is important because it reveals the hypocrisy of those who call for the regulation of others' private sex lives.

One of the casualties of scandals in the eighties and nineties was the feminist principle that the point of seeing private activity as political is to disarm sexism's power to subordinate women. "The personal is political" was not asserted in order to expand the realm of private life subjected to sensational and titillating surveillance. Activists asserted it in order to liberate women and others from oppressions that were hidden and unspoken. This principle has been muddled in the media-inspired voyeurism (in which "dutiful" wives often stand by their maligned husbands), manipulated for raw political advantage, or simply defeated (as in the Hill case). A second casualty is the gay rights claim that visibility is volitional and connected to empowerment. A feminist and gay rights political culture casts challenges to "private" acts of sexism and sexual harassment as part of a larger politics of liberty and equality. Crucially, those politics show a role for the state. A scandal and confessional political culture erases all that, substituting titillating entertainment—the old Victorian notion of scandal—and "gotcha" partisan politics. And, importantly, a scandal and confessional culture obviates any notion that rights or human freedoms that the state might protect are involved. Confessional culture is a market-oriented, antistatist culture and ultimately an anti-human-rights culture.

•

Echoing claims similar to those made in 1980, conservative evangelicals took credit for George W. Bush's reelection to the presidency in 2004. Tony Perkins, president of the Family Research Council, told reporters that opposition to gay marriage, in particular, was "the hood ornament on the family-values wagon that carried the president to a second term." Voters in eleven states, including the major presidential battleground states of Michigan and Ohio, considered ballot measures banning same-sex marriage. Convinced by organizations with names like Citizens for the Protection of Marriage and Ohio Campaign to Protect Marriage that they had to "protect" or "save" marriage, voters in all eleven states overwhelmingly approved the measures. The state ballot push was an extension of the presidential adviser Karl Rove's national political strategy. Earlier in 2004, Bush had endorsed the Federal Marriage Amendment, a constitutional amendment defining opposite-sex marriage as the only lawful kind.[37]

By 2004 this kind of political management had become a matter of course in the Republican Party. Journalists treated the development as unique largely because of the scale of the endeavor and the unsubtle targeting of Michigan and Ohio, two states poll watchers believed could decide the election. But it was merely an exaggerated version of the management of conservative pro-family and religious constituencies that had been a necessary part of Republican politics since 1980. As for its efficacy, scholars remain divided over whether or not the ballot measures made a conclusive difference in Bush's victory over John Kerry.[38]

More conclusive is the long view. The 2004 election was part of a national political and ideological realignment that was the dominant political story of American life in the last third of the twentieth century and much of the first decade of the twenty-first. The politics of gender, sex, sexuality, and family made possible that realignment, alongside and embedded within a racialized partisan reshuffling most evident in the South. The transformed national political debate halted the broad process of rights expansion that had begun under the Great Society and in its place substituted an antistatist, neoliberal formula of deregulation, reduced social welfare expenditure, and a redistribution of national wealth upward. Whether the liberal left can, or wishes to, revive the political symbols and popular support necessary to begin anew the process of democratizing rights and social costs remains to be seen.

Of course, in a nation of three hundred million people, of massive metropolitan global cities and untold thousands of small towns; of enormous regional, racial, and class diversity; and of equally great religious diversity, there is no single "realignment." There are only varieties of realignment. It would be a mistake to think that the strictly partisan component is even the most salient dimension of this process. Kansas, for instance, became increasingly conservative after the 1960s, shedding much of its tradition of progressive politics. Its *partisan* alignment changed relatively little, however, since it had long been a Republican-majority state. What changed was the ideology of the Republicans Kansans elected: moderates such as Bob Dole and Nancy Kassebaum have been replaced by far-right conservatives such as Sam Brownback. Pennsylvania, by contrast, is a swing state, where partisan politics has remained competitive. And yet Republicans have dominated state government. No state realignment looks quite the same, and the politics of gender, sex, sexuality, family, and race have played varied roles in different states.[39]

The South's realignment, in particular, cannot be attributed to an isolated gender and sexual politics. Resistance to racial desegregation and African American civil rights drove southern whites from the Democratic Party starting in 1964 (if not 1948). Nearly 80 percent of white southerners identified as Democrats in 1952, while fewer than 30 percent did in 2002. That historic shift did not, however, represent a significant ideological realignment because conservative southern Democrats in 1952 bore a striking resemblance to conservative southern Republicans in 2002. What stands out about the post-sixties South is the rise of evangelicalism in the rapidly expanding Sun Belt suburbs after the 1960s. For many southern evangelicals, a politics of nominal racial meritocracy (no affirmative action or busing) yoked to a politics of heterosexual family morality proved to be the ideological replacement for the raw white supremacy of much of the pre-1960s Democratic Party.[40]

While racial politics have an indisputable power of their own, they are also embedded in, and understood through, the gender and sexual components of citizenship. Breadwinner liberalism and breadwinner conservatism were gendered, sexual, *and* racial. When white supremacy gave way throughout much of the South (and nation) in the 1970s, to a nominally race-blind, meritocratic heterosexual breadwinner conservatism, this basic reality did not change. Indeed, breadwinner conservatism proved more deleterious to African Americans in certain specific ways than blatant white supremacy. Breadwinner conservatism offered a lens through which Americans could see black families as lacking the requisite values to succeed, while at the same time not seeming to be about race. A nominally race-blind conservatism proved as difficult to combat as, or even more than, an unapologetically white supremacist one.

Two additional arcs of realignment are striking. One is religious. For much of American history, religious denomination was a reliable predictor of political allegiance. Despite regional and class variations, Catholics tended to vote alike, as did white mainline Protestants and evangelicals. By the twenty-first century these religious blocs had divided along liberal-conservative lines. Conservative Catholics were much more likely to vote like conservative evangelicals, for instance. A second striking realignment is what has been called the gender gap. Only once between 1980 and 2010 did the Republican presidential nominee receive more than 50 percent of women's votes; this was George H. W. Bush in 1988. Ronald Reagan in 1984 received exactly 50 percent of the female vote. Aside from 1984 and 1988, the highest percentage of the female vote won by a Republican was George W. Bush in 2004 with 48. The gender gap has tended to range between 8 and 10 percent, striking evidence that post-1960s conservatism speaks more powerfully to men than women.[41]

The interplay between political and ideological realignment is the crucial dialectic with which this book has been concerned. The liberal-left insurgents of the 1960s and 1970s lost momentum, political allies, and purchase on crucial symbolic mythologies of the American family. Those insurgencies neither disappeared nor radically altered their political program. But by the early 2000s that program stood further and further to the left of the nation's political center. By that point a twentieth-century political movement, liberalism, whose two signal ambitions were to socialize public goods and the costs of capitalism and to expand rights to personal liberty and social equality for the nation's citizens, seemed to be in full retreat. In its place arose a neoliberal ideology of privatization and deregulation.

The major effect of this great realignment of American democracy has been to subject more and more aspects of national life to market forces. Here a return to the concept of the negative right of liberty and the positive right of equality is necessary. What has survived in the new political environment are a handful of abstract rights: women's market liberty, for instance, the constitutionality of abortion (barely), and sexual privacy, the latter embodied in *Lawrence v. Texas*, the 2003 Supreme Court decision that declared state sodomy statues unconstitutional. These are negative rights of liberty. But as the liberal-left insurgencies lost momentum and allies, and as conservative political programs gained traction in the 1980s and afterward, those rights were left almost entirely to the market. The positive rights necessary for those liberties to be meaningfully realized were absent. A painful and ironic truth became increasingly evident: meaningful rights varied with income and resources.

Three examples illustrate this reality. When the Supreme Court in *Wal-Mart v. Dukes* (2011) refused to certify more than one million female Wal-Mart employees as a class for the purposes of seeking redress for systematic wage and promotion discrimination at the company, it codified the new free market. Individual women could seek their own justice, but the state would not recognize or attempt to remedy systemic market bias. Given the realities of the American marketplace, where nonunion, low-wage labor remains the only option for the majority of women, including large majorities among women of color, decisions like *Wal-Mart* render women's market liberty increasingly less meaningful. And this is to say nothing of the absence of state-guaranteed child care or any of the other positive rights defeated in earlier political struggles. Take your right of liberty into the marketplace and see what you can do with it, Americans have increasingly told women.[42]

Reproductive rights too are increasingly subject to market forces. The "right of privacy" delineated by *Roe* had already been severely limited by the Helms and Hyde amendments, which banned all public funding of abortion, and by the prolonged battles over abortion provision at public hospitals, Planned Parenthood clinics, and doctors' offices. *Webster* and *Casey* allowed states to pass even more restrictive laws. Combined with clinic violence, the erosion of *Roe* has meant that the "right" to an abortion has grown even more closely dependent on money and other resources. By the first decade of the twenty-first century, across the United States, one-third fewer counties had an abortion provider than in the late 1970s. In 2005, 87 percent of all U.S. counties and 97 percent of all rural U.S. counties had no abortion provider. These counties were home to 35 percent of women aged fifteen to forty-four. The fissure in constitutional privacy, which many activists recognized at the time of *Roe*, has made reproductive rights far from universal; the costs of unwanted pregnancy are borne almost entirely by individual women.[43]

A third example, lesbian, gay, bisexual, and transgender rights, seemingly invites a paradox. With the slow emergence of marriage equality in a handful of states, lesbians and gay men have won a small measure of positive rights. In some legal instances, the "right" to marry is considered a liberty, but because marriage is a state-subsidized institution with an array of provisions—everything from tax advantages to spousal health insurance coverage—it behaves like a classic positive right. Marriage remains one of the few agreed-upon social goods that is broadly subsidized by the state. It is no irony that one of the few arenas in which positive rights have increased of late is marriage, the institution whose "sanctity" has been so crucial to conservative politics in the last decades—even as most conservatives have resisted marriage equality at every turn. Nevertheless, marriage rights remain far from universal, DOMA remains law, and LGBT people still inhabit a world in which only the smallest negative rights have been won and positive rights are confined to relatively few states. Raising families, finding health insurance, ensuring safe work and living spaces, and many other ordinary life pursuits are made more difficult as a result.[44]

None of the foregoing should be taken as evidence that the liberal-left insurgencies accomplished nothing. Nor is it to suggest that all those on the liberal left believed the state—what conservatives call the nanny state—could solve every social problem, though some liberals certainly placed too much faith in government. Rather, it is to make clear that if one of the signal ambitions of those insurgencies was to socialize the costs of public goods, including rights, much of that hope has gone unrealized. Neoliberalism requires that individuals, not states, bear social costs and pay market price for most social goods. Before anything like the revolution in liberty and equality, negative and positive rights, envisioned by people like Gloria Steinem, Shirley Chisholm, and Jean O'Leary was realized, it had been derailed and replaced with an unmistakable social and political movement toward neoliberal principles.

It has long been contended that the economic crisis in the industrialized West in the 1970s, and the failure of Keynesian adjustments to remedy this crisis in the short term, precipitated the shift toward market deregulation and social welfare contraction. That contention contains a great deal of truth and is sufficiently established in both scholarly and popular accounts. Observers have far less often recognized that the politics of gender, sexuality, and family shaped the rise of neoliberal free-market orthodoxy. In a nation that imagines that individuals rise solely by their own merits and the market follows its "natural" course, there is little room for an expanded social contract in which new gender and sexual rights—

or, increasingly, even hard-won race-based rights—are guaranteed by the state. There is even less room for such guarantees in a nation that imagines that its families require constant and vigilant protection from the moral harm allegedly caused by threatening gender and sexual values. This is another way of saying that the politics of gender, sexuality, and the family since the 1960s have not been injected, as if from some nonpolitical domain, into the public life of the nation. Rather, those politics have been one of the central grounds on which this public life itself has been constituted.

ABBREVIATIONS USED IN THE NOTES

MANUSCRIPT COLLECTIONS

ATLANTA, GEORGIA
JIMMY CARTER PRESIDENTIAL LIBRARY
BAB   Beth Abramowitz
JC   White House Central Files
MC   Midge Costanza Papers
RM   Robert Maddox Papers
RC   First Lady (Rosalynn Carter) Papers

AUSTIN, TEXAS
LYNDON BAINES JOHNSON PRESIDENTIAL LIBRARY
LBJ   White House Central Files
KC   Kerner Commission

BERKELEY, CALIFORNIA
BANCROFT LIBRARY, UNIVERSITY OF CALIFORNIA, BERKELEY
MCC   McCone Commission Collection

BOSTON, MASSACHUSETTS
JOHN F. KENNEDY PRESIDENTIAL LIBRARY
SR   Scott J. Rafferty Papers
SS   Robert Sargent Shriver Papers

CAMBRIDGE, MASSACHUSETTS
SCHLESINGER LIBRARY, RADCLIFFE INSTITUTE FOR ADVANCED STUDY, HARVARD UNIVERSITY
DB   Dolores Bargowski Papers
SB   Susan Brownmiller Papers
CB   Charlotte Bunche Papers
ME   Mary O. Eastwood Papers

BF   Betty Friedan Papers
SL   Shelah Leader Papers
LLH   Lucille Lord-Heinstein Papers
ERM   Edna Rankin McKinnon Papers
PM   Pauli Murray Papers
NARAL   National Abortion Rights Action League (NARAL) Records
NOW   National Organization for Women (NOW) Records
WAR   New York Women Against Rape
PCSW   President's Commission on the Status of Women Records
RPS   Ruth Proskauer Smith Papers
SHA   Society for Humane Abortion Papers
CSW   U.S. Presidential Commission on the Status of Women
WEAL   Women's Equity Action League Records

CHAPEL HILL, NORTH CAROLINA
UNIVERSITY OF NORTH CAROLINA MANUSCRIPTS, WILSON LIBRARY
SE   Sam Ervin Papers

CHICAGO, ILLINOIS
CHICAGO HISTORICAL SOCIETY
BE   Brenda Eichelberger papers

UNIVERSITY OF ILLINOIS, CHICAGO SPECIAL COLLECTIONS
LM   Lonny Myers Papers
NBFO   National Black Feminist Organization Papers

COLLEGE PARK, MARYLAND
NATIONAL ARCHIVES
PCB   Records of the Presidential Clemency Board (RG 429)
VWC   Records of the Vietnam War Crimes Working Group (RG 319)

RICHARD NIXON PRESIDENTIAL MATERIALS, NATIONAL ARCHIVES, COLLEGE PARK,
MARYLAND
CC   Charles W. Colson Files
JD   John Dean III Files
JE   John Ehrlichman Files
RN   President's Personal Files
RNWH   White House Central Files
[The Nixon Presidential Materials have since been moved to the Nixon Presidential
    Library and Museum in Yorba Linda, California.]

ITHACA, NEW YORK
DEPARTMENT OF SPECIAL COLLECTIONS, CORNELL UNIVERSITY
BB   Barbara Berger Eden Papers
CS   Citizen Soldier Records
GAG   Gay Alliance of the Genesee Valley Records
HRC   Human Rights Campaign Records

HL   Harry Langhorne Papers
NGLTF   National Gay and Lesbian Task Force Records
SHR   Sheldon Herman Ramsdell Papers
BV   Bruce Voeller Papers

LAWRENCE, KANSAS
ROBERT J. DOLE INSTITUTE OF POLITICS
RD   Robert Dole Papers

LITTLE ROCK, ARKANSAS
WILLIAM J. CLINTON PRESIDENTIAL LIBRARY
RB   Richard Beardsworth, National Security Council Records
EK   Elena Kagan, Domestic Policy Council Records
CR   Carol Rasco, Domestic Policy Council Records
BR   Bruce Reed, Domestic Policy Council Records
CS   Cliff Sloan, Counsel's Office

LOS ANGELES, CALIFORNIA
CITY OF LOS ANGELES, CITY RECORDS OFFICE
LACC   City Council Files
TB   Thomas Bradley Mayoral Files
JW   Joel Wachs Files

ONE INSTITUTE AND ARCHIVES, UNIVERSITY OF SOUTHERN CALIFORNIA, LOS ANGELES
ONE   ONE Archives
SDC   Stonewall Democratic Club Materials

DEPARTMENT OF SPECIAL COLLECTIONS, CHARLES E. YOUNG RESEARCH LIBRARY, UCLA
ACLU   ACLU of Southern California
TB   Mayor Tom Bradley Administrative Papers
CCTA   California Committee for Therapeutic Abortion
CDC   California Democratic Caucus
MK   Morris Kight Papers

SOUTHERN CALIFORNIA LIBRARY FOR SOCIAL RESEARCH
KC   Ken Cloke Papers
JK   Jim Kepner Papers

MADISON, WISCONSIN
WISCONSIN HISTORICAL SOCIETY
GW   George Wiley Papers
JJ   Joan Jordan Papers
MGF   Marlene Gerber Fried Papers
WRI   Workers' Rights Institute Papers

MINNEAPOLIS, MINNESOTA
UNIVERSITY OF MINNESOTA SPECIAL COLLECTIONS
JNT Jean-Nickolaus Tretter Collection in Gay, Lesbian, Bisexual, and Transgender
    Studies

NASHVILLE, TENNESSEE
VANDERBILT TELEVISION NEWS ARCHIVE, VANDERBILT UNIVERSITY
VTN Vanderbilt Television News Archive

NEW YORK, NEW YORK
COLUMBIA UNIVERSITY RARE BOOKS AND MANUSCRIPTS
BA Bella Abzug papers

LESBIAN HERSTORY ARCHIVES, BROOKLYN
DB Daughters of Bilitis Folder
BG Barbara Gittings Papers
IWY Houston National Women's Year Conference Folder
JL Julie Lee Papers
BS Barbara Smith Papers

NEW YORK PUBLIC LIBRARY
JNK Jonathan Ned Katz Papers
SD Stephen Donaldson Papers
MD Martin Duberman Papers
NYM Mattachine Society of New York Papers

TAMIMENT LIBRARY, NEW YORK UNIVERSITY
GI GI Newspapers Collection

NORTHAMPTON, MASSACHUSETTS
SOPHIA SMITH COLLECTION, SMITH COLLEGE
DA Dolores Alexander Papers
PB Phyllis Birkby Papers
HC Homosexuality Collection
IM Isabel Miller Papers
ES Ellen Shumsky Papers
GS Gloria Steinem Papers

PRINCETON, NEW JERSEY
MUDD LIBRARY, PRINCETON UNIVERSITY
GM George McGovern Papers

SAN FRANCISCO, CALIFORNIA
LESBIAN, GAY, BISEXUAL, AND TRANSGENDER HISTORICAL SOCIETY, SAN FRANCISCO
PL Phyllis Lyon Collection
LM Phyllis Lyon and Del Martin Papers

SAN FRANCISCO PUBLIC LIBRARY
ES   Evander Smith—California Hall Collection
FJ   Florence "Conrad" Jaffy Papers
HM   Harvey Milk Papers—Susan Davis Alch Collection

SAN MARINO, CALIFORNIA
HUNTINGTON LIBRARY
JH   James Hahn Collection

SANTA BARBARA, CALIFORNIA
UNIVERSITY OF CALIFORNIA, SANTA BARBARA SPECIAL COLLECTIONS
CF   Comisión Femenil Papers

SEATTLE, WASHINGTON
UNIVERSITY OF WASHINGTON SPECIAL COLLECTIONS
CH   Charles Harbaugh Papers
WH   William L. Harrington Papers
UWY   YWCA of the University of Washington

SIMI VALLEY, CALIFORNIA
RONALD REAGAN PRESIDENTIAL LIBRARY
CA   Carl Anderson Files
GB   Gary Bauer Files
MB   Morton Blackwell Files
RB   Ralph Bledsoe Files
JC   Jane Carpenter Files
BC   Bruce Chapman Files
JD   Juanita Duggan Files
SG   Stephen Galebach Files
DJ   Dee Jepsen Files
DM   Donald MacDonald Files
PMB   Patricia Mack Bryan Files
EM   Edwin Meese Files
NR   Nancy Risque Files
WR   William Roper Files

WASHINGTON, D.C.
LIBRARY OF CONGRESS
HB   Harry Blackmun Papers
TM   Thurgood Marshall Papers

WHEATON, ILLINOIS
WHEATON COLLEGE MANUSCRIPTS AND SPECIAL COLLECTIONS
NAE   National Association of Evangelicals Records

NEWSPAPERS, MAGAZINES, AND SERIALS

ADV   *The Advocate* (The *Los Angeles Advocate* until 1969)
AS   *The American Spectator*
BG   *The Boston Globe*
CDN   *Chicago Daily News*
CD   *Chicago Defender* (also *Chicago Daily Defender*)
CT   *Chicago Tribune*
CC   *Christian Century*
CHT   *Christianity Today*
CN   *Citizen News*
CONGD   *Congressional Digest*
COND   *Conservative Digest*
CR   *Congressional Record*
DMN   *The Dallas Morning News*
Drum
Ebony
EMM   *Eastern Mattachine Magazine*
GCN   *Gay Community News*
GSB   *Great Speckled Bird*
Harper's   *Harper's Magazine*
HALN   *Homophile Action League Newsletter*
HC   *Homosexual Citizen*
HE   *Human Events*
Jet
The Ladder
LCE News
LT   *The Lesbian Tide*
Liberator
Look
LADJ   *Los Angeles Daily Journal*
LAFP   *Los Angeles Free Press*
LAT   *Los Angeles Times*
MAP   *Mom's Apple Pie*
MLR   *Monthly Labor Review*
MMR   *Moral Majority Report*
MS   *Muhammad Speaks*
NATR   *National Review*
NR   *The New Republic*
NYT   *The New York Times*
NYTSM   *The New York Times Sunday Magazine*
Newswest
NMFG   *No More Fun and Games: A Journal of Female Liberation*
oob   *off our backs*
ONE
PSR   *Phyllis Schlafly Report*
Playboy

PT   The Plain Truth
Ramparts
Rat
RD   Reader's Digest
SPPP   St. Paul Pioneer Press/Dispatch
St. Petersburg Times
SR   Saturday Review
Tangents
TT   Town Talk
Valley Times
Vector
VV   The Village Voice
WSJ   The Wall Street Journal
WM   The Washington Monthly
WP   The Washington Post
WPTH   The Washington Post Times Herald
WE   The Wichita Eagle

NOTES

PROLOGUE

1. The equal rights framework itself was under constant contestation and was never precisely "settled." See Nancy MacLean, *Freedom Is Not Enough: The Opening of the American Workplace* (Cambridge, Mass.: Harvard University Press, 2006); Peniel E. Joseph, "Black Liberation Without Apology: Rethinking the Black Power Movement," *Black Scholar* 31/3–4 (Fall/Winter 2001): 2–17; Matthew J. Countryman, *Up South: Civil Rights and Black Power in Philadelphia* (Philadelphia: University of Pennsylvania Press, 2006); Thomas J. Sugrue, *Sweet Land of Liberty: The Forgotten Struggle for Civil Rights in the North* (New York: Random House, 2008). The term "sexual minorities" is inexact, but I use it here for shorthand to mean gay men, lesbians, and bisexuals. It describes transgender people least well, something taken up later in the book.
2. Here and throughout I see "citizenship" not as a fixed legal status but as a broader social and political category defined by the interplay of individual and communal rights, responsibilities, and authority in a democratic society. See Alice Kessler-Harris, *In Pursuit of Equity: Women, Men, and the Quest for Economic Citizenship in 20th-Century America* (New York: Oxford University Press, 2001); Gretchen Ritter, *The Constitution as Social Design: Gender and Civic Membership in the American Constitutional Order* (Stanford, Calif.: Stanford University Press, 2006); Lauren Berlant, *The Queen of America Goes to Washington City: Essays on Sex and Citizenship* (Durham, N.C.: Duke University Press, 1997).
3. In my use of terminology throughout the book, I have relied on the guidelines of the Gay & Lesbian Alliance Against Defamation and the Movement Advancement Project ("An Ally's Guide to Terminology: Talking About LGBT People & Equality," 2011). I have used historically specific terms, such as "homophile" and "transsexual," or "transexual," when appropriate.
4. Manning Marable, *Black American Politics: From the Washington Marches to Jesse Jackson* (London: Verso, 1985); Dan T. Carter, *The Politics of Rage: George Wallace, the Origins of the New Conservatism, and the Transformation of American Politics* (New York: Simon & Schuster, 1995); Robert O. Self, *American Babylon: Race and the Struggle for Postwar Oakland* (Princeton, N.J.: Princeton University Press, 2003);

Michelle Alexander, *The New Jim Crow: Mass Incarceration in the Age of Colorblindness* (New York: The New Press, 2010).

5. I stand on the shoulders of too many scholars to name here. They include Susan Faludi, *Backlash: The Undeclared War Against American Women* (New York: Crown, 1991); Dorothy Sue Cobble, *The Other Women's Movement: Workplace Justice and Social Rights in Modern America* (Princeton, N.J.: Princeton University Press, 2004); and Donald G. Mathews and Jane Sherron De Hart, *Sex, Gender, and the Politics of ERA: A State and the Nation* (New York: Oxford University Press, 1990).

6. See, for instance, Patricia Hill Collins, *Black Feminist Thought: Knowledge, Consciousness, and the Politics of Empowerment* (Boston: Unwin Hyman, 1990); Marc Stein, *City of Sisterly and Brotherly Loves: Lesbian and Gay Philadelphia, 1945–1972* (Chicago: University of Chicago Press, 2000); Nancy A. Hewitt, ed., *No Permanent Waves: Recasting Histories of U.S. Feminism* (New Brunswick, N.J.: Rutgers University Press, 2010).

7. Stephanie Coontz, *The Way We Never Were: American Families and the Nostalgia Trap* (New York: Basic Books, 1992); Nancy F. Cott, *Public Vows: A History of Marriage and the Nation* (Cambridge, Mass.: Harvard University Press, 2000); Susan Thistle, *From Marriage to the Market: The Transformation of Women's Lives and Work* (Berkeley: University of California Press, 2006).

8. My argument here derives from many sources, but one of the most thought-provoking is Michael Warner, *Publics and Counterpublics* (New York: Zone Books, 2002).

9. John D'Emilio and Estelle B. Freedman, *Intimate Matters: A History of Sexuality in America* (New York: Harper & Row, 1988); D'Emilio, "Capitalism and Gay Identity," in *Powers of Desire: The Politics of Sexuality*, ed. Ann Snitow, Christine Stansell, and Sharon Thompson (New York: Monthly Review Press, 1983), 100–113.

10. Isaiah Berlin, *Four Essays on Liberty* (New York: Oxford University Press, 1969); Kathleen M. Sullivan, "Constitutionalizing Women's Equality," *California Law Review* 90/3 (May 2002): 735–764.

1: ARE YOU MAN ENOUGH?

1. *Hearings Before the Subcommittee on the War on Poverty Program of the Committee on Education and Labor, House of Representatives* (Washington, D.C.: Government Printing Office, 1964), 64.

2. Ibid., 64.

3. Ibid., 114.

4. Morris Zelditch, "Role Differentiation in the Nuclear Family," in *Family, Socialization and Interaction Process* (Glencoe, Ill.: Free Press, 1955), 339; Linda Gordon, *Pitied but Not Entitled: Single Mothers and the History of Welfare, 1890–1935* (New York: Free Press, 1994).

5. Joan Williams, *Unbending Gender: Why Family and Work Conflict and What to Do About It* (Oxford, U.K.: Oxford University Press, 2000); Sidney M. Milkis and Jerome M. Mileur, *The Great Society and the High Tide of Liberalism* (Amherst: University of Massachusetts Press, 2005).

6. Eli Ginzberg, *Manpower Agenda for America* (New York: McGraw-Hill, 1968); Alice Kessler-Harris, *In Pursuit of Equity: Women, Men, and the Quest for Economic Citi-

zenship in Twentieth-Century America (New York: Oxford University Press, 2001), 211; Jennifer Mittelstadt, *From Welfare to Workfare: The Unintended Consequences of Liberal Reform, 1945–1965* (Chapel Hill: University of North Carolina Press, 2005).

7. Barbara Ehrenreich, *The Hearts of Men: American Dreams and the Flight from Commitment* (New York: Anchor, 1983), 11; Elizabeth Pleck, *Domestic Tyranny: The Making of Social Policy Against Family Violence from Colonial Times to the Present* (New York: Oxford University Press, 1987).

8. Stephanie Coontz, *The Way We Never Were: American Families and the Nostalgia Trap* (New York: Basic Books, 1992).

9. "Barriers to Employment, Advancement, and Equal Pay for Women Workers," Folder 14, Box 3, NOW.

10. White House memo, March 8, 1966, Box 7—Labor, LBJ.

11. Dorothy Sue Cobble, *The Other Women's Movement: Workplace Justice and Social Rights in Modern America* (Princeton, N.J.: Princeton University Press, 2004); Nancy F. Cott, *The Grounding of Modern Feminism* (New Haven, Conn.: Yale University Press, 1987); Nancy MacLean, *Freedom Is Not Enough* (Cambridge, Mass.: Harvard University Press, 2006), 117–127.

12. Dorothy Sue Cobble, "Halving the Double Day," *New Labor Forum* 12/3 (Fall 2003): 63–72; Brigid O'Farrell and Joyce L. Kornbluh, eds., *Rocking the Boat: Union Women's Voices, 1915–1975* (New Brunswick, N.J.: Rutgers University Press, 1996), 110–134.

13. *1960 Census Characteristics of Population*, vol. 1, Table 201.

14. Cott, *The Grounding of Modern Feminism*, 59–74, 120–142; Kessler-Harris, *In Pursuit of Equity*, 44–45, 205–217.

15. "Summary Report on Protective Labor Legislation," June 8, 1962, Box 1, Folder 3, PCSW. I owe this formulation to Sue Cobble.

16. Herbert Hill, "Racial Discrimination in the Nation's Apprenticeship Training Programs," *Phylon* 23/3 (Fall 1962): 216; Whitney Young, *To Be Equal* (New York: McGraw-Hill, 1964), 53.

17. *1960 Census Characteristics of Population*, vol. 1, Table 82; Sugrue, *Origins of the Urban Crisis: Race and Inequality in Postwar Detroit* (Princeton, N.J.: Princeton University Press, 1996), 144.

18. *1960 Census Characteristics of Population*, vol. 1, Table 213.

19. Murray quoted in committee transcripts, October 2, 1962, p. 333, Box 2, Folder 10, PCSW; her memo is in Box 8, Folder 61, PM; Cobble, *The Other Women's Movement*, 168–173; Serena Meyeri, *Reasoning from Race: Feminism, Law, and the Civil Rights Revolution* (Cambridge, Mass.: Harvard University Press, 2011).

20. Cobble, *The Other Women's Movement*, 175; Hugh Davis Graham, *The Civil Rights Era: Origins and Development of National Policy, 1960–1972* (Oxford, U.K.: Oxford University Press, 1990), 136.

21. Edith Green to Pauli Murray, April 27, 1964, Box 135, Folder 2456, PM; Caroline Bird, *Born Female: The High Cost of Keeping Women Down* (New York: David McKay, 1968), 1–6.

22. Pauli Murray to Edith Green, April 24, 1964; Murray to Marguerite Rawalt, April 14, 1964; Margaret Chase Smith to Murray, April 27, 1964, Box 135, Folder 2456, PM; Graham, *The Civil Rights Era*, 137.

23. *NYT*, April 9 and 12, 1964, 18 and 41; *NR*, September 4, 1965; *WSJ*, June 22, 1965, 1.

24. *Newsletter from the Equal Employment Opportunity Commission* (July–August 1965), Box 74, Folder 1298, PM.

25. Gerald Horne, *The Fire This Time: Watts and the 1960s* (Charlottesville: University Press of Virginia, 1995); Steve Estes, *I Am a Man!: Race, Manhood, and the Civil Rights Movement* (Chapel Hill: University of North Carolina Press, 2005), 87–130.

26. *Autobiography of Malcolm X* (New York: Grove Press, 1965), 221 (italics in original); Williams quoted in Estes, *I Am a Man!*, 66.

27. The PCSW meeting is recounted in Kessler-Harris, *In Pursuit of Equity*, 226–227; *Muhammad Speaks*, November 12, 1965, 16.

28. Alice O'Connor, *Poverty Knowledge: Social Science, Social Policy, and the Poor in Twentieth-Century U.S. History* (Princeton, N.J.: Princeton University Press, 2001), 74–124; Patricia Hill Collins, *Black Feminist Thought: Knowledge, Consciousness, and the Politics of Empowerment* (Boston: Unwin Hyman, 1990), 74–78.

29. Estes, *I Am a Man!*, 111; Lee Rainwater and William L. Yancey, *The Moynihan Report and the Politics of Controversy* (Cambridge, Mass.: MIT Press, 1967); Horne, *The Fire This Time*; *LAT*, January 29, 1967, A25.

30. Jerry Cohen and William S. Murphy, *Burn, Baby, Burn!* (New York: Avon Books, 1967).

31. Riot participant quoted in "Interview with Archie Hardwick," October 27, 1965, p. 4, vol. 15, *Testimony Before the Governor's Commission on the Watts Riots*, MCC; Rainwater and Yancey, *The Moynihan Report*, 413; on Malcolm X, see Joe Wood, ed., *Malcolm X: In Our Own Image* (New York: St. Martin's Press, 1992).

32. Mervyn Dymally, report dated October 11, 1965, Carton 18, Folder "Dymally-105," MCC; Governor's Commission on the Los Angeles Riots, *Violence in the City—an End or a Beginning? A Report* (Los Angeles, 1965), 8; Brown quoted in Thomas F. Jackson, *From Civil Rights to Human Rights: Martin Luther King, Jr., and the Struggle for Economic Justice* (Philadelphia: University of Pennsylvania Press, 2007), 239; Dr. H. H. Brookins, speech delivered to the Commonwealth Club of San Francisco, September 17, 1965, Carton 21, MCC.

33. Ira Katznelson, *When Affirmative Action Was White* (New York: W. W. Norton, 2005); Johnson quoted in Kent B. Germany, *New Orleans After the Promises: Poverty, Citizenship, and the Search for the Great Society* (Athens: University of Georgia Press, 2007), 43.

34. Michele Wallace, *Black Macho and the Myth of the Superwoman* (New York: Warner Books, 1978), 11; "A CORE Challenge to the White House Conference," Box 7, Folder 1, GW; Robert Staples, ed., *The Black Family: Essays and Studies* (New York: Wadsworth Publishing, 1978).

35. Rainwater and Yancey, *The Moynihan Report*, 136–138; *LAT*, August 14, 1965, 1; *NYTSM*, November 25, 1965, 52; Herbert Gans, "The Breakdown of the Negro Family: The 'Moynihan Report' and Its Implications for Federal Civil Rights Policy," Box 67, White House Conference folder, LBJ; Farmer quoted in *Chicago Defender*, December 20, 1965, 6; James T. Patterson, *Freedom Is Not Enough: The Moynihan Report and America's Struggle over Black Family Life from LBJ to Obama* (New York: Basic Books, 2010), 65–86; Anders Walker, "A Horrible Fascination: Sex, Segregation, and the Lost Politics of Obscenity," *Washington University Law Journal* 89 (2012): page numbers unavailable at press.

36. *Frontier*, October 1965, 13; Jean Carey Bond and Patricia Peery, "Has the Black Male Been Castrated?," *Liberator* 9/5 (May 1969): 4–8; LeRoi Jones, "American Sexual

Reference: Black Male," *Home* (New York: William Morrow, 1966); Daniel Matlin, "'Lift Up Yr Self!': Reinterpreting Amiri Baraka (LeRoi Jones), Black Power, and the Uplift Tradition," *Journal of American History* 93/1 (June 2006): 91–116.

37. Donna L. Franklin, *Ensuring Inequality: The Structural Transformation of the African American Family* (New York: Oxford University Press, 1997); Daryl Michale Scott, *Contempt and Pity: Social Policy and the Image of the Damaged Black Psyche, 1880–1996* (Chapel Hill: University of North Carolina Press, 1997); Martha Biondi, *To Stand and Fight* (Cambridge, Mass.: Harvard University Press, 2006). See also "Reconsidering Culture and Poverty," a special issue of *Annals of the American Academy of Political and Social Science* (May 2010).

38. See articles in *RD*, November 1965, 67–73; *Time*, August 27, 1965, 16–17; Daniel Patrick Moynihan, "The President and the Negro: The Moment Lost," *Commentary* (February 1960): 31–40.

39. *Ebony*, August 1966; Murray to William Yancey, January 25, 1966, 129/2339, PM; *The Church Woman*, November 1969, 11–12; Mary Ann Weathers, "An Argument for Black Women's Liberation as a Revolutionary Force," *No More Fun and Games: A Journal of Female Liberation* 1/2 (February 1969).

40. Chuck Stone, "The National Conference on Black Power," in *The Black Power Revolt*, ed. Floyd B. Barbour (New York: Macmillan, 1968); Peniel Joseph, *Waiting 'til the Midnight Hour: A Narrative History of Black Power in America* (New York: Henry Holt, 2006); Matthew Countryman, *Up South: Civil Rights and Black Power in Philadelphia* (Philadelphia: University of Pennsylvania Press, 2006), 258–260.

41. Stokely Carmichael and Charles V. Hamilton, *Black Power: The Politics of Liberation in America* (New York: Vintage, 1967), 44; Albert B. Cleague, Jr., *The Black Messiah* (New York: Sheed and Ward, 1968), 169; *NYTSM*, May 28, 1967, 15; Charles Lemert, *Muhammad Ali: Trickster in the Culture of Irony* (Cambridge, UK: Polity Press, 2003); Elliott Gorn, ed., *Muhammad Ali: The People's Champ* (Urbana: University of Illinois Press, 1995).

42. Nathan Hare, "The Frustrated Masculinity of the Negro Male," *Negro Digest* (August 1964): 5–9; Eldridge Cleaver, *Post-prison Writings and Speeches*, ed. Robert Scheer (New York: Random House, 1969), 112.

43. *NYTSM*, June 25, 1967, 3.

44. Carmichael and Hamilton, *Black Power*, 44; Cleague, *The Black Messiah*, 169; Malcolm X quoted in Estes, *I Am a Man!*, 92.

45. Ula Y. Taylor, *The Veiled Garvey: The Life and Times of Amy Jacques Garvey* (Chapel Hill: University of North Carolina Press, 2002); Countryman, *Up South*, 261–267; Komozi Woodard, *A Nation Within a Nation: Amiri Baraka (LeRoi Jones) and Black Power Politics* (Chapel Hill: University of North Carolina Press, 1999), 122–140; Imamu Ameer Baraka, "A Black Value System," *The Black Scholar* 1/1 (November 1969): 54–60.

46. Wallace, *Black Macho*, 60–61; Shirley Chisholm quoted in *NYTSM*, April 13, 1969, 32; *CR*, December 11, 1969, 38592–94; Chisholm, "Racism and Anti-Feminism," *Black Scholar* (January–February 1970): 40–47; Linda La Rue quoted in Jane Gerhard, *Desiring Revolution: Second-Wave Feminism and the Rewriting of American Sexual Thought, 1920 to 1982* (New York: Columbia University Press, 2001), 155.

47. Weathers, "An Argument for Black Women's Liberation as a Revolutionary Force"; Beverly Smith, notes, November 9, 1975, BS; Rosalyn Baxandall, "Re-visioning the

Women's Liberation Narrative: Early Second Wave African American Feminists," *Feminist Studies* 27/1 (Spring 2001): 225–245.

48. Kimberley Crenshaw, "Mapping the Margins: Intersectionality, Identity Politics, and Violence Against Women of Color," *Stanford Law Review* 43/6 (July 1991): 1241–1299; Hill Collins, *Black Feminist Thought*; Dayo Gore, *Radicalism at the Crossroads: African American Women Activists in the Cold War* (New York: New York University Press, 2011); Kimberly Springer, *Living for the Revolution: Black Feminist Organizations, 1968–1980* (Durham, N.C.: Duke University Press, 2005).

49. See *The Black Scholar*, November 1969, January–February and April 1970, September 1972; Paul Gilroy, *Small Acts: Thoughts on the Politics of Black Cultures* (London: Serpent's Tail, 1994), 192–207. In particular, see "The Black Woman and Women's Lib," *Ebony*, March 1971: 68–76; "Where Are All the Black Men?" *Ebony*, March 1972: 99–106.

50. Johnson speech before Congress, March 16, 1964, in *The War on Poverty and the Economic Opportunity Act: A Compilation of Materials Relevant to S. 2648* (Washington, D.C.: Government Printing Office, 1964), 39.

51. *MS*, December 25, 1965, 26; Johnson quoted in Germany, *New Orleans After the Promises*, 60.

52. *Hearings Before the Subcommittee on the War on Poverty Program of the Committee on Education and Labor, House of Representatives* (Washington, D.C.: Government Printing Office, 1964); *Examination of the War on Poverty: Hearings Before the Subcommittee on Employment, Manpower, and Poverty, U.S. Senate*, Part 1 (Washington, D.C.: Government Printing Office, 1967), 86–157.

53. Office of National Councils and Organizations, Office of Economic Opportunity, "Women in the War on Poverty," Conference Proceedings, May 8, 1967, 1–68.

54. Nixon quoted in Jill Quadagno, "Race, Class, and Gender in the U.S. Welfare State: Nixon's Failed Family Assistance Plan," *American Sociological Review* (February 1990): 15; John Campbell to Daniel Moynihan, n.d., Human Rights, Box 27, RNWH; Marisa Chappell, *The War on Welfare: Family, Poverty, and Politics in Modern America* (Philadelphia: University of Pennsylvania Press, 2010).

55. Melinda Chateauvert, "Framing Sexual Citizenship: Reconsidering the Discourse on African American Families," *The Journal of African American History* 93/2 (Spring 2008): 198–222; Mittelstadt, *From Welfare to Workfare*; Chappell, *The War on Welfare*.

56. American Civil Liberties Union, "Memorandum on the Rights of Welfare Recipients," March 1967, ACLU; "Goals for a National Welfare Rights Movement," August 6–7, 1966, Box 7, Folder 7, GW; Molly Michelmore, *Tax and Spend: The Welfare State, Tax Politics, and the Limits of American Liberalism* (Philadelphia: University of Pennsylvania Press, 2012).

57. Kornbluh, *The Battle for Welfare Rights*, 92–95; Johnnie Tillmon, "Welfare Is a Women's Issue," *Liberation News Service*, February 26, 1972; "The Poor People's Platform," n.d., Box 7, Folder 9, GW; NWRO, "Statement to the House Ways and Means Committee," October 27, 1969, Box 17, Folder 3, GW.

58. NYT, August 9, 1969, S6; "Fair Share Speech," Box 39, Welfare, JE; memo to the president from Moynihan, January 20, 1970, Box 38, Welfare, JE.

59. Mills quoted, January 25, 1970, clipping file, Box 38, JE; Kilpatrick quoted in *LAT*, January 15, 1970, C7; Patterson, *Freedom Is Not Enough*, 115–120.

60. Moynihan quoted in *NYT*, December 12, 1965, 74; letter from John Campbell to Moynihan, n.d., Box 27, Human Rights, RNWH; Rainwater and Yancey, *The Moynihan Report*, 452; Kornbluh, *The Battle for Welfare Rights*, 159. See also Willie Mae Reid, *Black Women's Struggle for Equality* (New York: Pathfinder Press, 1976).

61. Pete Hamill, "The Revolt of the White Lower Middle Class," *New York*, April 14, 1969.

62. Robert Wood, unpublished paper delivered at the National Consultation on Ethnic America, Fordham University, June 1968, quoted in Arnold Schuchter, *Reparations: The Black Manifesto and Its Challenge to White America* (Philadelphia: J. B. Lippincott, 1970), 97–98; letter to *NYT*, quoted in William W. Newman, "The Revival of Ethnic Consciousness," *Journal of Current Social Issues*, 10/3 (Summer 1972): 17; Matthew Frye Jacobson, *Roots Too: White Ethnic Revival in Post–Civil Rights America* (Cambridge, Mass.: Harvard University Press, 2006); Michael Novak, *The Rise of the Unmeltable Ethnics: The New Political Force of the Seventies* (New York: Macmillan, 1972); Joe Merton, "The Politics of Symbolism: Richard Nixon's Appeal to White Ethnics and the Frustration of Realignment," *European Journal of American Culture* 26/3 (2007): 181–198.

63. Barbara Ehrenreich, *Fear of Falling: The Inner Life of the Middle Class* (New York: Pantheon, 1989); Joshua B. Freeman, "Hardhats: Construction Workers, Manliness, and the 1970 Pro-War Demonstrations," *Journal of Social History* (Summer 1993): 725–744; Jefferson Cowie, "Nixon's Class Struggle: Romancing the New Right Worker, 1969–1973," *Labor History* 43/3 (2002): 257–283.

64. Hill quoted in MacLean, *Freedom Is Not Enough*, 91, and *The Philadelphia Plan: Congressional Oversight of Administrative Agencies, Hearings Before the Subcommittee on Separation of Powers, Committee on the Judiciary, U.S. Senate* (Washington, D.C.: Government Printing Office, 1970), 207; see the excellent anthology, David Goldberg and Trevor Griffey, eds., *Black Power at Work: Community Control, Affirmative Action, and the Construction Industry* (Ithaca, N.Y.: Cornell University Press, 2010).

65. NYTSM, September 14, 1969, 30; *CR—Senate*, December 18, 1969, 39950–39957.

66. Andrew W. Greeley, *Why Can't They Be Like Us? America's White Ethnic Groups* (New York: E.P. Dutton, 1971).

67. On EEOC cases, see James C. Harvey, *Black Civil Rights During the Johnson Administration* (Jackson: University and College Press of Mississippi, 1973); *CT*, July 23, 1969, B6; *America*, March 2, 1968, 285; *Business Week*, January 11, 1969, 88–92, and August 30, 1969, 22–24.

68. George Meany, "Labor and the Philadelphia Plan," address to the National Press Club, January 12, 1970; *New York Amsterdam News*, August 1, 1970, 16; November 18, 1972, D8; Thomas J. Sugrue, "Affirmative Action from Below: Civil Rights, the Building Trades, and the Politics of Racial Equality in the Urban North, 1945–1969," *Journal of American History* 91/1 (June 2004): 145–173.

69. *The Philadelphia Plan*, 61. Nicholas Pedriana and Robin Stryker, "Political Culture Wars 1960s Style: Equal Employment Opportunity—Affirmative Action Law and the Philadelphia Plan," *American Journal of Sociology* 103/3 (November 1997): 633–691.

70. Lyndon B. Johnson, "'To Fulfill These Rights': Address at Howard University, June 4, 1965," *Public Papers of the Presidents of the United States: Lyndon B. Johnson, 1965* (Washington, D.C.: Government Printing Office, 1965), 635–640.

71. Kerner Commission Report; *The Philadelphia Plan*, 207; NYTSM, May 21, 1972, 25.

72. For a deeper discussion of the relationship of the hard hat as symbol to real working-class communities, see Jefferson Cowie, *Stayin' Alive: The 1970s and the Last Days of the Working Class* (New York: New Press, 2010).

73. Cowie, *Stayin' Alive*; MacLean, *Freedom Is Not Enough*; Trevor Griffey, "'The Blacks Should Not Be Administering the Philadelphia Plan': Nixon, the Hard Hats, and 'Voluntary' Affirmative Action," in Goldberg and Griffey, eds., *Black Power at Work*, 134–160.

2: LAST MAN TO DIE

1. Philip Caputo, *A Rumor of a War* (New York: Holt, Rinehart, and Winston, 1977), xxi; George Q. Flynn, *Conscription and Democracy: The Draft in France, Great Britain, and the United States* (Westport, Conn.: Greenwood Press, 2002).

2. Benjamin L. Alpers, "This Is the Army: Imagining a Democratic Military in World War II," *Journal of American History* (June 1998): 129–163.

3. NYT, April 1, 1966, 5; CT, April 1, 1966, 12.

4. Andrew Meyers, *Black, White, and Olive Drab: Racial Integration at Fort Jackson, South Carolina, and the Civil Rights Movement* (Charlottesville: University of Virginia Press, 2006).

5. NYT, May 12, 1969, 4; NYTSM, May 18, 1969, 25; WP, June 4, 1969, 3; Fred Halstead, *Out Now: A Participant's Account of the American Movement Against the Vietnam War* (New York: Monad Press, 1978), 453; Fred Halstead, *G.I.s Speak Out Against the War: The Case of the Fort Jackson 8* (New York: Pathfinder, 1970); Derek Seidman, "The Unquiet Americans: GI Dissent During the Vietnam War" (Ph.D. dissertation, Brown University, 2010).

6. *The Ally*, April 1969; *About Face*, June 1969; *GI Press Service*, September 21, 1970, GI. See also David Cortright, *Soldiers in Revolt: GI Resistance During the Vietnam War* (Chicago: Haymarket, 2005, orig. 1975), 59–60.

7. Leisa D. Meyer, *Creating G. I. Jane: Sexuality and Power in the Women's Army Corps During World War II* (New York: Columbia University Press, 1996); Andrew Huebner, *The Warrior Image: Soldiers in American Culture from the Second World War to the Vietnam Era* (Chapel Hill: University of North Carolina Press, 2007).

8. Howard quoted in Wallace Terry, *Bloods: An Oral History of the Vietnam War by Black Veterans* (New York: Ballantine, 1985), 118; American Friends Service Committee, *The Draft?* (New York: Hill and Wang, 1968), 1–9; Jerome Johnston and Jerald G. Bachman, *Young Men Look at Military Service: A Preliminary Report* (Ann Arbor, Mich.: Institute for Social Research, 1970).

9. CONGD, October 1974, 198, 247.

10. President's Commission on an All-Volunteer Armed Force, *The Report of the President's Commission on an All-Volunteer Armed Force* (Washington, D.C.: Government Printing Office, 1970). For overall treatments of the draft, see George Flynn, *The Draft, 1940–1973* (Lawrence: University of Kansas Press, 1993); Robert K. Griffith, *The U.S. Army's Transition to an All-Volunteer Force, 1968–1974* (Washington, D.C.: U.S. Army Center for Military History, 1997); Beth Bailey, *America's Army: Making the All-Volunteer Force* (Cambridge, Mass.: Harvard University Press, 2009).

11. NYT, May 12, 1965, 46; Leslie S. Rothenberg, *The Draft and You: A Handbook on the Selective Service System* (Garden City, N.Y.: Anchor Books, 1968).

12. NYT, May 12, 1965, 46; *All Hands Abandon Ship!*, vol. 2, no. 9, p. 4, GI.

13. CONGD, October 1974, 202; *Review of the Administration and Operation of the Draft Law, Hearings by the Special Subcommittee on the Draft and the House Committee on Armed Services* (Washington, D.C.: Government Printing Office, 1970); James W. Davis and Kenneth M. Dolbeare, *Little Groups of Neighbors: The Selective Service System* (Chicago: Markham Publishing, 1968), 1–43; Roger W. Little, ed., *Selective Service and American Society* (New York: Russell Sage Foundation, 1969), 53–108; NYT, January 13, 1966, 18; Herman Graham III, *The Brothers' Vietnam War: Black Power, Manhood, and the Military Experience* (Tallahassee: University Press of Florida, 2003), 17; Ken Lawrence, "Thirty Years of Selective Service Racism," Box 15, Folder 3, KC.

14. Material on Armed Services Day, Box 3, Folder 2, NYM; Society for Individual Rights, *The Armed Services and Homosexuality* (San Francisco: The Society, 1968); Margot Canaday, *The Straight State: Sexuality and Citizenship in Twentieth-Century America* (Princeton, N.J.: Princeton University Press, 2009); Allan Bérubé, *Coming Out Under Fire: The History of Gay Men and Women in World War II* (New York: Free Press, 1990).

15. The President's Task Force on Manpower Conservation, *One Third of a Nation: A Report on Young Men Found Unqualified for Military Service* (Washington, D.C.: Government Printing Office, January 1, 1964), 2, 5–27; Steve Estes, *I Am a Man!: Race, Manhood, and the Civil Rights Movement* (Chapel Hill: University of North Carolina Press, 2005), 113.

16. President Johnson, "Message from the President of the United States: A Summary of Accomplishments for the Welfare of Veterans and Servicemen, Provisions of the 1969 Veterans' Budget," 4. See also Captain David A. Dawson, *The Impact of Project 100,000 on the Marine Corps* (Washington, D.C.: U.S. Marine Corps, 1995); Flynn, *The Draft*, 208–209.

17. McNamara quoted in *Readjustment of Project 100,000 Veterans: Hearing Before the Subcommittee on Oversight and Investigations of the House Committee on Veterans' Affairs*, February 28, 1990, 1; James Patterson, *Freedom Is Not Enough: The Moynihan Report and America's Struggle over Black Family Life from LBJ to Obama* (New York: Basic Books, 2010), 2–3, 12–13.

18. Graham, *The Brothers' Vietnam War*, 26–29; Rick Perlstein, *Nixonland: The Rise of a President and the Fracturing of America* (New York: Scribner, 2008), 97; *Freedomways* (Spring 1967), 101.

19. Stokely Carmichael, "Black Power" (speech, Chicago, July 28, 1966), Encyclopedia .com, accessed March 28, 2012, http://www.encyclopedia.com/doc/1G2-3401804839 .html.

20. César Chávez, "Speech at Exposition Park, May 2, 1971," in *The Words of César Chávez*, ed. Richard J. Jensen and John C. Hammerback (College Station: Texas A&M University Press, 2002), 63–64; Charles Ornelas and Michael González, "The Chicanos and the War: An Opinion Survey in Santa Barbara," *Aztlán: International Journal of Chicano Studies Research* 2/2 (Spring 1971): 23–35; Steven Rosales, "Soldados Razos: Chicano Politics, Identity, and Masculinity in the United States Military, 1940–1975" (Ph.D. dissertation, University of California, Irvine, 2007).

21. "Nation-Wide Protest," DB; "Armed Forces Day," Box 3, Folder 2, NYM; *ADV,* January 1970, 22, February 1970, 3, 8–21, July 1970, 7; Justin David Suran, "Coming Out Against the War: Antimilitarism and the Politicization of Homosexuality in the Era of Vietnam," *American Quarterly* 53/3 (September 2001): 452–488.

22. Flynn, *The Draft,* 209.

23. William A. Strauss, *Chance and Circumstance: The Draft, the War, and the Vietnam Generation* (New York: Knopf, 1978), 3–61; Michael S. Foley, *Confronting the War Machine: Draft Resistance During the Vietnam War* (Chapel Hill: University of North Carolina Press, 2003).

24. Sara M. Evans, "Sons, Daughters, and Patriarchy: Gender and the 1968 Generation," *American Historical Review* 114 (2009): 331–347.

25. President's Commission on an All-Volunteer Armed Force, *The Report of the President's Commission on an All-Volunteer Armed Force* (Washington, D.C.: Government Printing Office, 1970); NYT, January 2, 1966, 163.

26. WM, October 1975, 5–20.

27. NR, December 20, 1969, 9–11; NYT, August 4 and 6, 1965, 2 and 3.

28. Morley Safer, *Flashbacks: On Returning to Vietnam* (New York: Random House, 1990), 85–97; Marilyn Young, *The Vietnam Wars, 1945–1990* (New York: HarperCollins, 1991), 143–144; NYT, August 4 and 6, 1965, 2 and 3; letter from Mrs. Kenneth Brooks to President Nixon, March 31, 1971, Constituent Correspondence—Calley, RD.

29. Peter Barnes, *Pawns: The Plight of the Citizen-Soldier* (New York: Knopf, 1972), xix; Kennedy quoted in *American Experience: RFK,* directed by David Grubin (2004; Arlington, Va.: PBS, 2004), DVD, time stamp: 1:18:48.

30. NYT, April 29, 1967, 10; Jeffrey Clarke, *Advice and Support: The Final Years, 1965–1973* (Washington, D.C.: Center of Military History, 1988), 242.

31. NYT, October 24 and November 10, 1967, 5 and 21.

32. Ibid.

33. *Newsweek,* October 11, 1965, 44–48.

34. Michal Belknap, *The Vietnam War on Trial: The My Lai Massacre and the Court-Martial of Lieutenant Calley* (Lawrence: University Press of Kansas, 2002).

35. Seymour Hersh, *My Lai 4: A Report on the Massacre and Its Aftermath* (New York: Random House, 1970); United States Army, *The My Lai Massacre and Its Cover-up: Beyond the Reach of Law? The Peers Commission Report* (New York: Free Press, 1976).

36. *Time* quoted in "The Great Atrocity Hunt," NR, December 16, 1969, 1252.

37. Richard Hammer, *The Court-Martial of Lt. Calley* (New York: Coward, McCann & Geoghegan, 1971), 257. See also Lieutenant General W. R. Peers, *The My Lai Inquiry* (New York: W. W. Norton, 1979); NYT, September 10, 1970, 4.

38. Hammer, *The Court-Martial of Lt. Calley;* Peers, *The My Lai Inquiry.*

39. NYTSM, July 11, 1971, 6; Belknap, *The Vietnam War on Trial,* 23–36.

40. LAT, April 9, 1971, A7; Mayor Lillian Johnston, letter to Richard Nixon, Box 12, National Security—Calley section, Nixon subdivision, RNWH (hereafter Calley Letters); letter from Cecilia Porubsky to Senator Robert Dole, March 31, 1971, Constituent Correspondence—Calley, RD; The Calley Verdict: Right or Wrong?, Nixon Materials Tape No. 4259.

41. There are four large manuscript boxes (labeled "National Security—Calley Section") filled with letters to Nixon from defenders of Calley.

42. Donald W. Blue, mayor of Lafayette, to President Nixon, April 2, 1971, Box 12, Calley Letters.
43. *Commonweal*, April 30, 1971, 183–187; *Esquire*, September 1971, 85–98.
44. *LAT*, April 3, 1971, A9.
45. Christian G. Appy, *Patriots: The Vietnam War Remembered from All Sides* (New York: Penguin, 2004), 450.
46. Unnamed vet quoted in John Kerry and Vietnam Veterans Against the War, *The New Soldier* (New York: Macmillan, 1971), 134; *LAT*, April 24, 1971, 2A.
47. *Newsweek*, February 2, 1970, 24–30.
48. Gerald Nicosia, *Home to War: A History of the Vietnam Veterans' Movement* (New York: Crown, 2001), 73–93.
49. *CR*, April 5 and 6, 1971, E2825–E2935.
50. Vietnam Veterans Against the War, *The Winter Soldier Investigation: An Inquiry into American War Crimes* (Boston: Beacon Press, 1972), 16.
51. Ibid.
52. Quotes from ibid., 14, 16; Richard Stacewicz, *Winter Soldiers: An Oral History of the Vietnam Veterans Against the War* (New York: Twayne, 1997), 233–251.
53. Nicosia, *Home to War*, 96–157.
54. "The Testimony of Lieutenant John Kerry for the Vietnam Veterans Against the War," April 22, 1971, Box 1, SHR; *St. Petersburg Times*, April 24, 1971.
55. Andrew E. Hunt, *The Turning: A History of the Vietnam Veterans Against the War* (New York: New York University Press, 1999).
56. Peter Maslowski and Don Winslow, *Looking for a Hero: Staff Sergeant Joe Ronnie Hooper and the Vietnam War* (Lincoln: University of Nebraska Press, 2004), 359.
57. *NYT*, July 12 and September 10, 1966, 6 and 4; *The Bond*, November 24, 1972; *All Hands Abandon Ship*, September 1972; James Lewes, *Protest and Survive: Underground G.I. Newspapers During the Vietnam War* (Westport, Conn.: Praeger, 2003).
58. Graham, *The Brothers' Vietnam War*; Lea Ybarra, *Vietnam Veteranos: Chicanos Recall the War in Vietnam* (Austin: University of Texas Press, 2004); George Mariscal, ed., *Aztlán and Viet Nam: Chicano and Chicana Experiences of the War* (Berkeley: University of California Press, 1999); Steven Rosales, "Soldados Razos: Chicano Politics, Identity, and Masculinity in the United States Military, 1940–1975" (Ph.D. dissertation, University of California, Irvine, 2007).
59. William Hauser, *America's Army in Crisis: A Study in Civil-Military Relations* (Baltimore: Johns Hopkins University Press, 1973); Haynes Johnson and George C. Wilson, *Army in Anguish* (New York: Pocket Books, 1972); George Walton, *The Tarnished Shield: A Report on Today's Army* (New York: Dodd, Mead, 1973); U.S. Army War College, *Study on Military Professionalism* (Carlisle Barracks, Pa.: The College, 1970).
60. *NYT*, September 21, 1972, 40; *CONGD*, October 1974, 231; Nixon voter quoted in letter from Mrs. Pat Murphy to Richard Nixon, n.d., Box 4, Judicial—Clemency, RNWH; Lawrence M. Baskir and William A. Strauss, *Reconciliation After Vietnam: A Program of Relief for Vietnam Era Draft and Military Offenders* (Notre Dame, Ind.: University of Notre Dame Press, 1977), 6.
61. *Amnesty: An Unresolved National Question*, edited transcripts of a congressional conference, February 26, 1976 (Fund for New Priorities in America, 1976), 79.
62. Hendricks quoted in *NYTSM*, December 24, 1972, 6; Gruening quoted in "The Ad

Hoc Congressional Hearing on Unconditional Amnesty," May 24, 1973, 5, Box 9, CS; "Position Paper on Universal Unconditional Amnesty," Spring 1975, Amex-Canada, Box 10, CS; *Amnesty: An Unresolved National Question.*

63. *CONGD*, October 1974, 234; *NYTSM*, September 8, 1974, 98; *NYT*, February 15 and 20, 1973; *WSJ*, March 12, 1973, 10; Hendricks quoted in *NYTSM*, December 24, 1972, 6; Agnew quoted in *WP*, March 7, 1973, A12.

64. *CONGD*, October 1974, 234; *NYTSM*, September 8, 1974, 98.

65. *NYP*, September 16, 1974. The individual case files of all men who sought clemency under Ford's program can be found in Boxes 1–4, PCB.

66. Edward L. King, *The Death of the Army: A Pre-mortem* (New York: Saturday Review Press, 1972); Hauser, *America's Army in Crisis*; Murray Polner, *No Victory Parades: The Return of the Vietnam Veteran* (New York: Holt, Rinehart and Winston, 1971); *Soldiers in and After Vietnam*, special issue, *Journal of Social Forces* 31/4 (1975).

3: HOMOSEXUAL TENDENCIES

1. *ADV*, November 1969 and February 1970, 1 and 1; *NR*, May 21, 1966, 8–9; Colin J. Williams and Martin S. Weinberg, *Homosexuals and the Military: A Study of Less than Honorable Discharge* (New York: Harper & Row, 1971); Marc Stein, "*Boutilier* and the U.S. Supreme Court's Sexual Revolution," *Law and History Review* 23/3 (Fall 2005): 491–536. Despite official repression, a gay world existed within the military. See Margo Canaday, *The Straight State: Sexuality and Citizenship in 20th Century America* (Princeton, N.J.: Princeton University Press, 2009); Allan Bérubé, *Coming Out Under Fire: The History of Gay Men and Women in World War II* (New York: Free Press, 1990).

2. *Life*, June 11, 1965, 4; Society for Individual Rights et al., *The Challenges and Progress of Homosexual Law Reform* (San Francisco: SIR, 1968); Council on Religion and the Homosexual, *A Brief of Injustices: An Indictment of Our Society in Its Treatment of Homosexuals*, Box 232, ACLU; David K. Johnson, *The Lavender Scare: The Cold War Persecution of Gays and Lesbians in the Federal Government* (Chicago: University of Chicago Press, 2004), 76, 84, 88, 105, 123–138; George Chauncey, "'What Gay Studies Taught the Court': The Historians' Amicus Brief in *Lawrence v. Texas*," *GLQ* 10/3 (2004): 509–538; William N. Eskridge, Jr., *Dishonorable Passions: Sodomy Laws in America, 1861–2003* (New York: Viking, 2008).

3. Press releases and information bulletins, Box 8, Folders 5–6, NYM; *The Ladder*, July–August 1965, 23–25. On Kameny and the 1965 protests, see Johnson, *The Lavender Scare*, 179–185, 199–202. See also Eithne Luibhéid, *Entry Denied: Controlling Sexuality at the Border* (Minneapolis: University of Minnesota Press, 2002); Joyce Murdoch and Deb Price, *Courting Justice: Gay Men and Lesbians v. the Supreme Court* (New York: Basic Books, 2002).

4. On respectability, see Marc Stein, *City of Sisterly and Brotherly Loves: Lesbian and Gay Philadelphia, 1945–1972* (Chicago: University of Chicago Press, 2000), 11, 223, 226, 273–274, and Marcia M. Gallo, *Different Daughters: A History of the Daughters of Bilitis and the Rise of the Lesbian Rights Movement* (New York: Carroll & Graf, 2006), 18–24. On law reform, see William N. Eskridge, Jr., *Gay Law: Challenging the Apartheid of the Closet* (Cambridge, Mass: Harvard University Press, 1999).

5. Martin Meeker, "Behind the Mask of Respectability: Reconsidering the Mattachine Society and Male Homophile Practice, 1950s and 1960s," *Journal of the History of Sexuality* 10/1 (January 2001): 78–116. Terminology has its own history. Broadest and most inclusive is "sexual and gender difference," a designation that did not come into common usage until the 1990s. "Homosexuality" was used regularly by both homophile and early gay liberation activists. "Queer," a broader term with sharper political connotations, was also not commonly employed until the 1990s. See William B. Turner, *Genealogy of Queer Theory* (Philadelphia: Temple University Press, 2000).

6. Edward Alwood, *Straight News: Gays, Lesbians, and the News Media* (New York: Columbia University Press, 1996).

7. Foster Gunnison, "The Hidden Bias: The Homophile Movement and Law Reform," *HC*, March 1967, 11–12; *Vector*, December 1964, 6; *HC*, August 1966, 12; "An Overview of Legal Developments in Homosexual Rights," Congressional Research Service, April 16, 1985, Box 6, HRC. Karla Jay and Allen Young, eds., *Out of the Closets: Voices of Gay Liberation* (New York: Pyramid, 1974).

8. Jill Johnson, *Lesbian Nation: The Feminist Solution* (New York: Simon & Schuster, 1973); Melinda Chateauvert, "Framing Sexual Citizenship: Reconsidering the Discourse on African American Families," *The Journal of African American History*, 93/2 (Spring 2008): 198–222.

9. *Homosexuality and Citizenship in Florida: A Report of the Florida Legislative Investigation Committee* (Florida: Legislative Investigation Committee, 1964); "Florida Demagogury [*sic*]," *CN*, April 20, 1964; Dan Bertwell, "'A Veritable Refuge for Homosexuals': The Johns Committee and the University of South Florida," *Florida Historical Quarterly* 83/4 (2005): 410–431; Stacy Braukman, "'Nothing Else Matters but Sex': Cold War Narratives of Deviance and the Search for Lesbian Teachers in Florida, 1959–1963," *Feminist Studies* 27/3 (2001): 553–575; Gillian Frank, "Save Our Children: The Sexual Politics of Child Protection in the United States, 1965–1990" (Ph.D. dissertation, Brown University, 2009).

10. *The Ladder*, January 1966, 9; *EMM*, September/October 1965, 13; *Tangents*, November 1965, 10–13; letter from Kameny to Sargent Shriver, November 28, 1964, Box 1, NYM; Johnson, *The Lavender Scare*, 179–208.

11. K. A. Cuordileone, *Manhood and American Political Culture in the Cold War* (New York: Routledge, 2005), 167–236; Robert D. Dean, *Imperial Brotherhood: Gender and the Making of Cold War Foreign Policy* (Amherst: University of Massachusetts Press, 2001), 17–63.

12. Schlesinger quoted in Cuordileone, *Manhood and American Political Culture*, 31–32.

13. Society for Individual Rights et al., *The Challenges and Progress of Homosexual Law Reform*, 16–17; *San Fernando Valley Citizen-News*, February 1, 1963; Estelle Freedman, "'Uncontrolled Desires': The Response to the Sexual Psychopath, 1920–1960," *Journal of American History* 74/1 (June 1987): 83–106; George Chauncey, "The Postwar Sex Crime Panic," in *True Stories from the American Past*, ed. William Gnaebner (New York: McGraw-Hill, 1993), 160–178; John D'Emilio, "The Homosexual Menace: The Politics of Sexuality in Cold War America," in *Passion and Power*, ed. Kathy Peiss and Christina Simmons (Philadelphia: Temple University Press, 1989), 226–240. There is some debate about precisely when laws prohibiting (or penalizing) same-sex erotic behavior were put in place and how they were used. For a range of views, see Chauncey, "'What Gay Studies Taught the Court'"; William N. Eskridge, Jr.,

and Nan D. Hunter, *Sexuality, Gender, and the Law* (New York: Foundation Press, 2004), 1–112; Marc Stein, "'Birthplace of the Nation': Imagining Lesbian and Gay Communities in Philadelphia, 1969–1970," in *Creating a Place for Ourselves: Lesbian, Gay, and Bisexual Community Histories*, ed. Brett Beemyn (New York: Routledge, 1997), 253–288.

14. Andrea Friedman, "Sadists and Sissies: Anti-Pornography Campaigns in Cold War America," *Gender and History* 15/2 (2003): 201–227; Freedman, "'Uncontrolled Desires'"; George F. Gilder, *Sexual Suicide* (New York: Quadrangle, 1973).

15. Polak quoted in *Tangents*, August 1966, 5; Council on Religion and the Homosexual, *A Brief of Injustices*; Murdoch and Price, *Courting Justice*, 38–39.

16. *The Ladder*, September 1965, 4–7; *ADV*, April 1968, 2; Nan Alamilla Boyd, *Wide Open Town: A History of Queer San Francisco to 1965* (Berkeley: University of California Press, 2003), 120–162; David Carter, *Stonewall: The Riots That Sparked the Gay Revolution* (New York: St. Martin's Griffin, 2004), 30–55; "An Overview of Legal Developments in Homosexual Rights," Congressional Research Service, April 16, 1985, Box 6, HRC; Timothy Stewart-Winter, "Raids, Rights, and Rainbow Coalitions: Sexuality and Race in Chicago Politics, 1950–2000" (Ph.D. dissertation, University of Chicago, 2009), 39–86.

17. Siobhan Somerville, "Queer Loving," *GLQ* 11/3 (2005): 335–370; Stein, "*Boutilier* and the U.S. Supreme Court's Sexual Revolution"; Marc Stein, *Sexual Injustice: Supreme Court Decisions from Griswold to Roe* (Chapel Hill: University of North Carolina Press, 2010); Vincent J. Samar, *The Right to Privacy: Gays, Lesbians, and the Constitution* (Philadelphia: Temple University Press, 1991), 24–25.

18. Kameny letter to Shriver; *CN*, February 1966, 2; *EMM*, June 1965, 18; Kameny speech reprinted in Josh Gottheimer, ed., *Ripples of Hope: Great American Civil Rights Speeches* (New York: Basic Books, 2003), 293. John D'Emilio, *Sexual Politics, Sexual Communities: The Making of a Homosexual Minority in the United States, 1940–1970* (Chicago: University of Chicago Press, 1983); John Loughery, *The Other Side of Silence: Men's Lives and Gay Identities, a Twentieth-Century History* (New York: Henry Holt, 1998); Henry L. Minton, *Departing from Deviance: A History of Homosexual Rights and Emancipatory Science in America* (Chicago: University of Chicago Press, 2002).

19. *Vector*, December 1964, 1; "The Homosexual Citizen in the Great Society," 8–9. On San Francisco's new organizations, see D'Emilio, *Sexual Politics, Sexual Communities*; Boyd, *Wide Open Town*; Martin Duberman, *Stonewall* (New York: Plume, 1993), 110.

20. *Vector*, April 1966, 2, November 1966, 1, November 1965, 1–3, October 1966, 1–3, and September 1967, 26; *The Challenges and Progress of Homosexual Law Reform*; Society for Individual Rights, *The Armed Services and Homosexuality* (San Francisco: SIR, 1968); "Pocket Lawyer Ready," *Vector*, September 1965, 1–3; *ADV*, October 1968, 6.

21. A homosexual bill of rights was proposed as early as 1960 by *ONE* magazine. See *ADV*, March 1969, 3.

22. *Vector*, March and June 1966, 1, 1.

23. "Fourth Annual Reminder Day—Homosexual Rights," Box 2, NYM; *CDN*, June 20, 1966, 3; "ACLU Committee on Civil Liberties and Unusual Sex or Gender Behavior: Preliminary Report to Board of Directors," May 18, 1965, "Statement of ACLU

Policy Regarding Sexual Behavior," and ACLU Committee on Civil Liberties and Unusual Sex or Gender Behavior meeting notes, Box 232, ACLU; *EMM*, June 1965; *Vector*, February 1966, 1, 7; *ADV*, January 1968, 2; *SR*, October 9, 1965; David Eisenbach, *Gay Power: An American Revolution* (New York: Carroll & Graf, 2006), 7–10.

24. Audre Lorde, *Sister Outsider: Essays and Speeches* (Trumansburg, N.Y.: Crossing Press, 1984); Cherríe Moraga and Gloria Anzaldua, eds., *This Bridge Called My Back: Writings by Radical Women of Color* (Watertown, Mass.: Persephone Press, 1981); E. Patrick Johnson, *Sweet Tea: Black Gay Men of the South, an Oral History* (Chapel Hill: University of North Carolina Press, 2008).

25. *Vector*, October 1966, 8–9; *The Ladder*, February 1967, 2–5; *Concern*, January 1967, 2–4; Rodger Streitmatter, *Unspeakable: The Rise of the Gay and Lesbian Press in America* (Boston: Faber and Faber, 1995). Transsexuals too occupied a liminal place in early homophile activism. See Joanne Meyerowitz, *How Sex Changed: A History of Transsexuality in the United States* (Cambridge, Mass.: Harvard University Press, 2002). The centrality of lesbians to homophile politics is indisputable. But the major homophile publications in the mid-1960s—*Drum*, *Vector*, *The Los Angeles Advocate*, *LCE News*, *Eastern Mattachine Magazine*, *New York Mattachine Newsletter*, *Homosexual Citizen Tangents*, *ONE*—were overwhelmingly focused on men and men's issues, a point that lesbian activists constantly raised. Only the DOB's *The Ladder*, a specifically lesbian publication, gave anything like sustained attention to women.

26. On coming out, see "Toujours Gai," *Pursuit and Symposium*, March–April 1966, 3; Phoebe Christina Godfrey, "'Sweet Little Girls?': Miscegenation, Desegregation, and the Defense of Whiteness at Little Rock's Central High, 1957–1959" (Ph.D. dissertation, Binghamton University, 2001); Johnson, *Sweet Tea*; Horacio N. Roque Ramirez, "'That's My Place': Negotiating Racial, Sexual, and Gender Politics in San Francisco's Gay Latino Alliance, 1975–1983," *Journal of the History of Sexuality* 12/2 (April 2003): 224–258; Tomás Almaguer, "Chicano Men: A Cartography of Homosexual Identity and Behavior," *differences* (1991): 75–100.

27. Polak's advertisements quoted in Stein, *City of Sisterly and Brotherly Loves*, 232, 237. See also Loughery, *The Other Side of Silence*, 282–284. *The Los Angeles Advocate* began publication in 1967 and became simply *The Advocate* in 1969.

28. *ADV*, September 1967, 7; *Tangents*, June 1967, 2; *Vector*, March 1967, 10; Kameny speech, Gottheimer, ed., *Ripples of Hope*; *Vector*, September 1967, 15; "What Homosexuals Want," *Pursuit and Symposium*, June 1967, 31–36, JK; Craig Loftin, "Unacceptable Mannerisms: Gender Anxieties, Homosexual Activism, and Swish in the United States, 1945–1965," *Journal of Social History* 40/3 (Spring 2007): 577–596.

29. *ADV*, April 1968, 2–3.

30. Ibid.

31. *CDN*, June 20, 1966, 3; *CN*, n.d., vol. 4, no. 12, p. 7; *Vector*, December 1966, 2, April 1967, 17, May 1967, 13; *Harper's*, March 1963, 87; Homosexual Information Center, Newsletter No. 28, "Gay Community" Folder, Arthur Snyder papers, Box C-165, LACC.

32. W. E. Beardemphl, "President's Column," *Vector*, December 1966, 2; Homosexual Information Center, Newsletter No. 28, "Gay Community" Folder, Arthur Snyder papers, Box C-165, LACC; Rita Mae Brown quoted in David Allyn, *Make Love Not War: The Sexual Revolution, an Unfettered History* (Boston: Little, Brown, 2000), 251.

33. *ADV*, March 1970, 2; Kameny speech; Gottheimer, ed., *Ripples of Hope*.

34. *ADV*, September 1968, 5.

35. Ibid.

36. *The Ladder*, May and October 1965, 15, 10; "Draft of Letter to the Editor of the New York Times," written by Frank Kameny, n.d., FJ; *Time*, October 31, 1969, 56–67.

37. William Rubenstein, ed., *Lesbians, Gay Men, and the Law* (New York: New Press, 1993), 69–76; Stein, "*Boutilier* and the U.S. Supreme Court's Sexual Revolution." In order to emphasize the illness dimension of the *Boutilier* case, I have not discussed another important question raised before the Court: whether homosexuality constituted an act or a distinct identity. See Stein, *Sexual Injustice*, 57–207.

38. Socarides quoted in D'Emilio, *Sexual Politics, Sexual Communities*, 216; *Vector*, July 1968, 5; Minton, *Departing from Deviance*.

39. *The Challenges and Progress of Homosexual Law Reform*, Council on Religion and the Homosexual et al., 1968, 15; letter from Jo Regan to county supervisors, October 31, 1968, Folder 2.49.1, JH; *Life*, June 11, 1965.

40. *Victimless Crimes: A Research Project*, Los Angeles Police Department, May 1972, 23.

41. National Institute of Mental Health, *Final Report of the Task Force on Homosexuality*, Evelyn Hooker, chairman (Bethesda, Md.: NIMH, 1969), reprinted in Joseph A. McCaffrey, ed., *The Homosexual Dialectic* (Englewood Cliffs, N.J.: Prentice-Hall, 1972), 145–155; Minton, *Departing from Deviance*, 236–261.

42. Minton, *Departing from Deviance*, 236–261.

43. George Chauncey, "From Sexual Inversion to Homosexuality: Medicine and the Changing Conceptualization of Female Deviance," in *Passion and Power*, ed. Peiss and Simmons, 87–117.

44. *ADV*, June 1969, 16.

45. *ADV*, January, June, and August 1969, 16, 24, 5; *LAFP*, March 7 and May 16, 1969.

46. Johnson, *The Lavender Scare*, 189; *ADV*, March 1969, 1; Streitmatter, *Unspeakable: The Rise of the Gay and Lesbian Press in America*.

47. Johnson, *The Lavender Scare*, 189; *ADV*, March 1969, 1; Streitmatter, *Unspeakable: The Rise of the Gay and Lesbian Press in America*; Tracy Baim, ed., *Out and Proud in Chicago: An Overview of the City's Gay Community* (Chicago: Surrey Books, 2008).

48. *Vector*, January 1965, 4, December 1969, 7; *ADV*, August 1969, September 1 and 30, 1969, February 1970, 6.

49. *Vector*, September 1972, 38; "Bishop's Urban Coalition Hearings, February 16, 1978," Box 12, Folder 19, CH.

50. *ADV*, September 1969, 2, 4, March 1970, 1, May 27–June 9, 1970, 1, 3, 36; Johnson, *Lavender Scare*, 202; Alwood, *Straight News*, 120.

51. Johnson, *Lavender Scare*, 202; *ADV*, September 1969, 2, 4, March 1970, 1, May 27–June 9, 1970; Alwood, *Straight News*, 120.

52. *ADV*, September and October 1968, 2, December 1968, 30; *The Ladder*, August–September 1969, 16; Loughery, *The Other Side of Silence*, 305–307; "Report of the First National Conference of the Student Homophile League" and "The Homosexual Student on the College Campus," Box 8, Folder 3, MSNY.

53. There are dozens of accounts of the Stonewall riots. The brief account here is drawn from *ADV*, September 1969, 3 (reprinted from *New York Mattachine Newsletter*); Duberman, *Stonewall*, 167–213; Carter, *Stonewall*, 137–194.

54. *Esquire*, December 1969, 316–318.

4: THE WORKING MOTHER HAS NO WIFE

1. Jacqueline Jones, *Labor of Love, Labor of Sorrow: Black Women, Work, and the Family, from Slavery to the Present* (New York: Basic Books, 1985), 232–321; Dorothy Sue Cobble, *The Other Women's Movement: Workplace Justice and Social Rights in Modern America* (Princeton, N.J.: Princeton University Press, 2004), 69–144; Nancy MacLean, *Freedom Is Not Enough: The Opening of the American Workplace* (Cambridge, Mass.: Harvard University Press, 2006), 13–34, 117–154.

2. *Women's Role in Contemporary Society: Report of the New York City Commission on Human Rights,* 69; "Equal Rights for Women," CR 117/109 (July 15, 1971).

3. I owe the class formulation to a conversation with Dorothy Sue Cobble. For critiques of the wave metaphor for women's movements, see Nancy Hewitt, ed., *No Permanent Waves: Recasting Histories of U.S. Feminism* (New Brunswick, N.J.: Rutgers University Press, 2010); Patricia Hill Collins, *Black Feminist Thought: Knowledge, Consciousness, and the Politics of Empowerment* (Boston: Unwin Hyman, 1990).

4. Scholarship on transgender history suggests that even the biological category "woman" was not entirely coherent. See Joanne Meyerowitz, *How Sex Changed: A History of Transsexuality in the United States* (Cambridge, Mass.: Harvard University Press, 2002).

5. Joan Williams, *Unbending Gender: Why Family and Work Conflict and What to Do About It* (New York: Oxford University Press, 2001).

6. Stephanie Coontz, *The Way We Never Were: American Families and the Nostalgia Trap* (New York: Basic Books, 1992), 52–67.

7. *Wisconsin Women: The Second Major Report of the Governor's Commission on the Status of Women* (Madison, Wis.: The Commission, 1967), 28.

8. Jamakaya, *Like Our Sisters Before Us: Women of Wisconsin Labor* (Milwaukee: Wisconsin Historical Society, 1998), 46–49.

9. Women's Bureau, U.S. Department of Labor, *Negro Women in the Population and in the Labor Force,* n.d.; "To Fulfill the Rights of Negro Women in Disadvantaged Families," June 1–2, 1966, Box 129, Folder 2336, PM; Jones, *Labor of Love, Labor of Sorrow,* 301–310; U.S. Bureau of the Census, *Characteristics of the Population Below the Poverty Level* (Washington, D.C.: Government Printing Office, 1976), Table A.

10. Premilla Nadasen, *Welfare Warriors: The Welfare Rights Movement in the United States* (New York: Routledge, 2005), 19.

11. Frances Beal, "Double Jeopardy," in *The Black Woman: An Anthology,* ed. Toni Cade (New York: New American Library, 1970), 92–93, 95; Johnnie Tillmon, "Welfare Is a Women's Issue," *Liberation News Service,* February 26, 1972, quoted in Rosalyn Baxandall and Linda Gordon, eds., *Dear Sisters: Dispatches from the Women's Liberation Movement* (New York: Basic Books, 2000), 279–281.

12. Beal, "Double Jeopardy," 92–93, 95.

13. Martha May, "The Historical Problem of the Family Wage: The Ford Motor Company and the Five Dollar Day," *Feminist Studies* 8/2 (Summer 1982): 399–424; Nelson Lichtenstein, *State of the Union: A Century of American Labor* (Princeton, N.J.: Princeton University Press, 2002).

14. Robin Morgan (citing *U.S. Statistical Abstracts*), *The Word of a Woman: Feminist Dispatches, 1968–1992* (New York: W. W. Norton, 1992), 109.

15. *MLR*, February 1968, 1–12, April 1968, 14–22; U.S. Department of Labor, *1975 Handbook on Women Workers* (Washington, D.C.: Women's Bureau, 1975), 8–43; Kimberly Morgan, "A Child of the Sixties: The Great Society, the New Right, and the Politics of Federal Child Care," *Journal of Policy History* 13/2 (2001): 215–250.

16. U.S. Department of Labor, "The Negro Woman in the United States—New Roles, New Challenges," Box 140, Folder 2546, PM; Tillmon, "Welfare Is a Women's Issue."

17. *MLR*, February 1968, 1–12, April 1968, 14–22.

18. "Sex Discrimination and the Working Woman," unpublished report, Box 55, Folder 958, PM; "Proceedings: Equal Employment Opportunity: Its Evolvement, Its Enigmas, Its Orthodoxy," Box 86, Folder 1495, PM; memo from Pauli Murray and Mary Eastwood, February 9, 1968, Box 55, Folder 957, PM.

19. "Statement of the AFL-CIO on Methods of Removing Legal Discrimination Against Women," submitted to the Presidential Commission on the Status of Women, March 13, 1963, Box 55, Folder 956, PM; ACLU Memo, "ACLU Position on Sex Discrimination and Protective Legislation," March 17, 1970, Box 3, Folder 4, ME; Griffiths quoted in Pauli Murray and Mary Eastwood, "Jane Crow and the Law: Sex Discrimination and Title VII," *George Washington Law Review* 34/2 (December 1965): 248.

20. Pauli Murray letter to Kathryn Clarenbach, November 21, 1967, Box 51, Folder 899, PM; Serena Mayeri, *Reasoning from Race: Feminism, Law, and the Civil Rights Revolution* (Cambridge, Mass.: Harvard University Press, 2010), 44–63. On Murray's transgender identity, see Meyerowitz, *How Sex Changed*, 36–37.

21. Pauli Murray, "A Proposal to Reexamine the Applicability of the Fourteenth Amendment to State Laws and Practices Which Discriminate on the Basis of Sex per se," December 1962, Box 8, Folder 61, PCSW; Serena Mayeri, "'A Common Fate of Discrimination': Race-Gender Analogies in Legal and Historical Perspective," *Yale Law Review* 110/6 (April 2001): 1045–1087.

22. Murray, "A Proposal"; Murray, "The Legal Implications of Women-at-Work," October 12, 1965, Carton 1, Folder 34, ME (emphasis in original).

23. Remarks by Marjorie D. Tibbs, June 29, 1966, Box 49, Folder 877, PM; MacLean, *Freedom Is Not Enough*, 123; Nicholas Pedriana, "From Protective to Equal Treatment: Legal Framing Processes and Transformation of the Women's Movement in the 1960s," *American Journal of Sociology* 111/6 (May 2006): 1718–1761.

24. Martha Griffiths, speech before the House of Representatives, June 20, 1966, *CR*.

25. Pauli Murray letter to Kathryn Clarenbach, November 21, 1967, Box 51, Folder 899, PM.

26. Ibid.

27. Kathleen M. Barry, *Femininity in Flight: A History of Flight Attendants* (Durham, N.C.: Duke University Press, 2007); "DRAFT:SPressman," December 9, 1966, Box 39, Folder 685, PM.

28. "Status of the Mengelkoch Case," January 18, 1967; letter to Mr. Silver from Marguerite Rawalt, n.d.; NOW press release, August 7, 1968, Box 3, Folder: Mengelkoch Case, ME.

29. Betty Friedan to Attorney General Ramsey Clark, January 24, 1967, Box 51, Folder 898, PM; Aileen Hernandez statement, June 2, 1967, Box 3, Folder: Mengelkoch Case, ME; "Status of the Mengelkoch Case," January 18, 1967; letter to Mr. Silver

from Marguerite Rawalt, n.d.; NOW press release, August 7, 1968, Box 3, Folder: Mengelkoch Case, ME.

30. Mary Eastwood, "Constitutional Protection Against Sex Discrimination," November 1967, Folder 956, Box 55, PM.

31. Box 55, Folder 956, PM; *LAT*, December 2, 1971, A4; *WSJ*, December 2, 1971, 21, April 14, 1972, 23, and January 19, 1973, 3; *CT*, January 30, 1972, E4; MacLean, *Freedom Is Not Enough*, 124–126.

32. Hirma Hill Kay, "Ruth Bader Ginsburg, Professor of Law," *Columbia University Law Review* 104/1 (January 2004): 1–20; Elizabeth Duncan Koontz, "American Women at the Crossroads," June 12, 1970, 40/2548, PM.

33. Statement of Pauli Murray on the Equal Rights Amendment, submitted to the Senate Judiciary Committee, September 16, 1970, Folder 959, Box 44, PM; Murray to ACLU Equality Committee, March 30, 1970, Folder 959, Box 44, PM; MacLean, *Freedom Is Not Enough*, 124–126.

34. ACLU memo, "Sex Discrimination in Private Employment," December 21, 1967, Box 55, Folder 958, PM.

35. Katharine T. Bartlett, "Pregnancy and the Constitution: The Uniqueness Trap," *California Law Review* 62/5 (December 1974): 1532–1566; Jennifer Yatskis Dukart, "*Geduldig* Reborn: Hibbs as a Success (?) of Ruth Bader Ginsburg's Sex-Discrimination Strategy," *California Law Review* 93/2 (March 2005): 541–586; Diane L. Zimmerman, "*Geduldig v. Aiello:* 'Pregnancy' Classifications and the Definition of Sex Discrimination," *Columbia Law Review* 75/2 (March 1975): 441–482.

36. *Redbook* 34 (September 1970), 33–35.

37. Lauri Umansky, *Motherhood Reconceived: Feminism and the Legacies of the Sixties* (New York: New York University Press, 1996); Sylvia Ann Hewlett, *A Lesser Life: The Myth of Women's Liberation in America* (New York: William Morrow, 1986), 109–287; Jane J. Mansbridge, *Why We Lost the ERA* (Chicago: University of Chicago Press, 1986), 90–165.

38. Miss Rawalt, transcript, PCSW, February 11, 1963 (PCSW 2/11), 103; Carolyn Ware, transcript, PCSW, April 1, 1963, Box 2, Folder 12, PCSW.

39. Natalie Fousekis, *Demanding Child Care: Women's Activism and the Politics of Welfare* (Urbana: University of Illinois Press, 2011); Sonya Michel, *Children's Interests/ Mothers' Rights: The Shaping of America's Child Care Policy* (New Haven, Conn.: Yale University Press, 1999), 192–243. For an example of a local child care organizing project, see Box 1, Folders 40 and 43, Box 24, Folder 12, Box 25, Folder 1, UWY.

40. Targets for Action, 1966–1967, NOW, Box 50, Folder 894, PM.

41. *NYT*, August 26, 1971, 37; *Ms.*, 1/1 (July 1972): 56–59, 91–93; Betsy Warrior, "Housework: Slavery or Labor of Love," in *Radical Feminism*, ed. Anne Koedt et al. (New York: Quadrangle, 1973), 208–210; Pat Mainardi, "The Politics of Housework," in Baxandall and Gordon, eds., *Dear Sisters*, 255–257.

42. Patricia Coffin, "Memo to the American Woman," *Look* (January 11, 1966): 15–17.

43. *CT*, August 26, 1967, A13; *NYT*, August 22 and December 12, 1967, 36 and 46; Wiley quoted in Felicia Kornbluh, *The Battle for Welfare Rights: Politics and Poverty in Modern America* (Philadelphia: University of Pennsylvania Press, 2007), 9; "Interview with Mrs. J. L. Tillmon," November 2, 1965, Box 12, Folder 25C, MCC. The National Chicana Welfare Rights Organization, in the early 1970s, also opposed "denying the

NOTES TO PAGES 123–131

mother who is poor the right to stay home if she chooses." See "Chicana Caucus Resolutions," February 9–11, 1973, Box 168, Folder 8, GS.

44. *Ebony,* March 1971, 70; Beulah Sanders to the National Women's Political Caucus, 1972, Box 36, Folder 9, GW.

45. "Who We Are: Description of Women's Liberation Groups," Box 1, Folder 19, CB.

46. Toni Cade, *The Black Woman,* 166.

47. I owe the formulations in this paragraph to an exchange with Jane Gerhard. See also Robin Morgan, *The Word of a Woman;* Alice Echols, *Daring to Be Bad: Radical Feminism in America, 1967–1975* (Minneapolis: University of Minnesota Press, 1989).

48. Jane Gerhard, *Desiring Revolution: Second-Wave Feminism and the Rewriting of American Sexual Thought, 1920–1982* (New York: Columbia University Press, 2001).

49. Unpublished notes, Box 1, DB.

50. Janet Tenny, "Economics of Family and Abortion," Box 2, Folder: Women's Liberation, ME; *SR* (21 February 1970), 27.

51. Warrior, "Housework: Slavery or Labor of Love," in Koedt et al., eds., *Radical Feminism,* 208–210; *NYTSM,* March 10, 1968, 24; *NYT,* September 24, 1969, 93.

52. Sharon Deevey, "Such a Nice Girl," in *Lesbianism and the Women's Movement,* ed. Nancy Byron and Charlotte Bunch (Baltimore: Diana Press, 1975).

53. Wolfgang testimony, memo to ACLU, Box 55, Folder 956, PM.

54. *CT,* June 9, 1967, C15; Letty Cottin Pogrebin, "The Working Woman," *Ladies' Home Journal,* February 1972, 18 (emphasis in original).

55. Alice Kessler-Harris, *In Pursuit of Equity: Women, Men, and the Quest for Economic Citizenship in 20th-Century America* (New York: Oxford University Press, 2001); Suzanne Mettler, *Dividing Citizens: Gender and Federalism in New Deal Public Policy* (Ithaca, N.Y.: Cornell University Press, 1998); "Why Feminists Want Child Care," memo dated April 22, 1971, Box 42, Folder 34, NOW.

56. Abzug and Chisholm introduced an even stronger bill but settled on the CCDA out of political expediency. See the speeches, memos, and letters in Box 138, Folder: Child Care, 1970–71, and Box 140, Folder: Child Care: Speeches, BA; memos and letters, Box 30, Folder 57, NOW; *Texas Report of the Governor's Commission on the Status of Women,* 1967, 34; *Report of the Commission on the Status of Women to the Governor and General Assembly of Virginia,* 1966, 45; Chisholm quoted in *CR,* May 18, 1971, E4526.

57. *Comprehensive Child Development Act: Joint Hearings Before the Subcommittee on Employment, Manpower, and Poverty* (Washington, D.C.: Government Printing Office, 1971), vol. 2, 536–537; National Task Force on Child Care, NOW, July 31, 1970, assorted letters, minutes, and documents, Box 42, Folder 35, NOW.

58. National Women's Political Caucus Day Care Alert, July 30, 1971, Box 128, Folder 2333, PM; Michel, *Children's Interests/Mothers' Rights,* 248–251; Caputo, *Welfare and Freedom,* chap. 7; Kimberly Morgan, "A Child of the Sixties," 215–250; *Comprehensive Child Development Act: Joint Hearings Before the Subcommittee on Employment, Manpower, and Poverty* (Washington, D.C.: Government Printing Office, 1971), vol. 1, pp. 165, 366.

59. Phillips quoted in Morgan, "A Child of the Sixties," 232.

60. *NYT,* December 10, 1971, 20.

61. *Craig v. Boren* was the capstone decision in a series of Supreme Court rulings in the

early and mid-1970s that established the intermediate scrutiny test for laws that discriminated between men and women.

62. U.S. Department of Labor, *Women in the Labor Force: A Databook* (Washington, D.C.: U.S. Bureau of Labor Statistics, 2010), Tables 16 and 27.

63. *NYT*, December 14, 1967, 78; *NYTSM*, August 22, 1971, 14.

5: BODIES ON TRIAL

1. The letters to Maginnis, numbering in the hundreds, if not thousands, can be found in Boxes 5–7, SHA. Hunt's column ran in the *Defender* from 1964 through 1971. The ones cited come from issues dated November 7, 1964, February 27 and August 28, 1965, and May 6, 1967.

2. Claudia Dreifus, ed., *Seizing Our Bodies: The Politics of Women's Health* (New York: Vintage, 1977); Sandra Morgen, *Into Our Own Hands: The Women's Health Movement in the United States, 1969–1990* (New Brunswick, N.J.: Rutgers University Press, 2002); American Friends Service Committee, *Who Shall Live?* (New York: Hill and Wang, 1970). NARAL changed its name to National Abortion Rights Action League in 1973.

3. Samuel D. Warren and Louis Brandeis, "The Right to Privacy," *Harvard Law Review* 4 (1890): 193–220.

4. Abzug letter to Mr. Thomas and Ms. Nancy Renan, July 17, 1972, Folder: Abortion, 1971–1972, Box 600, BA; *oob*, February 26, 1971, 8.

5. Linda Gordon, *Woman's Body, Woman's Right: A Social History of Birth Control in America* (New York: Grossman, 1976).

6. David Garrow, *Liberty and Sexuality: The Right to Privacy and the Making of* Roe v. Wade (Berkeley: University of California Press, 1998; orig., 1994); Marc Stein, *Sexual Injustice: Supreme Court Decisions from Griswold to Roe* (Chapel Hill: University of North Carolina Press, 2010).

7. Assembly Interim Committee on Criminal Procedure, *Abortion Hearing AB 2614*, December 17 and 18, 1962, San Diego, Calif., 79–82.

8. Friedan quoted in Linda Greenhouse and Reva B. Siegel, eds., *Before Roe v. Wade: Voices That Shaped the Abortion Debate Before the Supreme Court's Ruling* (New York: Kaplan, 2010), 39; "First National Conference on Abortion Laws, February 14–16, 1969," Folder 196, Box 21, LM.

9. See Kristin Luker, *Abortion and the Politics of Motherhood* (Berkeley: University of California Press, 1984).

10. Leslie J. Reagan, *When Abortion Was a Crime: Women, Medicine, and Law in the United States, 1867–1973* (Berkeley: University of California Press, 1998), 161–192.

11. Letter to Allan Kahn from Ruth Roemer, December 23, 1968, Box 5, Folder: Post-Legislation CCTA, CCTA.

12. Marya Mannes, "A Woman Views Abortion," March 30, 1966, New York Academy of Medicine, Box 23, Folder 7, NOW; Gordon, *Woman's Body, Woman's Right*; Laura Kaplan, *The Story of Jane: The Legendary Underground Feminist Abortion Service* (New York: Pantheon, 1995).

13. *McCall's*, January 1971, 30–34; *Redbook*, April 1970, 78–79, 137–139; Tilda Norberg, "Abortion: A Human Choice," May 1971, United Methodist Church, Box 114, Folder

2043, PM; *Newsweek*, April 13, 1970, 53–61; *Guttmacher Report on Public Policy* 6/1 (March 2003); CC, May 20, 1970, 626.

14. American Friends Service Committee, *Who Shall Live?*, 26, 62–65; Ehrlich and Zero Population Control quoted in Greenhouse and Siegel, eds., *Before Roe v. Wade*, 55.

15. *Harper's*, January 1965; Harriet Pilpel oral history, March 20, 1972, Schlesinger Library; Serena Mayeri, "Constitutional Choices: Legal Feminism and the Historical Dynamics of Change," *California Law Review* 92 (2004): 757–840; Garrow, *Liberty and Sexuality*, 335–360.

16. Alan Charles and Susan Alexander, "Abortions for Poor and Nonwhite Women: Denial of Equal Protection?," *Hastings Law Journal* (1971–1972): 147–169; Greenhouse and Siegel, eds., *Before Roe v. Wade*, 269–282.

17. J. Harvie Wilkinson III, "The Supreme Court, the Equal Protection Clause, and the Three Faces of Constitutional Equality," *Virginia Law Review* 61/5 (June 1975): 945–1018.

18. Pauli Murray, "A Proposal to Reexamine the Applicability of the Fourteenth Amendment to State Laws and Practices Which Discriminate on the Basis of Sex per se," December 1962, Box 8, Folder 61, PCSW; Harriet F. Pilpel and Kenneth P. Norwick, "When Should Abortion Be Legal?," published in 1969 by the Public Affairs Committee, Box 114, Folder 2043, PM; Roy Lucas, "Federal Constitutional Limitations on the Enforcement and Administration of Abortion Statutes," *North Carolina Law Review* 46/4 (June 1968): 730–778; NYT, January 25, 1970, 200; *NARAL News*, Winter 1970.

19. "Modification or Repeal?," First National Conference on Abortion Laws, Box 1, Folder 1, NARAL; Midwest Strategy Conference, minutes, January 9, 1971, NARAL.

20. "The Story of California's Abortion Law," unpublished manuscript, Box 5, "Post-Legislation CCTA" Folder, CCTA; "Statement of Californians in the Social Services in Support of Proposed Humane Abortion Law," Box 7, Folder: CCTA, CCTA; Jerome M. Kummer, "New Trends in Therapeutic Abortion in California," *Obstetrics and Gynecology* 34/6 (December 1969): 883–887; *Newsletter*, Society for Human Abortion, Inc. 3/1 (January–February 1966/1967), Box 1, CCTA.

21. *Facts About Abortion: Women Have a Right to Know*, Box 1, Folder 6, SHA; *SFC*, July 22, 1966; letter to Lee Gidding from Don Frederick, May 26, 1969, Carton 2, Folder: Calif. 1968–1969, NARAL; Luker, *Abortion and the Politics of Motherhood*, 95–112.

22. "A Special Report on Therapeutic Abortion," *Pacific Churchman*, April 1967; "Profile of the Opposition," Box 1, Folder 10, NARAL.

23. *Public Hearings Before the Commission to Study the New Jersey Statutes Relating to Abortion*, November 13, 1968, Newark, and November 26, 1968, Camden, 3, 91, 99; *Michigan State Senate Committee on Abortion Law Reform Public Hearing*, December 12, 1969, Jackson, Michigan, 81; letter dated March 3, 1969, Folder NY 68–September 69, Carton 2, NARAL; assorted articles in "Redstockings Women's Liberation Archives for Action Project," Archives Distribution Project, Gainesville, Florida (hereafter RWLAAP).

24. Lonny Myers, "Abortion Is a Private Matter," 1967, Folder 196, Box 21, LM; "Executive Director's Report," September 27 and 28, 1970, Box 1, Folder 3, NARAL; "Minutes, Executive Committee Meeting," September 28, 1969, Box 1, Folder: Ex Com. Min-

utes, NARAL; NARAL, Statement of Policy and Program, March 27, 1969, Box 1, Folder 7, RPS; Friedan quoted in Greenhouse and Siegel, eds, *Before Roe v. Wade*, 39.

25. "The First Abortion Speakout," March 21, 1969, CD recording, RWLAAP; Diane Schulder and Florynce Kennedy, *Abortion Rap* (New York: McGraw-Hill, 1971), xii–88.

26. Linda Cisler, "Abortion Law Repeal (Sort of): A Warning to Women" (April 1970), in *Radical Feminism*, ed. Anne Koedt et al. (New York: Quadrangle, 1973), 151–164; Reagan, *When Abortion Was a Crime*, 230; Marya Mannes, "A Woman Views Abortion," speech to the New York Academy of Medicine, March 30, 1966, Box 23, Folder 7, NOW.

27. Robin Morgan, "Goodbye to All That" (1970), in Robin Morgan, *The Word of a Woman: Feminist Dispatches, 1968–1992* (New York: W. W. Norton, 1992), 57–69; Michele Wallace, "Anger in Isolation: A Black Feminist's Search for Sisterhood," *Village Voice* (1974), reprinted in Beverly Guy-Sheftall, ed., *Words of Fire: An Anthology of African-American Feminist Thought* (New York: New Press, 1995).

28. On the scope and aims of the new sexual politics, see virtually any issue, between 1970 and 1973, of *off our backs* (Washington, D.C.), *The Furies* (Washington, D.C.), and *No More Fun and Games* (Boston).

29. *NYT*, April 15, 1969, 44, 46.

30. "Current Status of Abortion Laws, August 1, 1970," Box 1, Folder 10, and "Abortion Law Gathers Speed," January 15, 1970, Box 2, Folder: Calif. January–September 1970, NARAL; Rosemary Nossif, *Before Roe: Abortion Policy in the States* (Philadelphia: Temple University Press, 2001).

31. NARAL, Statement of Policy and Program, March 27, 1969, Box 1, Folder 7, RPS; press release, September 29, 1969, Folder 18, Box 1, NARAL; "Modification or Repeal? First National Conference on Abortion Laws," February 14–16, 1969, Folder 1, Box 1, NARAL; Garrow, *Liberty and Sexuality*, 377, 382.

32. Vincent J. Samar, *The Right to Privacy: Gays, Lesbians, and the Constitution* (Philadelphia: Temple University Press, 1991).

33. Letter to Abzug from Emmalee B. Tarry, Folder: Abortion, 1971–1972, Box 600, BA.

34. *Ebony*, October 1973, 150–154.

35. Angela Davis, "On Black Women," *Ms.*, August 1972, 55. See Walter Wadlington, "The Loving Case: Virginia's Anti-Miscegenation Statute in Historical Perspective," *Virginia Law Review* 52/7 (November 1966): 1189–1223; Haywood Burns, "Black People and the Tyranny of American Law," *Annals of the American Academy of Political and Social Science* 407 (May 1973): 156–166; Peter W. Bardaglio, "Rape and the Law in the Old South: 'Calculated to Excite Indignation in Every Heart,'" *Journal of Southern History* 60/4 (November 1994): 749–772.

36. Herman Talmadge and Georgia legislator quoted in Ellen Reese, *Backlash Against Welfare Mothers, Past and Present* (Berkeley: University of California Press, 2005), 73; Edward L. Larson, *Sex, Race, and Science: Eugenics in the Deep South* (Baltimore: Johns Hopkins University Press, 1995).

37. Memorandum on Hartman Plan for Voluntary Sterilization, October 26, 1964, and news clipping, Box 1, Folder 5, RPS; Michele Mitchell, *Righteous Propagation: African Americans and the Politics of Racial Destiny After Reconstruction* (Chapel Hill: University of North Carolina Press, 2004); Gwendolyn Mink and Rickie Solinger, eds., *Welfare: A Documentary History of U.S. Politics and Poverty* (New York: New

York University Press, 2003); Robert Novak and Rowland Evans quoted in *WP*, December 10, 1965, A29.

38. *CD*, June 12 and 19, 1965. Dorothy Roberts, *Killing the Black Body: Race, Reproduction, and the Meaning of Liberty* (New York: Vintage, 1997).

39. *Relf v. Weinberger*, 372 F. Supp. 1196 [D.D.C. 1974]. Jeannie I. Rosoff, "Sterilization: The Montgomery Case," *Hastings Center Report* 3/4 (September 1973): 6; Patricia Donovan, "Sterilizing the Poor and Incompetent," *Hastings Center Report* 6/5 (October 1976): 7–8; Judith Coburn, "Sterilization Regulations: Debate Not Quelled by HEW Document," *Science* 183 (March 8, 1974): 935–939; Johanna Schoen, *Choice and Coercion: Birth Control, Sterilization, and Abortion in Public Health and Welfare* (Chapel Hill: University of North Carolina Press, 2005); *NYT*, July 2, 6, and 13, 1973, 10, 54, 43; "Statement of Carol Greitzer," Box 1, Folder 19, NARAL.

40. Jennifer Nelson, *Women of Color and the Reproductive Rights Movement* (New York: New York University Press, 2003), 85–111; *CD*, January 1, 1966, 10; Robert Staples, "The Myth of the Black Matriarchy," *Black Scholar* 1 (January–February 1970): 16.

41. Planned Parenthood Federation of America, *Birth Control Services in Tax-Supported Hospitals, Health Departments, and Welfare Agencies* (New York: PPFA, 1963); Mary Treadwell, "Is Abortion Black Genocide?," *Family Planning Perspectives* 4/1 (January 1972): 4–5; Chisholm quoted in *CR*, December 11, 1969, 38592–38594; remarks of Richard Austin before NARAL, October 7, 1972, Box 8, "Abortion," CCTA; "Black Feminist Attacks Myths," Box 1, Folder: writings as well as other materials in Folder 1, BE.

42. Frances Beal, "Double Jeopardy: To Be Black and Female" and Toni Cade, "The Pill: Genocide or Liberation?" in Cade, ed., *The Black Woman: An Anthology* (New York: New American Library, 1970), 90–100, 163–169; Linda La Rue, "The Black Movement and Women's Liberation," *Black Scholar* 1 (May 1970): 42; Chisholm quoted in Reagan, *When Abortion Was a Crime*, 232.

43. César Chávez quoted in Ana Raquel Minian, "'Indiscriminate and Shameless Sex': The Strategic Deployment of Sexuality by the United Farm Workers," unpublished paper in author's possession, 7; Alexandra Minna Stern, *Eugenic Nation: Faults and Frontiers of Better Breeding in Modern America* (Berkeley: University of California Press, 2005), 204; Francisca Flores, "Comisión Femenil Mexicana," *Regeneración*, n.d., 6; "Comisión Femenil Mexicana Nacional, Inc.," Box 2, Folder 7, CM; "Legislative Needs of Hispanic Women," Box 2, Folder 2, CM; "Comisión Femenil Mejicana de Los Angeles [*sic*], General Meeting" Box 1, Folder 18, CM. Gustavo Licón, "'¡La union hace la fuerza!' ('Unity Creates Strength!'): M.E.Ch.A. and Chicana/o Student Activism in California, 1966–1999" (Ph.D. dissertation, University of Southern California, 2009).

44. Alma M. García, *Chicana Feminist Thought: The Basic Historical Writings* (New York: Routledge, 1997), 153–171; "Is Abortion Genocide?," memo from Sharon Simms, July 1970, Box 4, Folder 62, NARAL. Welfare rights activists and their attorneys were able to win a measure of protection from indiscriminate state action. See Felicia Kornbluh, "Redistribution, Recognition, and Good China: Administrative Justice for Women Welfare Recipients Before *Goldberg v. Kelly*," *Yale Journal of Law and Feminism* 20/1 (2008): 165–194.

45. Greenhouse and Siegel, eds., *Before Roe v. Wade*, 19–21; "Draft: Reproductive Rights for Women," Box 49, Folder 23, NOW.

46. Garrow, *Liberty and Sexuality*, 484. "Report on the Third Annual National Right to Life Committee Meeting," Philadelphia, June 16–18, 1972, letter to NARAL from Helen Baer, December 1, 1970, "Right to Life Organizations," Box 8, Folder: Opposition, NARAL.

47. NYT, June 28, 1972, 21; *NYTSM*, August 20, 1972, 10–11, 34–35+; "Profile of the Opposition," Box 7, Folder: Legal, 1971–1972, NARAL.

48. *LAT*, April 9, 1972, A3.

49. *LAT*, November 1, 1972, C4; *CT*, November 5, 1972, B12; *oob*, November 1972. Rockefeller quoted in *NYT*, May 14, 1972, 62; Garrow, *Liberty and Sexuality*, 577. For Rockefeller's views on abortion, see his speech before the Association for the Study of Abortion, November 1968, Box 10, CCTA.

50. Abortion polls, Box 8, Folder: Orgzl. Position on Abortion, NARAL; "Opinion After the Supreme Court decision," Box 54, Folder 26, NOW; *oob*, December 1971; *PTA* magazine, May 1972, 13; "National Organizations Recommending Repeal of Abortion Laws," Box 1, Folder: Annual Meeting, 1971, NARAL Records; "Midwest Strategy Conference," January 9, 1971, Box 1, NARAL; Judith Black, "The Supreme Court's Abortion Decisions and Public Opinion in the United States," *Population and Development Review* 3 (March–June 1977): 45–62.

51. Memo to Executive Committee from Larry Lader, March 2, 1972, Box 7, Folder "NARAL Symposium," NARAL; memo to NECLC Executive Committee from Ramona Ripston, n.d., Box 8, Folder: Orgzl. Position on Abortion, NARAL; Garrow, *Liberty and Sexuality*, 414–415; Appendix A in Nanette J. Davis, *From Crime to Choice: The Transformation of Abortion in America* (Westport, Conn.: Greenwood Press, 1985).

52. NARAL memo, n.d., Box 4, Folder: NY State Campaign; "Profile of the Opposition"; letter to Margot Polevy from Lucinda Cisler, February 1, 1972, Box 600, Folder: Abortion, 1971–1972, BA.

53. NARAL memo, n.d., Box 4, Folder: NY State Campaign, "Profile of the Opposition," Box 7, Folder: Legal, 1971–1972, NARAL. McCorvey lived an interesting, bisexual life. See Garrow, *Liberty and Sexuality*, 402–403; Stein, *Sexual Injustice*, 125–127.

54. Garrow, *Liberty and Sexuality*, 405–429; Roy Lucas et al., *Brief for Appellants, Roe v. Wade*, No. 70-18, 1971; Clyde L. Randall et al., *Motion for Leave, Doe v. Bolton*, No. 70-40, 1971. On radical feminist amicus briefs and the heteronormative language of most of the briefs submitted in *Roe* and *Doe*, see Stein, *Sexual Injustice*, 128–130.

55. Garrow, *Liberty and Sexuality*, 588–597; Lynne Curry, *The Human Body on Trial: A Handbook with Cases, Laws, and Documents* (Santa Barbara, Calif.: ABC-CLIO, 2002).

56. Garrow, *Liberty and Sexuality*, 597.

57. James Buckley quoted in *Abortion—Part I: Hearings Before the Subcommittee on Constitutional Amendments of the Committee on the Judiciary, United States Senate, Ninety-third Congress* (Washington, D.C.: Government Printing Office, 1974), 41.

58. Harry Sidenstick to Bella Abzug, March 30, 1973, Box 600, Folder: Abortion, 1971–1972, Abzug Papers; Lawrence Lader to John Roberts, May 8, 1973, Box 6, Folder: ACLU and NARAL Lawsuits, NARAL; Chicago Women's Liberation Union, press release, August 16, 1973, Box 49, Folder 17, NOW; letter to Harry Blackmun from Fern Arpi, June 23, 1977, Box 1355, HB; WONAAC press release, January 12, 1972, Box 36, Folder 9, GW.

59. Guttmacher quoted in Reagan, *When Abortion Was a Crime*, 234.

60. Richard Lincoln et al., "The Court, the Congress, and the President: Turning Back the Clock on the Pregnant Poor," *Family Planning Perspectives* 9/5 (September–October 1977): 207–214; Mary C. Segers, "Abortion and the Supreme Court: Some Are More Equal than Others," *Hastings Center Report* 7/4 (April 1977): 5–6; J.K.W., "Doe v. Beal: Abortion, Medicaid, and Equal Protection," *Virginia Law Review* 62/4 (May 1976): 811–837; Wilkinson, "The Supreme Court, the Equal Protection Clause, and the Three Faces of Constitutional Equality."

6: AMERICAN SAPPHO

1. Susan Madden Johnson, "I Have Four Coming Out Stories to Tell," in *The Original Coming Out Stories*, ed. Julia Penelope and Susan J. Wolfe (Freedom, Calif.: Crossing Press, 1989), 124; Sidney Abbott and Barbara Love, *Sappho Was a Right-On Woman* (New York: Stein and Day, 1972), 45; *Ms.* 1/1 (July 1972): 74–77, 123.
2. Sarah Lucia-Hoagland and Julia Penelope, *For Lesbians Only: A Separatist Anthology* (London: Onlywomen Press, 1988); Cherríe Moraga and Gloria Anzaldúa, *This Bridge Called My Back: Writings by Radical Women of Color* (New York: Kitchen Table, Women of Color Press, 1984); Juanita Ramos, ed., *Compañeras: Latina Lesbians* (New York: Routledge, 1994).
3. Radicalesbians, "The Woman-Identified Woman" (1970), in *We Are Everywhere: A Historical Sourcebook of Gay and Lesbian Politics*, ed. Mark Blasius and Shane Phelan (New York: Routledge, 1997), 396–399.
4. Martha Shelley, "Stepin Fetchit Woman," *Come Out!*, November 1969. Stephanie Gilmore and Elizabeth Kaminski, "A Part and Apart: Lesbian and Straight Feminist Activists Negotiate Identity in a Second-Wave Organization," *Journal of the History of Sexuality* 16/1 (January 2007): 95–113.
5. *The Ladder*, January and September 1965, January 1966; Marc Stein, *City of Sisterly and Brotherly Loves: Lesbian and Gay Philadelphia, 1945–1972* (Chicago: University of Chicago Press, 2000), 220–245; Marcia M. Gallo, *Different Daughters: A History of the Daughters of Bilitis and the Rise of the Lesbian Rights Movement* (New York: Carroll & Graf, 2006), 100–120.
6. This is based on a systematic reading of ten years of *Vector* and fifteen years of *The Advocate* as well as a significant sampling of *Drum*. One of *Vector*'s own polls showed that 90 percent of its readership was male.
7. Vern L. Bullough, ed., *Before Stonewall: Activists for Gay and Lesbian Rights in Historical Context* (Binghamton, N.Y.: Harrington Park, 2002), 189–190; Stein, *City of Sisterly and Brotherly Loves*, 200–258.
8. Kay Lahusen was also known as Kay Tobin. Jaffy was also known as Florence Conrad. I have used their given names here, as has become custom. Gittings quoted in Eric Marcus, *Making History: The Struggle for Gay and Lesbian Rights, 1945–1990, an Oral History* (New York: HarperCollins, 1992), 119. Gittings to Jaffy, July 17, 1964; Jaffy to Gittings, July 22, 1964; see also Gittings to Jaffy, May 23, 1964, and August 11, 1964, FJ; *The Ladder*, September 1964, 25, June 1966, 8; Gallo, *Different Daughters*, 45, 95–96; Stein, *City of Sisterly and Brotherly Loves*, 52, 180–186. Stein uses the term "militant respectability" to describe the politics of the more aggressive mid-sixties male and female homophiles.

9. *The Ladder*, October 1966; Gallo, *Different Daughters*, 121–133; Nan Alamilla Boyd, *Wide Open Town: A History of Queer San Francisco to 1965* (Berkeley: University of California Press, 2003), 230–236; Lillian Faderman, *Odd Girls and Twilight Lovers: A History of Lesbian Life in Twentieth-Century America* (New York: Columbia University Press, 1991), 190–193.

10. Willer's speech originally appeared in *The Ladder* but can also be found, among other places, in Blasius and Phelan, eds., *We Are Everywhere*, 343–345. On Willer, see Marcus, *Making History*, 127–135; Bullough, *Before Stonewall*, 203–205.

11. *Vector*, October 1966, 8–9; *The Ladder*, February 1967, 2–5; *Concern*, January 1967, 2–4.

12. *The Ladder*, December 1966, 28, February and July 1967, 2, 11.

13. Anne M. Valk, *Radical Sisters: Second-Wave Feminism and Black Liberation in Washington, D.C.* (Urbana: University of Illinois Press, 2008), 155–157. There were a handful of women of color among lesbian homophiles, including Cleo Bonner in San Francisco and Ernestine Eckstein in New York.

14. "Bayamón, Brooklyn y yo," in Ramos, ed., *Compañeras*, 89–96.

15. *The Ladder*, June 1966.

16. Stein, *City of Sisterly and Brotherly Loves*, 270–280; Kristin G. Esterberg, "From Accommodation to Liberation: A Social Movement Analysis of Lesbians in the Homophile Movement," *Gender and Society* 8/3 (September 1994): 424–443. Willer's presidency set in motion enormous internal drama in the DOB that lasted until 1972. The full story is recounted in Gallo, *Different Daughters*, 146–157.

17. Albert Ellis to Barbara Gittings, December 24, 1963, FJ (italics added).

18. Irving Bieber, "Homosexuality," *American Journal of Nursing* 69/12 (December 1969): 2637–2641; *The Ladder*, August 1968, 7; William Simon and John H. Gagnon, "Femininity in the Lesbian Community," *Social Problems* 15/2 (Autumn 1967): 212–221; George Chauncey, "From Sexual Inversion to Homosexuality: Medicine and the Changing Conceptualization of Female Deviance," in *Passion and Power: Sexuality and History*, ed. Kathy Peiss and Christina Simmons (Philadelphia: Temple University Press, 1989), 87–117; John Loughery, *The Other Side of Silence, Men's Lives and Gay Identities: A Twentieth Century History* (New York: Henry Holt, 1998), 271.

19. *The Ladder*, August 1968, 7; NYT, December 23, 1973, 109. On the authority of postwar psychology, see Mari Jo Buhle, *Feminism and Its Discontents: A Century of Struggle with Psychoanalysis* (Cambridge, Mass.: Boston University Press, 1998).

20. *Homosexuality and Citizenship in Florida: A Report of the Florida Legislative Investigation Committee* (Florida: Legislative Investigation Committee, 1964); Stacy Braukman, " 'Nothing Else Matters but Sex': Cold War Narratives of Deviance and the Search for Lesbian Teachers in Florida, 1959–1963," *Feminist Studies* 27/3 (Fall 2001): 533–575; Gerard Sullivan, "Political Opportunism and the Harassment of Homosexuals in Florida, 1952–1965," *Journal of Homosexuality* 37/4 (1999): 57–81; Gittings to Florence Jaffy, July 17 and August 11, 1964, FJ; Donald Webster Cory, *The Lesbian in America* (New York: Citadel Press, 1964), 11, 73; Henry L. Minton, *Departing from Deviance: A History of Homosexual Rights and Emancipatory Science in America* (Chicago: University of Chicago Press, 2002), 246–250.

21. On the policing of these all-female networks, see Margot Canaday, *The Straight State: Sexuality and Citizenship in Twentieth-Century America* (Princeton, N.J.: Princeton University Press, 2009), 174–213; Braukman, "'Nothing Else Matters but Sex'"; Abbott and Love, *Sappho Was a Right-On Woman*, 58–60; Helen Lefkowitz Horowitz, *The Power and Passion of M. Carey Thomas* (New York: Knopf, 1994).

22. Gittings to Jaffy, February 14, July 17, and August 11, 1964, FJ; *The Ladder*, May 1965, 14–20, July–August 1965, 15–20.

23. Minton, *Departing from Deviance*, 256–262; Edward Alwood, *Straight News: Gays, Lesbians, and the News Media* (New York: Columbia University Press, 1996), 125–128; NYT, October 9, 1972, 32. Inside American psychiatry itself, figures such as Evelyn Hooker and Thomas Szasz had begun to chip away at the "sickness concept." See Ronald Bayer, *Homosexuality and American Psychiatry: The Politics of Diagnosis* (Princeton, N.J.: Princeton University Press, 1981), 59.

24. Melinda Relayne Michels, "Where the Girls Are: The Geographies of Lesbian Experience in Washington, D.C. During the Late 1960s and 1970s" (Ph.D. dissertation, American University, 2003), 65, 105; Elizabeth Lapovsky Kennedy and Madeline D. Davis, *Boots of Leather, Slippers of Gold: The History of a Lesbian Community* (New York: Routledge, 1993), 125–130.

25. Williams quoted in *What Is She Like? Lesbian Identities from the 1950s to the 1990s* (New York: Cassell, 1995), 35; Joan Nestle, *A Restricted Country* (San Francisco: Cleis Press, 1987), 44.

26. Nestle, *A Restricted Country*, 44.

27. John D'Emilio made this point in *Sexual Politics, Sexual Communities: The Making of a Homosexual Minority in the United States* (Chicago: University of Chicago Press, 1983).

28. Rochella Thorpe, "'A House Where Queers Go': African American Lesbian Nightlife in Detroit, 1940–1975," in *Inventing Lesbian Cultures in America*, ed. Ellen Lewin (Boston: Beacon Press, 1996), 40–61.

29. Perez quoted in *Compañeras*, 24; Saadat quoted in Lindsay Van Gelder and Pamela Robin Brandt, *The Girls Next Door: Into the Heart of Lesbian America* (New York: Simon & Schuster, 1996), 171; Lorde quoted in *Our Right to Love: A Lesbian Resource Book*, ed. Ginny Vida (Englewood Cliffs, N.J.: Prentice-Hall, 1978), 223.

30. Abbott and Love, *Sappho Was a Right-On Woman*, 95; Nestle quoted in Tracy Morgan, "Butch-Femme and the Politics of Identity," in *Sisters, Sexperts, Queers: Beyond the Lesbian Nation*, ed. Arlene Stein (New York: Plume, 1993), 39; Nestle, *A Restricted Country*, 93.

31. Nestle, *A Restricted Country*, 92–95.

32. Cherríe Moraga, *Loving in the War Years* (Boston: South End Press, 1983), iv, 36, 39, 55; Cherríe Moraga oral history, Sophia Smith Collection. Mears quoted in Michal Brody, ed., *Are We There Yet?: A Continuing History of Lavender Woman, a Chicago Lesbian Newspaper, 1971–1976* (Iowa City: Aunt Lute Books, 1985), 127–130; Lichty-Uribe quoted in Ramos, *Compañeras*, 32.

33. *The Ladder*, September 1964; Gittings to Jaffy, August 11, 1964, Jaffy to Gittings, August 22, 1964, FJ; Doris Lunden quoted in Vida, ed., *Our Right to Love*, 230.

34. Martha Shelley, Smith Oral History, 32–36. Shelley and Frank Kameny both penned articles entitled "Gay Is Good" within a year of each other in 1969 and 1970. Kameny's largely reiterates the liberal rights position; Shelley's is a direct and caustic

attack on heterosexuality. Both essays are reprinted in Blasius and Phelan, eds., *We Are Everywhere*, 366–376, 391–393.

35. Elizabeth A. Armstrong and Suzanna M. Crage, "Movements and Memory: The Making of the Stonewall Myth," *American Sociological Review* 71 (2006): 724–751.

36. Moraga, *Loving in the War Years*, v; Del Martin and Phyllis Lyon, "Lesbian Love and Sexuality," *MS* 1/1 (July 1972): 74; Del Martin and Phyllis Lyon, *Lesbian/Woman* (San Francisco: Glide Publications, 1972); Ann Ferguson, "Patriarchy, Sexual Identity, and the Sexual Revolution," *Signs: Journal of Women in Culture and Society* 7/1 (1981): 158–172.

37. Shelley, "Stepin Fetchit Woman"; Stephanie Gilmore and Elizabeth Kaminski, "A Part and Apart: Lesbian and Straight Feminist Activists Negotiate Identity in a Second-Wave Organization," *Journal of the History of Sexuality* 16/1 (January 2007): 95–113; Cheryl Clarke, "Lesbianism: An Act of Resistance," in *Words of Fire: An Anthology of African-American Feminist Thought*, ed. Beverly Guy-Sheftall (New York: New Press, 1995), 242–251.

38. "No More Dyke-Baiting," unpublished flyer, Box 2, ES; Flora Davis, *Moving the Mountain: The Women's Movement in America since 1960* (New York: Simon & Schuster, 1991), 267–268; Abbott and Love, *Sappho Was a Right-On Woman*, 109–130.

39. Karla Jay, *Tales of the Lavender Menace: A Memoir of Liberation* (New York: Basic Books, 1999), 143; Ann Aldrich, *Take a Lesbian to Lunch* (New York: Macfadden-Bartell, 1972), 9–12.

40. Rita Mae Brown, "Coitus Interruptus," *Rat*, February 1970: 12. The manifestos mentioned here can be found in dozens of publications, including (a short list): *Lesbians Speak Out* (Oakland, Calif.: Women's Press Collective, 1974); *Notes from the First Year* (New York: New York Radical Feminists, 1968); *Notes from the Second Year, Women's Liberation: Major Writings of the Radical Feminists* (New York: Radical Feminists, 1970).

41. *The Ladder*, December–January 1970–1971 and August–September 1971.

42. Barbara Grier to Dolores Alexander, June 14, 1969, Box 12, DA; Toni Carabillo and Judith Meuli, "Chronology of the Split," Box 12, DA; *LAT*, September 3, 1971, F1; Abbott and Love, *Sappho Was a Right-On Woman*, 109–130; "Friedan Is Not Our Leader" and other flyers and material in Box 12, Folder 37, UWY; *ADV*, April 11, 1973, 7.

43. NYT, December 18, 1970, 60; Carabillo and Meuli, "Chronology of the Split"; *The Lesbian Newsletter*, October 1971, Box 1, HC; Abbott and Love, *Sappho Was a Right-On Woman*, 124.

44. See the journals in Box 2, HC.

45. Wendy Cadden, in *Lesbians Speak Out*. On counterpublics, see Nancy Fraser, "Rethinking the Public Sphere: A Contribution to the Critique of Actually Existing Democracy," in *Justice Interruptus: Critical Reflections on the "Postcolonial" Condition*, ed. Nancy Fraser (New York: Routledge, 1997), 69–98.

46. *The Furies*, January 1972, 8; Martin and Lyon, *Lesbian/Woman*, 15; "Lesbian Separatism: An Amazon Analysis," Box 2, HC; Retter, "On the Side of the Angels"; Arlene Stein, "The Year of the Lustful Lesbian," in Stein, ed., *Sisters, Sexperts, Queers*, 17; Adrienne Rich, "Compulsory Heterosexuality and Lesbian Existence," *Signs: Journal of Women in Culture and Society* 5/4 (Summer 1980): 631–660.

47. Alice, Gordon, Debbie, and Mary, "Separatism," in Lucia-Hoagland and Penelope,

For Lesbians Only, 34; Zulma Rivera quoted in Vida, ed., *Our Right to Love*, 226; Barbry, "Taking the Bullshit by the Horns," *The Furies*, March–April 1972.
48. Brown, "Coitus Interruptus."
49. Cheshire Calhoun, *Feminism, the Family, and the Politics of the Closet: Lesbian and Gay Displacement* (New York: Oxford University Press, 2000).
50. Barbara Smith Oral History, Sophia Smith Collection, 30; Carmen Vázquez Oral History, Sophia Smith Collection, 32; *Come Out!*, December–January 1970, 16.
51. Mary Anne Sedey to Wilma Heide, October 13, 1971, Box 43/1528, BF.
52. Moraga, *Loving in the War Years*, 27.

7: WILD BEFORE THE FIRE

1. Garry Wills, *Nixon Agonistes: The Crisis of the Self-Made Man* (New York: Houghton Mifflin, 2002; orig., 1969), 52.
2. John D'Emilio and Estelle B. Freedman, *Intimate Matters: A History of Sexuality in America* (New York: Harper & Row, 1988); Alan Petigny, *The Permissive Society: America, 1941–1965* (New York: Cambridge University Press, 2009).
3. Helen Gurley Brown quoted in D'Emilio and Freedman, *Intimate Matters*, 304.
4. *NYT*, March 15, 1970, 230.
5. Robin Morgan, "Goodbye to All That," reprinted in *Feminism: The Essential Historical Writings*, ed. Miriam Schneir (New York: Vintage, 1994), 148–150.
6. David Allyn, *Make Love, Not War: the Sexual Revolution: An Unfettered History* (New York: Routledge, 2001), 21–22; Bill Osgerby, *Playboys in Paradise: Masculinity, Youth, and Leisure-Style in Modern America* (New York: Berg, 2001), 167–172.
7. Violette Lindbeck, "The Other American Dilemma: Sexual Apartheid and Separate but Not So Equal," Box 119, Folder 2132, PM; GSB, November 11, 1968; Toni Cade, "The Pill: Genocide or Liberation?" in Cade, *The Black Woman: An Anthology* (New York: New American Library, 1970), 166.
8. *NYTSM*, August 22, 1971, 14; Mary Ann Weathers, "Civil Rights and Women's Liberation" (1970), in *Words of Fire: An Anthology of African-American Feminist Thought*, ed. Beverly Guy-Sheftall (New York: New Press, 1995), 161; Elizabeth Martínez, "La Chicana," in *Chicana Feminist Thought: The Basic Historical Writings*, ed. Alma M. García (New York: Routledge, 1997), 33; "Exploitation of Women: The Chicana Perspective," Box 1, Folder 3, CF.
9. Jane Gerhard, *Desiring Revolution: Second-Wave Feminism and the Rewriting of American Sexual Thought, 1920–1982* (New York: Columbia University Press, 2001).
10. *LAT*, April 24, 1966, K1; GSB, August 14, 1969; Richard Meier, Donald Rollins, and Thomas Blush, *Elephants and Butterflies . . . and Contraception* (Chapel Hill, N.C.: ECOS, 1970); Linda Thurston, ed., *Birth Control, Abortion, and V.D.: A Guide for the B.U. Student* (Boston: University Student Union, 1970); Richard Feller, Elaine Fox, and Pepper Schwartz, eds., *Sex and the Yale Student* (New Haven: Student Committee on Human Sexuality, 1970).
11. Sadja Goldsmith, "San Francisco's Teen Clinic: Meeting the Sex Education and Birth Control Needs of the Sexually Active Schoolgirl," *Family Planning Perspectives* 1/2 (October 1969): 23–26.

12. *NYT*, January 14, 1973, 292; Jeffrey Escoffier, ed., *The Sexual Revolution* (New York: Thunder's Mouth Press, 2003), xxiv.
13. Vance Packard, *The Sexual Wilderness: The Contemporary Upheaval in Male-Female Relationships* (New York: David McKay, 1968). Harold T. Christensen and Christina F. Gregg, "Changing Sex Norms in America and Scandinavia," *Journal of Marriage and the Family* (November 1970): 616–627; Norval D. Glenn and Charles N. Weaver, "Attitudes Toward Premarital, Extramarital, and Homosexual Relations in the U.S. in the 1970s," *Journal of Sex Research* 15/2 (May 1979): 108–118.
14. Shere Hite, *The Hite Report* (New York: Dell, 1977), 11, 152.
15. *Playboy*, May 1965, 63–67, October 1974, 64, 68; *NMFG* 1/1 (October 1968); Osgerby, *Playboys in Paradise*, 6.
16. *LAFP*, March 11 and June 24, 1966, 1 and 6, February 28, 1969, 26.
17. *CT*, June 4, 1965, 36.
18. *CT*, May 7, 1965, 9–10, September 15, 1972, 38, June 6, 1975, 16; Packard, *The Sexual Wilderness*.
19. *CT*, July 19, 1968, 7; *PT*, December 1970, 18; Luther G. Baker, "The Rising Furor over Sex Education," *Family Coordinator* (1969): 210–217.
20. *CT*, August 16, 1968, 41–42; Allyn, *Make Love, Not War*, 110.
21. *Playboy*, April 1970, 63. Rose M. Somerville, "Family Life and Sex Education in the Turbulent Sixties," *Journal of Marriage and the Family* (February 1971): 11–35; Richard Kerckhoff, "Community Experience with the 1969 Attack on Sex Education," *Family Coordinator* (January 1970): 104–110; Mary Calderone, "Sex Education and the Roles of School and Church," *Annals of the American Academy of Political and Social Science* 376 (March 1968): 53–60; Jeffrey P. Moran, *Teaching Sex: The Shaping of Adolescence in the 20th Century* (Cambridge, Mass.: Harvard University Press, 2000), 156–193.
22. Roger Libby, "Parental Attitudes Toward Content in High School Sex Education Programs: Liberalism-Traditionalism and Demographic Correlates," *Family Coordinator* (April 1971): 127–136; Natalia Yael Mehlman-Petrzela, "Origins of the Culture Wars: Sex, Language, School, and State in California, 1968–1978" (Ph.D. dissertation, Stanford University, 2009), 185.
23. Baker, "The Rising Furor over Sex Education," 210–217; *LAT*, January 29, 1969, 7; Boris Sokoloff, *The Permissive Society* (New Rochelle, N.Y.: Arlington House, 1971), 16; SIECUS materials, Box 36, Folder 463, LM.
24. Kerckhoff, "Community Experience with the 1969 Attack on Sex Education," 105; *LAT*, April 16, 17, and 27, May 24 and 26, July 1 and 7, 1969, C1, F1, CS1, SG10, D22, A1, OC-A1; Mehlman-Petrzela, "Origins of the Culture Wars," 187–188.
25. Kerckhoff, "Community Experience with the 1969 Attack on Sex Education," 105; *LAT*, April 16, 17, and 27, May 24 and 26, July 1 and 7, 1969, C1, F1, CS1, SG10, D22, A1, OC-A1; *NYT*, April 13, 1969, 48; *HE*, June 28, 1969, 10; *COND*, April 1976, 24–25, July 1979, 10; letter, "Dear Pastor," December 31, 1979, Box 132, NAE.
26. *LAT*, January 29, 1969, 7.
27. Virtually any issue of *off our backs* and *The Furies* from 1970 to 1973 contains articles and/or essays raising these issues. On Chicana feminists and sex education, see conference notes, Box 1, Folder 13, CF.
28. Alix Kates Shulman, "Organs and Orgasms," in Escoffier, ed., *Sexual Revolution*, 111–121; *MS*, August 1972, 65–69.

29. Ellen Frankfort, "Vaginal Politics," in *Seizing Our Bodies: The Politics of Women's Health,* ed. Claudia Dreifus (New York: Vintage), 263–270; "Women's Sexuality Conference: To Explore, Define and Celebrate Our Own Sexuality," June 9–10, 1973 (National Organization for Women, New York Chapter, 1973).

30. *The Report of the Commission on Obscenity and Pornography* (Washington, D.C.: Government Printing Office, 1970), 74.

31. Whitney Strub, *Perversion for Profit: The Politics of Pornography and the Rise of the New Right* (New York: Columbia University Press, 2011); Edward de Grazia, *Girls Lean Back Everywhere: The Law of Obscenity and the Assault on Genius* (New York: Random House, 1992).

32. *LADJ* (n.d.), 3, 6, 7, Box 1, Folder 8, ACLU; Josh Sides, *Erotic City: Sexual Revolutions and the Making of Modern San Francisco* (New York: Oxford University Press, 2009); Susan M. Easton, *The Problem of Pornography: Regulation and the Right to Free Speech* (New York: Routledge, 1994).

33. *Harper's,* March 1965, 51–60; *Valley Times,* April 25, 1964; *LAT,* August 19, 1966, SF8; "Report on Pornography," 10. Whitney Strub, "The Clearly Obscene and the Queerly Obscene: Heteronormativity and Obscenity in Cold War Los Angeles," *American Quarterly* 60/2 (June 2008): 373–398.

34. Mrs. Phil Regan, "Let's Get Rid of the Smut Peddlers," and letter from Jo Regan to County Supervisors, October 31, 1968, Folder 2.49.1, JH.

35. *LAT,* October 16, 1966, W28; April 3, 1966, B1, 24; June 22, 1966, A4; September 12, 1966, A3.

36. *LAT,* February 17 and 25, F9 and G9, April 1 and 12, 1964, H11 and M5, November 14, 1965, M13; *NYT,* October 7, 1964, 48; *CT,* November 12, 1964, IND1.

37. Ibid.; Lane V. Sunderland, *Obscenity: The Court, Congress, and the President's Commission* (Washington, D.C.: American Enterprise Institute, 1974).

38. *CC,* November 11, 1970, 1339; *NATR,* October 22, 1971, 1179; *NYT,* October 2, 1970, 50; *The Report of the Commission on Obscenity and Pornography* (Washington, D.C.: Government Printing Office, 1970), 51, 53, 385, 517, 631; letter from Morton Hill to Guy Prescott, January 16, 1970, File No. 147700, sup. 12, LACC; Boxes 44–48, Commission on Obscenity and Pornography, LBJ, and Commission on Obscenity and Pornography, Box 1, RNWH.

39. William N. Eskridge, Jr., *Gaylaw: Challenging the Apartheid of the Closet* (Cambridge, Mass.: Harvard University Press, 1999), 95–120; Whitney Strub, "Lavender, Menaced: Lesbianism, Obscenity Law, and the Feminist Antipornography Movement," *Journal of Women's History,* 22/2 (2010): 83–107.

40. *NYT,* August 20 and December 20 and 30, 1972, 33, 56–57, and 22, January 4 and 21, 1973, 34 and E28.

41. Robin Morgan, "Theory and Practice: Pornography and Rape" (1974), in Morgan, *The Word of a Woman: Feminist Dispatches, 1968–1992* (New York: W. W. Norton, 1992), 88; *CC,* November 11, 1970, 1339; Carolyn Bronstein, *Battling Pornography: The American Feminist Anti-Pornography Movement, 1976–1986* (New York: Cambridge University Press, 2011); *LT,* October 1972, 4.

42. Morgan, "Theory and Practice: Pornography and Rape," 88–89; Andrea Dworkin, *Woman Hating* (New York: E. P. Dutton, 1974), 90, and *Pornography: Men Possessing Women* (New York: Perigree, 1981); Jeanne Cordova, *Sexism: It's a Nasty Affair* (Hollywood, Calif.: New Way Books, 1974), 68–69.

43. Gillian Frank, "Save Our Children: The Sexual Politics of Child Protection in the United States, 1965–1990" (Ph.D. dissertation, Brown University, 2009); Bronstein, *Battling Pornography*, 217–275.

44. Claire Bond Potter, "When Radical Feminism Talks Back: Taking an Ethnographic Turn in the Living Past," in *Doing Recent History: On Privacy, Copyright, Video Games, Institutional Review Boards, Activist Scholarship, and History That Talks Back*, eds. Claire Bond Potter and Renee C. Romano (Athens: University of Georgia Press, 2012), 155–172; Ann Ferguson, "Sex War: The Debate Between Radical and Libertarian Feminists," *Signs* 10/1 (Autumn 1984): 106–112; Catharine A. MacKinnon, *Feminism Unmodified: Discourse on Life and Law* (Cambridge, Mass.: Harvard University Press, 1987), 146–162; Lisa Dugan and Nan Hunter, *Sex Wars: Sexual Dissent and Political Culture* (New York: Routledge, 1995).

45. *Ramparts* 10/3 (September 1971), 26–35; Elaine Hilberman, *The Rape Victim* (New York: Basic Books, 1976); Lorenne Clark and Debra Lewis, *Rape: The Price of Coercive Sexuality* (Toronto: Women's Press, 1977); *Forcible Rape: A National Survey of the Response by Prosecutors* (Washington, D.C.: National Institute of Law Enforcement and Criminal Justice, 1977).

46. Diane Russell, *The Politics of Rape: The Victim's Perspective* (New York: Stein and Day, 1975), 87–96.

47. Kenneth E. Matthews, *Rape in Seattle: A Crime Impact Evaluation of the Seattle Rape Reduction Project* (City of Seattle, 1976), 6, 11; *Rape and the Treatment of Rape Victims in Georgia: A Study* (Atlanta: Georgia Commission on the Status of Women, 1975); County Council of Prince George's County, *Report of the Task Force to Study the Treatment of Victims of Sexual Assault* (March 1973); Carol Vidaros and the Center for Women Policy Studies, *Rape* (New Canaan, Conn.: Tobey Publishing, 1974); Brenda A. Brown, "Crime Against Women Alone: System Analysis of MPD Sex Crime Squad's 1973 Rape Investigations," May 18, 1974, Box 14, Folder 6, SB; "Rape: The Most Underreported Crime," Box 12, Folder 6, SB.

48. Unpublished manuscript, "Foreword," Box 1, Folder 1, WAR; Mary Ann Largen, "The Anti-Rape Movement: Past and Present," in *Rape and Sexual Assault: A Research Handbook*, ed. Ann Wolbert Burgess (New York: Garland Publishing, 1985), 1–13; Maria Bevacqua, *Rape on the Public Agenda* (Boston: Northeastern University Press, 2000), 18–43; Elaine Hilberman, *The Rape Victim* (New York: Basic Books, 1976).

49. "Seattle Rape Relief," Box 15, Folder 28, UWY; *oob*, February 1970, December 1972; Susan Brownmiller, *Against Our Will: Men, Women, and Rape* (New York: Simon & Schuster, 1975), xii.

50. Paula Giddings, *When and Where I Enter: The Impact of Black Women on Race and Sex in America* (New York: William Morrow, 1984).

51. Danielle L. McGuire, *At the Dark End of the Street: Black Women, Rape, and Resistance: A New History of the Civil Rights Movement from Rosa Parks to the Rise of Black Power* (New York: Knopf, 2010), 5–13, 135–140, 156–171; Lisa Lindquist Dorr, *White Women, Rape, and the Power of Race in Virginia, 1900–1960* (Chapel Hill: University of North Carolina Press, 2004); Alison Edwards, *Rape, Racism, and the White Women's Movement: An Answer to Susan Brownmiller* (Chicago: Sojourner Truth Organization, 1975); Patricia A. Schechter, "Unsettled Business: Ida B. Wells

Against Lynching, or, How Antilynching Got Its Gender," in *Under Sentence of Death: Lynching in the New South*, ed. W. Fitzhugh Brundage (Chapel Hill: University of North Carolina Press, 1997), 292–317. On black women's activism against racial and sexual violence, see Deborah Gray White, *Too Heavy a Load: Black Women in Defense of Themselves, 1894–1994* (New York: W. W. Norton, 1999) and Angela Y. Davis, *Violence Against Women and the Ongoing Challenge to Racism* (Latham, N.Y.: Kitchen Table, Women of Color Press, 1985).

52. Dawn Rae Flood, "'They Didn't Treat Me Good': African American Rape Victims and the Chicago Courtroom During the 1950s," *Journal of Women's History* 17/1 (2005): 38–61; National Alliance of Black Feminists, July/August 1979 Membership Letter, Box 2, Folder 1976A and "Everywoman's Bill of Rights," Box 4, Assertiveness Training Folder, BE; Anne M. Valk, *Radical Sisters: Second-Wave Feminism and Black Liberation in Washington, D.C.* (Chicago: University of Chicago Press, 2008), 170.

53. Barbara Mehrhof and Pamela Kearon, "Rape: An Act of Terror," *Notes from the Third Year: Women's Liberation* (1971), 80–81; Noreen Connell and Cassandra Wilson, *Rape: The First Sourcebook for Women* (New York: Plume, 1974), 3.

54. California Senate Judiciary Subcommittee on Violent Crime, *Hearing on Rape Reform Legislation and the Impact of the 1974 Robbins Rape Evidence Law*, Los Angeles, California, November 8, 1976, 2; California Assembly Criminal Justice Committee, "Findings and Recommendations for Revising California Law Relating to Rape," March 1974. See also A. Thomas Morris, "The Empirical, Historical and Legal Case Against the Cautionary Instruction: A Call for Legislative Reform," *Duke Law Journal* (1988): 154–173; *oob*, January 1972, 17.

55. Mary Ann Largen to Charles Mathias, April 29, 1974, Box 49, Folder 6, NOW; Largen to Dian Terry, September 21, 1973, Largen to NOW Members, n.d., CR, September 17, 1973, Box 31, Folder 5, NOW; Largen, "The Anti-Rape Movement: Past and Present"; *NYT*, December 24, 1974, 43, July 30, 1975, 69.

56. Committee on Judiciary, California Assembly, *SB 574 Rape Criminal Reform, SB 575 Rape Victim Reform* [transcript of hearing], Los Angeles, California, March 26–27, 1975; letters dated February 1974 and March 23, 1974, Box 1, Folder 8, WAR; Jeanne C. Marsh, "Criminal Sexual Conduct in Michigan: The Law Reform Solution," can be found in *Law Reform in the Prevention and Treatment of Rape: Final Report*, National Institute of Mental Health, July 1980; Gerald Bryant and Paul Cirel, *A Community Response to Rape: Polk County Rape/Sexual Assault Care Center*, March 1977; *NYT*, September 8 and December 1, 1974, 225 and 246.

57. Brownmiller quoted in *NYTSM*, January 30, 1972, 10; letter to members, July 30, 1974, Feminist Alliance Against Rape; Feminist Alliance Against Rape, *Newsletter* September–October 1974, Box 1, Folder 9, WAR.

58. Hare quoted in Valk, *Radical Sisters*, 171; Genna Rae McNeil, "The Body, Sexuality, and Self-Defense in *State v. Joan Little*, 1974–1975," *Journal of African American History* 93/2 (Spring 2008): 235–261. The chilling 1974 case of Joan Little, a black woman who murdered a white prison guard who tried to rape her in a jail in North Carolina, brought needed attention to black women's continued sexual vulnerability. That same year Inez Garcia, an American of Puerto Rican and Cuban heritage, shot and killed her rapist.

59. *VV*, April 15, 1971, 5.

60. *CT*, January 22, 1978, D1.

61. Carrie N. Baker, *The Women's Movement Against Sexual Harassment* (New York: Cambridge University Press, 2008); Catharine A. MacKinnon, *Sexual Harassment of Working Women: A Case of Sex Discrimination* (New Haven, Conn.: Yale University Press, 1979); Francis Achampong, *Workplace Sexual Harassment Law: Principles, Landmark Developments, and Frameworks for Effective Risk Management* (Westport, Conn.: Quorum Books, 1999); *LAT*, November 19, 1978, M25, December 25, 1978, D6, March 13, 1979, C1.

8: A PROCESS OF COMING OUT

1. Donn Teal, *The Gay Militants* (New York: Stein and Day, 1971), 271–272.
2. Ibid., David Eisenbach, *Gay Power: An American Revolution* (New York: Carroll & Graf, 2006), 149–51. I use "transsexual" and "transgender" here to be as inclusive as possible and to recognize that in the 1970s "transexual" was the dominant term of art.
3. Letter to Bruce Voeller and Howard Brown, February 12, 1974, Box 7, NGLTF. "Gay liberation" is a contested term. Generally, I prefer a usage that suggests the broader animating spirit of the whole lesbian and gay (and sometimes bisexual and transgender) community between 1968 and 1974 rather than the more limited usage confined only to the activities of the Gay Liberation Front (GLF). See Marc Stein, *City of Sisterly and Brotherly Loves: Lesbian and Gay Philadelphia, 1945–1972* (Chicago: University of Chicago Press, 2000), 313–387.
4. Transgender politics remained controversial, and often maligned or ignored, in lesbian and gay circles in these years. I have chosen not to use the contemporary term *LGBT* to refer to people who were the subject of gay politics in these years because I do not want to suggest an inclusiveness that was not present. See Susan Stryker, "(De)Subjugated Knowledges: An Introduction to Transgender Studies," in *The Transgender Studies Reader*, ed. Susan Stryker (New York: Routledge, 2006), 1–17.
5. *Rat*, August 1970; *The New Yorker*, July 15, 1972, 69.
6. *HALN*, February 1969, 1. On authenticity and identity, see Elizabeth Armstrong, *Forging Gay Identities: Organizing Sexuality in San Francisco, 1950–1994* (Chicago: University of Chicago Press, 2002).
7. Karla Jay and Allen Young, eds., *Out of the Closets: Voices of Gay Liberation* (New York: New York University Press, 1992; orig., 1972), lxii, 7, 31–33. On transsexuals, see Joanne Meyerowitz, *How Sex Changed: A History of Transsexuality in the United States* (Cambridge, Mass.: Harvard University Press, 2002), 231–245.
8. See, for instance, David Eisenbach, *Gay Power: An American Revolution* (New York: Carroll & Graf, 2006); David Carter, *Stonewall: The Riots That Sparked the Gay Revolution* (New York: St. Martin's Griffin, 2004); Teal, *The Gay Militants*; *ADV*, July 22, 1970, 1–6; *Come Out!*, November 1970. On media coverage, see *Time*, October 31, 1969, 56–57; *Newsweek*, August 23, 1971, 45–48; *Life*, December 31, 1971, 62–72; Edward Alwood, *Straight News: Gays, Lesbians, and the News Media* (New York: Columbia University Press, 1996).
9. *ADV*, February 1970, 1–9, 29; Terrence Kissack, "Freaking Fag Revolutionaries: New York's Gay Liberation Front, 1969–1971," *Radical History Review* (Spring 1995): 105–134.

10. *Newsweek*, February 26, 1973, 32; *ADV* (March 1970), 1, 15; Robinson quoted in Eisenbach, *Gay Power*, 155–156; Jim Owles letter to Bella Abzug, October 13, 1971, and other letters and flyers pertaining to Intro 175, Box 152, Folder: Gay Rights, 1970–74, BA.

11. Teal, *The Gay Militants*, 136, 271; Eisenbach, *Gay Power*, 146–181; *ADV*, June 24, 1970, 3.

12. *ADV*, February 17, March 17 and 31, April 28, May 26, June 9 and 23, 1971.

13. *ADV*, July 22–August 4, 1970, 1–5.

14. Del Martin, "If That's All There Is," in *We Are Everywhere: A Historical Sourcebook of Gay and Lesbian Politics*, ed. Mark Blasius and Shane Phelan (New York: Routledge, 1977), 352–354; Rita Mae Brown quoted in Anne M. Valk, *Radical Sisters: Second-Wave Feminism and Black Liberation in Washington, D.C.* (Urbana: University of Illinois Press, 2008), 141. See also Alice Echols, *Daring to Be Bad: Radical Feminism in America, 1967–1975* (Minneapolis: University of Minnesota Press, 1989), 228–238.

15. Jill Johnston, *Lesbian Nation: The Feminist Solution* (New York: Simon & Schuster, 1973), 165; *The Furies*, January 1972; Charlotte Bunch, *Passionate Politics: Essays, 1968–1986* (New York: St. Martin's Press, 1987).

16. Birdie MacLennan, "Traveling Lesbians or Sisters of the Road: The 1930s and the 1970s," December 1978, Box 1, HC; *GCN*, October 7, 1978, 9–12. On the lesbian press, collectives, and other aspects of this women's network, see Boxes 1–2, CB, and virtually any issue of *The Furies*, *Lesbian Feminist*, or *The Lesbian Tide* and the following issues of *GCN*: February 9, March 9, and September 7, 1975, October 7, 1978, 10–11; *LT*, May–June 1976, 13; Ginny Vida, ed., *Our Right to Love: A Lesbian Resource Book* (Englewood Cliffs, N.J.: Prentice-Hall, 1978), 13. For an example of a lesbian collective in Grants Pass, Oregon, see *Country Lesbians: The Story of the WomanShare Collective* (Grants Pass, Or.: WomanShare Books, 1976).

17. Radicalesbians, "The Woman-Identified Woman," in Blasius and Phelan, eds., *We Are Everywhere*, 396–399; Arlene Stein, *Sex and Sensibility: Stories of a Lesbian Generation* (Berkeley: University of California Press, 1997); Barbara Gittings and Kay Tobin, "Lesbians and the Gay Movement," Vida, ed., *Our Right to Love*, 151; Del Martin and Phyllis Lyon, *Lesbian/Woman* (Volcano, Calif.: Volcano Press, 1991; orig. 1972); *GCN*, February 9, 1974, 4.

18. "Gay Experiences—The Sisters Speak Out," reprinted in *Lesbians Speak Out* (1970), Folder 68, Box 2, CB; Adrienne Rich, "Compulsory Heterosexuality and Lesbian Existence," *Signs* 5/4 (Summer 1980): 631–660; *The Furies*, January 1972; Martha Shelley, "Gay Is Good," *Gay Flames Pamphlet No. 1*, Folder 27, Box 1, CB; *ADV*, February 14, 1974, 6; *LT*, September 1971; Phyllis Lyon, "Recognition NOW," speech delivered on May 25, 1974, reproduced in Josh Gottheimer, ed., *Ripples of Hope: Great American Civil Rights Speeches* (New York: Basic Books, 2003), 358–361; Yolanda G. Retter, "On the Side of the Angels: Lesbian Activism in Los Angeles, 1970–1990" (Ph.D. dissertation, University of New Mexico, 1999).

19. Sarah Lucia Hoagland and Julia Penelope, eds., *For Lesbians Only: A Separatist Anthology* (London: Onlywomen Press, 1988); *GCN*, March 9, 1974, 3–4; "Lesbian Separatism: An Amazon Analysis," Box 2, HC; Jane Gerhard, *Desiring Revolution: Second-Wave Feminism and the Rewriting of American Sexual Thought, 1920–1982* (New York: Columbia University Press, 2001), 150–153.

20. *LT*, October 1974, 3; Cheryl Clarke, "Lesbianism: An Act of Resistance," in *Words of*

Fire: An Anthology of African-American Feminist Thought, ed. Beverly Guy-Sheftall (New York: New Press, 1995), 242–251; Stein, *Sex and Sensibility*, 124; Barbara Smith, *Home Girls: A Black Feminist Anthology* (New York: Kitchen Table, Women of Color Press, 1983); Kimberly Springer, *Living for the Revolution: Black Feminist Organizations, 1968–1980* (Durham, N.C.: Duke University Press, 2005), 130–138. The first Black Lesbian Conference was held in San Francisco in 1980.

21. *ADV*, January 3, May 9, July 4 and 18, and November 7, 1973, 14, 4, 15, 21, 14. "Transgender" did not emerge as a term of art until the 1990s, and it should be noted that all these terms remain contested.

22. Sex change stories in the popular and gay press, as well as the increasingly out trans-gender community, also raised some of these issues. See Meyerowitz, *How Sex Changed*, 176–185.

23. *LT*, September 1971; Lyon, "Recognition NOW"; Karla Jay, *Tales of the Lavender Menace* (New York: Basic Books, 1999), 213; *ADV*, April 11, 1973, 1–6, July 17, 1974, 1–7.

24. Martha Shelley, "Notes of a Radical Lesbian," in *Sisterhood Is Powerful: An Anthology of Writings from the Women's Liberation Movement*, ed. Robin Morgan (New York: Random House, 1970), 306–311.

25. "The Custody Rights of Lesbian Mothers," unpublished manuscript in Box 136, Folder 6, LM; *LT*, September 1972, 13; *ADV*, October 22, 1975, 26; Mary L. Stevens, "Lesbian Mothers in Transition," in Vida, ed., *Our Right to Love*, 207–211; Benna F. Armanno, "The Lesbian Mother: Her Right to Child Custody," *Golden Gate Law Review* 4/1 (1973): 1–18; Patricia J. Falk, "Lesbian Mothers: Psychosocial Assumptions in Family Law," in *Lesbians and Child Custody: A Casebook*, ed. Dolores J. Maggiore (New York: Garland Publishing, 1992), 55–71.

26. Representative cases can be found in Box 196, Folder 8, Box 124, Folder 7 and 10, and Box 125, Folder 11, LM.

27. *ADV*, July 21–August 3, 1971, 16, June 7, 1972, 10; *BAR*, April 15, 1972; "Lesbian Mothers Union Formed," Box 124, Folder 2, LM; Ellen Lewin, *Lesbian Mothers: Accounts of Gender in American Culture* (Ithaca, N.Y.: Cornell University Press, 1993); articles in Box 125, Folder 12, LM; Stevens, "Lesbian Mothers in Transition." *The Lesbian Tide* and, to a lesser extent, *Gay Community News* and *The Advocate* seem to have covered these issues most carefully and extensively, outside of publications dedicated specifically to lesbian motherhood. See also Daniel Rivers, "Radical Relations: A History of Lesbian and Gay Parents and Their Children in the United States, 1945–2003" (Ph.D. dissertation, Stanford University, 2007).

28. *LT*, May–June 1976; Terry Arendell, *Mothers and Divorce: Legal, Economic, and Social Dilemmas* (Berkeley: University of California Press, 1986); Nan Hunter and Nancy D. Polikoff, "Custody Rights of Lesbian Mothers: Legal Theory and Litigation Strategy," *Buffalo Law Review* 25 (1976): 691–732.

29. *MS*, September 1976, 72–73; Stevens, "Lesbian Mothers in Transition," 208.

30. *MS*, September 1976, 72–73. The Risher case garnered an article in *People* magazine (January 19, 1976), inspired a book by Gifford Guy Gibson, in collaboration with Mary Jo Risher, entitled *By Her Own Admission: A Lesbian Mother's Fight to Keep Her Son* (New York: Doubleday, 1977), and was made into a television drama, ABC's *A Question of Love* (1978). All of Mary Jo's appeals were unsuccessful.

31. The psychiatrist's testimony in the case of *Sarah A. Hall v. David R. Hall* can be

found in Box 124, Folder 10, LM. For a different view, see Betty Berzon, "Sharing Your Lesbian Identity with Your Children: A Case for Openness," in Vida, ed., *Our Right to Love*, 69–77.

32. *ADV*, September 21, 1977, 35; *MAP*, June and November 1975.

33. "Lesbian Mothers" and "The Tired Old Question of Male Children," in *For Lesbians Only: A Separatist Anthology*, ed. Sarah Lucia Hoagland and Julia Penelope (London: Onlywomen Press, 1988), 305, 312–315; *MAP*, n.d., 1974; "Drawing Lines: Manhating," in *For Lesbians Only*, 329–348.

34. *GCN*, February 3, 1979; *Gaysweek*, March 13, 1978, 6; Jeanne Jullion, *Long Way Home: The Odyssey of a Lesbian Mother and Her Children* (San Francisco: Cleis Press, 1985); Ruth Mahaney, "In the Best Interests of the Children: Lesbian Mothers Speak Out," *Jump Cut* (December 1978), 6.

35. *MAP*, January 1970, May 1 and 3, 1978, October 1, 1978, July–August 1, 1979, n.p. Every issue of *Mom's Apple Pie* from 1977 to 1979 featured some report of a positive legal outcome.

36. *The Ladder*, April 1965, 4; *ADV*, April 28–May 11, 1971, 2.

37. *ADV*, October 28, 1970, March 31 and November 24, 1971; *Vector*, March and October 1971; *Gay*, February 15, 1971; *NYT*, June 29, 1970, 1; *LAT*, September 30, 1975, A1; Eisenbach, *Gay Power*, 154–156.

38. *ADV*, June 1969, October 28, 1970, September 15, 1971, January 17 and June 20, 1973; *Newswest*, March 17–31, May 12–26, June 9–23, 1977; "Stonewall Democratic Club," Box 253, MK; *Newsletter of the Stonewall Democratic Club*, SDC. On the gay alliance with Bradley, see Box 171, Folder 1, and Box 753, Folder 1, TB.

39. Kevin J. Mumford, "The Trouble with Gay Rights: Race and the Politics of Sexual Orientation in Philadelphia, 1969–1982," *Journal of American History* 98 (June 2011): 49–72; Timothy Stewart-Winter, "Raids, Rights, and Rainbow Coalitions: Sexuality and Race in Chicago Politics, 1950–2000" (Ph.D. dissertation, University of Chicago, 2009).

40. *Newswest*, May 28–June 11, 1976; *LAT*, September 30, 1975, A1; *ADV*, December 31, 1975; letter from Morris Kight, November 14, 1977, Box 256, MK.

41. *It's Time: Newsletter of the National Gay Task Force*, November 1975; *LAT*, September 7, 1980, E3. Lesbian migration and residence patterns were more complicated and have been less well documented. See Sy Adler and Johanna Brenner, "Gender and Space: Lesbians and Gay Men in the City," *International Journal of Urban and Regional Research* 16 (1992): 24–34; Yolanda Retter, "Lesbian Spaces in Los Angeles," in *Queers in Space*, ed. Gordon Brent Ingram et al. (Seattle: Bay Press, 1997), 325–339; Moira Rachel Kenney, *Mapping Gay L.A.: The Intersection of Place and Politics* (Philadelphia: Temple University Press, 2002).

42. *ADV*, February 28, 1972, 1, October 22, 1975, 11; Randy Shilts, *The Mayor of Castro Street: The Life and Times of Harvey Milk* (New York: St. Martin's Press, 1982).

43. *Newswest*, January 23, February 6–19, and March 19–April 2, 1976.

44. *Newswest*, December 12–25, 1975, March 19 and August 6, 1976; *ADV*, July 14, 1976, 6; "Gay Caucus," Folder 2, Box 15, CDC.

45. Craig A. Rimmerman, *From Identity to Politics: The Lesbian and Gay Movements in the United States* (Philadelphia: Temple University Press, 2002), 32; *ADV*, November 7, 1973, July 31, 1974; *It's Time*, November 1975; *GCN*, October 27, 1973, 1.

46. *ADV*, July 31, 1974; *GCN*, April 5, 1975, 1; O'Leary quoted in *GCN*, July 17, 1976, 1; *It's Time*, February 1976.

47. *ADV*, July 31 and December 4, 1974, June 1, 1977; *GCN*, September 15, 1973, 1, and January 26, 1974, 1.

48. Milk campaign letter, February 26, 1975, and letter to Milk (n.d.) from Bill Sunday, "Pre-1977 Letters" and "Correspondence, January 1978," Box 5, HM.

49. *ADV*, February 14 and July 18, 1973, 1, 2, December 31, 1975, 11; *GCN*, December 27, 1975, 3; *It's Time*, February 1976.

50. *Newswest*, November 14–27, 1975.

51. *LAT*, June 21 and July 22, 1975; *Newswest*, August 7, 1975, January 22, 1976.

52. *Newswest*, February 3–17, March 3–17, 1977; *Playboy*, May 1978, 73–97+; *Newsweek*, June 6, 1977, 16–26; NBC News, June 2, 1977, VTN 22, No. 494128.

53. NBC News, June 2, 1977, VTN No. 494128.

54. *LAT*, June 8, July 29, 1977; *Newswest*, July 23, 1977. See the Briggs material in Box 16, Folder 1, and Box 17, Folder 10, CDC. See also Gillian Frank, "Save Our Children: The Sexual Politics of Child Protection in the United States, 1965–1990" (Ph.D. dissertation, Brown University, 2009).

55. Shilts, *The Mayor of Castro Street*; *ADV*, May 21, 1975, October 18, 1975, 27–32, October 22, 1975, 10–11, April 7, 1976, 12–13.

56. *Newswest*, March 5–19, 1976, March 19–April 2, 1976; *ADV*, April 7, 1976, 12–13.

57. *LAT*, June 15 and 25, 1977; *Newswest*, June 23–July 7, July 29, 1977.

58. *ADV*, April 7, 1976, 12; *GCN*, November 3, 1979, 10–14.

59. *LAT*, March 22, 1978, A3, November 9, 1978, 21; *NYT*, March 22, 1978, A21; *ADV*, November 15, 1978, 11–12; *GCN*, November 4, 1978, 1; Box 16, Folder 1 and Box 17, Folder 10, CDC; Shilts, *The Mayor of Castro Street*, 238–250.

60. *SPPP*, April 19, 1978, 1, April 22, 1978, 38, April 26, 1978, 1; *WE*, May 3, 1978, 2C, May 6, 1978, 3C, May 7, 1978, 13G, May 10, 1978, 1; ABC News, May 8, 1978, CBS News, May 22, 1978, VTN Nos. 54153 and 257969.

61. Shilts, *The Mayor of Castro Street*, 257.

62. *NATR*, March 17, 1978, 344.

63. *CC*, August 3–10, 1977, 677–679.

9: NO STEELWORKERS AND NO PLUMBERS

1. Democratic National Committee, *The Party Reformed: Final Report of the Commission on Party Structure and Delegate Selection*, July 7, 1972; *LAT*, July 4, 1972, E7; "Morris Kight," Box 260, MK.

2. *WSJ*, June 30, 1972, 12; *ADV*, October 25, 1972, 3, 16, 28.

3. *The Official Proceedings of the Democratic National Convention, 1972*, ed. Sheila Hixson and Ruth Rose (Washington, D.C.: 1972).

4. Jane Mansbridge, *Why We Lost the ERA* (Chicago: University of Chicago Press, 1986), 11–12; *NYT*, May 4, 1971, 31.

5. NWPC, Newsletter, December 6, 1971, Box 170, Folder 2, GS; NWPC Statement of Purpose, Box 168, Folder 4, GS.

6. Ibid.

7. Newspaper clippings, Box 140, Folder 7, GS; NWPC Policy Council, Box 634, NWPC Folder, BS. Chana Kai Lee, *For Freedom's Sake: The Life of Fannie Lou Hamer* (Urbana: University of Illinois Press, 1999), 170–171; Chisholm quoted in NWPC, Newsletter, February–March 1973; *Jet*, February 3, 1972, 7; *NYT*, July 13, 1971, 37.

8. "National Women's Political Caucus" and "Black Caucus Resolutions," Box 168, Folder 4, GS; another women's political group, the Feminist Party, was founded in New York City by Ti-Grace Atkinson, Flo Kennedy, and Rosalyn Baxandall. See Maren Lockwood Carden, *The New Feminist Movement* (New York: Russell Sage Foundation, 1974), 139–140.

9. Alma M. García, *Chicana Feminist Thought: The Basic Historical Writings* (New York: Routledge, 1997), 142–165; Amelia Lorenzo Wilson, "Comisión Femenil Chicana, Nacional," July 10, 1973, Folder 18, Box 1, CF; *Jet*, February 3, 1972, 7.

10. Carol Greitzer, NYC councilwoman, president, NARAL, October 3, 1971, Box 1, Folder 5, NARAL; Friedan press release, June 7, 1972, Box 35, Folder 1206, BF.

11. *ADV*, February 17–March 2, 1971, 3; March 17–30, 1971, 1, 5; April 14–27, 1971, 1, 3; July 21–August 3, 1971, 1–4; September 15–28, 1971, 8, 11, 14; October 13, 1971, 1.

12. *The Militant*, March 10, 1972; *ADV*, March 15, 1972, 1, 6, 34; "National Coalition of Gay Organizations," Madeline Davis File, Lesbian Herstory; correspondence with Madeline Davis in author's possession.

13. Letter from Benjamin Spock to Betty Friedan, October 21, 1971, Box 35, Folder 1208, BF; *ADV*, March 15, 1972; *NYT*, February 12, 1971, 41, March 10, 1971, 48, November 28, 1971, 33; Bruce Miroff, *The Liberals' Moment: The McGovern Insurgency and the Identity Crisis of the Democratic Party* (Lawrence: University Press of Kansas, 2007), 2–26.

14. *LAT*, August 27, 1971, D4.

15. *Time*, January 5, 1970, 10–17; *LAT*, September 4, 1972, F1.

16. Brown quoted in "Abortion Makes Strange Bedfellows: GOP and God," *Commonweal*, October 9, 1970, 37–38.

17. *LAT*, July 26, 1970, F1, as well as *CT*, November 21, 1969, 7, and September 22, 1970, 10.

18. *Valley Times*, April 25, 1964; *LAT*, August 19, 1966, SF8; "Report on Pornography," 10. See also Whitney Strub, "Perversion for Profit: Citizens for Decent Literature and the Arousal of an Antiporn Public in the 1960s," *Journal of the History of Sexuality*, 15/2 (May 2006): 258–291; Michelle Nickerson, "Domestic Threats: Women, Gender, and Conservatism in Cold War Los Angeles, 1945–1966" (Ph.D. dissertation, Yale University, 2003).

19. Letter from Rev. John McCarthy, pastor of Saint Theresa Church, Houston, Texas, to Matthew Ahmann, The Liturgical Conference, U.S. Catholic Conference, August 29, 1972, Box 146, SS.

20. Letter from Benjamin Spock to Betty Friedan, October 21, 1971, Box 35, Folder 1208, BF; *ADV*, March 15, 1972; letter from McHugh re "Respect Life Week," August 3, 1972, Box 146, SS; Father Robert F. Drinan, "The State of the Abortion Question," *Commonweal*, April 17, 1970, 108–109.

21. Kevin P. Phillips, *The Emerging Republican Majority* (New Rochelle, N.Y.: Arlington House, 1969); Richard M. Scammon and Ben J. Wattenberg, *The Real Majority* (New York: Coward, McCann & Geoghegan, 1970), 71.

22. Msgr. Geno Baroni, "The Unmeltable American: He Will Be Heard," *Journal of Current Social Issues*, 10/3 (Summer 1972): 4–10; Buchanan quoted in Jefferson Cowie and Nick Salvatore, "The Long Exception: Rethinking the Place of the New Deal in American History," *International Labor and Working-Class History* 74 (Fall 2008), 19.

23. Humphrey quoted in *LAT*, June 20, 1972, A6. David Plotke, "Party Reform as Failed Democratic Renewal in the United States, 1968–1972," *Studies in Political Development* 10/2 (1996): 223–288.

24. *LAT*, July 20, 1972, A6.

25. *NYT*, June 29 and July 11, 1972, 28, 19–20; *LAT*, April 23 and July 3, 1972, B, A1–A3.

26. "A Proposal for Securing Full Participation by Women," Box 168, Folder 23, GS; memo from DNC to state party leaders, October 18, 1971, Box 8, SR; CR, 138/117, September 22, 1971.

27. See materials from the "Women's Education for Delegate Selection" project, Box 35, Folder 1207, BF; Chisholm campaign literature, Box 35, Folder 1211, BF; National Women's Political Caucus *Newsletter*, December 6, 1971, Box 170, Folder 2, GS; Box 634, Folder: NWPC, BA.

28. WP, July 9, 1972, B1; GSB, July 24, 1972, 5; *NYT*, June 29, 1972, 28; Hunter S. Thompson, *Fear and Loathing: On the Campaign Trail '72* (San Francisco: Straight Arrow Books, 1973), 281; Norman Mailer, *St. George and the Godfather* (New York: Signet, 1972).

29. CT, March 20, April 13, May 15, July 1, 1972, 3, B13, 3, S2; "Chicago Challenge," Box 35/1207, BF.

30. CT, July 1, 1972, S2; Royko quoted in Miroff, *The Liberals' Moment*, 193.

31. WP, July 14, 1972, A23.

32. "Delegate Statistics," July 9, 1972, Box 35, Folder 1207, BF. McGovern's forces arranged a tactical loss on the South Carolina vote in order to hold together the entire California delegation. This brazen and cynical political move, which violated the letter, if not necessarily the spirit, of the reforms he had championed, was widely criticized. See *Campaign '72: Press Opinions from New Hampshire to November*, 110–113.

33. Rick Perlstein, *Nixonland: The Rise of a President and the Fracturing of America* (New York: Simon & Schuster, 2008), 668.

34. "Equal Rights for Women," Box 35, Folder 1207, BF; ADV, March 1, 1972.

35. *LAT*, June 28, 1971; CT, June 25, 1972, 16.

36. WP, July 11, 1972, A12.

37. WP, July 11, 1972, A12; Shirley Chisholm, *The Good Fight* (New York: Harper & Row, 1973), 45.

38. Shirley Chisholm, "Racism and Anti-Feminism," *Black Scholar*, January–February (1970): 40–45; Jet, February 10, 1972, 14; *LAT*, January 16, 1972, SE5.

39. Chisholm, *The Good Fight*, 11, 25, 35–38; Jet, February 3, 1972, 12–18; *Life*, November 5, 1971, 58, 81.

40. *The Official Proceedings of the Democratic National Convention, 1972*, 294–297.

41. McGovern interview by John Hart, Washington, D.C., June 30, 1972, Vital History Cassettes.

42. *NYT*, November 21, 1971, 20.

43. *The Official Proceedings of the Democratic National Convention, 1972*, 310–312.

44. *WPTH*, July 13 1972, A1; *The Official Proceedings of the Democratic National Convention, 1972*, 310–328.

45. Letters, Box 146, SS; letter from Sara L. Elsea, Box 910, Folder: Misc. Letters, GM. Italics added for emphasis.

46. Miroff, *The Liberals' Moment*, 218.

47. National Coalition of Gay Organizations press release, July 12, 1972, and "A Final Message (We Think)," Madeline Davis File, Lesbian Herstory Archives; *The Official Proceedings of the Democratic National Convention, 1972*, 328–333.

48. National Coalition of Gay Organizations press release, July 12, 1972, and "A Final Message (We Think)," Madeline Davis File, Lesbian Herstory Archives; *ADV*, August 16 and 30, September 13, 1972.

49. *The Official Proceedings of the Democratic National Convention, 1972*, 401–405; *NYT*, October 3, 1971, 95.

50. *NYT*, September 21, 1972, 40.

51. Memo from Bruce Terris to David Marlin, n.d., Box 146, SS; *LAT*, July 20, 1972, A1; Jefferson Cowie, "Nixon's Class Struggle: Romancing the New Right Worker, 1969–1973," *Labor History* 43 (Summer 2002): 257–283; Richard A. McDonnell, "The Direction of the Wallace Vote in 1972 and 1976," *Presidential Studies Quarterly* 11/3 (Summer 1981): 374–383; Karen M. Kaufmann and John R. Petrocik, "The Changing Politics of American Men: Understanding the Sources of the Gender Gap," *American Journal of Political Science* 43/3 (July 1999): 864–887; Joe Merton, "The Politics of Symbolism: Richard Nixon's Appeal to White Ethnics and the Frustration of Realignment, 1969–72," *European Journal of American Culture* 26/3 (2007): 181–198.

52. *ADV*, October 25, 1972, 3, 16, 28.

10: A STRANGE BUT RIGHTEOUS POWER

1. *CR—House*, September 30, 1971, 34305, 34309; *CR—Senate*, September 9, 1971, vol. 117, Part 24, 31226.

2. George Gilder quoted in Pamela Abbott and Claire Wallace, *The Family and the New Right* (London: Pluto Press, 1992), 77–78.

3. Here I revise the assessments of scholars such as Michael Kazin and Lisa McGirr. While in a handful of places in the United States a populist conservatism had arisen prior to the 1970s, it remained local and weakly institutionalized. See Michael Kazin, *The Populist Persuasion: An American History* (New York: Basic Books, 1995); Lisa McGirr, *Suburban Warriors: The Origins of the New American Right* (Princeton, N.J.: Princeton University Press, 2002).

4. See Donald G. Matthews and Jane Sherron De Hart, *Sex, Gender, and the Politics of the ERA: A State and the Nation* (New York: Oxford University Press, 1990), x–xi, 28–53.

5. Shulamith Firestone, *The Dialectic of Sex: The Case for Feminist Revolution* (New York: Morrow, 1970), 89; Kate Millett, *Sexual Politics* (1969; repr., Urbana: University of Illinois Press, 2000), 36; Germaine Greer from *The Female Eunuch*, quoted in *Feminism: The Essential Historical Writings*, ed. Miriam Schneir (New York: Vintage, 1994), 345.

6. NYT, June 28, 1975, 14; CT, March 23 and June 1, 1975, F9 and D8; Helen B. Andelin, *Fascinating Womanhood: A Guide to a Happy Marriage* (Santa Barbara, Calif.: Pacific Press, 1974), 5, 7.

7. NYT, June 28, 1975, 14; CT, March 23 and June 1, 1975, F9 and D8; Marabel Morgan, *The Total Woman* (Old Tappan, N.J.: F. H. Revell, 1973); Maurine Startup and Elbert Startup, *The Secret Power of Femininity: The Art of Attracting, Winning, and Keeping the Right Man for Unmarried, Ex-married, and Married Women* (San Gabriel, Calif.: American Family and Femininity Institute, 1969).

8. NYT, June 28, 1975, 14; CT, March 23 and June 1, 1975, F9 and D8.

9. Jane J. Mansbridge, *Why We Lost the ERA* (Chicago: University of Chicago Press, 1986), 105–112.

10. LAT, November 23, 1969, H17; CT, March 22, 1970, F9; Lucianne Goldberg and Jeannie Sakol, *Purr, Baby, Purr* (New York: Hawthorn, 1971).

11. NYT, August 5 and December 5, 1971, 25 and BR78, March 21, 1973, 47; Midge Decter, *The Liberated Woman and Other Americans* (New York: Coward, McCann & Geoghegan, 1971) and *The New Chastity and Other Arguments Against Women's Liberation* (New York: Coward, McCann & Geoghegan, 1972).

12. Midge Decter interviewed by John Hart, November 2, 1972, Vital History Cassettes (New York: Encyclopedia Americana/CBS News Audio Resource Library, 1972).

13. Stacie Taranto, "Ellen McCormack for President: Politics and an Improbable Path to Passing Anti-Abortion Policy," *Journal of Policy History* 24/2 (Spring 2012): 263–287.

14. "Pro-Life Coalition Unanimously Adopts By-Laws, Statements of Belief and Purpose," "Abortion: A Collision of Rights," National Catholic News Service, Box 148, SS; *National Catholic Reporter*, March 26, 1971, 5; CC, May 20, 1970, 624–625, September 8, 1971, 1045–1048.

15. CC, February 26, 1969, 279; March 25, 1970, 348, January 21, 1970. David A. Hollinger, "After Cloven Tongues of Fire: Ecumenical Protestantism and the Modern American Encounter with Diversity," *Journal of American History* 98/1 (June 2011): 21–48.

16. CC, May 20, 1970, 624, 629, May 5, 1971, 556, April 25, 1973, 477.

17. CHT, December 22, 1972, 25; Lonny Myers, "Testimony for Family Study Commission," Folder: IL 68–July 69, Carton 2, NARAL.

18. "Abortion Dominates 'Respect Life Week,'" Box 148, SS; Kristin Luker, *Abortion and the Politics of Motherhood* (Berkeley: University of California Press, 1984).

19. Ms., January 1970, letter to Margot Polevy from Lucinda Cisler, February 1, 1972, Box 600, Folder: Abortion, 1971–1972, BA; NYT, October 3, 1972, 22; LAT, October 1, 1972, F6; "Respect Life Week: October 1–7, 1972" and letter from Most Reverend Cletus F. O'Donnell, September 26, 1972, Box 148, SS. On Catholic abortion rates, see "Portrait of the Opposition," Folder: Opposition, Box 8, NARAL.

20. CHT, December 22, 1972, 24; "Portrait of the Opposition," Folder: Opposition, Box 8, NARAL.

21. WPTH, January 23, 1973.

22. Ray White, executive director of National Right to Life Committee, quoted in *Abortion—Part I: Hearings Before the Subcommittee on Constitutional Amendments of the Committee on the Judiciary, United States Senate, Ninety-third Congress* (Washington, D.C.: Government Printing Office, 1974), 5 (hereafter, *Abortion Hearings—Part I*); Mildred Jefferson, chairman of the board of directors of NRTLC, quoted in *Abortion Hearings—Part I*, 8.

23. *Pittsburgh Press*, October 31, 1975, 26; letter to Birch Bayh from Glen Archer, June 7, 1973, Folder: Congress, June–November 1973, Box 7, NARAL.

24. Jesse Helms, "Statement," *Abortion Hearings—Part I*, 90; Engel, "Testimony on the Human Life Amendment," *Abortion Hearings—Part I* (emphasis in original). *Pro-Life Reporter* cited in Engel's testimony above, 74–76.

25. Bob Packwood, "The Rise and Fall of the Right-to-Life Movement in Congress: Response to the *Roe* Decision, 1973–1983," *Abortion, Medicine, and the Law*, ed. J. Douglas Butler and David F. Walbert (New York: Facts on File, 4th ed., 1992), 629–646; letter to John Roberts from Larry Lader, May 8, 1973, memo from Lader to ACLU and NARAL affiliates, June 28, 1973, Folder: ACLU and NARAL Lawsuits, Box 6, NARAL.

26. *ABC Evening News*, August 4, 1977, VTN, No. 50185. "A New (?) Approach to Abortion Cases," Box 140, 75-554, HB.

27. *National Pro-Life Journal* 4/1 (Winter 1979): 13–19, 7/2 (Spring 1982): 17–21; letter to NOW from Denise Spalding, August 2, 1974, Folder 32, Box 54, NOW; "Abortion Alert," *Newsletter of the American Civil Liberties Union of Oklahoma*, July 1973, Folder: ACLU and NARAL Lawsuits, NARAL.

28. Feminists for Life and Callahan quoted in *Abortion—Part IV: Hearings Before the Subcommittee on Constitutional Amendments of the Committee on the Judiciary, United States Senate*, Ninety-third Congress (Washington, D.C.: Government Printing Office, 1974), 122–123 (hereafter *Abortion Hearings—Part IV*).

29. M. J. Sobran, "Abortion: The Class Religion," *NATR*, January 23, 1976, 31; Fager quoted in *Abortion Hearings—Part IV*, 125.

30. Ervin quoted in Matthews and De Hart, *Sex, Gender, and the Politics of the ERA*, 39; *LAT*, July 13, 1975, SG1; Sam Ervin, "Why the Equal Rights Amendment Should Be Rejected," n.d., Folder 662, SE.

31. Dorothy Sue Cobble, *The Other Women's Movement: Workplace Justice and Social Rights in America* (Princeton, N.J.: Princeton University Press, 2004), 3–4, 60–68, 190–195; Nancy Elizabeth Baker, "Too Much to Lose, Too Little to Gain: The Role of the Rescission Movements in the Equal Rights Amendment Battle, 1972–1982" (Ph.D. dissertation, Harvard University, 2003).

32. For these and other explanations, see Gilbert Y. Steiner, *Constitutional Inequality: The Political Fortunes of the Equal Rights Amendment* (Washington, D.C.: Brookings Institution, 1985); Joan Hoff-Wilson, ed., *Rights of Passage: The Past and Future of the ERA* (Bloomington: University of Illinois Press, 1986).

33. *CT*, May 20, 1973, H12.

34. *PSR*, November 1972, March 1973, September 1986; Donald T. Critchlow, *Phyllis Schlafly and Grassroots Conservatism: A Woman's Crusade* (Princeton, N.J.: Princeton University Press, 2007).

35. *PSR*, November 1972, March 1973, September 1986.

36. *CR—Senate*, March 22, 1972, 9517–9520; letter to Ervin from Mrs. R. S. Coon, February 1, 1977, Folder 885, Ervin Papers; letter to Ervin from Patrick Craney, December 9, 1976, Folder 884, SE.

37. *WSJ*, July 26, 1974, 1; *ADV*, March 24, 1976, 12; letters to Ervin, Folders 882 and 884, SE; Stacie Taranto, "Defending 'Family Values': Women's Grassroots Politics and the Republican Right, 1970–1980" (Ph.D. dissertation, Brown University, 2010), 106–108.

38. Thomson's article, "The Equal Rights Amendment and Bible Principles," appeared in the Brethren Revival Fellowship newsletter *Witness*, March–April 1977, and is now available at http://www.brfwitness.org/?p=319 (accessed July 16, 2010).
39. Mansbridge, *Why We Lost the ERA*, 38–44.
40. NR, November 29, 1975, 20–24; Joan M. Krauskopf, "The Equal Rights Amendment: Its Political and Practical Contexts," *California Law Journal* (March–April 1975): 78–83, 136–141.
41. Fred R. Harris, *The New Populism* (New York: Saturday Review Press, 1973), 8.
42. *WSJ*, May 11, 1970, 10; *NYT*, May 9, 1970, 9.
43. Jefferson Cowie, "Nixon's Class Struggle: Romancing the New Right Worker, 1969–1973," *Labor History* 43/3 (2002): 257–283; Trevor Griffey, "'The Blacks Should Not Be Administering the Philadelphia Plan': Nixon, the Hard Hats, and 'Voluntary' Affirmative Action," in *Black Power at Work: Community Control Movements, Affirmative Action, and the Struggle to Desegregate the Construction Industry*, ed. Trevor Griffey and David Goldberg (Ithaca, N.Y.: Cornell University Press, 2011), 134–160.
44. *LAT*, May 27 and 28, 1970, 6, 1; *NYT*, October 15 and May 24, 1970, 52, E2; *CT*, May 12, June 8, and September 4, 1970, 7, 3, A3; *WPTH*, June 16, 1970, C1.
45. *LAT*, May 26, 1970, A9; Cowie, "Nixon's Class Struggle."
46. *CBS Evening News*, May 22, 1970, VTN, No. 209927.
47. *Hearings Before the Subcommittee on National Security Policy and Scientific Developments of the Committee on Foreign Affairs of the House of Representatives*, Ninety-first Congress, April 29, May 1, 6, 1970, Pt. 1, pp. 8, 30 (hereafter *1970 Hearings*).
48. *Hearings Before the Subcommittee on National Security Policy and Scientific Developments of the Committee on Foreign Affairs of the House of Representatives*, Ninety-first Congress, Part 2, June 29, August 3, September 28, 1971, pp. 5, 156–168 (hereafter *1971 Hearings*); Gerald Nicosia, *Home to War: A History of the Vietnam Veterans' Movement* (New York: Crown Publishers, 2001), 156.
49. *LAT*, May 25, 1973, A21. The best account of Operation Homecoming can be found in Natasha Zaretsky, *No Direction Home: The American Family and the Fear of National Decline, 1968–1980* (Chapel Hill: University of North Carolina Press, 2007), 38–50.
50. *NYT*, March 3, 1973, 16; letter from Mrs. Mizzi Campbell to Bella Abzug, February 26, 1973, Folder: Amnesty 1973, Box 423, BA.
51. *La Raza*, 1/10 (February 1973), 30–31.
52. U.S. Senate, *Hearings Before the Subcommittee on Administration and Practice of the Committee of the Judiciary*, second session, February 28, 29, March 1, 1972, 48, 58, 202, 214; "Announcement of Formation of FORA," Folder: Amnesty, Families of Resisters for Amnesty, Box 427, BA; VVAW/Winter Soldier Position paper on Amnesty, Box 425, Folder: Amnesty, 1973–1976, BA.
53. Ronald G. Bliss, "I'll Die If I Must," *V.F.W. Magazine*, n.d., Folder: Amnesty 1973, Box 423, BA; letters to Abzug re amnesty, Folder: Amnesty 1971–72, Box 423, BA; *PSR*, November 1973.
54. Robert Coles and Jon Erikson, *The Middle Americans: Proud and Uncertain* (Boston: Little, Brown, 1971), 130, 134.
55. Garry Wills, *Nixon Agonistes: The Crisis of the Self-Made Man* (New York: New American Library, 1971), 50; *NYT*, January 2, 1968, 36; *NYT*, August 22 and December 12, 1967, 38 and 46.

56. *LAT*, December 17, 1967, B10; Patrick J. Buchanan, *The New Majority: President Nixon at Mid-Passage* (Philadelphia: Girard Bank, 1973).

57. George C. Wallace, *Stand Up for America* (New York: Doubleday, 1976), 178; Kazin, *The Populist Persuasion*, 221–244; Stephan Lesher, *George Wallace: American Populist* (Reading, Mass: Addison-Wesley, 1993).

58. Jack Newfield and Jeff Greenfield, *A Populist Manifesto: The Making of a New Majority* (New York: Praeger, 1972), 12.

11: THE PRICE OF LIBERTY

1. *WSJ*, September 15, 1976, 26.

2. Ibid.

3. Rosemary Thomson, *The Price of Liberty* (Carol Stream, Ill.: Creation House, 1978), 9; Arlene S. Skolnick, *Embattled Paradise: The American Family in the Age of Uncertainty* (New York: Basic Books, 1991).

4. *NYT*, April 17, 1975, 41; *LAT*, April 26, 1975, 2; *CT*, June 21 and July 29, 1975, S1, 7.

5. Hanna Papanek, "The Work of Women: Postscript from Mexico City," *Signs* 1/1 (Autumn 1975): 215–226; Marjorie Spruill, "Gender and America's Right Turn," in *Rightward Bound: Making America Conservative in the 1970s*, ed. Bruce Schulman and Julian E. Zelizer (Cambridge, Mass.: Harvard University Press, 2008), 71–89; *CT*, December 28, 1975, A1.

6. Women's Resource Center memo, July–August 1977, National Commission on the Observation of International Women's Year, "Manual for State and Territorial IWY Coordinating Committees," November 1976, Box 139/10, GS.

7. Ruth Murray Brown, *For a "Christian America": A History of the Religious Right* (Amherst, N.Y.: Prometheus Books, 2002), 103–122; Rebecca Klatch, *Women of the New Right* (Philadelphia: Temple University Press, 1987), 119–153.

8. *PSR*, February 1974, June 1975, January 1976, August 1977; National Commission on the Observation of International Women's Year, memo, March 1, 1977, Box 11, DA; news clipping, Box 5, Folder 14, MC; memo from Birch Bayh, August 3, 1977, Box 104, Folder 2, MC.

9. *PSR*, May 1976; Klatch, *Women of the New Right*, 119–194.

10. *PSR*, October 1975; "Federal Festivals for Female Radicals Financed with Your Money," issue of *Citizens Forum*, Box 15/10, BAB.

11. Lawrence Mishel, Jared Bernstein, and Heidi Shierholz, *The State of Working America, 2008/2009* (Ithaca, N.Y.: ILR Press, 2009), 263–296; Susan Thistle, *From Marriage to the Market: The Transformation in Women's Lives and Work* (Berkeley: University of California Press, 2006), 99–132.

12. Harold Watts and Felicity Skidmore, *The Implications of Changing Family Patterns and Behavior on Labor Force and Hardship Measurement* (Washington, D.C.: National Commission on Employment and Unemployment Statistics, 1978), v; Frank Furstenberg, Jr., and Charles A. Thrall, "Counting the Jobless: The Impact of Job Rationing on the Measurement of Unemployment," *Annals of the American Academy of Political and Social Science* 418 (March 1975): 45–59.

13. Thomson, *The Price of Liberty*, 44.

14. *CT*, June 13 and 19, 1977, 3, D3; *LAT*, June 21, 1977, OC/A1; Schlafly, quoted in

Brown, *For a "Christian America,"* 105–106; Stacie Taranto, "Defending Family Values: Women's Grassroots Politics and the Republican Right, 1970–1980" (Ph.D. dissertation, Brown University, 2010), 167–171.

15. "Daily Breakthrough," November 18, 1977, 9, Box 11, DA; Elizabeth Anne Payne, Martha H. Swain, Marjorie Julian Spruill, and Brenda M. Eagles, *Mississippi Women, Vol. 1: Their Histories, Their Lives* (Athens: University of Georgia Press, 2003), 290–300.

16. Payne et al., *Mississippi Women*, 301–302; Atwater quoted in *NYT*, October 6, 2005, A37.

17. Shelton quoted in *Detroit News*, September 1, 1977, reprinted in *National Women's Conference Official Briefing Book: Houston, Texas, November 18–21, 1977* (Washington, D.C.: 1977), Box XX, SL (hereafter *Briefing Book*).

18. *CT*, April 14, 1977, 2.

19. *NYT*, October 29, 1977, 40.

20. Open letter to the lesbian caucus of the California IWY delegation, November 2, 1977, Box 51/12, LM; *LAT*, June 21, 1977.

21. *Redbook* and *Time* quoted in *Briefing Book*, 205–206; Caroline Bird, *What Women Want: From the Official Report to the President, the Congress and the People of the United States* (New York: Simon & Schuster, 1979), 11; Abzug quoted on ABC Evening News, November 18, 1977, Record No. 46577, VTN.

22. Bird, *What Women Want*, 7, 145–151, 160–164; *ABC Evening News*, November 18, 1977; Suzanne Braun Levine and Mary Thom, *Bella Abzug* (New York: Farrar, Straus, and Giroux, 2007), 210–211.

23.. "Pro-Family Rally" and flyers and reports in IWY; *LAT*, November 11 and 18, 1977, B16, H1; *NYT*, November 20, 1977, 32; CBS News, November 18, 1977, Record No. 249518, VTN; NBC News, November 18, 1977, Record No. 46577, VTN.

24. Schlafly quoted in *Eagle & Beacon*, August 3, 1977, reprinted in *Briefing Book*.

25. Bird, *What Women Want*, 79–80; "NGTF Action Report, October 1977," *On the Line: The Newsletter of the Gay Rights National Lobby*, n.d., vol. 1, no. 4; *It's Time: Newsletter of the National Gay Task Force*, January 1978, "A Brief History of Lesbian Organizing for IWY," by Charlotte Bunch, Folder 12, Box 51, LM.

26. *CT*, January 13, 1979, W18; *LAT*, January 14, 1979, 1; Levine and Thom, *Bella Abzug*, 214–225; "Briefing Paper on Family Policy," WE-16, JC; Executive Order Establishing a National Commission for Women, Box 15, Folder 9, BAB.

27. *LAT*, November 21, 1978, B6.

28. Thomson, *The Price of Liberty*, 35, 44.

29. Bird, *What Women Want*, 114; press release from McGovern Senate office, January 20, 1970, Box 30, Welfare, JE.

30. Ralph E. Smith, "The Movement of Women into the Labor Force," in *The Subtle Revolution: Women at Work*, ed. Ralph E. Smith (Washington, D.C.: Urban Institute, 1979), 1–29.

31. Watts and Skidmore, *The Implications of Changing Family Patterns and Behavior on Labor Force and Hardship Measurement*; Brian Cashell, *Inflation and the Family Budget*, Congressional Research Service Report No. 79-258 E, December 19, 1979.

32. Nancy MacLean, *Freedom Is Not Enough: The Opening of the American Workplace* (Cambridge, Mass.: Harvard University Press, 2006); Dorothy Sue Cobble, ed., *The*

Sex of Class: Women Transforming American Labor (Ithaca, N.Y.: ILR Press, 2007); Kathleen Gerson, *The Unfinished Revolution: How a New Generation Is Reshaping Family, Work, and Gender in America* (New York: Oxford University Press, 2010).

33. U.S. Bureau of Census, *U.S. Census of Population: 1960. Subject Reports. Occupation by Industry* (Washington, D.C.: U.S. Government Printing Office, 1963), Table 1; "Census 2000 Summary File 3, P49. Sex by Industry for the Employed Civilian Population 16 Years and Over," *Census 2000,* http://factfinder.census.gov, last accessed July 28, 2010.

34. David Caplovitz, *Making Ends Meet: How Families Cope with Inflation and Recession* (Beverly Hills, Calif.: Sage Publications, 1979), 9–10; Lawrence Mishel, Jared Bernstein, and Heidi Shierholz, *The State of Working America: 2008/2009* (Ithaca, N.Y.: Cornell University Press, 2009), 43–95, 227–261; Sheila B. Kamerman, *White House Conference on Families: Joint Hearings Before the Subcommittee on Child and Human Development, U.S. Senate, and the Subcommittee on Select Education, U.S. House,* February 2 and 3, 1978 (Washington, D.C.: Government Printing Office, 1978), 295.

35. Marisa Chappell, *The War on Welfare: Family, Poverty, and Politics in Modern America* (Philadelphia: University of Pennsylvania Press, 2010), 125–137; Hubert Humphrey, "Guaranteed Jobs for Human Rights," *Annals of the American Academy of Political and Social Science* 418 (March 1975): 17–25.

36. Press release from McGovern Senate office, January 20, 1970, Box 30, Welfare, JE; *Full Employment and Balanced Growth Act, 1976, Hearings Before the Subcommittee on Employment, Poverty, and Migratory Labor,* U.S. Senate, May 14, 17, 18, and 19, 1976 (Washington, D.C.: Government Printing Office, 1976), 44; *WSJ,* April 14, 1976, 16.

37. *WSJ,* May 20, 1976, 16.

38. *Economic Problems of Women: Hearings Before the Joint Economic Committee, Congress of the United States,* Part 1, July 10, 11, and 12, 1973 (Washington, D.C.: Government Printing Office, 1973), 128; *Hearings Before the Committee on Banking, Housing, and Urban Affairs, Senate of the United States,* May 20, 21, and 25, 1976 (Washington, D.C.: Government Printing Office, 1976), 277; MacLean, *Freedom Is Not Enough,* 289–290; Chappell, *The War on Welfare,* 127–129, 133.

39. Chappell, *The War on Welfare,* 129.

40. King quoted in *Full Employment and Balanced Growth Act, 1976, Hearings Before the Subcommittee on Employment, Poverty, and Migratory Labor,* 641; Full Employment and Balanced Growth Act of 1978, Public Law 95-523, October 27, 1978, Ninety-fifth Congress.

41. W. Carl Biven, *Jimmy Carter's Economy: Policy in an Age of Limits* (Chapel Hill: University of North Carolina Press, 2002); Andrew Levinson, *The Full Employment Alternative* (New York: Coward, McCann & Geoghegan, 1980).

42. Catherine Allen, "On the Importance to Policy of Defining the Family," WHCF Hearings, 178, 504–522; Mary Jo Bane, "Marital Disruption and the Lives of Children," *Journal of Social Issues* 32/1 (1976): 103–118; Kenneth Keniston and the Carnegie Council on Children, *All Our Children: The American Family Under Pressure* (New York: Carnegie Corporation, 1977).

43. Kamerman, prepared testimony, *White House Conference on Families,* 122–123;

Stephanie Coontz, *The Way We Never Were: American Families and the Nostalgia Trap* (New York: Basic Books, 1992), 263–264.

44. Andrew J. Cherlin, *The Marriage Go-round: The State of Marriage and Family in America Today* (New York: Alfred A. Knopf, 2009); Naomi R. Cahn and June Carbone, *Red Families v. Blue Families: Legal Polarization and the Creation of Culture* (New York: Oxford University Press, 2010); Kristin Celello, *Making Marriage Work: A History of Marriage and Divorce in the Twentieth-Century United States* (Chapel Hill: University of North Carolina Press, 2009).

45. CC, August 12–19, 1981, 794–799; Bob Frishman, *American Families: Responding to the Pro-family Movement* (Washington, D.C.: People for the American Way, 1984), 23–24.

46. For an interesting debate about "choice feminism," see the Symposium in *Perspectives on Politics* 8/1 (2010): 159–286.

47. Dorothy Sue Cobble, *The Other Women's Movement: Workplace Justice and Social Rights in Modern America* (Princeton, N.J.: Princeton University Press, 2003).

48. Robin Morgan, *The Word of a Woman: Feminist Dispatches, 1968–1992* (New York: W. W. Norton, 1992), 111.

49. Kamerman, prepared testimony, *White House Conference on Families*, 250.

50. Notes, Box OA 9101, SG.

51. Morgan, *The Word of a Woman*, 109; Kamerman, prepared testimony, *White House Conference on Families*, 107, 340–341, 430; Jane Mansbridge, *Why We Lost the ERA* (Chicago: University of Chicago Press, 1986), 20.

52. Letter from Kratzet to Stuart Eizenstat, September 3, 1976, "Daily Bulletin," September 21, 1976, WE-16, JC; "'Jimmy Carter's Catholic Problem—Not to Mention His Protestant One': The Democratic Coalition and the Struggle over Religious Liberty in the Late 1970s," *Journal of Church and State* 53/2 (Spring 2011): 183–202.

53. WP, February 27, 1980; *Newsweek*, January 28, 1980; clipping file, Box 18, RC.

54. "Family Working Overtime to Survive" and "Report of the WHCF," November 1979, Box 18, RC; *White House Conference on Families*, June 19, 1980, Box 104, Folder 11, RM; "Work and Families: A Report to Corporate Leaders on the White House Conference on Families," October 22, 1980, Box 104, Folder 12, RM.

55. MMR, March 14, May 26, and August 15, 1980, 2, 12, 15; NYT, July 14, 1980, B12; letter from Cindy Miller, n.d., Folder 12, Box 106, RM.

56. Remarks by Jim Guy Tucker, National Press Club, April 9, 1980, Box 26, RC; *Listening to America's Families: The Report to the President, Congress, and Families of the Nation* (Washington, D.C.: White House Conference on Families, 1980), 21–27.

57. MMR, March 14, 1980, 13.

58. Paul Weyrich, "A Blueprint for Destroying the Family," COND, January 1980, 4.

59. "Gallup Survey Data," Box 104, Folder 12, RM.

12: GO YE INTO ALL THE WORLD

1. Herbert Lee Williams, *D. James Kennedy and His Ministry* (Nashville, Tenn.: Thomas Nelson, 1990), 152–168; Susan Anne Cary, "The History of Coral Ridge Presbyterian Church, 1959–1994" (Ph.D. dissertation, Florida Atlantic University, 1994).

2. Williams, *D. James Kennedy and His Ministry*, 157–160; D. James Kennedy, *Evangelical Explosion* (Wheaton, Ill.: Tyndale House Publishers, 1970).

3. James Davison Hunter, *American Evangelicalism: Conservative Religion and the Quandary of Modernity* (New Brunswick, N.J.: Rutgers University Press, 1983); Neil J. Young, "We Gather Together: Catholics, Mormons, Southern Baptists, and the Question of Interfaith Politics, 1972–1984" (Ph.D. dissertation, Columbia University, 2008). The Mormon Church is not typically understood as belonging to the evangelical community, though it has fundamentalist tendencies and is a proselytizing faith.

4. Thomas C. Atwood, "Through a Glass Darkly: Is the Christian Right Overconfident It Knows God's Will?," *Policy Review* (Fall 1990): 44–50; *ABC Evening News*, July 7, 1980, Record No. 66905, VTN.

5. *NYTSM*, February 8, 1981, 64; Glenn H. Utter and John W. Storey, *The Religious Right: A Reference Handbook* (Santa Barbara, Calif.: ABC-CLIO, 1995), 83.

6. Hunter, *American Evangelicalism*; John C. Green, James L. Guth, and Kevin Hill, "Faith and Elections: The Christian Right in Congressional Campaigns, 1978–1988," *Journal of Politics* 55/1 (February 1993): 80–91; Lyman A. Kellstedt et al., "Religious Voting Blocs in the 1992 Election: The Year of the Evangelical?," *Sociology of Religion* 55/3 (1994): 307–326.

7. Linda Kintz, *Between Jesus and the Market: The Emotions That Matter in Right-Wing America* (Durham, N.C.: Duke University Press, 1997).

8. *NYTSM*, February 8, 1981, 64; Robison quoted on *ABC Nightly News*, September 23, 1980, Record No. 67666, VTN.

9. William F. Buckley, *God and Man at Yale: The Superstitions of Academic Freedom* (Chicago: Regnery, 1951).

10. Graham quoted in David Turley, *American Religion: Literary Sources and Documents*, vol. 3 (East Sussex, U.K.: Helm Information, 1998), 501; Jonathan Herzog, "America's Spiritual-Industrial Complex and the Policy of Revival in the Early Cold War," *Journal of Policy History* 22/3 (2010): 337–365.

11. James N. Gregory, *The Southern Diaspora: How the Great Migrations of Black and White Southerners Transformed America* (Chapel Hill: University of North Carolina Press, 2005), 223–227.

12. *COND*, January 1981, 38.

13. U.S. Commission on Civil Rights, "Discriminatory Religious Schools and Tax Exempt Status," December 1982; Joe Crespino, *In Search of Another Country: Mississippi and the Conservative Counterrevolution* (Princeton, N.J.: Princeton University Press, 2007); *Bob Jones University v. United States*, 461 U.S. 574 (1983).

14. Frank Van der Linden, "Secular Humanism: The Religion of the Public Schools," May 19, 1976, Box 132, NAE; "Contemporary Humanism," special issue of *Voice of Freedom*, July–August 1978; *COND*, November 1976; Seth Dowland, "Defending Manhood: Gender, Social Order, and the Rise of the Christian Right in the South, 1965–1995" (Ph.D. dissertation, Duke University, 2007); Francis Schaeffer, *How Should We Then Live?: The Rise and Decline of Western Thought and Culture* (Old Tappan, N.J.: Fleming H. Revell, 1976).

15. Steven P. Miller, *Billy Graham and the Rise of the Republican South* (Philadelphia: University of Pennsylvania Press, 2009), 7–10, 202–210; Duane Murray Oldfield,

The Right and the Righteous: The Christian Right Confronts the Republican Party (New York: Rowman & Littlefield, 1996), 16–29, 56–60; *CT*, May 10, 1974, 33; David A. Hollinger, "After Cloven Tongues of Fire: Ecumenical Protestantism and the American Encounter with Diversity," *Journal of American History* 98 (June 2011): 21–48; Dave Breese, "Directions for a New Decade," Box 65, NAE; "The Evangelical Challenge," "Evangelical Certainty in a World of Change," and "Saving the Seventies," annual convention programs, National Association of Evangelicals, Box 182, NAE.

16. George Gallup, Jr., and Jim Castelli, *The People's Religion: American Faith in the 90's* (New York: Macmillan, 1989), 15–20; Jeffrey K. Hadden and Anson Shupe, *Televangelism: Power and Politics on God's Frontier* (New York: Henry Holt, 1988), 177; Utter and Storey, *The Religious Right*, 80.

17. *COND*, August 1979, 48.

18. Bobby C. Alexander, *Televangelism Reconsidered: Ritual in the Search for Human Community* (Atlanta: Scholars Press, 1994), 103; Robison quoted on ABC *Nightly News*, September 23, 1980, Record No. 67666, VTN.

19. Alexander, *Televangelism Reconsidered*, 128–134.

20. Ezra Taft Benson, *God, Family, Country: Our Three Great Loyalties* (Salt Lake City: Deseret Book, 1974), 183.

21. *CT*, April 6, 1984, 12–17; Jerry Falwell, *Listen America!* (Garden City, N.Y.: Doubleday, 1980), 29; Anne C. Loveland, *American Evangelicals and the U.S. Military 1942–1993* (Baton Rouge: Louisiana State University Press, 1996).

22. Letter to "Christian Friend," October 18, 1972, Evangelical Welfare Agency, Box 3, NAE; *PT*, June 1972, 31–37; *CT*, May 23, 1975, 62–63.

23. *CT*, December 3 and 17, 1965, 35–36, 12–15; "The Continental Congress on the Family," October 13–17, 1975, Box 134, NAE.

24. James Robison, *Thank God, I'm Free: The James Robison Story* (Nashville, Tenn.: Thomas Nelson, 1988); James Robison, *God's Blueprint for Homes That Last* (Hurst, Texas: Life's Answer, 1979); James Robison, *Attack on the Family* (Wheaton, Ill.: Tyndale House, 1980); James Robison with Jim Cox, *Save America to Save the World: A Christian's Practical Guide to Stopping the Tidal Wave of Moral, Political, and Economic Destruction in America* (Wheaton, Ill.: Tyndale House, 1980).

25. Robison, *Attack on the Family*, 6–7, 29, 57.

26. Robison, *God's Blueprint for Homes That Last*, 2, 22, 25, 31, 45; Paul A. Kienel, ed., *The Philosophy of Christian School Education* (Whittier, Calif: Association of Christian Schools International, 1978); Rosemary Thomson, *The Price of Liberty* (Carol Stream, Ill.: Creation House, 1978); *CT*, January 18, 1974, 7–10.

27. Robison, *Thank God, I'm Free*, 118–128.

28. *COND*, June 1979, 14–15, August 1980, 34–39.

29. Robison, *Save America to Save the World*, 19–42, 102.

30. *CC*, October 8, 1980, 937–941.

31. *Sojourners*, April 1976, 5–12; *LAT*, July 25, 1976, F1; *Time*, October 4, 1976, 74–75; *Newsweek*, October 25, 1976, 68–77; CBS *Evening News*, September 21, 1976, Record No. 248065, VTN; Sara Diamond, *Roads to Dominion: Right-Wing Movements and Political Power in the United States* (New York: Guilford Press, 1995), 173–175, 368.

32. *COND*, June 1978, 24–25, May–June 1980, 15.

33. "The Presidential Biblical Scoreboard," 1980, 1984, 1988, 1992, Box 48, NAE; *LAT*, October 16 and November 1, 1980, OC/A1, C6; *NYT*, October 16, 1988, 44; *NBC Evening News*, August 19, 1980, Record No. 512071, VTN.

34. Albert J. Menendez, "Religious Lobbies," *Liberty*, March–April 1982, 2–20, Box 144, NAE; *NBC Evening News*, August 19, 1980, *ABC Evening News*, September 23, 1980, Record Nos. 512071 and 67666, VTN; *COND*, August 1979, 16–17, and January 1981, 2–7; Falwell quoted in *LAT*, September 7, 1980, E5.

35. Menendez, "Religious Lobbies"; "Washington PAC Spearheads Conservative Movement," *COND*, September 1978, 14–16; Oldfield, *The Right and the Righteous*, 95–119; *LAT*, May 19 and September 29, 1980, B1, C7; *NYT*, January 21, 1980, A21; *CT*, August 31, 1980, A1.

36. *COND*, September 1978, 14–16, August 1979, 14–19; Utter and Storey, *The Religious Right: A Reference Handbook*, 74.

37. Robison, *Save America to Save the World*, 13–18; *CT*, January 7, 1977, 26; "The Congressional Biblical Scoreboard," 1978, and "The Presidential Biblical Scoreboard," 1980, Box 48, NAE.

38. "Religion and Politics: Do They Mix?" NAE Women's Fellowship Report, March 1983, Box 182, NAE; *COND*, August 1979, 14–16.

39. *COND*, May–June 1980, 16–23; Samuel S. Hill, "Religion and Politics in the South," in *Religion in the South*, ed. Charles Reagan Wilson (Jackson: University Press of Mississippi, 1985), 139–153; Daniel K. Williams, "Jerry Falwell's Sunbelt Politics: The Regional Origins of the Moral Majority," *Journal of Policy History* 22/2 (2010): 125–147; Darren Dochuk, *From Bible Belt to Sunbelt: Plain-Folk Religion, Grassroots Politics, and the Rise of Evangelical Conservatism* (New York: W. W. Norton, 2010).

40. "Comparison of the Family Protection Act of 1981 and S. 1808" and "Family Protection Act Q&A," Box OA 9078, MB; A. James Reichley, "Religion and Political Realignment," *Brookings Review* (Fall 1984): 29–35; Samuel S. Hill, *Southern Churches in Crisis* (New York: Holt, Rinehart, and Winston, 1967); Edward L. Queen, *In the South the Baptists Are the Center of Gravity: Southern Baptists and Social Change, 1930–1980* (Brooklyn, N.Y.: Carlson Publishing, 1991).

41. James Melvin Washington, "Jesse Jackson and the Symbolic Politics of Black Christendom," *Annals of the American Academy of Political and Social Science* (July 1985): 89–105; Clyde Wilcox, "Blacks and the New Christian Right: Support for the Moral Majority and Pat Robertson Among Washington, D.C. Blacks," *Review of Religious Research* 32/1 (September 1990): 43–55.

42. *COND*, May–June 1980, 16–23.

43. *COND*, April, May, June, and October 1976, June 1979; Richard Viguerie, *The New Right: We're Ready to Lead* (Falls Church, Va.: Viguerie, 1980). Viguerie quoted in *LAT*, September 29, 1980, C7.

44. Anderson quoted in *CT*, September 30, 1980; Graham quoted in Miller, *Billy Graham and the Rise of the Republican South*, 207; Stephen D. Johnson and Joseph B. Tamney, "The Christian Right and the 1980 Presidential Election," *Journal for the Scientific Study of Religion* 21/2 (1982): 123–131.

45. CC, December 10, 1980; *NYT*, January 21, 1980, A21; *CT*, May 3, 1980, S15; Hatfield quoted on *ABC Evening News*, Record No. 67666, VTN.

46. *COND*, January 1981, 12, 20–21; Jerry Falwell to Morton Blackwell, March 30,

1982, Box OA 9079, MB (Blackwell's files in the Reagan Library contain much of the correspondence with disgruntled religious-right activists).

47. *CT*, April 6, 1984, 60–62, June 15, 1984, 30, October 5, 1984, 54–58; *COND*, October 1984, 47.
48. *COND*, October 1984, 47.
49. *CT*, August 9, 1985, 14–15.
50. Letha Dawson Scanzoni and Nancy A. Hardesty, *All We're Meant to Be: Biblical Feminism for Today* (Grand Rapids, Mich.: William B. Eerdman's Publishing, 1992; orig., 1974), x, 161, 211; *CC*, January 21, 1970, 73–77, February 7–14, 1979, 122–123, 141–146; Pamela Cochran, *Evangelical Feminism: A History* (New York: New York University Press, 2005).
51. *CT*, December 19, 1975, 36–37; Scanzoni and Hardesty, *All We're Meant to Be*, 1; Arthur P. Johnston, *The Battle for World Evangelism* (Wheaton, Ill.: Tyndale House, 1978).
52. *ADV*, June 9–22, 1971, 8; *CC*, June 23, 1972, 28, May 2, 1979, 500, September 30, 1981, 959; *CT*, January 31, 1975, 28–29, September 12, 1975, 14–17, March 4, 1977, 51–51, July 8, 1977, 36; Horace L. Griffin, *Their Own Receive Them Not: African American Lesbians and Gays in Black Churches* (Cleveland, Ohio: Pilgrim Press, 2006); Angelique C. Harris, "Homosexuality and the Black Church," *Journal of African American History* (Spring 2008): 263.
53. *CC*, November 7, 1979, 1085, October 13, 1976, 857–862, *CT*, February 16, 1968, 48–50, February 16, 1977, 137–142; *CT*, June 3 and July 8, 1977, 33–35, 36; *Record* (newsletter of Evangelicals Concerned, Inc.), Spring 1979, Box 146, NAE; Letha Dawson Scanzoni and Virginia Ramney Mollenkott, *Is the Homosexual My Neighbor?* (New York: Harper & Row, 1978); *CC*, May 2, 1979, 500; *CT*, July 8, 1977, 36; Carl Bean, *I Was Born This Way: A Gay Preacher's Journey Through Gospel Music, Disco Stardom, and Ministry in Christ* (New York: Simon & Schuster, 2010).
54. Bill J. Leonard, *God's Last and Only Hope: The Fragmentation of the Southern Baptist Convention* (Grand Rapids, Mich.: William B. Eerdman's Publishing, 1990); Nancy Tatom Ammerman, *Baptist Battles: Social Change and Religious Conflict in the Southern Baptist Convention* (New Brunswick, N.J.: Rutgers University Press, 1990); Barry Hankins, *Uneasy in Babylon: Southern Baptist Conservatives and American Culture* (Tuscaloosa: University of Alabama Press, 2002).
55. *LAT*, June 12, 1981, A7; William W. Finlator oral history, Southern Oral History Program, No. 4007, 17; McBeth quoted in Rob James, *The Takeover in the Southern Baptist Convention: A Brief History* (Decatur, Ga.: SBC Today, 1989), 21; Simmons quoted in Hankins, *Uneasy in Babylon*, 177; Harold Lindsell, *The Battle for the Bible* (Grand Rapids, Mich.: Zondervan Publishing House, 1976), *The Bible in the Balance* (Grand Rapids, Mich.: Zondervan Publishing House, 1979).
56. *LAT*, June 15, 1984, SD3; Hankins, *Uneasy in Babylon*, 165–239.

13: ANCIENT ROOTS

1. "Pro-family" is the name by which this movement came to be known. Sometimes I call its adherents family-issue conservatives, but pro-family is also used here in

deference to the movement's self-definition and the way it was recognized by conservatives and liberals alike in the 1980s.

2. *CBS Evening News*, August 9 and 29, November 13, 1978, Record Nos. 259494, 259370, 255466, VTN.

3. Donald S. Smith, "Pro-Life: What Is Our Timing and Strategy?," OA 9081, MB; "Abortion, 1981–1982: Public Opinion," OA 10773, DJ.

4. For a thorough treatment of McCormack's campaign, see Stacie Taranto, "Defending 'Family Values': Women's Grassroots Politics and the Republican Right, 1970–1980" (Ph.D. dissertation, Brown University, 2010); and Taranto, "Ellen McCormack for President: Politics and an Improbable Path to Passing Anti-Abortion Policy," *Journal of Policy History*, 24/2 (Spring 2012): 263–287.

5. *NYT*, August 30 and November 23, 1978, 14 and 18; *CT*, January 13, 1979, B16; *NYT*, January 7, August 15, and December 12, 1979, 36, D14, and B8.

6. Taranto, "Defending Family Values."

7. Untitled document on pro-life strategy, OA 9081, MB; Smith, "Pro-Life"; "Abortion, 1981–1982: Public Opinion."

8. *CBS Evening News*, November 13, 1978, Record No. 255466 VTN.

9. *NYT*, November 5, 1980, A21, A23; *CT*, October 26, 1980, 17; *LAT*, September 16, 1980, C5.

10. *COND*, July 1979; *NYT*, November 5, 1980, A21, A23; *CT*, October 26, 1980, 17; *LAT*, September 16, 1980, C5; "Who's Who—the Leaders, Their Organizations, Their Stands," OA 9081, MB; "Statement of Father Charles Fiore, Chairman," National Pro-Life Political Action Committee, June 3, 1981, OA 9079, MB.

11. *COND*, January 1980, 12–14 (italics added for emphasis); Center for Documenting the American Holocaust, "The American Holocaust," 1982, OA 9101, SG.

12. "Call to Action for Reproductive Rights," September 14, 1979, "Reproductive Rights Alerts," and untitled NOW memo on human life amendment, Folder 14, Box 95, NOW; "April 'Must Do' Activities to Stop HLA/HLB," March 20, 1981, Folder 14, Box 96, NOW.

13. "The 1980 Election: An Analysis," *Planned Parenthood–World Population Washington Memo*, November 14, 1980; *WP*, November 6, 1980, A22; *NYT*, November 6, 1980, A29; *CBS Evening News*, June 30, 1980, Record No. 271432, VTN; Richard P. Cincotta and Barbara B. Crane, "The Mexico City Policy and U.S. Family Planning Assistance," *Science*, New Series 294/5542 (October 19, 2001): 525–526.

14. "The 1980 Election: An Analysis"; *WP*, November 6, 1980, A22; *NYT*, September 15, 1980, A16, and November 6, 1980, A29; Gilbert Y. Steiner, ed., *The Abortion Dispute and the American System* (Washington, D.C.: Brookings Institution, 1983).

15. "Financial Activity of Anti-Choice and Conservative Political Action Committees," July 19, 1986, Folder 14, Box 95, NOW; *NARAL Newsletter*, September 1979.

16. *LAT*, August 4, 1982, SD10; "News from Senator Tom Eagleton," October 3, 1982, Box OA 9101, SG; *Lifeletter* #12, OA 9081, MB.

17. "The O'Connor Hearings: An Eyewitness Report," *Family Protection Report*, September 1981, OA 9081, MB; Ronald Reagan, "Abortion and the Conscience of a Nation," *Human Life Review*, Spring 1983.

18. White House Memo, "Meeting with National Leaders of Pro-Life Movement," January 23, 1984, OA 9079, MB; Barbara B. Crane and Jennifer Dusenberry, "Power

and Politics in International Funding for Reproductive Health: The US Global Gag Rule," *Reproductive Health Matters* 12/24 (2004): 128–137.

19. WP, November 6, 1980, A22; NYT, November 6, 1980, A29; *CBS Evening News*, June 30, 1980, Record No. 271432, VTN; Hyde quoted in Heather D. Boonstra, "The Heart of the Matter: Public Funding of Abortion for Poor Women in the United States," *Guttmacher Policy Review* 10/1 (Winter 2007): 12–16; NARAL News-letter, August 1979.

20. Boonstra, "The Heart of the Matter"; Guttmacher Institute Occasional Report No. 38 (January 2008). For state-level struggles, see Folder 14, Box 95 and Folder 14, Box 96, NOW Papers; on defensive campaigns, see "Call to Action for Reproductive Rights," September 14, 1979, Folder 14, Box 95, NOW, and "A Brief Chronology: Landmarks in America's Struggle for Reproductive Rights," Folder 14, Box 95, NOW; Women's Health and Abortion Project, "Women's Guidelines on Abortion," Box 4, Folder: NY Sutton's Abortion Hearings, NARAL.

21. COND, May–June 1980, 16–25.

22. "Comparison of the Family Protection Act of 1981 and S. 1808" and "Family Protec-tion Act Q&A," OA 9078, MB; memo to Morton Blackwell regarding Family Pro-tection Act, September 23, 1981, OA 90751, MB. Reagan advisers also targeted gay community centers with tax-exempt status; see "Homosexual Advocacy," OA 9078, MB.

23. Memo from Connie Marshner to Morton Blackwell, February 4, 1982, OA 9081, MB; NYT, May 31, 1981, E6, November 5, 1982, B1.

24. Unity '81 Press Release, September 11, 1981, OA 90751, MB; memorandum from Lyn Nofziger, January 21, 1981, memorandum from Howard Phillips, November 20, 1981, OA 9448, EM; COND, April 1981, 22–23.

25. See, for instance, "White Paper: Tax Payer Dollars (Federal Budget): Programs That Can Be Cut and at the Same Time Do a Great Deal to Advance the Family . . ." February 17, 1981, OA 9449, EM.

26. American Life Lobby, Inc., "Family Planning Briefing Paper: Title X of the Public Health Service," letter from Judie Brown to Richard Schweiker, November 19, 1982, letter from Howard Phillips to Richard Schweiker, December 7, 1982, OA 9101, SG; Richard Glasow, "Planned Parenthood's Abortion Crusade," Box 94, NAE.

27. "Spotlighting Federal Grants #3: Planned Parenthood of America," Heritage Foun-dation, August 1982, OA 10769, DJ; "HHS News," January 10, 1983, OA 9081, MB; NYT, April 16, 1984, A20, July 13, 1985, 6.

28. Ibid.

29. NYT, February 17, 1988, A10, May 24, 1991, A19; WSJ, August 31, 1987, 40, July 31, 1989.

30. WSJ, May 30, 1991, A14.

31. *The Family: Preserving America's Future, Report to the President from the White House Working Group on the Family* (Washington, D.C.: Domestic Policy Council, 1986), 4, 58–59.

32. Ibid., 8, 11, 16–25, 52.

33. LAT, June 22, 1983, C5; Josh Sides, *Erotic City: Sexual Revolutions and the Making of Modern San Francisco* (New York: Oxford University Press, 2009), 190; Dick Hafer, *Homosexuality: Legitimate, Alternate Deathstyle* (Boise, Idaho: Paradigm, 1986);

Jennifer Brier, "'Save Our Kids, Keep AIDS Out': Anti-AIDS Activism and the Legacy of Community Control in Queens, New York," *Journal of Social History* (Summer 2006): 965–987.

34. *NATR*, November 4, 1985, 11–13; speech by William Bennett at the Mecklenburg County Medical Society Dinner, January 19, 1988, OA 16939, PMB; letter to President Reagan from a group of congressional representatives, including Dannemeyer, Dornan, and Gingrich, November 22, 1985, OA 17012, RB.

35. *AS*, August 1984, 15–18; cartoon in OA 16934, PMB; Weyrich quoted in *NR*, November 4, 1985, 11; Gingrich quoted in Sides, *Erotic City*, 190.

36. David L. Kirp and Ronald Bayer, eds., *AIDS in the Industrialized Democracies: Passions, Politics, and Policies* (New Brunswick, N.J.: Rutgers University Press, 1992); *NYT*, May 1, 1986, A21; *LAT*, December 7, 1986, AF2.

37. Cindy Patton, *Inventing AIDS* (New York: Routledge, 1990) and *Sex and Germs: The Politics of AIDS* (Boston: South End Press, 1985). For the sake of space, I am bracketing the question of intravenous drugs users and other HIV/AIDS victims whose privacy was also compromised. See Brett C. Stockdill, *Activism Against AIDS: At the Intersections of Sexuality, Race, Gender, and Class* (Boulder, Colo.: Lynne Rienner Publishers, 2003).

38. *GCN*, May 14, 1983; Michael Callen and Richard Berkowitz, *How to Have Sex in an Epidemic: One Approach* (New York: News from the Front Publications, 1983); "Will 'Safe Sex' Education Effectively Combat AIDS?," Department of Education report, January 22, 1987, OA 17956, JD; Jennifer Brier, *Infectious Ideas: U.S. Political Responses to the AIDS Crisis* (Chapel Hill: University of North Carolina Press, 2009), 45–77.

39. Larry Kramer, "1,112 and Counting," reprinted in Kramer, *Reports from the Holocaust: The Story of an AIDS Activist* (New York: St. Martin's Press, 1994); Kramer quoted in *NYTSM*, February 6, 1983, 32; *NYT*, May 11, 1982, C1; Michael Bronski, "AIDing Our Guilt and Fear," *GCN*, October 9, 1982, 10; AIDS Behavioral Project quoted in Brier, *Infectious Ideas*, 33.

40. Geary quoted in *GCN*, October 9, 1982, 11; *GCN*, May 14, 1983; Callen and Berkowitz, *How to Have Sex in an Epidemic*; "Will 'Safe Sex' Education Effectively Combat AIDS?," Department of Education report, January 22, 1987, OA 17956, JD; Brier, *Infectious Ideas*, 45–77.

41. *GCN*, October 9, 1982, 11, and June 18, 1983, 7; *CT*, October 12, 1987, 1; Britt quoted on *CBS Evening News*, June 26, 1983, Record No. 524425, VTN.

42. Speech by William Bennett at the Mecklenburg County Medical Society Dinner; minutes, Working Group on Health Policy, September 20, 1985, OA 12733, WR; memorandum for the Domestic Policy Council, October 18, 1985, OA 17012, RB; Family Research Institute publications, OA 16934, PMB; letter to Gary Bauer re Surgeon General, n.d. OA 19222, GB.

43. "Congress Is Stalemated over AIDS Epidemic," 1987 *Congressional Quarterly* article in OA 16935, PMB; letter to President Reagan, November 22, 1985, OA 17012, RB; *BG*, October 30, 1986, 1; Ronald Bayer and David L. Kirp, "An Epidemic in Political and Policy Perspective," in *AIDS in Industrialized Democracies: Passions, Politics, and Policies*, ed. David L. Kirp and Ronald Bayer (New Brunswick, N.J.: Rutgers University Press, 1992), 7–48.

44. *LAT,* June 22, 1983, C5; Sides, *Erotic City,* 190. For antigay material in the Reagan archives, see OC 12399, JC; OA 14572, CA; OA 11295, SG; OA 9078, MB.
45. *NYT,* July 8, 1986, A21, and July 24, 1986, A24; *BG,* July 8, 1986, 15; *Bowers v. Hardwick,* 478 U.S. 186 (1986).
46. *NYT,* October 25, 1986, A26; Office of the Surgeon General, *Surgeon General's Report on Acquired Immune Deficiency Syndrome* (U.S. Public Health Service, Office of the Surgeon General, October 1986).
47. Koop had written *The Right to Live, the Right to Die* in 1976. *LAT,* February 7, 1987, 6; *WP,* March 24, 1987, H7 and September 22, 1988, A4; *NYT,* June 16, 1989, A14; *BG,* November 2, 1986, A1; *WSJ,* January 16, 1987, 1; *COND,* June 1987, 53–60; Family Research Institute material, OA 16934, PMB.
48. *GCN,* February 15–21 and March 22–28, 1987.
49. *BG,* October 30 and November 2, 1986, 1, 1; letter to executive director of the National Association of Evangelicals from Americans for a Sound AIDS/HIV Policy, August 24, 1992, Box 177, NAE; *LAT,* August 3 and 24, 1986, A3 and SD A1, September 3 and 21, 1986, 29 and E3, November 6, 1986, B5.
50. *WP,* October 9, 1987, 1; *CT,* October 12, 1987; *GCN,* December 7–13 and 21, 1986, 4–10, and January 18–24, May 24–31, August 2–8, and November 1–3, 1987.
51. Max Navarre, "Fighting the Victim Label," *October* (Winter 1987): 143–146.
52. *AIDS Federal Policy Act of 1987: Hearings Before the Committee on Labor and Human Resources, U.S. Senate* (Washington, D.C.: Government Printing Office, 1988), 9–20.
53. Letter to Carl Anderson from Judie Brown, president of American Life League, (n.d.), press release, "Comic Book brings threat of AIDS down to earth for parents and youth," April 7, 1987, "AIDS Is Looking for You," OA 14572, JC; American Legislative Exchange Council, "Homosexuals: Just Another Minority Group," Box 12399, JC.
54. Eric K. Lerner and Mary Ellen Hombs, *AIDS Crisis in America: A Reference Handbook* (Santa Barbara, Calif.: ABC-CLIO, 1998), 120; articles on the commission's report, OA 17756, DM; letter from NGLTF to Ian McDonald, July 13, 1988, OA 16757, DM.
55. Cindy Patton, *Last Served?: Gendering the HIV Pandemic* (London: Taylor & Francis, 1994); Cathy Cohen, *The Boundaries of Blackness: AIDS and the Breakdown of Black Politics* (Chicago: University of Chicago Press, 1999).
56. *CT,* September 4, 1987, 30–32, and May 13, 1988, 72; Lind quoted in Free Congress Research and Education Foundation, December 1, 1987, Box 54, NAE.
57. *COND,* February 1985.
58. *CT,* September 9, 1979, May 10, 11, and 14, 1980, 10, C1, October 12, 1980, B10, November 30, 1984, B1. Scheidler eventually published what became the movement's "manual," *Closed: 99 Ways to Stop Abortion* (Westchester, Ill.: Crossways Books, 1985).
59. "Anti-abortion Terrorism in the United States: Case Histories" and "Attacks on Abortion Facilities, 1984–1985," Folder 14, Box 95, NOW.
60. Terry quoted in Faye Ginsburg, "Rescuing the Nation: Operation Rescue and the Rise of Anti-Abortion Militance," in *Abortion Wars: A Half Century of Struggle, 1950–2000,* ed. Rickie Solinger (Berkeley: University of California Press, 1998), 227; Randall Terry, *Operation Rescue* (Springdale, Pa.: Whittaker House, 1988), 156, 195;

Robert A. Van Dyk, "Challenging Choice: Abortion Clinic Blockades and the Dynamics of Collective Action" (Ph.D. dissertation, University of Washington, 1995), 132–150.

61. Statements of Paul Weyrich and William Marshner, Free Congress Research and Education Foundation, December 1, 1987, Box 54, NAE; Jerry Falwell, "A Pragmatic Proposal," *Fundamentalist Journal*, March 1983, 8; *NYT*, November 30, 1987, B12; *COND*, October 1987, 17–22, and May–June 1988, 57–68; Matthew Moen, *The Transformation of the Christian Right* (Tuscaloosa: University of Alabama Press, 1992).

62. Robertson quoted on *NBC Evening News*, February 16, 1988, Record No. 560735, VTN; *COND*, August–September 1985, 13; January 1988, 5–14, March 1988, 27–32; letter to George H. W. Bush from Ad Hoc Coalition of Evangelical Leaders, August 8, 1988, Box 48, NAE; press releases and press clippings about the 1988 campaign, Box 65, NAE.

EPILOGUE

1. Jefferson Cowie, "Nixon's Class Struggle: Romancing the New Right Worker, 1969–1973," *Labor History* 43/3 (2002): 257–283; Trevor Griffey, " 'The Blacks Should Not Be Administering the Philadelphia Plan': Nixon, the Hard Hats, and 'Voluntary' Affirmative Action," in *Black Power at Work: Community Control Movements, Affirmative Action, and the Struggle to Desegregate the Construction Industry*, ed. Trevor Griffey and David Goldberg (Ithaca, N.Y.: Cornell University Press, 2011), 134–116.

2. *Time*, December 3, 1984.

3. Morris P. Fiorina, with Samuel J. Abrams and Jeremy C. Pope, *Culture War?: The Myth of a Polarized America* (New York: Pearson, 2006); *LAT*, May 18, 1995, 10; James Davison Hunter and Alan Wolfe, *Is There a Culture War?: A Dialogue on Values and American Public Life* (Washington, D.C.: Brookings Institution Press, 2006); Rhys H. Williams, ed., *Cultural Wars in American Politics: Critical Reviews of a Popular Myth* (New York: Aldine de Gruyter, 1997).

4. Letter to Patricia Ireland from Eleanor Holmes Norton, April 9, 1992, and Norton speech before Congress, April 7, 1992, Box 93, Folder 20, NOW.

5. *WP*, September 27, 1992, A21, and November 2, 1992, A7; *NYT*, August 16, 1992, 1; *DMN*, November 1, 1992, 28A; *National NOW Times*, August 1995. The antigay measure failed to receive enough signatures to make the ballot in ten states in 1994. See *LAT*, July 12, 1994.

6. Mark J. Rozell and Clyde Wilcox, *God at the Grassroots: The Christian Right in the 1994 Elections* (Lanham, Md.: Rowman and Littlefield, 1995); *WP*, August 16, 1992, C4.

7. *WP*, August 16, 1992, C4; "Evangelicals Evaluate Contract with America," *Baptist Press*, March 9, 1995, 1–6; *Contract with the American Family* (Nashville, Tenn.: Moorings, 1995).

8. *NYT*, November 14, 1992, 6.

9. Susan Faludi, *Stiffed: The Betrayal of the American Man* (New York: William Morrow, 1999), 359; Fred Turner, *Echoes of Combat: The Vietnam War in American Memory* (New York: Anchor Books, 1996), 63; Jerry Lembcke, *The Spitting Image: Myth, Memory, and the Legacy of Vietnam* (New York: New York University Press, 1998).

10. *CT,* May 23 and September 29, 1982, J46, D1; *NYT,* May 7, 1981, A20, October 7, 1982, C25; *LAT,* March 4 and 26, 1982, D6 and G1; *WSJ,* January 14, 1982, 29.

11. *WSJ,* January 14, 1982, 29; *CT,* May 23, 1982, J46.

12. *Newsweek,* November 22, 1982, 80–82; *NYT,* November 11, 1982.

13. *BG,* November 7, 1982.

14. *NYT,* November 11, 1982.

15. Jeff McMahan, *Reagan and the World: Imperial Policy in the New Cold War* (London: Pluto Press, 1984), 18–23; Marvin Kalb and Deborah H. Kalb, *Haunting Legacy: Vietnam and the American Presidency from Ford to Obama* (Washington, D.C.: Brookings Institution Press, 2011), 88–95; John Arquilla, *The Reagan Imprint: Ideas in American Foreign Policy from the Collapse of Communism to the War on Terror* (Chicago: Ivan R. Doe, 2006).

16. Beth Bailey, *America's Army: Making the All-Volunteer Force* (Cambridge, Mass.: Harvard University Press, 2009), 171–197; Charlotte Cahill, "Fighting the Vietnam Syndrome: The Construction of a Conservative Veterans Policy, 1966–1984" (Ph.D. dissertation, Northwestern University, 2008).

17. Peter Kornbluh and Malcolm Byrne, *The Iran-Contra Scandal: The Declassified History, a National Security Archive Documents Reader* (New York: New Press, 1993), 1–33, 379–411; Peter Hutchinson, *America's Splendid Little Wars: A Short History of U.S. Military Engagements, 1975–2000* (New York: Viking, 2003), 43–110.

18. *Joint Hearings Before the House Select Committee to Investigate Covert Arms Transactions with Iran and Senate Select Committee on Secret Military Assistance to Iran and the Nicaraguan Opposition: Testimony of Robert C. McFarlane, Gaston J. Sigur, and Robert W. Owen,* May 11–14 and 19, 1987 (Washington, D.C.: Government Printing Office, 1987), 440 (hereafter *Iran-Contra Hearings*).

19. Ibid., McFarlane, 31, 146; Secord, 40.

20. Bush quoted in *NYT,* March 3, 1991, 150; Zakheim quoted in *NYT,* March 4, 1991, A17; Steve A. Yetiv, *The Absence of Grand Strategy: The United States in the Persian Gulf, 1972–2005* (Baltimore: Johns Hopkins University Press, 2008), 76–90.

21. *LAT,* August 17, 2004, A1, and October 5, 2004, A4; *WP,* September 7, 2004, A2; *NYT,* May 23, 2004, 30, and August 20, 2004, 1; Kalb and Kalb, *Haunting Legacy,* 154–158.

22. Privatization was further accelerated in the 2000s with the military's use of corporate subcontractors, such as Kellogg Brown & Root (a division of Halliburton) and Blackwater USA (now Xe Services). See Congressional Budget Office, *Contractors' Support of U.S. Operations in Iraq* (Washington, D.C.: Government Printing Office, 2008).

23. News release, March 5, 1992, Box 93, Folder 22, NOW; Eleanor J. Bader, "March on Washington," Box 93, Folder 8, NOW; *WP,* April 6, 1992, A1; *LAT,* May 18, 1995, 10.

24. Letter to President Clinton from Edward Dobson, December 8, 1993, OA 7680, Box 1, Folder 1, CR.

25. Transcript of *Meet the Press,* March 21, 1993, 9, VOIA 2006-0227-F, Box 7, OA 3154, RB; reports on "Don't Ask, Don't Tell" can be found in Box 27, Folder 15, EK; the Meinhold case is documented extensively in FOIA 2006-0227-F, OA/ID 4658, Boxes 4–7, CS. See also Nathaniel Frank, *Unfriendly Fire: How the Gay Ban Undermines the Military and Weakens America* (New York: St. Martin's Press, 2009).

26. Press releases and press conference transcripts, "The Clinton/Gore Administration: A Record of Progress on HIV and AIDS," OA 21199, Box 98, BR; National

Commission on AIDS, "AIDS: An Expanding Tragedy" and "Recommendations to President Clinton," 1993, OA 7680, Box 2, Folder 3, CR; press release, June 15, 1995, OA 8688, Box 1, Folder 7, Press Release File; Eric K. Lerner and Mary Ellen Hombs, *AIDS Crisis in America: A Reference Handbook* (Santa Barbara, Calif.: ABC-CLIO, 1998), 120–132, 152.

27. Franklin Gilliam, Jr., "The 'Welfare Queen' Experiment: How Viewers React to Images of African American Mothers on Welfare," *Nieman Reports*, Summer 1999; "Punishment and Prejudice: Racial Disparities in the War on Drugs," *Human Rights Watch* 12/2 (2000): 1–28.

28. "The Values We Live By: What Americans Want from Welfare Reform," OA 18944, Box 28, Folder 7, BR; "Catholic Charities USA Targets AFDC Reform," OA 18939, Box 1, Folder 5, BR; memo and welfare reform talking points, May 4, 1994, OA 1894, Box 7, Folder 1, BR; "Welfare Reform," OA 18904, Box 7, Folder 5, BR.

29. Memorandum to President Clinton from Benjamin Barber, February 12, 1996, OA 2109, Box 127, Folder 10, BR.

30. *COND*, September 1987, 27–32; *LAT*, May 5, 1987, C1.

31. See the essays in Robert Chrisman and Robert L. Allen, *Court of Appeal: The Black Community Speaks Out on the Racial and Sexual Politics of Clarence Thomas vs. Anita Hill* (New York: Ballantine Books, 1992), and Toni Morrison, *Race-ing Justice, En-Gendering Power: Essays on Anita Hill, Clarence Thomas, and the Construction of Social Reality* (New York: Pantheon, 1992).

32. *NYT*, October 9, 1991, A25, October 13, 1991, 30; *WSJ*, October 11, 1991, A8, A10. Geneva Smitherman, ed., *African American Women Speak Out on Anita Hill–Clarence Thomas* (Detroit: Wayne State University Press, 1995); Paul Apostolidis and Juliet Williams, eds., *Public Affairs: Politics in the Age of Sex Scandals* (Durham, N.C.: Duke University Press, 2004), 1–35.

33. Nancy Fraser, "Sex, Lies, and the Public Sphere: Some Reflections on the Confirmation of Clarence Thomas," *Critical Inquiry* 18/3 (Spring 1992): 595–612; David Frye, "The Gendered Senate: National Politics and Gender Imagery After the Thomas Hearing," in *Outsiders Looking In: A Communication Perspective on the Hill/Thomas Hearings*, ed. Paul Siegel (Cresskill, N.J.: Hampton Press, 1996), 3–16. Anita Hill's own recounting of the events is fascinating and instructive. See Anita Faye Hill, "Marriage and Patronage in the Empowerment and Disempowerment of African American Women," in *Race, Gender, and Power in America: The Legacy of the Hill-Thomas Hearings*, ed. Anita Faye Hill and Emma Coleman Jordan (New York: Oxford University Press, 1995), 271–291. For Anna Quindlen's piece, "Listen to Us," see *NYT*, October 9, 1991, A25.

34. Bush quoted in Hill and Jordan, eds., *Race, Gender, and Power in America*, iv, x; Thomas quoted in James L. Nolan, Jr., "The Therapeutic State: The Clarence Thomas and Anita Hill Hearings," *Antioch Review* 56/1 (Winter 1998): 18. Thomas also famously appealed to a different racial narrative when he claimed that Hill's testimony constituted a "high-tech lynching," an updated version of the ultimate punishment for "uppity" blacks allegedly like him. See *NYT*, October 13, 1991, 30.

35. Alan M. Dershowitz, *Sexual McCarthyism: Clinton, Starr, and the Emerging Constitutional Crisis* (New York: Basic Books, 1998), 247–267.

36. Amelia Richards and Jennifer Baumgardner, "In Defense of Monica," *The Nation*, December 21, 1998, 6–7.

37. Daniel A. Smith, Matthew DeSantis, and Jason Kassel, "Same-Sex Marriage Ballot Measures and the 2004 Presidential Election," *State and Local Government Review* 38/2 (2006): 78–91.

38. James L. Guth et al., "Religious Influences in the 2004 Presidential Election," *Presidential Studies Quarterly* 36/2 (2006): 223–242.

39. Thomas Frank, *What's the Matter with Kansas?: How Conservatives Won the Heart of America* (New York: Metropolitan Books, 2004); Robert W. Speel, *Changing Patterns of Voting in the Northern United States: Electoral Realignment, 1952–1996* (University Park: Pennsylvania State University Press, 1998); Renée M. Lamis, *The Political Realignment of Pennsylvania Politics Since 1960: Two-Party Competition in a Battleground State* (University Park: Pennsylvania State University Press, 2009).

40. Merle Black, "The Transformation of the Southern Democratic Party," *Journal of Politics* 66/4 (November 2004): 1001–1017; Byron E. Shafer and Richard G. C. Johnston, "The Transformation of Southern Politics Revisited: The House of Representatives as a Window," *British Journal of Political Science* 31/4 (October 2001): 601–625; Matthew Lassiter, *Silent Majority: Suburban Politics in the Sunbelt South* (Princeton, N.J.: Princeton University Press, 2007).

41. Nancy J. Davis and Robert V. Robinson, "A War for America's Soul?: The American Religious Landscape," in *Cultural Wars in American Politics: Critical Reviews of a Popular Myth*, ed. Rhys H. Williams (New York: Aldine de Gruyter, 1997), 9–61; Center for the American Woman in Politics, "The Gender Gap Fact Sheet," 2008.

42. Lawrence Mishel, Jared Bernstein, and Heidi Shierholz, *The State of Working America, 2008–2009* (Ithaca, N.Y.: Cornell University Press, 2009), 213.

43. Gerber Fried, "Abortion in the United States: Barriers to Access"; Rachel K. Jones et al., "Abortion in the United States: Incidence and Access to Services, 2005," *Perspectives on Sexual and Reproductive Health* 40/1 (March 2008): 6–16; William Saletan, *Bearing Right: How Conservatives Won the Abortion War* (Berkeley: University of California Press, 2003).

44. I use "LGBT" here because this became increasingly standard usage in the early 2000s.

ACKNOWLEDGMENTS

I have long shared the sentiment that scholarship is a collective enterprise. This book confirmed and deepened that conviction. For reading all or significant parts of the manuscript, I would like to thank Ceren Belge, Margot Canaday, Nancy Cott, Jane Gerhard, Nancy Hewitt, Stephen P. Miller, Claire Potter, Marc Stein and Timothy Stewart-Winter. Sandy Zipp generously read, and greatly improved, much of the book. Nancy Cott and Mari Jo Buhle, in distinct but equally crucial ways, showed a great deal of early faith in the project. I hope the book honors that faith, even if they do not agree with everything in its pages. Two generous colleagues at Brown University, Maud Mandel and Ethan Pollock, read several chapters and kept me believing in the manuscript, even as they labored on their heavy second books. David Lobenstein read two-thirds of the manuscript and helped me improve virtually every page. My colleagues in the History Department at Brown have been phenomenally supportive, and I owe them a great deal. And many thanks to colleagues in History, American Studies, and Women's, Gender, and Sexuality Studies at the following institutions for providing me the opportunity to present portions of the manuscript and to receive critical feedback in workshops and other forums: Princeton University, Harvard University, Yale University, University of North Carolina, Chapel Hill, Brandeis University, and the University of Wisconsin, Milwaukee. Thomas LeBien, the superb former publisher at Hill and Wang, first believed in the book and then breathed life into its argument. Much of what is in these pages is a product of his prodigious efforts. It's hard to imagine a better editor. His newly arrived editorial assistant, Dan Gerstle, placed his own considerable skills in the service of the book and made it a great deal better. I owe the title to Donna Murch, who suggested it, as if to complete the circle, over lunch in Oakland. Errors of fact and interpretation are entirely mine.

Support and assistance from a range of institutions made the book possible. I want to thank the John Simon Guggenheim Foundation, the American Council of Learned Societies, the Radcliffe Institute at Harvard University, and Brown University, in particular. The labor of various staff members at Brown was essential to the book's evolution, and I thank them for their efforts: Julissa Bautista, Mary Beth Bryson, Cherrie Guerzon, and Karen Mota. Pembroke Herbert provided thoughtful assistance in locating photographs. Would that I could thank individually every archivist I encountered in the last six years, but their number and my poor memory would make a mockery of any attempt. I'll have to settle for a profound expression of gratitude collectively to the incredible staffs of the three dozen archives and special collections listed at the end of the book.

No collective was more essential to this project than my students, both undergraduate and graduate. I have benefited in countless ways from their extraordinary efforts. For research assistance, thank you to Kari Best, Casey Bohlen, Terah Crews, Christina Esquivel, Jan Foo, Ben Holtzman, Sam Oliker-Friedland, and Madeleine Rosenberg at Brown and Jessica Alvarez and April Wang at Harvard. Anya Goldstein, Chelsea Waite, and Heather Lee did particularly amazing work for which mere thanks seem insufficient. Derek Seidman, whose knowledge of the Vietnam-era GI movement far surpasses my own, and Stacie Taranto, whose research on antifeminism in New York State is nearing publication, helped and inspired me a great deal.

The emotional sustenance provided by friends and family, traditionally recognized last in acknowledgments, remains first in my heart. There is no way this book would have been possible without them. I do not list the enormous contributions of my friends one by one here only for fear that I would leave someone out. You know who you are, and my gratitude knows no bounds. I am a proud product of my family, and the book is dedicated to them.

INDEX

Abbott, Sidney, 161, 171, 173, 182
Abington School District v. Schempp, 344
abortion, 194; illegal, 138–40; self-induced, 140, 143; therapeutic, 139
Abortion (Lader), 142
"Abortion and the Conscience of a Nation" (Reagan, ghostwritten), 376
Abortion: A Reflection of Life, 339
abortion debate, 6, 82, 134–60, 197, 253, 258, 304, 335, 403, 411, 412, 423; African Americans and, 151; "baby killer" argument in, 155, 374; class in, 139, 377–78; in DNC (1972), 253, 258, 265, 269–71; as domain of women, 138, 139, 144–46; government intrusion issue in, 286–90; as key feminist issue, 371; Latinos in, 152–53; as male-dominated, 135–39, 144; moral opposition in, 143–44, 154–56, 159, 290–91; nonpartisan positions in, 371, 372; polarization of, 371; as public vs. private issue, 135–36, 140–43, 147–48, 153, 157–60; reform vs. repeal in, 137–45; *see also* antiabortion activism
"abortion on demand," 136, 158, 159, 286, 316, 376
Abortion Rights Act, 157
Abzug, Bella, 71, 128, 157, 200, 224, 252, 265–66, 269–70, 291, 312, 319, 320–21
ACT UP (AIDS Coalition to Unleash Power), 391–94
Advocate, The, 87, 88, 90, 93–95, 163, 236, 238–39, 241, 246, 275
affirmative action, 42–46, 131, 259, 325, 415

AFL-CIO, 21, 250, 261, 274
African Americans, 6–7; as breadwinners, 19–20, 27, 29, 30, 32, 36–37, 40; gay alliance with, 237; gender roles of, 32, 34–36; in HIV/AIDS crisis, 394, 413; men in workforce, 21, 23–36; in military, 48–49, 54, 68; urban population of, 45; and welfare, 39, 413–14; *see also* black freedom movement; black power
African American Unity Fellowship Church, 363
African Methodist Episcopal (AME) church, 363
Against Our Will (Brownmiller), 211–12
Agnew, Spiro, 41, 71, 256–57, 298, 303–304
AIDS Behavioral Research Project, 387
AIDS March on Washington, 391
AIDS quilt (Names Project AIDS Memorial Quilt), 392
Aid to Families with Dependent Children (AFDC), 38, 39, 149, 414
Ali, Muhammad, 33, 53, 59
Alice B. Toklas Democratic Club (Alice), 239, 242, 245, 251, 254
All We're Meant to Be (Scanzoni and Hardesty), 362, 363
Alliance for Black Social Welfare, 334
Alsop, Joseph, 263
American Civil Liberties Union (ACLU), 91, 156, 159, 233, 240, 381; Women's Rights Project, 117–18, 142, 289
American Dilemma (Myrdal), 28
American Family Association, 354–55